RIGHTS IN CONTEXT

Rights in Context
Law and Justice in Late Modern Society

Edited by

REZA BANAKAR
University of Westminster, UK

ASHGATE

Published by
Ashgate Publishing Limited
Wey Court East
Union Road
Farnham
Surrey, GU9 7PT
England

Ashgate Publishing Company
Suite 420
101 Cherry Street
Burlington
VT 05401-4405
USA

www.ashgate.com

British Library Cataloguing in Publication Data
Rights in context : law and justice in late modern society.
    1. Sociological jurisprudence. 2. Human rights advocacy.
    3. Human rights--Case studies.
    I. Banakar, Reza.
    340.1'15-dc22

Library of Congress Cataloging-in-Publication Data
Rights in context : law and justice in late modern society / by Reza Banakar.
        p. cm.
    Includes index.
    ISBN 978-1-4094-0739-3 (hardback) -- ISBN 978-1-4094-0740-9 (pbk.) -- ISBN 978-1-4094-0741-6
    (ebook) 1. Human rights. 2. Sociological jurisprudence. I. Banakar, Reza.
    K3240.R545 2010
    340'.115--dc22

                                                                                    2010006873

ISBN 9781409407393 (hbk)
ISBN 9781409407409 (pbk)
ISBN 9781409407416 (ebk)

Mixed Sources
Product group from well-managed
forests and other controlled sources
www.fsc.org Cert no. SA-COC-1565
© 1996 Forest Stewardship Council
FSC

Printed and bound in Great Britain by
MPG Books Group, UK

Contents

List of Figures and Tables

Figures

Tables

List of Contributors

Reza Banakar is Professor of Socio-Legal Studies at the Department of Advanced Legal Studies at the University of Westminster, London. He was previously the Paul Dodyk Research Fellow at the Centre for Socio-Legal Studies in Oxford. He has also taught at Lund University in Sweden and at the International Institute for the Sociology of Law in Oñati, Spain. Among his publications are *Merging Law and Sociology: Beyond the Dichotomies in Socio-Legal Research* (Gald & Wilch, 2003) and *Theory and Method in Socio-Legal Research*, co-edited with Max Travers (Hart, 2005).

Samia Bano is a lecturer in family law at the University of Reading. Her research interests include gender, migration, Islam, Muslim family law, human rights and multiculturalism and the law. She has worked on a number of research and policy initiatives in the areas of gender, migration and human rights. Her current work explores the relationships between informal religious legal systems, state law and gender relations within South-Asian Muslim communities in the UK and is due to be published as a book in Spring 2011 (Palgrave Macmillan).

Joxerramon Bengoetxea teaches comparative legal cultures, jurisprudence, sociology of law and history of European integration at the University of the Basque Country. After studying law and philosophy in Madrid and San Sebastian, he obtained his PhD in Edinburgh, under the guidance of the late Neil MacCormick. He has worked as legal secretary for Judge David Edward at the European Court of Justice and as Deputy Minister for Employment, Labour and Social Security at the Basque Autonomous Government. He has been Scientific Director at the Oñati Institute and member of the quasi-judicial Basque Electoral Board.

Bill Bowring is Professor of Law at Birkbeck College, University of London, where he teaches public international law and human rights. He has more than 70 publications: his recent book is *The Degradation of the International Legal Order?* (Routledge, 2008). As a practising barrister he has taken many cases to the Strasbourg Court. In 2003 he founded and is now Chair of the European Human Rights Advocacy Centre (EHRAC), representing many Chechen victims against Russia. He is also International Secretary of the Haldane Society of Socialist Lawyers and President of the European Association of Lawyers for Democracy and Human Rights.

Radha D'Souza is a reader in law at the University of Westminster, London. Her research interests include global and social justice, social movements, law and development, colonialism and imperialism, socio-legal studies in the Third World and water conflicts. She teaches law and development and has previously taught sociology, development studies, human geography, public law and legal theory. Earlier in her career she practised as a barrister at the High Court of Mumbai in India.

Sarah Dreier is a political science doctoral student at the University of Washington in Seattle. She previously served as a researcher for the Faith and Progressive Policy Initiative at the Center for American Progress, a progressive policy research institution in Washington, DC, where she conducted extensive research on religion in the public sphere, civil rights, and human rights. She holds an international Master of Arts degree from the Oñati International Institute for the Sociology of Law and a Bachelor of Arts degree in philosophy and legal studies from Northwestern University in Evanston, Illinois.

Susan Edwards is an activist engaged in a range of issues including Stop the War Coalition and the rights of the Palestinian people. She is a member of Amnesty International, Peace and Progress and the Bar Human Rights Group. She is actively involved in women's rights, especially domestic violence and international women's human rights. She has a BA, MA, PhD and LLM and teaches law at the University of Buckingham where she is also Professor of Law, Dean and Head of the Law School. She has published in the area of women's rights and women's issues, family law and criminal law. She is a practising barrister, a Door Tenant at Clarendon Chambers, Temple, London, and also a Member of the Expert Witness Institute.

Halleh Ghorashi holds the Chair in Management of Diversity and Integration at the Department of Culture, Organization and Management at the VU University Amsterdam, the Netherlands. She received her PhD in 2001 from the University of Nijmegen and is the author of *Ways to Survive, Battles to Win: Iranian Women Exiles in the Netherlands and the US* (Nova Science Publishers, 2003). She has several publications on topics such as identity, diasporic positioning, cultural diversity and emancipation issues both inside and outside the organizations. As an active participant in the Dutch public debates on diversity and integration she has received several awards.

Eric Heinze (Maîtrise Paris, JD Harvard, PhD Leiden) is Professor of Law at Queen Mary University, London. His books include *The Logic of Constitutional Rights* (2005); *The Logic of Liberal Rights* (2003); *The Logic of Equality* (2003); *Sexual Orientation: A Human Right* (1995) (Russian translation 2004), and *Of Innocence and Autonomy: Children, Sex and Human Rights* (2000). Book chapters appear in *Religious Pluralism and Human Rights* (2006) and *Minority and Group Rights* (1999). Recent articles appear in *Oxford Journal of Legal Studies*, *Modern Law Review*, *Harvard Human Rights Journal*, *Ratio Juris*, *Legal Studies*, *Michigan Journal of International Law*, *National Black Law Journal*, *Journal of Social & Legal Studies*, *Law & Critique* and *Law & Literature*.

Niilo Jääskinen is currently Advocate General at the European Court of Justice. Earlier in his career he worked as councillor of legislation and head of the European Law Section at the Finnish Ministry of Justice, as councillor of the Grand Committee of the Finnish Parliament and as justice at the Supreme Administrative Court of Finland. He was responsible for legal and institutional issues at the time of the negotiations for the accession of Finland to the European Union. His thesis for his doctorate of law discussed legal-theoretical questions relating to the Europeanization of law.

Paul Kearns read Jurisprudence at Jesus College, Oxford, where he was an Open Meyricke Exhibitioner from 1981 to 1984. He was awarded the Sankey Scholarship to assist him in being called to the Bar in 1985. From 1985 to 1986 he read for a Master's degree in Public International Law and Legal Philosophy at Jesus College, Cambridge; this completed, he read a for a doctorate at the European University Institute in Florence. A modification of his successful doctoral thesis was published by Hart under the title *The Legal Concept of Art*. From 1994 to 2000 he was a lecturer in law at the Faculty of Law, University of Leicester. In 2000 he joined Manchester University Law School where he is a senior lecturer. His main interests lie in the fields of human rights, public international law, and law, literature and art.

Emma McClean is a graduate of Trinity College Dublin and University College Cork, Ireland. She recently obtained her PhD from the University of Hull, UK for a thesis entitled 'Human Security in International Law: The Role of the United Nations'. Her thesis was highly commended in the 2007 annual dissertation award of the Academic Council for the United Nations System. In addition to being actively involved in a number of research projects in respect of human security, her current research focuses on the responsibility to protect, the nexus between human rights and security at a global level along with issues of governance, in particular the institutional aspects of implementing human rights norms. Emma currently holds the position of lecturer in law at the Law School, University of Westminster, London.

Daniel Moeckli is Oberassistent in Public Law at the University of Zurich and a Fellow of the University of Nottingham Human Rights Law Centre. His main research interests lie in the areas of constitutional law and human rights law, both international and national. He is the author of *Human Rights and Non-discrimination in the 'War on Terror'* (Oxford University Press, 2008) and co-editor (with Sangeeta Shah and Sandesh Sivakumaran) of *International Human Rights Law* (Oxford University Press, 2010). He has worked for Amnesty International and the Human Rights Institute of the International Bar Association and has trained UN and EU human rights field officers.

Kate Nash is Professor in the Department of Sociology at Goldsmiths College, University of London and Faculty Fellow at the Center for Cultural Sociology, Yale University. She has published widely on human rights, including *The Cultural Politics of Human Rights: Comparing the US and UK* (Cambridge University Press, 2009) and articles in *Sociology*, *The British Journal of Sociology, Economy and Society*, and *Citizenship Studies*. She is author of *Contemporary Political Sociology* (Blackwell, 2000); and co-editor (with Alan Scott) of *The Blackwell Companion to Political Sociology* (2001) and (with Alan Scott and Anna Marie Smith) of *New Critical Writings in Political Sociology* (Ashgate, 2009).

Hanne Petersen is Professor of Legal Cultures (from 2009) at the Centre for Studies of Legal Culture, University of Copenhagen. She was Jean Monnet Fellow from 1993 to 1994 at the EUI, Florence. From 1995 to 1999 she was Professor of Sociology of Law and Jurisprudence at Ilisimatusarfik, University of Greenland; from 2001 to 2006 Professor of Greenlandic Sociology of Law at UoCph; and from 2007 to 2010 she held an adjunct professorship at the University of Tromsø, Norway. She participated in international, Nordic, interdisciplinary research projects on issues concerning gender and law, legal pluralism and legal culture and from 2010 joined an EU project on religious and secular values in Europe.

Harriet Samuels is a senior lecturer at the University of Westminster. She teaches public law and human rights. Her writing and research have focused on feminist theory and human rights. She has co-authored *The Complete Public Law* (Oxford University Press, 2009, with Lisa Webley). She is Director of the Centre for Law, Gender and Sexuality at the University of Westminster.

Joseph Tanega, BA Philosophy Princeton University, MPhil Oxon Social Anthropology, St Antony's College, Oxford, Juris Doctor University of San Diego School of Law, is a Reader in International Financial Law and Course Leader to the LLM Corporate Finance Law, Department of Advanced Legal Studies, School of Law, University of Westminster, London. He was formerly Deputy Attorney General, State of Hawaii, an investment banker with Nomura Securities and Kleinwort Benson Securities, London, and a director of business risk consulting with Ernst & Young, London. He is the author of 23 articles on law, finance, banking and risk management and 16 books on law and finance. His latest book is entitled *Securitisation Law: EU and US Disclosure Regulations* (LexisNexis, 2009).

Max Travers is Senior Lecturer in the School of Sociology and Social Work, University of Tasmania. He qualified as a solicitor before completing a doctorate in sociology at the University of Manchester, UK examining the work of criminal lawyers from an ethnomethodological perspective. Publications include *The Reality of Law* (1997) and *The New Bureaucracy* (2007), a study of quality assurance regulation. He co-edited *An Introduction to Law and Social Theory* (2002) with Reza Banakar and has recently written a textbook, *Understanding Law and Society*, published by Routledge-Cavendish.

Acknowledgements

The editor acknowledges the kind permission of *Retfærd: The Nordic Journal of Law and Justice* to publish material from volume (2008) 3/122 which was originally published as 'Poetic Injustice'. He also acknowledges permission from *National Black Law Journal* to reprint sections from a paper originally published in volume (2008) 20 as 'Truth and Myth in Critical Race Theory and LatCrit: Human Rights and the Ethnocentrism of Anti-Ethnocentrism'.

Introduction: Snapshots of the Rights Discourse

Reza Banakar

We often hear that rights talk pervades politics, law and morality, that rights have never played a more decisive role in the formation of local and global relations, that rights are used more frequently than ever before to debate and resolve social, legal and political disputes, that rights emerge out of attempts to deal with or prevent injustice, and that rights can support strategies of emancipation. At the same time, we are warned that many of the rights we have been taking for granted are being undermined and their existence threatened by forces intent on recasting the domestic and international political order. These attempts to reorganize the political order by reconstructing rights are not, we are told, done in search of justice, but to enhance social control and political domination.[1] The volume at hand consists partly of attempts to examine such assumptions by exploring the role of rights in public political discourse, policy debates and legal decision making.

The collection of chapters presented here is the product of a workshop on rights discourse organized at the International Institute for the Sociology of Law in Oñati in May 2008. The first objective of the workshop was to bring together researchers from various fields to discuss how civil rights and civil liberties had been publicly debated in more recent years and to examine the impact of the rights discourse on the formation of law and politics. The workshop also asked if the events of 9/11 had been, as suggested by some analysts,[2] a watershed moment in the modern history of rights and used to justify a fundamental change of direction in the interpretation and application of certain rights used to debate politically sensitive issues such as multiculturalism, freedom of expression, war, torture and terrorism. How are legal and moral rights used to shape political debates and legal decisions and to justify controversial domestic and international policies? How do various approaches of law, social sciences and philosophy view and conceptualize the recent discourses on rights? These were some of the questions raised prior to the workshop.

The chapters presented in this volume provide snapshots of how rights are used and debated in Western democracies in the beginning of the twenty-first century. In addition, they bring to the fore a number of other issues which were not initially on the agenda of the workshop. For example, in the following pages the separation of positive law, rights, morality and justice is challenged, and it is suggested that whenever we explore the limits and applications of rights in specific social settings, we also become concerned with the possibility of delivering justice. In other words, an engagement with rights can also become an engagement with justice. Another issue concerns the role of law and the state in the global society. In the pages of this volume we

---

1 See, for example, A Dershowitz, *Rights From Wrongs: A Secular Theory of the Origins of Rights* (New York: Perseus, 2004); S Benhabib, *The Rights of Others: Aliens, Residents and Citizens* (Cambridge: Cambridge University Press, 2004); U Baxi, *The Future of Human Rights* (New Delhi: Oxford University Press, 2002); B Goold and L Lazarus (eds), *Security and Human Rights* (Oxford: Hart, 2007); C Douzinas, *Human Rights and Empire: The Political Philosophy of Cosmopolitanism* (London: Routledge-Cavendish, 2007).

2 See, for example, J Strawson (ed.), *Law after Ground Zero* (London: GlassHouse, 2004) and P Sand, *Lawless World: America and Making and Breaking of Global Rules* (London: Allen Lane, 2005).

find a concern with the inability of late modern states to provide adequate protection for individuals and groups who find themselves within their national borders. At the same time, as the role of the state appears to be undergoing a transformation, a new homogenizing and totalizing global order is emerging.[3] Transnational law, with human rights as its vanguard and the harmonization or unification of private international law as its core project, spearheads this new emerging order.[4] Human rights demand, if necessary through 'armed cross-border intervention',[5] that states comply with a standard set of values, which in the first place defines the rights of the individual. To borrow from Costas Douzinas, human rights have become the 'official ideology of the new world order after 1989', and it is 'in the name of human rights, democracy and freedom' that all recent wars and occupations have been wholly or partly carried out.[6] Correspondingly, Eric Hobsbawm refers to the international policies of great powers which 'selectively' (that is, in the Balkans but not in central Africa, in Iraq but not in Saudi Arabia or Pakistan) champion human rights, even though human rights are incidental to their objectives, as 'the imperialism of human rights'.[7] Private international law similarly demands and works towards the harmonization and unification of commercial relations across jurisdictions.[8] This form of transnational law, created and developed outside the institutions of the modern state, is becoming increasingly independent of the nation states,[9] and thus different from traditional international law, which regulates the relationship between states. At the same time, this emerging legal order poses a challenge to the legal pluralism associated with the globalization of law according to which law-making processes take place in multiple centres.[10] The drive towards establishing human rights and democracy and the urge to harmonize and unify commercial laws and practices across jurisdictions do not remove the multiple centres of normativity and their expressions in terms of plural legal orderings. They only indicate the internal contradictions of the new world order, which on the one hand continues to consist of decentralized law-making processes, while on the other is driven forward by incessant homogenizing forces that seek to reorganize the world under one single ideology.

Law is, thus, an integral component of the new world order, parts of which are not only currently under construction in places such as Iraq and Afghanistan, but also in chambers of commerce, mega law firms, the UN, the WTO, etc. The relationship between law and politics is, therefore, being reconsidered and reconstructed in such a way that it challenges law's traditional role in relation to society and the nation state. This, in turn, requires a recasting of the rights that have traditionally underpinned the concepts of Western law and democracy. The emerging global order is not, however, the primary focus of the collection of chapters presented in this volume; rather, it

---

3   Hardt and Negri use the concept of 'empire' to describe this emerging global force. See M Hardt and A Negri, *Empire* (Cambridge, MA: Harvard University Press, 2000).

4   M Goodale, 'Empire of law: Discipline and resistance within the transnational system', *Social and Legal Studies*, 14 (2005), 553–83, at 556.

5   E Hobsbawm, *Globalisation, Democracy and Terrorism* (London: Abacus, 2007), at 7.

6   Douzinas, above, n. 1, at 12.

7   Hobsbawm, above, n. 5, at 7.

8   This was already an established subject of debate in law and socio-legal research in the 1990s. See, for example, V Gessner and AC Budak (eds), *Emerging Legal Certainties: Empirical Studies on the Globalisation of the Law* (Aldershot: Ashgate, 1998); B de S Santos, 'Globalisation, nation-states and the legal field', in *Towards a New Common Sense: Law, Science and Politics in the Paradigmatic Transition* (London: Routledge, 1995); Y Dezalay and BG Garth, *Dealing in Virtue* (Chicago: University of Chicago, 1996); G Teubner, *Global Law Without a State* (Aldershot: Dartmouth, 1997).

9   Goodale, above, n. 4.

10   R Cotterrell, 'Spectres of transnationalism: Changing terrains of sociology of law', *Journal of Law and Society*, 4/36 (2009); G Teubner, *Global Law Without a State* (Aldershot: Dartmouth, 1997).

is the inevitable backdrop against which domestically organized efforts to employ and reconstruct rights unfold. Expressed differently, in the following we are interested in how rights are employed as part of the process that globalizes Western societies from within.

Contested Rights

Each chapter in this volume deals either with rights employed to challenge the state of affairs and demand changes in the way society is de facto organized, or with the legal and political strategies employed to curb the existing rights and duties utilized to shape and reshape existing relationships. It is, for example, about artists who employ their freedom of expression to astonish and shock their audience, and about those who mobilize the public's sense of morality and decency to curb the artists' rights of expression. It is about young British-born Muslim women, who use their freedom of religion and thought to return to the hijab, arguably, to reclaim their identity and autonomy, and about those who challenge them by banning the wearing of 'ostentatious' religious symbols in public places. The first group employs the existing rights and duties to support a claim, while the second group challenges the existing rights and duties in order to introduce new rights and corresponding duties. The former is used when the established order fails to deliver justice, that is, when individuals or groups rightly or wrongly feel that they have been unjustly treated and demand their rights. The latter is employed when practices and strategies of defiance emerge in opposition to established rights in an attempt to introduce a new order out of which a different sense of justice could flow.

It is equally important to consider what this collection is not about. The primary focus of the chapters that make up this volume is not on the role or implications of rights in our moral thinking and political history. In this sense, the discussions that follow are not in the first place concerned with the 'objective' aspects of rights that express a universal abstract proposition about the state of affairs, for example, all citizens have the right to freedom of expression. Instead, they are concerned with the 'subjective' sides of rights, which bring into focus the *relationship* between the individual or a social group and a particular state of affairs, for example, how the individual's rights to freedom of expression are exercised within a given legal and socio-political context.[11] Expressed differently, the emphasis of the collection is not on the moral content of rights as such, but on how rights are employed by various actors and interest groups as a strategic tool to create and recreate social relations and structures over time. In addition, the collection is substantively limited, addressing only a handful of issues related to multiculturalism, immigration, religion, terrorism, art and finance in Western democracies, leaving out a very large number of important areas such as environment, sexuality, development and issues such as the right to life. Notwithstanding this substantive limitation, we hope that the collection provides a series of interrelated and complementary snapshots of rights discourse in the beginning of the twenty-first century.

It should also be noted that 'late modernity' is employed here narrowly to explore how the spread of global market economy transforms the traditional social structures and institutions of modernity. This transformation brings about higher levels of socio-cultural diversity and uncertainty, but does not necessarily dissolve the apparently 'solid' structures of all social institutions.

---

11   For a discussion on the objective and subjective aspects of rights, see WA Edmundson, *An Introduction to Rights* (Cambridge: Cambridge University Press, 2004).

The Layout and Chapters

The collection of chapters presented in this volume may be grouped in several ways. Besides being concerned with how the notion of rights is applied and developed in public political discourses, many chapters either overlap in respect to their substantive focus or are linked through their theoretical concerns. These chapters could have been grouped according to, for example, their concern with culture, religion, gender, freedom of expression, security and terrorism. Irrespective of which type of classification we might choose to structure the collection, different chapters will inevitably overlap in more than one respect, indicating their embeddedness in a broader ongoing discourse on the relationship between law, morality and justice. The current grouping that the editor has opted for is a sociological one reflecting how rights *operate* in public political and legal discourses, that is, how they are *applied* by various individuals and groups as part of an ongoing dynamic socio-legal process to realize different aims. The keywords used to group the chapters into four sections are: critique, challenge, strategy and reconstruction.

The collection starts with five chapters that critically examine rights not only as part of the legal and political discourse, but also in the context of social theory. The second section, also containing five chapters, distinguishes itself from the first section by examining how rights are used to challenge and alter the state of affairs. The third section also deals with how rights are used in social and legal settings, but the three chapters placed in this section share the practising lawyer's concern with using rights as a legal strategy. The collection ends with four chapters that explore the reconstruction of rights.

The first chapter, written by the editor, aims to provide a preliminary theoretical framework for situating the various debates and issues in this volume. This chapter may be read at the outset as an extended introduction, which situates the debates in a broader theoretical perspective. It can equally be read at the end as the editor's reflection on how the disparate concerns of various chapters may be brought together under the theoretical umbrella of late modernity, which necessitates a re-examination of the concepts of law, society and the state. This chapter starts by introducing the notion of late modernity as the second stage in the development of modernity when many relationships – and their corresponding rights and duties, which are traditionally defined and regulated by the nation state – are undermined by the intensification and expansion of economic, political and cultural interrelationships across the globe. It will then explore how the intensification of interrelationships, a growing interdependence of people living in different parts of the world, and the changing character of the nation state influence and shape the ways in which rights are debated and employed. The central argument of this chapter is that, under late modernity and owing to the increased functional differentiation of social systems, moral concerns are increasingly marginalized and replaced by complex regulatory regimes, codes of ethics and a rights discourse that is drained from moral considerations and commitments. This chapter also hopes to show that the study of rights discourse can provide a standpoint from which to view how the relationship between law, justice, the state and morality is reconsidered and reconstructed under late modernity.

The Critiques

In Chapter 2, Max Travers presents his sociological critique of the concept of rights. Travers takes a debate between two prominent sociologists, Bryan Turner and Malcolm Waters, as his point of departure. Although Turner and Waters probably share the same general liberal views of political events and, more importantly for our purposes here, also agree that rights are necessary elements in the formation of modern societies, they nonetheless disagree on what sociology can say about rights. For Turner, the sociological scepticism of rights is no longer valid in the global world-system we find ourselves in today. The study of socio-political life in the global context (or within the 'world-system'), where people and states are becoming increasingly interdependent, requires concepts capable of transcending the socio-cultural and legal boundaries of national sovereign states; and 'universal rights' provide exactly one such concept. The fact that we are living in 'one-world' – as fragmented, diversified and antagonistic as this world might be – provides the sociological condition for 'removing the scepticism about a common ontology as a basis for human rights in the absence of a common law tradition'.[12] In contrast, Waters understands the nature of rights as socially constructed, arguing that an ontological theory of rights cannot possess any explanatory value for sociologists.

This is as much a debate concerning the ontology of rights as a debate on the limits of sociological enquiry. Is sociology capable of producing empirically-based value judgments, for example determining if and when freedom of speech trumps hate speech, or should it restrict its analysis to providing empirically-grounded descriptions of the social world, that is, how freedom of speech is de facto used in various cases to trump hate speech? Can empirically-informed sociological analyses determine if or when detention without trial is justifiable, or does it have to limit itself to describing the changing nature, causes and extent of detention without trial? Similar concerns with the relationship between the analytical, descriptive and evaluative aspects of socio-legal research have been raised since the 1960s. Some sociologists, such as Donald Black, have maintained that 'value judgments cannot be discovered in the empirical world' and are therefore irrelevant to the sociology of law.[13] Others, such as Philippe Nonet, have responded that law can benefit from the social scientific studies of the world it tries to govern, and employ empirical knowledge to improve its normative judgments.[14] Although values cannot be generated out of facts alone, accurate accounts of the relationship between law and society can lay the basis for addressing normative issues arising out of the law's operations in society.

Following Waters, Travers appears to be leaving the examination of the normative content of rights to moral and political philosophy. The next chapter by Radha D'Souza challenges this suggestion indirectly by criticizing the rights discourse for its political and philosophical poverty. The concept of rights, which played a decisive role in the seventeenth and eighteenth centuries, transforming European societies from feudal systems to modern capitalist economies, has, according to D'Souza, lost its transformative emancipatory momentum and become meaningless to the vast majority of the world's population. For D'Souza, rights for their own sake have no value; what counts in the final analysis is human emancipation, with or without rights. In other words, rights become significant once they articulate a realistic and plausible strategy for freedom and human emancipation.

The impotence of rights, according to D'Souza, partly indicates the poverty of philosophy in the current times and partly reveals the challenges of poverty in the contemporary world. The impasse of rights discourse, she writes, 'is felt most in the Third World where for the vast majority of the people dislocation and destitution is a regular feature of life'. Displacement is an ongoing phenomenon that parallels colonial history and continues through 'globalisation'. It illustrates how rights claims are used to defend and alter the status quo in places such as Palestine, where rights are used in relation to property and place by claimants – those who have it and those who desire

---

12   B Turner, 'Outline of a theory of human rights', *Sociology*, 27 (1993), at 499.

13   D Black, 'The boundaries of legal sociology', *Yale Law Journal*, 81 (1972), 1086–1092, at 1092.

14   P Nonet, 'For jurisprudential sociology', in WM Evan (ed.), *The Sociology of Law: A Social-Structural Perspective* (New York: Free Press, 1980), at 58.

it. However, the latecomer or the new claimant cannot claim on the basis of existing rights. He or she must challenge the validity of existing rights in order to replace them with new norms of property, which tilt the balance in favour of the newcomers. The displaced persons, groups and nations protest against displacement, against the new rights introduced by the usurper, ultimately asking and wondering 'Why *me*?' The rights discourse, writes D'Souza, provides no answers to the question of why the latecomer's claim trumps the existing claims. As it regards the law, D'Souza argues, it privileges the new norms to the old ones when the newcomer succeeds in evicting those who had prior entitlements and, thus, appropriating their property.

In Chapter 4, Kate Nash narrows down the discussion to human rights and the way the rights of citizens in particular are realized, explaining that 'the enjoyment of rights is never simply a matter of legal entitlement; it also depends on social structures through which power, material resources, and meanings are created and circulated'. Nash starts with a warning about the dangers associated with pursuing a human rights strategy and ends with the intriguing insight that 'human rights are dangerous'. While Travers sees rights from without, using sociological theory and method to describe and analyse rights as social facts, and D'Souza engages directly with their normative core, Nash's approach appears to suggest the possibility of bringing together the normative and descriptive components of rights in one single approach.

Following Arendt's critique of human rights in *The Origins of Totalitarianism*,[15] Nash argues that human rights are untenable 'because they are based on the abstraction of humanity rather than any possibility of participation, whether democratic or revolutionary'. Moreover, these are the 'inalienable' rights, which, as Arendt pointed out, are in practice 'enjoyed by citizens of most prosperous and civilised countries'.[16] By insisting on legally extending the rights of the citizens of prosperous states to all humans irrespective of race, creed, culture, nationality, country of residence and socio-economic situation, the well-meaning supporters of human rights create five categories of citizens: super-citizens, marginal citizens, quasi-citizens, sub-citizens, and un-citizens.

In conclusion, Nash advocates a form of cosmopolitan law, which I understand as a global form of humanitarian law that 'can only advance as a result of political mobilization' and by building support for human rights within political communities. She also argues that there appears to be nothing in the logic of state formation to prevent cosmopolitan law. Nash can, arguably, be challenged on this point. For cosmopolitan law to be truly cosmopolitan, it must sidestep the conventional theory of sources of law, challenge traditional state sovereignty and become independent of the existing hierarchy of legal institutions for its interpretation and application.[17] If traditional international law is primarily about law regulating the relationship between the states, then cosmopolitan law is a legal order above the states and concerned with the fate of the individual and humanity as a whole. Thus, cosmopolitan law cannot be constructed as a state-centred legal regime, and, as such (as we shall see futher on in Chapter 14), it challenges the traditional forms of state.

The scope of discussions is further narrowed down in the next chapter by Paul Kearns, who provides 'the first detailed critique of artists' human rights *simpliciter*'. This chapter is neither sociological in the sense that Max Travers was proposing, nor normative in a philosophical manner. Instead, it carefully maps law at the national, European and international levels, portraying a troubled image of the relationship between law and the rights of artists to freedom of artistic expression. Law and lawyers usually pay little attention to the legal status of arts in general or

---

15   H Arendt, *The Origins of Totalitarianism* (San Diego: Harvest Books, 1968).
16   Arendt, ibid., at 279.
17   P Eleftheriadis, 'Cosmopolitan law', *European Law Journal*, 9 (2003), 241–63.

the human rights of artists in particular. This is partly owing to the unwillingness of many artists to make legal claims or to get involved in litigation or other legal processes and partly a result of the ambiguity of modern art; that it is difficult to produce a universally valid definition of what art amounts to and how it may be identified legally. These two reasons do not, however, on their own provide an adequate explanation to the apparent disinterest of law and legal scholarship in the rights of artists. As Bill Bowring will explain in Chapter 13, 'terrorism' too is a multifaceted concept that is difficult to define legally. Yet, the difficulties associated with producing a definition of 'terrorism' have hardly hindered various governments in criminalizing it through anti-terrorism legislations. Cases from the UK, France and the US, discussed in this chapter, show that whenever artistic freedom and other legal rights, such as constitutional rights concerned with upholding morality, are brought face to face, artistic creativity is branded as seditious and, thus, illegal. Artists are often viewed as people who are 'in some ways conventionally immoral or simply unacceptable non-conformists'. As such, they are potentially dangerous to the stability of the society in which they live. That is perhaps why none of the national, European or international laws and conventions fully recognize or protect their autonomy of artistic expression and their rights of freedom of expression.

In Chapter 6, Eric Heinze questions some of the work produced by Critical Race Theorists and LatCrits for spreading a misleading and one-sided discourse about American law and the American civil liberties tradition. These critical scholars, according to Heinze, are right in criticizing the old myths of white America, which '[glorify] democracy where African-Americans, Latinos, Native Americans, Asians, women, sexual minorities and other outsiders have faced brutality and exclusion'. They are, however, disingenuous in their attempts to develop and spread their own 'fairytales', which are also based on simplification, myth-making and the exclusion of outsiders. On the one hand, 'they reject abstract, decontextualized or formalist interpretations of US law, insisting on a method of legal realism that would look to the brutal realities behind empty promises of "liberty" or "equal protection"'. On the other hand, 'in an effort to forge political alliances against US law [...] they then proceed to adopt wholly abstract, decontextualized and formalist readings of international norms'. As a result, they abandon their legal realism and instead end up supporting 'the empty promise of international norms'.

Critical theorists are known for their rights scepticism, which is rooted in their realist and social-scientific approach, discussed by Max Travers in Chapter 2. They are generally sceptical of dominant legal claims of neutrality and objectivity and insist on contextualized readings of law in its socio-political and historical contexts. It is perhaps not surprising that some Critical Race Theorists and LatCrits dismiss the American civil libertarian defence of free speech and argue that the failure of American law to ban and punish hate speech serves only to strengthen the political position of the privileged groups and enhance the liberty of the traditionally dominant sections of American society, that is, mainly middle-class white Americans, who are not the target of racist discourse and harm. If American law, in general, and the American civil liberties tradition, in particular, are as defective as these critical scholars appear to be suggesting, then why is it, asks Heinze, that Critical Race Theorists and LatCrits need to betray their own principles in order to prove their point? Heinze's sobering message is that 'in an age of growing internationalization of human rights, critical theorists must approach international norms with the same rigour they have applied to the bleak histories and manipulative formalisms of US law'.

The Challenges

In the next chapter, Susan Edwards discusses the debate on the rights of Muslim women to wear the veil, the jilbab and the headscarf against the background of a number of cases such as *Sahin*[18] and *Begum*.[19] In *Sahin v. Turkey* (2005),[20] the court ruled that a university student should not be permitted to wear the headscarf to attend university lectures.[21] Similarly, in *R (Begum) v. Headteacher and Governors of Denbigh High School*, Shabina Begum, a pupil at Denbigh High School, was not permitted to wear in school a specific variation of the school uniform – a long-sleeved, ankle-length, loose-fitting dress known as a jilbab – in manifestation of her religious belief. The question for the court was whether she had been denied her religious rights. The House of Lords, by a 3/2 majority, held that there had been no interference with the right to hold a religious belief or the right to manifest belief.

These legal decisions are embedded in the complex relationships that form and inform the debate on the hijab in the West, a context permeated by postcolonial assumptions about the 'other', the politics of fear spread through anti-terrorism measures introduced after 9/11 and Islamophobia. The Western rights discourse on the headscarf and the hijab, which transforms attire into a site for political struggle and resistance, is carried out in a climate of hostility against people regarded as Muslims. It is, thus, motivated by much more than determining the rights of Muslim women living in the West or liberating them from the yoke of tradition and the violence of patriarchy. Those Muslim women, who for various reasons wear the hijab or the headscarf in contemporary Britain and elsewhere in the Western world, serve as the obvious targets of the degrading discourse that depicts them as ignorant, sexualized, submissive, oppressed, dominated by traditional patriarchy and in need of emancipation. However, it is also their men and broader cultural identity as a group which are the targets of this instrument of social control.

Edwards explains that Muslim women wear the veil for a number of different religious, cultural and political reasons. They could, indeed, be wearing the hijab as a symbolic gesture of resistance to the forces of occupation, as in the Algerian war of independence, or, as it is arguably the case with some British-born Muslim women, as a gesture of defiance against the forces of assimilation (as in the UK), which deny their autonomy and degrade their cultural identity. As El Gundi pointed out, 'emancipation can be expressed by wearing the veil or by removing it. It can be secular or religious. It can represent tradition or resistance'.[22]

In her chapter, Samia Bano returns to the same concerns as discussed by Edwards regarding the feminist critique of Muslim female subject, the debate on the right to choose or reject wearing the veil, the significance of the socio-cultural conditions of Muslim women living in the West, and the contested issue of their sexual equality, autonomy, emancipation and agency. Bano, too, points out the 'hypervisibility of the women's bodies, which has led to extraordinary measures of stigmatization, surveillance and control'. However, while Edwards' approach is couched in the critical language of postcolonial studies, Bano discusses these issues from an angle sensitive to the dilemma of multiculturalism. How can we create a *universal* policy and a body of laws that recognize and accommodate rights claims to difference and equality and are at the same time

---

18   *Sahin v. Turkey* (2005) 41 EHRR 8.

19   *R (on the application of Begum (by her litigation friend, Rahman)) (Respondent) v. Headteacher and Governors of Denbigh High School (Appellants)* [2006] 2 All ER 487.

20   *Leyla Sahin v. Turkey* (Application no. 44774/98), Judgment of 29.6.2004 EHRR 8 [2004]; 10 BHRC 590 [2006] ELR 73.

21   See above, at 140.

22   F El Gundi, *Veil: Modesty, Privacy and Resistance* (Berg: Oxford, 1999), at 172.

rooted in the *particular* value systems of social groups and communities? This normative question cannot be answered in reference to the empirical reality of multiculturalism, that is, how gender, cultural, religious and ethnic relationships are de facto constructed in contemporary Britain. Yet, without an understanding of how the rights discourse is conducted on issues of multiculturalism – a discourse permeated by forms of power and dominance – we cannot possibly produce a practical solution to the dilemma posed by multiculturalism. This brings us back to the question we started with in section one: does sociology of law need a theory of rights and justice?

Chapter 9, by Halleh Ghorashi, focuses on the rights of migrants in the Netherlands and paints a disturbing picture of the growing ethno-cultural division in Dutch society following the events of 9/11. The so-called 'soft approach' of the 1980s, which emphasized the socio-economic integration of migrants, has given way to a 'tough approach' towards immigrants and their cultures, which demands cultural assimilation. According to this new approach, migrants' obligations, rather than their rights, define their relationship with Dutch society. Multicultural policies, which celebrated the right to preserve various cultural identities and languages, the right to be different and respected, have given way to demands that 'they' must learn Dutch and Dutch history, adopt Dutch customs and, in short, internalize the Dutch cultural identity.

Behind attempts to replace the rights of migrants with their obligation to Dutch culture and society lie an evil circle of fear, cultural racism, mistrust and insecurity. Since 9/11 and the subsequent terrorist attacks in Europe, not to mention the assassinations of Pim Fortuyn and Theo Van Gogh in Holland, the relationship between immigrant communities and mainstream Dutch society has rapidly deteriorated. Migrants have increasingly come to be perceived and depicted in the public political discourse as a single homogeneous cultural group. This culturalist thinking feeds into the climate of fear while, at the same time, its simplistic and sweeping generalizations gain currency and are publicly justified by the perception of the Islamic threat and the feeling of insecurity and fear in society. This growing sense of fear of the culture of migrants provides a basis for certain political groups (some, but not all, belonging to the far right of the political spectrum) to openly air sentiments and viewpoints that only a few years ago would have been dismissed as racist. This coalition of far right, anti-immigrant and populist political groups demands that migrants assimilate themselves into Dutch society. Assimilation, as propagated by these political groups, is a socio-culturally problematic and ethically questionable process, which often amounts to denouncing one's own cultural values and identity in the sense discussed in Chapter 7 by Edwards. The pressure to assimilate, in turn, increases the sense of political and cultural insecurity among migrant groups, who already find themselves in a socio-culturally vulnerable position, compelling them to regroup within their ethnic enclaves in order to defend their cultural identity and autonomy. This, however, provides one more reason to criticize the migrants as isolationists and their cultures as a growing ground for forms of deviance. This is the internal discourse of the majority about the 'other', about Muslims who are threatening the freedom and liberties of the Dutch people. The point made by Ghorashi is that it is a debate *about* and not *with* the Muslims living in the Netherlands; a debate that marginalizes their right to a democratic space – the space that allows 'otherness' and the right to be different. Ghorashi's message is that we need to challenge the dominance of the culturalist discourse wherever it occurs by using two interrelated methods that allow space for difference: first, by protecting the right to cultural difference and, second, by safeguarding the right to preserve one's own culture. The space for cultural recognition seems to be an essential precondition for individuals to feel secure enough to experiment with their culture and to initiate new connections with other cultures.

Chapter 10, by Sarah Dreier, is based on her master's dissertation (*Tesina*) written at the International Institute for the Sociology of Law (IISL). This chapter examines the debate that initially started in Denmark with the publication of 12 cartoons of the Prophet Muhammad by the daily newspaper *Jyllands-Posten* in September 2005, but soon spread to other parts of the world. In some ways the Danish cartoon incident is reminiscent of the Rushdie affair 15 years earlier, when the issues concerning the freedom of expression were challenged by some Muslims who saw the publication of *The Satanic Verses* as an affront to their religious beliefs. The Danish cartoons presented Islam as a violent and sexist religion and Muslim women as inferior and submissive. One of the cartoons depicted Muhammad with an ignited bomb in place of a turban, linking the Prophet to terrorism. *Jyllands-Posten* commissioned and published these cartoons for two reasons: first, to challenge what Flemming Rose, the newspaper's cultural editor, regarded as the tendency of mainstream media to self-censorship on issues related to Islam and Muslims from the fear of Muslim backlash; and, second, to force to the surface the tension between Islam and Western democracy. The publication of the cartoons was, thus, part of a carefully orchestrated, but politically risky and morally controversial, strategy to upset devout Muslims in order to provoke a public debate on the relationship between Islam and democracy. This was, however, not an attempt to have a 'dialogue' or a critical reflection on the issues involved. The Muslim sentiments were denounced from the outset by depicting Muhammad as a terrorist, while Islam was treated as one single monolithic cultural and racial entity.

Dreier's chapter focuses on the reception of the cartoons by the newspapers in the US. She argues that, although the Danish cartoon controversy was started and presented in terms of rights, the final decision of the US newspapers, many of which decided to report the debate but abstained from publishing the images, had little to do with their conception of the freedom of expression. It was, instead, motivated by the logic of the field of journalism in the US. According to this logic, a decision to publish an item is made on the basis of whether it is newsworthy and socio-politically important. By employing concepts and ideas from the reflexive sociology of Pierre Bourdieu, Dreier analyses and explains the decisions made by the majority of the US newspapers not to publish the cartoons in terms of the logic, the rules and the taken-for-granted values and assumptions that create journalism as a social field separate from other fields of activity such as politics, religion or education. The editors of the newspapers did not enter this controversy, writes Dreier, with a neutral mind and were not driven solely by a conception of freedom of expression; in fact, concerns with the freedom of expression might have been low on their list of priorities. Instead, they entered and dealt with the cartoons in accordance with the logic of the field of journalism that brought together the issues of newsworthiness and the responsibility to report events of importance. This responsibility, which is exercised in accordance with the US newspaper editors' general conception of appropriate reporting, amounted in this case to treating other people's religious sensibilities with a degree of sensitivity and respect.

This is an example of how rights are often explored sociologically as social facts and by focusing on the social mechanisms that mediate them, rather than as normative constructs in need of evaluation and assessment. The strength of the sociological approach lies in demonstrating, as Dreier accomplishes in her chapter, that the normative analysis of rights in itself can never offer a full understanding of why people involved in a dispute, such as the cartoon controversy, decide to act in a particular way. Rights become one of a number of factors employed in the struggles for 'stakes', which create any particular field of action. The issue that remains unanswered in this chapter is why the actors in such disputes nonetheless engage in rights talk and emphasize the concept of right. Is it simply because rights talk is the legitimate and politically correct form of argumentation within a liberal democratic polity, or is it because rights emphasize and make claims to correctness on the basis of one single universal standard, which is equally applicable to the claimant's and other people's actions? Once again, we are reminded of the sociological challenge of bringing together aspects of the rights discourse, one being empirically and the other normatively grounded.

In Chapter 11, Reza Banakar uses the cases of Mohammed Atif Siddique and Samina Malik, who became convicted on terrorism charges as starting points for exploring a range of issues related to the way rights discourse is employed in the UK to neutralize the threat of Islamic extremism through law. Malik was a 23-year-old British-born Muslim, who worked as a shop assistant at Heathrow Airport. The police arrested her at home, where she lived with her parents and siblings, in October 2006 after searching her room and finding her in possession of records likely to be used for terrorist purposes. This material, which had been downloaded and partly deleted, became the basis for the prosecution's prima facie evidence.[23] On the basis of this evidence, Malik was charged with two counts of offences contrary to sections 57 and 58 of the Terrorism Act 2000. At the Old Bailey, the court heard that Malik had posted poems on extremist websites under the screen name 'Lyrical Terrorist', 'praising Bin Laden, supporting martyrdom and discussing beheading'.[24] In addition, she had written on the back of a WHSmith receipt, 'The desire within me increases every day to go for martyrdom.'[25] She told the court that her poems were 'meaningless' and she had used the nickname 'Lyrical Terrorist' because she thought that it sounded 'cool'.[26] She was found guilty by the jury on one count of possessing material that could be used for terrorist activities, and sentenced by the court to a one and a half year suspended prison sentence. On 17 June 2008 the Court of Appeal quashed Malik's conviction after the Crown conceded that it was unsafe.[27]

Banakar argues that this case represents a general approach for dealing with internal ethno-cultural conflicts in British society, which are brought about as a result of the unresolved moral issues regarding Britain's foreign policy in general and its involvement in the Iraq war in particular. The law is used to limit the rights of British-born Muslims, to overlook their experience of living in what they consider as an Islamophobic environment and to dismiss their points of views as extremist ideology in service of Islamic terrorism. Banakar also points out that the general policy underpinning the legal regulation directed at the Muslim population in Britain is essentially informed by what David Garland called 'the culture of control', denoting the rise of punitiveness in late modern society and its corresponding change of policy from the ideology of rehabilitation and reforming of offenders to managing them as a source of risk.

The Strategies

The next two chapters deal with the problematic relationship between the 'the war on terror' and the rule of law illustrating how the discourse on rights is conducted at the level of international law and community, and how legal instruments such as 'terrorist lists' and legal spaces such as Guantánamo Bay are constructed beyond the rule of law. In Chapter 12, Daniel Moeckli takes issue with both liberal and critical scholars, arguing, firstly, that the problem with counter-terrorism measures devised to conduct the 'war on terror' does not lie in their being based on 'the state of exception', as described by Carl Schmitt. Secondly, Moeckli means that such constructs as

---

23   *R v. Malik* [2008] All ER (D) 201 (Jun).

24   *BBC News*, 8 November 2007.

25   *The Sun*, 8 November 2007.

26   *The Independent*, 11 November 2007.

27   *R v. Malik* [2008] All ER (D) 201 (Jun). I have discussed this case in some detail in 'Poetic Injustice: A Case Study of the UK's Anti-Terrorism Legislation', *Retfærd: The Nordic Journal of Law and Justice*, 3/112 (2008), 69–90.

Guantánamo Bay, which are administered by strict rules and regulations, can nonetheless render themselves susceptible to an internal legal critique by evoking the 'power-restraining' qualities of the rule of law. Guantánamo might be, as pointed out by various observers, 'full to the brim with rules and regulations', but it is not a place run according to the rule of law. In fact, one of the points made in this chapter is that precisely because the 'war on terror' is conducted through legal measures, its claim to legality renders its architects, to borrow a term from EP Thompson, 'prisoners of their own rhetoric'.[28]

Moeckli admits that the law is already implicated in human rights abuses and shows that detention without trial, far from representing an exceptional legal instrument in the US and UK, has a long history. Nonetheless, he proposes a strategy based on a more rigorous adherence to the rule of law as a means of ensuring the generality of the law, which utilizes the claims of legality of 'the war on terror' to challenge it on the procedural level. Moeckli's argument is that aspects of the rule of law as equality before the law may be effectively employed in harnessing the draconian measures introduced to prevent the threat of terrorism. Critical scholars might dismiss this stance by arguing that the rule of the law is a doctrine belonging to the same legal order already implicated in human rights abuses and warn us about being drawn into, and distracted by, litigation. If the rule of law could not prevent the construction of legal spaces such as Guantánamo to begin with, the critics would say, why should we trust it to remedy the wrongs, or prevent similar constructions and abuses from happening in future? However, Moeckli points out that the critics of the rule of law conduct their discourse at a theoretical level. Irrespective of whether they have a theoretically valid argument or not, the fact remains that all legal avenues open to a human rights lawyer need to be exhausted in order to protect the innocent people who end up at the receiving end of anti-terrorism measures.

In Chapter 13, Bill Bowring asks if 'the war on terror' constitutes a norm-free zone. In resolutions 1368 (of 12 September 2001) and 1373 (of 28 September 2001), adopted after 9/11, the UN Security Council condemned terrorism and urged states to combat it, but made no attempt to define what the term 'terrorism' entailed. This failure to produce a definition potentially legitimized the arbitrary actions of certain states against individuals and groups who opposed the authority of these states or threatened their interests. Expressed differently, the absence of an internationally valid definition of terrorism allowed the fight against terrorism to be conducted on terms decided by individual states. This freedom to combat terrorism was, in effect, realized by suspending the rule of law, that is, at the expense of safeguarding due process and the human rights of individuals and groups that became the target of the states' anti-terrorism measures.

As part of their anti-terrorism policy, many countries, including the UK and the US, and international organizations such as the UN and the EU, drew up their own 'terrorist lists' of organizations and individuals, which were subsequently subjected to restrictive measures such as asset freezing. Using case law of the European Court of Justice and the European Court of Human Rights, Bowring brings into sharp focus the gross violations of fundamental human rights that resulted from the operation of these 'terrorist lists'. Bowring shows that a person or a group designated as 'terrorist' loses the procedural rights that are not only fundamental human rights in themselves, but also provide the best protection against the arbitrary actions of the state. According to Bowring, 'the designation of a person or an organisation as "terrorist" opens up a chasm in the rule of law, a space defined by the absence of the procedural rights'. More importantly, Bowring argues that international organizations such as the UN, which is regarded as the bulwark against human rights violations, are influenced by the dominant states' interests.

---

28   EP Thompson, *Whigs and Hunters: The Origin of the Black Act* (London: Penguin Books, 1990), at 263.

In the next chapter, Emma McClean discusses the emergence of the idea of 'human security' as a post-Cold War humanitarian policy agenda aimed at promoting a people-centred conception of security. Human security attempts to go beyond the traditional understanding of security in terms of external military threats directed at nation states, and introduces into international law and politics an individual-centred understanding of the concept. The rationale behind the notion of human security is that 'states cannot be secured for long unless their citizens are secure'. More importantly, in order to effectively address many of the insecurities which threaten people in different parts of the world today, we need to eliminate their underlying causes, rather than reacting to their symptoms. The idea of human security, thus, responds to the shortcomings of the Westphalian state-centred conception of security by proposing an individual-centred approach capable of protecting citizens from a wide range of threats and harm – from fear, famine, ethnic conflicts and environmental threats to global terrorism.

For our purposes in this volume, human security represents a normative shift in the international landscape that has not emerged out of the actual legal and political practices of ordinary people, or the majority of states for that matter, but introduced from above by an international elite in response to such needs that are no longer satisfied by nation states. The question is, ultimately, whether human security as a social and political construct, which challenges the entrenched interests of sovereign states at the international level, can trickle down the structures of international organizations and penetrate the legal and policy practices of, for example, the Security Council. The rise of the discourse on human security must also be considered in the context of the changing role of the nation state.

The Reconstruction

In Chapter 15, Joxerramon Bengoetxea and Niilo Jääskinen examine how the rights of individuals and their legal positions are regulated by EU directives, which, in contrast to regulations, are not directly applicable to the legal order of the member states. In order for directives, which are not addressed to individuals but to the member states, to function adequately and effectively, they need to combine and coordinate the application of the supranational European Community legal order and those of the member states where the directive is transposed or transformed into legislative instruments typical of those legal orders. This coordination between legislators or regulators and the member states is necessary if the ultimate addressees of the norms contained therein are to enjoy their rights in a uniform way across the EU and govern their behaviour according to common, harmonized standards. The essence of such coordination consists in reaching a common view on harmonization through the 'Community method' at the supranational level, by adopting uniform norms and requiring the member states to ensure that their legal orders have incorporated those norms.

The main focus of this chapter is on the doctrine or principle of direct effect, which, together with other legal techniques, make it possible for individuals to benefit, under certain conditions, from the rights contemplated in non-transposed directives. This is a significant development that, once again, marks the changing role of the state, which can be best described in terms of the changing notions of law, regulation and society. According to Bengoetxea and Jääskinen, under certain circumstances, member states' jurisdictions are empowered to enforce certain rights in spite of the legislative inaction of their state. This raises a number of fundamental political and constitutional issues concerning the separation of powers, the federal distribution of competences and the powers recognised to judges.

Joseph Tanega's chapter explores the investor's rights to disclosure as a fundamental right underlying the entire structure of US and EU Securities Regulation by focusing on asset-backed securities and securitization, which are generally regarded as 'the catastrophic epicentre of the global credit crisis'. Tanega shows how investors' rights to asset-backed securities appear in a set of complex securities regulations in the US and the EU, and how information asymmetry has encouraged the production of ever-increasing, complex financial instruments. The unfolding of the credit crisis has revealed that this information asymmetry has the potential to undermine social cohesion by discrediting the financial system.[29]

One way to read Tanega's chapter, which to mainstream socio-legal readers might sound rather technical, is by placing it in the context of the discussions on late modernity developed in Chapter 1, where moral concerns are increasingly marginalized and replaced by complex regulatory regimes and codes of ethics. Admittedly, Tanega's starting point is not informed by assumptions regarding the relationship between the 'credit-crunch', morality and late modernity. Instead, he draws our attention to the liquidity problems and upheavals in the global financial markets, which were brought about by subprime mortgage lenders in the US and the UK, security-rating agencies and central banks. The so-called 'credit-crunch' is often discussed in economic terms and technical phrases, which mystify both ordinary people and those in charge of the economy, distracting them from the human dimension of the crisis, that is, that the crisis was ultimately brought about by the choices and decisions made by a small group of people within the financial system; a system designed to promote short-term profits. The actions of these financial actors were within the rules and in accordance with the objectives of the financial systems they operated in, that is, they worked to increase their own profit and produce wealth, which, in the first place, benefited them. This is admittedly their right within a capitalist system, yet they exercised their rights without any moral considerations or concerns for the long-term implications of their actions for other people. They could act in this way partly because such moral considerations are not part of the imperatives of the financial systems. These imperatives are concerned with calculating, managing and reducing the risks associated with making investments and transactions and ensuring profits, and not with critically reflecting on the nature of the good society. There is no solution to the financial crisis caused by the financial actors, and as we have seen in countries such as the US and the UK during 2009, taxpayers have had to foot the bill for the irresponsible actions of these financial actors. There are, however, signs that attempts will be made to regulate the financial markets in more detail than before, by setting up internal watchdogs. What is not on the agenda is a debate and reconsideration of the viability of a financial system that is based on an extreme form of instrumental rationality and, arguably, fosters egoism and greed and promotes courses of action, which are by implication imprudent and morally indefensible.

In Chapter 17, Harriet Samuels returns to some of the issues and types of case discussed in Chapter 6 by Susan Edwards. Samuels' point of departure is a critique of the postcolonial representations of women from non-Western cultures as the exotic 'other', which once translated into law and policy transforms them into 'subjects without agency'. Although Samuels' starting point is similar to that of Edwards, her primary intention is to go beyond the feminist critique of rights in order 'to re-emphasize human rights in any progressive feminist strategy'. Unlike Kate Nash, Samuels means that the universal norms of human rights have a role to play in constructing new rights aimed at protecting women from forms of violence. The question is how to preserve and effectively employ the positive aspects of rights, which, in practice, protect women, while isolating and neutralizing the negative consequences of human rights that vilify the culture of the 'other'.

---

29   For an examination of the root causes of the recent financial crisis see G Tett, *Fool's Gold: How Unrestrained Greed Corrupted a Dream, Shattered Global Markets and Unleashed a Catastrophe* (London: Little Brown, 2009).

One of the cases Samuels focuses on is *Fornah*,[30] a case concerning female genital mutilation (FGM), where we see how the universal norms of human rights are employed to develop 'a more gender-sensitive jurisprudence'. Fornah fled Sierra Leone and applied for refugee status in Britain to avoid being subjected to FGM. Her application was rejected on the basis that her claim could not be accommodated within the Refugee Convention, which defines a refugee as someone who 'owing to well-founded fear of being persecuted for reasons of race, religion, nationality, membership of a particular social group or political opinion, is outside the country of his nationality and is unable or, owing to such fear, is unwilling to avail himself of the protection of that country [...]'.[31] Samuels explains that sex does not provide a basis for establishing persecution within the Refugee Convention. Thus, in order to persuade domestic and international institutions and courts to interpret the Convention in such a way as to take account of gender persecution, one needs to establish that women are a 'particular social group'.

Fornah's initial appeal to an adjudicator was unsuccessful; the Immigration Appeal Tribunal could not identify a particular social group to which she belonged. However, the House of Lords, applying the doctrine of proportionality, which refers to 'the set of tests used to establish whether a limitation of rights is justifiable',[32] overturned the decision of the Court of Appeal and held that Fornah was persecuted as part of a 'particular social group', which consisted of 'uninitiated indigenous females in Sierra Leone'. Paradoxically, this is human rights in action at its best, for it helps to construct a new norm designed to protect a specific group of women against violence. At the same time, it is human rights at its worst, for by producing and spreading an understanding of a specific group of women as 'an essentialized, gendered and cultured subject', it, arguably, victimizes and deprives them of their agency while vilifying their cultural identity. Moreover, by focusing on and denouncing the culture to which these women belong, it underplays and obscures the central role of class, race, religion and other socio-culturally constructed categories in determining the existing differences between women in varying parts of the world. The question is whether the potential of legal tools such as proportionality or the doctrine of the margin of appreciation, which are part of the internal mechanisms of the law, allows positive law to reach beyond itself and ground its judgments ethically.

The final chapter in this volume, Chapter 18, by Hanne Petersen, contains an examination of the Danish discourse on rights, responsibility, identity, and nationhood. It is a discourse marked by a sense of anxiety connected with the loss of Danish 'land' and, thus, the additional loss of national identity. The context of this discourse is set by the disturbing transition from the local politics of rights, as defined by the welfare state, to the 'market state' and the global politics of fear. In this transition, the omnipotent Danish welfare state is increasingly marginalized by the transnational forces of globalization. What is left of the old traditional authority of the state can no longer be fully trusted by the citizens. This is also a move from industrial economy to information economy, and a move from an ethno-culturally homogenous Denmark to an ethnically and culturally pluralistic Denmark. The retreat of the welfare state in the face of globalization is to the advantage of those in possession of the appropriate resources, which enables them to adapt themselves promptly to the changing circumstances. Others, who neither possess the right resources nor can readjust themselves to the new conditions, are left behind. A widening gap is

30   *Secretary of State for the Home Department (Respondent) v. K (FC) (Appellant) Fornah (FC) (Appellant) v. Secretary of State for the Home Department (Respondent)* [2006] UKHL 46.
31   Article 1A(2) of the Refugee Convention 1951 as amended by the 1967 Protocol United Nations, *Treaty Series*, vol. 189, at 137 and 606 U.N.T.S. 267, *entered into force* 4 October 1967.
32   J Rivers, 'Proportionality and variable intensity of review', *Cambridge Law Journal*, 65/1 (2006), 174–207, at 174.

thus emerging between elite citizens, successful high-flying global citizens who feel responsible for little more than their own well-being and interests, and a local underclass consisting of those Danes who feel socio-economically vulnerable and culturally defenceless. The move from local politics to the global 'market state' brings insecurity for the latter group, making it increasingly isolationist and xenophobic.

Petersen takes her points of departure for discussing the anxiety arising out of the move from the local politics of rights to a global stage of uncertainty in Poul Anker Bech's painting 'The Lost Land' (see the cover), a poster by the far right Danish People's Party and the Danish cartoon controversy already discussed in Chapter 10 by Sarah Dreier. Beck's painting depicts a piece of landscape suspended in mid-air – a land no longer grounded but floating in the air, the poster shows a Muslim woman in a burka, residing as judge with the subtitle 'Give Denmark Back' – and the cartoons conflate Islamic symbols with the suppression of women and terrorism.

In Chapter 9, Ghorashi criticizes attempts to replace the rights of certain minorities such as immigrants to their cultural identity, with their duties to the Netherlands; a move that boiled down to immigrants being made responsible for assimilating themselves into the Dutch culture. In this final chapter, Petersen also talks about a move from rights to responsibility, but it is a move that responds to and compensates for the collapse of the welfare state in Denmark, which guaranteed a range of fundamental rights for all its citizens. For Petersen, this is a responsibility of the local space, its politics and normative orderings to care for what lies beyond local settings and to create a community that is capable of generating a sense of trust and security for all its politically confused and culturally uprooted and displaced citizens. It is in this sense that Petersen seeks a shift from the culture of rights to a culture of responsibility capable of responding to the ethical challenges of a pluralistic society. It is the sense of responsibility to the 'other', to the 'other's' cultural autonomy and the physical and psychological well-being. This sense of responsibility can provide the basis for a form of community to replace the notion of rights as defined by the relationship between the individual and the state of Denmark. More importantly, according to Petersen, although we find much isolationist talk in the public political discourse in Denmark, we also find evidence of a move from local rights of the individual to a sense of responsibility for what lies beyond the borders of Denmark.

Petersen's chapter allows us to end our discussions on an optimistic note and with a positive view of the thing to be. Her chapter is, nevertheless, a reminder that we are dealing with an ongoing debate that uses rights and responsibilities as part of the strategies of reconstructing the world we live in. Considering the social conditions of late modernity, characterized by an increased functional complexity of the environment of social systems, it is possible that reaching agreements on the content of universal rights and responsibilities may be an unrealistic expectation. Perhaps all we have left is the debate itself, and what we ought to protect is not the content of rights, which appear to withstand neither the pace of time nor the change of social and cultural space, but the right to debate openly, the democratic space Ghorashi was discussing in her chapter, the space which allows the expressions of otherness through an open political discourse on rights and responsibilities. Is it possible to construct this democratic space in such a way that it allows all voices to be heard equally? And can we confidently move from the political culture of rights to the politics of responsibilities (in Petersen's sense of the word) in the context of existing global relations defined by the imbalance of economic and military power? It is true that we are all collectively responsible for the problems we confront today, problems ranging from environmental threat, disease and war in places such as Afghanistan and Iraq. Nevertheless, we are not equally responsible for creating these problems. In a world that continues to be shaped by economic disparity and military force, would we not run the risk of collectively taking responsibility for the consequences of the actions of global powers, which in the first place aim to secure their short-term interests? The democratic space for airing and debating our differences and disagreements and the shift from the politics of rights to the global politics of responsibility sound promising only when we disregard the imbalance of power that defines global relationships. Many such issues need to be discussed further and many questions remain to be debated and addressed. All we can hope is that this collection provides useful snapshots of this debate and a starting point for considering further the role of socio-legal research in this debate.

Chapter 1

Law, Rights and Justice in Late Modern Society: A Tentative Theoretical Framework

Reza Banakar

The rights discourse is an integral part of the highly dynamic social process through which the content and boundaries of social norms are negotiated, and social relations, practices and institutions are created over time. These norms, relations, practices and institutions are parts of the interconnected networks of socio-cultural communications, economic exchanges and political and military interdependencies that transcend the traditional national and cultural boundaries and spaces of sovereign states. Various chapters in this collection bear witness that the rights discourse is no longer contained by local conditions and factors belonging to one society, one culture or one nation state. Today, states no longer hold the monopoly on regulating many of the social and economic relationships that traditionally fell within their jurisdiction,[1] which has long-term implications for the way we conceive of, define and study the relationship between law (in terms of the sovereign state) and society (in terms of locally constructed relationships, practices, cultures and institutions).[2] As William Twining points out, we can no longer offer an adequate account of law in the modern world without paying 'some attention to the significance of transnational non-governmental organisations [...] to people that are nations without states [...] to organised crime, liberation movements, multi-national companies, transnational law firms and significant classes such as herds of displaced persons [...]'.[3]

The chapter by Hanne Petersen, in which she suggests that responsibility to others outside our own locality, community and country should replace the traditional forms of rights, and the discussions by Emma McClean regarding human security, provide clear examples of how rights are used to reconstruct new global societies or, to put it differently, to globalize societies internally. Similarly, the rights of terrorism suspects, the right to wear the hijab in public institutions or the need to protect victims of genital mutilations, discussed in several chapters, bring into sharp focus the cross-cultural and cross-national aspects of many of the moral and political issues in our contemporary societies. Under late modernity, most locally debated political and moral issues have global dimensions, which require taking into consideration other people with divergent socio-political systems in other places. This does not mean that any conversation about rights is necessarily of global or international character, but that the intensification of interrelationships, the growing interdependence of people living in different parts of the world and the changing character of the nation state influence and shape the way in which rights are debated and employed. Neither does this imply that universal solutions can be devised to tackle

---

1   See AC Cutler, 'Constituting capitalism: Corporations, law and private transnational governance', *St Anthony's International Review*, 5/1 (2009), 99–115; A-M Slaughter, 'Disaggregated sovereignty: Towards the public accountability and global governance networks', *Government and Opposition*, 39/2 (2004), 159–90.

2   R Cotterrell, 'Transnational communities and the concept of law', *Ratio Juris*, 21 (2008).

3   W Twining, *Globalisation and Legal Theory* (London: Butterworths, 2000), at 10.

social problems at local levels. Instead, as this collection demonstrates, the rights discourse needs to be socio-culturally contextualized.

Notwithstanding the importance of the notion of rights in potentially linking the spheres of law, politics and justice, the sociological studies of law have traditionally been hesitant in conceptualizing and exploring rights as a normative construct.[4] The sceptical attitude of sociology towards rights is demonstrated in Chapter 2, where Max Travers examines the debate between Turner and Waters, and further illustrated in Chapter 10, where Sarah Dreier describes social structures and existing interests and relationships, rather than a consideration of normative claims raised by rights, as the primary justification and motivation for decision making. Sociology might, as it is argued by Travers, run into difficulties when constructing an ontological theory of rights, but it remains in need of a general theory that explains the varying functions of rights in the global settings of late modernity.

What follows is an attempt to produce a tentative theoretical framework for situating and interpreting the various debates we encounter in this collection. This chapter starts by introducing the notion of late modernity as the second stage in the development of modern society, when the foundations and the structural makeup of industrial society are transformed and a radical form of modernity is born. At this stage, many relationships and their corresponding rights and duties, which are defined and regulated traditionally by the nation state, are undermined by the intensification and expansion of economic, political and cultural interrelationships across the globe. It then goes on to argue that since social systems such as law, polity and economy can no longer fully respond to the moral diversity in their environments, rights are increasingly invoked through law to replace the discourse on moral issues that question the foundations of our form of social organization. However, rights employed through law become 'juridified', losing their emancipatory power and moral significance for reconsidering social relationships. The chapter ends by returning to various discussions in this volume, demonstrating the need to study the rights discourse in the context of ongoing political resistance and struggles in society.

As pointed out in the introduction, 'late modernity' is employed here in a narrow sense to explore the consequences of the conquest of neo-liberalism and the spread of global market economy. Our focus will be on how globalisation brings about higher levels of uncertainty and gives rise to new forms of inequality, while transforming the ostensibly solid and timeless social structures of early modernity (those of the state in particular). This chapter recognises the growing 'liquidity' in society and the dissolution of certain (but not all) social relationships and structures of early modernity, but does not assume that 'liquid society' provides an adequate description of the present society where many social institutions retain their apparent 'solidity' and durability.

Late Modernity and its Threats

The collection of chapters in this volume reflects, momentarily as it might be, how policy-makers, lawyers, journalists and citizens negotiate and renegotiate the normative content, boundaries and forms of rights in political and legal settings, which are characterized by increased cultural diversity, the social breakdown of traditional social class structures and identities, and the changing

---

4   For a discussion on the sociological viability of rights, see L Morris, *Rights: Sociological Perspectives* (London: Routledge, 2006). On legal sociology's limited grasp of justice, see G Teubner, 'Self-subversive justice: Contingency or transcendence formula of law', *Modern Law Review*, 72/1 (2009), 1–23. For a typical treatment of rights and justice in sociology, see D Black, *Sociological Justice* (Oxford: Oxford University Press, 1989) and *The Social Structure of Rights and Wrongs* (San Diego: Academic Press, 1998).

role of the nation state. One way to examine and understand these negotiations in their totality is to place them in the context of late modernity, when territorially-based social relations, networks and communications distinctive of a nation state are undermined by 'a new kind of capitalism, a new kind of economy, a new kind of global order and a new kind of personal life'.[5] Late modernity draws our attention to the socio-political consequences of the world economy's shift from local manufacturing economies to global service economies. This shift is made possible by two apparently unrelated events: the advancements in electronic technology that facilitate and enhance communications across national borders and cultural boundaries; and the collapse of the East European socialist economies, which gave free reign to market economy forces. Worldwide marketplaces have, thus, emerged over the last few decades, as national policies restricting the movement of capital and labour across borders have been either removed or liberalized, allowing firms to base 'individual productive activities at the optimal world locations for the particular activities'.[6] The globalization of production has, in turn, triggered off several interrelated processes at the local level, transforming many of the operations performed by nation states.

As transnational and global forces emerge and reshape political and legal landscapes across nations, we observe a move from the welfare-oriented social and legal policies of the 1960s and 1970s, when an excessive 'juridification of the social sphere'[7] was carried out in many Western countries in order to reform social conditions, to legal forms of regulation more concerned with managing risks than addressing the causes of social problems. The shift to risk management strategies is often explained by reference to the inability of late modern social systems and institutions (such as law, economy and polity) fully to respond to and control the increasing complexity of moral conflicts arising out of the 'unforeseen consequences of functional differentiation' by further functional differentiation.[8] Parallel to this development, we witness the rise of global problems such as environmental pollution, climate warming, war, terrorism, famine and pandemics, to mention a few. These are caused by anonymous transnational forces that do not lend themselves to simple risk calculations or policy regulation and, as pointed out by von Wright, lack an obvious unity or purposeful coordination – 'do not form a unified system or order' – and are subsequently difficult to identify.[9] Hence, for Bauman, they represent the 'new world disorder':

> [N]o one seems to be in control. Worse still – it is not clear what "being in control" could, under the circumstances, be like. As before, all ordering initiatives and actions are local and issue-oriented; but there is no longer a locality arrogant enough to pronounce for mankind as a whole. Or to be

---

5   U Beck, *World Risk Society* (Cambridge: Polity, 1999), at 2. In an earlier publication Beck described late modernity in terms of 'reflexive modernization' indicating 'a *radicalization* of modernity, which breaks up the premises and contours of industrial society and opens paths to another modernity'. This second stage of modernity marks the transition from industrial society to 'risk society'. U Beck, 'The reinvention of politics', in U Beck et al. (eds), *Reflexive Modernity: Politics, Tradition and Aesthetics in the Modern Social Order* (Cambridge: Polity Press, 1994), at 3–5.

6   See P Dicken, *Global Shift – The Internationalization of Economic Activity* (New York: Guilford Press, 1992), at 25; and CWL Hill, *International Business: Competing in the Global Market* (Chicago, IL: Irwin, 1997, 2nd edn), at 5.

7   G Teubner (ed.), *Juridification of Social Spheres* (Berlin: de Gruyter, 1987).

8   Beck, above, n. 5, ibid.

9   GH von Wright, 'The crisis of social science and the withering away of the nation state', *Associations*, 1 (1997), 49–52.

listened to and obeyed by mankind when making the pronouncements. Neither is there a single issue which could grasp and telescope the totality of global affairs while commanding global consent.[10]

A decade after Bauman wrote these lines, we could witness the unfolding of one aspect of this 'new world disorder' in the events leading to the recent global economic meltdown, the so-called 'credit crunch', discussed by Joseph Tanega in Chapter 16. In *Fool's Gold*,[11] Gillian Tett, a social anthropologist working as a financial journalist who was given access to the inner circles of the elite bankers, describes how the 'tribe' of young traders at JP Morgan unleashed forces that caused the near collapse of the global financial system. This young group of investment bankers was largely responsible for engineering a sophisticated financial product that came to be known as the credit derivative, which enabled them to reduce the capital reserves required for lending money to investors. The innovative use of derivatives took risk off their books, packaged it as 'securities' and then sold it on in the market for high fees, thus dispersing the risk of financial system excesses around the globe. Derivatives were a form of financial instrument capable of bringing security to global finance. However, as their application spread across the sector and other banks such as Citigroup, USB, Deutsche Bank and Merrill Lynch also adopted them, this instrument inevitably got into the wrong hands and was perverted by arrogant, reckless, deluded and greedy investment bankers. The largest application of derivatives was in sub-prime mortgages, which allowed the repackaging of loans to homeowners who failed to meet the usual requirements into bonds for sale on an industrial scale. What was started by a group of young traders at JP Morgan quickly cascaded into a full-scale financial crisis of global dimensions, a crisis no one had any control over, least of all the governments of the US and West European countries. They could only step in once the international economic crisis was in full bloom to bail out the investment banks with hundreds of billions of dollars of taxpayers' money to avoid a collapse of their national economies.

The notion of late modernity as it is employed in this chapter refers to this new sense of (dis)order, the realization that no single nation state or specific interest group is any longer in charge. No single nation state was in control under the first stage of modernity either, but ideological polarization at international level, confrontation between the socialist and capitalist models of economy that united and divided many countries under one or the other ideological banner, together with locally-based production and policy-making, gave the appearance of direction and purpose to national and international forces.[12] It is this sense of direction, purpose and control over one's jurisdiction that has been lost under late modernity.

---

10   Z Bauman, *Globalisation: The Human Consequences* (Cambridge: Polity Press, 1998), at 58.

11   G Tett, *Fool's Gold: How Unrestrained Greed Corrupted a Dream, Shattered Global Markets and Unleashed a Catastrophe* (London: Little Brown, 2009). For a discussion of *Fool's Gold* see J Flood, 'Book reviews', *Journal of Law and Society*, 36/9 (2009), 579–84.

12   Following the collapse of the Soviet Union, the United States has become the dominant force in the international arena. As we have seen in Iraq and Afghanistan, the United States does not hesitate in bringing its military might to bear on local developments that challenge its interests, and uses its diplomatic influence to lean on governments (such as Iran), which refuse to fall in line with US foreign policies. Although the United States' global hegemony, in particular its military supremacy, is beyond doubt, it does not have total control over the way the new global order develops. Its lack of control is clearly demonstrated in its inability to reshape Iraq and Afghanistan in its own image. As Stephen Gill argues, intensification of the globalization of power and capital is met with new forms of political resistance and struggle, 'many of which seek a more just, sustainable and democratic world order'. See S Gill, *Power and Resistance in the New World Order* (London: Palgrave, 2008, 2nd edn), at xv.

The nation state has not withered away and national borders continue to pose obstacles to the movement of people, yet their operations have changed qualitatively; they impede the movement of migrants from the South while facilitating the movement of labour, capital and tourists. How the nation state changes in response to the emerging international and transnational forces it partly promotes (for example, in the cases of trade, movement of capital and labour) and partly impedes (in the cases of anti-globalization movements, terrorism and migration from the South) is discussed in several chapters in this volume. Hanne Petersen discusses, for example, the inability of the Danish state to continue guaranteeing the welfare rights of its citizens; Emma McClean criticizes the inadequacy of nation states in protecting individuals from fear and want, and Joxerramon Bengoetxea and Niilo Jääskinen examine how, under certain conditions, EU directives circumvent the authority of member states, regulating the rights and legal positions of the citizens of EU member states.

At the local level, late modernity marks and explains the failure of welfare ideology, which originally required an omnipotent nation state to realize its vision of a better society, that is, a welfare society that guaranteed a minimum standard of living, education, health care and employment for all its citizens. At the risk of oversimplification, the modern welfare state was characterized by governmental *regulation*, often carried out by introducing legal measures aimed at enhancing *social integration* through a fair allocation of resources, duties and responsibilities. The state was seen as a potential force for good, capable of reorganizing social conditions for the better by legally regulating social and economic relationships. In contrast, late modernity is characterized by governmental *deregulation* and system integration through the market economy, which is achieved by facilitating two apparently separate, but on closer inspection interrelated and corresponding, processes. These are achieved at global and local levels by: 1) promoting the rise of transnational relationship networks in production, global finance and trade; and 2) passing on responsibility for the general welfare of citizens, that is, for employment (benefits), health care, retirement, education, housing, etc. to the individual citizens themselves.[13] We also see a move from policies designed to promote social integration through participation and mutual recognition to one based on cultural *assimilation* (for example, in respect to immigrants and ethnic and religious minorities), social *exclusion* (reflected, for example, in the emergence of criminal policies aimed at prevention, preferring to build more prisons to house an ever-growing number of inmates for longer periods instead of attempting to rehabilitate them) and political *neutralization* (for example, in respect of the way that moral issues are politically marginalized). Assimilation, exclusion and neutralization provide the bases for developing forms of social control, which are exercised through an ever-increasing machinery of surveillance, ultimately motivated by the belief that the risk posed by various threats can be calculated and pre-empted.

To grasp late modernity, one needs to consider globalization,[14] that is, the intended and unintended consequences of the advancement of electronic technology, the intensification of social relations

---

13　The welfare state model developed in different ways and to different degrees in some Western European countries, Australia, North America (Canada in particular) and other places, but not in countries that lacked either the necessary resources or the political motivation. Although the spread of welfare ideology did not occur everywhere and cannot be regarded as a global development, the move to deregulate and privatize public services appears to be quite widespread across the countries in both the North and the South. Even in countries such as Iran, which has not experienced a welfare system, there is move to privatize public services.

14　Globalization is a contested concept. Many scholars have argued that the globalization of trade is nothing new and that the consequences of the global prevalence of capitalism were already predicated and discussed by scholars such as Karl Marx. For a discussion see M Travers, *Understanding Law and Society*

and communications across political and cultural boundaries, the global expansion of markets, the transformation of the nation state, the reshaping of the social institutions of modernity, and the rise of new social movements and forms of resistance. Globalization transforms and integrates the world into a global marketplace, bringing humanity closer together without necessarily creating a sense of solidarity at the global level. It does, admittedly, bring the peoples of the world closer together by creating if not a 'global village' then at least a 'global neighbourhood', which, however, reflects in the first place a physical proximity caused by the growing movement of capital, labour and technology across national borders, not the enhancement of cultural understanding and recognition of the 'other'. Societies become increasingly pluralistic in social, religious, cultural and political terms, while at the same time they also become more divided and fragmented. When we say that Britain, Denmark and Holland are multicultural societies, we do not mean that they are cultural melting pots, but that various people belonging to different ethnic and cultural backgrounds live side by side. Globalization can alienate people from one another in human and cultural terms; for the form of rationality that underpins the operations of the global marketplace is 'instrumental', reflecting the operational imperatives of the economic system.[15] However, humans remain *social* beings in need of communities to which they can belong and which support and acknowledge their identities – communities that can exist only through intersubjectively shared values and worldviews, mutual trust, respect, and a sense of duty and responsibility towards each other. The theoretical framework suggested here helps to explore moral concerns with the loss of trust and the uncertainties associated with duties and responsibilities under late modern conditions by focusing on the rights discourse.

Contesting and Subverting Rights

The rights discourse is understood here in terms of the ongoing negotiations, deliberation and contentions utilized to establish the content, form and boundaries of the *permissions* and *prohibitions* that protect individuals or social groups, allowing them to pursue their personal projects against encroachments of the state, other individuals and groups. Whether we define rights as 'natural' or 'positive', they are normally 'related logically to *duty* and *obligation* and also to the concept of law-like rules and principles'[16] devised to govern the relationship between the right holder and other individuals against whom the rights are held. In this sense, rights exert a constraining influence on our moral capacity to act by replacing our moral hesitations and dilemmas, which may arise out of our deliberations on how to act in a particular situation with certainty. An understanding of rights in terms of normative rules designed to enhance moral certainty depicts them as a set of fixed, perhaps even immutable, concepts and relationships. However, in everyday social reality, rights are fluid and open-ended. Rights do constrain the scope of moral action and help to form our decisions, but they are externally contested and internally subverted. Externally, individuals

---

(London: Routledge, 2009), at 165–88. In addition, there are disagreements as to whether globalization brings about convergence or a divergence of cultures (including legal traditions). For a discussion see W Twining, 'Globalisation and comparative law', in E Örücü and D Nelken (eds), *Comparative Law: A Handbook* (Oxford: Hart, 2007). For a discussion on the significance of law and lawyering in the creation and reproduction of the global business order see J Flood, 'Law and globalisation', in R Banakar and M Travers (eds), *An Introduction to Law and Social Theory* (Oxford: Hart, 2002), at 311–28.

15   Instrumental rationality is here contrasted with communicative rationality, as described by Jürgen Habermas. See J Habermas, *The Theory of Communicative Action*, vol. I (Boston, MA: Beacon Press, 1984).

16   J Waldron (ed.), 'Introduction', in *Theories of Rights* (Oxford: Oxford University Press, 1984), at 2.

and groups debate and question the validity, applicability and enforceability of the moral content of rights, while internally, rights can be interpreted and implemented in such ways as to produce an effect very different from, and at times in conflict with, what was originally intended. As Kate Nash, Susan Edwards and Harriet Samuels show in their chapters, this is true even in regard to our most established regimes of rights, such as human rights.

As a result of rights being contested externally and subverted internally, a chasm opens up between the rules and principles that mediate moral or legal rights and how these are unfolded in everyday life or legal practice. In his discussions on human rights, Christopher McCrudden distinguishes between 'theories supporting human rights – including the *general principles* of human rights – and their *application* in specific situations'.[17] There is, admittedly, much agreement on the principles of human rights internationally, but little consensus on why, how and where these principles should be applied. Consequently, '[a]ll that is left is an empty shell of principle, and when principle comes to be applied, the appearance of commonality disappears and human rights are exposed as culturally relative, deeply contingent on local politics and values'.[18]

The global forces briefly discussed above are primarily economic, but their impact is hardly limited to global finance and trade. Besides promoting global trade, these transnational forces also enhance mobility across cultural and national boundaries, increasing the diversity of local cultures and influencing the formation of values, worldviews, perceptions and expectations in new directions. Put differently, global forces influence local conditions beyond the economic sphere, diversifying them socio-culturally and politically. As a result, the rights discourse we encounter under these socially and culturally diverse conditions is increasingly fragmented, and at the level of legal and political organization internally subverted, that is, it carries with it the kernel of its own negation. Much of this could be said about the rights discourse under modernity, but the point made here is that today the rights discourse has – more than ever before – become the catalyst of internal tensions and conflicting ideologies. The discourse deals, on the one hand, with public political debates that introduce a new treatment of individuals and groups in law such as the right to detain terrorism suspects without trial, and, on the other, questions the legitimacy of such a treatment (see the chapters by Bill Bowring, Daniel Moeckli and Reza Banakar). It extends human rights to an increasing number of people and groups and unwittingly creates groups of sub-citizens and non-citizens, who fall outside the protection of the state and whose basic human rights are therefore denied (see the chapter by Kate Nash). On the one hand, it mediates between the state (including the institutions of law, polity and economy that underpin the state) and the needs and aspirations of citizenry, while, on the other, it questions and undermines the sovereign state's traditional role by drawing attention to its inability to provide security for its citizens against fear, want, disease and environmental disasters (see the chapters by Emma McClean, Hanne Petersen and Halleh Ghorashi). Furthermore, it emphasizes gender equality and freedom of religion while, conversely, it deprives the most vulnerable women of their agency and cultural identity (see the chapters by Susan Edwards, Samia Bano and Harriet Samuels). Additionally, it promotes and protects the freedom of expression, yet suppresses civil liberties and freedoms (see, for example, the chapters by Paul Kearns, Sarah Dreier and Eric Heinze).

Perhaps more importantly, as many chapters in this collection demonstrate, the applications and effects of rights need to be assessed (inter-)contextually and examined from different standpoints representing the different objectives, interests and worldviews of those who interact with each other

---

17   C McCrudden, 'Judicial comparativism and human rights', in E Öröcu and D Nelken (eds), *Comparative Law: A Handbook* (Oxford: Hart, 2007), at 372.

18   McCrudden, ibid., at 372.

over time to create a specific context. The case of *Fornah*, discussed in Chapters 6 and 16, concerning an asylum seeker from Sierra Leone who fled her country in fear of female genital mutilation, exemplifies this need to consider different standpoints and their specific contexts. In *Fornah*, rights operate paradoxically by confronting three standpoints embedded in different contexts: the first is the UK's immigration policy, the second is the discourse of Western feminist activists, and the third reflects the specific socio-cultural conditions of women such as Fornah. *Fornah* demonstrates how the encounter between these three standpoints is realized through the rights discourse and how a new legal norm is subsequently constructed as the result of this encounter to protect a specific category of women against violence, while at the same time victimizing them and depriving them of their agency. It also shows that Fornah's legal, cultural and socio-political dimensions are interconnected, thus requiring the inter-contextualization of various aspects of her case. *Fornah* needs to be placed and discussed in the context of the struggles of Western feminists and their use of the law as a site of struggle for political emancipation (this reflects the confrontations between the first and the second standpoints mentioned above). The feminists' struggles and their use of law must, however, be further contextualized by understanding, acknowledging and respecting Fornah as a social and cultural being in her own right (this reveals a tension between the second and the third standpoints). *Fornah* demonstrates that the content, interpretation, application and socio-political effects of rights are necessarily seen and experienced differently by different groups and individuals.[19] Does this mean that rights in general – and universal rights in particular – are obsolete and incapable of delivering justice? Or is it instead that in conditions specific to late modernity, where societies are increasingly pluralistic and diverse, we need to reconsider our understanding and expectations of rights in action? After all, rights are used to negotiate and renegotiate, define and redefine, create and recreate socio-political relations.

Two tentative assumptions can be made at this stage, which will help to grasp rights in socio-legal terms. Firstly, rights consist of normative rules (often recognized in law)[20] intended as standards that can guide us in our deliberations concerning the correct form of action in a particular situation. They are yardsticks that can be employed when making decisions and assessing the *correctness* of our own and other people's actions and situations. Secondly, how rights are interpreted and implemented is dependent on the political, legal and socio-cultural forces that interact to provide the social context in which our decisions are made and our actions played out.[21] These forces are no longer limited to specific localities or jurisdictions of specific nation states, and also include anonymous transnational forces, which operate at the global level without any apparent unity of action or purpose. These two assumptions can also be regarded as the basis for a socio-legal framework within which the various contributions in this volume may be read and analysed.

---

19   I have discussed the importance of standpoints elsewhere. See R Banakar, 'Studying legal cases empirically', in R Banakar and M Travers, *Theory and Method in Socio-Legal Research* (Oxford: Hart, 2005).

20   According to Jeremy Bentham, to talk of rights such as natural or moral rights, which do not have positive law as their source, is meaningless. See W Twining, *General Jurisprudence* (Oxford: Oxford University Press, 2009), at 189.

21   Here I am drawing on and extending Denis Galligan's discussion of legal rules to an understanding of rights, which also consist of rules. See D Galligan, *Law in Modern Society* (Oxford: Oxford University Press, 2006), at 57. While legal rules provide in the first place a source of 'validity' for making legal decisions, rights provide a source of 'correctness', potentially linking the spheres of positive law and morality.

The Juridification of the Moral Sphere

Rights often contain a moral element, which derives its authority from various sources such as 'moral reason' and the social mechanisms of 'persuasion, appeals to conscience, "naming and shaming" and threats of exclusion'.[22] To ensure their efficacy, rights have become increasingly incorporated into positive law, which is backed by the threat of violence against those who transgress their limits. Once the moral imperatives underpinning rights are expressed in terms of legal rules and doctrine they cease to require moral justification for their validity or enforcement.[23] This can be viewed in two ways: first, in terms of positive law's tendency to enhance its autonomy; and, second, as an attempt to use law as a political instrument to neutralize moral conflicts. The first approach highlights how law deals internally with the moral diversity in its environment, while the second approach explains the effects of law on its environment. These two points of views are, however, dialectically related.

The Internal Standpoint

Modernity's separation of law and morality was a step towards securing law's relative autonomy from polity and other centres of power and normativity. It aimed at enhancing the objectivity of legal decision making and ensuring a greater degree of certainty and continuity in the outcomes of legal processes. According to Luhmann, social systems enhance their autonomy by normative closure, which allows them to reproduce themselves self-referentially and in relation to their environment. Their normative closure increases their operational consistency and system stability while allowing them to become cognitively open towards their environment.[24] However, social systems such as law can only respond in a limited fashion to the moral diversity in their environment if they are to operate in a coherent and stable fashion. The normative closure of the legal system excludes morality as a valid criterion for decision making within the legal system, but this exclusion is compensated by law internally constructing 'programmes' (such as justice, legitimacy, welfare and efficiency), which, per definition, cannot recognize, accommodate or address all moral issues and points of view. Luhmann's notion of justice, 'a programme of (all) programmes',[25] is thus constructed by law internally. It is 'self-reference in the form of observation, but not in the form of an operation; not on the level of the codes, but on the level of programmes; not in the form of theory, but in the form of (disappointment-ridden) norm. All this means that there are unjust (or more or less just) legal systems'.[26]

Both Moeckli's and Samuels' arguments in their chapters can be seen as attempts to produce internal solutions to the problem of justice. They do not refer to Luhmann, but Luhmann's notion of justice as an internal construct of the legal system captures the essence of their arguments. Moeckli regards constructs such as Guantánamo, which are administered by a strict regime of rules, susceptible to an internal legal critique that evokes the power-restraining qualities of the

---

22   C Smith, 'The sequestration of experience: Rights, talk and moral thinking in "late modernity"', *Sociology*, 36/1 (2002), 43–66, at 47.

23   See Smith, 2002, ibid.

24   According to Luhmann, a 'system constitutes its unity and its environment in a certain domain through operative closure'. N Luhmann, *Law as a Social System* (Oxford: Oxford University Press, 2004), at 105.

25   Luhmann, ibid., at 213.

26   Luhmann, ibid., at 214. For a discussion see G Teubner, 'Self-subversive justice: Contingency or transcendence formula of law', *Modern Law Review*, 72/1 (2009), 1–23.

rule of law. Similarly, Samuels indicates that legal tools such as proportionality or the doctrine of the margin of appreciation, which are parts of the internal mechanism of law, may be employed effectively to allow positive law to protect vulnerable groups of women, without depriving them of their autonomy and agency.

The External Standpoint

The need to preserve law's autonomy remains high on the agenda of late modern legal systems, for only an autonomous legal order can operate efficiently in a functionally differentiated society. However, as pointed out by Carole Smith, while modernity excluded moral issues by emphasizing the sovereignty of reason, late modernity achieves this 'through the enormous and ever-expanding invocation of *rights* in the governance and mediation of human affairs'.[27] Once these rights are imported into the legal system, the collective moral conflicts they were intended to address become juridified, that is, transformed into individual legal disputes, which the political/administrative system can then deal with as regulatory dysfunctions. The conflict of values arising out of the very organization of society is in this way decontextualized and transformed into individual disputes requiring the corrective (de)regulation of actions, entitlements and responsibilities. Clearly this increased juridification of rights has wider normative implications for the way society is developed and governed through law, for it neutralizes the collective moral force of rights, thus marginalizing moral concerns in public political debates.[28] The increased juridification of rights can politically marginalize and even temporarily neutralize moral concerns, relieving policy-makers, the media and the public from the burden of dealing with the complexity of moral questions emerging out of our collective actions;[29] however, it does not eliminate the moral conflicts, as their root causes remain intact. Radha D'Souza's critique of rights in Chapter 2, where she argues that they have lost their emancipatory power, could also be seen as making the point that rights drained of their moral content can no longer be employed as agents of social change.

To borrow from Smith again, rights discourse in late modernity leads to the 'colonization' of morality, which, through the invocation of rights, happens whenever 'rights and duties are locked together in the governance of reciprocity or when rights become dislocated from a sense of responsibility for others'.[30] We find several examples of this type of colonization in this volume. In Chapter 9, Ghorashi's description of the shift in the Netherlands from a policy based on the social integration of migrants to one based on their cultural assimilation, according to which the relationship between Dutch mainstream culture and migrant minorities is defined by the rights of the former to demand of the latter to assimilate themselves into mainstream Dutch culture, is one such example of the colonization of morality by invoking rights. Insisting on exercising one's freedom of expression, without concern for the social consequences of one's actions, is one such dislocation of the sense of responsibility (see, for example, the debate in Chapter 9 by Sarah Dreier on the Danish cartoons of the Prophet Muhammad, and discussions regarding responsibility in Chapter 18 by Hanne Petersen). A different form of colonization of the rights discourse is found in Chapter 5 by Paul Kearns, in which the courts 'consistently enforce public-moral interests to the unequivocal sacrifice of artistic freedom'. The colonization in this case takes place by regarding the

---

27   Smith, above, n. 22, at 46.

28   According to Smith 2002, above, n. 22, this process drains rights of their moral meaning.

29   Smith 2002, above, n. 22, and J Raz, 'Right-based moralities', in J Waldron (ed.), *Theories of Rights* (Oxford: Oxford University Press, 1984), 182–200.

30   Smith, above, n. 22, at 46.

public sense of morality as a homogeneous standpoint and a yardstick for assessing and censuring artistic freedom.

In short, rights potentially link law and polity on the one hand, with ethics and justice on the other. However, self-referentially-closed systems such as law, economy and polity, owing to their operational limitations, find it difficult to respond to the changing character of morality and the conflicting moral concerns and claims voiced by different socio-cultural groups in society. As a result, the invocation of rights has come to replace these concerns with moral issues, but the juridification of rights drains them of their moral and emancipatory powers.

The Marginalization of Morality

Three recent events in Britain illustrate how moral issues evolving out of the organization of contemporary society can be marginalized in public political discourse. The first event concerns the revelations made by *The Daily Telegraph* regarding the expense claims of Members of Parliament (MPs). Many MPs represent constituents outside London and therefore need to maintain a second home near Parliament for which they may claim a 'second home allowance'. In addition, they may claim expenses incurred in the course of performing their parliamentary duties. In a series of articles published during 2009, *The Daily Telegraph* revealed that a large number of MPs across all parties had exploited their right to the second home allowance and misused the expense system for personal gain. Some MPs who had used the 'additional cost allowance' to buy or rent their designated second home from a close relation or company they own faced having to repay up to £100,000, while others were forced to pay back various expenses they had claimed, which included bills for excessive gardening costs, cleaning, improper mortgage claims, decorating, house repairs, insurance, mobile phones, electricity, council tax, and so on. Some had claimed twice for the same expense. Others had 'flipped their second home so that they could claim for renovations on house after house', potentially making 'hundreds of thousands of pounds of profit through taxpayers-subsidized property market speculation'.[31] In their own defence, the MPs repeatedly pointed out that the claims were strictly within the rules set by Parliament, which did little to calm public outrage over the way some had exploited the system. However, beside four cases of alleged abuses of parliamentary expenses that were referred to the Crown Prosecution Service, the majority of MPs who had made excessive claims were not suspected of breaking any laws. Instead they were thought to have acted without moral consideration and to have done so because they operated within a system in which moral considerations are marginalized and replaced by codes of conduct. A similar problem is discussed in Chapter 15 by Joseph Tanega concerning the recent financial crisis, which caused the 'credit crunch' and the collapse of a number of investment banks. The 'tribe' of investment bankers we discussed earlier in reference to Gillian Tett's study were also acting within a system which marginalizes moral considerations and promotes profiteering. However, while the financial sector operates to maximize profits, the political system sets the standards of conduct in various walks of life and, thus, politicians are expected by the public to show greater moral integrity than other groups – hence the public's outrage at discovering that their political representatives enriched themselves at taxpayers' expense by manipulating the system of rules they had devised themselves. The public's outrage also demonstrated that, although late modernity might marginalize moral considerations at the macro level of systems and governance for the reasons we noted above, concerns with morality remain a force to reckon with and continue to shape opinions and mobilize people.

---

31 *The Daily Telegraph*, 'Brown heckled by his angry MPs', 14 October 2009, at 5.

Not surprisingly, to resolve the MPs' expenses scandal and to restore public trust, an Independent Parliamentary Standards Authority (IPSA) was created on 20 May 2009, a new parliamentary 'watchdog to regulate the allowances and create criminal offences which could see errant MPs facing jail'.[32] The new watchdog, to borrow from Luhmann, represents an enhanced 'programme' of self-observation, expected to ensure parliamentary conduct in respect to MPs' expense claims and – in theory – bring transparency to how taxpayers' money is used by MPs. The public has a *right* to know how their representatives conduct themselves in respect to the official duties for which they are elected. Although an enhanced programme of self-observation might indeed bring about a greater degree of compliance with parliamentary codes of conduct among MPs, it does not resolve the moral issue concerning the public's lack of trust in their representatives. Instead, it transforms the moral issues related to lack of trust into the right of the public to know the details of their MPs' expenses. This illustrates that 'solutions' to moral issues, such as programmes of self-observation, which are generated internally within a system such as law or politics, are often exceptionally limited in their scope and instead work towards an avoidance of moral problems (especially by managing risks and pre-empting threats associated with social conflicts) rather than resolving the internal contradictions of social systems. It is within this scheme of avoiding rather than resolving moral issues that the rights discourse is employed and rights are colonized. This insight is in line with the sociological studies of dispute resolution, which demonstrate that instead of resolving social conflicts, legal processes often neutralize them, for example, by redefining and processing them in terms other than those originally used by the parties to the dispute, helping the disputing parties to 'lump' their grievance.[33] In a similar fashion, the legal system appears to be using rights to neutralize moral concerns (which also represent forms of social conflict) by discussing them in terms other than those of morality and ethics.

The second event concerns the case of Baby P, a toddler who sustained more than 50 injuries at the hands of those responsible for his care, including his mother. Although Baby P was on the Child Protection Register, he 'was allowed to stay in the care of his mother, her boyfriend and their lodger', who were later found guilty of 'causing or allowing the death of a child or vulnerable person'.[34] The public political debate following this case, which was, incidentally, not without precedence in Britain,[35] focused on the role of social workers and other professionals, such as the doctor who had examined Baby P prior to his death and failed to report his injuries as signs of possible abuse, in order to allocate blame. Thus, a moral issue facing the whole of society was transformed into the failings of individual doctors and social workers. Although there are good reasons for examining the failings of these professionals, and especially the role of the social workers who neglected Baby P's need for protection, such examination will only distract us from questioning the type of society we have collectively created, in which children are abused by those who are responsible for their care. Furthermore, the media attention devoted to Baby P's case draws our attention away from the widespread character of child abuse in Britain. A helpline

---

32   *Telegraph.co.uk*, 'MPs' expenses: scandal damage "cannot be underestimated" says Electoral Commission', published 1 July 2009, posted at <http://www.telegraph.co.uk/>.

33   See WLF Felstiner 'Influences of social organization on dispute processing', *Law & Society Review*, 9 (1974), 631; WLF Felstiner, RL Abel and A Sarat, 'The emergence and transformation of disputes: Naming, blaming, claiming', *Law & Society Review*, 15 (1980–81), 63 and R Banakar, *The Doorkeepers of the Law* (Aldershot: Ashgate, 1998).

34   *Telegraph.co.uk*, 'Baby "used as punch bag" died despite 60 visits from social services', 11 November 2008.

35   For an earlier, similar incident which led to public debate, see Victoria Climbie's case: *The Victoria Climbie Inquiry*, at <http://publications.everychildmatters.gov.uk/eOrderingDownload/CM-5730PDF.pdf>.

set up by the NSPCC, which allows the public to report child abuse to the authorities, passed on 11,243 suspected child protection cases to the police and social services between April 2008 and March 2009.[36] In addition, *The Guardian* reported that 'at least 30 children have been murdered as a result of abuse since the death of Baby P two years ago'.[37] The responsibility for Baby P's death was passed on to the child protection services of the London borough where he lived and a policy debate was initiated on how to minimize the risk of similar neglect happening again. Subsequently, extra recourses were made available to identify and remove children being abused or neglected in time. This is an example of how contemporary society marginalizes the moral dimensions of social organizations by seeking to manage the risks of social problems rather than resolving their underlying social causes.

The third event concerns the teenager Hammaad Munshi, the youngest British-born Muslim to be convicted of offences under the Terrorism Act 2000.[38] Munshi, who was just 16 when he was arrested, had, according to the media, 'led a double life' for over a year, attending lessons by day at the local comprehensive and 'surfing jihadist sites' by night, 'distributing material to others' as part of 'a "worldwide conspiracy" to wipe out non-Muslims'.[39] The schoolboy had been recruited and radicalized when he was 15 by Aabid Khan, a 23-year-old British-born Muslim, who was also found guilty of four counts of offences under section 57(1) of the Terrorism Act 2000. Khan wanted to arrange Munshi's passage to Pakistan to 'fight jihad'.[40] The prosecution told the court that the schoolboy was in fact a dangerous individual 'dedicated to the cause of al-Qaeda'.[41] Khan was sentenced to 12 years and Munshi to two years in a young offenders' institution. While sentencing Munshi, the judge told him that he had brought 'great shame' on himself, his family and his religion. The judge admitted that Munshi, being naïve and vulnerable, had been misled by Aabid Khan's 'malign influence', but there was no doubt that Munshi was 'aware of the nature of the record of information' on deadly chemical weapons that he had collected and sent to Aabid Khan.[42] In such a case, the judge added, 'a custodial sentence is inevitable and unavoidable'.[43]

In an earlier case, discussed in Chapter 10, Samina Malik, a 23-year-old British-born Muslim who worked as a shop assistant at Heathrow Airport, became the first woman convicted under the Terrorism Act 2000.[44] Despite the rising number of such cases, we find no public political debate on the possibility that perhaps British society as a whole might have some moral responsibility in

---

36   BBC News, 'Baby P case sees abuse calls rise', posted at <http://www.newsvote.bbc.co.uk/> [accessed 4 August 2009].

37   Guardian.co.uk, 'Baby P warning still ignored', posted at <http://www.guardian.co.uk> [accessed 4 August 2009].

38   Munshi was convicted on 18 August 2008 of offences under sections 57(1) and 58(1) of the Terrorism Act 2000 for possession of an article which gave reasonable suspicion that it was for a purpose connected with the commission, preparation or instigation of an act of terrorism. Section 57(1) – possessing an article for a purpose connected with terrorism – carries a maximum sentence of 10 years. Section 58 (1) – making a record of information likely to be useful in terrorism – also carries a maximum sentence of 10 years.

39   *Timesonline*, 'Britain's youngest terrorist, Hammad Munshi, faces jail after guilty verdict', posted at <www.timesonline.co.uk>, 18 August 2008. *The Daily Telegraph*, 'Britain's "youngest terrorist" jailed', posted at <www.telegraph.co.uk>, 18 August 2008.

40   Ibid.

41   *AFP*, '"Youngest terrorist" jailed', posted at <http://afp.google.com/article/ALeqM5hGpT5sFYk Srb5Bta7mQAdiFAaU5w>, 20 August 2008.

42   *Daily Mail*, 'Schoolboy terrorist locked up: The teenager who at 15 joined Islamic fanatics targeting the Royal Family', 20 September 2008.

43   *Daily Mail*, ibid.

44   *R v. Malik* [2008] All ER (D) 201 (June). This case is discussed in Chapter 11.

respect to British-born Muslims who are drawn to terrorism. Instead, authorities draw the attention of the public to factors external to British society and culture, such as international terrorism. For example, an Islamic think-tank set up by the Government explained recently in its report that 'young Muslims are pushed towards extremism because their mosques are run by elderly and out of touch cliques'.[45] Such reports locating the root of Islamic extremism among British-born Muslims outside the UK's national, political and cultural borders do surface on regular intervals in the British media. However, those arrested for terrorist activities are often more likely to be independent individuals with a mind of their own, and more likely to have been radicalized at school, university or in cyberspace than in a mosque run by Urdu-speaking, elderly mullahs from the rural backwaters of Pakistan. By blaming the mosques and the elderly Pakistani mullahs, British society exonerates itself from any responsibility and avoids acknowledging and discussing the moral issues related to the marginalization of Muslim youth caused by what they, rightly or wrongly, perceive as the demonization of Islam and Muslims after 9/11. The very application of the labels 'radical', 'extremist' and 'jihadist', intended as an explanation to the threat of terrorism by British-born Muslims, hides more than it reveals. It hides the uncertainty, confusion and alienation that underpin their radicalization, as well as the feeling of social exclusion felt by many young British Muslims whose voices, concerns and first-hand experiences of social justice, both at home and overseas, are marginalized in public political discourse in Britain or misplaced in the context of an increased threat of terrorist attacks. It hides the existing power relationships and modes of cultural domination in Britain, which makes essential the discourse on Islam, portrays it as a threat to democracy, stigmatizes Muslims in public opinion, and dismisses the concerns and experiences of the likes of Munshi and Malik.[46] Finally, it hides the fact that the involvement of many young British-born Muslims in terrorist activities, destructive, misguided and deluded as these individuals and their involvements might be, is part of their resistance to what they perceive and experience as a form of domination pitched against their ethno-cultural identity. To borrow from Michel Foucault, 'where there is power, there is resistance' and, arguably, 'this resistance is never in a position of exteriority with respect to power'.[47] It means that the forms of 'resistance' posed by Munshi and Malik are, as argued above, not inseparable from the form of power and domination that permeates the social context of their existence within British society.

Power and Resistance

The above discussion regarding the rise of terrorism among young British-born Muslims demonstrates that an understanding of the power relationships in society is a precondition for making sense of the cases of Munshi and Malik. It allows us to introduce into the equation their viewpoint, that is, the experience of living in contemporary Britain as a Muslim, and take into account how the discourse on rights is unfolded partly by marginalizing and colonizing moral conflicts. The understanding of power in terms of discourse is also central to the other two cases concerning the MPs' expenses scandal and Baby P, the former representing a group in society with access to the political apparatus and the latter representing one of the most vulnerable groups in society with no access to the public political forum or competence to defend

---

45   *Daily Mail*, 24 February 2009.

46   For a discussion on the relations of power and domination in relation to Western Muslims see J Cesari, *When Islam and Democracy Meet: Muslims in Europe and the United States* (New York: Palgrave Macmillan, 2006).

47   M Foucault, *The History of Sexuality*, *Part I* (New York: Random House, 1978), at 94–95.

or express its own interests. However, these three cases were presented above without explaining exactly who is in charge of this discourse, who has the authority to make decisions within the public political forum, who is responsible for the colonization of moral conflicts, and who dominates whom objectively (materially or economically) and subjectively (psychologically or culturally). In short, the question still remains: who should take moral responsibility for the marginalization of young British-born Muslims, the thousands of children who are condemned to a life of poverty and neglect in a prosperous Britain, the global financial crisis, or the MPs' abuse of their expenses claim system? Are we individually responsible for our predicaments or, as suggested above, should society as a 'whole' take responsibility for social wrongs and harm?

Invoking the idea of the 'whole' becomes increasingly difficult under social conditions characterized by growing discontinuity and fragmentation. In other words, there is no empirically identifiable single social entity, or 'whole', capable of decision making or taking responsibility for social problems. Even governments and supreme courts are incapable of speaking with one voice at all times, and are often divided internally on how to deal with socio-political issues. This is why, as pointed out by Bauman, within the 'new world disorder' no one appears to be in control, and it is unclear 'what "being in control" could, under the circumstances be like'.[48] It is, therefore, easier to attach responsibility for wrongful actions and social problems, which are otherwise rooted in the constitution of our society, to individuals. Criminal law achieves and legitimizes this by introducing the idea of the "legal subject as a responsible agent' through doctrines such as *mens rea* and *actus reus*.[49] As also argued in Chapter 11, this amounts to abstracting agency from 'the context of social conflict and deprivation which generates crime', excluding 'that context from the judicial gaze'[50] and, instead, providing a partial and mystified image of the individual and society. In short, under late modernity it is as problematic to attach moral responsibility to the 'whole' of society as it is to take the individual social actor responsible for wrongful and harmful actions. The latter is, nonetheless, taken as being responsible in law and, thus, in public political discourse, because by focusing on individuals' responsibility alone we avoid questioning the constitution of our society and the structural inequalities that generate social wrongs and harms.

This does not mean that we cannot empirically explore power relationships under late modernity. Instead, it means that the scope of such an analysis can no longer limit itself to the individual actor's ability to make choices and act intentionally in order to secure and promote his/her interest in the face of resistance by other actors. That is why many chapters in this collection raise the issue of *access* to the public political domain – 'access' as a structural precondition for claiming or defending one's rights publicly. Powers should be, therefore, viewed and studied as a fluid property of social positions, relationships, institutions and fields of action, rather than a property of individual actors. Admittedly, various social positions, relationships, institutions or fields are not endowed equally with power – some carry more power and responsibility, while others are subjected more to the exercise of power than others. However, although individuals can make a difference to how social processes evolve over time by influencing the processes through which power is exercised, social positions, relationships and institutions, such as law, politics and finance, which provide access to forms of power, remain independent of the will, aim or interest of any individual actor.

Instead of focusing on individual actors' exercise of power, we need to consider power as one of the primary defining properties of social contexts within which action and interaction

---

48   Bauman, above, n. 10, at 58.
49   A Norrie, *Law and the Beautiful Soul* (London: GlassHouse Press, 2005), at ix.
50   Ibid., at 30.

are played out – a property that permeates all social relationships and processes *unequally* and *asymmetrically*. That is also why power should not be defined only in terms of taking actions and pursuing one's interests or, as in the case here, in terms of effectively claiming or defending one's rights. A different manifestation of power is revealed contextually as the *non-invoking* of rights. For example, the socio-economically privileged categories of citizens, such as the high-flying elite discussed in Chapter 3 by Kate Nash and in Chapter 18 by Hanne Petersen, which are produced by, and thrive on, transnational forces, do not have the same need as the local underclass to claim their rights or feel threatened by what the rights of others (such as immigrants or refugees) might entail for them. Other forms through which power is exercised are discussed in the chapters by Daniel Moeckli, Bill Bowring, Samia Bano and Susan Edwards.

The voices of the vulnerable can be excluded from public political discourse in many ways, some of which appear unintentional and result from the institutional fragmentations of late modernity. Daniel Moeckli points out in his chapter, for example, that human rights organizations have paid disproportionate attention to human rights abuses resulting from the introduction of draconian anti-terrorism laws and policy measures. As a result, they have neglected other types of similar human rights abuses that have been taking place on a considerably larger scale. Since September 11, Human Rights Watch has, for example, issued approximately 550 news releases, reports and other publications on the human rights impacts of counter-terrorism, compared to 51 publications on 'health and human rights' and approximately 170 on 'labor [sic] and human rights' and 'treatment of prisoners'.[51] Moeckli writes:

> It is, above all, the degree of attention that Guantánamo Bay has attracted over the last few years that is, in my view, out of all proportion. All international (and countless national) human rights organisations have been running major campaigns against Guantánamo for several years. There have been films, demonstrations, readings of poems and even a "virtual flotilla" to Guantánamo. The secretary general of Amnesty International justified the considerable resources and efforts invested by her organisation by claiming that Guantánamo is "the Gulag of our time".[52] But if one was to make this kind of historical comparison (which I do not think one should), then surely "the Gulag of our time" is not Guantánamo with its now approximately 270 detainees, but the worldwide web of immigration detention centres holding tens of thousands of people who have not committed any criminal offence.

Several issues are combined to create this situation. First, detainees in the immigration detention centres are among those with the least access to the public political forum. Not even the most liberal sections of the media are interested in reporting the wretched conditions of immigration detention centres, which as a news item fails to entertain newspaper readers and TV viewers. Second, the rights discourse is conducted within a social context already structured by asymmetrical power relations representing different dominant groups' interests. Even when rights are used to challenge existing power constellations, rights talk can be influenced by existing views and ongoing political discourses in society. Guantánamo, with 270 detainees, appears a much graver problem because these detainees are presented individually as highly dangerous men and collectively as the growing threat to the foundations of Western civilization. At the same time, they are seen by the critics of US foreign policy (including some human rights organizations) as a symbol of neo-imperialism, as a sign of things to come, and how the US and its allies view and treat those who dare challenge their

---

51   See <www.hrw.org> [accessed 20 May 2008].
52   R Norton-Taylor, 'Guantánamo is Gulag of our time, says Amnesty', *The Guardian*, 26 May 2005.

rule. Perhaps understandably, most human rights organizations fall into the trap of blindly following the political agenda set by governments and, subsequently, they too make (counter-)terrorism their top priority, even though there are other human rights issues that are equally pressing.

Another example of the significance of power is pointed out by Bill Bowring. In his chapter he argues that international organizations such as the UN, which are taken as the bulwark against human rights violations, are influenced by dominant state interests:

> It now tends to be forgotten that international law recognises the legal right of peoples to self-determination; this applies especially to peoples resisting occupation and tyranny, and was recognised during the period from the 1960s until the end of the Cold War in the case of the National Liberation Movements. Thus, armed struggle was by no means prohibited by international law.[53] But under the proscription regimes adopted by the EU, UN, USA, UK and other states, armed struggle in self-defence has been criminalised as "terrorism" and the solidarity of the so-called "international community" lies increasingly with the oppressor.[54]

Yet another power-related question is examined in Samia Bano's chapter concerning the way in which UK law has been employed in regulating and banning forced marriages. Some Muslim women apparently 'consent to marriage in the face of coercive social, cultural and structural forces', which has often been interpreted as evidence of their submission to the patriarchal authority exercised by Muslim men within the traditional (in contrast to modern) framework of their culture (which is in turn understood as a monolithic entity and a function of Islam). At the same time, agency is equated with women's declared resistance, often through the strategy of exit, which is also why measures introduced by the authorities in Britain to curb forced marriage and to protect women, such as the Forced Marriage (Civil Remedies) Protection Act 2007, are pivoted on 'the right to exit' the marriage. However, this 'right to exit' often amounts to denouncing their own identity by physically fleeing their cultural space. What is often neglected in this equation is the role of structural inequalities, that is, particular circumstances shaped by a combination of factors such as education, employment, class, racism and so on in the way women's agency is realized and, subsequently, in their choice of marriage partner. Many women have no alternative but to act within the constraints and possibilities presented by the social and cultural context in which they find themselves. Furthermore, as Bano points out, 'not all Muslim women seek to exercise their agency as understood by Western feminists in order to enhance Western feminist interpretations of their autonomy'. Agency is, admittedly, necessary, but in itself is not a sufficient condition for achieving emancipation. Within the structural constraints of a patriarchal system, many women exercise their autonomy and agency in order to, for example, reproduce 'gendered norms, such as beauty culture, or adopt disciplinary bodily technologies like elective cosmetic surgery', while others may choose not to opt for their 'right to exit' for a variety of reasons, for example, because it might not appear to them as a legitimate course of action. Bano writes:

> Women exercise their agency in complex and often contradictory ways, as they assess the options that are open to them, weigh the costs and benefits of their actions, and seek to balance their

---

53   See H Wilson, *International Law and the Use of Force by National Liberation Movements* (Oxford: Clarendon Press, 1988).
54   See B Bowring, 'Self-determination – the revolutionary kernel of international law', in *The Degradation of the International Legal Order? The Rehabilitation of Law and the Possibility of Politics* (Abingdon: Routledge Cavendish, 2008), at 9–38.

often competing needs with the expectations and desires. While there remains a need to recognise gendered power imbalances, at the same time there also remains a need to respect women's exercise of agency.

Similarly, Susan Edwards points out in her chapter that legal decisions on cases such as *Begum* are embedded in the context of relationships that form and inform the debate on the hijab in the West; a context permeated by post-colonial assumptions about the 'other' – the politics of fear spread through the anti-terrorism measures introduced after the terrorist attacks of 9/11 – and Islamophobia. Edwards writes:

> The hijab, jilbab and veil as items of women's clothing are not under attack per se. It is the cultural and social groups who wear these items of clothing, and their marginalisation, that have become the primary targets for governments and the general public. The racism driving these attitudes, which would otherwise have been considered unacceptable, is now repackaged and reconfigured, supported by a justificatory rationale about the need to protect the community from terrorism, and, reduction ad absurdum, Muslims. (Interestingly, the IRA even at its height never provoked an anti-terrorism backlash resulting in the control or vilification of all Catholics or of all Christians worldwide, or the control of their churches or religious practices etc.). The visibly hidden face is seen to challenge and resist, and the veil, once regarded as a symbol of women's oppression, as discussed by Saadawi above, is now regarded as emblematic of women's defiance. The recent desire to unveil women is an attempt to bring these women under control to make them submit.

A sociological theory of right must be sensitive to power structures and the economic, socio-political and cultural inequalities that hinder the access of some groups to the public political sphere, while facilitating the access of others. Such a theory will be concerned ultimately with the notion of justice and have both a normative and descriptive dimension – it will throw light on how individuals and interest groups employ rights in everyday life without losing sight of the ethical dimension of rights, that it has a claim to correctness which transcends the scope of mere legality. Justice, as used here, is therefore not limited to 'programmes' devised internally by the legal system to observe its operations, as suggested by Luhmann, and as pointed out above in connection with the discussions regarding parliamentary watchdogs, such internal constructions provide a very limited form of justice.[55] Instead, justice is understood here as a form of ethical judgment, which lies beyond the legal system and positive law.[56] Positive law needs to transcend its own system-specific boundaries and reach out in order to access the sphere of justice. At the same time, law has no alternative but to reach out, for law without justice, that is, unjust law, which admittedly can enjoy legality, will never satisfy the fundamental requirement of legitimacy. Put simply, law divorced from justice will not have the support of the ordinary men and women whose lives it affects. Thus, although positive law and justice are apparently two separate domains of action and decision making, law cannot function satisfactorily, efficiently and reliably without anchoring its operations in the *experience* of justice, which it can only produce by ethically grounding its judgments. Thus, as I have argued elsewhere,[57] and as is amply exemplified by various contributions in this volume,

---

55   Luhmann is not alone in understanding justice as an internally constructed condition: legal theorists with theoretically different points of departure, such as Robert Alexy, also conceptualize justice as an internally constructed category. For a critique see R Banakar, 'Whose experience is the measure of justice?', *Legal Ethics*, 10 (2008), 209–22.

56   Norrie, above, n. 49.

57   See Banakar, above, n. 55.

we need to consider justice from various standpoints belonging to various social agents, reflecting different socio-political and cultural contexts and personal experiences. By regarding justice as a criterion in need of the contextual validation of its substance, which consists of claim rights, that is, by treating justice not as a universal category but as a social process dependent on time and socio-cultural space, this approach responds to the diversity and fragmentation characteristic of late modern conditions. Expressed differently, *a link between spheres of law and justice may be created by the rights discourse* by mediating the experience of the exercise of power – political as well as legal – from the level of the individual citizens and groups to the institutional level of law and polity. This link would operate only when the rights discourse is not colonized as discussed above, as colonization can take place once there is an asymmetry in the power structures. This volume is, thus, as much about the rights discourse as it is about the troubled relationship between law and justice.

To sum up the discussion, this chapter has tried to show that social systems and institutions such as law, polity and the economy are no longer capable of responding fully to the complexity of moral conflicts arising out of the socio-cultural diversity of their environment. As a result, moral issues are increasingly juridified and expressed in terms of legal rights and codes of conduct. This process of juridification marginalizes moral concerns in public political discourse, thus relieving citizenry and authorities of the burden of debating the morally intricate and socially complex dimensions of wrongful and harmful actions and events that are born out of structural inequities in late modern societies. In law, wrongful and harmful actions are treated as the responsibility of legal subjects, that is, the individual actors dislocated and judged in isolation from their socio-cultural context. At the level of social policy, risk management strategies are devised to contain social and political problems by pre-empting conflicts that threaten the normal operations of social systems instead of recognizing their moral dimensions and addressing their root causes. Most moral issues and social problems are not confined locally and are parts of processes that transcend national boundaries and cultures. This means that a much higher degree of contingency characterizes social conditions, which in turn makes risk calculations almost impossible. Although the late modern strategies of risk management might work in the short term, they are bound to fail long term, as unresolved moral conflicts accumulate in the environment of social systems, undermining the legitimacy and authority of social institutions.

PART I
The Critiques of Rights

Chapter 2

A Sociological Critique of Rights

Max Travers

Introduction

Although sociologists, historically, have been sceptical towards the idea of universal human rights, there has recently been increasing recognition and acknowledgement that they are important and necessary for achieving a good society. This has partly resulted from the efforts of Bryan Turner, a British social theorist associated with the journal *Theory, Culture and Society*, to advance a serious argument as to why sociologists need an 'ontological theory of rights' and to explain why they have been neglected or discounted by classical thinkers.[1] There have also been many sociologists who have been associated with campaigns to achieve global human rights, just as they were previously associated with movements seeking citizenship rights within nation states. Moreover, the diverse, critical traditions that constitute mainstream sociology and critical jurisprudence, whether they are influenced by Marxism, feminism or postmodernism, often support obtaining rights as a means of achieving social justice, even though they continue to promote the utopian dream of a society in which minorities no longer need the protection of rights or law. Far from being critical of rights, it would appear that sociology has finally accepted them as necessary for a good society, and that many contemporary sociologists participate in the rights discourse of legislators, jurists and political scientists without striking a discordant note.[2]

Sociology as an academic discipline does, however, persistently ask difficult questions or, to put this differently, has at least from the late nineteenth century identified problems and dilemmas in the aspirations and achievements of the modern, industrialized, democratic societies that were founded on the belief that individuals should have rights. It always generates debate rather than consensus about fundamentals, so there should be no surprise that Malcolm Waters has argued, without qualification, that it makes no sense from a sociological perspective to talk of universal human rights. Instead, they are 'historically contingent and culturally relativised'.[3] Moreover, because sociologists conduct empirical research based on understanding historical processes, interviewing social actors or observing what happens on the ground, they are better equipped than legal theorists or philosophers to see the problems behind the optimistic claims and hopes expressed by human rights advocates.[4]

This chapter will review the debate between Turner and Waters, siding with Waters' view, which is consistent with the methodological position of Max Weber[5] but also with symbolic

1   B Turner, 'Outline of a theory of human rights', *Sociology*, 27 (1993), 489–512.
2   The British Sociological Association Study Group on Human Rights, established in 2007, has adopted a generally positive, rather than sceptical or debunking, view of rights.
3   M Waters, 'Human rights and the universalisation of interests: Towards a social constructionist approach', *Sociology*, 30 (1996), at 593.
4   L Morris (ed.), *Rights: Sociological Perspectives* (London: Routledge, 2006).
5   M Weber, *Economy and Society* (London: Routledge, 1978).

interactionism,[6] that rights are socially constructed rather than universal, and reflect interests and power relations rather than the evolution of legal instruments that represent the underlying, ontological needs of humanity. It will do so through considering, using historical and contemporary examples, how rights arise, disputes about rights and the problem of realizing rights. In considering how rights arise, it will look at the United Nations system of treaties and international organizations that developed during the twentieth century and its limitations. In looking at disputes, it will review recent debates about employment legislation and the rights of indigenous peoples in Australia. In considering the realization of rights, it will discuss the effectiveness of the 1951 UN Convention on Refugees in giving asylum-seekers the right to claim protection in a different country.

The next part of the chapter will discuss how to develop this constructionist agenda for studying rights. It will start by arguing that there are resources in modern and contemporary sociological theory, and in particular in the interpretive tradition of symbolic interactionism, that make it possible to advance beyond the classics, through investigating political debates about rights and how institutions realize rights claims, using a variety of empirical methods. It will also discuss the problem of relativism as it is understood by Weber and interactionists, suggesting that it is only possible to advance a persuasive moral viewpoint by acknowledging and properly describing different political or institutional perspectives.

This realistic or even pessimistic view of rights may appear unconstructive and perhaps even disrespectful towards institutions such as the United Nations, and those many policy-makers and academics who believe that it is possible to build a better world through more effective and wide-ranging legal and administrative regulation. The constructionist tradition in sociology does not pretend that it offers solutions to unnecessary suffering caused by human actions and institutions (which confront us each time we watch the evening news). It is, however, good at dispelling comforting illusions, or those that serve the interests of powerful nations, groups or institutions.

Does Sociology Need a Theory of Human Rights?

Although sociologists have written on rights from a variety of theoretical perspectives, in recent years there has been relatively little consideration of the philosophical assumptions informing rights claims.[7] Bryan Turner is an important exception since his 1993 paper addresses the foundational issue of whether sociology needs a theory of rights.[8] Turner argues, against the discipline, that it needs an ontological foundation that recognizes the existence of universal rights. By contrast, Malcolm Waters has argued from a constructionist perspective, influenced by Weber, that no theory is needed other than the recognition that rights arise through the mobilization of human interests.[9] These theorists are debating the nature of sociology as an academic discipline (whether it should or

---

6   H Blumer, *Symbolic Interactionism: Perspective and Method* (Berkeley, CA: University of California Press, 1968).

7   See, for example, C Smart, *Feminism and the Power of Law* (London: Routledge, 1989); R Connell, 'Sociology and human rights', *Journal of Sociology*, 31 (1995), 25–28; S Roach Anleu, 'Sociologists confront human rights: The problem of universalism', *Journal of Sociology*, 35 (1999), 198–212; A Woodiwis, *Human Rights* (London: Routledge, 2005); Morris, above n. 4; K Plummer, 'Rights work: Constructing lesbian, gay and sexual rights in late modern times', in Morris, ibid., at 152–67; and T Benton, 'Do we need rights? If so, what sort?', in Morris, ibid., at 21–36.

8   Turner, above, n. 1.

9   Waters, above, n. 3.

can make moral or political judgments and, if so, what moral or political project should be pursued) as much as how to conceptualize rights.

Bryan Turner's Search for Foundations

Turner contrasts sociology with jurisprudence and political science in not having conducted much empirical research or developed a theory of human rights. He provides a critical discussion on the neglect or dismissal of rights by the classical sociologists, which, while inevitably contentious, provides a good starting point for thinking about wider issues in sociology. Turner notes that Emile Durkheim, as a positivist, produced a scientific theory of how laws develop and their relationship to social solidarity. This methodological position precluded him from making overt value statements about the justice or fairness of particular laws.[10] Karl Marx, on the other hand, was explicitly hostile and sceptical towards rights as representing the interests of bourgeois property owners.[11] According to Turner, Weber had an even more thoroughly sceptical or constructionist view of law. He saw the decline of the natural law tradition in jurisprudence (the belief in universal rights) as a negative aspect of rationalization. He also saw the granting of rights as one means in which ruling elites maintained legitimacy given the decline of traditional sources of authority:

> Dominant social groups attempt to legitimise their monopolistic enjoyment of resources by an appeal to religion, tradition, ideology or whatever, but secularisation and rationalistic scepticism have meant that the dignity of traditional systems of belief, by which power can be legitimised, had been brought into question. "Law" and "rights" are part of this class struggle whereby classes appeal to substantive law to justify their claim to resources.[12]

Although it is not entirely clear from this article why Turner objects on moral or philosophical grounds to this constructionist position,[13] he is worried that sociology has lost its way and no longer speaks with moral authority about important social issues. He is particularly interested in globalization as a feature of our times, and the increasing importance of the United Nations in international politics. He notes that 'human rights debates and legislation are major features of the

---

10 E Durkheim, *The Division of Labour in Society* (London: Macmillan, 1984). This seems rather an unfair criticism, given that Durkheim was asking larger questions about the nature of modern societies than whether particular laws are fair. He shows, for example, how individualism as a set of ideas, which includes legal protection for individual rights, arises from industrialization. This generally benefits human beings, but can also create social and cultural problems such as anomie.

11 There are many positions in Marxism, as in any other sociological tradition. Some thinkers have argued forcefully that rights and legal protections are needed to protect vulnerable groups. See, for example, E Thompson, 'The poverty of theory', in E Thompson, *The Poverty of Theory and Other Essays* (London: Merlin, 1978), 193–406 and R Fine, 'Marxism and the social theory of law', in R Banakar and M Travers (eds), *An Introduction to Law and Social Theory* (Oxford: Hart, 2002), 101–18. Others have argued that rights are always a fiction or sham, and that engaging in rights discourse strengthens the underlying economic system that produces inequality. See, for example, A Buchanan, 'The Marxian critique of justice and rights', in A Buchanan, *Marx and Justice: The Radical Critique of Liberalism* (New Jersey: Rowman and Littlefield, 1982) and S Zizek, *Violence* (London: Profile, 2008). Similar debates have taken place in feminism. Compare, for example, C Mackinnon, *Toward a Feminist Theory of the State* (Cambridge, MA: Harvard University Press, 1989) and Smart, above, n. 7.

12 Turner, above, n. 1, at 494.

13 See the debates in M Krauz (ed.), *Relativism: Interpretation and Confrontation* (Notre Dame, IN: University of Notre Dame Press, 1989).

socio-political processes and institutions of modern societies, but sociology apparently possesses no contemporary theory of rights'.[14]

Following a familiar route in classical and contemporary sociological theorizing, Turner argues that the reason why sociology should change its key concepts or address new questions is because society has also changed. In his view, the subject matter for sociology is modernization, including the breakdown of traditional communities and the growth of the modern state, which is based on respect for individual rights and freedoms. Whereas in his earlier writings he had argued that sociologists needed to take the idea of citizenship seriously as a central feature of the modern world, today we are living in a world-system that requires concepts extending beyond the nation state:

> If sociology is the study of the transformation of *gemeinschaft* (organic and particularistic values and institutions) into *gesellschaft* (associations which are more universalistic in their definition of social membership) as a consequence of modernisation, we can conceptualise human-rights solidarity as a historical stage beyond citizenship solidarity.[15]

Although Turner admits that globalization is not a smooth process, he sees the rise of international organizations as inevitable in addressing transnational problems and, like other globalization theorists, believes that people and states recognize their interdependence more than in previous stages of world history. This means that sociological scepticism towards universal values may be outdated:

> Thus, consciousness of the possibility of "one world" (however, diversified and antagonistic) might create the sociological conditions in which the conventional sense of anthropological relativism might decline, thereby removing the scepticism about a common ontology as a basis for human rights in the absence of a common law tradition.[16]

In the remainder of his article, Turner advances a possible ontology, drawing on political theorists such as Leo Strauss and the philosophical anthropologist Arnold Gehlen, and considering a number of counter-arguments, based on the recognition that human life is inherently precarious. This was the case before industrialization, but Turner, like Ulrich Beck, sees technology as creating new risks, such as 'pollution, environmental disaster, a scarcity of resources [created by human institutions] and chronic diseases of civilisation'.[17] Because it is grounded in an analysis of how the world is changing, Turner sees this ontology as preferable to natural rights theory, and as one that will 'prepare the ground for a genuinely sociological account of human rights, which will counteract the largely negative view of rights which we have inherited from the classics within mainstream sociology'.[18]

Malcolm Waters' Constructionist Response

Perhaps the most provocative part of Turner's argument is that sociology, which normally has no time for universal values or institutions, needs to make an exception in the case of rights. It

---

14   Turner, above, n. 1, at 490.
15   Turner, ibid., at 498.
16   Turner, ibid., at 499.
17   Turner, ibid., at 501.
18   Turner, ibid., at 509.

should be remembered that the discipline began by opposing religious or political institutions that presented themselves as god-given or representing the natural order, and that most varieties of sociology, including positivist traditions that seek to emulate natural science, do so without making assumptions about human nature. Turner concentrates on providing a thoughtful and nuanced critique of Marx, Durkheim and Weber (the classical sociologists who have so far dominated discussion in the rights literature) either for not adopting a value position or for encouraging a sceptical view of rights. He also blames Mannheim for establishing a tradition 'in the sociology of knowledge which has a relativistic reaction to rights claims'.[19]

The most forceful, constructionist response to Turner to date has been made by Malcolm Waters. He has argued that 'an adequate sociological theory of human rights must [...] take a social-constructionist point of view, that human rights is an institution that is specific to historical and cultural context just like any other, and that its very universality is itself a human construction'.[20] Waters identifies some internal problems or contradictions within Turner's assumption that rights arise when the strong are led to help the weak through some moral imperative arising from the precariousness of human existence. Why is it that only modern societies have rights? Why is it that historically rights have been advanced by rising groups, such as the bourgeoisie, rather than those that are weak or threatened?

Waters also notes that there seems ample historical evidence that political interests are involved in advancing and contesting rights. One example is that the Universal Declaration of Human Rights in 1948 represented a variety of interests reaching a political accommodation, rather than arising from a collective recognition of human frailty. He argues for a 'social constructionist theory of rights' that will be more effective in explaining the 'historical origins of human rights institutions' and 'historical and cultural variation in the prosecution of claims'.[21] This is not, however, a new theory, as much as a call to acknowledge that an ontological theory of universal rights has no explanatory value for sociologists. He suggests that 'history is filled with institutions that failed because some prophet or intellectual claimed to have discovered a natural or supernatural universal foundation that could underpin them'.[22] Although human rights talk might be in the ascendant now and might seem self-evidently correct or progressive, there is no guarantee that this will always be the case. Presaging current fears of environmental and economic collapse and possible global fragmentation into 'isolated political entities', Waters suggests that 'human rights would be the first casualty'.

The Realities of Rights

Since Turner and Waters agree that rights are needed and probably have similar liberal political views, it can be difficult to see what is at issue in these debates. These theorists are not engaging in political debate about rights as these go on in human societies and to which sociologists sometimes contribute on behalf of different social movements. Instead, they advance philosophical arguments about the nature of sociological explanation: whether it should be normative or value free in describing the social world. Moreover, Turner does not dispute that what actually happens in creating and enforcing rights involves political struggles: instead, like many legal and political philosophers, he does not see this as relevant to the underlying ontological principle that leads

---

19   Turner, ibid., at 493.
20   Waters, above, n. 3, at 593.
21   Waters, ibid., at 599.
22   Waters, ibid., at 598.

social actors and groups, in different ways, towards the need for rights. Nevertheless, Turner probably does have the concern, attributed to him by Waters, 'that if we theorise rights as fragile constructions then they become vulnerable to attack and dismantling',[23] and that dwelling in too much detail on the imperfections and realities will damage the authority and legitimacy of rights.

Many sociologists who support progressive causes might view this call for restraint as unhelpful in that we cannot establish rights or improve their effectiveness without engaging in empirical and, where necessary, muck-raking research. However, from another perspective it seems to exaggerate the importance of the intellectual or sociologist in either national or international politics. One does not, after all, need to be a sociologist to have sceptical views about human rights, or for that matter the ability of the legal system to deliver justice. Many surveys have shown that there is a large degree of scepticism, particularly about the United Nations, even though ordinary citizens believe on balance that it benefits the world community. Most academic and intellectual writers on human rights, although they acknowledge the problems, never describe these in great detail, perhaps because when one does so there is such a large gap between the ideal of rights protections and the realities. This can be illustrated by briefly considering some examples of how rights are made, disputes and the problem of realizing rights.

How Rights are Made

In the teleological model of history favoured by many advocates of the UN system, the human rights we enjoy today have a lineage going back to antiquity, and emerged as intellectuals and politicians developed a sense of responsibility to the whole of humanity.[24] An alternative model is that they have resulted from political struggle by marginalized groups over a long period. In fact, the present system of protection was only established after the massive economic and social dislocation arising from the Second World War, and from political struggles between powerful states seeking to advance their interests. As often happens in international politics, the great powers came together to make a noble statement in the 1948 Declaration of Human Rights about protecting individual freedoms and outlawing war, while creating a system that has allowed them to do exactly what they want and has had only limited success in preventing human suffering.

Anyone with a general knowledge of recent historical events can contrast the aspirations with the reality, in a way that makes the United Nations system appear ineffectual and even hypocritical in allowing abuses to take place in the interest of good international relations. Article 1 of the Declaration of Human Rights, which echoes the language of the 1789 Declaration of the Rights of Man, proclaims that 'all human beings are born free and equal. They are endowed with reason and conscience and should act towards one in a spirit of brotherhood'.

This declaration has not, however, prevented the subsequent mass detention and murder of Soviet dissidents in concentration camps, the United States' use of depleted uranium in recent wars against Iraq, terrorism by numerous groups against civilians, dispossessions, ethnic cleansing and other forced population movements, apartheid, child slavery, the international drugs trade, the worldwide subordination of women and other minority groups, the suppression of free speech in many countries, unsafe working conditions, 'man-made' famine, and at least two cases of genocide on a scale that rivals the Second World War in Cambodia and Rwanda. There was no intervention

---

23   Waters, ibid., at 599.

24   J Donnelly, *Universal Human Rights: In Theory and Practice* (Ithaca, NY: Cornell University Press, 2003).

in these well-documented cases of genocide because Rwanda was of no economic or strategic interest to the great powers, and because Cambodia is within the Chinese sphere of influence.

Without going into detail, one can give a taste of the institutional constraints, built into the system, that have permitted non-intervention. After much political wrangling, two covenants were completed in 1954, but not ratified until 1974. The International Covenant on Civil and Political Rights (ICCPR) provides protection from torture and arbitrary arrest, and the rights to press freedom and to practice your religion. Breaches are monitored by the Commission on Human Rights, a sub-committee of the United Nations that can consider complaints by member states (the 1503 procedure) or appoint a country rapporteur (the 1235 procedure). For enforcement, the General Assembly has to pass a resolution, and then the Security Council can authorize sanctions and the use of force to maintain peace and security, or establish war crimes procedures. These powers, inevitably, have been used selectively and reflect political considerations. To give one example, there will be no UN resolution passed against the alleged use of waterboarding as a means of interrogating terrorist suspects, or rendition, or detention without trial, since any resolution authorizing sanctions can be vetoed by the United States as a member of the Security Council. The International Court of Justice in the Hague can arbitrate in disputes concerning human rights between member states but has no enforcement powers.

The International Covenant on Economic, Social and Cultural Rights (ICESCR) was also ratified in 1974 and establishes rights to just and favourable conditions at work, to form trade unions and to an adequate standard of living and education. There is, however, no means of enforcement. These rights are often promoted by countries in the developing world which argue that breaches of political freedoms are justified in the interests of development. A 1991 Chinese white paper argued that 'it is a simple truth that for any country or nation, the right to subsistence is the most important of all human rights without which all other rights are out of the question'.[25] The whole area of human rights and which rights are enforceable has always been highly politicized, and since there are rarely resolutions or enforcement actions there is a lot of rights talk in various United Nations public fora and among non-governmental organizations (NGOs), without this leading to action by states or the international community against breaches of either covenant.

Disputes Over Rights

Those who present rights in universal terms accept that there must always be a trade-off between competing rights, even if they do not dwell on the difficulties. Turner sees this as a problem particular to late modernity because of the risks created by technological progress. He gives the example of how some rights might need to be curtailed to combat the AIDS pandemic (there is a potential conflict between the right to freedom of movement versus the right to health). However, one can agree with utilitarian thinkers that conflicts arise whenever a right is claimed, without accepting that there is a simple calculus that can allow governments to make wise and fair decisions.

The courts in Western democracies have traditionally favoured the right of free speech over the right to be free from the harms caused by racial vilification or pornography, but ethnic minorities and feminists profoundly disagree with the fairness or disinterested character of these judgments. All the major political debates of our own times concern conflicts over rights. Is it justifiable, for example, to detain people without a right to legal representation for long periods in order to protect the population from potential acts of mass terrorism?

---

25   S Angle and M Svenson (eds), *The Chinese Human Rights Reader: Documents and Commentary 1960–2000* (New York: ME Sharpe, 2001), at 358.

In Australia, there are equally compelling examples of political disputes over rights. The struggle between business interests and the labour unions over Work Choices, a piece of legislation enacted by the Liberal Government and subsequently repealed after Labour won the 2007 election, was a dispute over competing rights. Employers wanted the right to dismiss workers more easily, which they argued would benefit employment and the economy. The unions wanted to protect the rights and conditions of employees.[26] Similarly, the controversial Emergency Intervention in which the Federal Government has taken control of indigenous communities in the Northern Territory has been justified and opposed using the discourse of rights.[27] Proponents believe that intervention is necessary to protect the rights of children from abuse and that this justifies draconian measures such as mandatory health checks on those at risk. Those who demonstrated against the measures across Australia recently complained that indigenous peoples have the right not simply to an apology for the injustices that followed colonization and dispossession (an apology that was made by the Labour Government in February 2007) but also to financial compensation and equal treatment in terms of access to basic services. Although the concept of universal human rights is often used in these debates, it is hard to see how this helps in choosing between competing rights. Certainly, the sociologist or critical legal scholar is no better placed than anyone else to find solutions to these difficult, and often intractable, problems.

Realizing Rights

Even when a right has been established that everyone accepts as genuinely universal and of benefit to the world community, there is still the problem of implementation and enforcement. A good example is the right to claim protection as a political refugee in a safe country, which was established by the 1951 Convention with the aim of assisting displaced people after the Second World War. One can argue that the right should be drafted in broader terms, so that it allows anyone who has been displaced by war or environmental disaster, or minority groups such as women or homosexuals to claim protection. One can also argue that the requirement for asylum claims to be made inside the safe country prevents most people who experience persecution from making claims, or encourages people trafficking. Most people would agree, however, that this is a well-intentioned attempt to support democracy and protect individuals who experience persecution on the grounds of their political beliefs. It can, in theory, protect dissidents who face persecution under any political regime and supports rights established in other covenants supporting free speech and the right of political association.

The problem of implementing rights has arisen following the dramatic rise in asylum claims from the developing world during the 1980s.[28] Britain was particularly affected as a country that had closed other routes to immigration in the late 1960s, when it was perceived as an attractive and tolerant land of opportunity for migrants, and where there were already communities with family and cultural ties to many of its ex-colonies. The number of claimants rose from a few thousand each year in the 1980s to a peak of 100,000 in the 1990s. Because no new resource was put into the Home Office or appeals system there was a large backlog, so in some cases asylum-seekers waited several years for an appeal hearing. A large proportion of these appeals failed in that an immigration appeals tribunal, after considering the evidence, either felt that it was safe for the

---

26   A Stewart and G Williams, *Work Choices: What the High Court Said* (Sydney: Federation Press, 2007).

27   J Altman and M Hinkman (eds), *Coercive Reconciliation: Stabilise, Normalise, Exit Aboriginal Communities* (Melbourne: Arena, 2007).

28   D Joly and R Cohen (eds), *Reluctant Hosts: Europe and its Refugees* (Aldershot: Avebury, 1989).

asylum-seeker to return to his or her original country, or that the applicant lacked 'credibility'. The Government took this to mean that tens of thousands were claiming asylum each year who had made up stories of persecution to get into Britain.

As a consequence, there was a tough policy of preventing people reaching the country, detaining some asylum-seekers, usually on arbitrary grounds as a deterrent, and removing the right to welfare benefits. These policies had the unfortunate side-effect of stirring up racism, and were partly designed for political reasons to make the Government look tough on immigration. At the same time, very few asylum-seekers were, or continue to be, deported, so although individuals experienced great hardship and were forced to join the illegal economy, as far as one can tell, most stayed in the country. Some may have lived for years fearful of a knock on the door from the Immigration Service, which protested throughout this period that the system was ridiculously weak and sought greater powers and resources.

Although this remains a politically contentious topic, where statistics can be manipulated (for example, by allowing more asylum-seekers to stay on temporary permits) and where there is no agreement on how many false claims are made, it seems likely that hearing many weak appeals has led the adjudicators (now immigration judges) who decide appeals to become case-hardened towards some claims that may well be genuine. It is worth noting here that, in most cases, there is no evidence that the appellant has a right to asylum, on the grounds for example of being tortured, other than his or her word. Consider, for instance, the following December 1996 appeal made by a Kurd, who claimed that he had been given fallaca, a method of torture that involves beating the soles of the feet but if done skilfully leaves no marks.[29] He argued that he had a well-founded fear of persecution from being arrested and tortured, after distributing leaflets for the TKPMLH, the political wing of a militant Kurdish organization. He claimed to have a stammer as a result of the torture and submitted a 12-page psychological report that concluded he was suffering from post-traumatic stress disorder.

The Home Office, however, argued that he had fabricated the story to join his family who were already in the country. The application was refused, among other reasons, because when interviewed he demonstrated only a 'basic understanding' of the TKPMLH rather than that of 'someone who was actually involved'. Moreover, even if he was telling the truth about being detained, but had exaggerated the torture, it was a case of legitimate 'prosecution' rather than 'persecution'. One can get a sense of how asylum claims are actually decided, and what adjudicators have to work with, from this attempt by his representative during examination-in-chief to demonstrate that he was a political activist:

R: Can you tell us what the TKPH is?

W: They defend TKPMLH actions. They defend the rights of workers, the rights of arrested people, and their aim is to stand by such oppressed people from whom their rights have been taken away.

R: And who founded the TKPMLH?

W: His name is Ibrahim Kaypakaya.

R: Can you spell his second name?

---

29   This is one of a number of appeals documented in M Travers, *The British Immigration Courts: A Study in Law and Politics* (Bristol: Policy Press, 1999).

W: K A Y P A K A Y A.

R: And if I said to you which concept of communism do the TKPMLH follow, what would you say?

W: There are no different concepts in communism.

R: So, what do you mean by that?

W: Communism is a worldwide system of labourers and peasants.

This asylum appeal was given careful consideration by the adjudicator concerned because Turkey at the time was a country in which the tribunal accepted that political persecution did take place and that it was not safe to return there. One can see, however, that the ideal of giving protection to victims of political persecution can only be realized by people making difficult decisions through exercising interpretive judgment about accounts given by appellants with no corroborative evidence.

This asylum-seeker may have known the name of the leader of this political party as a member or because he had prepared for this question. The court may have had accurate information about what members of the party understood by communism, or this may have been simplistic or inaccurate. He may have suffered from post-traumatic stress disorder, but there was no hard scientific basis to that finding, which was, in any case, made by a psychologist who had himself been an asylum-seeker and who specialized in providing expert evidence for appellants. As the adjudicator admitted when interviewed after the hearing, reaching a decision in Turkish cases was difficult:

> They are very difficult cases. Very often you will find yourself having some sympathy. Then you will find they are not considered to be persecuted per se, although it's close. They tend to be taken in and beaten on the soles of their feet (it's called fallaca), and they tend to exaggerate. There are never any documents they can produce but an abundance of background information. It all comes down to credibility. They all want to come to the UK. The question is if they are telling a pack of lies.

Although the outcome of this appeal is unknown, one can see that mistakes must be made, and individuals treated with great unfairness, simply by having to wait for years before an appeal.[30] There is, moreover, no rational or scientific method of demonstrating whether an asylum-seeker is genuine: given that there is no hard evidence, it depends on whether the asylum-seeker gives a convincing and sufficiently detailed account, and how this is received. Whatever the quality of the evidence, a representative can often predict the outcome by knowing whether a 'hard' or 'soft' adjudicator will be hearing the appeal.

Decisions about entitlement to protection made in these messy, practical circumstances requiring imperfect human judgment, are far removed from the abstract principles discussed by philosophers and political theorists, including the issue of whether a state is entitled to close borders to immigrants.[31] One cannot even make a clear contrast between the forces of good and evil, or

---

30   There were 1,820 asylum applications from Turkey in 1995, out of a total of 43,965 applications, most of which were refused and appealed. According to research conducted by one NGO, only 5.4 per cent of appeals from Turkey were allowed.

31   A Dummett, *Towards a Just Immigration Policy* (London: Cobden, 1986).

the moral judgments about states which seem to flow easily in human rights talk. One civil servant pointed out that any increase in budget for the immigration appeals system, including giving legal aid for legal representation outside government-funded agencies (mainly staffed by non-lawyers) has to come from some other area of expenditure.

Studying Rights: A Sociological Agenda

Although Turner, in his search for an ontology to underpin sociological research, acknowledges that rights arise through a political process, he does not dwell on the difficulties, or see these as threatening the value or legitimacy of rights talk. Like philosophers, political theorists, socio-legal researchers and sociologists arguing in favour of human rights and, more generally, the value of regulation, he tends to assume that institutions work properly or that problems can be remedied given sufficient resources or political will. Waters, on the other hand, sees the political character of rights as requiring a constructionist theory. Even Waters, however, says little about what actually happens in this political process, or suggests how one might study this as a sociologist. In fact, most sociological discussion on rights stays at this general level, partly because contributors usually only discuss classical sociology. There are, however, some long-established and theoretically developed twentieth-century traditions that go further than Weber in pursuing a constructionist agenda. This section will consider how the interpretive traditions of symbolic interactionism and ethnomethodology could be used to investigate the politics of rights and rights talk. It will also consider the charge, made implicitly at least by Turner, that such approaches lead to relativism and are not sufficiently respectful to human rights institutions.

Interpretive Sociology and Human Rights

Alison Morris, in the introduction and conclusion to her recent collection,[32] advances what sounds like an interactionist approach to rights even though, like many theorists, she does not acknowledge the source or explore the methodological basis of this position. Ken Plummer, a British sociologist whose work about homosexuality has combined interactionist and critical approaches, goes further by listing a set of principles that derive from the social problems tradition, a productive empirical programme in American sociology that grew out of labelling theory in the 1970s.[33] He notes, for example, that from an interactionist perspective 'rights are inventions'. They 'come into being through the interpretivist and activist work of social movements and a diverse range of moral crusaders and entrepeneurs'.[34] They should be analysed as moving through certain stages from discovery to institutionalization. There is also advice to the sociologist, based on Herbert Blumer's methodological writings,[35] to study rights empirically, through conducting inductive, naturalistic research:

> Although rights can be analysed abstractly, the task for sociologists is to become intimately familiar with the crusaders, their claims and the social processes through which rights emerge. They need

---

32 Morris, above, n. 4.
33 K Plummer, 'Rights work: Constructing lesbian, gay and sexual rights in late modern times', in L Morris (ed.), *Rights: Sociological Perspectives* (London: Routledge, 2006), 152–67.
34 Plummer, ibid., at 153.
35 Blumer, above, n. 6.

to see "rights" as part of the day-to-day world of lived meaning, and not simply belonging to the theoretical and philosophical or even legal heavens.[36]

In discussing rights for homosexuals, Plummer takes a long historical view rather than drawing on ethnographic research inside rights organizations. However, there are many empirical studies about social problems that illustrate that the approach is fruitful, even or perhaps because it reveals political debates within social movements that are not always reported in official histories. Plummer also notes that one should expect to find 'schisms and fracturings' within rights movements, which is certainly evident in divisions between radicals and liberals in campaigns for homosexual rights. There seems ample scope for ethnographic research that interviews social actors in the environmental movement, indigenous groups, the feminist movement, the animal rights movement and many others, and describes these processes.[37]

Although interactionism has so far had most influence on mainstream sociology, it is not the only interpretive tradition that could be used in studying rights talk and organizations. Ethnomethodology and conversation analysis are also productive and diverse research traditions that have already contributed to our understanding of law through looking in more detail at action and meaning. Ethnomethodological ethnographies have looked at decision-making processes within the police, prosecution offices and law firms.[38] Richard Harper employed this approach while working as an IT consultant for the IMF, looking at how mission teams reached judgments about economic performance when conducting in-country visits.[39] Given access to an international or state agency, it might be possible to describe the practical and political reasoning used in determining whether countries have an acceptable human rights record. There is already some ethnographic and anthropological research on decision making by administrative and legal institutions in asylum appeals,[40] and there is scope for similar research in other organizations and agencies concerned with protecting human rights. Then there are the various organizations, including the committees and General Assembly of the United Nations, in which rights issues are publicly debated and resolutions made for intervention in countries that have breached the conventions. Even without needing permission to go behind the scenes or obtain access to confidential information, conversation analysts, or other traditions in discourse analysis, could examine the language used in these debates, which often involve a conflict between competing rights.

The Problem of Relativism

Although Turner does not consider these modern sociological approaches, it seems likely that he might object that they make it difficult to study or appreciate rights because they have relativist epistemological assumptions. The constructionist position seems to undermine the pursuit of a

---

36   Plummer, above, n. 32, at 153.

37   See, for example, A Riles, *The Network Inside Out* (Ann Arbor, MI: University of Michigan Press, 2000) and S Hopgood, *Keepers of the Flame: Inside Amnesty International* (Ithaca, NY: Cornell University Press, 2006).

38   For example, A Cicourel, *The Social Organisation of Juvenile Justice* (New York: Wiley, 1967).

39   R Harper, *Inside the IMF: An Ethnography of Documents, Technology and Organisational Action* (London: Academic Press, 1998).

40   Travers, above, n. 28; T Spijkerboer, 'Stereotyping and acceleration: Gender, procedural acceleration and marginalised judicial review in the Dutch asylum system', in G Noll (ed.), *Proof, Evidentiary Assessment and Credibility in Asylum Procedures* (Dordrecht; Martinus Nijhoff, 2005); A Good, *Anthropology and Expertise in the Asylum Courts* (London: Routledge, 2006).

just world through suggesting that there are no universal standards. It even makes it difficult for the sociologist to advance a moral or political position, since one presumably has to accept that opposing views (even those advanced by dictatorships) are equally valid, and attempt to give these equal weight in research studies. These are, however, misunderstandings that arise during the often heated debates that take place between sociological paradigms, since the interpretivist position falls short of saying that academics are not permitted to hold moral or political views. Weber argued, forcefully and explicitly, that the sociologist cannot avoid adopting a value position, even in choosing which problems to investigate, but that it is also important to acknowledge your own bias and other political and moral viewpoints (he was a critic of false objectivity in academic writing about political topics).

Howard Becker within the interactionist tradition has also argued that the researcher cannot avoid taking sides when describing any group or organization in which there are different viewpoints.[41] However, the objective should be to give a scientific, balanced account. Becker also advised researchers troubled by these problems that it is difficult to avoid offending someone (consider the various factions in a social movement), but that one consolation is that, over time, there could be several studies offering a multi-faceted view of any organization:

> What do we do in the meantime? I suppose the answers are more or less obvious. We take sides as our personal and political commitments dictate, or use theoretical and technical resources to avoid the distortions that they might introduce into our work, limit our conclusions generally [...] and field as best we can the accusations and doubts that will surely be our fate.[42]

The problem of relativism raises difficult issues that affect all sociological paradigms. There is still no agreement on whether the sociologist should aspire to a form of objectivity, as against advancing a one-sided or emotional viewpoint. Those, like Turner, who promote a particular moral viewpoint often seem to stay at the level of general principles rather than addressing the complexity of political disputes or what actually happens inside institutions. In any case, both Plummer and Waters object to the view that seeing rights as constructed weakens their moral authority, especially if the alternative is accepting a version of natural law theory (subjecting ourselves uncritically to some higher moral power).

Conclusion: A Realist View of Rights

This chapter has been critical towards the idea that sociologists need an ontological theory of rights, and has instead favoured a constructionist understanding of rights that sees them as arising from political struggle and as being implemented through imperfect human institutions. This does not prevent the sociologist from believing in rights as an ideal worth pursuing, but allows a realistic appreciation of the political, material and interpretive difficulties inherent in making and realizing rights. The chapter has given a taste, for example, of how there are usually competing views of rights, so that governments argue on principled, moral grounds in favour of practices, such as torture, which liberal intellectuals see as completely indefensible. It has also shown in the case of the right of asylum that realizing rights may be no easy matter without spending more money to

---

41　H Becker, 'Whose side are we on?', in H Becker (ed.), *Sociological Work* (Chicago, IL: Aldine, 1970), 123–34.

42　Becker, above, at 134.

create a faster appeals process (at a time when British governments are trying to contain public spending). And it has suggested at a methodological level that good sociological work should always address and respect different perspectives and viewpoints, even though the sociologist advances a particular value position.

Although advocates including Turner acknowledge the political, and to some extent the material and organizational, problems surrounding rights, they do not usually dwell on the difficulties, and often suggest or imply that there are solutions. There is also a tendency among both liberal and critical sociologists to assume that there are easy solutions to social problems, even though this is not usually the case. To give an example, chosen because it is highly controversial, there is no obvious or easy solution to the Palestinian-Israeli conflict. Most liberal commentators side with the Palestinians, objecting to the occupation and Israeli policies on moral and political grounds, in the same way and for the same reasons that they opposed apartheid in South Africa. This includes opponents of the occupation within Israel, including the criminologist Stan Cohen, who despaired before eventually leaving the country at the level of injustice routinely inflicted on the Palestinians. He used this example in *States of Denial*,[43] urging liberals not to turn a blind eye to human rights abuses. On the other hand, Cohen recognized that there are competing rights in the case of Israel/Palestine, and that a settlement will only take place with considerable compromise on each side. One can, therefore, argue that the expression of moral outrage towards hard-liners in Israel or for that matter the Palestinians for not respecting human rights, while understandable and necessary in political debate, is not helpful in achieving a solution. This is because in negotiations, the general principles expressed in United Nations resolutions, and the parties' deeply felt sense of what is right, can only be a starting point: the hard work of reaching an agreement involves working through practical and mundane issues, such as the shape of borders.

As Morris has observed, 'there is scope for a considerable gap between recognition of the need for protection and its achievement in practice, and this is arguably a gap that sociology as a discipline is well placed to address'.[44] Although it is perhaps even more difficult than in previous decades to obtain access to the 'backstage' work of institutions or agencies concerned with sensitive political issues,[45] there is still a need for empirical research that tests the claims made in the name of human rights against the realities and, because of this, has a 'moral sting' to it.[46] Although it is important to debate general principles, including whether sociologists and socio-legal researchers need a theory of rights, we may learn most through examining what actually happens inside social movements and human rights institutions.

---

43   S Cohen, States of Denial: Knowing about Atrocities and Suffering (Cambridge: Polity Press, 2001).
44   Morris, above, n. 4, at 2.
45   E Goffman, *The Presentation of Self in Everyday Life* (Harmondsworth: Penguin, 1959).
46   H Becker, *Outsiders* (New York: Free Press, 1973), at 206.

Chapter 3

The 'Rights' Conundrum:
Poverty of Philosophy amidst Poverty

Radha D'Souza

You are not my fellow traveller,
Tread your own path.
May you be affluent,
And I, downtrodden.
(Hazrat Nizamuddin Awlia [d. 1325 AD]
Chishti Order of Sufis, South Asia)

1

The rights discourse has exhausted itself. The last drop has been squeezed out of the concept discursively and in praxis. Yet, the discourse continues to haunt like a disembodied ghost. When ideas capture popular imaginations they acquire a material force, so Marx argued. The idea of rights became a material force in the anti-feudal revolutions of Europe in the seventeenth and eighteenth centuries; it lost its power to inspire thereafter but bounced back after it was reformulated in the course of the anti-capitalist, anti-colonial revolutions of the early twentieth century. Since the end of the Second World War, and especially since the end of the Cold War, the rights discourse has presented itself as a conundrum in theory and in praxis: doomed with rights and doomed without them. Nobody today, not even its most ardent advocate, argues that the idea of rights, reformulated or otherwise, has the potential to shake the world order in the way that the capitalist, socialist and national liberation revolutions did.

The discourse has worked itself out through a number of familiar dualisms: moral rights versus legal rights, economic rights versus human rights, institutionalized rights versus right claims in praxis, rights under capitalism and socialism, Eurocentric right concepts versus non-Eurocentric rights, the Asian values discourse or indigenous discourses, for example, but, whatever the starting point for the discourse or the preferred theoretical framework, attempts to ground it in the materiality of the contemporary world order entangles the discourse in a conundrum of one type or another. Yet, if not grounded in the materiality of the contemporary world the rights discourse loses its meaning, as the very idea of rights is tied inextricably to its sociality.

In part the rights impasse is symptomatic of the poverty of philosophy in current times. In part it is the manifestation of challenges of poverty in the contemporary world. Since its reformulations in the course of the socialist and national liberation movements of the early twentieth century, the rights discourse has become embroiled, willy-nilly, in problems of poverty within Third World states and inequality between states. To ignore these realities is to render the rights discourse meaningless to the vast majority of the world's populations. To take into account the realities invites us to confront the theoretical challenges for human emancipation with or without rights.

Necessarily generalizing the rights discourse has two broad orientations: immanent discourses that interrogate the conceptual and philosophical aspects of rights and sociological discourses that seek to evaluate rights in terms of what they do in the real world. In this essay both types of argument are used to locate the rights discourse within a wider problematic: that of emancipation and freedom.

2

The socialist and national liberation struggles of the early twentieth century forced people to reconsider the rights discourse in terms of classical liberal theory because of the challenges posed by polarization within and between societies; and because of the widespread dislocation of people from economic, political, social, and cultural institutions. The dislocation demonstrated the failure of the narrow individualistic orientation of classical liberal theory and the praxis that followed from it. The reformulation revolved around the tension between economic rights and political rights in liberal theory. After the end of the Second World War three types of social formation emerged: socialist states, neo, post/colonial states, and welfare democratic states. Each social formation was based on the specific forms that the reconciliations between the economic and political domains to address social polarization and dislocation took. At the heart of the rights conundrum today is the breakdown of that reconciliation, the effects of which are felt most acutely in one region in particular: the Third World.

Increasingly it is apparent that while the rights discourse touches people in the three worlds differently, the impasse in the discourse is felt most acutely in the Third World where for the vast majority of its people dislocation and destitution are a regular feature of life. In the Third World the problem of displacement more than any other issue poses a challenge to the rights discourse. The 'economic versus human rights' dichotomy is mirrored in the way displacements are characterized: some, like wars and ethnic discrimination, are considered 'human rights' issues, properly speaking, rendering their economic underpinnings opaque at best; and others, like urbanization and industrialization, flow from 'economic' rights as by-products, seen only indirectly, if at all, as 'human rights' issues. According to the World Bank's World Development Report 2009, out of the world population of over six billion, one billion live in slums, one billion in what the World Bank calls 'fragile lagging areas within countries' and another one billion 'at the bottom of the global hierarchy of nations'.[1] The vast majority of displaced people are internally displaced. Thus, according to the World Bank, one out of five persons from rural China migrates to cities in search of jobs. According to UN estimates about 1 per cent of the world's population is internally displaced owing to wars, development projects and natural disasters each year. The World Bank estimates that at least 10 million people are displaced each year to make way for development projects like roads, railways, dams and such. In India alone 33 million people have been displaced by development projects. These involuntary displacements occur almost entirely in the Third World skewing the geographies of rights in ways that are seldom acknowledged within the discourse. Statistics in these regions are likely to be underestimates for sociological and institutional reasons that need not be gone into here. In reality the displaced populations could be much higher. Legal definitions of voluntary and involuntary displacement, the device by which the 'economic versus human rights' differentiation is sustained, obfuscate a large grey no-man's-land where myriad social, economic, political, and cultural pressures operate in ways that leave people with no choice but to succumb to pressures of displacement. The rights discourse today offers two solutions out of the impasse: a return to classical liberal theory; or to

---

1   The World Bank, *World Development Report 2009: Reshaping Economic Geography* (Washington, DC: The World Bank, 2009), at 5.

attempts to reconstruct the broken relationship between the economic and the political. Both of these courses offer a return to failed conceptions. Hence the conundrum.

A closer examination reveals that displacement is an ongoing phenomenon that parallels colonial history and continues through 'globalization' today. Displacement has always involved complex social, military, cultural, economic, and human causes and effects. From Palestinians' right of return to road, dam, and bridge projects undertaken in the name of 'development'; from the colonization of the Americas and Australasia to the social impact of the World Trade Organization's free trade policies in the Third World, displacement is a question that appears to embody all that is entailed in imperialism and colonialism.

Probing displacement further reveals that it is integral to processes of modernity itself and parallels the emergence and growth of capitalism as exemplified by the enclosure movements in Britain and the peasant wars in Germany and France in the eighteenth centuries which were responses to displacement from land and place. In the nineteenth century 40.9 per cent of the population of the British Isles, 30.9 per cent of Norway, 30.1 per cent of Portugal, 29.2 per cent of Italy and 23.2 per cent of Spain migrated to colonize and settle in different parts of the world as a result of domestic turmoil.[2] That history is one of double displacement – the displaced at home displacing people in distant places. Bauman (2004) refers to 'the production of wasted humans' as an inevitable by-product of modernity.[3] The production of 'wasted humans' occurs through displacement.

The modernist discourse of rights in philosophy, political and legal theory parallels large-scale displacement of people. Each slum dweller, each migration, whether owing to economic or political causes, whether historically or at present, tells a story of displacement. The focus of this chapter is not on particular stories of displacement: their histories, empirical realities, anthropology or sociology. There is, by now, a significant body of work with different disciplinary orientations on various types of displacement. This chapter focuses instead on the *concept* of 'displacement' and its relationship to the rights discourse with which it co-exists as its 'other': as its underbelly, its necessary precondition and inevitable consequence. What then is the nexus between the reality of displacement and the discourse of rights, if there is one?

3

Displacement is conceptually simple to grasp. A Tamil proverb says that a visiting ghost drives away the resident ghost of the village. The property or place occupied by a person, group, community or nation on the basis of prior entitlements (whatever they may be) is usurped by another, a latecomer. The question that arises is this: why should the later claimant have preference over the existing claimant? This question is at the heart of displacement issues everywhere throughout history: why should *I* be uprooted to make way for a newcomer? Why should the Palestinians be expelled from their homes to compensate for injustices that occurred in distant Europe? Why should the Kurds have to leave their homes because the Turkish state wants to build a dam? Why should the Aborigines be displaced to accommodate Britain's poverty and population problems? Why must a subsistence farmer be evicted from his little farm to make way for a bridge or highway? Why *me*?

The problem of displacement is thus one of contesting claims to property and place, one prior, the other posterior in time. Both claimants uphold the sanctity of property and place in principle, except that one has it and the other desires it. The usurper, as the later claimant, cannot claim on

---

2   The World Bank, ibid.

3   Z Bauman, *Wasted Lives: Modernity and its Outcasts* (Cambridge: Polity Press, 2004).

the basis of existing norms because the existing occupier occupies the property or place on the basis of those very norms. The new claimant must therefore articulate his or her claims on some other grounds. Equally, the later claimant must claim in the name of all if he or she wishes to inscribe their claims as the *new* norm. If later claims are articulated too narrowly the old norms will continue to operate and the usurper will at best have gotten away with breaking the norms and at worst be penalized for it. For example, if a subsistence farmer is forcibly evicted from her land by a company wanting to set up a chemical factory on her farm, existing property laws will protect the farmer against the company. But if many companies can claim through the state in the name of nation building, the new norm of nation building becomes wide enough to include the farmer in principle, as citizen. Nevertheless, the farmer must first be evicted from her existing land and must rearticulate her claim for a place in the new normative order, in this case in terms of the benefits of economic development that the chemical factory will bring, preferential claims to employment in the factory and such. The farmer's displacement, just as that of the Aborigines, or Palestinians, or whoever, becomes the basis of a new normative order, call it nation building, modernization, collectivization, the New World, a New World Order, whatever. The new claimants, thus, do not claim on the basis of existing rights.

Quite naturally the displaced persons, groups and nations protest against displacement. This is the 'Why *me?*' question. Between these competing claims, an existing one and a new one, the rights discourse acts in curious ways. It represents the protests against displacement in the language of rights: political rights, cultural rights, democratic rights, human rights, whatever, in other words, as claims by people for land, homeland, livelihoods, property, culture and such. In actual fact, by opposing displacement, the protestors are not claiming anything new; their demand is rather to remain where they are without interference from the new claimants. Their protest is against the new rights *proposed* by the usurper. A banner at the World Social Forum 2004 in Mumbai captured this sentiment in its slogan – 'We do not want development. We want to live' – a slogan against those seeking to establish 'globalization' as the new normative order.

In contrast, the rights discourse abstains from answering the question: why are later claimants' claims preferable to those of existing claimants? This temporal question falls outside the scope of the rights discourse properly speaking. Instead, the rights discourse refers metonymically to philosophy, political theory and legal theory for justifications. In philosophy discourses about change, history and time emphasize the inevitability of subsequent usurpers evicting existing ones. The Hegelian spirit advances to Europe leaving ancient civilizations by the wayside because history works in teleological ways. In political theory ideals of progress, modernization, freedom and nationhood emphasize the need for people to break the existing structural constraints of political economy and institutions but obfuscate the new structural constraints and institutions that they propose to replace it with, or the larger reality that all social life involves constraints in some form. In legal theory not only are property relations privileged over all other social, cultural and political relations, but, more importantly, newer rights are privileged over older ones: a later statute prevails over an earlier one, statute law prevails over common law and, in the non-European societies, colonial modern law prevails over traditional law making it possible for new usurpers to articulate newer forms of property rights and rights to justify displacement and new settlements.

The new claimant invokes philosophy, political theory or legal theory as superior reason in terms antithetical to mundane existing entitlements inscribed in everyday rights. This way of rationalizing new claims introduces a hiatus between Rights with a capital 'R' and really existing entitlements in everyday life, a hiatus that manifests as a disjuncture between the ideal and the real in the rights discourse. It obscures the spatio-temporal dimensions of rights and the pain and suffering necessarily entailed in replacing old claims with new ones. Whatever the merits or demerits of philosophical and theoretical ideas of change, history, the linearity of time, progress, or freedom, the pain and upheavals of displacement remain real for the displaced. It means that the 'Why *me*?' question chases the rights discourse like a dark shadow.

In pre-modern times the 'Why *me*?' question was answered by invoking a divine will or a supernatural or cosmological order. The Book of Matthew says: 'For unto every one that hath shall be given, and he shall have abundance: but from him that hath not shall be taken away even that which he hath'.[4] It has to be accepted without question because divine will imposes limits on what human agents can do. The modernist discourse of the inevitability of history, progress, change, etc. seeks to remove God and a predetermined cosmological order and puts human beings in charge of their destinies; indeed it commands them to become self-conscious agents of change. At the same time modernist discourses retain the inevitability of history, progress, development, whatever.

This change in the place of human beings within the world and of human agency within modernist thinking means the 'Why *me*?' question *must* be answered as a matter of necessity. To the extent that the rights discourse can never satisfy this question sufficiently for the displaced, and to the extent that new claimants always come out winners, the rights discourse inevitably carries dissent, adversarial attitudes and the terms of its undoing within itself. The World Bank may say winners and losers are inevitable in a world guided by the invisible hand of the market, but the losers are bound to query their position. 'Pain' and 'suffering' become more than the empirical experiences of the displaced, assuming a non-factual transcendental character of the type entailed in the concept of *dukkha* in Indian and Buddhist philosophical traditions. This concept will be discussed further in the concluding section but for now it suffices to say that the pain principle is inscribed in the attributes of rights, its very make-up in modernist thought such that the rights discourse follows the suffering caused by displacement. Yet the rights discourse holds out rights as the means to freedom from constraints. Much of the focus of the rights discourse therefore centres on ways of eliminating the perceived obstructions to its fulfilment.

Two objections are possible to the proposition that displacement entails privileging a later claimant over the existing one and therefore causing suffering in the broadest sense of the term to the existing claimants. First, one may argue that displacement is at heart an economic question whatever the political, social or cultural manifestations, and ask whether the above account of displacement and rights does not amount to repackaging the old antinomies of 'economic versus human rights' arguments in the rights discourse? Second, it could be said that something more is needed to establish a causal link between displacement and rights such that it becomes its inevitable 'other'. The sections that follow examine these aspects of displacement and the rights discourse.

4

The 'economic versus human rights' framework in the rights discourse misrepresents the problem of displacement. The misrepresentation lies in that it represents human dis*placement* as dis*possession*. The 'economic versus human rights' strand in the rights discourse frames economic rights in antithetical terms to human rights and argues that economic rights, particularly property rights, erode human rights and make their actualization difficult, if not impossible. In as much as the economic *is* human (socio-political-cultural) and the human (socio-political-cultural) *is* economic, the framework introduces an analytical distinction between economy and humanity in ways that reify a wider epistemological problem in modernist thought, which I call *epistemological economism*.

---

4 Matthew 25:29, King James Bible.

Epistemological economism refers to a merchant's world view inscribed in the very structure of reason such that it extends an accountant's logic to every sphere of human life. Statistical reasoning, empiricism, cost–benefit enumerations resembling ledger-book classifications – costs in one column, benefits in another – become integral to the way socio-political-cultural questions are analysed. The merchant world view is no longer limited to trade and commerce but extends to all spheres of social and cultural life. Labour, an attribute of being human, is transformed into a tradable commodity like shoes or furniture. Social problems are aggregated numerically to become comprehensible, as in statistical analysis.[5] Even philosophical arguments must be 'weighed' so that they may 'profit' society in definite ways.

Douzinas argues that the rights discourse (in Western philosophy) underwent a shift from a moral/ethical idea in natural philosophy to a legal idea underpinned by the institution of the state.[6] The shift *is* the modernist moment. The epistemic break in the rights discourse is underpinned by the analytical separation of 'the economic' and 'the socio-political' as distinct realms with different logics. The analytical separation of economic relations from other social relations is necessitated by the development of capitalism spearheaded initially by merchants but this necessity leaves us with profound epistemological consequences that cannot be contained in the 'moral/ethical versus legal' framework for rights, nor in the 'economic versus human rights' framework.

The analytical separation of 'the economic' from 'the socio-political' is made possible by liberal theory. Classical liberalism, the philosophy of capitalism, naturalized property by putting it on a par with life and liberty. It was the analytical separation of economic relations from other social relations that made this naturalization possible however. The 'economic versus human rights' strand in the rights discourse acknowledges this tension between naturalized property on the one hand and life and liberty on the other. The tension is interrogated in the Marxist tradition, in particular, in Marx's essays 'On the Jewish question' and 'The Eighteenth Brumaire of Louis Bonaparte', written in 1843 and 1851/52 respectively. Marx's critique of rights was based on three arguments, summarized elsewhere as:

> [...]: (a) the "empty shell" argument, i.e. liberal rights are negative endowments that promise the possibility of their fulfilment but do not create the conditions for their fulfilment; (b) the "preconditions for liberty" argument, i.e. that individualism, commodification and production relations of capitalism do not create the real social conditions necessary for flourishing of human freedoms, if anything the conditions of capitalist production create bondage and oppression. Therefore real freedoms require a radically different type of production relationships as the basis of social organisation; (c) the "means to an end" argument, i.e. that while bourgeois democracy may free labouring people from old feudal oppression, they do not liberate them from capitalist oppression and have limited value to the extent they allow limited political space for labouring people to pursue their own political emancipation; therefore bourgeois democracy is a means to freedom and not an end in itself.[7]

For Marx the binary opposition between the economic and the human (socio-political) must be overcome through political action in praxis supported by explanatory critique in theory that exposes the actors behind the naturalization of property, that is, the interests of merchant classes

---

5   See, for example, TM Porter, *Trust in Numbers: The Pursuit of Objectivity in Science and Public Life* (Princeton, NJ: Princeton University Press, 1995).

6   C Douzinas, *The End of Human Rights* (Oxford: Hart Publishing, 2000).

7   R D'Souza, 'Liberal theory, human rights and water-justice: Back to square one?', *Law, Social Justice & Global Development Journal*, 1 (2008), 1–15, at 7.

and capitalists who benefit by putting tradable property in the form of property rights on a par with life and liberty. In classical liberalism the relationship between the economic and human (socio-political-cultural) realms is treated as non-adversarial. The Marxist critique, by exposing what is entailed in the separation, that is, an exploitative capitalist system, casts the relationship in adversarial terms. The Marxist critique acknowledges the constraints on human action: 'Men make their own history, but they do not make it as they please; they do not make it under self-selected circumstances, but under circumstances existing already, given and transmitted from the past.'[8] Marx's vision of a communist society is one where the economic versus human binary is transcended. Nevertheless, the philosophical and epistemological grounds for the transcendence remain implicit and underdeveloped in Marxist theory, as shall be discussed further on. The Marxist critique continues to have a profound influence in social justice movements that impugn and de-legitimize the political, normative and juridical discourses of rights. This is especially so in the Third World where the gaps between the claims of the rights discourse and the reality of displacement is stark. The interplay of the rights discourse with displacement in the twentieth century widened and exacerbated the analytical separation of economic relations from socio-political relations in ways that reified epistemological economism.

Naturalizing property alongside life and liberty makes violations of life and liberty compensable in principle. Retribution takes a property form. The accountant's logic articulates justice in money terms. This can be seen in the most ordinary incidences in daily life: police abuse, state violence, war crimes, indeed even slavery and colonization can be compensated in principle. Reparation claims for slavery,[9] against displacement by World Bank projects,[10] and for military invasions,[11] point to the extension of the accountant's logic to questions of life and liberty. Displacement can be *righted* if the usurper pays compensation. The rights discourse asserts the intrinsic worth of life and liberty but allows the 'trade-off' (to use a mercantile phrase) between the economic and the human by remaining silent on the compensation principle.

By establishing equivalence between property on the one hand, and life and liberty on the other, epistemological economism transforms the meaning of justice to a mercantile view of justice. The meaning of justice is the restoration of equivalence between 'the economic' and 'life and liberty'. If the displaced are compensated adequately, reparations are paid for upheavals caused by wars, and historical justice is achievable by expropriating the expropriators as in socialist revolutions, the equivalence between the economic and the human can be restored. Epistemological economism is reified and returned to more secure foundations as a result.

The equivalence erodes the intrinsic worth of the 'self' in its particularities: individuals – people in time/place contexts – as well as the 'Self' in its universality – the human, the eternal. Epistemological economism renders empirically specific humans (with a small 'h') valuable depending on their economic worth, and, at the same time exorcises Humans (capital 'H') as the abstracted subjects of life from economic values, making them pristine and untainted by the grit and grime of the economic world. However, as law and justice allow a 'trade-off' between the two it becomes necessary to retain the differentiation between 'human' and 'Human'.

---

8   K Marx, 'The eighteenth brumaire of Louis Bonaparte', in D Fernbach (ed.), *Karl Marx: Surveys from Exile Political Writings*, vol. 2 (Harmondsworth: Penguin Books, 1977 [1851–1852]).

9   See, for example, S Winter, 'What's so bad about slavery? Assessing the grounds for reparations', *Patterns of Prejudice* (2007), 373–93.

10   See the guidelines in the World Bank Involuntary Resettlement Sourcebook: Planning and Implementation in Development Projects (Washinton, DC: The World Bank, 2004).

11   For example, see L Turgeon, 'The political economy of reparations', *New German Critique*, 1 (1973), 111–25.

The relationship between the human with a small 'h' that is embroiled in the economic, political and social turmoil of everyday life and the Human with a capital 'H' that informs normative, ethical and moral life is a two-way traffic however. It is more generally accepted that the rights discourse is informed by conceptualizations of the eternal, the intrinsic, the Human. It is equally true that the treatment of human beings in everyday life informs the ethical/moral normative conceptualization of the Human. The 'down-payments' we are prepared to make to return Palestinians their homeland, Third World peasants their right to live, indigenous peoples their right to be a nation, and workers in Third World sweat shops their rights to fair wages and such colour the rights discourse in direct and indirect ways. The equivalence of 'the economic' with 'life and liberty' therefore qualifies and colours our conceptions of what it is to be human.

Epistemological economism leaves the strident critic of economic rights with nothing more than the human will; and the strident Marxist with collective political will as the means to overcome the hiatus between the economic and human dimensions of social life. Voluntarism, however, embeds rather than overcomes epistemological economism and generates yet another binary in the rights discourse: the moral/ethical versus the legal.

Above all epistemological economism misrepresents displacement as dis*possession* in that it presents human dislocation as loss of *possession*. The 'possession' in dis*possession* anchors human displacement to property relations in the economy. Dispossession is but displacement through the lens of epistemological economism. It produces the rights discourse as its inevitable 'other'. This transformation of human dislocation into dispossession compensatable in principle requires consideration of place and possession in modernist thought, a point addressed in the next section.

5

The modernist moment when rights as a moral/ethical idea became a legal idea alluded to by Douzinas is also the moment when modernist thought transformed place into possession as property. As Roy Bhasker points out, society is unilaterally dependent on nature.[12] The unilateral dependence on nature makes place an ontological attribute and a condition for life. According to Edward Casey, '[…] place, by virtue of its unencompassibility by anything other than itself, is at once the limit and the condition of all that exists. […] place serves as the *condition* of all existing things'.[13]

Human relationships with nature are, however, socially negotiated and sustained through social structures, epistemology, ideology and the materiality of human life, including the economic activities of production, all of which occur in places. The transformation of place into possession is accomplished in classical liberalism by reformulating conceptions of time and space and their relationship in ways that dismiss place and render time and space as linear abstractions. The reformulation was brought about in the fields of science and technology, in particular navigation technologies, important for merchants, but also in the fields least constrained by moral/ethical norms prevailing in society. Casey provides a phenomenological account of the processes through which this transformation is brought about and, quoting Cisco Lassiter, states that '[…] for the modern self, all places are essentially the same: in the uniform, homogeneous space of a Euclidean-

---

12   R Bhaskar, *Reclaiming Reality: A Critical Introduction to Contemporary Philosophy* (London, Verso, 1989).

13   ES Casey, *Getting Back into Place: Toward a Renewed Understanding the Place-World* (Bloomington and Indianapolis, IN: Indiana University Press, 1993), at 15.

Newtonian grid, all places are essentially interchangeable. Our places, even our places for homes, are defined by objective measures'.[14]

The homogenonization and objectification of place in ways where it can be measured and exchanged makes possible the transformation of place into property and possession. For the possibility to be actualized as a feature of everyday social life, though, something more than philosophical reworking and technological innovations is needed.

Advances in positive law made the transformation of place into possession a reality by embedding the idea in everyday social transactions. Positive law removed place from cosmology and culture, and from supernaturally sanctioned entitlements, divine rights, animistic conceptions of human nature unity or whatever, and anchored it to law analogous to merchant law such that places made measurable and interchangeable by theory and technology could be traded like possessions and chattels through property rights.[15] Entitlement to place, exorcised of any supernatural or ancestral claims, in other words natural right claims, now needed to be made through rights claims in law as ownerships, permits, titles, licences, leases, tenancy or whatever. The unilateral contingency of human life on nature must be mediated through property rights: laws inspired by merchant law and mirroring merchant's conception of agency.

Notwithstanding the widespread displacement and social upheaval and misery that came in its wake, the idea of rights acquired a material force in the anti-feudal revolutions spearheaded by merchants because it held out to society at large expectations of emancipation and freedom from the constraints imposed upon society by the feudal order. As Jewei Ci points out, liberal theory conceptualizes freedom as absence of restraint – through the fact that 'something is allowed to happen' liberal theory invites us to conclude that 'it is likely to happen or even cause it to happen'.[16] Liberalism sees the economy as morally neutral and generates a human rights discourse that is related to but independent of the economy. According to Ci, liberalism:

> [...] redescribes the existing behaviour of economic actors within morally neutral framework of capitalist ethic. What happens here may be described as willing after the fact. [...] that [c]apitalism, as a system of contractual freedom and technical innovation, historically required the weakening of rigoristic morality and the toleration of external effects. Willing after these facts is willing one's self-interest, not willing moral freedom. It testifies to the power of bourgeois ideology that the case is often thought to be otherwise, that the positions of horse and carriage are reversed without being noticed most of the time.[17]

This 'willing after the effect' necessitates the rights discourse *after* displacement occurs. The expectation generated by the rights discourse proved false in the face of the widespread dislocation of people and the economic polarization occurring everywhere after the anti-feudal revolutions succeeded in establishing a capitalist order. The Marxist critique arose in response to the displacement and inequities of the capitalist order, but the primary focus of the critique was human freedom and emancipation, not rights for their own sake. Freedom was freedom from a capitalist economy that dehumanized people and alienated them from place, people, labour and self. At the

---

14   Casey, ibid., quoting C Lassiter, 'Relocation and illness', at 38.

15   For an account of the influence of merchant law and merchant practices, such as jury systems for modern law, see ME Tigar and MR Levy, *Law and the Rise of Capitalism* (New York: Monthly Review Press, 1977).

16   J Ci, 'Justice, freedom, and the moral bounds of capitalism', *Social Theory and Practice*, 25/3 (1999), 409–38, at 416.

17   Ci, ibid., at 432–33.

same time Marxist critique saw modern technology and positive law as emancipatory when used by a different set of actors: the dispossessed. Later Marxists extended the concepts of political freedom to colonized societies. By articulating a wider freedom for all, the Marxist movements subordinated the rights discourse to emancipation from capitalist and colonial oppression. But it did this by *reversing* the emphasis from the economic to the socio-political domain and by replacing collective popular political will with the will of capitalist actors. In other words, the aim was to capture economic institutions to *implace* those previously displaced, in Marx's words 'expropriating the expropriators'. The result was the revolutionary upheavals of the early twentieth century, which had profound effects in shaping the structure of the New World Order at the end of the Second World War. The upheavals of the twentieth century did not *transcend* the economic versus human binary; it only reversed the emphasis.

The expectations generated by the socialist and national liberation struggles went thus far and no further in their ambition to overcome economic oppression using collective political will. This state of affairs calls for rethinking human emancipation and freedom, but rethinking it from the point when the trajectory of the rights discourse reached an impasse. Since the revolutionary upheavals of the early twentieth century no new *conceptual* development has occurred in the rights discourse capable of anchoring the discourse to human emancipation and freedom. Generally, the rights discourse remains trapped in concepts and ideas from classical liberalism, or classical Marxism, or an eclectic mix of both by grafting different strands of thought in the two schools.

David Harvey's 'accumulation by dispossession' thesis, now part of the critical vocabulary in academic scholarship, reveals how the rights discourse fetishises displacement and reifies the hiatus between the economic and political domains.[18] Briefly, Harvey's thesis is that under neo-liberal states capitalist accumulation occurs through new means of dispossession such as privatization, financialization, innovations in crises management and changes in the state's role relating to re-regulation and the maldistribution of wealth. Harvey's 'accumulation by dispossession' thesis reworks Marx's thesis on 'primitive accumulation' in ways that exacerbates rather than transcends the economic/political rights divide in the rights discourse. For Marx 'primitive accumulation' is a primeval moment when capitalist relations penetrate a society. The merchant classes which spearheaded capitalism made claims to land, evicted populations en masse and de-legitimized their claims to place by transforming land into a commodity amenable to merchants' laws of sale and contracts. The primeval displacement is also 'alienation': a rupture with human ties to nature, labour, culture and self. In the Marxist discourse once the primeval dis*placement* was accomplished the stage of 'primitive accumulation' ended and made way for industrial capitalism. Thereafter people were dis*possessed*. This account of displacement obfuscates the distinction between 'place' and 'possession' by postulating a temporal distance between 'displacement' and 'dispossession'. Harvey's thesis exacerbates the temporally mediated hiatus further by introducing a spatial dimension to the hiatus. Harvey differentiates between the 'logic of capital' and the 'logic of territory' as two distinct logics that must be overcome by political action articulated through rights discourses that affirm the claims of the dispossessed to economic equity and distributive justice. We are trapped in the same economic versus political rights framework.[19]

It is important to note here that historically the primeval displacement in primitive accumulation is also the moment of the modernist discourse of rights. The moot question is what happens once this primeval eviction takes place that alters the character of displacement such that it appears as

---

18   D Harvey, *The New Imperialism* (Oxford: Oxford University Press, 2003).

19   For an overview of different strands of Marxist theory on primitive accumulation and political action see J Glassman, 'Primitive accumulation, accumulation by dispossession, accumulation by extra-economic means', *Progress in Human Geography*, 30/5 (2006), 608–25.

perpetual dispossession thereafter? Equally, if displacement as reality and the discourse of rights have been co-extensive for centuries can we continue to assume that the relationship between the two is an unfortunate coincidence? May we not ask if there is a causal connection between the two such that rights discourse inevitably exists with displacement as its 'other'?

The primeval moment of capitalism displaces people from supernaturally sanctioned relations to place and *implaces* them in market institutions. To be 'in place' means to have 'a place' within market institutions. People's 'place' within market institutions, including the nation state, is secured and sanctioned through 'rights': right of citizenship, to own property (including one's labour, therefore the 'right' to be a 'wage slave'), to trade capital, labour, and environment. Right to place is secured through property rights. Thus, the primeval displacement is followed by implacement in economic institutions sanctioned through a regime of economic rights.

Nonetheless people must still live and work in real physical places. Within market institutions sanctified by economic rights the contingency of human life on place can be fulfilled only by finding a 'place' in economic institutions. Unlike supernaturally sanctioned entitlements to place, economic rights make it possible to take away rights to place through institutional captures legitimated by rights discourses in politics. Whichever group/class captures the institutions to 'implace' themselves can do so only by 'displacing' existing incumbents who must then take recourse to the rights discourse to reclaim their 'places' within economic institutions.

Implacement in market institutions like labour markets and property markets does not take away the ontological contingency of human life on nature and therefore the need for social life to be played out in places. Market institutions are based on voluntarist conceptions of human agency that take contract forms: collective or individual. Market institutions therefore do not guarantee places to everyone or for that matter, permanency to those already 'implaced'. Dispossession from market institutions hovers as a possibility at all times as a permanent existential condition of life. The ontological contingency of society on nature and place means the trauma of dispossession is experienced as displacement, as dislocation from places and people where lives are lived out. The displacement, when it occurs, is not any less primeval or painful because people are rendered potentially 'placeless' at all times; because place is transformed into a conceptual place within market institutions, and a 'possession' which can be traded and compensated. The rights discourse offers to overcome the trauma of displacement and dislocation caused by dispossession through another rights framework: 'moral versus legal rights'.

The 'moral versus legal rights' framework in the rights discourse effectively claims that socio-political considerations have a superior moral worth and therefore must have primacy over existing rights inscribed in the law. In effect, it implies that another group, class, nation or whatever must be allowed to partake in the property relations, whether as redistributive justice, revolutionary expropriation, or by other means. The 'moral versus legal rights' framework thus allows the later claimant to make rights claims and argue that they are superior. It does not show the way out for transcendence from the economic/human binary in the rights discourse.

In this displacement-implacement-displacement game the 'economic versus human rights' framework and the 'moral versus legal rights' framework (and other types of binaries in the rights discourse) become necessary as arguments about ways in which possession and dispossession are rationalized. The rights discourse generates displacement, which in turn generates a new round of rights discourse, each mutually entailing the other as cause and consequence in a vicious displacement-rights claims cycle; a perpetual conflict between the reality of displacement and the ideals held out by the discourse of rights, leaving the world in a perpetual state of suffering, upheaval and pain caused by dislocation.

As Jewei Ci argues, the rights discourse is intrinsically reifying and ideological; and the three generations of rights that the discourse identifies – individual, economic, and cultural – are not, in fact, advancements in rights discourse but exist as incompatible discourses in ways that sustain gaps between the ideal and the real.[20] Furthermore:

> […] the concept of rights fits with the conditions of life of the well-off much more accurately (and conveniently) than those of the badly off, reflecting the contingent fact that all *they* need is the protection of "human rights" understood centrally as rights to non-interference. That this concept of human rights is so dominant and reified and couched in unabashedly universalistic terms bespeaks a specific set of power relations – the power of the well-off vis-à-vis the badly off, and the power of the West vis-à-vis the rest of the world. After all, it is the powerful who are in the habit of speaking, and are able to speak, in universalistic terms, as if their condition of life were true of humanity as such.[21]

The causal nexus between displacement and the rights discourse and their mutual entailment necessitates bringing freedom and human emancipation back to centre stage in theory and practice. The concluding section reflects on the scope and ambit of human agency, which is pivotal to any conception of freedom and emancipation.

6

Following Ci, if we are to break out of the rights conundrum it is important that we take the reasons for human rights seriously. The idea of human agency is at the heart of the rights conundrum, for as Ci writes, '[…] all sufficiently deep reasons for human rights either appeal directly to the idea of human agency or rely on ideas that presuppose human agency'.[22]

The rights discourse envisages human agency as unfettered freedom where constraint is undesirable and is to be minimized to the extent possible. This representation helps to identify direct coercion, but fails to identify indirect coercion dictated by social institutions. Further, conceptualizing agency as unfettered freedom prevents a fuller understanding that includes other ways of envisioning it. Agency is an essential attribute of being human. As Ci writes:

> […] any adequate picture of human existence must take this feature [human agency] into account, even in forms of life in which people ostensibly deny power to themselves. Thus, the key to understanding so-called collectivist societies is not to avoid explanations in terms of agency but to see how attributions of power are possible, even if not made through such values as freedom and autonomy, and how subjectivity is possible, even if not formed through attributions of power to oneself.[23]

And, more importantly:

> A human society in which no attribution of power and hence no formation of subjectivity ever take place is not a recognizably human society, as distinct from the natural world, and a human being

---

20   J Ci, 'Taking the reasons for human rights seriously', *Political Theory*, 33/2 (2005), 243–65.
21   Ibid., at 259.
22   Ibid., at 251.
23   Ibid., at 252.

who neither attributes power to himself nor identifies with possessors of power and is therefore unable to become a subject is not recognizably human being, as distinct from a mere object.[24]

Equally, any ideas of human agency must conceptualize constraints. Conceptions of freedom as absence of constraints in liberal theory do not provide a way of conceptualizing constraints, except as an obstacle, a hindrance that must be removed so that freedom can be enjoyed without impediments. Consequently, the freedom/bondage binary in liberal theory diverts attention from another necessary attribute of human life: its sociality. The contingency of human life on its sociality (and its unilateral dependence on nature) calls for recognition that human life is dependent on social institutions and social structures without which human life is impossible. The question that presents itself is this: if human life is contingent on society, and, if social institutions and structures are necessarily constraining, how may we conceptualize constraint such that it is possible to sustain human agency? Can we conceive of structural constraints, not in antithetical terms to agency, but rather as facilitative of human agency?

In many ways the concept of *dukkha* in Indian intellectual traditions does just that.[25] *Dukkha* recognizes constraints (pain/suffering) as an ontological attribute of human life, thus directing human agency to seek freedom through actions. *Dukkha* is a central concept in Indian philosophical thought. *Sarvam dukham* – the idea that everything is suffering/pain – forms the guide for *karma*, or action/deeds. It is now generally accepted that *dukkha* is much more than the common European translation of 'suffering' or 'pain' which has a strong empirical orientation. Indeed, the limited meaning of 'pain' and 'suffering' in English misrepresents the philosophical significance of *dukkha*. Besides, the translation of 'suffering' or 'pain' suggests its opposite – 'happiness' or 'pleasure', or *sukha* – which is an empirical/existential idea and is unhelpful in understanding the deeper and broader scope of *dukkha* as a guide to *karma* in Indian thought. 'There is no word in English covering the same ground as Dukkha does in Pali. Our modern worlds are too specialised, too limited, and usually too strong. [...] Dukkha is equally mental and physical.'[26]

Dukkha is an empirical as well as a metaphysical concept. As Bimal Krishna Matilal points out, one cannot understand Indian thought without understanding what *dukkha* means.[27] It is both a description of the world comparable to the empirical/existential 'pain' and 'suffering', the opposite of which is *sukha* or pleasure/happiness in Western thought, as well as a prescriptive term that guides moral/evaluative action or *karma*, how to be in the world. It also encompasses a transcendental category about the nature of reality and 'truth', which is the ontological contingency of human life on society. It is non-factual and factual, fact and value.[28] The dominant structure of thought in the Indian intellectual tradition is non-dualistic (not be be confused with 'monistic'

24 Ibid., at 252.

25 Indian intellectual traditions are used here in the broadest possible sense. Concepts like *dukkha*, *karma* and *dharma* are interpreted differently in different schools of Indian philosophy, with many variations and nuanced arguments. To the extent that certain concepts inform all schools of Indian philosophy they form part of the structure of Indian thought, much like the Greco-Roman and Judea-Christian conceptual frames that inform Euro-American thinking. See AK Ramanujan, 'Is there an Indian way of thinking? An informal essay', in V Dharwadker (ed.), *The Collected Essays of AK Ramanujan* (New Delhi: Oxford University Press, 1999).

26 GJ Larson, 'The relations between "action" and "suffering" in Asian philosophy', *Philosophy East and West*, 34/4 (1984), 351–56, at 351.

27 BK Matilal, *Logical and Ethical Issues: An Essay on Indian Philosophy of Religion* (New Delhi: Chronicle Books, 2004), ch. 2.

28 Ibid.

in the Western tradition). Non-dualistic intellectual traditions developed ontologically informed, open-ended conceptual categories that take meaning from context. *Dukkha* is one such conceptual category which in a given context becomes capable of guiding action.

One way of understanding *sarvam dukham*, everything is suffering/pain, is to read it as a statement recognizing the ontological contingency of human life as constrained in some way or other. The idea of unfettered freedom is ontologically false. Therefore in the Indian tradition we are invited to consider human freedom within the overarching reality that, ontologically, all human life is constrained. This approach makes it easier to trace empirical suffering/pain to multiple sources of suffering/pain including social institutions, limits imposed by nature, and by psychological life without reducing one to the other or deriving one from the other. In other words, the recognition of constraint as an attribute of being itself frees epistemology and sociology to pursue human well-being without being limited by antithetical binaries.

Marx and Engels refer to the relations between necessity and freedom in different texts and different ways in political, economic and philosophical writings. Marx's communist eudemonia is premised on transcending the economic/human and moral/legal binaries. But within the conceptual resources provided to them by Western intellectual thought dominated by philosophical dualism, Marx and Engels were unable to anchor their intuitive understanding that 'knowledge of necessity gives freedom for action' to more reliable philosophical foundations.

Philosophical dualism views the world through binary conceptual categories: good versus evil, god versus devil, heaven versus hell, body versus mind, materialism versus spiritualism, mind versus matter, thought versus action, the ideal versus real, subjective versus objective, Socratic justice versus injustice, Aristotelian particular versus universal – the list could be extended endlessly. Such is the dominance of binary categories that even dualism produces its binary: monism in the Western tradition as opposed to non-dualism in other philosophical traditions.

Binary categories provide linear scales between which various shades of the same concepts are differentiated. The closures inherent in binaries make transcendence illusory. Where transcendence is attempted it must be through human will mediated through adversarial social processes, which usually replace one type of suffering with another while holding out unfettered freedom. Philosophical dualism promotes binary concepts that have a tendency to reduce complexity and promote adversarial relations between nature, society and people as relations between the universal and particular, the ideal and the real, must be bridged by conceptions of human agency unfettered by context.[29] In the triad of nature-society-individuals constitutive of all societies and social life, binaries subsume one or the other category or relation.

In contrast, in the Indian tradition where the dominant structure of thought is non-dualistic, the centrality of constraints, *dukkha*, rather than freedom informs human agency. Non-dualistic intellectual traditions view the world through conceptual categories that contain their negations. Thus in 'white-not-white', 'not-white' could be black but could also be anything else. Non-dualistic conceptions of agency involve going from an unwanted to a wanted source of determination without holding out absolute ideals or goals. Action, or *karma*, is also an ontological attribute of human life that follows from *dukkha*. It is not an inevitable bother, a burdensome or onerous duty that must be borne with fortitude, as in the Western traditions where freedom is an unfettered ideal. If both *dukkha* and *karma* are attributes of social and human life, the impulse for action is always *dukkha*.

---

29   On context-sensitive and context-free thinking in the Indian intellectual traditions see Ramanujan, above, n. 22.

This way of conceptualizing constraints allows us to examine a wide range of sources of *dukkha* from social institutions to psychological, natural and supernatural worlds, what J.P.S. Oberoi calls the esoteric and exoteric dimensions of human life and well-being in ways that enhance freedom in a given context. Equally, when constraint is recognized as an ontological attribute of human life, far from promoting pessimism, as many Western commentators have suggested, it provides the psychological *attitudes* necessary for transcendence in a given context, the energy that freedom demands of us.[30]

In the present context, can we even imagine the freedom and emancipation that might follow if the 'wasted humans' comprising half of humanity, instead of clutching on to a jaded rights discourse, said:

> *You are not my fellow traveller,*
> *Tread your own path.*
> *May you be affluent,*
> *And I, downtrodden.*

---

30   D'Souza (2011, forthcoming), 'What Can Activist Scholars Learn from Rumi', in Ananta Kumar Giri (ed.), *Pathways of Creative Research: Towards a Festival of Dialogues* (Chennai, India: Madras Institute of Development Studies).

Chapter 4

Dangerous Rights: Of Citizens and Humans

Kate Nash

Barely Human or Global Citizen?

Writing of the treatment of stateless persons, refugees and minorities without powerful governments to protect them between the two world wars, which culminated in the genocide of Armenians and Jews, Hannah Arendt famously criticized 'the efforts of well-meaning idealists who stubbornly insist on regarding as "inalienable" those human rights [...] which are enjoyed only by citizens of the most prosperous and civilized countries'.[1] Arendt saw human rights as untenable because they are based on the abstraction of humanity rather than on any possibility of participation, whether democratic or revolutionary, in a concrete political community. She noted that:

> The conception of human rights, based upon the assumed existence of a human being as such, broke down at the very moment when those who professed to believe in it were for the first time confronted with people who had indeed lost all other qualities and specific relationships – except they were still human. The world found nothing sacred in the abstract nakedness of being human.[2]

When Arendt wrote these words in the late 1940s she was looking back to what she saw as the making of a new world of chaos and catastrophe as a result of the disintegration of empires with the First World War. In terms of human rights, however, at the time she was writing the world was at another beginning, that of the global regime of human rights that started with the Universal Declaration of Human Rights (UDHR) on 10 December 1948. Arendt's reading of historical evidence led her to scepticism regarding the future of human rights. We are now in a position to reflect on how far the potential of this new global regime has been realized.

In more recent times, Arendt's understanding has inspired Georgio Agamben's critique of human rights. He argues that human rights are impossible because the 'bare life' (bios) of humanity, where it does not vanish into the figure of the national citizen, is the constitutive 'other' on which national political community is founded: the bare life of humanity is precisely what must be excluded from the political life (zoe) of citizens.[3] It is unclear whether this exclusion is, for Agamben, historically, or logically – even metaphysically – necessary. Agamben maintains that the gap between citizens and non-citizens is opening still more widely under the pressure of what he (like Arendt in her time) sees as the symptomatic element of contemporary politics: the fact of growing numbers of refugees that put pressure on state sovereignty. As Agamben sees it, non-nationals permanently resident within industrialized countries today are de facto stateless – they thus 'unhinge' the trinity

1 H Arendt, *The Origins of Totalitarianism* (San Diego, Harvest Books, 1968).
2 Ibid., at 299.
3 G Agamben, *Homo Sacer: Sovereign Power and Bare Life* (Stanford, CA: Stanford University Press, 1995) and G Agamben, 'Beyond human rights', in P Virno and M Hardt (eds), *Radical Thought in Italy: A Potential Politics* (Minneapolis, MN: University of Minnesota, 1996).

of state-nation-territory, and the formation of detention camps soon follows.[4] However, Agamben does not reflect on the progressive potential of the UN regime of human rights – not to mention that of Europe, which is derived from it – focusing rather on what was already evident, according to his analysis, at the time of the French Revolution.

Since the great national declarations of human rights in the eighteenth century, the French and the American, and since Arendt wrote in the 1940s, there has been a major shift in human rights: the increasing legalization of international human rights that cross, contest, and even reconfigure jurisdictional borders.[5] 'Legalization' refers to the way in which international human rights agreements are becoming more detailed, precise and binding; and the way in which law that draws on and invokes human rights is increasingly being used and applied in both national and international courts.[6] The legalization of international human rights treaties and conventions is precisely aimed at effectively abolishing the distinction between citizens and 'barely human' non-citizens.

Traditionally international law concerned only relations between sovereign states. After the Second World War, liberal internationalism began more systematically to challenge the distinction between citizens and non-citizens on which state sovereignty was based. These changes to international law are sometimes known as the 'Nuremberg principles' because they were initially developed in the Nuremberg trials that followed the Second World War. Two major changes in international law came together in the legal aftermath of this war. Firstly, individuals became criminally accountable for violations of the laws of war ('just obeying orders' was no longer a legitimate legal defence, however lowly a position the accused held in the military or state hierarchy). Secondly, principles of human rights began to be developed, which prescribed limits to a government's conduct towards its own citizens, to apply in times of peace and war.[7] This second principle was carried forward and extended with the UDHR, beginning international human rights law in the UN human rights system. According to the UDHR, and subsequent international human rights law based on it, individuals have human rights, and also the responsibility to uphold human rights, *regardless of citizenship status or residency*. As Article 2 of the UDHR has it:

> Everyone is entitled to all the rights and freedoms set forth in this Declaration, without distinction of any kind, such as race, colour, sex, language, religion, political or other opinion, national or social origin, property, birth or other status. Furthermore, no distinction shall be made on the

---

4   Agamben, 1996, above, n. 3.

5   The focus is on legalization here for reasons of space, but elsewhere I have analysed how human rights are becoming 'intermestic' along a number of other dimensions too. The legalization of human rights complicates the international/domestic division assumed by conventional legal scholarship; in addition, political use of the language of human rights is increasingly important in the rhetoric both of state elites and of NGOs (which themselves cross borders, often having ambiguous status in relation to the international/ domestic distinction) to justify action at home and abroad; and – as will be seen later in this chapter – human rights are contested in the cultural politics of the mediated public sphere in popular terms as well (see Nash 2007, 2009, below, n. 15).

6   K Abbott et al., 'The concept of legalization', in *Legalization and World Politics* (Cambridge, MA: MIT Press, 2001).

7   S Ratner and J Abrams, *Accountability for Human Rights Atrocities in International Law: Beyond the Nuremberg Legacy* (Oxford: Oxford University Press, 2001), at 4; and D Held, *Democracy and the Global Order: From the Modern State to Cosmopolitan Governance* (Cambridge: Polity Press, 1995), at 101–2.

basis of the political, jurisdictional or international status of the country or territory to which a person belongs, whether it be independent, trust, non-self-governing or under any other limitation of sovereignty.[8]

However, with the partial exception of the European system of human rights, the balance of powers until the end of the Cold War meant that international law effectively maintained classic state sovereignty, being overwhelmingly concerned with keeping the peace between states.[9]

Since the Cold War, however, some argue that we are now seeing the beginning of cosmopolitan law. In contrast to international law, and building on the 'Nuremberg principles', cosmopolitan law reaches inside states, piercing nominal state sovereignty and enforcing claims against human rights violators.[10] Undoubtedly the best example of cosmopolitan law is European human rights law: the European Court of Human Rights is effectively 'the constitutional court for civil and political rights' in Europe, hearing complaints from individuals, who may be citizens or non-citizens, as well as from member states.[11] Another good example of cosmopolitan law is customary international law, defined as established state practice, which states understand to be followed 'from a sense of legal obligation'.[12] The sources used to establish customary international law include such a diverse array as 'newspaper reports of actions taken by states [...] statements made by government spokesmen [sic] to Parliament, to the press, at international conferences [...] a state's laws and judicial decisions' and multilateral treaties.[13] They also include judicial decisions and the teachings of highly qualified legal experts, and the resolutions and declarations of international governmental organizations like the General Assembly of the UN.[14] Customary international law is increasingly drawn upon in national as well as international courts; celebrated examples include the extradition case against General Pinochet and cases that use the Alien Tort Claims Act in the US.[15]

The aim of human rights activists and legal innovators who support and extend cosmopolitan law is that each and every individual should become legally responsible for the rights of each and every other individual, regardless of nationality or residency, and regardless of internal domestic politics, even where there are clashes between international human rights norms and national law. In this respect, cosmopolitan law is intended to create a new political community to replace nations organized around states, a global community that is set up to abolish the distinction between citizen and non-citizen on which national states are founded. Global citizens happen to be resident in

---

8   The UN system replaced the failed Minorities Treaties of the League of Nations, which Arendt writes of in terms of human rights. In contrast to the protection of minorities afforded by the League of Nations, the UN system was designed as formally universalist, set up to protect the rights of all individuals (not some groups) in all states (not just those selected for the patronage of the Great Powers). See M Mazower, 'The strange triumph of human rights, 1933–1950', *The Historical Journal*, 47/2 (2004), 379–98.

9   D Held, 'Law of states, law of peoples: Three models of sovereignty', *Legal Theory*, 8/1 (2002), 1–44.

10   Held, ibid.; D Hirsh, *Law against Genocide: Cosmopolitan Trials* (London: GlassHouse, 2003).

11   T Burgenthal et al., *International Human Rights* (St Paul, MN: West Publishing, 2002), at 172 and M Dembour, *Who Believes in Human Rights? Reflections on the European Convention* (Cambridge: Cambridge University Press, 2006).

12   H Steiner and P Alston (eds), *International Human Rights in Context: Law, Politics, Morals* (Oxford: Oxford University Press, 2000, 2nd edn), at 70.

13   Steiner and Alston, ibid., at 73.

14   H Charlesworth and C Chinkin, *The Boundaries of International Law: A Feminist Analysis* (Manchester: Manchester University Press, 2000).

15   See K Nash 'The Pinochet case: Cosmopolitanism and intermestic human rights', *The British Journal of Sociology*, 58/3 (2007), 417–35 and K Nash, *The Cultural Politics of Human Rights: Comparing the US and UK* (Cambridge: Cambridge University Press, 2009).

particular states, because there is no world state, but, according to this vision, we all have rights and responsibilities created by cosmopolitan law.

This chapter explores the discrepancy between Arendt's and Agamben's pessimism concerning human rights, and the determined optimism of human rights activists. It explores the cosmopolitan project to abolish the distinction between citizens and non-citizens through human rights from a sociological perspective. As sociologists we are well-equipped to study how the legalization of human rights works in practice. The following section considers how the legalization of human rights is working in terms of what sociologists have traditionally seen as the three dimensions of citizenship within national states: civil, political and social rights. It then considers in more detail a critical example concerning the civil rights of non-citizens, looking at the relationship between national civil liberties and human rights in the case of terrorist suspects detained without charge or trial in the UK. It concludes by considering the dangers and the potentialities of human rights today.

Citizenship and Human Rights: A Question of Status

I follow TH Marshall's classic definition of citizenship as according civil rights of individual freedom, political rights of participation and social rights to basic levels of provision for education, housing, health care and welfare.[16] Although Marshall's model of citizenship is undoubtedly flawed, it is still the common reference point for sociologists working in this area.[17] In order to explore the relationship between citizenship and human rights, David Lockwood's work on civic stratification is a useful starting point.[18] Lockwood argues that the actual enjoyment of rights depends on two interlinked axes of inequality: the presence or absence of legal, bureaucratic rights; and the possession of moral or material resources, which generally operate informally.

From a sociological perspective, then, the enjoyment of rights is never simply a matter of legal entitlement; it also depends on social structures through which power, material resources and meanings are created and circulated. As we shall see, in relation to non-citizens, citizenship, as membership of a national political community, is itself a material and a moral resource as well as one permitting individual citizens legal entitlements. The interplay of the two axes of legal entitlement and material and moral resources means that legal claims to human rights that are intended to 'humanize' states are actually tending to produce new types of formally and substantively unequal status. An analysis of different types of status produced with respect to citizenship and human rights would have to include at least the following five distinctions.[19]

Firstly, within the legal status of 'full citizenship' there is a marked difference between what we might call 'super-citizens' and 'marginal citizens' in relation to human rights. Super-citizens have all the rights of citizens but, increasingly, in a globalizing, de-regulated political economy, citizenship does not tie them to states because they own the means of production or are in possession of secure employment or marketable skills that enable mobility across borders. Super-citizens are Craig Calhoun's 'frequent flier' elite cosmopolitans.[20] This group has very little material interest as

---

16   TH Marshall and T Bottomore (eds), *Citizenship and Social Class* (London: Pluto Press, 1992), at 8.

17   B Turner, 'Outline of a theory of citizenship', *Sociology*, 24/2 (2002), 189–217.

18   L Morris, 'Sociology and rights: An emergent field', in L Morris (ed.), *Rights: Sociological Perspectives* (London: Routledge, 2006).

19   For a fuller discussion of this typology see 'Between citizenship and human rights', *Sociology*, vol. 43, no. 6, pp. 1067–1083.

20   C Calhoun, 'The class consciousness of frequent travellers: Towards a critique of actually existing cosmopolitanism', in D Archibugi (ed.), *Debating Cosmopolitics* (London: Verso, 2003).

a group in human rights except insofar as human rights policies may succeed in making the world generally more stable and profitable. Their protected mobility comes from their citizenship status as well as from their wealth and/or skills. When faced with unstable or dangerous political conditions, super-citizens are more likely to fly home or appeal to the authorities of the states to which they belong to intervene on their behalf than they are to claim human rights. As individuals, members of this group may be involved in the extension of human rights as professionals – especially as lawyers, leaders of international non-governmental organizations (INGOs), or researchers – but they would not generally expect to see themselves as the subjects of human rights claims.

Super-citizens can be compared with a second status group, 'marginal citizens', who have full citizenship rights but who either do not have paid work, or who have insecure, low paid or only partial participation in the labour market. This group enjoys full citizenship rights to a variable degree, according to different dimensions of inequality and subordination. As a category these people have civil rights to protect them from state force in a reasonably functioning multi-party democracy. However, young black and Muslim men and women, for example, are more likely to be discriminated against if they need positively to exercise those rights than are others.[21] Moreover, it is increasingly the case that the social and economic benefits of citizenship to which marginal citizens have been entitled are under attack as the regulation of capitalism is altered through globalization.[22] The growth of the global human rights regime is, of course, an aspect of gobalization, but in terms of deteriorating social citizenship, human rights are of little interest to marginal citizens.

The history of social and economic rights has been very different from that of civil rights in terms of legalization. In principle, social and economic rights have been part of the core schedule of international human rights since the UDHR. Article 22 of the UDHR, for example, which is just one of many that specify core welfare rights, states that everyone is entitled to realization 'through national effort and international co-operation' of his economic, social and cultural rights. What this should mean in practice was spelled out in still more detail in the International Covenant of Economic, Social and Cultural Rights (ICESCR), which entered into force in 1976, signed and ratified by most states (with the notable exception of the US). Nevertheless, a clear distinction was drawn between social and economic rights and civil and political rights from the very beginning of the global human rights regime, with socialists and liberals opposed over which set of rights should be ideologically and strategically prioritized.[23] Since the end of the Cold War, economic and social rights are often compared to civil rights in respect of the logical possibilities of legalization: it is hard to specify clear, detailed state obligations to meet social needs (especially where resources are lacking) in comparison with the specific obligations on the part of specific agents to *stop* acting in certain ways that characterise civil rights.[24] This argument has become somewhat less compelling since social and economic rights were made justiciable in India and South Africa, where the state has been called to account in its national courts for violations of the social and economic rights of people under its jurisdiction.[25] In the North, however, the term 'human rights' is still used almost

---

21 B Bowling and C Phillips, 'Disproportionate and discriminatory: Reviewing the evidence of stop and search', *Modern Law Review*, 70/6 (2007), 236–961.

22 B Turner, 'The erosion of citizenship', *British Journal of Sociology*, 52/2 (2001), 189–209.

23 D Forsythe, *Human Rights in International Relations* (Cambridge: Cambridge University Press, 2000).

24 J Donnelly, *Universal Human Rights in Theory and Practice* (Ithaca, NY: Cornell University Press, 1989), at 33–34 and M Dembour, *Who Believes in Human Rights? Reflections on the European Convention* (Cambridge: Cambridge University Press, 2006).

25 M Olivier and L Jansen van Rensburg, 'South African poverty law: The role and influence of international human rights instruments', in L Williams (ed.), *International Poverty Law: An Emerging Discourse* (London: Zed Books, 2006); and S Shankar and PB Mehta, 'Courts and socioeconomic rights

exclusively in the mainstream mediated public to mean the civil rights covered by the International Covenant of Civil and Political Rights (ICCPR).[26] Claims to economic and social human rights have been effective for some migrants within existing, deteriorating state regimes of welfare – as we shall see in the case of quasi-citizens below – but human rights language has not been developed to address issues of welfare more generally. There is, for example, no provision in the system of European human rights law for economic and social rights. The European Social Charter of the Council of Europe is policy-oriented, relying on the supervision of practices through scrutiny of reports and complaints submitted to the European Committee of Social Rights, which may recommend that states should bring national law and practice into conformity with the Charter. It does not allow for adjudication in the European Court of Human Rights. Despite the apparent importance of economic and social human rights in terms of international agreements, then, they have not become cosmopolitan law in the same way as civil rights, and they do not provide protection for marginal citizens in the North. They appear rather, to be irrelevant to the welfare of these citizens.

Thirdly, outside these unequally positioned citizens, there are 'quasi-citizens'. Quasi-citizens are denizens or long-term residents in a state who have access to employment and who have gained social and even economic rights as a result of relatively secure employment, long-term residence and political mobilization. They have organized politically to put pressure on states to recognize their human rights in order to gain access to education, health care, housing and other welfare rights on the same basis as citizens.[27] Quasi-citizens do not, however, have political rights to vote in the national elections of states in which they are resident, though they may, in some cases, have rights to vote in local elections.[28]

The category of quasi-citizens contains a diverse group of people. It includes some EU citizens – those from less powerful states who are employed in unskilled work – guest-workers, and also those who have been granted refugee status. Whilst, as Soysal has argued, what she calls 'postnational citizenship' has been an important advance for migrants in terms of institutionalizing their human rights, the relative instability of their legal status (as they are 'not-citizens') and the dangers it creates for securing other fundamental human rights on which they may need to depend is becoming clearer. An excellent example of the dangers of quasi-citizenship for human rights in this respect comes from the UK state's treatment of those who have been granted asylum because of well-founded fears of persecution in the states of which they are nationals, and who have subsequently been arrested and detained without charge on suspicion of terrorist activities. These cases will be examined more closely in the following section.

If quasi-citizens are in a precarious position with regard to their fundamental human rights, sub-citizens routinely face even greater difficulties. Sub-citizens are those who do not have paid employment in the country in which they are resident, nor any entitlement to state benefits there. This category includes those who are waiting to have asylum cases heard and who may be detained indefinitely in camps whilst that process is going on. It also includes those considered to be adult

---

in India', in V Gauri and DM Brinks (eds), *Courting Social Justice: Judicial Enforcement of Social and Economic Rights in the Developing World* (Cambridge: Cambridge University Press, 2008).

26   For example, the Make Poverty History campaign that was so popular in 2005, and that continues today, never used the term 'human rights' (see Nash 2009, above, n. 15).

27   Y Soysal, *Limits of Citizenship: Migrants and Postnational Membership in Europe* (Chicago, IL: University of Chicago Press, 1994).

28   E Balibar, *We, the People of Europe? Reflections on Transnational Citizenship* (Princeton, NJ: Princeton University Press, 2004) and S Benhabib, 'Twilight of sovereignty or the emergence of cosmopolitan norms? Rethinking citizenship in volatile times', *Citizenship Studies*, 11/1 (2007), 19–36.

dependents of quasi-citizens – wives and other family members – who have no independent right to residence and who are, therefore, potentially subject to violence and abuse within the home (without real possibility of redress), as well from their home states. The category of 'sub-citizens' is literally *created* by international human rights law as it is administered through state-specific policies. The status of refugees in the country in which they are detained or resident is based on international law concerning the human rights of refugees, derived from the 1951 UN Convention Relating to the Status of Refugees, and on national regulations concerning the administration of that law. Sub-citizens who are the dependants of quasi-citizens have virtually no legal status in international law as individuals, but only that which has been won through national political mobilization, usually by women's groups. In the UK, for example, it was as a result of such campaigning that the Government finally lifted the rule which meant that a wife could not leave a husband who abused her during their first year of residence without being immediately removed from the country – though the type of evidence of abuse that is admitted in these cases is still unacceptably restricted.[29]

Finally, even sub-citizens are in a better position than 'un-citizens'. This group includes undocumented migrants who have no recognized status in receiving countries and who may, therefore, be immediately deported, unless they are permitted to apply for asylum. It also now includes people detained in the 'war on terror' in newly created 'non-places', which are outside national territories and therefore somehow also outside the jurisdiction of sovereign states, whilst being under their administration. The most famous example here is Guantánamo Bay, though there are also other such camps containing suspected terrorists in Bagram, Kandahar and elsewhere. These un-citizens are in a legal 'black hole' because of the special status they have been assigned as 'illegal combatants' and the extraordinary lengths to which the US executive has gone to deny them access to lawyers and to keep them out of US courts.[30] Interestingly, with regard to Arendt's suspicions concerning human rights, it is citizenship status, combined with diplomatic relations between allies, and not claims for human rights, which has enabled relief for some of the detainees in Guantánamo Bay. For example, all those holding British passports were sent back to Britain and released without charge in 2005, but it was not until 2007 that the UK Government, under legal pressure from the detainees' families and following changes in US policy with regard to Guantánamo, requested the return of non-citizens resident in the UK. The last British resident, Binyam Mohamed, was finally released in 2009.

For quasi-citizens, sub-citizens and un-citizens, then, what we see is not so much the unfolding achievement of global citizenship, but rather a paradox: gross violations of fundamental human rights may be perpetuated because of the legal enforcement of other human rights. Human rights that are ideally inviolable, universal, indivisible and protective of all human beings, citizens and non-citizens alike, are actually creating groups of persons whose rights are extremely fragile and insecure. The insecure position of these people with regard to their legal status and also their access to material and moral resources is, on occasion, resulting in violations of the dignity, freedom and bodily integrity of those who have nothing but their human rights. The increasing legalization of human rights has led, then, neither to guarantees of human rights commitments, nor to an end to human rights violations. It has, however, led to a great deal of legal and political creativity.

---

29   See 'Campaigns', <www.southallblacksisters.org.uk> [accessed 27 November 2007].
30   J Steyn, 'Guantánamo Bay: The legal black hole', *International and Comparative Law Quarterly*, 53/1 (2004), 1–15.

Citizens versus Humans

This section looks more closely at one particular situation of quasi-citizens in the UK, in order to explore in detail exactly how and why the legalization of human rights is failing to secure the abolition of the distinction between citizens and humans. The cases of the Belmarsh detainees are critical as an example of the paradoxes of legalization because they concern human rights law which is very well-established internationally and which covers fundamental civil rights. In addition, we are dealing here with European human rights law, which is the most thoroughly institutionalized human rights system in the world. If legalization leads to paradoxes in securing human rights in the European system, it is unlikely to have a happy outcome elsewhere.

What this example shows is the way in which, when cosmopolitan law is relatively successful in abolishing the distinction between citizens and non-citizens in controversial cases, human rights come under increased political pressure. In the case of the arbitrary detention of terrorist suspects with which we are concerned here, there has been a political struggle, played out between politicians, the judiciary, human rights activists and journalists, in both formal and informal political spaces. This struggle has concerned how human rights figure, and should figure, in imagining the political community. In concrete terms it has been fought out over the meaning of the terms 'human rights' and 'civil liberties' as they are used by the judiciary, human rights activists and politicians.

Cosmopolitan human rights law was relatively effective in abolishing the distinction between citizens and humans in the Belmarsh detainees' case. In order to detain suspected terrorists without charge, the UK Executive declared 'a public emergency facing the nation' to derogate from Article 5 of the European Convention on Human Rights. Article 5 forbids arbitrary detention, requiring that proper procedures of law should be followed if a person is detained, including telling them the reasons for their detention, charging them and bringing them 'speedily' before a judge.[31] The details of who has been held under the subsequent Anti-Terrorism, Crime and Security Act (ATCSA) are secret but it seems that, according to the categories outlined above, most are quasi-citizens, granted leave to remain in Britain as refugees from persecution in the states of which they are nationals – which is why they cannot be returned to those countries; and un-citizens, failed asylum-seekers who have not left the country or been deported but who presumably also cannot be returned because they face persecution in the countries of which they are nationals.

In December 2004 the Law Lords heard the Belmarsh detainees' case on appeal against the decision of a lower court that their detention was lawful, despite the fact that none had been charged or had any prospect of being tried (*A v. Home Secretary* (2004)).[32] Although they refused to judge the declaration of public emergency as such in *A v. Home Secretary* – citing 'traditional deference' of the courts to an Executive decision to declare a public emergency – the Law Lords (the UK Supreme Court) nevertheless ruled that the detentions were unlawful. They found that ATCSA was disproportionate – arbitrary detention was a poor solution to the threat posed by the suspected terrorists; and discriminatory because it targeted only non-citizens. In this sense, the logic of human

---

31   The UK remained bound by the ECHR, even as it opted out of certain key Articles of the Convention. When the UK incorporated the ECHR into domestic law as the Human Rights Act in 1998, the Law Lords (the UK Supreme Court) became legally bound to judge whether the Executive decision to declare a state of exception was justified. Derogation from the ECHR must be lawful according to the ECHR itself: the measures that are put in place to deal with the dangers presented must be *proportionate* to the situation; and they must be *compatible* with other human rights obligations under international law (Article 15 ECHR). The Law Lords are also legally bound to judge whether the exceptional measures the UK Government put in place in ATCSA were proportionate and consistent with the UK's other human rights obligations.

32   *A and others v. Home Secretary* (UKHL 56 2004).

rights was effective: all the judges agreed that it was not legal for the Executive to treat non-citizens differently from citizens even under the exceptional circumstances of an officially declared, and legally sanctioned, state of emergency. In response to the Lords' ruling, Parliament passed the Prevention of Terrorism Act (PTA), which granted the Executive the power to keep suspected terrorists under 'control orders' if the authorities had 'reasonable suspicion' about their activities based on secret evidence (which neither they nor their lawyers were allowed to see). The PTA put an end to discrimination against non-citizens by sanctioning the violation of the fundamental rights of citizens too: all are potentially equally subject to a range of punitive measures without ever having been charged with a crime or having had the chance to defend themselves in court.[33]

The case was highly politicized. 'Human rights' was used to refer to and to make sense of the law regulating arbitrary detention in technical terms. However, from the very beginning of debates over the suspension of fundamental rights, it was not the term 'human rights' but rather 'civil liberties', sometimes qualified as 'British civil liberties' or 'centuries old liberties', that mobilized political passions. Opposition to the Executive decision to suspend rights was very frequently made, across the political spectrum, in terms of the glorious history of British freedoms. Such sentiments were resoundingly invoked in arguments by both major political parties, by the leader of Liberty,[34] and, most notably, and at some length, by Lord Hoffman in the Belmarsh detainees' case. In what one commentator has described as 'tabloid history',[35] Lord Hoffman constructed the European Convention as a modern-day protection of ancient British liberties, arguing that:

> Freedom from arbitrary arrest is a quintessentially British liberty, enjoyed by the inhabitants of this country when most of the population of Europe could be thrown into prison at the whim of their rulers. It was incorporated into the European Convention in order to entrench the same liberty in countries which had recently been under Nazi occupation. The United Kingdom subscribed to the Convention because it set out the rights which British subjects enjoyed under the common law.[36]

We see here a strategy on the part of human rights supporters to join human rights and British traditions together in an appeal to national pride. This strategy can be understood as an attempt to translate human rights into the vernacular of British political life. Sally Engle Merry has shown how cultural politics are necessary to bring human rights from the transnational sphere of global elites into local, everyday life. In order for human rights to make sense to ordinary people in a society, they must be translated into terms that enable them to judge their situation in human rights terms, to see it as unjust and to take action against that injustice. Merry calls this process of translation and framing 'making human rights vernacular'.[37]

---

33   The Government has appealed various High Court rulings that control orders are not compatible with human rights, depriving individuals of liberty and of rights to due process that require derogation from the ECHR (Joint Committee on Human Rights Eighth Report 2007). On 31 October 2007, the Law Lords basically endorsed the control order regime, though they set limits to the curfews that could be imposed and ruled that suspects should have access to 'key evidence' against them (case reference). There will undoubtedly be further legal challenges to that ruling.

34   For example, S Chakrabarti, 'Anti-terror laws ride roughshod over human rights' (2003), <www. poptel.org.uk/scgn/issues/0502.htm> [accessed 25 May 2007].

35   T Poole, 'Harnessing the power of the past? Lord Hoffman and the *Belmarsh Detainees* Case', *Journal of Law and Society*, 32/4 (2005), 534–61.

36   *A and others v. Home Secretary* (UKHL 56 2004).

37   S Merry, *Human Rights and Gender Violence: Translating International Law into Local Justice* (Chicago, IL: University of Chicago Press, 2006).

The strategy to make human rights vernacular through an appeal to national pride was not successful. On the contrary, rather than sharing in, or borrowing from, the passion aroused by commitment to fundamental 'civil liberties', the meaning of 'human rights' became all the more clearly separated and even opposed to 'civil liberties' in many sections of the media. Outside liberal and legal circles, in fact, European human rights were increasingly understood as *threatening* the ancient civil liberties of British citizens. On the one hand, human rights were seen as responsible for letting terrorist suspects loose in the country because the Government was not allowed to deport them; on the other, human rights were perceived as responsible for overturning centuries of entrenched liberties for British citizens.

Political opposition to human rights came from all quarters. It came, for example, from the Prime Minister responsible for the Human Rights Act that incorporated the ECHR into British law in 1998. In a speech following the terrorist attacks of 7/7, in which Tony Blair declared that 'the rules of the game have changed', he stated that human rights were creating obstacles to safeguarding national security.[38] He proposed that foreigners suspected of terrorism should simply be deported. It is in contravention of European human rights law to send a person to a state where they are at risk of torture.[39] Blair's suggestion in this speech that human rights law must be altered so that government measures to deal with terrorist threats are not judged to be in violation of human rights has been widely taken up. Reforming or 'scrapping' the Human Rights Act, which incorporates the ECHR into British law and which was passed by the Labour Government in 1998, became part of the Conservative Party's election manifesto in 2005. *The Sun*, the newspaper with the widest circulation of any paper in the UK, went so far as to run a campaign soliciting readers' votes to demand that the HRA should be repealed.[40]

Although Parliament can, in principle, repeal or alter the HRA, the UK must still comply with the ECHR, from which the HRA is derived. To avoid European censure for not complying, the UK would have to leave the 47 states of the Council of Europe and also the European Union (because signing the ECHR is a condition of joining). The UK would effectively become a pariah state in Europe.[41] This seems a very unlikely course of action for any government. What the newly revived, and oft-repeated, opposition between 'our' security and 'their' rights does mean, however, is that although human rights are embedded in law in the UK, they are far from becoming part of the vernacular of political life. Human rights are themselves now in need of defence, as well as those unpopular non-citizens accused of terrorist activities which human rights are supposed to protect.

Conclusion

Human rights are dangerous. Human rights innovators and activists try to abolish the distinction between citizens and others, but in practice the legal extension of human rights is, paradoxically, producing categories of people who are vulnerable to human rights abuses precisely because of their insecure status in countries – or sometimes in specially designed 'non-places' – in which they live or are detained as non-citizens. This does not mean that the legalization of human rights as such is problematic. On the contrary, as it is the situation seems rather to require that the reach of

---

38 PM's press conference, 5 August 2005, <www.number10.gov.uk/output/Page8041.asp> [accessed 23 June 2010].

39 *Chahal v. United Kingdom* (Application 22414/93) ECHR 54 (1996).

40 *The Sun*, 'Time to stop the madness', 12 May 2006.

41 V Bognador, 'Judges and the Constitution', speech at Gresham College, London, 30 May 2006 and F Klug, 'A bill of rights: Do we need one or do we already have one?', *Public Law* (2007), 701–19.

cosmopolitan law should be extended and deepened. The creation of a genuinely global citizenship of duties and entitlements would seem to be necessary in an unevenly globalizing world in which people are increasingly mobile, whether they are forced to move countries to escape poverty or persecution, or whether they are simply taking opportunities to change their lives that present themselves as a result of increased flows of communication and possibilities of transportation across borders.

It is important, therefore, that we take heed of Arendt's scepticism concerning human rights. As we have seen, legalization is only partially achieved, even when, on the face of it, the law itself seems to be quite clearly established. Once human rights law is put into practice in controversial cases, it is contested precisely around *safeguarding* the opposition between citizens and humans. Human rights were designed, in principle, to protect vulnerable people faced with the most difficult circumstances, whether of state persecution or of poverty. As we have seen in the example discussed here of the Belmarsh detainees, however, it is precisely when fundamental civil rights are most needed that they are most highly politicized.

It is clear, then, that cosmopolitan law as a project can only advance as a result of political mobilization. It is necessary to find a way to build support for human rights *within* what have historically been constituted as national political communities. The legalization of human rights is not a technical matter; it is not a matter of simply applying the letter of the law as it already exists in international agreements, or even of extending it through national legislation. Cosmopolitan law will only progress as a result of politics, and it is closely tied to the formation of political community transformed by human rights. Agamben is wrong: though states have historically been formed around the opposition between citizens and non-citizens, there appears to be nothing in the *logic* of state formation to prevent cosmopolitan law; if the distinction between citizens and non-citizens were fundamentally necessary to state formation, how is it that statuses that complicate and confound this opposition have proliferated in recent times as a result of cosmopolitan law?

Of course, the difficulties of mobilizing politically in order to extend cosmopolitan law towards achieving global citizenship are considerable. This chapter has explored nationalism as one of the main obstacles to gaining popular consent for the abolition of the distinction between citizens and non-citizens. In the case of the Belmarsh detainees, as a response to violations of human rights by state elites, human rights innovators in the judiciary and human rights activists tried to build pride in human rights into nationalism itself; they tried to turn sentiments concerning the exclusivity of national citizenship into sentiments of pride in the *inclusivity* of the political community, into pride in the nation because it upholds universal norms of human rights. While it seems likely that at least some super-citizens will be attracted to the cosmopolitan idealism of this project, it is difficult to imagine that it would gain popular support from marginal citizens who may fear losing not only the material benefits of citizenship, including the security that is supposed to be assured by a well-functioning state, but also its relative moral status in comparison with quasi-, sub- and un-citizens. The moral status of citizenship was at least as much in question in this case as were legal entitlements to human rights; the Government was unwilling, initially, to extend measures to detain citizens without charge that it did not hesitate to apply to non-citizens. I have suggested that as human rights are currently conceived in the North, in terms of the civil rights that most citizens feel they already enjoy quite securely, citizens apparently have little to gain from the extension of human rights. Indeed, as we have seen, in ruling discrimination between citizens and non-citizens illegal in the Belmarsh case, a judgment which was correct in terms of cosmopolitan law paved the way for the Government to remove fundamental civil rights from citizens.

In order to construct popular support for human rights, which is the only way to achieve their secure legalization in the most difficult political circumstances, it is necessary to show how human rights are relevant and necessary to *citizens*. The energies of the cosmopolitan project have been put, quite reasonably, into extending the law and building support for the human rights of vulnerable non-citizens in order to 'protect the human'. In order to break down the dichotomy between citizen and non-citizen, it may, however, be necessary also to foreground how human rights can be used to protect the freedom and well-being of citizens *as well as* non-citizens. This most certainly will not be easy. It is very doubtful that it can be achieved through an appeal to nationalism which, by definition, divides the world into 'insiders' and 'outsiders'. As there is, however, no going back to a world of closed borders, in a globalizing world the 'well-meaning idealism' of human rights innovators and activists has become absolutely necessary.

Chapter 5
The Neglected Minority:
The Penurious Human Rights of Artists

Paul Kearns

Introduction

Artists are not renowned for their business acumen, and it is not just a romantic notion that artists are usually oblivious to the law and their rights. Copyright inheres in created objects automatically, right from the moment of their physical manifestation. Artists are therefore saved the trouble of formally registering their central intellectual property right by courtesy of this deliberately helpful and paternalistic gesture on the part of the law. In other respects, it is arguable that, although artists who achieve some popular acclaim are frequently lauded for their creativity, they are habitually denied financial benefits commensurate with such encomium. In the postmodern environment, this is not the case with multi-millionaire artists such as Damien Hirst, but it certainly was the case with earlier artists like Van Gogh, who famously sold only one painting during his lifetime, and who would now be considerably wealthier given the extravagant sums paid nowadays for his works. Why acknowledged art ultimately possesses significant fiscal worth as well as social allure is a matter of debate, but, as a matter of popular sociology,[1] it is sometimes alleged that artistic creation is understood in terms of some kind of magical process, which consequently attracts great attention. To pursue sociological assumptions further, it is also commonplace to generalize about the personal nature of artists as a distinct breed. They are alleged to be unconventional creatures living on a higher plane of reality than ordinary folk, an image that rehabilitates them in the eyes of society, which might otherwise protest about their radical individualism. This almost surreal mystique acts as an excuse for the liberties artists tend to take, and justifies them ontologically as having a common essence housing all manner of peculiarity, that is fortuitously offset by a sort of charismatic, intangible, transcendent power.

So how does law accommodate these intractable eccentrics? In the world of rights, artists' general legal interests are bifurcated but are not then neatly congregated within the two separate streams. However, some generalizations can be made. The first set of relevant rights falls into the broad category of freedom of artistic expression; the second set of artists' rights exists in the law of intellectual property. Following a Hohfeldian classification of rights, the first set is 'liberty-rights', and the second set is 'claim-rights'. The first set concerns artistic choice of subject-matter, the second artists' economic interests in their products. The central investigation of this chapter is whether artists' liberty-rights in the form of human rights are adequately legally-protected. Liberty of artistic expression is protected in provisions sometimes within national constitutions or national laws lower in the domestic hierarchy, and sometimes within international human rights treaties. Contrastingly, artists' intellectual property interests are more straightforwardly preserved within a wide ambit of usually only national copyright laws. Ideologically and practically, a basic

---

1   J Duvignaud, *The Sociology of Art* (London: Paladin, 1972).

conflict can arise between the prevention of copying others' work and artistic liberty, a tension that is somewhat inevitable. However, there is a correlation in Western thought between genuine creativity and the presence of originality, so few artists aim in their practices to borrow from others' work in fashioning their own art, though some artworks, notably collages, involve a collation of pre-constituted materials that may contain others' art.

In the broader scheme of things, it is infrequently that art attracts legal attention, and the human rights of artists, as adverted to above, are seldom grouped together as a specific homogeneous body. It may not then be surprising that this chapter encompasses the first detailed critique of artists' human rights *simpliciter*. By way of contrast, much academic attention has been focused on the law of intellectual property, which, as well as affording basic copyright protection to artistic works, includes what are termed 'moral rights', and a right comparable to a moral right, namely the 'droit de suite' (the artists' resale right). All these rights exist for authors of original works and, as previously mentioned, have been the subject of much careful analysis by copyright lawyers. In this specialized area, artists' rights are clearly prescribed in many legal jurisdictions. However, in other legal subject areas, notably the law of human rights, artists' rights are comparatively under-researched and indistinct. Another principal broad object of this chapter, accordingly, is an examination of the specialized juridification of art issues in the context of freedom of expression, and the degree to which artists' rights are identified and effectively protected in that legal sphere. The classic scenario here involves the confrontation between artistic freedom and the legal, often constitutional, enforcement of morality; sometimes, though, artistic creativity can also be claimed to be illegal because seditious. The chapter therefore involves an analysis of the interaction of art with the laws of obscenity and blasphemy together with sedition. This can be succinctly characterized as the relationship between artistic freedom and certain libel laws (which will also involve referring briefly to the law of defamation so as to be a holistic study of art's treatment within the collective law of libel). A key feature of this theme is art's heteronomous position when placed in a legal arena, and the way this conflicts with the philosophically-recognized autonomy of art ontologically, and as a cultural phenomenon in society. Another central concern here is the determination of the quality of appropriate legal skill in courts to deal with the specialized character of art when art is engaged by the legal process. This will involve an assessment, for the purposes of rights discourse, in particular, of the efficacy of the judicialization of art in terms of juridical fairness to art, as identified in relevant legal judgments. Attention must also be paid to the era in which the art-law relation occurs, because in classical and mediaeval times art was a rule-based activity. The then strict canons of the artistic process meant that art was comparatively recognizable once produced, in accordance with its own methodological strictures. In the postmodern époque, contrastingly, art is identified merely by what can be termed self-legitimation.[2] In essence, the current position is that all practising artists need to do for the identification of their vocation is to proclaim themselves artists, and their product art, so that society is then obliged to be infinitely flexible regarding the definition of who is a bona fide artist and what, definitionally, constitutes art. As far as law is concerned, this position is unsatisfactory because law relies heavily on conceptual certainties to render clear and consistent justice. The ambiguity of art in the postmodern era confounds law's more stable internal points of reference and the efficiency of its habitual operation. This in part explains what we will discover to be a judicial reluctance to acknowledge artists' rights within a reciprocal dialogue of understanding, which supplements a judicial tendency to non-engagement with habitual, as well as complex, artistic terms of reference that find themselves usually unwelcome within law's definitive and incisive mechanism for categorical, binary, unequivocal dispute resolution. This phenomenon

---

2   See, further, F Jameson, *Postmodernism* (London: Verso, 1991).

is compounded by an antagonism between art's prospective, usually avant-garde, modus operandi, and law's reflex to the past, including its systemic use of precedents.

The Legal Positions in England, France and the United States of America

In England art is sometimes the object of prosecution for obscenity. Under the Obscene Publications Act 1959 the relevant legal test is whether the publication has a tendency to deprave and corrupt. It amounts to being a strict liability offence. If a jury is satisfied that the tendency exists, there is a conviction. However, if the object under legal scrutiny is art or literature, for example, a defence of artistic or literary merit for the public good is available under the 1959 Act's section 4. If that defence is successfully made out, it cancels the obscenity, and the creative work is exonerated. This happened in the first major case under the 1959 legislation involving DH Lawrence's novel, *Lady Chatterley's Lover*.[3] This case of 1960 is representative of most judicial attitudes in this context. The judge in the *Chatterley* case was Byrne J, and he was aggressively antagonistic towards the novel because of its erotic qualities and 'immoral' messages. He treated the novel as if it were ordinary prose rather than a work of fiction and imagination. He treated its details as literal fact. He was dismissive of the expert witnesses who had come to court to defend the novel as having artistic merit, evidence explicitly provided for as relevant under the 1959 Act. He displayed virtually no knowledge of this genre of creative writing and was blinkered by his obsession with the immoral nature of the storyline. There was no suggestion in his judgment condemning the novel that artists/ creative writers had a unique mode of working that entailed creating *oeuvres* that had only an oblique and symbolic relation to real-life matters. Moreover, no judicial cognizance was taken of the argument that such people have a right to express what they wish in the artistic realm, and that the societal recognition of their culturally-distinct role underlines their indisputable value. Fortunately for the novel's publishers, the jury ignored Byrne J's hostility to art and found in their favour. This artistic triumph was achieved despite the absence of judicial attention to the relevance of a right to free speech. The situation could be different today courtesy of the Human Rights Act 1998, which came into force in 2000. That legislation ensures that a relevant rights-based approach is to be entertained, if not always expected, in such circumstances.

In the later English case of *Lemon*,[4] another morality-related offence threatened artistic freedom. At the instigation of the late Mary Whitehouse, there was the prosecution for blasphemy of a poem, plus accompanying illustration, which had featured in the journal *Gay News*. The items allegedly vilified the Christian religion by the depiction of homosexual interference with Christ's dead body. The offence was again one of virtually strict liability. Again no mention was made of freedom of artistic expression. The question was simply put to the jury whether these publications were blasphemous. The jury held that they were. No investigation of artistic intent was involved. No judicial attempt was made to appreciate the artistic relevance of the artworks for a gay or bisexual readership. The case was insulated from art-pertinent concerns by the strict application of draconian censorship. Artists' rights were again ignored and the House of Lords was blithely impervious to their relevance.

In 1989 a summons was sought to charge the award-winning novelist Salman Rushdie with, inter alia, blasphemous libel in relation to certain passages in his novel *The Satanic Verses* that

---

3   See, further, P Kearns, 'Obscenity law and the creative writer: The case of DH Lawrence', *Columbia-VLA Journal of Law and the Arts*, 22/4 (1998), at 525.

4   [1979] AC 617, [1979] 1 All ER 898, [1979] 2 WLR 281.

could be classified as anti-Islamic. The court of first instance refused the application and had its decision affirmed by the English Divisional Court.[5] Both courts based their decisions on the fact that in England the crime of blasphemy pertained only to the Christian religion, the inference being that the novel was only potentially blasphemous in the eyes of Muslims as an affront to Islam, a matter to which the courts held English blasphemy law to be indifferent. This stance ignored the relevance of Christ as a prophet (though not the Messiah) in Islamic religious doctrine. No mention was made at either court level of *The Satanic Verses* being a work of the creative imagination. No question was raised as to whether an artistic statement, in contradistinction to a literal one, could ever be literally blasphemous. Again, notions such as artists' rights were kept extrinsic to the legal proceedings.

In the same year, 1989, the artist Richard Gibson was prosecuted for outraging public decency, a little-used English offence at common law.[6] This visual artist had constructed a model's head on the ears of which were earrings made out of real human foetuses. Unlike under the 1959 obscenity legislation, no artistic merit defence obtains to counteract outraging public decency. By the police's utilization of this particular offence of strict liability, there was therefore no way that the artist could convey to the court artistic intentions that could feasibly redeem him. Gibson could have been self-consciously lamenting in his art the lack of respect for human life to the degree of its being used as mere ornament, for example. However, art matters were excluded from the jury's purview and the jury found against Gibson forthwith. The lack of availability of artistic discourse in the courtroom precluded freedom of artistic expression to be aired as a relevant juridical concern in the case. Again an artist was condemned by a jury that remained ignorant about the modus operandi of his creative vocation and profession. It is clearly arguable that such crucial detail should be provided by the judge, if the trial is to be fair and publicly perceived to be fair.

In France the approximate equivalent to our obscenity law is *l'outrage aux bonnes moeurs*.[7] Historically, this law has been used to suppress obscenities but from the mid-nineteenth century, after the famous cases involving Flaubert and Baudelaire, no art has been legally challenged as immoral. Art is viewed in France as an *oeuvre d'esprit* (a work of the mind or spirit) and is now elevated above the possible constraints of censorship. One exception relates to violent films; another is based on the uncontested need for the protection of children. Sexual representations in art for adults go unprosecuted. This is unsurprising since so much highly explicit pornography is available freely on the Internet, which has none of the dignity and aesthetic allure that art possesses. The French intellectual legal approach is very satisfactory to the minds of art-appreciating individuals. It escapes criticism for not differentiating between art and literal facts, and obviates the need for the provision of legal defences for artists whose work is morally controversial. There is no law against blasphemy in France.

---

5   [1990] 3 WLR 986.

6   [1990] 2 QB 619, [1990] 3 WLR 595.

7   It translates as the 'outraging' of good morals. A comparable law in England is outraging public decency, which is ancient and which rests uneasily with the 1959 Act on obscene publications as a measure of contemporary application. An irregularity emergent from the archaic offence's current prosecution is based on the fact that outraging public decency can be used, arguably wrongly, to circumvent the 1959 Act's section 4 artistic merit defence to an obscenity charge, even though this is clearly legally antinomic. The two offences, used as alternatives, should not be allowed to so overlap to the detriment of the protection of artists under section 4. The practical impact of this was shown in July 2008 when a private prosecution for outraging public decency was launched against the Baltic Centre for Contemporary Art in Gateshead, in relation to a Terence Koh statue exhibited there, which comprised a sexually provocative representation of Christ. No artistic merit defence could be utilized by the gallery.

In the United States of America the legal stance adopted is formalistic. All obscenity falls outside the protection of the First Amendment, which protects freedom of expression. A constitutional standard operates to determine whether something is or is not obscene.[8] Art which has 'serious artistic value' is deemed not to be obscene.[9] As with 'artistic merit' in English obscenity law, 'serious artistic value' is very difficult to evaluate, and the legal task of such evaluation cannot fail to be executed subjectively. This clearly clashes with the general legal principle that judges are not legally permitted to be arbiters of taste. In copyright law, this hurdle is overcome to some degree by the legal search for the presence of the more objectively-determinable quality of 'artistic character' as the legal litmus test for what is or is not an 'artistic work'. This approach could be adopted and modified profitably in the context of obscenity law: all works of objectively-apparent artistic character could be insulated against prosecution for immorality on the basis of their inclusion in an objective artistic category that is beyond the strictures of moral concern because based simply on a definition of the character of art as legally amoral. In America there is no blasphemy law, because that would be contrary to the First Amendment. Removing all art from the constraint of obscenity laws would also be consonant with the spirit of the First Amendment.

As well as concerns about obscene and blasphemous libel and their detrimental effects on artistic creativity and freedom, there is also a debate, most prevalent in the USA, about whether an artwork could, in theory, or in practice, or in both, defame. For example, if fictional characters in a novel are based on real-life models and those fictional characters are full of vices, to what degree is this circumstance of legal relevance to the real-life models if readers identify the notorious fictional characters with them? In such circumstances, could the real-life models (individually) bring successful actions against the novelist for defamation? This legal and factual conundrum is resolved in the defamation law of the United States of America by the use of a doctrine known as 'defamation by fiction'. This is very complex and its effects on artists' rights are readily apparent: writers of fiction often draw on real-life characters as the raw material for artistic inspiration; it is arguable that to do otherwise would be to present artistically just useless fantasies instead of instructive commentaries on real-life matters. In brief, the law in this area should be governed by the concept of malice. It is submitted that it must be demonstrated by the plaintiff that the creative artist bore ill will towards him in so unpleasantly fictionally characterizing him in his novel. In more succinct terms, a legal test could be effectively phrased based on the question: did the novelist *intend* to harm the plaintiff by such a depiction? Although other approaches abound, this appears to be the fairest. You cannot intend to harm a plaintiff you do not know, and evidence of artistic concealment of the fictional character's real-life model in the novel clearly militates against a finding of malice towards him. The suggested approach also has the advantage of being easily applicable to all types of fiction. As a matter of the rights of artists, it is indisputable that an artist should not be deprived of source material that fuels his legitimate vocation if it is clear that art rather than spite was his motivating force. However, again we find that, in the field of defamation in most jurisdictions, little, if anything, is said about an artist's genuine professional needs except occasionally in the many-faceted, and variously-formulated, instances of defamation by fiction, as judicially construed in the American jurisdiction.[10] In this context, too, though, the radicalization of fiction and its concomitant increased difficulty have not improved the quality of judges' art discourse in the course of art's judicialization. For that quality to be ameliorated, there must be a

---

8   *Roth v. US*, 354 US 476, 1 L Ed 2d 1498, 77 S Ct 134 (1957).

9   *Miller v. California*, 413 US 15 (1973).

10   See, generally, F Schauer, 'Liars, novelists, and the law of defamation', *Brooklyn Law Review*, 51 (1985), at 233; and P Kearns, *The Legal Concept of Art* (Oxford: Hart, 1998), ch. 4, 86–113.

less inartistic judicial approach to the specialized area of art. Indeed, judicial experts on art would be especially welcome in this highly conceptually-complicated field of libel.

The European Convention on Human Rights

The rights of artists are sometimes specifically legally protected in national constitutional laws, such as, notably, in Austria and Germany, which establish the possibility for an artist, as a distinct entity, to found a legal action on the positive right constitutionally guaranteed.[11] This also, in effect, creates a preliminary positive 'presumption' in favour of artistic expression when that value competes with other societal interests such as the need to protect public morality. However, another important source of artistic rights in the human rights field is provided by international human rights instruments. Arguably the most significant of these is the *European Convention on Human Rights*. Article 10 of that treaty sets out the general right of freedom of expression in all the contracting states.[12] Unfortunately for artists, the rubric of Article 10 does not make explicit provision for the protection of artistic freedom. Instead, political, artistic and commercial freedoms of speech are informally distinguished by the judiciary of the European Court of Human Rights. It is arguable that a hierarchy of protection operates favouring political expression first, followed by artistic freedom, then, finally, freedom of commercial expression.[13] However, it is submitted that this does not reflect the real judicial priorities indicated by the Strasbourg jurisprudence. Of key concern to us is the fact that artistic freedom has *never* been judicially preferred in practice to the need to protect morality. This is shocking. Another disturbing feature about judicial practice under the Convention is that the subtleties of the interaction of art and morality go unexplored. The established judicial habit is to simply rubber-stamp its previous decisions in this area without due attention being paid to the delicate problems raised by concepts such as art, pornography, obscenity and harm. There is no system of precedent in the Court's regimen and it is arguable that cases involving artistic freedom and public morality should be decided afresh in each new case, such is the conceptual complexity of the legal problematic in such cases. More worryingly, it is the Court's primary job in this context to uphold conscientiously all freedoms related to expression and to accommodate restrictions on such freedoms comparatively reluctantly. At present what the Court does is consistently to enforce public-moral interests to the unequivocal sacrifice of artistic freedom. This is arguably a dereliction of duty, given the Convention's foundational remit

---

    11   On domestic constitutional legal provisions generally, including a comparative legal analysis, see E Barendt, *Freedom of Speech* (Oxford: Clarendon Press, 1985).
    12   Article 10 provides: 1. Everyone has the right to freedom of expression. This right shall include freedom to hold opinions and to receive and impart information and ideas without interference by public authority and regardless of frontiers. This Article shall not prevent states from requiring the licensing of broadcasting, television or cinema enterprises; 2. The exercise of these freedoms, since it carries with it duties and responsibilities, may be subject to such formalities, conditions, restrictions or penalties as are prescribed by law and are necessary in a democratic society, in the interests of national security, territorial integrity or public safety, for the prevention of disorder or crime, for the protection of health or morals, for the protection of the reputation or rights of others, for the disclosure of information received in confidence, or for maintaining the authority and impartiality of the judiciary.
    13   This is an informal arrangement that has been inferred from the case law by many commentators, its habitual reassertion proving to be in some respects misleading. See, further, C Munro, 'The value of commercial speech', *Cambridge Law Journal*, 62 (2003), 134–58; and I Hare, 'Is the privileged position of political expression justified?', in Beatson and Cripps (eds), *Freedom of Expression and Freedom of Information* (Oxford: Oxford University Press, 2000), 105–21.

of fundamental rights protection. It is also a very surprising form of institutional laxness, given that freedom of expression is often quoted as being the cardinal democratic right that the Convention is designed to protect.

The starting point of relevant Convention case law is the seminal case of *Handyside v. United Kingdom*.[14] The applicant published *The Little Red Schoolbook*, a book for children that, amongst other things, advised them on sexual matters. He was convicted for publishing an obscene libel under the Obscene Publications Act 1959 and the European Court of Human Rights judged that there was no breach of Article 10 of the Convention. It considered that a subsidiarity principle should operate that makes certain decisions the prerogative of the contracting states alone; and this judicially-created latitude given to the individual states, notably, for our purposes, in moral areas, is termed 'the margin of appreciation'. This doctrine will be analysed more closely later in this chapter. In *Handyside*,[15] the Court reasoned that because there was no uniform conception of morals in the contracting states, they should be a matter of local concern only. It added that local authorities were in a superior position to itself in being able to gauge local moral feeling. Prima facie, such an approach by the Court is logical. However, a unifying standard of morality formulated by the Court would eradicate the injustices of the inconsistent local decisions on moral matters and encourage contracting states to improve their standards by following an optimal one put forward by the Court. To avoid such an approach jeopardizes artistic freedom, because artists who produce morally-controversial work may be at the mercy of narrow, parochial moral decisions at the local level. Art is famous for being at the cutting-edge of moral development and reflects critically on the moralities of the status quo. It has a moral function in this regard that the Court in *Handyside* ignores.[16] This function of art should not be made vulnerable at the hands of village moral politics. Artistic vision tends to transcend petty scruples and synthesizes different concepts of morality in its own unique presentations. This generic artistic method of creating original moral directions is invaluable for society, not least in assisting it to challenge and undo the evil of moral stagnation.

In the next case chronologically, *X and Y v. United Kingdom*,[17] the European Commission of Human Rights reviewed the *Lemon* case adumbrated above.[18] It decided that the allegedly anti-Christian poem and illustration in *Gay News* was a proper object of control by blasphemy law, and that, consequently, there was not a breach of Article 10. The Commission ignored the fact that there might be an artistic right to be unconstrained as to subject-matter in the course of genuinely artistic endeavour and failed to appreciate that the likely audience of the offending items was small and specialized and unlikely to be corrupted or depraved by encountering the admittedly sensationalist artwork. In the subsequent case of *Muller et al. v. Switzerland*,[19] the European Court of Human Rights applied similar reasoning to the application of obscenity law by a contracting state. It considered that the applicant's pictorial art might well offend the sensibilities of an averagely sensitive person, depicting as it did graphic sexual practices. However, it failed to find relevant that the person who brought the offensiveness of the art to the relevant authorities was a teenage girl. It is clearly arguable that artists should not have to pander to the sensitivities of a minor when exhibiting their work in an adult environment that her father wrongly estimated would be innocuous for her. Moreover, the artist had exhibited the same work in other parts of Switzerland

---

14   E Ct HRR A 24 (1976), 1 E.H.R.R. 737.
15   Ibid.
16   Ibid.
17   28 DR 77 (1982).
18   Above, n. 4.
19   E Ct HRRA 113 (1991), 13 EHRR 212.

without official interference with it. Again we witness a provincial approach adopted by the Court as its own. The Court, in being supranational, should make correspondingly elevated decisions.

In *Choudhury v. United Kingdom*,[20] the European Commission of Human Rights held that Article 9 on freedom of religion was not breached by the United Kingdom. The United Kingdom was entitled to protect only Christians under its blasphemy law even though the state is religiously plural. This has relevance for freedom of artistic expression because if the Commission had found otherwise it may have then been obliged to examine whether or not Salman Rushdie's novel, *The Satanic Verses,* could in theory contravene the law even though the alleged blasphemy appeared only within imagined dream sequences in a work of art. It is still not clear whether characters in art are capable of having their allegedly blasphemous statements attributed to their creator, which is one step removed from literal blasphemy. Now that blasphemy law has been abolished in the United Kingdom, the answer will have to emerge from Convention cases involving an application from one of the other contracting states that continue to operate a blasphemy law. It is to be hoped that the essential ingredients of artistic creativity that rest in the case of a novel on, inter alia, the autonomy of the opinions of characters within a novel will not be undermined by a ruling that a novelist can blaspheme via those imagined protagonists. Otherwise, the very essence of one of creative writing's time-honoured mechanisms would be violated: the fictive would be being treated as the factual.

In a later important case under the Convention, *Otto-Preminger Institute v. Austria*,[21] the likely approach of the European Court of Human Rights to putative blasphemy expressed by characters in novels may be able to be predicted if an analogy with the Court's approach here to putative blasphemy in films is appropriate. In the instant case, a religiously controversial film, caricaturing iconic Christian figures, was to be shown at the named Institute. Despite the fact that Article 17a of the Austrian Basic Law expressly protects artistic freedom, the relevant film, *Das Liebeskinzil*, was seized and forfeited by the local provincial authorities on the grounds that cherished religious doctrines had been disparaged. Considering Article 10's possible violation, the Court in Strasbourg supported the contracting state's censorious stance: the offensiveness of the film outweighed any artistic virtue it had, and so Article 10 had not been breached, the imposed restriction on freedom of artistic expression being quite legitimate. This decision was made despite the fact that no one who did not wish to see the film was in any way obliged to see it. In addition, the film was to be shown in what was described as an 'art cinema', so only the art-interested would have been attracted to see it in its natural setting as an 'art film'. The clear principal focus of the film was artistic stimulus, not religious irreverence. Yet again we find artistic freedom swept aside by the overwhelming force of local moral indignation at its practice. The artist Karel Appel said that 'art must shock'.[22] Ignoring the imperative, the legal acceptance that it merely has the right to would be welcome.

The final case relating to the art versus morality debate is *Wingrove v. United Kingdom*.[23] This case was heard over a decade before the law of blasphemy was repealed in the United Kingdom. The applicant, Nigel Wingrove, was denied a certificate for his video-film to be shown, first by the British Board of Film Classification and then by the Video Appeals Panel, on the grounds that

---

20   *Human Rights Law Journal*, 12 (1991), 172.

21   E Ct HRR A 295-A (1994), 19 EHRR 34, E Ct HR.

22   Karel Appel was born in 1921 and became a member of the Cobra movement, which was constituted in 1948 by a group of artists from Copenhagen, Brussels and Amsterdam who were united in rejecting passive and lifeless art in favour of more violent subjects. Highly expressionistic, Appel painted in thick, naive strokes and with very lurid colours, paying attention to astonishing brutal effects above formal perfection of technique.

23   24 EHHR 1 (1997).

it potentially contravened United Kingdom blasphemy law. The film, *Visions of Ecstasy*, was an erotic interpretation of the story that Saint Teresa of Avila had ecstatic visions of Christ. It is not feasible that this video was as offensive as much that is legally available in the pornographic field on the Internet. No one suggested that the film was in anyway comparable in severity to routine hard-core pornography. Despite this, the European Court of Human Rights held that Article 10 had been violated. The Court used its habitual, non-reflective argument that a standard of morality was best adjudged in the region where it was allegedly upheld. It also approved again the national operation of a blasphemy law as a legitimate restriction on artistic freedom. Again it was unwilling to formulate a supranational meta-standard of morality of its own; it was content to remain consistent with its policy of abandoning artistic freedom when confronted by very limited tolerance towards it, as demonstrated, for example, at varying levels of regulation by the contracting state in relation to the blasphemy issue at hand. In short, and with respect to the artistic freedom and morality cases in general, the Court is revealing priorities that are inimical to its rights-advancing role. It is bewildering that its constant omission to protect artistic freedom in favour of moral censorship has not been challenged and rectified.

The protection of artistic freedom when threatened by countervailing moral concerns is jeopardized in particular by the Court's subsidiarity tool, the margin of appreciation. Basically, the Court upholds a certain amount of discretion on the part of the contracting state when it comes to controversial or delicate matters of specifically local concern. The idea behind this mechanism, as propounded by the Court, notably seminally in *Handyside*,[24] is that local authorities are in a better position to evaluate the moral climate, inter alia, in the local environment than is the comparatively distant Strasbourg Court. The argument is prima facie appealing. But what it in effect involves is the Court relinquishing its supervisory role in deference to local moral opinion as determined by local bodies. What is the point of someone making an application to the Court if the Court does not pronounce its own ethical judgment that is substantively separate from the local ruling against which such an application is made? In the area of morality, the margin of appreciation is said by the Court to be 'wide', a concession to the varying local-moral standards that exist in the allegedly morally disparate contracting states. However, the Court gives no scientific evidence for such a disparity and engages in no comparative law analysis, for example, to support its view that where morals are concerned there is no moral 'objective character' discernible across the contracting states. Moreover, when so many contracting states now have very morally plural societies, a decision on what is a state's moral position as a singular corpus may be even empirically impossible to ascertain. In addition, if in the art versus morality cases the Strasbourg Court observes only local mores rather than an international moral meta-standard, morally controversial art is judged by more conservative parochial values than the cosmopolitan ones habitually found in a large metropolis where morally cutting-edge artists enjoy greater moral freedom. Finally, the European Convention on Human Rights is meant to be used as a 'living instrument' and interpreted 'dynamically'. This entails provision for the morality of art to be assessed by the most contemporary value-judgments. With due respect, such judgments are seldom found to be initiated and sustained in a regional village atmosphere that the margin of appreciation permits to dictate moral imperatives.

Yet, in another sphere of rights protection, the European Court of Human Rights has commendably demonstrated a greater awareness of art-relevant issues. This is the area of sedition. Whereas the Court has been markedly disinclined to defend artists against the charge of immorality, it has seen fit to protect artists from condemnation for more serious crimes akin to seditious libel. This stance is somewhat paradoxical, and the cases concerning art and sedition have received little

---

24 Above, n. 14.

attention in comparison to the cases concerning art and immorality. One unreported case of 1999 on art and sedition is *Karata v. Turkey*.[25] The applicant in this case was a Turk of Kurdish origin. He published a collection of poetry called *The Song of a Rebellion*. At the national level, he was convicted of disseminating separatist propaganda and imprisoned. His poetry was confiscated. The applicant made an application against Turkey to the European Court of Human Rights. Had there been a legitimate restriction of the artist's freedom of artistic expression under Article 10? The Court emphasized that the material concerned comprised poetry, which, it said, reached a very small readership, and that the poet's punishment by the Turkish authorities was disproportionate. It focused its judgment on the limited potential impact of the verse in issue on national security, territorial integrity and public order. The poet explicitly stated that the poetry was not a reflection of his own political opinions; but no argument was put forward based on the autonomy of art. Such an argument might have immunized the poetry from inartistic interference from the outset but at least the Court in this case acknowledged in the course of its deliberations that the poetry collection was primarily a literary, as opposed to a political, work. Strangely, the European Commission of Human Rights, prior to the Court's decision making, had sided with the Turkish authorities. This is surprising because in the art and immorality cases the Commission had steadfastly defended artists against censorship, whereas the Court had, in that context, opposed such arguments. It is surprising that the Commission and the Court failed to cross-reference the immorality and sedition cases to make their different overall stances on artistic freedom consistent in both contexts. This omission reveals an unholistic institutional approach to artistic freedom. This is antithetical to a consistent juridical awareness, and associated doctrinal development, of the legal distinctiveness of artistic freedom under Article 10. However, in *Karata*,[26] the Court is to be commended for its specialistic recognition of the uniquely artistic context of any apparent aggression towards the integrity of Turkey as a sovereign state that the applicant's poetry could have been interpreted as exhibiting.

In this respect, the Court has been reassuringly consistent. In *Alinak v. Turkey*,[27] a 2005 case, the applicant had written a novel, using fictional characters, that criticized hostility generated by Turkish security forces against residents of an actual village. The Turkish Security Court seized the book. The European Court of Human Rights noted that the medium of the criticism was artistic and that a novel reached a smaller readership than the mass media. It duly held that the seizure of the work of fiction was not a proportionate reaction to the alleged political abuse of the right to freedom of expression by its author. It is perhaps significant that, whereas in the art versus morality cases the facts involve visual art, in the art versus sedition cases the facts involve creative writing. Given the reasoning in its sedition judgments in favour of artistic freedom, and against it in the immorality cases, it could be that the Court is of the opinion that visual art tends to reach a wider audience than creative writing, and is therefore more extensively harmful than the written word could be. The demographic validity of any such assumption is a matter of conjecture.

International Human Rights Instruments, Universal and Regional, Excluding the European Convention on Human Rights

There is, of course, international concern for the human rights of artists beyond the European Convention. A fundamental question of global interest is whether, theoretically, legal constraints

---

25   [1999] ECHR 23168/94.
26   Ibid.
27   Judgment of 29 March 2005 (unreported).

can be imposed on artistic freedom given that the nature of artistic enterprise necessarily implies in theory, and reinforces in practice, the notion of the transgression of limits, as part of the very essence of art, in terms of such ideas as creative inventiveness, novelty, inspiration and adventure. Historically, the Universal Declaration of Human Rights recognized first the need to internationalize the relation between art and liberty.[28] In its Article 19, the Declaration protects freedom of expression in general, then paragraphs 1 and 2 of its Article 27 preserve, respectively, the right of everyone to participate in the cultural life of the community, and the right of every author to secure protection of his/her moral and material interests resulting from literary and artistic production. Artistic liberty per se is not explicitly referred to but is implicitly protected under both paragraphs. The Declaration, however, is not a binding international human rights instrument, which restricts its practical if not iconic value: even though merely rhetorical, it has been a catalyst for two binding international covenants on artistically-related matters. The first of these, the International Covenant on Civil and Political Rights, in its Article 19, paragraph 2, reiterates the commitment to the international protection of freedom of expression in general, and, though not recognizing that some art is non-cognitive but simply affective, it proceeds to protecting, specifically, inter alia, the imparting of information and ideas in the form of art. Though this binding provision is helpful to artists, the paragraph emphasizes only the furtherance of art's incidental function, sometimes, of ideation, rather than the promotion and protection of art in all its ontological complexity. Moreover, there is no detail given in the broad and open-textured language of the provision that assists the recognition of art for protective purposes. An important feature of paragraph 3 of the law here is the prescriptive accommodation of others' competing interests with those of the artist, which must be strictly observed under Article 19 as a contrasting priority in the form of a list of legitimate restrictions on artistic freedom. This countervailing set of interests, which includes the rights and reputations of others and the need for the more communal protection of national security, public order, public health or public morals, places a significant, and arguably draconian, practical limitation on artistic liberty that also appears in the European Convention on Human Rights. However, these conflicting restrictions must not undermine the essence of the right to artistic freedom within the range of the cardinal basic human right of freedom of speech, including symbolic speech. In the International Covenant on Civil and Political Rights, there is no reference made to democratic society, which is a central feature of the European Convention, because of the Covenant's hybrid political global context. This begs the question as to whether the true observance of human rights can work successfully only in a democratic framework, as some commentators on rights insist. In ignoring the arguably necessary democratic medium for rights, the Covenant expediently avoids antagonizing non-democratic states. To do the contrary would be to impose on them, in the universal Covenant's terms and interpretation, a key plank in the traditional Western theoretical structure, and political value-system, of rights protection.

The sister instrument of the International Covenant on Civil and Political Rights is the International Covenant on Economic, Social and Cultural Rights. This human rights covenant, in

---

28   The initial enthusiasm for freedom of expression of all types was exhibited in such eighteenth-century documents as the First Amendment of the US Constitution and the French Declaration of 1789. It is instructive that whereas the Americans favoured an absolute conception of expressive freedom, the French preferred a relative concept of liberty based on the writings of Rousseau. The international human rights instruments that evolved much later than these seminal national approaches still reflect subtle aspects of this dichotomic thinking but in a much more complex way. This variation results from the necessity for significantly more philosophical and practical compromise at the international legal level, where a relative conception of freedom of speech is more generally favoured, to accommodate, as diplomatically as possible, international political and moral diversity.

its Article 15, paragraph 1, does not stress artistic freedom as a primary issue. Instead, it points to the importance of participation in cultural life, the benefits of scientific progress and the intellectual property rights resultant from authorship in the scientific, literary and artistic fields. It is only belatedly, in its Article 19, paragraph 3, that freedom of artistic expression is implied by the nebulous if imperative nomenclature involving the 'indispensable' freedom of 'creative activity'. As in its partner covenant, the instrument on economic, social and cultural rights attempts to synthesize the freedom and solitude of the artist and the values involved in his/her public usefulness and participation. It is submitted that this exaggerates the importance of state control over the necessary privacy of creative endeavour and its personal rewards; and, in general, the International Covenant on Economic, Social and Cultural Rights mistakenly sees the role of the artist as one of public service rather than individual fulfilment. This underestimates the tension between the right of artists to shock and the accepted moral standards of a given, basically inartistic, community setting.[29]

As well as universal arrangements for the protection of human rights, regional arrangements comparable to the European Convention system also exist in America and Africa. The American Convention on Human Rights, 1969, reflects the terms of the International Covenant on Civil and Political Rights. Its Article 13, paragraph 1, protects freedom of expression in general, including in the form of art. The Article's paragraph 2 bans prior censorship as a leading principle but recognizes that artistic freedom can be compromised by others' interests, much as conveyed in the legitimate restrictions placed on freedom of expression in general in the European Convention on Human Rights. These include concessions to such interests related to defamation, national security, public order, public health, public morals and unspecified 'rights of others'. This last residual category is potentially threatening to artistic freedom because of its vagueness, which could conceal various justifiable counter-claims to the exercise of artistic liberty that an artist cannot foresee. Article 13, paragraph 4, stipulates that another restriction on artistic freedom, inter alia, pertains to the moral protection of childhood and adolescence. It is submitted that this stance is uncontroversial except that the rule here could have provided for the use of warning signs at art exhibitions as a paternalistic solution to the situation of minors, instead of possible legal action on their behalf by their parents or guardians. Another international regional arrangement for the protection of human rights is the African Charter on Human and Peoples' Rights, 1981, which has idiosyncratic provisions on freedom of expression. This charter begins conventionally by protecting the right to express and disseminate opinions in its Article 9, paragraph 2, and by providing for free participation in the cultural life of the community in its Article 17. However, it also affirms the duty of the state to protect the morals and traditional values recognized by the community, a duty the performance of which may restrict free speech. Individuals are also oppressed in Article 27, paragraph 2, by a host of onerous duties to respect the rights of others (the rights being unspecified) and to have due regard for collective security, morality and the common interest. There is no recognition of the autonomy of artists as, under Article 29, paragraph 7, they and their fellow citizens must preserve and strengthen 'positive African cultural values' and promote the moral well-being of society.[30] This

---

29   The dynamic created by the reception of art in society often involves an uncomfortable interaction of opposing moral positions. In Hartian terms, this can be accurately expressed as a reaction of society's 'accepted' morality to art's 'critical' morality. The difficulty for art here is that 'society' is usually unaware that art has a moral purpose at all, let alone one that impacts on accepted morality as a catalyst for that morality to evolve according to change in societal attitudes. This lacuna in societal awareness makes art vulnerable to maltreatment by establishment norms that are misconceived to be superior and static.

30   This political stance misconceives art as being comprised of moral opinions. Art is a specialized form of cultural value, not a vehicle of opinion; and any morality involved in it is not political engineering, nor is it designed to wield political influence. Sometimes, as an incidental and often unintended reflection of

is virtually a prescription for an official literature even though the measures may have been well-intentioned in being designed to cultivate a post-colonial communal spirit of solidarity. There is the strong intimation that anything that could be judged negative or amoral art, or any other type of offending unofficial 'message', could be censored in a typically totalitarian fashion. This possibility is obviously inimical to the true spirit of freedom of expression, and its products' sometimes critical approach to the status quo, quite properly within the poetic canons of artistry. Any alleged offensiveness by an artist is misunderstood if taken as literally, rather than symbolically, real, and the African Charter's restrictive elements militate against the very essence of art's ontological, and culturally-recognized, oblique and independent, and thus syncretically conceptually-insulated, relationship with the real-life, extrinsic brouhaha of ordinary, and interpersonally consequential, human affairs. Instead of accusing artists of being in some way conventionally immoral or simply unacceptable non-conformists, there should be a general legal recognition of art's moral autonomy in accordance with its own internal specialist criteria of reference. Having proceeded to acknowledge and respect artistic autonomy, legal systems involving human rights can attribute to art a particularly elevated type of esteemed *virtue*, which can be legally and morally identifiable as indelibly associated with creative virtuosity, a word with the same semantic root.[31]

Artistic freedom should be secured based on two arguments, one from the standpoint of individual self-fulfilment, which is self-evident, and (in the case of cognitive art, in particular, which communicates ideas) another that maintains that artistic expression can comprise or generate information that can lead to the ascertainment of truth. Moreover, an argument exists that art should be insulated from legal purview entirely, in accordance with the fact that art is a *sui generis*, culturally-acknowledged, unique form. In addition, as well as art being independent based on its own ontology as an autonomous product, aesthetic perceiving or dwelling upon an art-form gives autonomy to the self-activating interplay that can be termed 'the art experience'.

It is to the benefit of society in general for art to be produced: creativity is a noble and commendable exercise at all levels, and the most highly-prized examples of art lift humanity to heights of awe and pleasure, and contribute to what is worthwhile and creditable about human civilization. This fact should find reflection in the recognition of artists as rights-holders in all spheres of their artistic activity, including their role as critical-moral agents. This critical-moral capacity involves the presentation of new moral stimulus or insights that challenge the societal-moral status quo, albeit with the subtlety sometimes of an inherently ambiguous medium. The exclusive focus of the law should be extreme 'worthless' pornography, such as that associated with the exploitation of children and with the portrayal of serious violence, examples of which occur on the Internet. This argument is supported by theoretical reasons why individuals should not be limited in their artwork on account of an allegation that a given product's showing is detrimental to public-moral standards. One such reason is that obscenity as a phenomenon can only emanate from a non-artistic medium. Only when art is viewed out of context can obscenity result, because, if the viewer adopts the appropriate art-appreciative attitude, that specialized psychic approach denudes the art of any potentially offensive literal impact. Moreover, if something is displayed as art in an art gallery, there is a natural and necessary presumption that the object is art. The oblique communication of art militates against its having detrimental literal effects; it is symbol, not quotidian fact; its physical position in an art gallery affirms its artistic status unqualifiedly. In addition, if one espouses the theory that the viewer co-creates an artwork in the course of that

---

its aesthetic function, a political message of sorts can be inferred, but art is not involved in literal argument, being an autonomous symbolic medium.

31　We can return to Van Gogh. In his case, there is a particularly potent argument that his life and art had an essentially sacred dimension.

object's mental reception, obscenity is necessarily excluded from the viewer-to-object interaction since the creative liaison between viewer and object does not allow for anything extrinsic to interfere with the culturally-specialized purity of that relation, which can be broadly described as aesthetic.

Unlike the ontology of pornography, the ontology of art presupposes the culturally-valued autonomy of a privileged class of imagery. This is an ineluctable and inevitable insularity that the law, virtually uniquely, frequently disrespects, usually because of law's a priori schemas and a habitual element of prejudication based on a conservative adverse reaction to charges of immorality in general. Moreover, the judicialization of art sometimes conjures up institutional prejudices about 'ivory-tower' approaches and their juridical insignificance. The appreciation of art is not a rarefied pursuit and it is in the interests of civilization in general that artists have rights to engage in critical-moral activity that shifts understanding on accepted, complacent or demoded moral practice. To misunderstand art's intrinsic moral role leads to injustice to artists, and this is indefensible as a common legal phenomenon.

For law to maintain its image of being a neutral, fair and refined culture, it must desist from revealing itself as unsophisticated in its dealings with controversial but ultimately edifying art. To demand of art that it has a uniform moral pallor in conformity with the comparatively dull complexion of allegedly accepted moral mores is to make artists restrict themselves to creating works that merely replicate the attitudes that congregate to form what could even be a *fictive* censorious consensus (because there is no empirical evidence to suggest that 'accepted morality' is other than a mistaken legal presupposition in the first place). Some, but too few, written national constitutions offer as a counter-proposition that art should be free as the primary presumption when art is confronted by what is often its public-moral nemesis. To prosecute artists and to deny them their rights qua artists leads not only to injustice but also to autocensorship; more worryingly, it is the prelude to the prescription of an official art and that art's close association with totalitarianism.

Chapter 6

Truth, Myth and Critical Theory

Eric Heinze

Introduction[1]

Once upon a time there lived some pious souls. They desired only the freedom to follow their conscience. They were industrious, yet thrifty; prosperous, yet humble. Persecution made them abandon their English homeland. They sailed the stormy Atlantic in quest of the sacred birthright of all mankind: democracy. Yet the English tyrant still blighted them in America, as he had done in England. So they mustered a ragtag army, whose sparse but brave men at first seemed no match for the vast empire. Clever and agile, and with right on their side, they nevertheless threw off the English despot. They founded a new nation, indivisible, with liberty and justice for all.

That schoolroom fairytale was once ubiquitous in the United States. It is by no means dead today. It is anathema for Critical Race Theorists[2] and LatCrits.[3] It lies, because it glorifies democracy where African-Americans, Latinos, Native Americans, Asians, women, sexual minorities and other outsiders,[4] have faced brutality and exclusion. It lies by silencing as much as it tells. It tells the conquerors' story. The conquered go unnamed, their story untold. It lies because it is a myth that speaks of 'liberty and justice for all', while disguising a political history that long favoured a straight, white, male elite. It lies by parading the dominant group's ideals as the American reality; by proclaiming the very partial and particular ideals of one American group as the universal ideals held equally by all American groups, even those who were systematically barred from sharing in that ideal. A cardinal task of Critical Race Theorists and LatCrits has been to explode that kind of American myth in order to unmask the politics behind it.

But here's another fairytale. Once upon a time, children from around the globe, of all races, creeds and colours, with brightly beaming faces, gathered together and joined hands. Adults looked on in tearful joy and *learned their lesson*, as the children's voices sang out in gleeful counterpoint: 'It's a small world after all.' In demolishing the American fairytale, have some Critical Race Theorists and LatCrits merely adopted that internationalist one? Are they making their own choices about which partial ideals they will universalize and which embarrassing truths they will silence, in order to promote platforms that do not even reflect the interests of the outsiders for whom they speak?

---

1   This chapter draws from sections I–IIIb of my article 'Truth and myth in Critical Race Theory and LatCrit: Human rights and the ethnocentrism of anti-ethnocentrism', *National Black Law Journal* (Columbia Law School), 20 (2008), 107–62. Those sections are reprinted here with the kind permission of the *NBLJ* editors. Further analysis of Delgado, Romany and others can be found in the remainder of that article.

2   For examples of leading contributions see, generally, M Matsuda et al. (eds), *Words that Wound* (Boulder, CO: Westview Press, 1993) [hereinafter *Words*]; R Delgado and J Stefancic (eds), *Critical Race Theory: The Cutting Edge* (Philadelphia: Temple University Press, 2000) [hereinafter CRT].

3   For examples see, generally, Harvard Latino Law Review, La Raza Law Journal or Chicano Latino Law Review.

4   On the concept of outsider groups and outsider jurisprudence, see M Matsuda, 'Public response to racist speech: Considering the victim's story', in *Words*, above, n. 2, at 17, 18–20.

Critical Race Theory and LatCrit might at first appear to be distinctly American movements, insofar as their criticisms have largely focused on US law. Their analyses of history and culture draw strongly upon the experiences of minorities in the United States. Their exponents are generally based in US universities, and the movements have arisen from their teachings and publications within the American academic establishment.[5] However, problems of domination, marginalization, exclusion or inter-ethnic conflict resonate throughout the post-colonial world, and throughout the international human rights movement. Several Critical Race Theorists and LatCrits have looked beyond US shores, seeking solutions within international law and institutions.

In some of their work, however, these scholars have played the same game of simplification, myth-making and exclusion-of-outsiders that they rightly condemn when it is played to spread the old myths of white America. They claim to reject abstract, decontextualized or formalist interpretations of US law, insisting on a method of legal realism that would look to the brutal realities behind empty promises of 'liberty' or 'equal protection'. However, in an effort to forge political alliances against US law – in particular, against the American civil liberties tradition – they then proceed to adopt wholly abstract, decontextualized and formalist readings of international norms. They endorse the empty promises of international norms while abandoning the same legal realism that would reveal brutal realities waged against non-American outsider groups. Having examined such scholars elsewhere, the focus in this chapter is on the work of Mari Matsuda.

A legal realist approach prompts Matsuda to reject any idealism about what US law promises by condemning what it has actually delivered. However, she then claims an ally in a mythical international 'community',[6] applauding what it has promised while resorting to equally idealized legal formalisms in order to ignore what that 'community' has actually delivered. Instead of seeking a balanced assessment of the US in light of other societies of comparable history and demographics, she merely replaces the old American myths with new internationalist ones.

In an age of growing internationalization of human rights, American critical theorists must approach international norms with the same rigour they have applied to the bleak histories and manipulative formalisms of US law. This chapter argues that, by doing so, their work will provide more accurate insight, not only into the ideals and realities of the United States, but also into the ideals and realities of the so-called 'international community'.

The first section of this chapter suggests that two principal trends have emerged in the relationships between those two critical movements and international law. On the one hand, some Critical Race Theorists and LatCrits suggest a thoroughgoing harmony between their movements and international law. That tendency can be called the 'alliance trend'. On the other hand, many scholars, particularly among Critical Race Theorists, have ignored international law altogether. That tendency is the 'neglect trend'. This section looks first to the neglect trend, examining but rejecting the reasons why Critical Race Theorists might be thought to share little common cause with international human rights law, and arguing that their overlaps are important. Following that is a discussion of the alliance trend, equally rejecting suggestions of straightforwardly allied positions between these critical movements and international law. The chapter advocates critical scholars' return to their own critical and realist approach, that is, to a 'critical trend', whereby they might scrutinize the professed norms of international law with the same rigour that they have applied to US law. The discussion briefly proposes some alternative principles that might guide future critical approaches to outsider jurisprudence in an age of globalization.

---

5   See, above, text accompanying n. 2 and n. 3.
6   See, below, text accompanying n. 91.

The Two Principal Trends

Critical Race Theorists and LatCrits have suggested two general kinds of relationship between their movements and international human rights law, 'alliance' and 'neglect'. These two trends are compared briefly here, before being examined individually.

The Alliance Trend

Some Critical Race Theorists and LatCrits suggest a straightforward, essentially unproblematic alliance between their theories and international human rights law. They argue, for example, that racist invective causes as much harm as the batteries, assaults or illicit speech acts (for example, fraud, criminal solicitation or conspiracy) that domestic legal systems have traditionally outlawed.[7] They maintain that the American failure to punish hate speech, on grounds of abstract, universalist understandings of liberty, serves only to enhance the liberties of traditionally dominant groups. The disempowered then become further marginalized.[8]

In an article entitled 'A shifting balance: Freedom of expression and hate speech regulation', Jean Stefancic and Richard Delgado review the international consensus in favour of hate speech bans, in order to reject American civil libertarian defences of free speech.[9] Mari Matsuda reaches similar conclusions in 'Public response to racist speech: Considering the victim's story', published in the frequently cited collection *Words that Wound*.[10] The analyses of Stefancic, Delgado and Matsuda join those of many other Critical Race Theorists[11] and human rights advocates.[12]

Stefancic and Delgado's analysis is comparative. They review hate speech bans in various countries, often adopted pursuant to international treaty obligations. As I have already commented on that approach elsewhere,[13] the focus in this chapter will be on Matsuda's piece. Matsuda does not analyse domestic jurisdictions. Instead, she explores bans on hate speech advocated at the United Nations during the drafting of the International Convention on the Elimination of All Forms of Racial Discrimination.[14]

The alliance trend has emerged more prominently in LatCrit. LatCrits are concerned with ethnic minority communities whose experience, albeit sharing important similarities with African-American communities, have also had distinct experiences and problems. Berta Esperanza Hernández-Truyol sees LatCrit as interested in 'the Latina/o multidimensional experience within

---

7   For a recent discussion with reference to international norms, see E Heinze, 'Viewpoint absolutism and hate speech', *Mod L Rev*, 69/4 (2006), 543, 577–78 [hereinafter Heinze 'Viewpoint absolutism'].

8   See generally *Words*, above, n. 2.

9   J Stefancic and R Delgado, A shifting balance: Freedom of expression and hate speech regulation, *Iowa L Rev*, 78 (1992–93), 737.

10   Matsuda, above, n. 4, at 17.

11   See generally *Words*, above, n. 2. See also R Delgado, 'About your masthead: A preliminary inquiry into the compatibility of civil rights and civil liberties', *Harv CR-CL L Rev*, 39 (2004), 1 [hereinafter Delgado 'About your masthead'] (reviewing arguments in favour of hate speech bans).

12   See K Boyle, 'Hate speech: The United States versus the rest of the world?', *Me L Rev*, 53 (2001), 487; S Colliver (ed.), *Striking a Balance: Hate Speech, Freedom of Expression and Non-Discrimination* (Human Rights Centre, University of Essex, 1992).

13   See Heinze 'Viewpoint absolutism', above, n. 7 (arguing that, within the mature, stable and prosperous liberal democracies of Western Europe, hate speech bans do not and cannot fulfil their aims).

14   Convention on the Elimination of All Forms of Racial Discrimination, 21 December 1965, 660 UNTS 195 (entered into force 4 January 1969).

the *fronteras estadounidenses* [US borders – EH] [...] multiracial, multicultural, multilingual, multiethnic, and even multinational'.[15]

Unlike much Critical Race Theory, international perspectives have become central to core LatCrit concerns. LatCrits' interest in immigration, cross-border employment, or economic development in the Americas, has led them to look beyond US law when international law offers attractive solutions.[16] The experience of being defined by identities reaching beyond US frontiers has also led some LatCrits to a more deeply existential identification with international human rights law – to a sense that only a legal system recognizing individual and collective identities beyond national borders can embrace their experience of multiple and conflicting selves.[17] The alliance trend, then, encompasses both Critical Race Theorists and LatCrits who not only reject fundamental elements of US law, but also claim to find superior alternatives within international law.

The Neglect Trend

Within Critical Race Theory, those approaches by Matsuda, Stefancic and Delgado still represent the exception more than the rule. Unlike LatCrits, most Critical Race Theorists have paid little attention to international law, having generally confined their analyses to US law and history.[18] It is always difficult to analyse a negative – in this case, to ask why most Critical Race Theorists have *not* turned their attention to international human rights law. But it is important to ask that question. Have they neglected international law because of some fundamental incompatibility between Critical Race Theory and internationalism? Or does the neglect arise more from pragmatics than from principle? Those two questions provide a starting point. We must first establish *whether* there is a genuine relationship between these two critical movements and international human rights law before we ask what that relationship should be.

The Failure of the 'Neglect' Trend

This discussion begins, then, with the neglect trend, arguing that some critical theorists have indeed tended to overlook international law, but only for pragmatic, and not theoretical, reasons. The theoretical and historical relationships among Critical Race Theory, LatCrit and international human rights law are crucial – but, as will be explained later, not for the reasons suggested by many Critical Race Theorists and LatCrits.

Critical Race Theory and Rights Scepticism

Because its authors see hate speech as broadly reflecting the outsider status of ethnic minorities, *Words that Wound* became more than a book about hate speech. The book has become a landmark text in critical theory. It stands among Critical Race Theorists' first attempts to characterize outsider jurisprudence in general terms. While noting a diversity of approaches to outsider jurisprudence,

---

15   B Esperanza Hernández-Truyol, 'Building bridges IV: Of cultures, colors, and clashes – Capturing the international in Delgado's chronicles', *Harv Latino L Rev*, 4 (2000), 115, 118.

16   See the various contributions in a special issue on LatCrit published in *U Miami Inter-Am L Rev*, 28 (1996–97).

17   See C Romany, 'Claiming a global identity: Latino/a critical scholarship and international human rights', *U Miami Inter-Am L Rev*, 28 (1996–97), 215.

18   See generally CRT, above, n. 2.

the authors set forth six 'defining elements'. Two are particularly relevant to understanding rights and, in particular, to understanding the kinds of formal proclamations of rights that we find in national instruments, such as the US Bill of Rights,[19] as well as international instruments, such as the Universal Declaration of Human Rights[20] (read 'element' for the letter 'E'),

> [E]2. Critical Race Theory expresses scepticism toward dominant legal claims of neutrality [and] objectivity. [...] These claims are central to an ideology of equal opportunity [which] tells an ahistorical, abstracted story of racial inequality as a series of randomly occurring, intentional, and individualized acts.

> [E]3. Critical Race Theory challenges ahistoricism and insists on a contextual/historical analysis of the law. Current inequalities and social/institutional practices are linked to earlier periods in which the intent and cultural meaning of such practices were clear. [...][21]

Critical Race Theorists maintain that legal norms cannot be read off the page. They are meaningful only in historical and social contexts. We can read in the US Declaration of Independence that 'all men are created equal', or in the Constitution's Fourteenth Amendment that the individual states shall guarantee 'equal protection of the law' or 'due process' to all citizens. For Critical Race Theory, however, those formally declared norms have systemically worked out to be the exclusive privileges of white males.[22] In *Dred Scott v. Sanford*, the Supreme Court used the discourse of higher-law rights not to defeat slavery but to affirm whites' property interests in their slaves.[23] In *Plessy v. Ferguson*, the Court cited separate but 'equal' facilities for whites and blacks, not as evidence of unconstitutional discrimination, but as evidence that blacks were being treated equally to whites.[24]

Accordingly, it might at first seem that Critical Race Theorists' general neglect of international human rights law arises from an overall scepticism about formal proclamations of rights. Critical Race Theorists might seem justified in keeping some distance from the leading international human rights instruments, like the Universal Declaration of Human Rights or the International Covenant on Civil and Political Rights,[25] in view of the historical failures of individual rights promulgated in abstract, universalist terms.

That rights scepticism, however, cannot really explain the neglect trend. In *The Alchemy of Race and Rights*, Patricia Williams famously rejects the scepticism about rights that had characterized the Critical Legal Studies movement of the 1970s and 1980s. Williams certainly acknowledges that white Americans had benefited from rights far more than African-Americans. At the same time, she notes that the limited access to rights that African-Americans have enjoyed has often provided real empowerment.

In discussing her search to rent an apartment, Williams concedes that white males (such as those who formed the American Critical Legal Studies movement) might, through their inherited social

---

19   US Const. Amend I–X.

20   GA RES 217A (III), AT 71, UN DOC A/810 (10 December 1948) [Hereinafter GA RES. 217A].

21   CR Lawrence et al., 'Introduction', in *Words*, above, n. 2, at 6.

22   See generally CRT, above, n. 2, pts I–IV.

23   *Dred Scott v. Sanford*, 60 US 393, 450, 451, 453 (How) (1856). Cf. also ibid. at 408, 410, 411, 414, 415, 435, 444, 446, 447, 448, 449.

24   *Plessy v. Ferguson*, 163 US 537, 544, 548-9, 550-1 (1896).

25   International Covenant on Civil and Political Rights, 16 December 1966, 993 UNTS 3 (entered into force 3 January 1976) [hereinafter ICCPR].

privilege, feel secure in 'overcoming' the impersonal and adversarial nature of contract rights, by striking a friendly, informal, oral agreement. She, however, as an African-American woman, felt more secure with a formal, written agreement that she could wave in court if she were cheated, as ethnic minorities and women had been cheated in the past.[26] The would-be radicalism of the Critical Legal Studies movement suddenly looked like an elitist, white, middle-class pastime. Traditional individual rights could be seen as constructive for outsider groups, as long as they remained vigilant about the ease with which rights had been turned against their interests in the past.[27]

Other Critical Race Theorists have taken similar positions, rejecting simple dualisms between 'rights are good' and 'rights are bad'. They acknowledge the empowering potential of rights, but warn that formal proclamations must not be taken at face value. Another 'defining element' of Critical Race Theory set forth in *Words that Wound* states:

> [E]5. Critical Race Theory is interdisciplinary and eclectic. It borrows from several traditions, including liberalism, law and society, feminism, Marxism, poststructuralism, critical legal theory, pragmatism and nationalism. This eclecticism allows Critical Race Theory to examine and incorporate those aspects of a methodology or theory that effectively enable our voice and advance the cause of racial justice even as we maintain a critical posture.[28]

It would be misleading, then, to believe that Critical Race Theorists had bypassed international human rights because of their rights scepticism. Critical Race Theorists' rights scepticism is generally a vigilance about rights discourse, not a rejection of it.

Critical Race Theory and Anti-Universalism

International human rights must apply to people in particular places at particular times. For the most part, however, the norms of human rights law have been formulated not in local but in global terms. They attempt to generalize about all people everywhere,[29] or, at least, about whole categories of people, such as women,[30] children,[31] or workers.[32] Much of international human rights law speaks about *the* human being, about *the* individual *as such*.[33] The Universal Declaration of Human Rights proclaims the 'inherent dignity and [...] the equal and inalienable rights of *all* members of the human family'.[34]

---

26   PJ Williams, *The Alchemy of Race and Rights* (Cambridge, MA: Harvard University Press, 1991), 147–65.

27   See also K Crenshaw, 'Race, reform and retrenchment: Transformation and legitimation in anti-discrimination law', *Harv L Rev*, 101 (1988), 1331.

28   Lawrence et al., above, n. 21, at 6.

29   See Universal Declaration of Human Rights, GA Res 217A (III), at 71, UN Doc A/810 (10 December 1948); see ICCPR, above, n. 25.

30   See 'Convention on the Elimination of All Forms of Discrimination against Women', 1249 UNTS 513 (entered into force 3 September 1981).

31   See 'Convention on the Rights of the Child', 20 November 1989, S1577 UNTS 3 (entered into force 2 September 1990).

32   See 'Discrimination (Employment and Occupation) Convention', 25 June 1958, 362 UNTS 31 (entered into force 15 June 1960).

33   Cf. MJ Sandel, *Liberalism and the Limits of Justice* (Cambridge: Cambridge University Press, 1998, 2nd edn) (criticizing abstract-universalist concepts of the human subject as a basis for politics or justice).

34   See GA Res 217A, above, n. 20.

Critical Race Theory has moved in the opposite direction. Its 'vigilant' rights scepticism calls for a cautious approach to abstract and universalist claims about human beings or human experience. That scepticism is illustrated through storytelling, a crucial innovation of Critical Race Theory. Storytelling focuses on the complexities of individually lived experiences that cannot be grasped either through terse and highly generalized norms, or through traditional, abstract, 'disembodied' legal theory. 'For many minority persons', writes Richard Delgado, 'the principal instrument of their subordination [...] is the prevailing *mindset* by means of which members of the dominant group justify the world as it is'.[35]

That mindset, its assumptions and attitudes can be said to pervade not only mass culture, but also the more rarefied discourses of traditional legal culture and analysis. It may indeed be overtly racist: 'with whites on top and browns and blacks at the bottom'.[36] However, it can also be more diffuse. It often persists within a society whose formally adopted norms include universalist values of 'liberty', 'democracy', 'due process' or 'equal protection'.[37] Those norms may have been legislated with the best will in the world by a liberally minded elite. In reality, however, they apply without regard to subtler relationships of power and subordination that systematically pervert the very fairness that those norms are designed to promote.

Cases such as *Washington v. Davis*,[38] or *McCleskey v. Kemp*,[39] suggest that racism more deeply seated within social attitudes may threaten justice, even as judges insist that the universalist norms of equal protection and due process are adequate to assure fairness. Racism can, then, be disempowering, despite formal, abstract, universalist promises of empowerment. Disempowerment, in turn, signifies alienation and exclusion. Where, then, can outsider groups draw strength? How do they empower themselves? Delgado continues:

> The attraction of stories should come as no surprise, for stories create their own bonds, represent cohesion, shared understandings, and meanings. The cohesiveness that stories bring is part of the strength of the outgroup. An outgroup creates its own stories, which circulate within the group as a kind of counter-reality.[40]

If we care not only about abstract ideals, but also about concrete reality, then that vigilance towards formal, abstract, universalist concepts can be applied to the Universal Declaration of Human Rights. The Universal Declaration purports to speak equally for 'all members of the human family', yet continues to do so in a world of flagrant inequalities.

International human rights law relies on global organizations and institutions. The latter are, in turn, influenced by powerful states. One could argue, then, that human rights law serves not to challenge existing arrangements of global exploitation, but merely to legitimate them through a hollow universalist discourse. This is precisely what Critical Race Theorists often accuse US law of having done.[41] Critical Race Theorists remind us that pseudo-cosmopolitan notions of American

---

35   R Delgado, 'Storytelling for oppositionists and others: A plea for narrative', *Mich L Rev*, 87 (1989), 2411, 2413 [hereinafter Delgado 'Storytelling'] (original emphasis).

36   Ibid.

37   See K Karst 'Integration success story', *S Cal L Rev*, 69 (1996), 1781, 1783 (book review).

38   *Washington v. Davis*, 426 US 229 (1976) (rejecting claims that examinations for admission into police force contained racist bias).

39   *McCleskey v. Kemp*, 481 US 279 (1987) (rejecting claims that death penalty sentencing contained racist bias).

40   Delgado, above, n. 35, at 2412.

41   See, below, Part III.

federal sovereignty, vested in 'We the People',[42] turned out to exclude slaves, who had counted as only three-fifths of a person,[43] and then segregated blacks, who were 'separate but equal'.[44] Accordingly, the neglect trend might appear to stand as a rejection of those abstract concepts of 'the human being' or 'the human family', which, like promises of 'equal protection' or 'due process', have served as means of oppressing society's outsiders.

That conclusion, however, also fails to explain the neglect trend. While remaining cautious about conceptual abstractions, critical theory cannot avoid them. No clear lines can be drawn between 'abstract' and 'concrete' expressions of social problems or legal interests. Ethnic differences in the US have spread over too many populations, too many situations, too broad a geography and too long a time to warrant any understanding of Critical Race Theory as merely 'local', 'immediate' or 'concrete'. One need merely compare Soujourner Truth to Clarence Thomas, Billie Holliday to Will Smith, to recognize that 'the African-American', let alone 'the outsider', can only ever be a vast, diverse, inevitably abstract category. That is why storytelling can only ever tell part of its story. If law is to be transformed into a means of empowerment for such a large and diverse population, we cannot eschew its abstractions and generalities. No less than black-letter human rights lawyers must critical theorists deal in conceptual abstractions and generalized human categories.

Accordingly, just as with Critical Race Theorists' approach to rights, their approach towards abstract human classifications is one of vigilance, not outright rejection. Higher and lower levels of abstraction inevitably blend to shape any movement dealing with vast and complex issues: terms like 'black', 'African-American', 'Latina/o', 'women', 'minority', 'gay' and 'sexual minority' are all abstractions, covering people in different circumstances. Internationally, the term 'American' may be the opposite of 'global'; nationally, however, 'American' – along with 'African American', 'gay American', and so on – is surely the opposite of 'local'. Critical Race Theorists' neglect of international human rights law cannot, then, be attributed to the levels of conceptual abstraction at which the two movements approach the human being. Both deal with the human being at significant levels of abstraction, and can scarcely do otherwise.

Pragmatics

The tendency of many Critical Race Theorists to neglect international law cannot be explained, then, on the foregoing theoretical grounds – neither in terms of their caution towards rights discourse, nor in terms of their caution towards abstract or universalist discourses. Rather, the neglect trend arises from purely practical constraints. In paying little attention to international law, Critical Race Theorists are no different from many other US public interest lawyers and legal scholars (the LatCrits are an unusual exception, in view of the more immediately transnational character of many of their communities and legal problems). US public interest lawyers who seek real reforms have long recognized the limited force of international human rights on domestic US law, at federal and state as well as local levels.[45] High-profile civil rights battles in the United States show that international human rights law, albeit occasionally mentioned, is rarely decisive for US courts.

---

42   US CONST preamb.
43   US CONST art I, § 2, cl. 3.
44   See above text accompanying n. 24.
45   See generally, HJ Steiner and P Alston, *International Human Rights in Context 1029–48* (Oxford: Oxford University Press, 2000, 2nd edn) for the limited influence of international human rights law on US law. See also DQ Thomas, 'Advancing rights protection in the United States: An internationalized advocacy strategy', *Harv Hum Rts J*, 9 (1996), 15, 19–22.

Consider the Civil Rights movement of the 1950s and 1960s, the death penalty, religious freedom, free speech, women's rights, or abortion rights. Some scholars have pointed to occasional initiatives by US civil rights organizations to bring action against the United States within the United Nations.[46] None, however, have argued that those initiatives ever amounted to a central pillar of legal or political strategy. Within US legal practice, such attempts tend to be notable as rare exceptions, and not as routine practice.[47] For Critical Race Theorists and most law reform movements in the United States, the thickets of the federal and case-law system have been dense enough, without their having to face the complications of legal norms that have heretofore carried little weight in domestic US law.

Overall Affinities

If the neglect trend arises, then, from pragmatic constraints, it becomes that much clearer that there is no *conceptual* barrier between the fundamental concerns of Critical Race Theory and those of international human rights law. The two movements share deep affinities.[48] Many international norms and proclamations concerning racism could easily have been penned by Critical Race Theorists. The International Convention on the Elimination of All Forms of Racial Discrimination (CERD),[49] for example, condemns 'colonialism and all practices of segregation and discrimination associated therewith' (preamb. para. 4). States Parties proclaim themselves '[c]onvinced that any doctrine of superiority based on racial differentiation is scientifically false, morally condemnable, socially unjust and dangerous, and that there is no justification for racial discrimination, in theory or in practice' (preamb. para. 6). They further declare themselves '[c]onvinced that the existence of racial barriers is repugnant to the ideals of any human society' (preamb. para. 8) and '[a]larmed by manifestations of racial discrimination still in evidence in some areas of the world and by governmental policies based on racial superiority or hatred' (preamb. para. 9). Those thematic overlaps between Critical Race Theory and international human rights law are no coincidence. American racism arose entirely within the context of history's first great calamity of globalization, the trans-Atlantic slave trade. The roots (recalling that word's rich significance in recent years[50]) of American racism were nothing if not international.

During the Cold War, when human rights activity within the United Nations was largely immobilized by political differences, South African apartheid became one of the few situations that commanded broad consensus. Sufficient anti-apartheid sentiment in both East and West fostered a mighty global response. Apartheid became the paradigm of a global human rights issue.[51] Further norm creation within the United Nations was often far reaching. Article 2(2) of the Declaration on Race and Racial Prejudice (DRRP),[52] for example, depicts racism in expansive terms:

---

46 See Thomas, above, n. 45, at 17.

47 In a 2005 case, the Supreme Court referred to international standards in striking down the death penalty for persons who were juveniles at the time the crime was committed. *Roper v. Simmons*, 543 US 551, 604 (2005). That decision was chastised for being highly unusual for, if not patently incompatible with, American law.

48 See Hernández-Truyol, above, n. 15, at 122.

49 Convention on the Elimination of All Forms of Racial Discrimination, 21 December 1965, 660 UNTS 195 (entered into force 4 January 1969).

50 See A Haley, *Roots* (30th anniversary edn, 2007).

51 See International Convention on the Suppression and Punishment of the Crime of Apartheid, 18 July 1976, 1015 UNTS 243.

52 E/CN4/Sub.2/1982/2/Add.1, annex V (1982).

Racism includes racist ideologies, prejudiced attitudes, discriminatory behaviour, structural arrangements and institutionalized practices resulting in racial inequality as well as the fallacious notion that discriminatory relations between groups are morally and scientifically justifiable; it is reflected in discriminatory provisions in legislation or regulations and discriminatory practices as well as in anti-social beliefs and acts; it hinders the development of its victims, perverts those who practise it, divides nations internally, impedes international co-operation and gives rise to political tensions between peoples; it is contrary to the fundamental principles of international law and, consequently, seriously disturbs international peace and security.

DRRP's normative recommendations follow that ambitious sweep. According to Article 3:

Any distinction, exclusion, restriction or preference based on race, colour, ethnic or national origin or religious intolerance motivated by racist considerations, which destroys or compromises the sovereign equality of States and the right of peoples to self-determination, or which limits in an arbitrary or discriminatory manner the right of every human being and group to full development is incompatible with the requirements of an international order which is just and guarantees respect for human rights; the right to full development implies equal access to the means of personal and collective advancement and fulfilment in a climate of respect for the values of civilizations and cultures, both national and world-wide.

An instrument like the Convention Concerning Indigenous and Tribal Peoples in Independent Countries,[53] which must deal with wholly distinct and highly contested concepts of ethnic and minority identities,[54] takes a further step. It declares the aims of 'removing the assimilationist orientation' of earlier international documents. It proclaims 'the aspirations' of indigenous and tribal peoples 'to exercise control over their own institutions, ways of life and economic development and to maintain and develop their identities, languages and religions, within the framework of the States in which they live' (preamb. para. 9).

The writings by Matsuda, Stefancic and Delgado on hate speech further confirm that Critical Race Theorists have identified issues of immediate concern within international human rights law. The UN Committee on the Elimination of Racial Discrimination, responsible for supervising state compliance with CERD obligations, devoted its first general recommendation to the problem of hate speech, criticizing states parties that had failed to adopt appropriate national legislation.[55]

---

53   Convention Concerning Indigenous and Tribal Peoples in Independent Countries, ILO No. 169, 27 June 1989, 72 ILO Official Bull 59 (entered into force 5 September 1991).

54   See E Heinze, 'The construction and contingency of the minority concept', in B Bowring and D Fottrell (eds), *Minority and Group Rights Towards The New Millennium*, 25–74 (Leiden: Nijhoff, 1999) [hereinafter Heinze 'Construction and contingency'].

55   Committee on the Elimination of Racial Discrimination, General Recommendation 1, States parties' obligations (1972), reprinted in Compilation of General Comments and General Recommendations Adopted by Human Rights Treaty Bodies, UNDoc. HRI\GEN\1\Rev.6, at 195 (12 May 2003) [hereinafter Compilation].

It has reiterated that concern in two subsequent recommendations,[56] and in comments on individual state practices.[57]

The Failure of the 'Alliance' Trend

There can be no doubt, then, about the themes that link critical theory to international human rights law. The next question is, what relationships should emerge among Critical Race Theory, LatCrit and international human rights law? Are they all fully allied – merely different ways of saying the same things? This section argues that they are not; that critical theorists must retain the same critical, vigilant attitude towards international law that they apply to US law. In failing to do so, they have betrayed the outsiders for whom they purport to speak.

When *Words that Wound* was published, in 1993, the Cold War had just ended. The first President Bush had called for a 'New World Order', and international human rights law was enjoying a fresh start after decades of inertia. The treaty-based committees of the United Nations, including the Committee on the Elimination of Racial Discrimination (UN-CERD) and the Human Rights Committee (UN-HRC), found their activity increased. States newly embracing democracy submitted declarations of intent[58] to adhere to individual complaints procedures.[59] It may be no coincidence that writings by Critical Race Theorists and LatCrits examining international human rights began to emerge at that time of renewed vigour.

The fact that Critical Race Theory, LatCrits and international human rights law share common concerns does not mean, however, that they share common understandings. International human rights law is largely the creation of states and power blocs, who often pursue the interests of those in power. As we have seen, its documents are expressed through the same kinds of abstract, universalist formalisms as the US Bill of Rights, which has provoked such concern for critical

---

56 'Committee on the Elimination of Racial Discrimination', General Recommendation 7, Measures to Eradicate Incitement to or Acts of Discrimination, 32nd Sess, UN Doc A/40/18 at 120 (1985), reprinted in Compilation, above, n. 55, at 199; 'Committee on the Elimination of Racial Discrimination', General Recommendation 15, Measures to Eradicate Incitement to or Acts of Discrimination, 42nd Sess, UN Doc. A/48/18 at 114 (1994), reprinted in Compilation, above, n. 55, at 204.

57 See Committee on the Elimination of Racial Discrimination, Conclusions and Recommendations of the Committee on the Elimination of Racial Discrimination, United States of America, 391, UN Doc A/56/18 (8 September 2001) (criticizing US constitutional protections of hate speech); Committee on the Elimination of Racial Discrimination, Conclusions and Recommendations of the Committee on the Elimination of Racial Discrimination, Denmark, A 3, UN Doc. CERD/C/304/Add.2 (28 March 1996) (criticizing interview with racists broadcast on Danish television).

58 See Office of the United Nations High Commissioner for Human Rights (UNHCRH), Statistical Survey of Individual Complaints Considered Under the Procedure Governed by Article 14 of the International Convention on the Elimination of All Forms of Racial Discrimination (31 March 2004), available at <http://www.unhchr.ch/html/menu2/8/stat4.htm> [hereinafter Office of the United Nations High Commissioner].

59 See Office of the United Nations High Commissioner for Human Rights (UNHCHR), Statistical Survey of Individual Complaints Considered Under the Procedure Governed by Article 14 of the International Convention on the Elimination of All Forms of Racial Discrimination, For CERD art. 14, available at <http://www.ohchr.org/english/bodies/cerd/stat4.htm> [hereinafter Survey of CERD article 14]. See also Office of the United Nations Commissioner for Human Rights (UNCHR), Statistical survey of individual complaints dealt with by the Human Rights Committee under the Optional Protocol to the International Covenant on Civil and Political Rights, available at <http://www.ohchr.org/english/bodies/hrc/ stat2.htm> [hereinafter Survey of ICCPR Optional Protocol] (for the 'Optional Protocol to the International Covenant on Civil and Political Rights', 23 March 1976, 999 UNTS 302).

legal theory. Here it is argued that an approach such as Matsuda's merely generates myths about international law. Insisting upon legal realism for US law, while abandoning any realist analysis of international law, Matsuda constructs wholly misleading notions about both US and international norms and realities.

Formalism and Realism

In her discussion of hate speech, Matsuda recalls the drafting and ratification of Article 4 of the International Convention on the Elimination of All Forms of Racial Discrimination (CERD), which provides that state parties:

(a) Shall declare an offence punishable by law all dissemination of ideas based on racial superiority or hatred, incitement to racial discrimination, as well as all acts of violence or incitement to such acts against any race or group of persons of another colour of ethnic origin. […]

(b) Shall declare illegal and prohibit organizations, and also organized and all other propaganda activities, which promote and incite racial discrimination, and shall recognize participation in such organizations or activities as an offence punishable by law.

Matsuda praises what she calls an international 'consensus' favouring the elimination of racist hate propaganda.[60] She rejects the US Government position, which was, and to this day remains,[61] isolated at the UN in its opposition to Article 4. The US position reflected increasingly strong protections of speech and association that had been pushed by US civil libertarians, and began to triumph in the Supreme Court during the 1960s.[62] Most importantly, Matsuda proposes what she calls a 'bipolar'[63] distinction between (a) the 'first amendment story of free speech', which, in her view, disregards 'the victims' experience';[64] and (b) the international 'consensus' behind CERD Article 4, which, in her view, illustrates '[t]he emerging acceptance of the victim's story'.[65]

    That is where the myth-making begins. I shall now argue that Matsuda first embraces a myth of an essentially benign 'international community', from which she derives her 'bipolar' distinction. Her concept of an international community is a myth, because it depends upon the same kind of naïve anti-realism, the same ignoring of brutal realities that propelled the old myths of white America. She achieves her bipolar analysis only by turning the same blind eye towards the atrocities of the 'international community' that she condemned when it was turned towards American atrocities. She then devises a story of an essentially oppressive US, which she constructs in 'bipolar' opposition to that mythical international community. She attacks the old, uninformed myths of US-is-good, not in a quest for a more nuanced and balanced assessment – for example, an understanding that US-is-complex, based on a critical exploration of the actual realities of *both* US *and* international law and institutions – but in a quest for an equally simplistic myth of US-is-bad. She in no way challenges the international power politics that betray human rights in the way she and other Critical Race Theorists attack American politics that have betrayed American legal norms. She advances American outsider groups only at the price of ignoring non-American

60   Matsuda, above, n. 4, at 27.
61   See Boyle, above, n. 12, at 497.
62   Notably confirmed by *Brandenburg v. Ohio*, 395 US 444, 447–48 (1969).
63   Matsuda, above, n. 4, at 17.
64   Ibid., at 50.
65   Ibid., at 26.

ones. By using international law not to overcome American parochialism but to recapitulate it, she exhibits what can be called an 'anti-ethnocentric ethnocentrism'.

Matsuda notes that, during the drafting phases of CERD in 1964, the United States, the United Kingdom and the USSR jointly with Poland each submitted a draft to the UN Sub-Commission on Prevention of Discrimination and Protection of Minorities[66] (now the Sub-Commission on the Promotion and Protection of Human Rights[67]). The British proposal[68] generally represented approaches of Western European states in endorsing limited bans on hate speech. Elsewhere I have criticized the shortcomings of the Western European approaches.[69] However, in view of the numbers and influence of socialist states during the drafting and signatory phases of CERD, crucial to building the supposed international 'consensus', their role in the process now merits equal examination.

Matsuda specifically applauds the USSR-Poland draft for overcoming the 'individualistic, civil libertarian conception of free speech'.[70] She notes: 'The USSR/Poland draft would have banned all "propaganda" of "superiority" and would have criminalized participation in any organization that discriminated or advanced discrimination. In obvious contrast to the US view, the socialist nations proposed direct action against hate messages […].'[71] Matsuda praises the Soviet-Polish proposal's black letter without posing a single question about how the Soviet Union and its satellites were actually treating their minorities at the time of the proposal. Principles E2 and E3 from *Words that Wound* effectively exhort: *Don't just look at the black-letter norms of the US Constitution. Look also at the brutal histories behind them.* We might therefore expect Matsuda to apply precisely that critical realist method to the Soviet-Polish proposal.

But she does nothing of the kind. The Sovietologists Barghoorn and Remington write that, throughout its existence, the Soviet Union alone had included 'well over one hundred indigenous nationalities, of which twenty-two contain[ed] at least one million people'.[72] Both the Soviet and the Chinese (two dominant socialist spheres of influence by the 1960s) included states that had crushed vast numbers of minority ethnic and outsider groups, and were continuing to do so through the 1980s, that is, through the periods relevant to the emergence of the UN human rights work to which Matsuda refers. Chechens, Ingush, Balkars, Baltic peoples, Roma, Jews, Muslims, Romanian ethnic Hungarians, Tibetans or Uighurs represent only a very few of the many groups that were often harshly, even murderously, repressed both preceding and during the very period in which the USSR and Poland were pushing their strong version of Article 4.[73]

Despite the claims of E2 and E3, Matsuda never asks why the Soviet proposal for CERD Article 4 was so far reaching, nor who was paying the price of the international 'consensus' with which she associates it. As the Sovietologist Henry Huttenbach notes, the story of national and

---

66   Matsuda, above, n. 4, at 27.
67   See GA Res 60/251, UN Doc. A/RES/60/251 (15 March 2006).
68   Matsuda, above, n. 4, at 30.
69   See Heinze 'Viewpoint absolutism', above, n. 7.
70   Matsuda, above, n. 4, at 28.
71   Ibid., at 28.
72   FC Barghoorn and TF Remington, *Politics in the USSR* (Boston, MA: Little, Brown, 1986, 3rd edn), 71–72.
73   See generally HR Huttenbach (ed.), Soviet Nationality Policies: Ruling Ethnic Groups in the USSR (New York: Mansell, 1990) [hereinafter Soviet Nationality Policies].

ethnic diversity in the Soviet Union was little more than the continuation of outright conquests during the Tsarist periods.[74]

> Though Stalin initially promoted the Leninist policy of *sblizhenie* ["merging" or "drawing together" – EH] by relying mostly on cadres drawn from the indigenous minority populations (a policy known as *korenizatsiia*), by the late 1930s he embarked on an open course of blatant Russification as a way to Sovietization and denationalisation, thereby running counter to Lenin's original course, which sought to steer clear of the shoals of overt Russification, a danger [that Lenin] had condemned with one of his more famous aphorisms: "Scratch a Russian Communist and you will find a Russian chauvinist."[75]

Far from downplaying its repression of ethnic identities, Soviet policy proudly and actively pursued their dissolution. Soviet authorities avowedly deemed 'the elimination of national customs and culture in the creation of a homogeneous Soviet nation' to be a 'process of protracted duration'.[76]

Matusda, then, does precisely what *Words that Wound* had condemned the dominant American civil liberties tradition for doing. She takes the high-minded pretensions of black-letter norms on face value, overlooking the brutal realities lurking behind them. That choice is disturbing from an author who purports to overcome a narrowly American focus in order to seek 'a just *world* free of existing conditions of domination'.[77] It is particularly disquieting for a chapter that, in Matsuda's words, 'focuses on the phenomenology of racism',[78] with reference to a supposed global 'consensus'. Matsuda's chapter is sprinkled with quotations from or about victims of racism, including sinister phrases like 'everywhere the crosses are burning',[79] or 'a noose was hanging one day in his work area'.[80] Such passages rightly humanize the targets of oppression, giving them a voice that cold facts and figures can never impart. Sadly, however, for a scholar purporting to situate the US within a global context, Matsuda selects only passages concerning victims of US oppression.[81] She cites not one victim within those socialist states whose proposals she applauds.

A recurring theme for Critical Race Theory is the necessity of listening to unheard voices.[82] Elsewhere I have objected that, in the context of hate speech, critical theorists turn mysteriously deaf when some of society's weakest groups are concerned, such as the physically or mentally disabled, whom Critical Race Theorists, feminists, queer theorists and others have often excluded from their proposed hate speech bans.[83] Similarly, we find Matsuda's listening disturbingly selective, cleanly divided between the voices of US minorities, which are named and heard, and those of non-US minorities, which are excluded while Matsuda embraces their governments' official positions.

---

74   HR Huttenbach, 'Introduction: Towards a unitary Soviet state: Managing a multinational society, 1917–1985', in Soviet Nationality Policies, above, n. 73, at 1, 3–4.

75   Ibid., at 5.

76   Barghoorn and Remington, above, n. 72, at 74.

77   Ibid., at 19 (emphasis added).

78   Ibid., at 22.

79   Matsuda, above, n. 4, at 24.

80   Ibid., at 20.

81   Except for one passage that cites Matsuda's personal experience in Australia. Ibid., at 17.

82   See generally ibid.

83   The whole concept of 'outsider' is introduced in *Words* to stress that the book is not only about race, but also includes, say, Jews or gays. See above, n. 4. However, categories such as physical or mental disability show how theorists of the 'outsider' select their own insiders and outsiders from the moment that a favoured norm, like a hate speech ban, simply cannot accommodate all long-standing victims of hate speech.

If, during the drafting period of CERD, the great numbers of oppressed ethnic and national groups in the socialist states received nothing near the attention that had been focused, both in the US and abroad, on US racism, it was not because of their great empowerment under socialist rule, but because of a disempowerment so massive, so systematically repressive of dissenting voices, and so entirely overlooked by Western intellectuals,[84] that we find a putatively critical theorist like Matsuda endorsing the official line of the socialist states as the worthy and principled position.

As late as 1990, Huttenbach could still show how scholars purporting to do critical analysis had bought into socialist states' official self-image:

> Unfortunately, the multinational and hence multicultural character of the Soviet Union and the obvious difficulties of governing a heterogeneous population has not been the central concern of most scholars of the Soviet Union, perhaps, in part, because the Bolsheviks themselves and their heirs also did not stress the highly visible fact of the multifariousness and potential divisiveness of the composition of their citizenry. (From the outset, an optimistic emphasis was placed upon the singleness rather than the plurality of the post-Revolution Soviet population.) Even the more recent publications place little or no emphasis on the Soviet Union as a multinational entity.[85]

Huttenbach criticizes Western scholars for having effectively recapitulated official Soviet policy through their failure to examine ethnic and national groups, even when issues of inter-ethnic tension have been central to the problems those authors are discussing.[86]

Adherence to complaint and reporting procedures was crucial to the credibility and authority of CERD and of the UN treaty system during those formative years. There could be no effective international human rights law without the cooperation and support of UN member states. How successful were those arrangements? Matsuda endorses what she sees as the progressive Soviet stance. While insisting that we must examine states' actual adherence to the norms they profess, however, she fails to explain why, throughout the Cold War period, the USSR and its allies systematically sabotaged UN human rights work, for example, by refusing to submit to CERD Article 14(1),[87] which provides, in part:

> A State Party may at any time declare that it recognizes the competence of the Committee to receive and consider communications from individuals or groups of individuals within its jurisdiction claiming to be victims of a violation by that State Party of any of the rights set forth in this Convention.

The United States, too, can be accused of having failed to subscribe to Article 14(1). However, any legal-realist analysis would show that, by the 1960s, US federal and state legislatures and courts were beginning to secure far better protections for ethnic minorities than anything to be found throughout much of the Soviet, Chinese or non-aligned spheres. Meanwhile, free speech was paving the way for the breaking of taboos around other outsiders, such as women, immigrants or sexual minorities, in a way that was unthinkable in socialist states at the time. Figures as different as Martin Luther King, Cesar Chavez, Angela Davis, Betty Friedan and Gloria Steinem knew well

---

84   Cf. C Fourest, *La Tentation Obscurantiste* (Paris: Grasset, 2005), 9–13 (criticizing traditional leftist sympathies for totalitarianism).

85   Huttenbach, above, n. 74, at 2.

86   Ibid., at 2–3.

87   See Survey of CERD article 14, above, n. 59.

what it meant for themselves and their supporters to be mistreated by both law and society. But free speech, secured through the now-dominant First Amendment civil liberties jurisprudence, carried their messages into millions of homes. That possibility was unimaginable for outsiders and dissidents in socialist states. Under Soviet rule, publication of even the most anodyne works in many minority languages was rigidly controlled as a means of suppressing non-Russian identities.[88] In an era when the US Black Panther leader Eldridge Cleaver enjoyed the freedom to condemn US oppression in *Soul on Ice*, Lithuanians could not even publish an automotive magazine in their own language: 'the Russian-language *Za rulem* was supposed to fill the gap'.[89]

Matsuda rests the authority of her analysis on a normative framework advanced by states that were crushing anything remotely resembling civil rights movements among their own ethnic minority groups (let alone the remotest analogue of a Critical Race Theory within their universities).[90] Non-US ethnic minorities, whose interests were as much at stake in CERD as US ones, are, to use the language of Critical Race Theory, the unseen, unheard absences of Matsuda's commitment to the sanitized black letter of CERD Article 4 and to what she mythically constructs as a fundamentally benign 'community of nations' standing behind it.[91]

Matsuda praises the achievements of the United Nations on racial discrimination. However, the Human Rights Commission,[92] a notoriously cynical political body throughout the Cold War, never condemned the treatment of ethnic minorities by the Soviet Union or other socialist states. Those states systematically prevented examinations of their human rights records. Neither UN-HRC nor UN-CERD could exert real influence. The socialist states' refusal to adhere to complaints procedures and the opacity of socialist regimes allowed only limited monitoring of the treatment of ethnic minorities and of human rights by either outside or even inside observers. For all its defects, a US-style civil liberties approach would have been a boon to minorities, dissidents and outcasts under socialist rule.

It is disconcerting that a scholar who trumpets the imperative of critical realism, and of analysing law in historical and contextual terms, would have overlooked socialist states' sheer self-interest in pushing for strong limits on expression and association. Matsuda's suggestion that the socialist states made an essentially good-faith contribution to CERD presupposes that those states saw CERD as a genuine commitment to the prosperity and autonomous empowerment of their ethnic minorities.

But that would be quite a claim. The benefits to totalitarian regimes of the broadest possible wording for limits on expression and political organization were obvious enough. Article 4 bans not merely the hardest core of racist speech, but, on the Soviet-Polish approach, would have banned massive amounts of speech that socialist states saw as politically destabilizing, including legitimate criticism by minority ethnic groups about ethnic *majority* practices running from the Tsarist through to the Soviet periods.[93] Totalitarian dictatorships rarely see restrictions on speech that they do not like. They gleefully draft them in the broadest terms, and can always do so in the

---

88   See generally *Soviet Nationality Policies*, above, n. 74.

89   RJ Misiunas, 'Baltic nationalism and Soviet language policy', in *Soviet Nationality Policies*, above, n. 74, at 206, 210.

90   See generally *Soviet Nationality Policies*, above, n. 73.

91   Matsuda, above, n. 4, at 29.

92   Now replaced by the Human Rights Council. See GA Res 60/251, UN Doc A/RES/60/251 (15 March 2006) (establishing the Human Rights Council to replace the Commission); CHR Res. 2006/2, UN Doc E/CN4/2006/L.2 (27 March 2006) (closing the work of the Commission).

93   For example, UN Comm. on the Elimination of Racial Discrimination [hereinafter CERD], Conclusions and recommendations of the Committee on the Elimination of Racial Discrimination: Russian

name of some vague (that is, wholly formal) ideal, such as 'peace' or 'stability' or 'security' or even 'tolerance'. The more we look at international reality, the more Matsuda's tidy 'bipolar' scheme crumbles.

Dubious commitments to human rights have not come only from socialist states. Japan ratified the International Covenant on Civil and Political Rights (ICCPR) in 1979, though it did not become party to CERD until 1995.[94] Over decades, however, it has taken few steps to combat systemic discrimination against Ainu, Buraku or ethnic Koreans.[95] Japan still declines to accede to the ICCPR and CERD individual complaints procedures,[96] despite ample prosperity and resources to meet its obligations. India ratified CERD in 1968 and acceded to ICCPR in 1969,[97] but has also failed to adhere to those treaties' individual complaint procedures.[98] Although massive and brutal ethnic and caste discrimination has claimed millions of victims over generations, government action against it has long proved inadequate.[99]

Of course, many members of non-US ethnic minority groups would certainly have been sympathetic to the *values expressed* in CERD Article 4. More recently, for example, there was broad participation by non-governmental organizations in the drafting of the 2001 Report of the World Conference against Racism, Racial Discrimination, Xenophobia and Related Intolerance adopted in Durban, South Africa (also called the Durban Declaration and Programme of Action).[100] Yet many US minorities, too, have long been sympathetic to the *values expressed* in the US Constitution and Declaration of Independence. Once again, E2 and E3 teach that the task of critical theory is to look beyond official proclamations, condemning hypocrisies and abuses.

If the international 'consensus' against racism really represented '[t]he emerging acceptance of the victim's story', it is hard to understand why not even a dozen states adhered to CERD's individual complaint procedure – which does not even endow the Committee (UN-CERD) with any compulsory enforcement power – during the Cold War, and why less than a quarter of UN member states adhere to it even today.[101] Even that increase is owing largely to the democratization of former socialist states, pushed by the US in the years immediately following the Cold War.

So, Matsuda's internationalist myths renounce traditional American ethnocentrism in order to create what can be called an 'anti-ethnocentric ethnocentrism'. 'Ethnocentrism' has been described as a 'view of things in which one's own group is the center of everything, and all others are scaled and rated with reference to it'.[102] Let us recall a standard type of ethnocentrism before considering Matsuda's variation.

Ordinarily, we would associate American ethnocentrism with a powerful white, Anglo-Protestant elite, viewing the rest of the world through a lens of US superiority. Other cultures might be seen

---

Federation, 16, UN Doc CERD/C/62/CO/7, 16 (21 March 2003) notes the ongoing hostilities between Cossacks and ethnic minorities.

94   See UNHCRH, above n. 58; UNHCRH, above n. 59.

95   As recently as 2001, these problems had not yet been satisfactorily remedied. See Report of the Comm. on the Elimination of Racial Discrimination, Conclusions and Recommendations of the Committee on the Elimination of Racial Discrimination: Japan, 14, 16, 18, UN Doc A/56/18 (8 September 2001).

96   See Survey of CERD article 14, above, n. 59; Survey of ICCPR Optional Protocol, above, n. 59.

97   See UNHCRH, above n. 58; UNHCRH, above n. 59.

98   See Survey of CERD article 14, supra note 59; Survey of ICCPR Optional Protocol, above, n. 59.

99   See UN Human Rights Comm. Concluding Observations of the Human Rights Committee: India, 15, UN Doc CCPR/C/79/Add.81 (4 August 1997).

100   UN Doc A/CONF 189/12 (31 August to 8 September 2001).

101   See Office of the United Nations High Commissioner, above, n. 58.

102   M Festenstein and M Kenny (eds), *Political Ideologies* (Oxford: Oxford University Press, 2005), 142.

as scaled and rated as 'high' or 'low' depending on the degree to which they embrace US values or practices.[103] In the late twentieth and early twenty-first centuries, high marks might go to Margaret Thatcher's or Tony Blair's Britain; low marks to Mahmoud Ahmadinejad's Iran, or to Kim Jong Il's North Korea. Such a view is ethnocentric, then, because those societies are understood entirely in terms of US values, and not with reference to their own histories and cultures. Their identities are constructed wholly with respect to the extent to which they appear to accept or reject the values of US-is-good. Matsuda's internationalism purports to do the opposite, but ends up doing the same. Failing to recognize the grim realities of human rights lurking behind her 'international community', her 'UN', or her 'socialist nations', she constructs their views as essentially correct solely insofar as they reject US views. She recognizes in them no reality aside from the negatively defined reality of not-being-the-US. No other identity, no other brutality, no other victims matter. Her supposed anti-ethnocentrism is wholly ethnocentric.

Critical Race Theorists have, admittedly, branched off in various directions. They cannot always be assumed to be speaking for each other. Nevertheless, Matsuda's contributions, and *Words that Wound* generally, have counted among the most frequently cited works within the movement. No one has seriously challenged Matusda's 'bipolar' scheme. It would be difficult, for example, to distinguish Matsuda's approach from that of Stefancic and Delgado. Although they do not analyse the genesis of international norms, 'A Shifting Balance' and other of their comparative arguments mirror Matsuda's underlying dichotomy. They equate the American civil liberties position with an oppressive US approach, and international hate speech bans with the plight of the victims.[104]

As recently as 2000, Hernández-Truyol endorsed a similar approach. She praised the 'vision [...] of communist States [...] that the masses could and would be liberated only by the grant of positive social and economic rights'.[105] Missing from her view is any trace of critical realism, which might have explained exactly what kind of 'vision', what kind of 'liberation', and what kinds of social and economic rights were actually provided for tens of millions of lives killed, ruined or culturally suppressed through mass deportations, farm collectivizations, agro-industrial complexes, political purges, state-generated famines or religious persecution. Her work provides another example of a critical theorist abandoning the approach taken to the US, asking us to look only at the lofty promises of socialist states and not at their bleak realities.

Matsuda's strategy is clear. Having seen that a realist jurisprudence reveals much of the evil of US law, she assumes that, by broadening her scholarly context to situate US law within international human rights law, US law will look that much more aberrant when measured against international standards. And US law does indeed pale when, precisely at the point of introducing international law, Matsuda's goalposts suddenly shift from hard-nosed realism to idealized, black-letter formalism. By that point in her analysis, she is forced to take that regressive step: she had failed to anticipate the embarrassment that, by applying the critical-realist approach to the socialist countries with which she was comparing the US position, the US would start to look *better*. Had Matsuda taken her movement's critical, contextual approach to international human rights law, she would have been forced into the rather less dazzling, rather more humdrum conclusion that the US, when compared to countries of generally similar complexity and demographics, has, at worst,

---

103   See D Rumsfeld, 'United States Secretary of Defence, Security in the Middle East: New Challenges for NATO and EU', address at the Munich Conference on Security Policy (2 February 2005), <http://www.securityconference.de/konferenzen/rede.php?id=144&sprache =en&>.

104   Cf. Hernández-Truyol, above, n. 48 (noting the essential similarity between Delgado's positions and those of international human rights law).

105   Ibid., at 127.

delivered a mixed bag: undeniable abuses coupled with important advances. American ideals only emerge as signally dystopian when compared with a wholly utopian 'international community'.

The story of a uniquely deviant US has undeniable appeal for those who purport to do progressive politics. In its policies and practices, the United States has defied many black-letter international norms governing, for example, social and economic rights, environmental protection,[106] the death penalty,[107] or international law of armed conflict.[108] However, that narrative of a distinctly aberrant US often turns out to rely more on formalism than realism.

Consider an analogy to the problem of climate change. A formalist can readily condemn the United States for its defiant stance in refusing to sign the Kyoto agreement on climate change. The realist, however, must ask whether those countries that *did* sign it, particularly wealthy and powerful states, have in fact been progressing towards their targets. As of this writing, European Union states with a combined wealth greater than that of the United States have largely failed to do so.[109] The realist picture of adherence and defiance on climate change (what states are actually doing) differs markedly from the formalist one (what they are officially proclaiming). Indeed, American exceptionalism runs both ways. As of this writing, for example, US Government condemnation of genocide in Darfur has gone largely unheeded in Europe, the UN and much of the world.[110]

Striking a balance between deontology (an ethics based on the intrinsic value of some act x, or on some specific duty to undertake or to refrain from committing x) and consequentialism (an ethics based on the value of a specific outcome of act x, as distinguished from its intrinsic value or its specific intent) within critical theories is no easy task. Noting the various intellectual movements that inform Critical Race Theory, E5 strongly suggests an agnostic or eclectic stance. Wholly fallacious, however, is a methodology that applies a strict consequentialism to condemn US law, while praising an international human rights regime on grounds of an utterly idealized deontology, expressed solely through states' formal proclamations of their obligations. Matsuda, Stefancic and Delgado, and Hernández-Truyol are not alone in constructing their myths under the guise of progressive politics. When it comes to the United Nations and the patina of internationalism associated with it, the historian Perry Anderson has noted, generally, the same kinds of 'mind-numbing pieties from assorted well-wishers in the universities'.[111]

Ironically, on hate speech, it is the conventional, black-letter international lawyer, and not the critical realist, who ends up better equipped to depict the US as uniquely deviant, since the black-letter lawyer by definition avoids questions of historical, political or social context. In an article drawing normative conclusions similar to those of Matsuda or Delgado and Stefancic, the black-letter human rights lawyer Kevin Boyle criticizes American exceptionalism and the US position on hate speech, advocating instead the international 'consensus' reflected in CERD Article 4.[112] Boyle can do so plausibly because he never purports to embrace a method that looks behind norms to the actual attitudes and practices of the governments who draft them. It simply does not matter to his

---

106   See below text accompanying n. 109.

107   See Amnesty International, United States, in Report 2006, at <http://web.amnesty.org/report2006/usa-summary-eng>.

108   See *Hamdan v. Rumsfeld*, 126 S Ct 2749 (2006) (examining rights of detainees at the Guantánamo Bay detention facility).

109   See D Gow, 'Figures reveal Europe falling far short of climate targets', *The Guardian*, 28 October 2006, at 1.

110   See US Dept St, 'United States Policy in Sudan' (6 May 2006), at <http://www.state.gov/r/pa/prs/ps/2006/65973.htm> (specifically referring to genocide in Sudan).

111   P Anderson, 'Our man', *London Review of Books*, 10 May 2007, at 9, 29.

112   See Boyle, above, n. 12 at 496–97, 502.

analysis that the Soviet Union and its satellites advocated strong versions of CERD Article 4 while crushing many of their own minorities, or that the corresponding limitations on speech strongly supported Soviet restrictions on free speech and expression. All that matters is that we accept the norms of human rights instruments at face value, and then proceed to apply them mechanically. For the black-letter lawyer there would be no inconsistency in claiming that socialist states' formal proclamations amounted to an 'emerging acceptance of the victim's story'.[113] However, if we care about what those states were actually doing, if we care about 'real harm to real people',[114] then Matsuda's fantasy of an 'international community' that 'listens' to the 'victims' story' becomes downright Orwellian.

Matsuda claims that Critical Race Theory rejects 'falsely universalist' norms through an approach that is 'realist' and that 'accepts the standard teaching of street wisdom: Law is political'.[115] That is no small claim for someone embracing international human rights law – rarely drafted on the streets – and for which universalist concepts are core components. If law is political, always at risk of betraying justice by serving dominant interests, then what gives the purely formal proclamations of international human rights law and institutions the high authority that Matsuda accords them? The black-letter of the Universal Declaration of Human Rights (UDHR) Article 1 tells us that '[a]ll human beings are born free and equal in dignity and rights'.[116] We have seen, however, that the UN General Assembly adopted the UDHR and subsequent instruments with the votes of some of history's most oppressive regimes. If UDHR Article 1 is 'truly' universalist, on what grounds does Matsuda ignore such contexts? And if it is 'falsely' universalist, then why would its black letter, and that of its progeny, carry any greater authority than key provisions of the US Constitution?

Matsuda's concept of 'false universalism' is altogether opaque. It presupposes either of two spurious concepts. Either she means that some universalist claims or assumptions are true and others false, or that all are false. If she means that all are false, then it becomes difficult to understand how international human rights law would provide any authority at all, let alone the peremptory role it plays in her analysis. By contrast, if she means that some universalist claims or assumptions are true and others false, then she would have to explain which belong to which category, and why. In particular, she would have to explain how a realist analysis shows the international human rights norms to be truly universal and the US ones to be falsely universal.

In discussing the three drafts that the US, the UK and USSR-Poland submitted to the UN Sub-Commission, Matsuda writes that 'the sub-commission [sic] had the benefit of vastly different ideological views as well as a basic consensus on the necessity of combating discrimination'.[117] Vastly different ideological views? Of all Matusda's claims, this one is perhaps the most offensive to any global or historically sensitive notion of legal outsiders. Predictably, the US advocated a more classical, liberal view of free speech, while Western European social democracies advocated greater restrictions. As to the socialist states, it remains unclear what 'ideology' Matsuda thinks they represented, in good faith or otherwise. To place Matsuda's argument in the best light, however, let us assume that they represented something good. As we have seen, Matusda's strategy then becomes obvious enough: the more the 'international consensus' can be shown to unify 'vastly different' ideologies, the more deviant the dissenting US position will appear.

We might have expected to read the view that the three drafts represented 'vastly different ideological views' in conventional textbooks on international human rights law, which generally

---

113   See, above, n. 65.
114   Matsuda, above, n. 4, at 50.
115   Ibid., at 19.
116   See GA Res 217A, above, n. 20, at art. 1.
117   Matsuda, above, n. 4, at 27.

discuss the views advanced by various states during the Cold War without any deep inquiry into their political or historical origins, or indeed into the sincerity with which they are made.[118] But we should hardly expect to read it from someone who insists on placing official proclamations in their historical context.

So let us take a longer view of history. If those were indeed the three 'ideological views' that happened to be presented to the UN Sub-Commission, it is not so much because they were 'vastly different', but because they represented the official statements of power blocks that had come to dominate the world after centuries of imperial extinction or subjugation of countless peoples who *genuinely had* represented 'vastly different' world views – views so different from those familiar to Western legal scholars, different at the most fundamental linguistic and cognitive levels, that our minds would require years to begin to understand just one of them, let alone to generalize so glibly about all of them.

If we follow Critical Race Theorists' advice to examine law and society historically, then arguably the Cold War emerges as one of the most intellectually ('ideologically') impoverished periods in human history. An internationalist fairyland may indeed tell us that the UN emerged out of 'vastly different ideological views'. But history recites a rather bleaker tale. The idea of an overarching system of international law replete with a 'United Nations', and a sufficiently shared set of norms and concepts, surfaces only at that moment in world history when sufficient human diversity has been either exterminated or subordinated by big powers. The fewer than 200 seats representing the member states of the United Nations pay tribute not to the countless distinct peoples that have populated the earth, but to their systematic elimination and subordination over centuries of big-power politics. The three draft proposals for CERD Article 4, far from representing 'vastly different ideological views', reflected entirely run-of-the-mill debates about the extent and limits of individual rights. They assume post-Westphalian, post-Enlightenment, Eurocentric approaches to law, largely overlooking any number of fundamentally distinct ethical, political or legal 'ideologies'.

Matsuda's uncritical acceptance of the power politics of the Cold War, whereby an international 'consensus' is praised while not a single ethnic group outside the US is even named, along with the hackneyed internationalist myth of the Cold War's 'vast' ideological diversity, wholly betrays history's extinguished and marginalized outsiders. E3 turns out to apply only to US outsiders, not to others. Historical memory becomes historical manipulation. Matsuda does not lead us out of US-ethnocentrism. She crudely recapitulates it. The fact that someone, somewhere, safely ensconced within the sterile chambers of the UN, said 'No' to the US, meant that the world contained 'vastly different ideological views'.

That point also responds, if not to an affirmative defence of Matsuda's position, then to an objection that could be brought against mine. Major powers did play a leading role in drafting CERD, but by no means an exclusive one. Many states, including various developing or unaligned states, participated as well. It might be thought that, by emphasizing the Soviet Union and socialist states, I retain the same kind of narrow big-power focus that I reproach Matsuda for adopting. Certainly, there can be no doubt that participation in the drafting was broad, and much of it made in good faith by states and independent experts genuinely concerned about racism. The important point, however, is that such participation took place within the confines of political and legal discourses and ideas already strongly defined, throughout decades, even centuries, by dominant powers.

---

118 See AH Robertson and JG Merrills, *Human Rights in the World*, 4th ed. (Manchester, UK: Manchester University Press, 1996), pp. 83–89.

Objections and Replies to My Analysis of Matsuda

A difficulty in assessing Matsuda's contribution to *Words that Wound* is that she shows little critical awareness of the historical and geopolitical assumptions that she is making, or expects the reader to supply. Does she neglect the abuses of the USSR, and of other oppressive states that supported CERD Article 4, because she thinks the readers will have already understood the shortcomings of the UN and its member states? If so, why wouldn't they also have already understood the shortcomings of the US, particularly in view of the book's wholly American focus? As no close reading of her views is possible without some attention to those issues, some discussion of them is appropriate.

Instrumentalist approaches to rights   In praising international human rights, perhaps Matsuda was merely assuming an instrumentalist conception, whereby only certain ends of social justice are important, regardless of the conceptual means employed to achieve them. That approach might well reflect the intellectual eclecticism of E5, which can be read to suggest the importance of achieving certain concrete ends, regardless of the vocabulary or concepts ('rights', 'fairness', 'utility', etc.) used to achieve them. That instrumentalist interpretation, however, would scarcely fit Matsuda's 'bipolar' scheme, which she conspicuously embraces as a matter of fundamental normative principle. More importantly, that approach would only beg the questions: an instrument of *which* substantive political or legal values – that is, which values pursued *not* for other ends but as ends in themselves – and how does Matsuda think the 'international community' is promoting *those* values? In sum, it is unlikely that an instrumentalist reading of Matsuda would yield very different results.

The overall role of international law in Matsuda's analysis   In Matsuda's defence it might be suggested that she never intends her discussion of international human rights to occupy centre stage; that she remains focused on specific problems within American society, making no claim to solve problems beyond US borders. She might be said to cite international law as only one ingredient in a complex blend.

But that defence, too, would be unpersuasive. Recall that Matsuda equates the dichotomy between regressive US practice and a progressive international consensus with her 'bipolar' distinction between 'the victim's story of the effects of racist hate messages' and 'the first amendment story of free speech' in order to explain 'different ways of knowing to determine [sic] what is true and what is just'.[119] Accordingly, she equates the 'international law of human rights' with 'the emerging acceptance of the victim's story'.[120] Any attempt to diminish that recourse to international law would contradict E2 in suggesting that international human rights can be thrown into the overall argument as an essentially neutral, background element of analysis.

Alternatively, it might be argued that Matsuda keeps her discussion of international law brief as a purely practical matter. After all, it is rarely possible for an author to cover all points exhaustively, so some points must inevitably be omitted or condensed. Yet that suggestion, too, would be unpersuasive. Neither the book nor Matsuda's chapter is long. Even a few sentences acknowledging the historical price paid by ethnic minorities in those states whose positions Matsuda praises would have differed from her stone silence.

---

119   Matsuda, above, n. 4, at 17.
120   Ibid., at 26.

The history of Cold War rhetoric   It might be argued that, by the time *Words that Wound* appeared, the Soviet Union and its satellites had already collapsed. There was no longer any point to fighting old cold war battles. But that view would contradict Critical Race Theorists' insistence on the role of long histories of oppression, and their view that oppression does not suddenly end through a handful of constitutional or legal changes. Under the historical readings required by E3, Critical Race Theorists forbid us from looking at US law only from the time of *Brown v. Board of Education*,[121] when the US began moving more decisively against discrimination. The memories of slavery, *Dred Scott*, *Plessy*, Jim Crow, segregation and indeed the entire colonial enterprise since the early modern period are kept alive on the view that those strands of history continue in the form of ongoing injustices. That is why '[c]urrent inequalities and social/institutional practices are linked to earlier periods in which the intent and cultural meaning of such practices were clear'.[122]

Matsuda, however, looks only at the Soviet-Polish proposal and at international law and institutions from the time of CERD's drafting in the post-Stalinist 1960s. She ignores the histories of the USSR and other socialist states. She also ignores the entire positivist heritage of earlier international law, whereby states' treatment of their own nationals (up to and including genocide) was deemed a purely internal affair[123] – a position maintained by totalitarian regimes through the Cold War to the present day, and which has hardly been overcome, in view of the ongoing human rights records of states like China,[124] Russia,[125] Iran,[126] Saudi Arabia,[127] and many others.[128]

Some LatCrits do gingerly mention that flawed history of international law.[129] It cannot seriously be suggested, however, that they apply to it the unrelenting rigour that they direct at US law. Many international lawyers, acknowledging the pernicious and ongoing legacy of classical positivism, might argue that international law can be no more humane, and no more effective, than states allow it to be. That explanation is plausible, but can hardly satisfy a critical realist: it only reinforces the suggestion that many of the *realities* behind international human rights norms must be examined with reference to the actual practices of states, and not in an idealizing vacuum. The fundamental international human rights framework is a product of a long positivist heritage and of the Cold War, which are no more redundant than are slavery and Jim Crow. Critical theorists must decide: either both histories are dead and are superseded by current improvements, or both histories are living and are germane to current forms of injustice. We cannot claim that Stalin and Mao are dead, while insisting that *Dred Scott* lives on.

It might be argued that the atrocities of socialist states have been so well publicized in the West, and were such staples of Cold War rhetoric, that they could be taken as read in Matsuda's

---

121   See *Brown v. Board of Education*, 347 US 483 (1954) (striking down laws requiring racially segregated schools).

122   Cf. Lawrence, above, text accompanying n. 21.

123   See Malcom Shaw, International Law 200 (4th edn, 1997). Cf. ibid., at 201–2 (discussing special regimes including humanitarian law and protection of minorities and workers).

124   See Amnesty International, China, Report 2005, at <http://web.amnesty.org/report2005/chn-summary-eng>.

125   See Amnesty International, Russian Federation, Report 2005, at <http://web.amnesty.org/report 2005/rus-summary-eng>.

126   See Amnesty International, Iran, Report 2005, at <http://web.amnesty.org/report2005/irn-summary-eng>.

127   See Amnesty International, Saudi Arabia, Report 2005, at <http://web.amnesty.org/report2005/sau-summary-eng>.

128   See generally Amnesty International at <http://www.amnesty.org/ailib/aireport/index.html> [accessed 26 January 2008) for annual worldwide reports.

129   See Hernández-Truyol, above, n. 15, at 232.

analysis, requiring no special attention. But that suggestion would be equally unconvincing. If the attention due to a problem is inversely proportional to the publicity it has already received, then one might wonder why critical scholars would be concerned with the United States at all. Surely, the volume of ink spilled, celluloid shot, broadcasts transmitted, cases litigated and courses taught on American racism far exceeds that spent on all ethnic minorities of all former and current socialist states combined. Have the major Russian or Chinese media outlets produced anything like, say, Tibetan, Chechen or Baltic counterparts to *Roots*, *The Colour Purple*, *In the Heat of the Night*, *Mississippi Burning* or even *Uncle Tom's Cabin*, which captured both national and international audiences from the moment they were released? If we are to set up an international pecking order based on publicity already received (precisely the kind of 'more victim than thou' trap that I have rejected as a danger inherent in the analyses of some critical theorists[130]), then minorities of former and current socialist states would have to take clear precedence.

A variation on that theme would be the view that anti-communism was a well-worn tool of US conservatives and of US governments throughout the Cold War. The task of Critical Race Theorists and LatCrits, one might argue, is not to echo but to challenge dominant and establishment attitudes from the perspective of the outsider. But that argument also fails. Critical theory is hardly served when, in order to challenge one 800 pound gorilla, it uncritically endorses the stance of another. Perhaps we should condemn Pericles for warfare, slavery or misogyny; but we should think twice before heralding Xerxes as the voice of the voiceless. If Matsuda needed a bipoloar structure (though we might question whether she did), she should have placed *all* states and state-directed bodies on one side, and the real outsiders, including non-US as well as US minorities, on the other. If institutional allies were required, they should have been sought among such non-governmental organizations as Minority Rights Group International[131] or SOS-Racisme,[132] who cooperate with intergovernmental organizations when it is productive to do so, while maintaining a critical distance from them.

The specific claims of American democracy   The Cold War derived largely from US claims to promote democracy and to oppose those who repressed it. In Matsuda's defence one might argue that it was legitimate to hold the US to a higher standard. In other words, we would *expect* the Soviet Union to oppress its people; yet we would be legitimately outraged by a US government, so-called leader of the free world, that promises rights while practising discrimination. That double standard, however, contradicts core tenets of the same human rights law that Matsuda invokes. It would be sordid indeed to suggest that the most brutal, even genocidal, regimes should be held to a lower standard simply because they make no pretence of being democracies. Human rights law requires that all governments be held accountable for human rights,[133] in proportion to the abuses for which they are responsible. No doctrine of human rights law suggests that democracies carry an additional burden. Quite the contrary. Lack of democracy is ordinarily seen as an aggravating, not an ameliorating, factor in assessing a state's human rights record, not only because it denies fundamental human rights of political participation, but also because non-democracies tend to curtail the media in ways that make their overall human rights situations more difficult to monitor.[134]

---

130   Heinze 'Viewpoint absolutism', above, n. 13, at section II.B.

131   See Minority Rights Group International, <http://www.minorityrights.org/> [accessed 26 January 2008].

132   See SOS Racisme, <http://www.sos-racisme.org/> [accessed 26 January 2008].

133   UN Charter, art. 1, 3, art. 55–56.

134   See Human Rights Committee, 'General Comment 25 (57): General Comments under article 40, paragraph 4, of the International Covenant on Civil and Political Rights, UN Doc CCPR/C/21/Rev.1/Add.7 (12 July 1996).

Moreover, that double standard overlooks the fact that all governments justify their hold on power in the name of purportedly beneficial ideals. That strategy has never been the particular preserve of democracies. The USSR had promised to be 'a socialist state of the whole people, expressing the will and interests of the workers, peasants, and intelligentsia, the working people of all the nations and nationalities of the country'.[135] Similarly, China promises to be a 'People's Republic'.[136] North Korea promises to be a 'Democratic People's Republic'.[137] Iran promises to be an 'Islamic Republic'.[138] The United Nations, despite having constantly shielded the world's most brutal regimes,[139] promises to 'promote social progress and better standards of life in larger freedom'.[140] Like any number of Western constitutions, the constitutions of the USSR and its allies had promised regimes of rights, liberties and equalities.[141] Why would we hold only the US, and no other power, to its proclaimed ideals? Miss Russia's plea to stop world hunger scarcely shows up Miss America's call for world peace. (Nor can the United States be accused of dominance over UN human rights policy in the present case, and many like it, as Matsuda's whole point is to condemn US *deviance* from the dominant norms and policies, that is, from norms and policies that have been adopted despite rigorous US opposition.)

In the same year that Matsuda published her account of the specifically deviant US approach, the human rights scholar Scott Davidson embraced a diametrically opposed thesis: '[T]he denial of human rights stands in direct proportion to the denial of democratic participation in a government.'[142] Davidson's proportionality test in no way denies human rights abuses or institutional lapses, even grave and systemic ones, in a democratic nation such as the US. It does, however, suggest an assessment of human rights contrary to Matsuda's suggestion of a distinctly aberrant US deviating from an essentially benign international community.

Perhaps the best demonstration of Davidson's proportionality test can be found in the actual work of the better non-governmental organizations (NGOs). For example, in Amnesty International's 2006 Annual Report, even well-performing states like Finland[143] or Sweden,[144] let alone the United States,[145] faced sharp criticism, and earlier reports have done the same. No state or government anywhere is a priori immune from suspicion of human rights abuses. Potential to commit abuse inheres in the very fact of political power and is therefore common to all regimes.[146]

---

135   Konstitutsiia SSSR, chs 6–7 (1977) [Konst SSSR][USSR Constitution] (adopted at the Seventh (Special) Session of the Supreme Soviet of the USSR Ninth Convocation, 7 October 1977).

136   Xian Fa (1982) (PRC Constitution).

137   DPRK Socialist Constitution (1998) (Constitution of the Democratic People's Republic of Korea).

138   Oanuni Assassi Jumhuri'I Isla'mai (1979) (Constitution of the Islamic Republic of Iran).

139   See supra text accompanying note 92.

140   UN Charter, preamb. 4.

141   Konstitutsiia SSSR, chs 6–7 (1977) [Konst. SSSR][USSR Constitution] (adopted at the Seventh (Special) Session of the Supreme Soviet of the USSR Ninth Convocation, 7 October 1977).

142   S Davidson, *Human Rights* (London: Open University Press, 1993), 165.

143   Amnesty International, Finland, in Report 2006, at <http://web.amnesty.org/report2006/fin-summary-eng>.

144   Amnesty International, Sweden, in Report 2006, at <http://web.amnesty.org/report2006/swe-summary-eng>.

145   Amnesty International, above, n. 107.

146   See, generally, *Ludger Kühnhardt, Die Universalität Der Menschenrechte* (Munich: Olzog, 1988) (critical of claims about the universality of human rights, but recognizing attempts to curb abusive government power as a foundation for such claims).

At the same time, reports on states such as China[147] or Saudi Arabia,[148] suggest scales of abuse altogether surpassing Finland, Sweden or even the United States. No state is to be presumed free from suspicion. Every state should be condemned, as nearly as possible, in proportion to its overall levels of abuse.

Some have claimed that organizations like Amnesty or Human Rights Watch place too much focus on the US and other Western states, making them appear to be on a par with far more abusive, non-Western states or entities.[149] Having examined the problem of even-handedness elsewhere,[150] I shall not consider it here. Even if that claim has merit, the principle evident in their work overall, as illustrated particularly in Amnesty's annual reports, is a principle of even-handedness, that is, of condemnation generally proportionate to abuse. It is contrary to the aims of human rights law, and to the interests of outsiders, for critical theorists to overlook the abuses of dictatorial states simply because they posture as an 'ideological' counter-weight to the United States.

International law and critical realism   Even as a prima facie matter, Matsuda's praise for the 'emerging acceptance of the victim's story' within the UN is puzzling. Despite much of the excellent work of human rights experts, particularly those appointed in their independent capacities,[151] the promulgation of norms, positions and procedures on human rights at the UN have always remained subject to individual states' self-interest. No one, for example, seriously claims that appointees from states such as Burma, China, Cuba, Iran, Libya, North Korea, Saudi Arabia, Russia, Sudan, Syria, Tunisia or Zimbabwe have generally spoken out against their governments' dictates. Even on face value, it is bizarre for Matsuda to equate official government positions proclaimed within the UN with any 'emerging acceptance of the victim's story'.

The word 'emerging' might be taken to mean that Matsuda seeks to describe only an encouraging trend rather than a *fait accompli*. But that interpretation is implausible. If she intends the word in a strong sense, to mean 'already substantially emerged', then we are still left with a gaping divide between proclaimed norms and actual practice. Yet she cannot mean it in a weak sense, as merely an 'embryonic leaning' towards emergence, as that would suggest that she thinks the *dominant* international reality to be something very different, which she never suggests, and which would defeat her belief in a distinct 'bipolarity' between US and international approaches.

Conclusion: Back to Critical Theory

We have seen how *Words that Wound* attempted to ground Critical Race Theory by setting forth a list of six principles. In view of the foregoing analysis, I would recommend three more, as principles for critical theory in an era of globalization, not negating so much as applying E1–E6 with greater consistency. They propose a movement away from the bipolar, 'US versus the

---

147   See Amnesty International, China, in Report 2006, at <http://web.amnesty.org/report2006/chn-summary-eng>.

148   Amnesty International, Saudi Arabia, in Report 2006, at <http://web.amnesty.org/report2006/sau-summary-eng>.

149   See 'Many rights, some wrong', *The Economist*, 24 March 2007; also Alan Dershowitz, 'What are they watching?', *The New York Sun*, 23 August 2006, available at <http://www.nysuncom/article/38428>.

150   See E Heinze, 'Even-handedness and the politics of human rights', *Harvard Human Rights Journal*, 21 (2008), 7–46.

151   Both CERD art. 8(1) and ICCPR art. 28(3) provide that members of their respective supervisory committees shall serve not as official representatives of their governments, but 'in their personal capacity'.

world' view, towards a critical, historical and realist analysis of the totality of international norms, institutions and processes:

7. International human rights norms, like those within many national legal systems, are often formulated in abstract terms. Critical theory must resist purely surface readings of their black-letter content. It must analyse such norms precisely as it has analysed them in US law, within the context of their overall genesis, interpretation and implementation.
8. Human rights standards impose obligations on all states.[152] The vices of one must not be silenced solely for the purpose of condemning those of another. Many states, not limited to liberal democracies, preach norms that they fail to practise, often with devastating consequences for their populations and for outsider groups. States should be condemned in proportion to their levels of abuse.
9. Popular and scholarly attention to oppression inevitably depends on relative freedom of the media, with the result that human rights abuses in societies with a free press attract the greatest attention. Lack of publicity must never be equated with lack of abuse. Critical theorists must recall their pledge to listen to voices where they are least heard.

How might we apply these principles? To take one example, as noted earlier, the global struggle against apartheid, waged largely through UN-coordinated action, became one of the few relative successes of the Cold War period. But can a critically-minded theory be fully satisfied? Again, during that same period, many regimes were committing equal and worse acts of genocide and brutality, often with ethnic dimensions. They, however, were exempt from condemnation because of their powerful or strategic positions at the United Nations. From the point of view of those victims, the struggle against apartheid became more of an international foil for avoiding their plight than a credible expression of a deep commitment to human rights; a way of making the 'international community' look like it was *doing something* about violations, while it was systematically ignoring some of the worst of them.[153]

In the 1980s, college campuses and public commons throughout the Western world became venues for energetic anti-apartheid campaigns. To remain silent *about apartheid* – to plead for 'quiet diplomacy' – was to be complicit with it. No such grass-roots activism was, in the late twentieth and early twenty-first centuries, directed against Robert Mugabe's abuse of millions of Zimbabweans,[154] nor against South Africa's ruling ANC and its 'quiet diplomacy'. One might argue that Critical Race Theory or LatCrit are bound to focus on white, Western oppression. However, that choice would raise some moral dilemmas. Leaving aside the question of whether murder, torture or rape *hurt more* when committed by someone with whiter skin, any choice to focus exclusively on the colonial, white-on-black dynamic departs from approaches actually adopted within the UN. UN-CERD, for example, has declined to treat 'race' and 'ethnicity' as distinct categories, having recognized inter-ethnic oppression and discrimination as falling within the scope of norms governing racial discrimination under CERD. The former UN Secretary General Kofi Annan recently stated that 'Africans must guard against a pernicious, self-destructive form of racism that unites citizens to rise up and expel tyrannical rulers who are white, but to excuse tyrannical rulers who are black'.[155]

---

152   Limited only, where appropriate, by those states' ability to fulfil those obligations.

153   See Robertson and Merrills, above, n. 118, at 83–89.

154   See Amnesty International, Zimbabwe, in Report 2005, at <http://web.amnesty.org/report2005/zwe-summary-eng>.

155   See C Jacobson, 'Annan: Zimbabwe spiral down intolerable' (ABC News broadcast, 23 July 2007), available at <http://abcnews.go.com/International/wireStory?id=3403445>.

Similarly, the gestational years of African human rights law and institutions were marked by both highly politicized and almost deliberately ineffective approaches. Instruments like the Declarations of the First and Second Conferences of Independent African States or the Resolutions of the First Assembly of the Heads of State and Government of the Organization of African Unity overwhelmingly condemned only oppression by whites.[156] They remained silent about brutal and dictatorial practices that often claimed far more black-on-black, albeit commonly inter-ethnic, victims. Perhaps another foil to deflect attention from human rights than any kind of commitment to them?[157] There can be no internationally-minded critical theory without a review of such attitudes, and of their persistence and consequences in today's world.

---

156   First Conference of Independent African States, Accra, 15–22 April 1958; Second Conference of Independent African States, Addis Ababa, 15–24 June 1960; Resolutions of the First Assembly of the Heads of State and Government of the Organization of African Unity, Cairo, July 1964.

157   Cf. Steiner and Alston, above, n. 45, at 920–37.

PART II
The Challenges of Rights

Chapter 7

Defacing Muslim Women:
Dialectical Meanings of Dress in the Body Politic

Susan Edwards

Introduction

Body apparel has become the site of contemporary political struggle. In a world where the master signifier is considered by the super powers to be the events of 9/11, and where those considered responsible for that attack were from Saudi Arabia and Morocco and also of the Islamic faith, the pariah in our midst is identified as Islam. The West, in its quest to protect its citizens from such random crime, responds by mounting its own jihad and confronting, in every way possible, what it perceives as the enemy in its midst. To this end it introduces counter-terrorism legislation and develops a panoply of measures that, in particular, marginalize and criminalize Islamic communities and controls the way of life of those communities it targets, by amongst others attacking their cultural identity and religious faith. The first strategy is characterized by the development of counter-terrorism legislation and the creation of a raft of entirely new offences, including, for example, the glorification of terrorist related activity,[1] and the prohibition of certain political organizations through the use of proscription orders.[2] At the same time erstwhile canons of liberty have been compromised. On the one hand derogating from Article 5 (the right to liberty) and Article 6 (the right to a fair trial) of the European Convention on Human Rights (ECHR) is permitted and considered justified, on the grounds that the nation is under threat.[3] The second strategy includes measures to restrict immigration by tightening immigration control.[4] The third strategy involves attacks on the very personality and identity of Islamic communities, including an assault on dress forms, which is legitimated by ensuring that the observers' stereotypical interpretation of these forms of dress, seen as representing either subjugation or strident militancy,[5] take precedence over the wearers' definitions. Here, body apparel, and especially 'her' Islamic body, is the target of

---

1   Under the Terrorism Act 2000, section 57 states: '(1) A person commits an offence if he possesses an article in circumstances which give rise to a reasonable suspicion that his possession is for a purpose connected with the commission, preparation or instigation of an act of terrorism.' Samina Malik was found not guilty under this section but convicted of an offence under section 58 of the act, later quashed on appeal on 17 June 2008.

2   The Terrorism Act 2000, section 3 provides for criminalization of being a member of certain political organizations if that organization is deemed by the UK Government to be 'terrorist'.

3   The Human Rights Act 1998 (Designated Derogation) Order 2001.

4   A Mooney, 'Citizens, immigrants, anarchists and other animals', in A Wagner, T Summerfield, and F Vanegas (eds), *Contemporary Issues in the Semiotics of Law* (Oxford: Hart, 2005), at 35–55. And by employing persons and giving contracts to convicted violent criminals to deport asylum seekers. *Daily Mail*, 2 June 2008; *The Daily Telegraph*, 2 June 2008; see the case of Mark Ayres.

5   B Parekh, *Rethinking Multiculturalism, Cultural Diversity and Political Theory* (Cambridge, MA: Harvard University Press, 2000) lists 12 practices or customs that lead to multicultural conflicts. The dress of Muslim women is one.

imperialist scrutiny, regulation, condemnation and, at times, vilification. Dress form has been reified and made a fetish. It has also been regarded as the embodiment of either a gendered oppression or else a threatening force. Yet dress styles such as hijab (head scarf), jilbab (long tunic) and niqab (face veil) – all of which are the objects of this gaze, control and scorn[6] – when viewed from the standpoint of the wearer embody a multiplicity of meanings, some religious, some not, some strident, some oppressive, some passive, some subversive, some celebratory and some lost in translation. These several meanings must each be understood and located in their specific historical and materialist context. The binary presentation and crude over-determination of the imperialist interpretation merely obscures and eschews these complexities and contradictions.[7]

Body Apparel as Text-Signifiers

The hijab (head scarf), niqab (face veil) and jilbab (long tunic) are but three forms of cultural dress that are currently under the scrutiny of the imperialist gaze. McGoldrick, in trying to grapple with the real and material complexity of meaning attached to wearing the hijab, not only by the wearer but also as it is understood by the observer, writes: 'Because of the way it is perceived and understood, the symbolism attached to this simple piece of clothing worn by women has managed to place it within a series of major contemporary issues – identity, multiculturalism, liberalism and religious fundamentalism.'[8] The head scarf/hijab worn by women at the centre of this most recent fixation carries a multiplicity of meanings. It is presently worn by Muslim and non-Muslim women in much the same manner and style as it was worn, for example, by the late Jackie Onassis and, in the UK, by, amongst others, the present Queen and the late Princess Margaret, when it was considered haute couture and an emblematic icon of fashion. This recent fixation by the West with the headscarf is less about the 87 grams of square cloth which incites so much excitement, and more about its perceived signification. Certainly the Queen, for example, has never incited so much interest for wearing a head scarf on windy days or whilst horse riding at Windsor. A similar point can also be made with regard to the face covering of the veil. In England, for example, from the mid-Victorian era to the end of the nineteenth century the veil was often worn as a bridal headdress covering the bride's face prior to the wedding ceremony. No debate attached to this practice. Yet today the niqab when worn by some women arouses indignation and sometimes anger and hatred.

Body apparel cross-culturally and throughout history is encoded with a particular meaning for both the wearer and also for the observer. These meanings are often in conflict and a struggle ensues between the wearer of the dress form and the observer. How the West, as observer, constructs, projects and cliches other cultures including their dress form is central to its imperialist colonialist project. The construction of non-Western and in this case Arab/Islamic, otherwise 'Oriental' women has been central to both ancient and modern colonization. Whilst today the projection of 'Oriental' women is as a subjugated group, one of the earlier and enduring projections of 'Women of the

---

6   Reminiscent of Charles De Gaulle who in 1962 said: 'Muslims, have you seen them with their turbans and djellabas?', cited in JW Scott, *The Politics of the Veil* (Princeton, NJ: Princeton University Press, 2007), at 61.

7   L Althusser, 'Contradiction and overdetermination', in *Lenin and Philosophy and Other Essays* (New York and London: Monthly Review Press, New Left Books, 1971).

8   D McGoldrick, Human Rights and Religion: The Islamic Headscarf Debate in Europe (Oxford: Hart, 2006), at 308.

Orient',[9] as constructed in and by the Western psyche, is their inherent eroticism. This perception says more about the sexual desire of Western men for women who are unattainable than it does about the women themselves. This sexualized imagery has been constructed by a masculinist, predatory, imperialist desire. This projection of erotic imaginings are redolent in nineteenth- and twentieth-century art, which attempted to capture the characteristics of a different people. Leighton's 'Light of the Harem' (1880) and the paintings of Eugene Delacroix and Jean-Auguste Dominique Ingres play on these projections and desires. It is also conceded that by the early twentieth century there was an attempt to present a more realistic, albeit still stylized, portrayal of 'the Orient' found in the paintings of Mariano Fortuny and in the photography of the period brought together by Ken Jacobson[10] and more recently by Owen Logan.[11] Contemporary fiction, however, perpetuates this sexualized projection where 'Oriental women' are eroticized in Richard Manton's novel, *The Odalisque*.[12] In all these representations the veil (niqab/burqa) assumes a sexual significance.

The same item of dress, across time and cultures, carries and conveys a multiplicity of different meanings.[13] Drawing on the work of Ferdinand de Saussure[14] body apparel can be read as text. Thus hijab, veil or jilbab is the sign. The signifier is the concept, construct or the idea that situates the meaning of the sign in its place and time. What is manifestly apparent is that the hijab, veil or jilbab has a multiplicity of signifiers and is never fixed in its meaning.[15] Sawchuk writes that '[…] events, objects, images, as cultural signs or allegories [which] do not have one fixed or stable meaning, […] derive their significance […] from their place in a chain of signifiers, a chain which is itself unstable because of the constant intervention of [this] theoretical change'.[16] Thus, body apparel, like the body itself, cannot escape being a vehicle of history and a veritable metaphor and metonym in time.[17] Body apparel becomes a site of power, as contested meanings struggle for their placement where selected meanings become primary definers within a multiplicity of meanings. Sawchuk refers to the way in which 'the body bears the scatalogical marks, the historical scars of power'.[18] This is also true of dress form that bears the scars of struggle and, depending on context, can represent both powerlessness and power. In this interrelationship between sign and signifier the individual is constituted through words and language. 'Whether in the order of spoken or written discourse, no element can function as a sign without referring to another element which itself is not simply present. This interweaving results in each element – phoneme or grapheme – being

9   I am relying on Edward Said's use and meaning of the term 'orient' here, as in E Said, *Orientalism* (London: Penguin, 1978).

10   K Jacobson, *Odalisques and Arabesques: Orientalist Photography 1839–1925* (London, Quaritch, 2007).

11   See O Logan, *Al Maghrib: Photographs from Morocco* (Edinburgh: Polygon, 1988).

12   R Manton, *The Odalesque* (London: Running Press Books, 1999).

13   S Forbes Bliss, 'Clothing arguments', *Life*, 181 (2008), 36–39.

14   F De Saussure, *Course in General Linguistics* (London: Duckworth, 1995). See also P Thibault, *Re-reading Saussur : The Dynamics of Signs in Social Life* (London: Routledge, 1996).

15   H Sedghi, *Women and Politics in Iran: Veiling, Unveiling, and Reveiling* (Cambridge: Cambridge University Press, 2007); see also MMJ Fischer, 'On changing the concept and position of Persian women', in L Beck and N Keddie (eds), *Women in the Muslim World* (third printing 1980) (Cambridge, MA: Harvard University Press, 1978), at 189–215.

16   K Sawchuk, 'A tale of inscription: Fashion statements', in A Kroker and M Kroker (eds), *Body Invaders: Sexuality and the Postmodern Condition* (Basingstoke: MacMillan, 1988), at 67.

17   See J Comaroff and J Comaroff, 'Bodily reform as historical practice', in *Ethnography and the Historical Imagination* (Oxford: Westview Press, 1992), at 79.

18   Sawchuk, above, n. 16, at 72.

constituted on the basis of the place within it of the other elements of the chain or the system.'[19] Women who wear the hijab, veil (niqab) or jilbab are constituted by others through this dress form, and in and by this dress form, and in resisting these imposed definitions must engage in a struggle to constitute and project themselves in accordance with the meanings the particular dress form holds for them.

Historical, Cultural Signifiers

The hijab, veil and jilbab, and the meanings these dress forms hold, and the language that expresses the signification of these meanings, has been constructed, severally, by amongst others Western commentators, most notably Western Orientalists: by those mimicking the West and living in false consciousness: by women trying to free themselves from at least the fixity of the veil when it functions as a vehicle of their oppression and subordination to men within their own cultures: and paradoxically by women, in recent history, who in resisting modern colonialism and assimilation, as well as negative ascriptions of their culture imposed by super powers have reveiled. In the first category writers like Qasim Amin[20] criticized the Western Orientalists' misconception of the veil. In the second category, without wishing to oversimplify the nationalistic struggles, some believed that emancipation and progress depended on adopting Western practices. Turkey, for example, banned the headscarf in the 1920s[21] and in Iran the veil was banned in 1936.

In the third category, Egyptian feminist Nawal El Saadawi[22] recognized (like Hoda Sha'arawi Pasha who in 1923 abandoned the veil)[23] that the veil has often, although not always, been a symbol and a vehicle of patriarchal oppression. It is apparent, as Ebert articulates, that 'women are produced differently as women in each system, and in relation to the differences in the other systems. For the specific position of each woman is "overdetermined" in that she is produced differently in conjunction with the other systems acting on her in terms of class, race, and nationality'.[24] History, time and the specificities of the cultural context are all relevant to understanding the fluidity of signification of dress form, and realization that the cultural sign of the veil, or hijab, is not fixed in its meaning. In analysing the meaning and signification as well as exploring the ambiguity of the veil, Saadawi writes that the veil is variously 'one of the most visible aspects of Islamic fundamentalism', 'a fashion now among upper-class women', a dress form for women 'to protect themselves from men on the street', and is also worn as 'an anti [W]estern protest'.[25] Minces, in her work, also identifies the veil's ambivalence when she writes:

---

19   J Derrida, *Positions* (Chicago, IL: University of Chicago Press, 1981), at 26.

20   Q Amin, *The Liberation of Women: Two Documents in the History of Egyptian Feminism* (Cairo: The American University in Cairo Press, 2000).

21   E Hughes, 'The secularism debate and Turkey's quest for European Union membership', *Religion and Human Rights*, 3/1 (2008), 15–32.

22   N El Saadawi, *The Hidden Face of Eve* (London: Zed Press, 1980), at 176.

23   SA Al Kader, *The Status of Egyptian Women 1900–1973* (Cairo: The American University in Cairo, Social Research Center, 1973), at 14. On this point discussions were had by the author and Al Kader at the American University in Cairo in 1978. See also S Abd al-Kader, *Egyptian Women in a Changing Society, 1899–1987* (Boulder, CO: Lynne Rienner Publishers, 1987).

24   TL Ebert, 'Writing in the political: Resistance (post) modernism', in J Leonard (ed.), *Legal Studies as Cultural Studies: Reader in Post Modern Critical Theory* (New York: State University of New York Press, 1995), at 356.

25   N El Saadawi, *The Nawal El Saadawi Reader* (London: Zed Books, 1990), at 96. It is also worthy of note that during my own research fieldtrip to Egypt, Cairo in 1977, funded by the Social Science Research

On the one hand, the veil is falling into disuse as a result of women's schooling, work and greater participation in public life. On the other, and in the same countries, some women are ostentatiously taking up the veil for political reasons, as a matter of choice rather than in response to family or social pressures. It symbolizes their demand for a more "moral" economic, political and social life, as prescribed by Islam; a return to the wellsprings of Muslim identity and a new fundamentalism [...].[26]

Seyla Benhabib also recognizes that the veil signifies a complexity of meaning including submission, ambivalence, freedom, protection from intrusion of men, and a powerful statement of opposition.[27] El Gundi similarly acknowledges that 'the veil is a complex symbol of many meanings. Emancipation can be expressed by wearing the veil or by removing it. It can be secular or religious. It can represent tradition or resistance.'[28]

Situating these meanings within the historical and political context is fundamental, as 'veiling is a much more complex social phenomenon [. For example ...] in post independence Algeria and Morrocco, the veil has both spread to the new classes and been contained among the urban bourgeoisie, among whom it is felt to be, in part, nationalistic or Islamic reaction against French ways and the denigration of Islamic customs'.[29] The dialectical working of the 'veil' is a significant characteristic feature of its power of transformation.[30] The meaning and importance of the veil, hijab or more recently jilbab, from the viewpoint of the Western eye, can be seen as a story of the West imposing and validating its own determination of what these dress forms mean. It is a determination informed by values that enabled empire, colonialism, post-colonialism and super power dominion, 'including and especially those ideas that underdeveloped countries and the third world were something inferior'.[31] In this context, the 'Islamic woman' has been essentialized and constructed as sexualized (discussed above) as unemancipated and oppressed. It is in this sense that Saadawi is suspicious of, and rejects as essentially imperialist, those attempts of Western feminists to understand the Arab and Islamic woman and her dress form: 'Of course I oppose the desire of certain religious leaders in Iran to see women covered in the chador or deprived of the civil rights they have gained over the years'.[32] She continues, however, 'in underdeveloped countries, liberation from foreign domination [...] still remains the crucial issue'.[33] It is important to recognize that Saadawi's and Mernissi's rejection of the veil is a rejection that is located in a time when the veil was predominantly a signifier and metonym of the subjugation of women.

More recently, the veil, hijab and niqab have become, for some women who wear them, a visible symbol of political positionality and an expression of resistance to Western foreign policy.

Council, I never saw a veiled woman. The few women wearing a hijab were women working in the finance and banking industry who incidentally wore a beautifully crocheted version of the headscarf, of which I purchased several for my own use in England as they transcended any fixed meaning.

26   J Minces, *The House of Obedience:Women in Arab Society* (London, Zed Books, 1982), at 51.

27   S Benhabib, *The Claims of Culture Equality and Diversity in the Global Era* (Princeton, NJ: Princeton University Press, 2002), at 95.

28   F El Guindi, *Veil: Modesty, Privacy and Resistance* (Oxford: Berg, 1999), at 172.

29   Beck and Keddie, above, n. 15, at 7–8.

30   *Franz Fanon: Black Skin, White Mask*, directed by Isaac Julien (Video Pal Format) 1996; SA Djebar, F Fanon and R Faulkner, 'Women, veils and land', *World Literature Today*, 70 (1996); NC Gibson, *Rethinking Fanon: The Continuing Dialogue* (Prometheus Books, 1999); A-E Berger, 'The newly veiled woman: Irigaray, specularity and the Islamic veil', *Diacritics*, 28/1 (1998), 93–119.

31   E Said, *Orientalism* (London: Penguin, 1978).

32   See above, at viii.

33   See above, at ix.

So, for example, in the context of Iran's more recent history: 'Significant metaphorically and literally, veiling, unveiling, and re-veiling illuminate the contest for political power in the course of Iran's development.'[34]

Lifting the Veil: Dress Codes, Context and Connotations

Why has the hijab (headscarf), the jilbab and, more recently, the veil become of such supreme political importance in the UK in the last decade? Certainly, in the UK there is plenty of evidence that politicians have become excited and distracted by dress. Jack Straw in 2004, in responding to the French ban on headscarves in state schools, said: 'I would like to say that we will never ever ban any hijabs in schools. We must learn to celebrate the fact that we have state funded religious schools.'[35] However, too soon afterwards, in response to veiled women in his own political constituency of Blackburn, he said that he asks Muslim women who visit him in his constituency office to unveil themselves as such dress forms are a '[...] visible statement of separation and difference' and the veiling by women 'made it harder to bring communities together'.[36] Other Western leaders have also made items of Muslim women's clothing their target. Jacques Chirac, in a speech he made in Tunisia in December 2003, said: 'Wearing the veil [...] is a kind of aggression.'[37] Harriet Harman, in 2006 when a cabinet minister, fell into the all too familiar encoding of the veil as a metonym of women's subordination when she said that it was 'an obstacle to women's participation, on equal terms, in society'.[38] And in 2009, in France once again, the veil (niqab/burqa) described as the *voile integral* assumed an omnipotent importance. The right wing deputy Jacques Myard presented a draft bill prohibiting the wearing of the niqab (face veil), making it an offence carrying a sanction of two months' imprisonment and a fine for a first offence, and one year's imprisonment and a fine for a second offence. France decides on this matter in July 2010.

   The hijab, veil and jilbab as items of women's clothing are not under attack per se. It is the cultural and social groups who wear these items of clothing that have become the primary targets for the aggression of Western governments and the populace. An indirect racism underpins and drives these attitudes, which is now repackaged, reconfigured and legitimated, supported by a justificatory rationale in the need to protect the community from terrorism and, reductio ad absurdum, Muslims. (Interestingly the IRA, even at its height, never provoked an anti-terrorism backlash resulting in the control or vilification of all Catholics or of all Christians worldwide, or indeed the control of their churches or religious practices etc.) The visibly hidden face behind the veil is in the modern era a banner of challenge and resistance, and, whilst once regarded as a symbol of women's oppression (as discussed by Saadawi above), is now regarded somewhat schizophrenically as giving meaning to the conception of the Orient as backward, primitive and oppressive, whilst also being considered

---

   34   Sedghi, above, n. 15.
   35   UK Newsquest Regional Press, *This is Lancashire*, 15 April 2004.
   36   Jack Straw provoked an angry reaction after he revealed that he asks Muslim women to remove their veils when they visit his constituency surgery (*The Times*, 6 October 2006). Saima Shah, a student at Blackburn College in Jack Straw's constituency, presented a photographic exhibition of positive images of women and dress codes to try to educate and challenge the meanings imputed to the sign of the face veil and hijab in contemporary Britain. See <http://www.asianimage.co.uk/news/education/display.var.2040312.0.0.php>.
   37   JW Scott, *The Politics of the Veil* (Princeton, NJ: Princeton University Press, 2007), at 84.
   38   H Harman, *Why I want to see the veil gone from Britain*, at <www.newstateman.com/200610160019>. See also T Welch, 'The prohibition of the Muslim headscarf: Contrasting international approaches in policy and law', *Denning Law Journal*, 19 (2007), 181–217.

as emblematic of women's defiance, power and threatening force. Recent concerted efforts to unveil women are an attempt to bring 'these' women under control. Jack Straw (the Member of Parliament for Blackburn) not only wanted to unveil Muslim women; he went further to say that unveiling was good for them. The colonialist male always knew what was best for the colonized female. He claimed with some pride that in unveiling women in the confines of his constituency office the women really wanted to be unveiled. She was waiting for a man like him to unveil her! The overlaying/underlaying of male sexual desire and control in the seduction of women, and his projection of 'her' as wanting to yield and surrender, are obvious.[39] Such forcible tactics of stripping women bare have frequently been deployed against immigrant and marginalized women, and in so many ways. Take, for example, the treatment of women who, in a witch-obsessed medieval Europe, were stripped by men and their body hair shaved as part of an investigation for moles or blemishes that were considered to be the visible signs of consorting with the devil.[40] Take, for example, the scandalous methods used to control immigration in the 1970s, when the migration of women from the Asian sub-continent was policed by forcibly subjecting women to a vaginal examination for 'virginity testing' at Heathrow airport, based on the assumption that no Asian woman could have sex before marriage and, therefore, if discovered not to be a virgin, must be already married.[41] This was taken as sufficient evidence to refuse a woman entry; whilst, on the other hand, if she was a virgin it was presumed that she would find a fiancé and stay to get married in the UK.[42]

The politics of lifting the veil, or forcibly unveiling women,[43] has of course been a deliberate colonialist strategy for years and has been critiqued specifically by Franz Fanon. Fanon analysed the meaning of forcible unveiling for Algerian women in *Studies in a Dying Colonialism* in 1959. In exploring the forcible unveiling of Algerian women by the French occupiers he wrote: 'There is also in the European the crystallisation of an aggressiveness, the strain of a kind of violence before the Algerian woman. Unveiling this woman is revealing her beauty; it is baring her secret, breaking her resistance [to colonial rule …]. There is in it the will to bring this woman within his reach, to make her a possible object of possession.'[44] Fanon clearly understood the ambivalence of the veil for Muslim women in occupied Algeria. Fanon observed that prior to the war for independence the veil was 'invisible', yet during the resistance it became a potent symbol of national liberation and identity. He concluded that women wore the veil as a visible sign of defiance and in solidarity. In turn women were forcibly unveiled as a way of destroying not only them as women, but also the group to which they belonged; therefore it was an integral tactic of the genocide strategy.

---

39   J Bourke, *Rape: A History from 1860 to the Present* (London: Virago, 2007).

40   J Sprenger and H Kramer, H Institoris (1486–87) *The Malleus Maleficarum*, trans. and ed. Rev. Montague Summers (London: John Rodker, 1928).

41   Immigration (Gynaeclogical Practice) HC Deb 9 February 1979, vol. 962 cc 312-3W. 'Mr Bidwell asked the Secretary of State under what rule virginity testing of immigrant women was undertaken. Mr Merlyn Rees Secretary of State: The medical examination in the recent case which my learned hon. Friend has in mind was sought to establish whether the passenger concerned has borne children., The authority for the medical examination of any person subject to immigration control who seeks to enter the United Kingdom is contained in paragraph 2 schedule 2 to the Immigration Act 1971 […].'

42   This practice was stopped in 1979. See *The Associated Press*, 2 February 1979. Virginity testing was described by the British Medical Association as an 'abomination', *Manchester Guardian Weekly*, 4 January 1981.

43   R Rabhari, 'Unveiling Muslim women: A trajectory of post colonial culture', *Dialectical Anthropology*, 25/3–4 (2000).

44   F Fanon, 'Algeria unveiled', in *Studies in a Dying Colonialism*, reprinted in *The Fanon Reader* (ed.), A Haddour (New York: *Monthly Review*, 1990); see also F Fanon, *The Wretched of the Earth* (London: Penguin, 1990); see also McGoldrick, above, n. 8.

French soldiers forcibly 'unveiled' Algerian women during the war, raping and torturing them as a deliberate policy. 'If we want to destroy the structure of Algerian society, its capacity for resistance we must first of all conquer the women.'[45] Fanon explores this stripping, not only at the political level, but also at the level of the sexual psyche of the occupying power: 'Thus the rape of the Algerian woman in the dream of a European is always preceded by a rending of the veil.'[46] '[I]t was the colonialist's frenzy to unveil the Algerian woman, it was his gamble on winning the battle of the veil, at whatever cost, that were to provoke the native's bristling resistance.'[47]

Sedghi, writing about Iranian women in the 1980s identifies the self-same motivation in more recent efforts to unveil women. She writes that the strategy and purpose of unveiling women is to 'intrigue and conquer women'. Women's modesty, she maintains, is embodied in the hijab; if the 'hejab [sic] is dismantled, women are dismantled [...]'.[48]

From Latent Orientalism to the Politics of Reveiling

In the present moment it is women especially who are at the receiving end of imperialist control through dress and body apparel. Latent Orientalism,[49] in the form of the feigned obsequious claims by Jack Straw and others that their intention is to liberate the 'subordinated Islamic woman', is reminiscent of the French colonial masters' strategy in Algeria to forcibly 'Westernize' Algerian women. McClintock identifies such practices as a 'colonial masquerade' for achieving 'a real power over the man' through women.[50] Such obsequious claims to protect the equality and human rights of women become a masquerade when promoted by those who have inexorably eschewed the human rights of women from the subaltern.

Over the last two decades, women in Islamic communities are reveiling and returning to the head scarf as a form of revolutionary protest and assertion of cultural identity and in opposition to the West's totalizing occupation of media, minds and culture.[51] This revivalism in dress form is happening in Egypt, in Iran, in Bahrain, in Pakistan, in Blackburn, in Bradford, and in London, but it is not simply a return to religious Islamic orthodoxy. Anyone who attributes this practice purely to religious revivalism misses its wider purpose. Again, as Sedghi notes:

> Active women are diverse and their activities intersect with their class background, ideology, the degree of their religious identity, and the geographical setting of their environment. More secular and middle-class, many urban opponent women redefine veiling practices and gender policies almost daily.[52]

The reality is that those who choose to reveil do so as a symbol of resisting psychological occupation and forced assimilation and acculturation practices, and not because they are oppressed in their communities, nor as a mark of religiosity. The failure of the UK and other Western countries to

---

45   F Fanon, *Black Skin White Masks* (London: Pluto, 1986), at 37–38.
46   F Fanon, 'Algeria unveiled', ibid., at 107.
47   See above, at 109.
48   Sedghi, above, n. 15, at 262.
49   Said, above, n. 9, at 207.
50   A McClintock, *Imperial Leather* (London: Routledge, 1995), at 363.
51   K Bullock, *Rethinking Muslim Women and the Veil* (London: The International Institute of Islamic Thought, 2003).
52   See Sedghi, above, n. 15, at 246.

understand the complexity of this new posture, and the centrality of reveiling, along with the return to the hijab and jilbab, to women's identity and group identity, is at their peril. The UK, in its own efforts to forcibly unveil, depicts the veil as obstructing communication and assimilation, and furthering separation. These rationales and justifications, which acclaim the human rights moral high ground, are, however, not the trajectory of a movement towards the liberation of woman or towards multiculturalism and assimilation, for there has been no supporting evidence whatever of any such a movement at local or governmental level. Historically the experience of women from Asia, Africa and the Arab world in the UK has been one of deliberate marginalization from Grunwick onwards.[53] Policies that demand unveiling are not about equality: they can be seen as yet another example of a strategy of destroying identity, faith, culture, and the ethnicity of the individual and of the group, in whole or in part, through humiliation and undressing, which is a state-orchestrated and validated 'violence against women'.[54] This state violence has in France become legitimated through the ploy of the sacred cow of secularism. France obsesses over the head scarf worn by Maheanor Ozdemir (which is confused with the burqa). Ozdemir is the first 'veiled' woman in the Belgian Parliament. Because she wears the head scarf she has been reified and fetishized. She explains: 'Unfortunately I was reduced to nothing more than this veil [head scarf].' To argue, as many have done already, that this strategy of unveiling is to protect women from oppressive practices within their own communities, or else to comply with the international minimum requirement of respecting the human rights of women and the promotion of their equality with men, is fatuous and entirely disingenuous. One must ask the question, when has the UK ever been interested in the human rights of women from Arab countries or the Asian sub-continent? One must ask what is the basis of this recent concern for veiled women and women wearing the head scarf who are resident in the UK. At the same time one might also ask what lies at the basis of the recent concern of the situation of women living under, for example, the Taliban.

Law in the Control of Muslim Dress Forms

What part, if any, does the law play in this wider dynamic of the control and policing of dress code? It is true that the law has always controlled and regulated particular social groups and communities by regulating dress form in education and employment. Legal argument controlling dress form has expressly been articulated around contractual requirements in the workplace, which have been presented as concerns around health and safety requirements. More recently, in the human rights age, such arguments have centred around balancing the rights of individuals, where the claim to wear a form of dress has been advanced as part of an integral aspect of the right to freedom of expression against the rights of others. Prior to the advent of human rights, the dress and body style of immigrant and marginalized communities have always been the target of control and discrimination both direct and indirect.[55] Their dress styles and body styles (hair,[56] piercing and scarification[57]) amongst other practices including, for example, the slaughter of animals for

---

53 *The Great Grunwick Strike 1976–1978*, Director Chris Thomas, Brent Trade Union Council.

54 Such strategies of getting to a group through its women were adopted in Bosnia where Muslim women were raped with the object of deliberately impregnating them with Serb babies.

55 *Dress Discrimination*, State Legislatures, April 2008, vol. 34, I.

56 See K Owusu, *Black British Culture and Society* (London: Routledge, 1999).

57 *R v. Adesanya* (1974) [1975] 24 ICLG 136 noted.

meat,[58] have become anthropomorphized into the subaltern and the 'other'.[59] Since dress code and body style is a potent and visible expression of identity and self-determination, the control and regulation of dress and body styles has been regarded as a deliberate attempt to control particular social groups. The regulation of this self-expression has also been regarded as an attempt to destroy the identity of the group.[60]

'The way people clothe themselves, together with the traditions of dress and finery that custom implies, constitutes the most distinctive form of society's uniqueness, that is to say the one that is the most immediately perceptible.'[61] The annals of public policy in the UK, as elsewhere, are replete with attempts to regulate dress code and body style. Some of the earlier expressions of regulation were directed at both men and women. Earlier battles were waged in the education and employment contexts and engaged the Race Relations Act (RRA) 1976 section 3,[62] which provided for the protection against discrimination of those who are considered to be outsiders, including those of colour, race, nationality or ethnic or national origins (it did not offer protection from religious discrimination per se, nor did it offer protection for Muslims, who were not considered a racial, national or ethnic group).[63] For example, the piece of cloth, when not arranged into a cap on a man's head, has been the site of struggle for identity and also a target of discrimination. In *Mandla v. Dowell Lee* (1983),[64] a boy of the Sikh faith, who wore a turban covering his hair required of him by his faith, was refused entry into a private school unless he removed his turban. Lord Denning, in the Court of Appeal, had ruled that they – Sikhs – were not a racial group and therefore not protected under the RRA. The House of Lords did not agree and found that Sikhs were members of a particular racial group protected by the Race Relations Act of 1976: 'Section 3(1) of the Act defines racial group as "a group of persons defined by reference to colour, nationality or ethnic or national origins" […].' Similar struggles have taken place in the workplace. For example, a Sikh trainee nurse who sought employment in the National Health Service and wanted to dress (as she saw it) modestly in trousers and not in the regulation above-knee or knee-length skirt required of British nurses at the time found that the employment appeal tribunal upheld the decision of the

---

58   S Poulter, *Ethnicity and Human Rights* (Oxford: Clarendon Press, 1988).

59   Said, above, n. 9.

60   In 1998, Article 7 of the Rome Statute of the International Criminal Court expanded the definition of 'crimes against humanity': '[T]he following acts when committed as part of a widespread or systematic attack directed against any civilian population, with knowledge of the attack: (a) Murder; (b) Extermination; (c) Enslavement; (d) Deportation or forcible transfer of population; (e) Imprisonment; (f) Torture; (g) Rape, sexual slavery; (h) Persecution against any identifiable group or collectivity on political, racial, national, ethnic, cultural, religious, gender … grounds; (i) Enforced disappearance of persons; (j) The crime of apartheid; and (k) Other inhumane acts of a similar character …'.

61   Fanon, above, n. 44, at 100.

62   (1) In this Act, unless the context otherwise requires – 'racial grounds' means any of the following grounds, namely colour, race, nationality or ethnic or national origins; 'racial group' means a group of persons defined by reference to colour, race, nationality or ethnic or national origins, and references to a person's racial group refer to any racial group into which he falls.

63   See *Nyazi v. Rymans*, EAT 10 May 1988 unreported; *Tariq v. Young*, Birmingham IT, 19 April unreported; *Commission for Racial Equality v. Precision Manufacturing Services*, Sheffield IT, 26 July 1991 unreported. See *JH Walker Ltd v. Hussain* (1996) IRLR 11 reported at n. 155, p. 354 in S Poulter, *Ethnicity, Law and Human Rights* (Oxford: Clarendon Press, 1988).

64   *Mandla v. Dowell Lee* (1983) IRLR 209 (HL).

health authority and refused her leave to appeal to the House of Lords.[65] Today, trousers are the preferred form of dress worn by all nurses. Some comfort, but too late for Ms Tajwinder Kaur.

Body styles, especially the arrangement of hair on the head or face, have also been the site of discrimination and struggle. In the case of *Singh v. Lyons Maid Ltd* (1975)[66] Mr Singh, a Sikh, was dismissed from his job as a production worker in an ice cream factory for refusing to remove his beard, although it was a symbol of his faith. The court found it a reasonable condition of his contract of employment to require him to do so. Afro-Caribbean hairstyle, in the form of dreadlocks, has also been a site of conflict and discrimination. In *Dawkins v. Department of the Environment* (1993)[67] a prospective employee did not wish to cut his dreadlocks, since as a Rastafarian it was a sign of his culture and faith, and so he was refused employment as a van driver. The Court of Appeal held that Rastafarians did not constitute a racial group. This ruling was upheld by the House of Lords. In the recent anti-terrorism climate of hysteria and rage, almost any method of control of marginalized communities is claimed to be justified. For example, a Sikh was asked to remove his turban at an airport, even though the sophisticated electronic detection equipment was capable of detecting devices, liquids, etc.[68]

If You Could See Her through My Eyes – Post 9/11

It is women who, post 9/11, have been the primary target of control with regard to dress and it is through women that men and entire communities are targeted and controlled. The meaning attributed to dress form has been dictated by the observer, and it is his/her definitions that have been privileged. Fanon explains how the powerful discourses define the 'other', the subaltern. 'The customs of the colonized peoples, their traditions, their myths – above all, their myths – are the very sign of that poverty of spirit and of their constitutional depravity.'[69] Cannadine writes in a similar vein: 'The hegemonic imperial project was primarily concerned with the production of a derogatory stereotype of other, alien, subordinated societies.'[70] Islamic women, in the post 9/11 era, are represented as something to be controlled in their own right. What is new is others' perception of these dress codes, not just as signifying subordination (which was hitherto the perception), but also as signifying a stance of subversion and anti-West posture. It is important to consider the context of these particular significations, a context, characterized by the rise of Islamaphobia, where latent Orientalism is condoned and justified by the threat of terrorism. Edward Said, in exploring the extent and manifestation of this hostile misunderstanding of Islam even prior to 9/11,[71] said: '[W]hat is said about the Muslim mind, character, and religion cannot be said in

---

65   *Kingston and Richmond Area Health Authority v. Kaur (Tajwinder)* (1981) ICR 631. See also AD Renteln, 'Visual religious symbols and the law', *American Behavioural Scientist*, 47 (2004), 1573–96.

66   *Singh v. Lyons Maid Ltd* (1975) IRLR 3285. In Sikhism the beard is a requirement for the orthodox follower.

67   *Dawkins v. Department of the Environment* (1993) IRLR 284.

68   See the case of Jaswant Singh Judge, *The Times of India*, 12 July 2008, where he was asked to remove his turban at the airport.

69   Fanon, above, n. 44, *Wretched of the Earth*, at 32

70   D Cannadine, *Ornamentalism: How the British saw their Empire* (London: Allen Lane, Penguin Press, 2001), at xvi.

71   Said, above, n. 9, at 209.

mainstream discussion about Africans, Jews, other Orientals or Asians.'[72] Edward Said's thesis is that there is no correspondence between what he calls the Orientalist articulation of Islam and the reality of its diversity or polysemicity; that Islam is overused and caricatured; and that essentialist theorizations eschew local articulations. Islam has become essentialized, and misunderstandings promulgate spurious generalizations. Indeed, to use and apply the label Christianity, in the same way as Islam is being applied, is to essentialize, rendering the description incomprehensible whilst residing in a place somewhere between discriminatory speech and hate speech. Indeed, in this wider discussion (beyond the scope of this presentation) we need to consider why 'Islam' has operated as a master signifier.[73]

In understanding contemporary readings of the text of the hijab, veil and jilbab, the contemporary context of the construction of Islam, Islamic fundamentalism and the counter-terrorism response is central. The events of 9/11 unleashed legislation in the UK in the form of the Terrorism Act 2000, the Prevention of Terrorism Act 2005 and the Terrorism Act 2006, expanding the spectre of counter-terrorism law – this includes, inter alia; proscribing of certain political organizations,[74] proscribing the wearing of particular uniform,[75] proscribing fund-raising in connection with certain organizations,[76] and making illegal the possession of an article considered to be 'involved in terrorism';[77] and under the Terrorism Act 2006,[78] encouragement[79] and the entirely novel offence of 'glorification of terrorist activity'.[80] On 16 December 2004, the House of Lords, in *A and others v. Secretary of State for the Home Department*,[81] ruled that indefinite detention of non-UK nationals,

---

72   E Said, *Covering Islam: How the Media and the Experts Determine How We See the Rest of the World* (London: Vintage, 1997), at xii.

73   B Sayyid, *A Fundamental Fear: Eurocentrism and the Emergence of Islamism* (London: Zed Books, 1997), at 46.

74   Terrorism Act 2000 section 12. See also *R v. F*, Court of Appeal (Criminal Division) 16 February 2007 [2007] EWCA Crim 243 [2007] 2 All ER 193, in which it was held that, '... in interpreting the meaning of "proscribed organisation" under section 58 of the Terrorism Act 2000, F was not entitled to argue that the provision permitted him to advance as a "reasonable excuse" for possessing the relevant documents that they had 'originated as part of an effort to change an illegal or undemocratic regime'.

75   Terrorism Act 2000 s 13.

76   Terrorism Act 2000 s 15.

77   Terrorism Act 2000 s 57. See also *R v. M* [2007] EWCA Crim 298, Crim LR [2008] 71, *R v. Rowe* [2007] EWCA Crim 635, Crim LR [2008] 72.

78   The Terrorism Bill 2007 (commons 2nd reading stage, April 2008) seeks to extend the range of current offences.

79   Terrorism Act 2006 s 1.

80   Terrorism Act 2006 s 1(3)(a) 'For the purposes of this section, the statements that are likely to be understood by members of the public as indirectly encouraging the commission or preparation of acts of terrorism or Convention offences include every statement which – (a) glorifies the commission or preparation (whether in the past, in the future or generally) of such acts or offences; and (b) is a statement from which those members of the public could reasonably be expected to infer that what is being glorified is being glorified as conduct that should be emulated by them in existing circumstances.' 'Glorification' is defined in s 20(2) as including 'any form of praise or celebration, and cognate expressions are to be construed accordingly.' *Yorkshire Post*, 20 March 2008, reported that a trader from Yorkshire who sold extremist Islamic videos glorifying terrorist activities that amounted to recruitment propaganda to young Muslims had been jailed for three years.

81   [2004] UKHL 56 [2005] 3 All ER 169 [2005] 2 AC 68. Appeals allowed. Human Rights Act 1998 (Designated Derogation) Order 2001 quashed. A declaration was made that s 23 of the Anti-Terrorism, Crime and Security Act 2001 was incompatible with Articles 5 and 14 of the European Convention for the Protection of Human Rights and Fundamental Freedoms 1950.

without charge or trial, was incompatible with the protection of liberty afforded by Article 5 of the European Convention of Human Rights (ECHR). In *A and others v. Secretary of State for the Home Department* (No. 2),[82] Lord Carswell said that '[…] no court will readily lend itself to indefinite detention without charge, let alone trial'.[83] Following the House of Lords ruling and the subsequent release of the Belmarsh prisoners,[84] the government responded, and, on 11 March 2005, introduced the Prevention of Terrorism Act 2005 (PTA), which provided for a new and novel legal mechanism, that of non-derogating and derogating 'control orders'. This inhabits a newly emerging area of law, a veritable 'no man's land' neither criminal nor civil,[85] whereby a person suspected of terrorist activity, although not sufficiently so to be able to charge him or her with any criminal offence, can be detained, under curfew, for up to 14 hours a day. And the order, which lasts for either six or 12 months, can be renewed again and again. The power to impose a control order turns on the definition of 'terrorist related activity'.[86] This phrase is insufficiently defined. It embraces under its banner a band-wagon of ills and misdemeanours, which depend entirely on the authorities' suspicion and anxiety, such that ways of thinking and feeling, that is, intellectual and emotional moods, as well as actions or contemplated actions that are considered to be terrorist related, are all included. As a result, for example, individuals who resist oppressive regimes may be defined as terrorists. Conor Gearty has recently warned:

> […] the definition of "terrorism" in the 2000 Act is far wider than is popularly assumed, covering politically, religiously or ideologically motivated serious violence to the person and serious damage to property but also similarly motivated conduct creating either "a serious risk to the health or safety of the public or a section of the public", or which is "designed seriously to interfere with or seriously to disrupt an electronic system" and that this means these control orders will be far wider than is generally understood.[87]

---

82   *A and others v. Secretary of State for the Home Department* (No. 2) [2005] UKHL 71 [2006] 1 All ER 575. 'The appeals would be allowed and the cases remitted to the SIAC for reconsideration.'

83   See above, at para. 164.

84   Detained in HMP Belmarsh without charge.

85   The House of Lords did not resolve this matter. See *Secretary of State for the Home Department v. MB; Secretary of State for the Home Department v. AF* [2007] UKHL 46, para. 17, per Lord Bingham: '… in this country … judges have regarded the classification of proceedings as criminal or civil as less important than the question of what protections are required for a fair trial'. Further, in *Customs and Excise Commissioners v. City of London Magistrates' Court* [2000] 4 All ER 763, it was held: 'criminal proceedings involve a formal accusation made on behalf of the state or by a private prosecutor that a defendant has committed a breach of the criminal law, and [that] the state or the private prosecutor has instituted proceedings which may culminate in the conviction and condemnation of the defendant'.

86   'Terrorism' is defined by the several offences created, and in the Terrorism Act 2000, s 1. (1) In this Act 'terrorism' means the use or threat of action where – (a) the action falls within subsection (2) (b) the use or threat is designed to influence the government or an international governmental organisation or to intimidate the public or a section of the public, and (c) the use or threat is made for the purpose of advancing a political, religious or ideological cause (2) Action falls within this subsection if it – (a) involves serious violence against a person, (b) involves serious damage to property, (c) endangers a person's life, other than that of the person committing the action, (d) creates a serious risk to the health or safety of the public or a section of the public, or (e) is designed seriously to interfere with or seriously to disrupt an electronic system.

87   Current Legal Problems Public Lecture, University College London, 3 March 2008.

The Terrorism Acts of 2000 and 2006 introduced and later amended the notion of proscription of terrorist organizations[88] and left the courts to decide what the term terrorism means.[89] In *R v. K* (2008),[90] the appellant appealed against a decision of the judge alleging offences under section 58 of the Terrorism Act 2000. K was charged with three counts of possessing material containing information 'likely to be useful to a person committing or preparing an act of terrorism'. The first count involved a copy of the Al Qaeda training manual; the second count related to a text about Jihad movements; the third count related to a text about the duty of a Muslim to work for an Islamic state. Whether such material is 'likely to be useful' is a matter for the jury, a jury whose mind and impressions of Islam and/or terrorism may have been fuelled by fear and prejudice. The Terrorism Act 2006 section 1(3) criminalizes glorification and statements that are likely to be understood, by members of the public, as indirectly encouraging the commission or preparation of acts of terrorism. Such offences include every statement which (a) glorifies the commission or preparation (whether in the past, in the future or generally) of such acts or offences; and (b) is a statement from which those members of the public could reasonably be expected to infer that what is being glorified is being glorified as conduct that should be emulated by them in existing circumstances. 'Glorification' includes any form of praise or celebration, and cognate expressions are to be construed accordingly'.[91] This is the context which drives the unveiling and undressing of Muslim women, not the desire to emancipate. It is this context that directs the observer's gaze and quest to control, and it is this context which erases the wearer's meaning and her agency.

Rising Tide of Hostility

Judge Tulkans in her dissenting judgment in the *Sahin*[92] case (below) (decided a few weeks before the House of Lords in *Begum* (below))[93] articulated the rising tide of hostility towards Muslims.

> I end by noting that all these issues must also be considered in the light of the observations set out in the annual activity report published in June 2005 of the European Commission against Racism and Intolerance (ECRI), which expresses concern about the climate of hostility existing against persons who are or are believed to be Muslim, and considers that the situation requires attention and action in the future. Above all, the message that needs to be repeated over and over again is that the best means of preventing and combating fanaticism and extremism is to uphold human rights.[94]

---

88   See section 21: Grounds of proscription. 'In section 3 of the Terrorism Act 2000 (c. 11) (proscription of organisations), after subsection (5) – (5A) The cases in which an organisation promotes or encourages terrorism for the purposes of subsection (5)(c) include any case in which activities of the organisation – (a) include the unlawful glorification of the commission or preparation (whether in the past, in the future or generally) of acts of terrorism.'

89   M Muller, 'Terrorism, proscription and the right to resist in an age of conflict', *Denning Law Journal* (2008), 113–31.

90   EWCA 185.

91   Terrorism Act 2006.

92   *Sahin v. Turkey* (2005) 41 EHRR 8.

93   *R (on the application of Begum (by her litigation friend, Rahman)) (Respondent) v. Headteacher and Governors of Denbigh High School (Appellants)* [2006] 2 All ER 487.

94   Per Tulkens *Sahin v. Turkey* (2005) 41 EHRR 8, at para. 20. See also Polly Toynbee. *The Independent*, 23 October 1997, who wrote: 'I am an Islamophobe, and proud of it.' Robert Kilroy Silk wrote in *The Daily*

The law has been coopted as a vehicle for controlling women's dress code on the grounds that its objective is to protect the liberty of Muslim women. Law feigns the objectives of freedom and equality that have been used and abused in a war on Islam. Throughout Western Europe this feigned desire to protect Muslim women has spread throughout, inter alia, France, Denmark and Holland, forcing a vulgarized version of very questionable sexual freedom on Muslim women. Women who do not regard pornography or G-strings as liberating (a group that includes this author) are women who are deemed to be in need of rescue and liberalization. The bigotry is barefaced, as the Dutch Government, for example, requires of those applying for citizenship a tolerance of homosexual kissing and nudity in public. In the same breath the Dutch Government proposes a ban on wearing burqas/face veils in public.[95] France follows suit and denies citizenship to Faiza Mabchour because her face veil was regarded as emblematic of a failure to integrate.[96] Faiza Mabchour is no outsider, however: she speaks French fluently, is married to a French citizen and is mother of three French citizens. Part of the reasoning was that she had 'adopted a radical practice of her religion, incompatible with the essential values of the French community, and particularly with the principle of sexual equality'.[97]

Two legal cases in the UK in the educational arena have brought the discussion of the jilbab (dress) and the niqab (face veil) into the public domain. Consider the case of *R (on the application of Begum) v. Head Teacher and Governors of Denbigh High School*,[98] in which an adolescent wanted to wear a long loose-fitting dress (a jilbab) to school in conformity with, as she saw it, the requirements of her religious faith. This case has been the subject of numerous legal[99] and academic commentaries[100] and feature articles[101] throughout its journey from the High Court to the House of Lords. In *Begum*, the House of Lords ruled upon the interpretation and application of Article 9 of the Human Rights Act 1998:

(1) Everyone has the right to freedom of thought, conscience and religion; this right includes freedom to change his religion or belief and freedom, either alone or in community with others and

---

Express, 25 February 1991; '... they (Muslims) are backward and evil, and if it is being racist to say so then I must be and happy and proud to be so'.

95   M Corder, Associated Press Writer, 8 February 2008.

96   *The Times*, 17 July 2008.

97   *The Star-Ledger* (Newark, New Jersey) 24 July 2008 .

98   *R (on the application of Begum (by her litigation friend, Rahman)) (Respondent) v. Headteacher and Governors of Denbigh High School (Appellants)* [2006] 2 All ER 487.

99   L Lundy, 'Family values in the classroom? Reconciling parental wishes and children's rights in state schools', *International Journal of Law Policy and Family*, 23 (2005), 331; A Blair (2005), 'Case Commentary: *R (SB) v. Head teacher and Governors of Denbigh High School* – human rights and religious dress in schools' CFLQ 17 3 (399); T Linden and T Hetherington, 'Schools and human rights: The Denbigh High School Case', *Education Law Journal*, 6/4 (2005), 229. See also G Davies (2005) 'Banning the Jilbab: Reflections on Restricting Religious Clothing in the Light of the Court of Appeal in *SB v. Denbigh High School*'. Decision of 2 March 2005 *European Constitutional Law Review* (EuConst), vol. 1 (3), 511.

100   I Ward, 'Shabina Begum and the headscarf girls', *Journal of Gender Studies*, 15/2 (2006), 119–31; E Tarlo, 'Reconsidering stereotypes: Anthropological reflections on the jilbab controversy', *Anthropology Today*, 21/6 (2005), 13–17; A Syed, 'Why here, why now? Young Muslim women wearing hijab', *Muslim World*, 95/4 (2005).

101   'A Victory for common sense' (2006) 4687 *Times Educational Supplement*, 4687 (2006), at 22; (AN 21030159) D Lepkowska, 'School wins jilbab battle', *Times Educational Supplement*, 4678 (2006), at 7; T Dalrymple, 'Wrong from head to toe', *National Review*, 57/5 (2005), at 30–34; I Ahmad, 'Islamic dress code', *Education Journal*, 82 (2005), at 19.

in public or private, to manifest his religion or belief, in worship, teaching, practice and observance. (2) Freedom to manifest one's religion or beliefs shall be subject only to such limitations as are prescribed by law and are necessary in a democratic society [...] for the protection of the rights and freedoms of others.

Ms Shabina Begum, a pupil at Denbigh High School, was not permitted to wear in school a specific variation of the school uniform, a long-sleeved, ankle-length, loose-fitting dress, known as a 'jilbab', in manifestation of her religious belief. The question for the courts was whether she had been denied her religious right. The House of Lords in a 3/2 majority (Lord Bingham of Cornhill, Lord Hoffmann, and Lord Scott of Foscote) held that there had been no interference with the right to hold a religious belief or the right to manifest belief. Baroness Hale of Richmond and Lord Nicholls dissenting held that there had been interference but that in interpretation of Article 9(2) such a limitation was justified to 'protect the rights of others'. The judges in deciding this case at every stage could not avoid the wider meanings, which predefined particular aspects of this case as they were played out on the public concourse of debate. The courts at each stage resisted any engagement with the wider public debate around Islam or fundamentalism:[102] 'I will avoid the use of the term.'[103] Islam was binarized by the court into 'very strict' and 'liberal' Muslims.[104] These impressions of Islam, and especially of Islamic fundamentalism, were advanced by Denbigh High School witnesses, each of whom regarded his or her school as a recruitment ground for Muslim extremism.[105] The jilbab was perceived by the school witnesses, a perception accepted and endorsed by the courts, as the standard-bearer of Islamic fundamentalism. Miss Begum was perceived as being, at the least, manipulated, if not, indeed, recruited by others.[106] This case unfolded in a particular situation where anti-Muslim feeling was strong, where malicious generalizations of Islam became accepted and considered justified following 9/11 and 7/7.[107] The judges were all agreed that interference was necessary for the protection of the rights of others at the school and, more specifically, protecting other young Muslim adolescent women from feeling pressurized into wearing the jilbab, not appearing to favour any one religion, preserving the multicultural mix of the school, and avoiding divisiveness.

All courts, High Court, Appeal Court and House of Lords imagined Islam through their silence about Islam, their ellipsis and their exaggerated misapprehension. The Court of Appeal avoided the use of the term 'fundamentalism', preferring instead the nomenclature of 'moderate' and 'very strong religious beliefs',[108] explaining:

---

102   [2005] 1WLR 3372, CA *Begum* 3390H.

103   See above.

104   See above 3380H – 3381A at para. 31.

105   *R (on the application of Begum) v. Headteacher and Governors of Denbigh High School* [2004] EWHC 1389 (Admin)QBD Begum para. 41 [15] [16], para. 82 [16].

106   Said, in his book *Orientalism*, says of such similar images 'lurking behind all of these images is the menace of the jihad', p. 287 above, n. 9.

107   As Jonathan Freedland wrote: 'The first three items on the radio news yesterday morning were the verdict in the Abu Hamza trial; the ongoing, and increasingly lethal, row about the Danish cartoons of Mohammed; and a new statement from the Palestinian Islamist movement, Hamas. One way or another, how the West encounters Islam is looking like the central challenge of the age' (*Evening Standard*, 9 February 2006).

108   Above, n. 101, CA Begum 3376A, para. 8.

For the purposes of this judgment, because the epithet "fundamentalist" has resonations which it would be inappropriate to carry into the discussion of the issues in this difficult case, I will refer to those Muslims who believe that it is mandatory for women to wear the jilbab as "very strict Muslims", and those Muslims who consider it inappropriate dress for a woman as "liberal Muslims", while being conscious that experts might find these epithets equally inappropriate.[109]

Ms Begum said of the case and the context:

> As a young woman growing up in a post-9/11 Britain, I have witnessed a great deal of bigotry from the media, politicians, and legal officials [...]. This bigotry resulted from my choice to wear a piece of cloth, not out of coercion, but out of my faith and belief in Islam. It is amazing that in the so-called free world I have to fight to wear this attire.[110]

As Shabina Begum herself recognized and articulated in interviews with the media, her case was set against a landscape in which Islam was 'a target for vilification in the name of the War on Terror'.[111]

The Begum case was followed by the case of *R (on the application of X) v. The Headteacher of Y School and another.*[112] Miss X, a 12-year-old Muslim girl, attended a selective all girls' grammar school. At the start of her second year she wore the niqab (veil) when male teachers were present. The first defendant headteacher told X that the wearing of the veil contravened school uniform policy, and that if she continued to wear it she would be excluded. X contended that she wore the veil for religious reasons. Meetings to resolve the matter were not successful, and the parents of X removed her from the school. Another girls' school with similar academic standing, which permitted the veil, had offered her a place, but she wanted to stay at the original school. Her father wrote to the governors explaining that her older siblings, who had completed their education at the same school, had been allowed to wear the veil. The governors said that it would not become involved in a decision about school uniform. X, by her father as her litigation friend, applied for judicial review. Counsel on Miss X's behalf submitted that the headteacher and governors had acted unlawfully in refusing X to wear the niqab (veil) at school, that the refusal breached X's rights under art. 9 of the ECHR, that she had a 'legitimate expectation' that she would be permitted to wear the niqab (veil), since her sisters had done so, and that there had been no proportionate or objective justification for the school's change of policy so as to frustrate that expectation. It also submitted that X had been in a 'similar position' to that of her siblings who had previously attended, and, given that it was axiomatic to rational decision making for 'like cases to be treated alike', unless some good reason dictated otherwise, since no good reason had been provided for the school's change of policy, X should have been entitled to wear the veil. The application was dismissed. The court ruled on these three questions in this way. First, although Article 9 of the Convention had been engaged, the school had not interfered with X's Article 9 rights. Even if X's Article 9 rights had been interfered with, any interference would have been justified under Article 9(2) of the Convention. Second, the claim based on 'legitimate expectation' could not be sustained and would fail, given that there had not been a 'practice', let alone any 'regular practice'. Third, the school was pursuing legitimate aims, which were in the public interest, and a proportionate response, which could not be criticized.

---

109 CA Begum 3380G, para. 31. See also above, n. 101.
110 *The Times*, 3 March 2005.
111 *The Independent*, 3 March 2005.
112 [2007] EWHC 298 (Admin) [2007] All ER (D) 267 (Feb) (approved judgment).

Breaking Muslim Women, Erasing Identity

Global intolerance in the name of global understanding, and secular fundamentalism in the name of freedom, together with feminist fundamentalism in the name of gender equality, now wage their wars on minority women, both in the UK and also elsewhere. In Switzerland, for example, the case of *Dahlab v. Switzerland* (1996)[113] upheld the prohibition imposed on teachers preventing them from working if they refused to remove the hijab, and can be seen as another attempt to unveil women on the grounds of 'protecting pupils by preserving religious harmony'. In *Dahlab*, as McGoldrick points out, the real truth was that the hijab was perceived as a 'powerful external symbol'.[114] In Turkey, which is 99 per cent Muslim, there is also a ban on the hijab in schools and in higher educational establishments. In 1934 the Dress Regulations Act imposed a ban on the wearing of religious attire, and in the case of *Karaduman v. Turkey* (1993), where a university student who had completed her degree was refused her certificate because, in the photograph she submitted of herself, she was wearing a headscarf,[115] this refusal was upheld by the court on the grounds that she had failed to comply with university regulations. The court held that such a prohibition did not constitute an interference with her freedom of religion. Similarly, in *Sahin v. Turkey* (2005),[116] the court ruled that a university student should not be permitted to wear the headscarf to attend university lectures.[117]

These attacks on women, as the West becomes increasingly obsessed with dress styles, are difficult to sustain and, since dress codes contain a multiplicity of meanings that are not all Islamic, indefensible. Ethnic minority women have always been the primary target, since they are seen as crossing the line in defiance and turning the tables. It is, thus, increasingly difficult to justify the attitude to women's dress as being founded on reason. However, not all religious dress code cases have followed suit. In the case of *R (on the application of Watkins-Singh) v. Governing Body of Aberdare Girls' High School*,[118] a young school girl, Sarika Watkins-Singh, has been allowed to wear a kara, which is a bracelet worn by those of the Sikh faith. Mr Justice Silber in this case ruled in her favour for the following reasons:

> The first is the honest belief of the claimant, justified by objective evidence that the wearing of the article is of exceptional importance to her for racial or religious reasons. The second factor is the unobtrusive nature of the Kara being 50 mm wide and made of plain steel. The fear of the school that permitting the claimant to return to school wearing her Kara will lead to an end of its uniform policy with many other girls wearing items to show their nationality or political or religious beliefs is totally unjustified.[119]

But the Watkins-Singh decision flies in the face of public opinion and the public face of intolerance remains fixed and resolute in its condemnation of Islamic dress, together with a voracious anti-Muslim-women tide washing over Western Europe and on to its shores and into its estuaries, a tide that cannot be held back. There is no desire to liberate here, only a determination to control

---

113   *Dahlab v. Switzerland* (Application no. 42393/98), ECHR 2001-V.

114   See, above, at 131.

115   See, above, at 137.

116   *Leyla Sahin v. Turkey* (Application no. 44774/98), Judgment of 29.6.2004 EHRR 8 [2004]; 10 BHRC 590 [2006] ELR 73.

117   See, above, at 140.

118   [2008] EWHC 1865 (Admin) Queen's Bench Division, Administrative Court.

119   See, above, para. 162.

and break, and thereby destroy. Muslim women are being deliberately defaced in a new form of state-sponsored violence. Fanon, in *Racism and Culture*, reminds us of the colonial imperative, a colonial imperative that is being resuscitated:

> We witness the destruction of culture, values, ways of life. As language, dress, and techniques are devalorized [...]. We witness the setting up of archaic, inert institutions, functioning under the oppressor's supervision [...]. These bodies appear to embody respect for the tradition, the cultural specificities, and the personality of the subjugated people. This pseudo-respect, in fact, is tantamount to the most utter contempt [...].[120]

> Rediscovering tradition, living it as a fence mechanism, as a symbol of purity, of salvation, the decultured individual leaves the impression that the mediation takes vengeance by substantializing itself [...].[121]

---

120   F Fanon, 'Racism and culture', in *The Fanon Reader*, see, above, n. 44, at 20–21.
121   Ibid., at 28.

Chapter 8

Beyond the Sacred and Secular:
Muslim Women, the Law and the Delivery of Justice

Samia Bano

The veiled woman troubles feminism and secularism in much the same way. Both feminism and secularism face a problem of finding a consistent position that respects individual autonomy, and simultaneously sustains a conception of politics freed from heteronomous determination. (Stewart Motha)[1]

The Muslim woman has not been waiting in pained silence for the law to liberate her. (Olivier Roy)[2]

Introduction

The question of Muslim integration into Western European societies remains at the forefront of current social and political analyses. At the heart of these debates lie questions over the limits of multiculturalism and a rights discourse that seeks to reconcile the integration of minority ethnic communities into mainstream liberal societies with the values of democratic citizenship, belonging and nation building. It has also become increasingly apparent that the place of religion and religious practice in civic society raises fundamental conflicts-type questions regarding the rise of a specific form of Muslim religiosity and subsequent state response. Underlying this discourse is the problematic that liberal feminist scholars have been grappling with for the past two decades, namely the Susan Okin inspired debate over the perceived polarity of equality versus difference,[3] and the conflicts generated by demands for cultural and religious recognition and the effects upon minority women.

Increasingly the role of law has also become critical to understanding how groups and communities demonstrate both their commitment and loyalty to the state, to universal principles of rights, justice and equality and to the limits of cultural and religious recognition. In the UK the legal sphere is the site upon which commitment to Britishness and citizenship is presented and where debates on whether it is possible to reconcile Islam with Western secular values are increasingly discussed. In this chapter I argue that recent claims for cultural uniformity, constructions of the 'secular' and secularism, and constructions of 'common citizenship' and 'equality before the law' must be understood in relation to the complex lived realities that Muslim identity entails. Drawing upon the work of a number of scholars,[4] I hope to locate this cultural and religious lived experience

---

1 S Motha, 'Veiled women and the affect of religion in democracy', *Journal of Law and Society*, 34/1 (2007), 138–61, at 140.

2 O Roy, *Globalised Islam: The Search for a New Umma* (Cambridge: Cambridge University Press, 2004), at 6.

3 SM Okin, 'Is multiculturalism bad for women?', *Boston Review*, 22 (1999), 25–28.

4 T Asad, *Formations of the Secular: Christianity, Islam, Modernity* (Stanford, CA: Stanford University Press, 2003); S Mahmood, *Politics of Piety: The Islamic Revival and the Feminist Subject* (Princeton, NJ: Princeton University Press, 2006).

within the wider socio-historical process of migration, belonging and settlement, and unpack the current discourses of demands for cultural and religious rights as part of a broader system of meaning and lived experience.

The place of Islam in Europe continues to be subject to enormous social and political commentary. In particular the visible presence of Muslims in public is deemed so problematic that political initiatives have begun to limit this presence. In November 2009 a new crisis erupted when an estimated 57.5 per cent of Swiss voters voted in favour of a ban on building minarets in Switzerland.[5] This result was all the more remarkable for the facts that Switzerland currently has only four minarets and that Swiss Muslims are described as being extremely well integrated into Swiss society. Although this result itself produced wide-spread condemnation both from religious and secular authorities (including the Vatican and various human rights organizations) it also reflects the continuing and strained relationship in Western European societies over the management of ethnic diversity and the regulation of religious communities. In France the issue of veiling and, in particular, the extent to which full face veiling transcends French values of republicanism and sexual equality currently dominate political discussion. On Tuesday 13th July the Lower House of the French Parliament approved a ban which would make it illegal for women to cover the full veil in public. The measure now goes to the senate in September 2010.[6] In Britain the place of Islam in British society continues to be debated in the contexts of free speech, education, employment rights and the accommodation of Sharia law into English law. On 16 January 2010 *The Times* newspaper reported that the UK Independence Party is to call for a ban on the burka and niqab, claiming that they are an affront to British values.[7] In February 2008 the controversy surrounding the comments made by the Archbishop of Canterbury, Dr Rowan Williams, on civil and religious law in England continue to reflect the current consensus among many Western commentators that Islam and Islamic religious practice can serve to undermine the principles upon which liberal democracy and liberal legality are based.[8] During this episode, for example, Western liberal commentators were quick to point to the adverse consequences of demands made by Muslims regarding the introduction of parallel legal systems into English law. It was, for example, claimed that the consequences of this 'imposed Islamism' threatened not only the social and legal foundations of liberal legality, but also the very Enlightenment values (including democracy, reason, equality, autonomy and individual choice) upon which Western democratic societies are built. Underlying this argument was also the claim that Islamic law is unreasonable and patriarchal, whereas Western law is both secular and egalitarian. The debate became closely associated with an agenda of law reform to accommodate the needs of Muslims in the UK but which also relied somewhat heavily upon a fixed and determinate vision of Muslim identity that was itself reproduced in extensive public and mainstream discussion. Needless to say this debate was devoid of Muslim 'voice' and 'agency', with little if any discussion on whether British Muslims themselves were in favour of such developments. And it is important to remember that there are many complex and deeply entrenched cultural, religious and philosophical assumptions about Islam and Muslims that are both reinforced and mediated via different social relations.

5   See, 'Swiss voters back ban on minarets', *BBC News*, Sunday 29 November 2009. A copy of this report can be accessed at <www.news.bbc/minarets>.

6   'Why must I cast off the Veil?', *The Telegraph*, 17 July 2010. A copy of this article can be accessed at <www.telegraph.co.uk>.

7   See 'UKIP woos white working lass with call for total ban on burkas', *The Times*, 16 January 2010. A copy of this article can be accessed at <timesonline.co.uk/news/politics>.

8   A speech made to the Royal Courts of Justice in February 2007. A copy of this speech can be accessed at <www.archbishopofcanterbury.org/1580>.

Unsurprisingly such debates on the place of Islam in Western European societies are often expressed via the site of gender and gender relations and the 'subordinating' effect Islam is perceived to have upon Muslim women. Western women are often presented as 'enlightened' and the bearers of liberal legal ideals such as equality and non-discrimination; and the Muslim female subject is presented as the 'other', a victim to cultural and religious practices in violation of her human rights. Law thus becomes the site upon which constructions of Muslims as the 'other' take shape, where internal traditions of dissent within Islam are sidelined and deemed anathema to Western intellectual thought and reason. This is why, at present, the dominant view of Islamic legal tradition and human rights is presented as incompatible, in opposition and at best producing an uneasy tension with Western liberal values of human rights.[9] Indeed, the very idea of Islam embodying the universalism of human rights, justice and equality as discussed in mainstream multicultural and political theory seems at odds with its presentation as a culturally relativist ideology that emphasizes the impossibility of individual free will, consent and reason. I suggest that the current totalizing of Islam is not only dangerous in its explicit Islamophobic tone but that the relationships between religious legal practice and the rights discourse surrounding faith, freedom, democracy and equality are a lot more complex than the integrated/separated trajectories currently presented.

The implications of presenting Islam as a unified monolithic entity are not only intellectually problematic but raise the question of what we understand as truth and authority in law (and Islam). What I mean is that if there appears to be little space for genuine political and cultural contestation and exchange in the forming and reforming of a community then we are left with the dichotomies of modern versus traditional, West versus non-West, liberal and secular versus undemocratic and religious, which do not reflect the complexity that identity and religious identity within minority diasporic communities entail. Yet the 'problem of Islam' in Europe brings to the fore the classic liberal dilemma of individual choice versus community autonomy. Demands made by Muslim communities for the right to self-regulation in matters of family law and increased visual symbolization of Muslim dress and attire in the public space mean that such discussions often revolve around conflicts generated by liberal conceptions of community and community claims-making, with the Muslim community of believers (Umma) in turn raising questions on the extent to which Muslims are *truly* loyal to the state.

The current discourses on the clash of secularism versus the rise of religiosity among Muslims and the perceived social conservatism among Muslims fit in neatly with a specific understanding of multiculturalism and constructions of belonging and 'otherness'. One way of better understanding the relationship between identity and group rights is to draw upon feminist scholarship, which in turn draws upon the notions of agency, *habitus* and subjectivity to better understand the relationship between identity, religious practice, authority and belonging. However, and just as importantly, this scholarship analyses how the rights discourse frames tolerance as espoused in policies of multiculturalism in particular anti-discrimination legislation. It raises the key question of how we deal with sections of the community who wish to use such legislation for protection when they may not embrace notions of justice, equality before the law and citizenship.[10]

---

9   This is not of course to underestimate the wealth of literature challenging such interpretations. See, for example, S Ali, *Gender and Human Rights in Islam and International Law: Equal Before Allah, Unequal Before Man?* (The Hague: Kluwer Law International, 2000).

10   See, for example, Davina Cooper, *Challenging Diversity: Rethinking Equality and the Value of Difference* (Cambridge: Cambridge University Press, 2004) and Iris Young, *Justice and the Politics of Difference* (Princeton, NJ: Princeton University Press, 1990).

The Rise of Muslim Religiosity in the West?

There are a number of studies arguing that the modern rise of Muslim religiosity in Western European societies is both a product of and a reaction to Westernization. The French sociologist Olivier Roy, for example, describes the current religiosity within Muslim populations as a new form of Islamic religiosity, which he maintains has parallels with similar quests for new forms of spirituality in the secular environments of the West. 'Islam', he writes, 'cannot escape the New Age of religion or choose the form of its own modernity'.[11] In this way new forms of Muslim religiosity cannot be understood with reference to the traditional portrayal of Islam as bounded, fixed with immutable categories of belonging in the distant past. Roy also insists that the continual portrayal of Islam as a single culture serves an important purpose to preserve the mythical notion of Western civilization and progress. If Muslim populations are expressing new forms of religiosity then the contexts in which they are doing so need to be better understood and explained. Various judicial and legislative decrees in Western Europe, prominently among them the French law banning Islamic headscarves, are examples of this objectification.

So what is the relationship between Islam and civil society? This is a complex question but many commentators draw upon Gellner and Huntington,[12] the two key proponents of the 'clash of civilizations' discourse who argue quite simply that Islam is a dangerous ideology that undermines both liberal democracy and civil society. Yet civil society is just as much a contested terrain as that which is understood as Islam.[13] Turam points out that:

> Islam's role in either propelling or undermining civil society is largely assumed to occur through a struggle with the secular state. While some of these accounts have been normative rather than descriptive, the post-September 11 climate has reinforced the predominant assumptions of clash, hostility and distrust as essential qualities of the Islamic revival.[14]

This raises the question of the extent to which Islam and Islamic practice in the West can be understood as part of the social, political and civic process in Western liberal societies. In Britain, for example, the greater visibility of religious symbols in the public space has led to a sustained argument that we are witnessing a rise in religiosity. Unsurprisingly, perhaps, the focus has been largely on Muslim communities and their demands to practise their faith in the public sphere, which may conflict with British norms, values and customs. Debate on Islam in the West is also closely linked to questions of immigration, loss of cultural identity for majority societies and constructions of Muslims as the 'other' and contemporary discussion focuses on the idea that Islam is incompatible with modernity. In this way, as Savage points out, the increasing Muslim presence in Europe has reopened debates on several issues: the place of religion in public life, social tolerance in Europe, secularism as the only path open to modernity, and Europe's very identity.[15] One of the ways European countries respond to this 'Muslim factor' is by effectively nationalizing, if not secularizing Islam. Savage adds: 'These governments are trying to foster nationally oriented Islam

---

11   Roy, above, n. 2, at 15.

12   S Huntington, *The Clash of Civilizations and the Remaking of World Order* (New York: Simon and Schuster, 1996).

13   B Bryant, *Nationalism and Orientalism* (New York:, Greenwich Press, 1993).

14   B Turam, 'The politics of engagement between Islam and the secular state: Ambivalences of "civil society"', *The British Journal of Sociology*, 55/2 (2004), 259–81, at 242.

15   TM Savage, 'Europe and Islam: Crescent waxing, cultures clashing', *Washington Quarterly*, 27 (2004), 25–50.

as subordinate to the state as well as to European norms stretching back to the Treaty of Westphalia, the Enlightenment, and Napoleonic rule.'[16]

The nature of Muslim settlement in Western Europe is both diverse and complex. In his work, Saeed outlines four types of Muslim settlement: isolationist, semi-isolationist, non-ideological isolationist and participant.[17] Within each category there are multiple identifications of what it means to be a Muslim. For example, he describes the participant Muslims as

> [...] dealing with areas such as rethinking Islam; Muslim identity, Islamic norms and values in the [W]estern context, itjihad and the re-interpretation of key Islamic texts, citizenship, functioning in a secular environment, and what it means to be both [W]estern and Muslim. Their familiarity with the institutions culture, values, norms and history of the [W]estern country they find themselves in makes them an important intermediary between Muslims and non-Muslim mainstream [W]estern society. They are not necessarily attached to particular theologians, religious leaders or foreign imams. They do not want to be affiliated with a particular transnational movement or legal or theological school.[18]

This analysis of the participant Muslim living in the West describes a form of privatization of religion and the increasing secularization of Muslims. The idea of an emergence of a European Muslim identity has been developed by the Muslim scholar Tariq Ramadan.[19] He puts forward the questions of dual identity, dual language and the reformation and reformulation of Islam in the West in order to provide 'Western Muslims' with a coherent set of tools to live as believers in non-Muslim societies.

Religious Difference and Muslim Women's Agency

Over the past three decades feminist theorists have grappled with the question of how to reconcile Western interpretations of sexual equality and the autonomy of women's agency with cultural and religious difference.[20] Debates have been largely focused on a clash of values scenario, where liberal notions of equality, free will and free choice have been deemed 'progressively modern' and open to all, whereas the continued adherence of women belonging to minority communities with religious and traditional ties is presented as illiberal, backward and a barrier to the enhancement of women's rights. Yet feminist writing also provides a clearer conceptual understanding of the relations of multiple identities and multiple forms of inequality.[21] For Nancy Fraser the issue raises a number of key questions: '[W]hich identity claims are rooted in the defense of social relations of inequality and domination? And which are rooted in a challenge to such relations? [...] Which differences [...] should a democratic society seek to foster, and which, on the contrary should it aim

---

16   Ibid., at 32.

17   A Saeed, 'Muslims in the West and their attitudes to full participation in western societies: Some reflections', in G Levey and T Modood (eds), *Secularism, Religion and Multicultural Citizenship* (Cambridge: Cambridge University Press, 2009), at 200–15.

18   Ibid., at 206.

19   T Ramadan, *Western Muslim and the Future of Islam* (Oxford: Oxford University Press, 2004).

20   The concept of agency is often understood in relation to concepts of the individual, the person and the self. This chapter will not engage in these discussions.

21   D Cooper, *Challenging Diversity: Rethinking Equality and the Value of Difference* (Cambridge: Cambridge University Press, 2004), at 41.

to abolish?'[22] Thus, for many feminist theorists claims of cultural and religious difference – part of a pluralist model of power that affords minority groups limited yet significant autonomy – can be recognized only if they do not involve the oppression and subordination of women. A particular cause for concern for liberal feminists has been whether the practice of personal laws within the family context leads to the unequal treatment of women within these communities.[23] It has led to interesting scholarly debates regarding the question of female oppression and personal agency. The influential scholar Iris Young, in her book *Justice and the Politics of Difference*, provides five criteria of oppression: exploitation, marginalization, powerlessness, cultural imperialism and violence.[24] She draws upon the category of 'woman' as the social constituency in which to understand how the different dimensions of oppression may affect different groups of women and this can be better understood in relation to other groups such as the elderly or gay and lesbian groups. In contrast, Nancy Fraser approaches oppression as a process whereby social collectivities operate along a spectrum from injustices of distribution to those of recognition. In this way Fraser links particular social relations to distinct societal structures (economic and cultural) on the one hand and forms of redress (recognition and redistribution) on the other.

For many feminist legal scholars the focus has been on the question of equality and on the need to provide a critique of the ways in which legal regulations construct, and respond to, intersecting orders of inequality.[25] This approach draws upon the work of Catherine MacKinnon,[26] namely that the law tends to reflect masculine values: many of the values around which the law is built, including its assumption of an individualistic 'reasonable' person are those used and valued by men. Scholars such as Patricia Williams[27] and Kimberley Crenshaw[28] draw upon intersecting identities (in this case race, class and gender) to illustrate how the law and legal relations fail to grasp the complexities of black women's lives. For example, juridical liberalism expressed via legislation such as anti-discrimination legislation remains inadequate in understanding the position of minority ethnic women who may be situated in multiple social locations. As such these laws simply fail effectively to redress the claims of discrimination.

More recently feminist legal scholarship has identified and critiqued the hierarchical positions of power that many Western feminists occupy in equality debates. For example, Gayatri Spivak[29] and Mohanty[30] have challenged the representations about non-Western women made by both liberal inclusionist and structural bias approaches to women's human rights. As Engle points out, there is an urgent need to attend to cultural and religious differences and to see similar types of

----

22   N Fraser, *Unruly Discourses: Power, Discourse and Gender in Contemporary Social Theory* (Cambridge: Cambridge, Polity Press, 1989), at 65.

23   Thus, more recently, ideas of gender equality, justice and the limits of liberal multiculturalism have emerged from within the discipline(s) of political theory, ethics and philosophy and have been couched within the context of tensions between feminism and multiculturalism.

24   I Young, *Justice and the Politics of Difference* (Princeton, NJ: Princeton University Press, 1990), at 64.

25   Cooper, above, n. 17, at 45.

26   C MacKinnon, *Feminism Unmodified* (Cambridge, MA: Harvard University Press, 1987).

27   P Williams, 'On being the object of property', *Signs*, 14 (1988), 5.

28   K Crenshaw, 'Demarginalizing the intersection of race and sex: A black feminist critique of antidiscrimination doctrine, feminist theory and antiracist politics', *University of Chicago Legal Forum* (1989), 139.

29   G Spivak, *The Postcolonial Critic: Interviews, Strategies, Dialogues* (New York: Routledge, 1990).

30   C Mohanty *Feminist Genealogies, Colonial Legacies, Democratic Futures* (New York: Routledge, 1997).

oppression in both majority and minority communities.[31] In addition to questioning First World feminist understandings of culture and religion, such critics also challenge the structural bias, with its focus on culture, as the principal site of women's oppression. As Obiora puts it, '[t]he truth of the matter is that, despite popular feminist discourses, culture may not be the dispositive influence on the responses of women'.[32]

So how does such scholarship help us to better understand the question of religious difference and the expression of Muslim women's agency and choice as members of religious communities in the UK? Feminist analysis of the public and private divisions offers important insights into the feminist goals of autonomy, equality and women's capacity for decision making. Feminist interpretations of autonomy encourage women to make personal choices that include the autonomy of being and the right to go against what is considered as the norm. This raises a number of important questions relating to how we understand autonomy, choice and agency and whether ultimately autonomy and equality can ever be reconciled. As Charusheela questions: 'Can we conceive of worlds in which women act differently from men, attain different outcomes based on criteria we do not ourselves agree with, and yet do so as autonomous choosing beings expressing a desired identity for themselves?'[33] She goes on to list a number of questions that lie at the heart of current feminist debates:

> [W]hat do we do when women in a foreign culture assert as a choice actions or behaviours that do not lead to equality? What do we do when women in asserting their right to autonomy of cultural identity and national self-determination do not attack a social construction of gender we deem patriarchal, nor seek to replace it with notions of human autonomy or choice that we consider marks of female emancipation?[34]

Many have focused on the issue of internalized oppression – the barriers, boundaries and divisions that suggest that such women are part of a pattern of social coercion versus false consciousness, as they are unable fully to understand what is truly in their best interests. Understood in this way many women are simply unable fully to exercise their choice and autonomy. Women's apparent consent to marriage in the face of coercive social, cultural and structural forces has often been broadly interpreted as acquiescence to patriarchal authority, whereas agency is equated with women's declared resistance, often through the strategy of exit.[35] Others have argued that the very idea of choice in the context of more overarching systems and networks of power and domination is problematic.[36] Inter-generational changes among British Asian communities in the UK have also been interpreted as evidence of the rational exercise of agency by young British Asian women through strategic manoeuvres, and through compromise and negotiation within structural

---

31   SE Merry, *Human Rights and Gender Violence: Translating International Law into Local Justice* (Chicago, IL: Chicago University Press, 2006), at 61.

32   CO Obiora, 'Legitimate governance in Africa: International and Domestic Legal Perspectives', in SE Merry, *Human Rights and Gender Violence: Translating International Law into Local Justice* (Chicago, IL: University of Chicago Press, 2006), at 60.

33   S Charushleea and Eiman Zein-Elabdin (eds), *Postcolonialism Meets Economics* (London: Routledge, 2004), at 197.

34   Charushleea, ibid., at 197.

35   V Goddard (ed.), *Gender, Agency and Change: Anthropological Perspectives* (New York: Routledge, 2000), at 3.

36   A Wilson, *Dreams, Questions, Struggles: South Asian Women in Britain* (London: Pluto Press, 2006).

constraints.[37] As we can see from the brief discussion above, feminist engagements with issues of choice and definitions of agency can be underpinned by broad and sometimes false distinctions. The scepticism of either/or choices of belonging to families and communities is now well documented and for the past two decades feminist theorists have been grappling with the criticism that their analyses of women's oppression are ethnocentrically universalist. As Anne Phillips points out, while there is broad agreement in principle that ethnocentric universalism is to be avoided, there is also much disagreement about how this can be achieved without falling into debates on cultural relativism.[38]

The Right to Veil Debates

Contemporary discussions on the right to veil go to the heart of current feminist concerns on whether veiling acts as a *constraint* that limits the choice of Muslim women. The discussions on the veil and veiling in the UK do focus on the autonomy of Muslim girls and women *freely* to veil themselves; and thus such discussions embrace ideas that Muslim women have little choice but to veil and therefore displace any notions of autonomy and decision making in the process of choosing to veil.[39] For Barlas, the veil 'has become so overinvested with meaning that one can no longer speak of it in any simple way'; in Western societies it has become a 'Muslim cultural icon'.[40] In 2006 Jack Straw expressed his discomfort at meeting with Muslim female constituents who wear the veil (with their face covered), and stated that he was in the habit of asking women to remove their veil in his office. He further stated that women should not wear veils that cover their face. Characterizing the veil as 'a visible statement of separation and of difference', he said that, above all, his discomfort lay in the fact that the veil, in his view, prevented him from having a truly 'face-to-face' encounter with his constituent.[41] Drawing upon this example and the Government Green Paper entitled 'The Governance of Britain', published in July 2007, Bhandar points out that Jack Straw's comments reflect anxiety about the issue of social cohesion and the perceived need for common British values.[42] So on what basis has this specific form of clothing become a symbol for constraint and disempowerment of Muslim women. As Charusheela quite rightly points out:

> Unless one decides that all social markers of gender-difference are always and everywhere constraints, there is no intrinsic aspect of the veil that can make us decide to locate it as constraint while we leave out stockings and skirts and all other markers of female-male difference in apparel norms in other societies.[43]

---

37 Y Samad and J Eade, *Community Perceptions of Forced Marriage* (London: Foreign and Commonwealth Office, 2002).

38 A Philips, *Multiculturalism without Culture* (Princeton, NJ: Princeton University Press, 2007).

39 B Bhandar, 'The ties that bind: Multiculturalism and secularism reconsidered', *Journal of Law and Society*, 36/2 (2009).

40 A Barlas, *Believing Women in Islam: Unreading Patriarchal Interpretations of the Qur'an* (Austin, TX: University of Texas Press, 2006), at 57.

41 He first made the comments in his weekly column in a newspaper in his Blackburn constituency, which was followed by radio interviews in which he reiterated his comments <http://news.bbc.co.uk/1/hi/uk_politics/5413470.stm>.

42 Bhandar, ibid.

43 Charusheela, ibid., at 201.

Thus not all Muslim women seek to exercise their agency as understood by Western feminists in order to enhance Western feminist interpretations of their autonomy. Within the context of a patriarchal system, women will often act to uphold gendered norms, such as beauty culture, or adopt disciplinary bodily technologies like elective cosmetic surgery.[44] Most feminist celebrations of women's agency are in service of the politics of emancipation, and such accounts interpret women's lack of autonomous impulses as acquiescence to patriarchal power structures, and see women's desires as informed by 'oppressive norms of femininity'.[45] Waggoner discusses the question of ethics in discussions of agency and draws upon the notion of 'ethical embodiment'. He explains:

> The idea it preserves is that a strong model of agency (as radically autonomous) is a fiction, since subjects are always formed and shaped by conditions not of their making, but there is nonetheless more to subjectivity than those conditions and their effects alone. Causal conditions are capable of giving rise to undetermined moments of self-reflection, self-interrogation, openness to the unforeseeable [...].[46]

One argument that does not conceptualize agency as oppositional has been discussed extensively in Mahmood's account of women's piety movement in the mosques of Cairo, which uncouples agency from liberatory politics.[47] Thus the complexity of women's actions in different contexts can be understood in multiple ways. Wendall points to the role of structural inequalities while retaining a strong sense of respect for women's agency and responsibility to act within the constraints and possibilities presented by their context.[48] That this agency, which has been defined as 'the socio-culturally mediated capacity to act',[49] can emerge in particular situations and places and at particular times has been noted in research examining the impact of education, employment, class and the perception and reality of racism on women's marriage choices.[50] However, there has been far less exploration of how personal histories, emotions, motivations and institutional arrangements, as well as practical concerns such as access to information and perceived access to services, all have a bearing on women's agency and the language they use to talk about it.

More recently, in Britain, there have been two high-profile cases that seem best to illustrate this conflict between Islamic religious practice and public space, both involving Islamic dress code for Muslim women and the use of the Human Rights Act 1998. In *Begum v. Denbigh High School Governors*,[51] the House of Lords ruled that the exclusion of Sabina Begum for her unwillingness to comply with school uniform requirements was not in violation of Article 9 of the Human Rights

---

44   K Frank, 'Agency', *Anthropological Theory*, 6/3 (2006), 281–302.

45   K Morgan, 'Women and the knife: Cosmetic surgery and the colonization of women's bodies', *Hypatia*, 6/3 (1991), 25–53; N Wolf, *The Beauty Myth: How Images of Beauty are Used against Women* (New York: Doubleday, 1991).

46   M Waggoner, 'Irony, Embodiment and the critical attitude: Engaging Saba Mahmood's critique of secular' in (2005) *Culture and Religion*.

47   See Mahmood, above, n 4.

48   S Wendell, 'Oppression and victimization: Choice and responsibility', *Hypatia*, 5/3 (1990), 15–46; C Chetkovich, 'Women's agency in a context of oppression: Assessing strategies for personal action and public policy', *Hypatia*, 19/4 (2004), 12–141.

49   L Ahearn, 'Language and agency', *Annual Review of Anthropology*, 30 (2001), 109–37, at 112.

50   For example, A Bredal, 'Arranged marriages as a multicultural battlefield', in M Andersson, Y Lithman and O Sernhede (eds), *Youth, Otherness and the Plural City: Modes of Belonging and Social Life* (Gothenburg: Daidalos, 2005).

51   1 A C 100 (2006) UKHL 15HL.

Act 1998. *In R (on the Application of Begum) v. Head Teacher and Governors of Denbigh High School*[52] (hereinafter '*Begum*'), the claimant Shabina Begum, a young Muslim woman, sought the right to wear a jilbab as part of her school uniform. Her insistence on wearing the jilbab meant that she contravened official school policy and was excluded from her local school, Denbigh High. She claimed that the school was in breach of Article 9 of the ECHR: the right to freedom of thought, conscience and religion. She challenged the decision of her school and the majority judgment found that her right had not been infringed, on the basis that in the interests of social cohesion, the school had legitimately infringed her right to wear the jilbab. Relying on the Grand Chamber of the Strasbourg Court's judgment in *Sahin v. Turkey* (2005) 19 BHRC 590, the majority recognized:

> [T]he need in some situations to restrict freedom to manifest religious belief; the value of religious harmony and tolerance between opposing or competing groups and of pluralism and broadmindedness; the need for compromise and balance; the role of the state in deciding what is necessary to protect the rights and freedoms of others; the variation of practice and tradition among member states; and the permissibility in some contexts of restricting the wearing of religious dress. (*Begum*, paragraph 32)

The *Azmi v. Kirklees* (2007) case involved a Muslim woman who worked as a school teaching assistant and refused to follow an instruction not to wear a full-face veil when assisting a male teacher in class. She was suspended and brought claims for direct and indirect religious discrimination and harassment on the ground of religion or belief. Again the appeal was dismissed, as the tribunal found no indirect discrimination and that the local council's ways of achieving its aim was proportionate.

These cases have led to increased discussions on questions of Islam, identity, belonging and citizenship in multicultural societies. Western commentators and legal scholars now discuss at length the limits of religious practice and belief and many query the need to accommodate and respect cultural and religious diversity in Western societies. For some the politics of multiculturalism and the recognition of cultural difference has led to rise in a politics of cultural separatism; but for others the liberal principles of justice, equality and human rights justify the protection of all cultural and religious minority communities. As Bhandar points out:

> The contestations over the rights of girls and women to wear (various forms of) the veil has been articulated in a discourse of rights, recognition and plurality in the UK context. While the juridification of the conflicts in the cases of Shabina Begum and Aisha Azmi necessarily meant the framing of a range of issues in the language of rights, the broader discussions, such as those mentioned above, as well as subsequent discussions about Britishness and British values ha[ve] for the most part remained within the realm of legal rights, social policy, and the political ethos attached to a desire to establish a particular nationalist vision. In other words, the contestation over the *appropriateness* and *permissibility* of girls and women to engage with certain types of veiling has been situated in the juridical-political sphere of individual legal rights, multiculturalism and national identity.[53]

In these cases there is an explicit desire to protect social harmony and pluralism from religious extremism, which the jilbab and niqab have come to represent in the social imaginary. Culture,

---

52   [2006] 2 All ER 487.
53   Bhandar, ibid.

race and religion are all at play here, but the UK is seen as a defender of difference for those 'reasonable' Muslims who fit within the limits of British tolerance.

The Sharia Debate in Britain

In Britain the controversy surrounding the comments made by the Archbishop of Canterbury on civil and religious law in England reflects the current consensus among many Western commentators that Islam and its legal principles (sharia) threaten the very foundations upon which Western democratic societies are built. Liberal commentators were quick, for example, to point to the consequences of demands made by Muslims for the introduction of parallel legal systems into English law. It was claimed that the consequences of this 'imposed Islamism' threatened not only the social and legal foundations of liberal legality but also threatened the Enlightenment values – democracy, reason, equality, autonomy and individual choice – upon which Western legal systems are based. Underlying this argument was also the claim that Islamic law is unreasonable and patriarchal whereas Western law is both secular and egalitarian. Unsurprisingly, perhaps, these tensions were expressed via the site of gender and gender relations and the 'subordinating' effect Islam has upon Muslim women. As stated earlier, Western women were presented as 'enlightened' and bearers of liberal legal ideals, such as equality and non-discrimination, while the Muslim female subject was presented as the 'other', a victim to cultural and religious practices in violation of her human rights. Law thus became the site upon which constructions of Muslims as the 'other' took shape, where internal traditions of dissent within Islam were sidelined and deemed anathema to Western intellectual thought and reason. Subsequently at present the dominant view of Islamic legal tradition and human rights is presented as incompatible, in opposition and at best producing an uneasy tension.[54] Indeed, the very idea of Islam as embodying the universalism of human rights, justice and equality as discussed in mainstream multicultural and political theory seems at odds with its presentation as a culturally relativist ideology that emphasizes the impossibility of individual free will, consent and reason. I suggest that the current totalizing of Islam is not only dangerous in its explicit Islamophobic tone, but that the relationships among religious legal practice, rights, faith, freedom, democracy and equality are a lot more complex than the integrated/separated trajectories presented currently.

The primary outcome of this response has been to strike a note of caution concerning calls for the recognition and/or accommodation of sharia into English law. Apart from the significant practical difficulties inherent in giving legitimacy to sharia councils, I argue that the narratives of Muslim women must underpin such discussions and that debates on the accommodation of sharia must at their very centre place the experience of Muslim women, who are the primary users of sharia councils and the ones most likely to be affected by any form of accommodation.

Typically there has been much discussion on the motivations behind the Archbishop's lecture and much of this relates to what some commentators identify as his real desire to enhance the role of Christianity in public life.[55] Others, such as Tariq Modood, argue that a new form of 'practical multiculturalism' must allow 'for a nuanced understanding of the inter-relationship of "secular"

---

54   This is not, of course, to underestimate the wealth of literature challenging such interpretations. See, for example, AA An-Naim, *Toward an Islamic Reformation: Civil Liberties, Human Rights and International Law* (Syracuse: Syracuse University Press, 1990); S Ali, *Gender and Human Rights in Islam and International Law: Equal before Allah, Unequal before Man?* (The Hague: Kluwer Law International, 2000); E Mayer, *Islam and Human Rights* (Boulder, CO: Westview Press, 1999).

55   See a range of interesting discussions on Open Democracy at <http://www.opendemocracy.net/>.

and "religious" notions in civic life'.[56] He supports the accommodation of sharia in the form of recognizing sharia councils as official arbitration bodies as long as they are consistent with English law, human rights, gender equality and child-protection legislation. Yet even such thoughtful responses must draw upon the experiences of Muslim women, who are reluctant for such bodies to be formally accommodated in English law.

The Archbishop should be applauded for tackling a complex and difficult topic and for his thoughtful insight both into the heterogeneity of Muslim communities settled in British society and into the complexity of Islamic jurisprudence and sharia as evolving and dynamic rather than as fixed and prescriptive. The lecture critiqued the cultural essentialism inherent in state law and articulated a sophisticated understanding of the ways in which power and dominance have shaped the ideals of 'equality before the law'. The rule of law can legitimate dominant social and political discourse and practice, which may exclude individuals and communities from equal access to the law and forms of justice. However, I also believe that this spirit of complexity and heterogeneity underpinning the lecture is somewhat undermined by assumptions that most, if not all, Muslims are in favour of the accommodation of sharia into English law and the implicit presentation of a unified Muslim community, the Muslim umma. Clearly this is not the case, and what such arguments succeed in doing is privileging a particular religious practice as part of a specific Muslim identity. The problem with this approach is that it tends to ignore the possibility of alternative narratives within the Muslim community. Evidently there is a sense of belonging to a Muslim community, which Muslim women express. Yet descriptions of belonging and community were often articulated in different ways. Some women are marginalized, while others occupy a position closer to the acceptable dictates of community expectations. Such discussions must therefore recognize the complex lived reality that Muslim identity entails. To simply analyse the relationship and conflicts between secular law and religious practice in relation to sharia misses out the key issues of conflict, change and diversity within the Muslim communities in question. The Archbishop was clear in his understanding of Islamic law, embodying traditions of reason, critique and pluralism over the past 1,200 years. However, we must be cautious in not conflating developments surrounding sharia in Muslim countries to how such processes develop and operate within minority diasporic communities as part of multicultural British society. This conflation, however small, also runs the risk of not understanding how these religious laws and cultural customs are reformulated within a British context to suit the specific Muslim community in question.[57]

Religious arbitration bodies may provide spaces for new forms of governance to resolve marital disputes away from the context of a Western secular framework but this does not imply that these local settings predetermine a more suitable outcome for the parties involved. For example, religious and socio-cultural terms of reference often marginalize women. Furthermore the space(s) inhabited by these bodies is neither distinct from local communities nor in totality separate from state law. Instead, it is a space that intersects with contested sites of local communal power and state law, and in this way is a unique formation of a British diaspora. Trying to understand these socio-legal processes requires a critique of the underlying power relations within family, community and state and to recognize that dialogue is often imbued with power relations. The dichotomous approach that posits 'law' and unofficial law as opposite and in conflict consequently fails to explore the spaces 'in between', the sites of resistance and change. Furthermore, as Sunder points out, 'more and more people on the ground are challenging traditional cultural and religious leaders to incorporate norms

---

56   Part of the Open Democracy discussions. This response was entitled 'Multicultural citizenship and the anti-sharia storm'. See <http://www.opendemocracy.net/>.

57   Similarly, discussions on the Muslim 'umma' and the presentation of a community of believers simply does not exist in the uniform way in which it was presented.

of equality, reason and liberty into the private spheres of religion and culture';[58] but this does not itself mean that Muslim women wish to formalize these bodies. This space is only used to obtain a Muslim divorce and the women are fully aware of the need to utilize state law to deal with issues concerning access, custody and financial settlements.

The angry reactions sparked by the Archbishop's lecture have also led to discussions on ways in which we can develop a constructive dialogue with those representing the Muslim faith. Although in favour of such developments, I also stress the need to include Muslim women in such debates and this requires a critique of the underlying power relations within family, individual and community bodies. We must recognize that dialogue is often imbued with power relations and is constituted in relation to controlling family and communal boundaries, and we must strive to develop an inclusive dialogue that includes the narratives of minorities within minority group. As Anthias points out, 'effective dialogue requires an already formulated mutual respect, a common communication language and a common starting point in terms of power'.[59] It is the 'common starting point in terms of power' that raises the dilemma of the multicultural question of how the particular and the universal, the claims of both difference and equality, can be recognized. We must also address the potential conflicts and tensions that arise in different and at times conflicting social contexts, including intra-family relations. Experiences of marriage, divorce, family and community relationships for many women tend to be messy, fragmented and complex. During the process of resolving marital disputes women cannot be stereotyped as requesting no family support or going down the road of nothing but family support. Instead they are themselves negotiating the outcomes of their disputes. Muslim women have complex views about who they are and thus identity cannot be understood as a dichotomous variable of insider/outsider, Muslim/non-Muslim or resistance versus victim. Instead the narratives produced by the women themselves justify attention to their participation, interaction and outcomes with these 'unofficial' bodies.

The troubled reception of the lecture by Dr Williams also identifies the ways in which contemporary liberal thinkers continue to be challenged with questions of how to manage cultural, religious and ethnic diversity in multicultural Britain. Such questions of religious identity, belonging and citizenship in multicultural societies now dominate social, political and academic thought. Western commentators and legal scholars discuss at length the limits of religious practice and belief and many query the need to accommodate and respect cultural and religious diversity in Western societies at all. For some the politics of multiculturalism and the recognition of cultural difference has led to a rise in a politics of cultural separatism, but for others the liberal principles of justice, equality and human rights justifies the protection of all cultural and religious minority communities.[60] Undoubtedly we need to address these issues in the light of empirical findings rather than solutions based upon abstract theoretical discussions. We need to incorporate debates on complexity, difference and diversity to understand the realities of Muslim women's lives. Women feel the contradictory pulls that these forces exert but their narratives must be heard. Some are happy to conform, others are not; some trade identities but for others there is a primacy of a Muslim identity. Many are suspicious of state intervention that challenges cultural norms deemed oppressive, because the state has not historically acted as the neutral arbiter of disputes.[61] Furthermore, some women see 'themselves strictly bound to submit to the dictates of Islamic law and the commands of

---

58   See M Sunder, 'Enlightened constitutionalism', *Connecticut Law Review*, 37 (2005), at 896.
59   See F Anthias, 'Beyond feminism and mutliculturalism: Locating difference and the politics of location', *Women's Studies International Forum*, 25/3 (2002), 275–86.
60   Refer to the cases of Sabina Begum and Aisha Azmi discussed earlier.
61   S Hall, 'Conclusion to the multi-cultural question', in B Hesse (ed.), *Unsettled Multiculturalisms: Diasporas, Entanglements, Transruptions* (London: Zed Books, 2000).

the authorities charged with its execution';[62] and we must recognize this as their lived experience. The real conflicts are over power and how those competing voices for power and representation ignore the internal voices of dissent and change, most often the voices of women.

My concern focuses on three key issues: first, the claim that seeing culture and forms of religious practice as a mode of legitimating claims to power and authority dramatically shifts the way we understand the universalism/relativism debate. Thus, the view that Muslims increasingly seek the freedom to live under sharia is not only problematic but fails to capture the complexity of British Muslim identity as fragmented, porous and hybrid. Second, anthropological scholarship points to the importance of locating gender and gender relations as key sites to the debate, thus *seeing* the ways in which Muslim women engage with sharia councils in Britain illustrates how processes and concepts of sharia law are mobilized, adopted and transformed: Muslim women's agency. Underlying this process are power relations that define the nature of the interaction, define the meanings of sharia within the sharia councils, and constructs the possibilities of change and action. Finally, an essentialized understanding of Muslim religious practice does not reflect the experience of Britain Muslim women. A more dynamic understanding of British Muslim identity is needed, which does not label the needs of Muslims to accommodate sharia as fixed, but understands this process as temporal, shifting from cultural to religious practice and vice versa.

Conclusion: The Rise of a Secular Imaginary?

One of the most enduring ideas of the Enlightenment and the process of modernization was the claim that the rise of secularism will eventually bring about the (inevitable) decline of religion and religious practice among believers. The failure of this claim and the need to understand the rise of religious fundamentalisms is now extensively discussed among sociologists, anthropologists, political theorists and, increasingly, legal scholars. Thus, more recently, the relationship between religion and the state in modern liberal societies has taken an interesting turn, focusing on the current process of secularization and the rise of a secular imaginary in the West complemented with a critique of the liberal paradigm of church–state relations. Scholars such as Talal Asad put forward the compelling argument that secularism is one way in which the modern state secures its own power and actively produces the citizen whose loyalty to the state.

Undoubtedly, contemporary Western societies today remain secularized. However, secularized Europe also remains deeply Christian; and this is often understood as part of a complex process of social and cultural relations upon which religion translates itself to wider society. For example, in the UK, although church and state remain firmly established there is no constitutional guarantee of religious liberty – civil society does not define itself through faith and religious practice but the relationship between law and religion increasingly dominates and underpins the liberal rights discourse.

Attention is once again focused on the public/private divide where the 'other' is expected to confine any 'un-British' values to the private space. In this context the question of whether religious practice can ever be confined to the private sphere takes on a greater urgency.

Does secularism have anything to do with shared values? The term secularism is both contested and fraught with definitional tensions. A basic definition defines secularism as the principle of public policy for organizing the relationship between religion and the state in very specific contexts. As Roy points out:

---

62   E Mayer, *Islam and Human Rights* (Boulder, CO: Westview Press, 1999), at 35.

Secularization brings about the loss of the prominent social presence of religion and the obligation to define oneself explicitly as a believer (or non-believer), not because the non-believer campaigns against the religious community but because the conditions for belonging to the religious group have become stricter: one's faith must be displayed.[63]

It is noteworthy that recent case law mirrors intellectual arguments over a crisis of multiculturalism and the failure of Muslims to integrate into British society.[64] The social anxieties about Muslim bodies is two-fold: the Muslim male is constructed as a dangerous threat in the battle with the 'war on terror'; and the Muslim female is deemed a victim, without autonomy, choice and personal subjectivity against the patriarchal customs of Islam and especially Muslim fathers, brothers and uncles who are deemed the custodians of this culture.

The recent controversy generated by the Archbishop of Canterbury's comments cannot be seen in isolation. The centrality of gender to the debates is crucial. There is an interesting continuum to the debates – in France the banning of the headscarf and religious symbols in public and in Britain conflicts over the hijab, jilbab or nikab and now the possibility of the recognition of parallel legal systems in Britain all point in the same direction – the need to save Muslim women from fathers and brothers, from Islam itself. We can understand their motivations for subjecting themselves to such oppression only in relation to the opposing frameworks of social coercion versus free will and false consciousness, West and non-West. The agency, autonomy and choice of Muslim women as active agents of their families and communities is lost and we see a resurgence of the frameworks of secularism versus religious practice. As Badiou asks, why this insistence that the Muslim girl must disrobe, must show herself?[65] In actual fact many Muslims have adapted well to secularization and many define themselves as secular Muslims. According to Ramadan, '[i]ntegrated Muslims have [...] increasingly reformulated their beliefs according to the terms of the Western debate'.[66] Instead the rise of a specific version of secularism has led to considerable regulation and surveillance of Muslims.

Similarly the recent sharia debate in England produced what I can only describe as moral panic. The idea that sharia law might be implemented in England and Wales propelled many Western intellectuals and commentators to pre-empt this threat by the projection of Muslim men as dangerous, Muslim women as shackled and subjugated, and the European as the defender of the values of Western civilization and democracy.

There are porous spaces between the law and religion that provide sites for engagement and contestation. Empirical research demonstrates that the complex lived reality of Muslims challenges the dichotomy of separated/integrated, free will versus social coercion. A rights discourse that seeks to protect the rights of all subjects must challenge all dominant and subordinate groups, both at a national and global level, as well as inequality within groups. For example, there is a tendency to

---

63   Roy, above, n. 2, at 2.

64   An-Na'im explores the possibility of developing a theoretical model that explores the synergy and interdependence of human rights, religion and secularism. He points out that, '[...] historical experience has shown that the exclusivity of religion tends to undermine possibilities of peaceful co-existence and solidarity among different communities of believers, secularism has evolved as the means for ensuring the possibility of pluralistic political community among different religious communities. The key feature of secularism is its ability to safeguard the pluralism of political community, subject to significant differences as to how that might be achieved in practice'. See AA An-Na'im, *Islam and the Secular State: Negotiating the Future of Shari'a* (Cambridge, MA: Harvard University Press, 2008), at 2.

65   Quoted in Motha, above, n. 1, at 1.

66   Ramadan, above, n. 19.

critique a 'Muslim culture' and speak about the 'Muslim community' where a specific aspect of an Islamic identity comes to symbolize the essence of the religious identity in question. One starting point in which to (re-)examine the relationship between the current rights discourse, religious demands and individual agency is the law and legal relations. Legal knowledge increasingly plays a pivotal role in framing religious and cultural practices, which seeks to emphasize law's heteronomy but which often distorts the ways in which cultural and religious practices are mediated via different and conflicting social relations.[67] The current rights discourse as mediated through the law not only depends upon reified notions of cultural and religious practice but also provides for a partial understanding of the perceived rise of a Muslim religiosity (and social conservatism) within Muslim diasporic communities.

Many feminist critiques continue to place gender in opposition to culture; and, for the Muslim woman, her exit out of this culture and her community is represented as the only way in which she can achieve modernity. In turn the security of the modern nation state is construed in part through the surveillance and discipline of the Muslim man. Muslims are increasingly presented as the 'other', with very little attention paid to what Muslim identity in the West actually entails. My current work with Muslim women in England demonstrates that membership of the Muslim community is complex, fragmented and messy. Razack concludes that a critique of the current liberal rights discourse must include the urgent question of how feminists can avoid being drawn into the framework of the superior, secular women, saving their less enlightened and more imperilled sisters from religion and community, and still respond to the dangers at hand.[68]

---

67   S Motha, 'Veiled women and the effect of religion in democracy', *Journal of Law and Society*, 34/1 (2007), 138–61, at 143.

68   SH Razack, *Casting Out: The Eviction of Muslims from Western Law and Politics* (Toronto: University of Toronto Press, 2008), at 20.

Chapter 9

The Right to be Different: The Position of Muslim Migrants in the Netherlands

Halleh Ghorashi

Introduction

For many in the West, the cultures of migrants from Islamic countries became a source of discomfort and fear after the events of 9/11, which were followed by a number of attacks in Madrid, London and elsewhere. This sense of apprehension had a significantly negative impact on how many people in Western countries view Islam and Muslims, despite the fact that one of the major impacts of globalization has been the emergence of new forms of identities within nation states. To borrow a phrase from Stuart Hall, 'modern nations are all cultural hybrids'.[1] Another scholar, Robert Young, believes that 'heterogeneity, cultural interchange and diversity have now become the self-conscious identity of modern society'.[2] This may still be a fair assessment of a globalized society, yet in the years following the events of 9/11, the growing fear of migrants from Islamic countries has led to an urgent appeal for the assimilation of their culture into that of the dominant host society. This has resulted in a widening gap between migrants (even those born in the country adopted by their parents) and the rest of society. This new *culture* promises to be the source of many challenges in the coming years. The UNDP (United Nations Development Programme) report of 2004 cites the growing gap combined with the lack of cultural recognition of migrants as one of the major challenges and dangers that new multicultural societies face.[3]

In this time of omnipresent cultural diversity, we are witness to contradictory processes: inclusion and exclusion; sensitivity and misunderstanding; curiosity and resistance. On the one hand, there is an increasing demand for culturally sensitive measures and cultural recognition. On the other, we see a growing resistance towards *culturalization*. By culturalization, I mean a tendency to explain social problems mainly in terms of the cultural differences between various ethnic groups in society. Verena Stolcke has earlier referred to this culturist presence as 'cultural fundamentalism', a term which she explains as a new form of exclusion rhetoric in the West, and which is based on a homogeneous, static, coherent and rooted notion of culture.[4] This time it is not the race that needs to be protected but the assumed historically rooted homogenous culture of the nation:

---

1   S Hall, 'The question of cultural identity', in S Hall, D Held and T McGrew (eds), *Modernity and its Futures* (Cambridge: Polity Press, 1992), at 297.

2   See RJC Young, *Colonial Desire: Hybridity in Theory, Culture and Race* (London: Routledge, 1995), at 4.

3   UNDP, Human Development Report 2004: Cultural Liberty in Today's Diverse World (New York: United Nations Development Programme, 2004).

4   V Stolcke, 'Talking culture: New boundaries, new rhetorics of exclusion in Europe', *Current Anthropology*, 36/1 (1995), 1–24.

'racism without race'.[5] The recent developments and public debates in various European countries, in particular in the Netherlands, prove Stolcke's point.

The question becomes how to deal with the paradox of the growing fear of the 'other' alongside the increasing necessity to recognize the space and right of the 'other' to be different. This chapter focuses on both the necessity and the limitations of a space in which groups with different cultural identities could flourish in a multicultural society such as the Netherlands.

The Background of Culturalist Thinking

The dominant discourse in the Netherlands in regard to new migrants from Islamic countries has been culturalist right from the start.[6] The culture of these migrants was considered to deviate from Dutch norms. This is founded on a static and essentialist approach to culture, in which cultural content is considered the determining factor for all actions perpetrated by individuals. Such an approach leaves little space for individual interpretations and creativity with regard to cultural background.

This discourse – as expressed in policies, political debate and public discussion – has shifted several times in recent decades. In the 1970s it focused on the preservation of the cultures of migrants. Later it shifted to integration while preserving the cultures of migrants. At present the central idea is that of attacking the so-called 'culture-based crime' and making civic integration mandatory. It seems, therefore, as though the dominant discourse has had a complete makeover in terms of content. It is widely believed that the much criticized approach of 'indifference' prevalent in the 1970s and 1980s has been abandoned, and that a shift has taken place from socio-economic to socio-cultural aspects of integration issues. However, despite the changes of direction that have taken place, the content of this dominant discourse on migrant issues has hardly changed. This is because thinking in terms of absolute categories, in particular cultural categories, has remained a crucial feature of debating and presenting migrant issues in the Netherlands.

In order to understand the dominant culturalist discourse in Dutch society, we need to situate it within the context of 'pillarization'. The construction of pillars – 'own worlds' – along the lines of religious denomination and political ideology has long provided the dominant framework within which differences in the Netherlands are considered. Studies of the pillars are too diverse and numerous to allow us to present an all-encompassing overview of them in this chapter.[7] Still, a short outline is necessary for my further argumentation. According to Pennings, pillars consist of 'separated institutional complexes of religiously or ideologically motivated institutions and members, which are marked along the same boundaries in different social sectors'.[8] He describes pillarization as 'the process in which after 1880 Catholics, orthodox Protestants and social democrats have gradually institutionalized their mutual differences'.[9] Regardless of whether the

---

5   Ibid.

6   See, for more, H Ghorashi, *Paradoxen van culturele erkenning: Management van diversiteit in nieuw Nederland* (Inaugural lecture at VU University Amsterdam, 2006).

7   See H Blom, 'Vernietigende kracht en nieuwe vergezichten', in JHC Blom and J Talsma (eds), *De verzuiling voorbij: godsdienst, stand en natie in de lange negentiende eeuw* (Amsterdam: Het Spinhuis, 2000), at 204–87.

8   P Pennings, *Verzuiling en ontzuiling: De lokale verschillen* (Kampen: Kok, 1991), at 21 (translation is mine).

9   Ibid.

pillars have been shaped by the elites in the service of national pacification,[10] or have developed within an (already) existing pluralistic political culture,[11] they have had a channelling effect on cultural differences, as a result of which 'its supporters remained separated while the pillar-elites maintained contact with each other'.[12] Despite the variation within the pillars – the 'own worlds' – the concept conveyed to the members that the boundaries of the pillars indicated who belonged and who did not. This distinction, which was assumed to be clear, was used subsequently to organize many social activities within one's own pillar. This represents a dichotomy between 'us' and 'them', which stems from an essentialist approach towards the own group and the others, something which has latently shaped the way in which new migrants have been approached in the Netherlands.

It is very likely that the habitus[13] of pillarization continued when the new migrants came to the Netherlands, bringing with them cultures that were presumed to be entirely different from the country in which they were settling. Koopmans holds that the relationship between Dutch society and its migrants is strongly rooted in the pillarized tradition.[14] The pillarized system, which in the early twentieth century was a successful pacifying element in the conflicts between local religious and political groups, has been re-employed as an instrument of integration.

The influence of this pillarized history on migrants is witnessed clearly on those from Islamic countries. Policy-makers and academics considered this group to be a new kind of pillar. Based on a thorough examination of the multiple studies on pillarization, Blom concludes that it is best – despite the amount of criticism concerning the term – to 'again let pillarization become a metaphor' for new social developments.[15] Here we encounter contrary processes: after the welfare state made pillars redundant, we now observe the creation of a new pillar in a relatively de-pillarized Netherlands. In addition, the continuous influence of pillarization did not suddenly disappear owing to the realization that it was no longer necessary; the effect of pillarization on various social fields has continued, be it in a less explicit form.[16]

This has caused new migrants from Islamic countries to find themselves in a confusing area of tension. The historical habit of thinking in terms of pillars was translated into the migrants' condition, and left – even created – space for these migrants to preserve their cultures. Paradoxically, this happened in a de-pillarized Netherlands in which individual autonomy was seen as prevalent and protected. Thinking in terms of pillars has had a much wider effect than on Muslim migrants alone, as, to a certain extent, it has demarcated thinking about cultural differences and ethnic boundaries. This has led to the creation of cultural contrasts that make it virtually impossible to consider the individual migrant as separate from his or her cultural or ethnic category.

---

10 Referring to Lijphart 1968 (see Pennings 1991, above, n. 8, at 8–9).

11 Referring to Daalder 1891 (see Pennings 1991, above, n. 8, at 8–9).

12 Pennings 1991, above, n. 8, at 17.

13 Habitus in Bourdieuian sense is a set of socialized dispositions that shapes practices and perceptions.

14 R Koopmans, 'Good intentions sometimes make bad policy: A comparison of Dutch and German integration policies', in R Cupeurs, KA Duffek and J Kandel (eds), *The Challenge of Diversity: European Social Democracy Facing Migration, Integration, and Multiculturalism* (Innsbruck: StudienVerlag, 2003), at 166–67.

15 Blom (2000), above, n. 7, at 236.

16 See also J Rath et al., *Nederland en zijn islam: Een ontzuilde samenleving reageert op het ontstaan van een geloofsgemeenschap* (Amsterdam: het Spinhuis, 1996), at 240.

So What Has Changed?

What has changed considerably, however, since 2000 is the tone, demanding that 'we must be allowed to say what we think'. Baukje Prins calls this period the era of 'the new realism'.[17] The new realist is someone with guts, someone who dares to call a spade a spade, someone who sets himself up as the mouthpiece of the common people, and then puts up a vigorous fight against the so-called leftists and the 'politically correct' views of cultural relativism.[18]

In retrospect, the culturalist statements made in the early 1990s by Frits Bolkestein, the leader of the Liberal Party (VVD), can be seen as the start of the period of new realism.[19] Pim Fortuyn took it to the next level by radicalizing new realism into a kind of hyperrealism in which 'the guts to tell the truth' became an end in itself, irrespective of the consequences.[20] Once a scholar and publicist, Fortuyn became remarkable when he was chosen as the leader of the newly established party, Leefbaar Nederland (Liveable Netherlands), and succeeded in increasing the party's popularity among the Dutch people. This, together with the prominence he gained in the media, shocked old school politicians. His success with the Dutch public was greatly enhanced by the events of 9/11. In the minds of many, the potential enmity of Muslim migrants that Bolkestein discussed in the 1990s had become a reality. In the US, but also in other countries, the events of 9/11 were explained and analysed by reference to Samuel Huntington's 'Clash of Civilizations', which made it easier for Fortuyn to express publicly his concerns that had earlier been implied, but never made explicit. In an interview in *de Volkskrant* on 9 February 2002,[21] Fortuyn used phrases such as 'Islam is a backward culture' or 'the real refugees do not reach Holland'; comments that unsettled the foundation of Dutch politics.

The result of this new era – which was marked by the 9/11 attacks and the assassinations of Fortuyn and Van Gogh – was that the political climate in the Netherlands hardened considerably. As a result, thinking in terms of cultural contrasts became linked more than before to feelings of fear and discontent; any statement was allowed, irrespective of consequences, while guts and decisiveness became the new show-qualities of the political leaders. Not only were the new political commentators allowed to utter anything they wished in respect to immigrants and immigration, but also they could claim to be cleaning up the mess left behind by the previous government. As a reaction to the so-called 'soft approach' of the 1980s, a 'tough approach' towards migrants was introduced in which the notion of obligations, rather than rights, became the keyword. They (with an emphasis on 'they', meaning 'entirely different') should learn the language, study Dutch history, adapt to Dutch customs and wholly embrace Dutch identity by giving up their original identity. In contemporary Dutch dominant discourse, assimilation – although not always formulated in this way – is seen as the solution to all social problems. This idea is strongly rooted in the assumed superiority of European culture, which rates migrant cultures as lower on the scale.[22] As a result,

17   B Prins, *Voorbij de onschuld: het debat over integratie in Nederland* (Amsterdam: Van Gennep, 2004 [2000]), at 35–36.

18   Ibid.

19   This period goes together with the start of the era of political populism in France (Jean Marie La Pen), but also in other West European countries. The populist right made a breakthrough in both Danish and Norwegian politics during the 1990s.

20   Prins (2004), above, n. 17, at 43.

21   One of the influential Dutch newspapers.

22   R Gowricharn, *Het omstreden paradijs: Over multiculturaliteit en sociale cohesie* (Tilburg: Inaugural lecture at the University of Tilburg, 2002), at 6.

it is perfectly acceptable nowadays to express publicly the idea that migrant cultures are not only different, but also inferior. As a consequence, migrants and, hence, migrant cultures and religion are now viewed with aversion and mistrust, and these views are being translated into policy and public debate. The question here is how can migrants assimilate into a new culture that does not want them to begin with?

Ayaan Hirsi Ali added a gender component to this new realist discourse. She became famous for her radical standpoints against Islam in general and the Islamic community in the Netherlands in particular. In the film *Submission*, she and Theo Van Gogh (who was the producer of the film) chose a tack of confrontation by showing verses from the Qur'an on the naked body of a molested woman. The most recent event in this vein has been the critical film about the Qur'an made by a member of the Dutch Parliament and the leader of the Party for Freedom (Partij voor de Vrijheid), Geert Wilders, which made world news.

The post-2000 emergence of these events in the public space of the Netherlands, particularly after Van Gogh's assassination and the continuous death threats issued against Hirsi Ali and Geert Wilders, among others who publicly insulted Islamic fundaments, threw new light on the existing culturalist discourse. The extreme construction of otherness, as totally different from us, gained a new core subject, namely 'tolerance of criticism'. It is argued that people in the West are much more tolerant towards criticism of their religion and culture, whereas Muslim individuals and communities do not tolerate any kind of criticism of their religion or religious figures. In addition, it is claimed that they do not have a sense of humour. Violent images of Muslims throughout the world burning flags or attacking embassies are used to portray the violent potential of Muslims in general, but Muslim migrants living in the Netherlands in particular. In all these discussions we see the Western majority's claim to their right of free speech, emphasizing that this right is endangered by the low tolerance of criticism and high potential of violence of Muslims, both outside and inside their territorial borders.

Surprisingly, there has been no comprehensive debate on the effects of this negatively loaded culturalist discourse on the positioning of migrants in the Netherlands and their right to be different and respected. Every single attempt to raise this issue in the public sphere faces reactions such as: 'But Muslim migrants had enough space in the 1980s, and they have misused that space; now it is time that they adjust to the Dutch society.'[23] The recent presentation (5 April 2008) by Rita Verdonk (previously Minister of Integration for the Liberal Party VVD) of her new political movement (TON, Trots op Nederland, or 'Proud of the Netherlands') is an example of this viewpoint. One of the main topics in her speech was concerned with defending Dutch cultural norms and values in addition to the basic right to the freedom of speech. She blames Prime Minister Balkenende for not defending this right, referring to Balkendende's press conference (29 March 2008) when he requested Wilders not to show his film.

Portraying the Muslim other as 'uncritical and violent' brings a new dimension to the debates in the Netherlands. Although this new approach occurs within the culturalist and new realist discourses of the last decades, it shows an even blunter construction of otherness which deepens the assumed contrast between 'us free and critical Dutch' and 'the Muslim other: the uncritical, the threat to our freedom and democratic space and rights'. Emphasizing this contrast, supported by the mainstream media in the Netherlands, carries within it the danger of undermining democracy using the same tactics with which it is defended.

---

23   This remark is based on my personal experience during my participation in public debates in the Netherlands.

Shaping a Democratic Culture

Democracy goes far beyond the right to vote. In contrast to what is often maintained, democracy is not simply about the majority, but it is particularly about the space for the minority to voice its views and concerns. This is exactly what constitutes the difference between a constitutional democracy and a populist democracy: in the latter, the voice of the majority is given relatively free reign while the voice of the minority is not. Democracy without political opposition is, consequently, not democracy.

Samuel IJsseling argues that democracy is not primarily about similarity but rather about the recognition of difference or being different.[24] This important aspect of democracy requires a democratic culture that creates space for difference, yet it is precisely this aspect of democracy that is in danger of being overlooked by predominating economic interests. This is why Giddens advocates the 'democratisation of democracy', in which greater attention is paid to a democratic culture.[25] According to de Tocqueville, democracy is not only a form of government, but is also a way of life, which implies a change in social relations. Proponents of 'deliberative' democracy underscore the public forum, in which citizens are empowered in a free and open dialogue to translate their personal preferences into more public objectives.[26]

Critics of this approach feel that democracy is reduced to being a dialogue and that it fails to take into account power relations and their impact on access to major public platforms. In this process the notion of justice seems to be crucial. Iris Young emphasizes in this regard two ideals of social justice: the rights of self-determination and self-development. The first ideal concerns the opportunities of citizens – in spite of their differences – to gain equal access to societal resources, while the second concerns the freedom of a person to pursue life in his/her own way. Pursuing one's way of life is not absolute and has to be within a certain legal and/or moral framework that ensures that it does not bring harm to others. When we talk about 'real' freedom within a democratic system it means that there is an absence of the institutional relations of domination of certain values above others.[27] Nevertheless, we also know that what we ask for is impossible in its absolute sense; a perfectly just democracy is impossible, since power relations, structural inequality and the domination of certain economic processes and value systems above others, which exclude groups of people, remain in all societies. Accepting these limitations, I agree with Young when she proposes that '[p]olitical mobilization within formally democratic institutions and norms is usually the only realistic option for oppressed and disadvantaged people and their allies to improve social relations and institutions'.[28]

Theorists from the 1970s and the 1980s mainly emphasized what Rawls called 'the basic structure' of society, meaning the constitutional rights, political decision-making processes and social institutions that make democracy possible. By now it has become widely accepted that, in addition to this basic structure, attention should be given to the qualities and attitude of citizens operating within these basic structures.[29] This 'basic attitude' – what de Tocqueville calls lifestyle

---

24   S IJsseling, *Macht en onmacht* (Amsterdam: Boom, 1999).

25   A Giddens, *The Third Way: The Renewal of Social Democracy* (London: Polity Press, 1999).

26   M Janssens and C Steyaert, *Meerstemmigheid: Organiseren met verschil* (Leuven: Universitaire Pers Leuven, 2001), at 204.

27   See IM Young, *Inclusion and Democracy* (Oxford: Oxford University Press, 2002 [2000]).

28   Young (2002), above, n. 27, at 35.

29   W Kymlicka and W Norman, 'Citizenship in culturally diverse societies: Issues, contexts, concepts', in W Kymlicka and W Norman (eds), *Citizenship in Diverse Societies* (Oxford: Oxford University Press, 2000), at 6.

– is mandatory for maintaining and protecting a culture of democracy. Democracy in this sense is more than simply a dialogue; it comprises a culture, an outlook and a way of life. A democratic outlook implies accepting from the very start the existence of different positions in life and being conscious about the working of the processes of power of exclusion and domination. A democratic structure does not amount to much without a democratic culture, and a democratic culture is only feasible if it takes not the *I* but the *other* as its starting point.[30]

In a democratic state such as the Netherlands that respects the rule of law, the culture of democracy is enhanced by the tension between its two major components, namely the state-form and the societal-form or 'civil society' (citizens' initiative). There is no doubt that the constitutional framework should be unequivocal, but this by no means entails a mono-cultural state. The constitutional state should instead guard and facilitate the culture of democracy, in other words the diversity of public space, including cultural diversity. Within this space, freedom of opinion becomes possible, but there is also room for dialogue in which ideas and beliefs can meet. Citizens play a large role in this; they maintain a culture of democracy through their daily words and actions. The role of the state is also indispensable in creating a framework that furthers and guarantees these individual actions. Apart from the citizens and the state, the social midfield (in the form of democratic institutions, interest groups and self-organizations) plays a key role in providing citizens with an opportunity to make themselves heard, as well as to meet and encounter each other. In short, an inclusive society guards both its basic structure (in the form of justice, freedom of opinion and equal rights) and basic attitude (in the form of social virtues such as respect, tolerance, curiosity, and openness) with democratic institutions and citizens. The authorities should not compel, but rather facilitate and protect the democratic space.[31]

Yet, in our late modern societies, we are facing new kinds of 'situatedness' when it comes to individual freedoms and rights. Late modern societies are characterized by many scholars as being in a condition of fluidity,[32] greater reflexivity,[33] and concerned with perceived risks.[34] Bauman, for example, argues that each of the once solid aspects of society has become liquid, and that patterns of dependency are thrown into the melting pot.[35] What is left is individuality in its most extreme form; unattached and fully responsible for its actions. In this condition, highly individualized societies require even more urgent protection of the democratic lifestyle or culture. As mentioned before, in the context of an extreme fixation on individual rights and spaces we see now that the space for minorities becomes marginalized so that the rights of majorities are protected. This is especially the case when this space is assumed to present a threat to the democratic structure of societies. The result of this process is, in Bauman's words, that the individual becomes the worst enemy of the citizen. The citizen is the one whose well-being is connected to that of the 'city', while the individual is only after self-satisfaction. Inspired by Bauman's line of thinking, I argue that extreme individualization could lead to a slow disintegration of citizenship. The consequence is that the 'public' becomes colonized by the 'private'.[36] The greatest challenge of second modernity will be to learn collectively to tackle public issues without reducing them solely to private needs.

---

30 For this I have been inspired tremendously by the work of Emmanuel Levinas.

31 See B Parekh, *Rethinking Multiculturalism: Cultural Diversity and Political Theory* (Basingstoke: Palgrave, 2000).

32 See Z Bauman, *Liquid Modernity* (Cambridge: Polity Press, 2000).

33 A Giddens, *Modernity and Self-Identity: Self and Society in the Late Modern Age* (Cambridge: Polity Press, 1991).

34 U Beck, *Risk Society: Towards a New Modernity* (London: Sage Publications, 1992).

35 Bauman (2000), above, n. 32.

36 Bauman (2000), above, n. 32.

Protecting a democratic culture that is inclusive towards diversity is one of the features of pursuing communality without overruling diversity. One of the basic preconditions for this democratic culture is tolerance, yet, in the Netherlands, tolerance in terms of *allowing space* for otherness has proven to promote indifference in the last few decades. Thus, society does not tackle collective issues through difference. This is also what de Tocqueville warned us about: 'Setting people free makes them indifferent.'[37] The result of this kind of tolerance is paradoxical, by both strengthening the individualization of a society and essentializing difference on a group basis. What is lacking is a growing sense of the collective notion of citizenship. What individuals need to do to become citizens is to take an additional step: not only *of allowing* space, but also *of making space*. This is about the will to meet the other, which, over and above a convincing plea, requires the ability to make space or to step aside. This step to the side is an important and inevitable move in creating a common shared space between cultures, in which we can admit, meet and connect with the other. The next step in a democratic outlook would then be one towards *guarded space*, which means preparing to make an effort to guard and, if necessary, defend another person's liberty and space. Adopting these steps of toleration brings the individual closer to the citizen, which is particularly interesting when taking the dominance of 'the freedom of speech' as an example. Based on the above-mentioned, it should be clear that this freedom cannot be defined solely through what an individual wants or needs to say, as it should also be through how one's expression relates to the city. This does not mean that societal tensions grow less, but that the approach towards these tensions becomes different. The way citizens relate to these tensions will no longer be based solely on individually motivated actions, but informed by a relational responsibility of the citizen to his/her city. This is the only way in which the public can be freed from what Bauman termed the 'colonisation of the private'.

However, in our everyday practices we are far from making a space for otherness, let alone guarding it. Owing to the dominance of the culturalist discourse, the frightening and threatening elements of cultural difference have been so overemphasized that little space is left for cultural recognition or identifying points of commonality. Instead of solving problems, this focus on culture has contributed to a growing gap in various European societies between the European self and the migrant other. The main explanation for this is that when culture is presumed to be a problem, and debated and presented only in terms of cultural contrasts, the culturalist discourse may cause migrants to regroup increasingly within their ethnic boundaries to defend that culture. Feelings of social insecurity and lack of recognition tend to encourage the radicalization of both majorities and minorities; when people feel threatened, they will go to extremes to defend their boundaries. The growing threat of extreme Islamic and extreme right-wing groups is a case in point here.

The Way Forward

My main criticism of the culturalist approach does not concern the categorizing itself. It is impossible to conceive of life without categories. The criticism is about cultural categories being made into absolute contrasts. In social sciences, this type of conceptualization of culture has been criticized since the 1960s, when the anthropologist Fredrik Barth argued that ethnic boundaries are

---

37   Bauman (2000), above, n. 32, at 36.

not created and preserved by cultural content, but are constructed in search of 'political' goals.[38] Cultural characteristics are thrown into sharp relief precisely when they can be used to mark a difference between *us* and *them*, which means that ethnic boundaries between groups should chiefly be considered as constructions that are situational, contextual and changeable, rather than entities that are inherent in the essence of the cultures.

This non-essentialist approach to identity leaves greater scope for analysing individual action with regard to the individual's own culture. The ways in which individuals perceive their culture and give meaning to it are diverse and variable. People are capable of criticizing their cultural habitus and opening themselves up to innovation and supplementation with new cultural elements, which often leads to constructing diverse forms and connections. What is needed, however, for such reflection and innovation to be admitted is a feeling of security. The general precondition for reflection, therefore, is a safe space. When people feel threatened and coerced, they generally respond reactively, which considerably narrows down the space for making connections, for it causes them to cut themselves off from rather than open themselves up to potential new contacts and combinations. For people to open themselves up to new ideas and connections, they need to feel recognized as who they are: cultural recognition is of paramount importance for human development.[39]

For this sense of recognition to grow, the steps mentioned above are essential; we as citizens should not only leave space for the other, but also should make space and protect that space. In a society where the democratic structure and culture are in balance, citizens protect the public space as an open and free space, which enables individuals to feel safe in making their choices. This space also grants minorities a free choice and practice of their cultural and religious identity. This freedom of public space means that people should feel free to both criticize and hold on to their cultural and religious backgrounds. Individuals need to feel that the public space is open enough to shape and reshape their identities, which is only possible if their identities are not fully defined by others, especially by those who enjoy dominant places in the public space. The dominance of strict boundaries between 'us, as civilized' and 'them, as uncivilized' within the public space limit the room for minorities – in this case migrants with Islamic backgrounds – to feel the openness of the public space. When in the public domain dominant voices appear to attack their cultural and religious identity, insulting them on a daily basis without the opportunity to offer a balanced counter-discourse, minorities start to consider this public domain as closed and normatively pitched against them. In that case, the logical reaction of minority groups is to claim their difference, and by doing so essentializing identities. The dominant assimilative discourse becomes a self-fulfilling prophecy leading to the very situation it aims to prevent, which is the formation of segregated cultural identities. In terms of public space, we need to make a distinction between incidents and a dominant pattern. When the dominant pattern in a society in terms of utterances in the public space seems to be normative in a negative sense – even to the point of insulting minorities – it forces minorities on to the offensive and jeopardizes democratic culture in the sense of the right to be different. Therefore, the core issue here is that we cannot talk about democratic rights – the freedom of speech, for example – without democratic culture; the responsibility of society to deal with that freedom in a way that does not suppress the minority. When a democratic state fails to strike a balance between these two basic elements of democracy, the only room left will be occupied by those who propagate extreme essentialized positions. These positions are taken, on

---

38 F Barth, *Ethnic Groups and Boundaries: The Social Organization of Cultural Difference* (Boston, MA: Little, Brown, 1969).

39 See C Taylor, *Multiculturalism* (translated by Tine Ausma) (Amsterdam: Boom, 1995 [1994]).

the one side, by the native Dutch who want to protect their culture, along with some ex-Muslims who denigrate other Muslims, and, on the other side, by cultural and religious radicals who claim the most traditional patterns of their background to be the source of their struggle for justice. In this unbalanced society there is no room for nuances or dynamic interplays between cultures and religions.

The next section will elaborate on the possibilities for combating the essentialized-based positionings.

Creating Space for a Diversity of Cultural Expressions in the Public Domain

A feeling of connectedness can only come into being if the new Dutch get space to experience their symbols, rituals and cultural formation, although this cultural freedom should not be confused with a defence of tradition per se.[40] When people feel free to express their cultural identity, they often also feel safe enough to distance themselves from subjugating practices within their own culture. More importantly, when people feel that their cultural identity is recognized and protected by the Dutch democratic state, this can lead to an emotional connectedness to the Netherlands. In my earlier work, which was in a different context, I showed that, when this connectedness is present, migrants are able to realize new creations in which they link their cultural ceremonies from the past to the new context in which these ceremonies take place.[41] Thus, out of their diverse cultural/ religious backgrounds, people can become Dutch citizens and also feel emotionally connected to the Netherlands. In this way, being Dutch would not exclude, for example, being a Muslim. Dutchness can thus include the cultural and/or religious background of the new Dutch, so that new creations can come into being such as Dutch Muslims. The following quote describes this multiple positioning in a strong manner:

> I hate the word "allochthonous [non-native Dutch citizens – HG]". I'm Dutch. Often, people don't know if you ask them what Pentecost means. I'm a Muslim and yet I have to explain that it means the descent of the Holy Spirit. [...] As if being a Muslim, you are less Dutch. I would fight for this country. I have the Dutch nationality and the Islamic faith.[42]

Making Space for Cultural Hybrids

By making space for cultural diversity – the basic principle of a culture of democracy – individuals are able to shape their culture more freely, which can lead to different forms of extended linkages between cultures and to new connections between identities. Many who belong to the growing middle class of new Dutch are even more Dutch than they would like to admit. Some were born and raised here, while others have accustomed themselves to all sorts of Dutch patterns, yet they still do not feel connected to the Netherlands or call themselves Dutch. Some are able to combine their different identities when they feel safe enough for reflection. This road is not for all to take, however,

---

40   See also UNDP 2004, above, n. 3.

41   See H Ghorashi 'How dual is transnational identity? A debate on duality of transnational immigrant organizations', in H Dahles and L Stobbe (eds), *Managing Cohesion in Transnational Organizations*, in an special issue of *Culture & Organization*, 10/4 (2000), 329–40.

42   L Çakir, in C Pektaş-Weber, *Moslima's: Emancipatie achter de dijken* (Amsterdam: Bulaaq, 2006), at 22.

as every society has groups that are antagonistic and prefer to remain marginal. Nonetheless, a society must create conditions that are favourable to those who do not wish to isolate themselves and who do opt for change. In concrete terms, I am referring to the group of new Dutch nationals that has the potential of being hybrid or hyphenated Dutch and position themselves as Differently Dutch.[43] These 'cultural hybrids' are not rooted in who they are, but actively give shape to who they want to be. These people symbolize what modern societies embody – freedom – because they are capable of preserving the best of different worlds without getting enmeshed in the givens of their own culture. By making space for these new Dutch citizens and by making sure they receive the recognition they need to shape their identities in liberty, it will be possible to marginalize radical groups. These new hybrid Dutch citizens are not enemies of Dutch society, but allies of the 'native' Dutch, who also need to have the courage to change for the future.

Making Space for Social Dialogue and Encounter

The major conditions for a social encounter proceeding from difference are openness and curiosity.[44] Unfortunately, recent social developments in the Netherlands, instead of encouraging people to come closer to each other with cultural openness and curiosity, have frightened them away from cultural contacts. In the Netherlands today, it requires courage to run counter to the dominant discourse of categorical thinking and to convert abhorrence and fear of the other into curiosity and openness. For a more profound encounter with the other, however, yet another step must be taken – the step that the Dutch philosopher Theo de Boer considers as the first prerequisite for intercultural dialogue.[45] This step is called *epochè*, which is a temporary suspension of the truth of one's own judgment. We cannot listen to another person without temporarily putting a question mark over our own conviction. This does not involve casting doubt on our own ideas, but rather creating a common space in which we can listen to the other and get closer to him or her. What is salient in de Boer's view is that, without this suspension, discussion is pointless; without conviction, there is nothing at stake.

For a social encounter to take place we should be able to approach, look at and listen to the other. For this to happen, it is important to create an interspace by stepping aside temporarily to make space for the other, before we judge or condemn him or her. Importantly, making space is the only way to counter the dominant discourse. By encountering each other in as open an atmosphere as possible, and by virtue of the courage to step aside, we can create a temporary interspace that could lead to a real dialogue and connection. Thus, it becomes possible to overcome, to a certain extent, the self-evident power of the dominant discourse. It is exactly this interspace which gives us the opportunity to adopt new ideas and creations, and to forge new connections.

Making Space for a New Kind of Dutchness

The idea of the migrant as a guest has long since lost its currency in the Netherlands, but the idea that a migrant's most 'natural' link is his or her country of origin continues to persist in the

---

43   I use this term to refer to all those Dutch nationals who hyphenate their identities, as in Moroccan-Dutch, Turkish-Dutch, or Iranian-Dutch.

44   J Tennekes, 'Communicatie en cultuurverschil', *M&O, Tijdschrift voor organisatiekunde en sociaal beleid*, 48/2 (2000), 130–44.

45   T de Boer, *Tamara A, Awater en andere verhalen over subjectiviteit* (Amsterdam: Boom, 1993).

majority's discourse about migrants. Within this essentialist view of the concept of 'home', it is self-evident that migrants' loyalty and connectedness remain with their 'home country', even if they have, for example, been born in the Netherlands. This obvious link between migrants and their home countries is not only made in the Netherlands; it can be witnessed in most European countries. The often-told joke by Ulrich Beck explains this point: A black man in Germany is asked: 'Where are you from?' He answers: 'From Munich.' Q: 'And your parents?' A: 'Also from Munich.' Q: 'And where were they born?' A: 'My mother in Munich.' Q: 'And your father?' A: 'In Ghana.' Q: 'Ah, so you're from Ghana.'

This joke clearly shows the obvious link that is made between identity and home country. One's identity, therefore, becomes a fixed and clearly demarcated piece of baggage that is carried around from one place or generation to the next. Departing from this idea, migrants will always be misplaced in their new country, because they *in fact* belong somewhere else and will therefore never be considered 'real Dutch'. Hence, it is no coincidence that recent debates around migrants concentrate either on their return or on mandatory integration. In both cases, the starting point is that migrants feel connected mainly to their country of origin, the idea behind this being that they should either return to their 'homeland', or, if they want to stay here, adapt.

The second idea is that migrants will not integrate out of their own free will, because of this strong connectedness to their country of origin. This is evidently an either/or mode of thought – in order to join us, you must renounce the other. The recent debate on double nationality is a clear example of such an either/or way of thinking in which a set of basic assumptions leaves little space for newly created identities that hold out possibilities for new combinations and new ways of being a Dutch national.

A telling example is the striking remark with which a Dutch friend once confronted me. During the first year of my studies in anthropology, I regularly visited a Dutch fellow student, Ellen, but in the second year personal circumstances forced her to give up her studies. Next, she moved to another town and we lost touch. After a five-year interval we caught up again. She said to me: 'Halleh, in the time I haven't seen you, you've really changed; you've become both more Dutch and more Iranian.' I was flabbergasted. I could not grasp her observation. What was she getting at? The observation bugged me for years, and it was only later that I understood it to be the perfect and/and scenario, or example of hybridity.

This example shows how a life can be enriched by an encounter, and this is not because one gives up one's own identity to become the other. That person becomes richer because she/he becomes more of both, not only by making another culture into one's own, but also because one can reflect on one's original customs through the lens of this new culture. Furthermore, the way in which one acquires the new culture will be influenced by the frame of reference from one's other culture. Unfortunately, a result of the dominant mode of thinking in terms of dichotomies or contrasts is that policies often become limited to an instrumental approach to issues of integration, and are thus incapable of developing a broader vision for the future. To enable this future vision, these basic assumptions should be put up for debate in order to make the necessary space for the construction of a new form of Dutchness that is diversity-inclusive.

In my earlier work, I showed that the Dutch national identity is too 'thick',[46] which renders it not comprehensive enough to be able to embrace the diversity of cultures present in the Netherlands.

---

46   In making a distinction between 'thin' and 'thick' constructions of national identities, I was inspired by Rawls' (1971, 1980) distinction between thin universalism and thick particularism in relation to pluralism. In addition, Stratton and Ang's (1998) work also helped me to get a handle on the relation between cultural diversity and national identity. See H Ghorashi, *Ways to Survive, Battles to Win: Iranian Women Exiles in the Netherlands and the United States* (New York: Nova Science Publishers, 2003).

Until recently, the Dutch national identity was barely explicit, though there were implicit and unspoken notions about codes of conduct and appearance that established who was and who was not a 'real' Dutchman or Dutchwoman. The Dutch citizen is expected to be white and Judeo-Christian. In line with categorical thinking, it has become self-evident that migrants, with their 'deviating' cultures, do indeed live in the Netherlands but can never be 'truly' Dutch – at the very most, they can hope to be assimilated into the community of 'solid citizens' that the Netherlands will tolerate.

This unspoken, but all the same 'thick' notion of Dutch national identity has become more explicit over the past few years, recent debates about the Dutch historical canon being a case in point.[47] These developments might serve mainly to further the assimilation of difference rather than help to open up a space for creating the kind of unity in diversity that does justice to a democratic culture. The result of this exclusive construction of Dutchness is that even migrants who have been born and raised here do not feel able, or inclined, to position themselves as Dutch, which shows that an essentialist approach to identity and cultural experience in the Netherlands stimulates a static and clearly demarcated form of identity-construction, both in migrants and in Native Dutch. As a result, the divide between us (the 'real' Dutch) and them (the 'others') runs deeper and deeper, which constitutes the greatest danger for new multicultural states, as was signalled by the UN Human Development Report of 2004. If the construction of the other as completely different prevails, it becomes nearly impossible to stimulate people to work together. Neither is the strong pressure on migrants to adapt themselves particularly realistic. The Netherlands of the twenty-first century is completely different from what it used to be, thus calling for an 'ability to adapt' on all sides, as much from the migrants as the Native. The Netherlands will never find a peaceful solution for the culturally complex country it has become if it is incapable of putting its own basic assumptions and self-concept up for discussion.

In order to create a new unity in the Netherlands, it is therefore essential for the Dutch national identity to be constructed as 'thinly' as possible, which would allow for differences to be included. This emphasis on diversity, though, is not about *preserving* culture or creating a new pillar. In the new Netherlands, with its traditional barriers broken down, this notion of unity in diversity should be about creating space where connections can be made between diverse cultures, a space in which cultural innovation and experimentation will be allowed to flourish. This requires a redefinition of the Dutch national identity in which identity can function as a web that ties differences instead of excluding them.[48] The main condition for establishing a common basis in the Netherlands is to take steps to create interspaces and, subsequently, to redefine what it means to be a Dutch national.

Emancipation from the Culturalist Discourse

In order to regain the balance between democratic structure and democratic culture, it is necessary to mirror the right of the individual to the freedom of expression and, thus, the right to be different. Above all, we need to challenge the dominance of the culturalist discourse in the Netherlands and in other Western European societies. Protecting the right to cultural difference and the claim to producing one's own culture are, in my view, two essential ways to tackle the dominance of

47 For an elaborate criticism of these developments see M Grever, 'Nationale identiteit en historisch besef: de risico's van een canon in de postmoderne samenleving', *Tijdschrift voor Geschiedenis*, 119/2 (2006), 160–77.

48 In this vein, see T Modood, 'Muslims and the politics of difference', *The Political Quarterly*, 74/1 (2003), 100–15, on redefining being British.

the culturalist discourse. In both instances, allowing space for difference appears essential. As the 2004 UNDP report shows, when individuals have the space and the right to their cultural identity, they feel safe enough to change and reshape their culture. In other words, the space for cultural recognition seems to be an essential precondition for individuals to feel secure enough to experiment with their culture and to initiate new connections with the diversity of cultures in them, or with other cultures. In addition to the right to cultural difference, it is essential to create space for producing cultural identity in the margins as a precondition of emancipation from the dominant discourse. Within this created safe space, self-narratives and self-appreciation seem to be crucial in resisting the negative images produced by the dominant discourse. In other words, we are dealing with a paradox and what we need is more culture to resist the culturalist discourse. Nevertheless, we need a different kind of culture: a culture of our own production.

In summary, I have undertaken to show in this chapter that the culturalist approach, combined with a new attitude that allows 'everything to be said, never mind the consequences', has reached a point where it is beginning to erode the most valuable foundations of Dutch society. Many have already jettisoned one of the most important Dutch virtues, tolerance. The paradox, then, is that, at a time when an attempt is being made to construct an essentialist Dutch identity with a canon of morals and values at its core, important historical Dutch virtues such as openness and tolerance are being violated. The breaking of taboos has tipped to such a point that Dutch communities find themselves pitted one against the other, which is where I see danger for the future of the Netherlands. It is imperative, therefore, for the new Netherlands to prioritize the development of a perspective that seeks to promote *new sources of communality and conditions for encounter and openness*.

To begin with, we need to stop exaggerating the negative aspects of cultural difference that are so prevalent within the dominant discourse, in order to be able to create space for cultural differences. We need to refocus towards those situations and realms in which people actually meet and in which *cultural differences play a part*. If culturally sensitive behaviour is our goal, we must first create an interspace for people to meet, recognize and acknowledge their similarities and differences. In a proper balance between being similar and being different, dialogue, encounter and innovation may arise. With the awareness that culture is only one aspect of our being together, working together and living together, ethnicity-transcending connections can be made.

Chapter 10

It's Not about Free Expression: A Sociological Examination of the Danish Cartoon Controversy

Sarah Dreier

Introduction

In 2005 a Danish newspaper demonstrated its panegyric for free expression by publishing 12 caricatures of the Muslim Prophet Muhammad, despite the belief held by many Muslims that the Prophet should not be depicted. The publication of the cartoons offended some Muslims and caused a political debate in Denmark reminiscent of the 1989 controversy in Britain sparked by Salman Rushdie's critique of Islam in *The Satanic Verses*. The debate, which started locally, soon spread to other countries in Europe, the Middle East, Asia, Africa and North America, and transformed into an international conflict of startling magnitude and deadly consequences.

This cartoon controversy is often discussed in a rather abstract way, as a conflict between the right to free expression and the related civic responsibility to respect religion. But a rights-based approach to the controversy fails to explain why the case spread internationally as it did and why it became such a sensitive political issue around the world. Rather than addressing this case as a conflict of rights and values, this chapter explores the events arising out of the original publication of the cartoons in terms of spaces of confrontation, where agents compete for power and prestige. Pierre Bourdieu's approach to reflexive sociology suggests that an agent's actions and intentions have political dimensions; agents are constantly struggling to maintain and increase their own positions of power, according to their specific, socially-structured perspectives and intentions. Even an agent's dynamic sense of what is 'good' and 'right' is shaped within this constant struggle.

Based on research conducted at the Oñati Institute, this chapter adopts Bourdieu's reflexive sociology as a framework through which to examine and consequently re-conceptualize the cartoon controversy. First, it briefly describes the Danish cartoons and the ensuing controversy. Second, it introduces Bourdieu's trio concepts of habitus, practice and field as a three-part lens through which to approach and re-conceptualize the cartoon controversy. Third, the chapter examines the international reaction to the cartoon controversy within the field of journalism in the United States and posits that Bourdieu's sociological approach provides a more meaningful explanation for what motivated and justified the US journalists' reaction to the controversy than does a rights-based discussion that is most directly concerned with the moral content of the rights. The final section suggests that there is a newly-emerging international space of confrontation that can be understood as a field of terrorism.

Bourdieu's conceptualization allows a sociological interpretation of the power dynamics that fuelled the controversy, and therefore a more comprehensive understanding of the real consequences at stake in this controversy that goes beyond the analysis of conflicting – or clashing – ideas. By exploring the social factors and processes through which the discourse on the Danish cartoons were mediated, this chapter sheds new light on the controversy.

The Cartoon Case

In September 2005 Denmark's largest daily newspaper, *Jyllands-Posten*, commissioned and published 12 original editorial cartoons depicting provocative interpretations of the Muslim Prophet Muhammad. *Jyllands-Posten*'s Cultural Editor Flemming Rose published the cartoons in reaction to several recent instances of self-censorship in Europe, which he believed were motivated by fear of Muslim retaliation.[1] Flemming considered it inappropriate that Muslims would retaliate against the public free expression of ideas. He published the cartoons to challenge what he considered to be a tenuous relationship between liberal democracy and Muslim culture and values, explaining that

> [s]ome Muslims reject modern secular society. They demand a special position, insisting on special consideration of their own religious feelings. It is incompatible with contemporary secular democracy and freedom of expression, where one has to be ready to put up with scorn, mockery and ridicule.[2]

Some Muslims regard any depiction of the Prophet Muhammad blasphemous and, therefore, considered the cartoons as intrinsically offensive. A few provocative cartoons represented Muhammad as violent or abusive, thus causing more widespread offence among Muslims. One image, considered among the most inflammatory, depicted Muhammad with an ignited bomb in place of a turban and carried an inscription in Arabic: 'There is no god but God, Muhammad is the messenger of God.'[3] Some Muslims saw these images, which were designed to present Islam as a violent religion, as an affront to Islam and Muslims worldwide.[4] Reminiscent of the Rushdie affair over 15 years earlier, the nascent controversy started locally. Those Danish Muslims who felt deeply offended organized public, peaceful protests against the publication of the cartoons. However, a few went further and resorted to attacks and violent threats.[5] In the weeks following the original publication, Danish Muslim groups requested an apology from *Jyllands-Posten*, a meeting with Danish Prime Minister Anders Fogh Rasmussen to discuss their grievances,[6] and a ruling from the Director of Public Prosecutions that the cartoons had violated Danish anti-blasphemy laws.[7] And like Rushdie before them, all these requests were denied. A group of angry Danish Muslims brought the cartoon controversy to the Organisation of the Islamic Conference

---

1   F Rose, 'Why I published those cartoons', *Washington Post*, 19 February 2006, available at <http://www.washingtonpost.com/wp-dyn/content/article/2006/02/17/AR2006021702499.html>.

2   F Rose, 'Muhammeds ansigt', *Jyllands-Posten*, 30 September 2005, available at <http://multimedia.jp.dk/archive/00080/Avisside_Muhammed-te_80003a.pdf>.

3   For descriptions of the cartoons, see H Fode, 'Decision on possible criminal proceedings in the case of Jyllands-Posten's article "The Face of Muhammed"', in *Danish Public Prosecutions, File No. RA-2006-41-0151*, 15 March 2006, available at <http://www.rigsadvokaten.dk/media/bilag/afgorelse_engelsk.pdf>.

4   See V Cornell, 'The face of the Prophet: Cartoons and Chasm', in Krista Tippett (interviewer), *Speaking of Faith,* American Public Media (16 February 2006).

5   'News Alert 2006: Danish newspaper receives bomb threat for cartoons of Muhammad', *Committee to Protect Journalists*, 1 February 2006, available at <http://www.cpj.org/news/2006/europe/denmark01feb06na.html>.

6   'Muslim Anger at Danish Cartoons', *BBC News*, 20 October 2005, available at <http://news.bbc.co.uk/2/hi/europe/4361260.stm>.

7   Fode, above, n. 3.

(OIC) meeting that December.[8] The OIC issued a statement declaring that the cartoons desecrated Muhammad and represented a 'rising hatred against Islam and Muslims in the world'.[9]

Despite subsequent reconciliatory statements from Rasmussen[10] and *Jyllands-Posten*,[11] the cartoon controversy spread internationally and became increasingly inciting.[12] European media began reprinting the cartoons to support *Jyllands-Posten* and free speech.[13] Leaders of several Islamic countries publicly condemned the cartoons and their subsequent re-publication.[14] Cartoon-related protests spread throughout the Muslim world,[15] where the cartoons were seen as a deliberate affront to Islam.[16] Aggrieved Muslim consumers boycotted Danish goods, costing businesses 134 million euros.[17] At least 139 people died in cartoon-related protests in countries including Nigeria, Afghanistan, Pakistan and Libya, and the Danish embassies in Damascus, Beirut and Tehran were attacked.[18] During the height of the conflict, Hezbollah leader Hassan Nasrallah assailed the cartoons and declared that only violent retribution would deter future affronts to the Prophet Muhammed: 'If there had been a Muslim to carry out Imam Khomeini's *fatwa* against the renegade Salman Rushdie, this rabble who insult our Prophet Mohammed in Denmark, Norway and France would not have dared to do so.'[19]

The cartoon controversy Provoked deeply-rooted cultural and political tensions amongst diverse populations within Denmark. For many, the cartoons were a lauded paragon of free speech,[20] and the protests indicated that Islam was incompatible with the values underpinning Western

---

8   HM Fattah, 'At Mecca meeting, cartoon outrage crystallized', *New York Times*, 8 February 2006, available at <http://www.nytimes.com/2006/02/09/international/middleeast/09cartoon.html>.

9   M Al-Mukarramah, '2005 Public Statement: Final Communiqué of the Third OIC Summit', *Organisation of the Islamic Conference*, 8 December 2005, available at <http://www.saudiembassy.net/2005News/Statements/StateDetail.asp?cIndex=568>.

10   'Response by the Danish Government to Letter of 24 November 2005 from UN Special Rapporteur on Freedom of Religion or Belief, Ms Asma Jahangir, and UN Special Rapporteur on Contemporary Forms of Racism, Racial Discrimination, Xenophobia and Related Intolerance, Mr Doudou Diéne, Regarding Cartoons Representing the Prophet Mohammed Published in a Newspaper', 23 January 2006, available at <www.um.dk/NR/rdonlyres/00D9E6F7-32DC-4C5A-8E24-F0C96E813C06/0/060123final.pdf>.

11   C Juste, 'Honourable fellow citizens of the Muslim world', *Jyllands-Posten*, 8 February 2006, available at <http://www.jp.dk/udland/artikel:aid=3544992:fid=11328/>.

12   See L Harding, 'How one of the biggest rows of modern times helped Danish exports to prosper', *The Guardian*, 30 September 2006, available at <http://www.guardian.co.uk/world/2006/sep/30/muhammadcartoons.lukeharding>.

13   Several editors were fired for this decision. For example, 'French editor fired over cartoons', *BBC News*, 2 February 2006, available at <http://news.bbc.co.uk/2/hi/europe/4672642.stm>.

14   Fattah, above, n. 8.

15   Fattah, above, n. 8.

16   For example, Vice-Chairman of the Central Council of Muslims in Germany, Mohammad Aman Hobohm, said: 'It was done not to defend freedom of the press, but to spite the Muslims.' 'Muhammad cartoon row intensifies', *BBC News*, 1 February 2006, available at <http://news.bbc.co.uk/1/hi/world/europe/4670370.stm>.

17   'Cartoon row hits Danish exports', *BBC News*, 9 September 2006, available at <http://news.bbc.co.uk/2/hi/europe/5329642.stm>.

18   'Muslim cartoon row timeline', *BBC News*, 19 February 2006, available at <http://news.bbc.co.uk/2/hi/middle_east/4688602.stm>.

19   'Hezbollah: Rushdie death would stop Prophet insults', *AFP*, 2 February 2006, available at <http://www.natashatynes.com/newswire/2006/02/hezbollah_killi.html>.

20   In fact, newspapers around the world republished the cartoons at their one-year anniversary to demonstrate the importance of free expression.

democratic traditions;[21] they concluded that 'Islam hates freedom'. For others, the cartoons were an unnecessary and unacceptable affront to Islamic values and a case that stepped beyond the appropriate bounds of free expression; they concluded that 'the West hates Islam'. Some international leaders took a more moderate stance: Participants in the 2006 United Nations Commemoration on World Press Freedom Day exalted the media's potential power to kindle dialogue and expose injustice,[22] and expressed dismay that, in the case of these cartoons, the media had instead become a globalized vehicle for incitement, degradation, alienation and Islamophobia.[23]

This chapter addresses important questions about the negotiations between freedom and civil responsibility. At the same time, it takes into account the unique and differing perspectives and premises from which each actor approached the controversy and the perceived stakes that each actor believed the controversy to implicate. To understand why the case moved and spread as it did, this chapter explores the social factors and processes through which the discourse on the Danish cartoons was mediated. This sheds new light on the controversy by identifying the type of rationality that each agent brings to the case. An analysis that does not take these vantage points into account quickly leads to sweeping, ineffectual conclusions, such as those described above.

Bourdieu's Reflexive Sociology

Bourdieu's approach to reflexive sociology suggests that agents' actions and intentions be examined against the backdrop of the objective relations between institutions and individuals and the specific historical development of rationality.[24] An agent (whether a journalist, policy-maker, religious leader, Muslim protestor, or newspaper reader) experiences the world as if it consisted of objective relations existing outside of, and independent from, her own vantage point. In contrast to this objective assumption, Bourdieu posits that every agent is oriented according to a particular habitus, that is, a dynamic perspective that develops within an historical and cultural context:

> The habitus is a structure of dispositions of thought and action which the actor acquires as a member
> of a social group or class. It is something like a mental and behaviour set (as psychologists would
> say), which the actor takes for granted and which structures her or his experience of things.[25]

A person's habitus serves as an orientation; it is socially acquired and provides a socially shared way of thinking about and acting toward the world.[26] Expressed differently, it is an internalized scheme, a shared set of dispositions, which orient and guide the agents of a particular group.[27] It is

---

21   See S Huntington, *The Clash of Civilizations and the Remaking of World Order* (New York: Simon & Schuster, 1996).

22   Statement given by Shashi Tharoor at the United Nations' World Press Freedom Day Commemoration, New York, 3 May 2006, available at <http://www.un.org/News/Press/docs/2006/obv555.doc.htm>.

23   Statement given by Kofi Annan at the United Nations' World Press Freedom Day Commemoration, New York, 3 May 2006, available at <http://www.un.org/News/Press/docs/2006/obv555.doc.htm>.

24   P Bourdieu and LJD Wacquant, *An Invitation to Reflexive Sociology* (Chicago, IL: University of Chicago Press, 1992), at 48.

25   EC Cuff et al., *Perspectives in Sociology* (New York: Routledge, 4th edn, 1998), at 320.

26   Ibid.

27   Bourdieu and Wacquant, above, n. 24, at 192–93.

the unified logic of practice, the 'socially-constituted "sense of the game"'.[28] Logically, any given habitus lends itself to specific practices that reflect a group's common experience, perspective and assumptions. A group's practices create its habitus, while at the same time mediating between its habitus and the social world in which the group is located. However, practices

> are not to be thought of in terms of means-end rationality, i.e. as the most efficient or effective means for attaining some goal, since each practice has its own endogenous (i.e. intrinsic or built-in) logic. Each social group therefore has a body of practices which are simply "what one does".[29]

Bourdieu's concept of practice reminds that objects of knowledge are socially constructed and are acquired in practice and also constantly aimed at these practical functions.[30] The field is an arena of struggle, a competitive social space where different forms of capital (economic, cultural, social or symbolic) are engaged by various actors; it is a dynamic space that is occupied by agents or institutions which share a specific habitus:

> These are social environments inhabited by one or more, usually by several, groups. A group is constituted as such by virtue of its location within the field, which typically involves competitive relations with other groups in the same field.[31]

These trio concepts (habitus, practice and field) are employed in the following pages to shed light on to how, and why, the cartoon case led to such contentious results – people approached the 'objective' world from that perspective which they considered to be true (habitus) and acted accordingly (practice).

From this lens, all agents are engaged in a constant struggle for legitimacy – or a negotiation for power – within their own field and between other fields. This struggle defines and dictates an agents' actions within the field, as they struggle to maintain and increase their own power within their field. This power, or legitimacy, within the field is measured in terms of the degree of social capital (whatever social capital is valued in that field) that any given agent possesses. Therefore, power is defined in terms of *objective structures*:

> These positions are objectively defined, in their existence and in the determinations they impose upon their occupants, agents or institutions, by their present and potential situation (situs) in the structure of the distribution of species of power (or capital) whose possession commands access to the specific profits that are at stake in the field, as well as by their objective relation to other positions (domination, subordination, homology, etc.).[32]

The habitus develops within this struggle. Agents struggle according to, and at times against, the accepted objective structures and habitus of the field in order to maintain or improve their own position within the objective structures of the field. As such, the habitus structures the struggles for power, and is also structured by the struggles. The habitus is therefore a dynamic orientation that reflects both past struggles and anticipated tensions.

---

28 Ibid., at 120–21.
29 Cuff et al., above, n. 25.
30 Bourdieu and Wacquant, above, n. 24, at 121.
31 Cuff et al., above, n. 25.
32 Bourdieu and Wacquant, above, n. 24, at 97.

This concept of habitus allows us to examine agents as *reasonable* – acting relationally within an historical moment and the specific logic of their field, according to (and even trapped within) what has been constructed as their rules of conduct:

> We must [...] seek the origins of reason not in a human "faculty", that is, a *nature*, but in the very history of these peculiar social microcosms in which agents struggle, in the name of the universal, for the legitimate monopoly over the universal, and in the progressive institutionalization of a dialogical language which owes its seemingly intrinsic properties to the social conditions of its genesis and of its utilization.[33]

The next section discusses the reaction to the Danish cartoon controversy by agents within the US journalism field from the lens of Bourdieu's trio concepts of habitus, practice and field, and in terms of their struggles for power within the journalism field.

The Pervading Logic of the US Journalism Field

In the original publication of the cartoons, *Jyllands-Posten* called upon – and indeed challenged – journalists to express their ideas freely rather than cater to specific Muslim values for fear of retaliation or retribution. As the cartoon conflict developed, one could argue that the republication of the cartoons was all the more merited: The ensuing controversy not only demonstrated *Jyllands-Posten*'s original assertion, but the cartoons had themselves become newsworthy. Although the cartoons could be seen to represent foundational principles of the journalism logic (unfettered expression and newsworthiness), the vast majority of newspapers in the United States refrained from republishing them. This research found only 27 US print publications (mainly local, alternative and/or university student newspapers) that reprinted any of the cartoons.

Many lauded US editors for respecting Muslim sensitivities. For example, US Assistant Secretary of State for European Affairs Daniel Fried attributed this overwhelming consistency to a consensus among US editors that free speech should be exercised in a context of respect:

> In the United States because of our own history there are certain editorial taboos, usually having to do with race, and they're not enforced by government edicts. They're enforced by a kind of social consensus [... I]n the United States on these matters our social consensus is very strong. But we also value freedom of the press, and in a free society editors, people work these things out in an atmosphere of freedom and respect.[34]

Yet others accused US editors of compromising free expression by succumbing to fear-based self-censorship. For example, an episode of the satirical television cartoon *South Park* critiqued the US media for compromising free expression in order to accommodate Muslim sensitivities:

> Freedom of speech is at stake here, don't you all see? If anything, we should all make cartoons of Muhammad and show the terrorists and the extremists that we are all united in the belief that every person has a right to say what they want. Look, people, it's been real easy for us to stand up for

---

33   Ibid., at 48.

34   D Fried, 'Interview with Danish TV2: The US-Danish Relationship' in *US Department of State*, 7 June 2006, <http://www.state.gov/p/eur/rls/rm/67731.htm>.

free speech lately. For the past few decades, we haven't had to risk anything to defend it. But those times are going to come, and one of those times is right now. And if we aren't willing to risk what we have, then we just believe in free speech, but we don't defend it.[35]

But the priorities and commitments of US news editors in this case cannot be understood exclusively in terms of rights (and of constraints on free expression) or responsibilities (and social consensus). These editors did not enter into the cartoon controversy debate with a neutral mind influenced only by their legal and moral values. Rather, they encountered this particular controversy as they are embedded in complex social mechanisms that objectively and subjectively define their 'rules of the game' and their positions of power within that game.

Bourdieu's approach and conceptualization allows a nuanced understanding of this consistent choice that neither of the two perspectives on rights and responsibilities can provide. Since each newspaper editor was acting within the habitus of the journalism field, her individual practice must reflect her specific social capital (among the most prominent being the publication's readership and circulation) and the correlating degree to which the agent subscribes to the logic of the field (a commitment to 'objectivity' which, Bourdieu posits, 'distinguishes "news" from the mere "stories" of tabloids'[36]). The empirical evidence suggests that the decisions and explanations presented by these editors can best be understood in terms of their negotiation for power and struggle for legitimacy within the journalism field and the dynamic habitus that has developed amid this struggle.

The 'Newsworthy' Logic

By the time US news editors were engaged in the Danish cartoon controversy, the cartoons had already incited Muslims around the world. These editors employed the logic of the field of journalism, avoiding the conflicting ideas of the case and the high stakes involved (among those stakes: causing offence, attracting criticism and protests, and loss of readership), by reaffirming their position as strictly objective news agents and their exclusive responsibility to relay the news. In December 2005 the *Associated Press* (AP, the world's largest news organization) decided not to distribute the cartoons because '[W]e don't distribute content that is known to be offensive, with rare exceptions. This is not one of those exceptions.'[37] *AP* revisited and reaffirmed that decision during the first week in February 2006, when the cartoon controversy attracted prime-time coverage in international news. By revisiting and rejecting the decision when the cartoons were most newsworthy, *AP* indicated that it was not necessary for them to reprint the cartoons in order to fulfil their responsibility to relay the news; the decision to print the cartoons was now their *choice*, rather than their obligation, one that they could frame in terms of a desire to be morally responsible.

By February 2006 the highest circulating newspapers (with one noted exception)[38] in the United States, including the *New York Times*, the *Wall Street Journal*, the *Washington Post*, the *Los Angeles Times* and the *Chicago Tribune*, announced that they would fully inform their readers of

---

35 'Cartoon Wars Part 1', in *South Park*, episode 142, Comedy Central, 5 April 2006.
36 Bourdieu and Wacquant, above, n. 24, at 101.
37 'Controversial cartoons stir worldwide media debate', *Associated Press*, 7 February 2006, available at <http://www.firstamendmentcenter.org/news.aspx?id=16430>.
38 The *Philadelphia Inquirer*.

the controversy with written descriptions of the images. Like *AP*, they avoided unnecessary offence without compromising their responsibility to relay the news.[39] See Table 10.1 for examples.

Table 10.1 Statements from representatives of nationally-circulating US news sources

New York Times editor: Bill Keller	[Publishing would be] perceived as a particularly deliberate insult [by Muslims]. Like any decision to withhold elements of a story, this was neither easy nor entirely satisfying, but it feels like the right thing to do.[1]
Wall Street Journal spokesman: Robert Christie	Readers were well served by a short story without publishing the cartoon … We didn't want to publish anything that can be perceived as inflammatory to our readers' culture when it didn't add anything to the story.[2]
Chicago Tribune managing editor: James O'Shea	We can communicate to our readers what this is about without running it.[3]
Chicago Tribune editor's note:	The Tribune chose not to publish the cartoons because editors decided the images inaccurately depicted Islam as a violent religion, and that it was not necessary to print the cartoons in order to explain them to readers.[4]
USA Today deputy world editor: Jim Michaels	We concluded that we could cover the issue comprehensively without republishing the cartoon, something clearly offensive to many Muslims. It's not censorship, self or otherwise.[5]
USA Today editor's note:	USA TODAY has not published the cartoons, preferring to describe their content instead. In political cartoons as in other content, the newspaper seeks vibrant commentary on issues of public interest, including those with a religious component, but it avoids symbolism likely to be perceived as gratuitously offensive to readers' religious beliefs.[6]
CBS Evening News producer: Rome Hartman	[This] should not be seen as somehow sanctioning or kowtowing to a violent minority, since the vast majority of Muslims would find the depictions of Mohammed inherently offensive.[7]

Note: [1] P Johnson, 'Media draw the line on running cartoons' in *USA Today*, 7 February 2006, available at <http://www.usatoday.com/life/columnist/mediamix/2006-02-07-media-mix_x.htm>; [2] Brinkley and Fisher, n. 39; [3] Ibid; [4] M Ramirez and MA Brachear, 'Why cartoons sparked furor', *Chicago Tribune*, 7 February 2006, available at <http://pewforum.org/news/display.php?NewsID=6322>; [5] Johnson, note 1; [6] K Parker, 'Faith, free speech: Where to draw the line?: Shameful appeasement' in *USA Today*, 8 February 2006, available at <http://www.mywire.com/pubs/USATODAY/2006/02/08/1187971?extID=10051>; [7] Johnson, note 1.

With notable exceptions,[40] all regional, local and even alternative newspapers and magazines in the United States similarly opted against republishing the cartoons. These news agents – with less access to social capital and therefore less power within the objective structures of the journalism field – had less power and access to influence the habitus of the field. Once the powerful agents set the standard for approaching the case, these agents were not in an objective position to go against that logic. But these objective struggles within a field also structure (and are structured by) the

---

39   J Brinkley and I Fisher, 'US says it also finds cartoons of Muhammad Offensive', *New York Times*, 4 February 2006.

40   This research identified 27 publications that reprinted one or several of the cartoons.

norms, morals and rationality of the field. Subjectively, each newspaper editor was acting according to the habitus which historically structured, and continues to be structured by, the struggles of the field.[41] Less powerful agents were, in effect, trapped by the existing habitus of the field, which was reinforced by the actions of the objectively powerful agents as 'that which "has" to be done or said'.[42]

Even among those 27 publications that acted against the consistent reaction of the mainstream agents, 14 of them did so according to the existing logic of the field. They explained that, contrary to the opinions of the mainstream agents, the cartoons were in fact key components of this important news story, and that they therefore had a journalistic responsibility to print the images for their readers. The *Philadelphia Inquirer* wrote: 'You run it because there's a news reason to run it.'[43] These agents who struggled against the mainstream agents accepted the responsibility that the mainstream media had 'failed' to realize. Student editors of Northern Illinois University's *Northern Star* said: 'Many American newspapers have yet to run these images, and we feel it is unfair to send our readers on a chase through Google to find the cause of such a newsworthy event.'[44]

But even in this example, the student editors acknowledged (and acted in line with) their comparatively low position of power within the objective structures of their field. As the evidence suggests, these 14 agents struggled in opposition to the mainstream agents, 'only to the extent that they concur[red] in their belief (*doxa*) in the game and its stakes'.[45] See Table 10.2 for more examples.

Table 10.2 Statements from news sources:
     'Newsworthy' justifications for running the cartoons

Phil. Inquirer	[W]hen a use of religious imagery that many find offensive becomes a major news story, we believe it is important for readers to be able to judge the content of the image for themselves, as with the 1987 photograph by Andres Serrano of a crucifix in urine.[1]
Mobile Press-Register	Now that the cartoons have become the story itself and are in the public domain, however, curious American readers have a reasonable expectation to see what is causing all the fuss.[2]
Northern Star	[The cartoons are] ignorant, tasteless, inappropriate and offensive [but readers deserved to know the] cause of such a newsworthy event.[3]
ABC News	You couldn't really explain to the audience what the controversy was without showing what the controversy was.[4]
Fox News	[Running the bomb/turban cartoon] doesn't mean you're being insensitive. It means you're a journalist and you're telling the story.[5]

Note: [1] Maykuth, n. 43; [2] 'Editorial: There's No Excuse for Cartoonish Violence' in *Mobile Press-Register*, 9 February 2006; [3] Roy, n. 44; [4] Brinkley and Fisher, n. 39; [5] Johnson, note 1, Table 10.1.

---

41   Bourdieu and Wacquant, above, n. 24, at 120–21.

42   Ibid., at 130.

43   A Maykuth, 'A Media Dilemma: The Rest of a Story', *Philadelphia Inquirer*, 4 February 2006, available at <http://www.philly.com/mld/inquirer/news/front/13788640.htm>.

44   L Roy, 'More than cartoons', *The Northern Star*, 13 February 2006, available at <http://www.star.niu.edu/articles/?id=19272>.

45   Bourdieu and Wacquant, above, n. 24, at 98.

The 'Free Expression' Logic

Other editors lamented that free expression has been endangered in the last few decades by a fear of causing offence.[46] Twenty newspaper agents positioned themselves at the dynamic, peripheral edge of the journalism field by republishing one or several of the cartoons as a celebration and defence of free expression against a controversy that was threatening its scope (the commentaries from several of these newspapers fit into both this category and the 'newsworthy' category). They were supporting the important right to publish content that may be considered offensive. The editor of one local, alternative news source wrote that America's self-censoring newspaper editors have compromised liberty:

> Free speech is like a Ferrari: What good is it if you don't use it or if you barely use it, only driving it in town, in stop-and-go traffic? It's useless until you can head out to the Arizona desert and push it past 150 mph. Short of libel, slander and impersonation, anything goes – that is, if you believe in the First Amendment.[47]

That fear of offence has allegedly led to journalistic immorality, for the most immoral action in public discourse is to 'declare a given topic "off limits"'.[48] Some asserted that journalists should not be intimidated by the threat of violence,[49] and the editors of the *Harvard Salient* even contended: 'The freedom to offend is far more important than the freedom from being offended.'[50] These agents were acting against the journalism habitus in order to restructure and reorient the logic and the stakes of the field as it was modelled by *Jyllands-Posten*, from compromising objectivity and respectability to compromising free expression itself. By presenting this reorientation, they struggled to assert themselves as the legitimate, responsible agents dedicated to the reoriented stakes of the field.

The 'Clash of Civilizations' Logic

Twelve US newspapers published the cartoons and said that the controversy indicated an irreconcilable 'clash of civilizations' between Muslim protestors and Western democracy. Most of these newspapers were alternative university student newspapers or local – often alternative – publications. Some of these agents said the Muslim world's reaction to the controversy indicated that Muslim extremism is an evil social force that threatens democracy, and made inflammatory and dehumanizing comments about either radical Islam or Islam as a whole. The *Austin American-Statesman* said that the 'violent, bloodthirsty, intolerant and [medieval] Muslim extremists' knife at the throat of European nations is real'.[51] The alternative university student publication *Tiger Town*

---

46   A Spiegelman, 'Outrageous cartoons and the art of outrage', *Harper's Magazine*, June 2006, at 46.

47   T Rall, 'The bland leading the blind: The nanny press and the cartoon controversy,' *Columbia City Paper*, 9 February 2006, at 12.

48   'Comics kill! … but words still leading cause of hurt feelings', *Oregon Commentator*, March 2006, at 4, available at <http://www.oregoncommentator.com/pdf/vol23_issue05.pdf>.

49   JK Wilson, 'The world of cartoon violence', *Indy* (Bloomington-Normal, IL), 15 February 2006, at 7.

50   SK Mahtani, 'The need for liberalism: Offensive cartoons and the purpose of freedom', *Harvard Salient*, 8 February 2006, available at <http://www.hcs.harvard.edu/~salient/issues/060208/060208_mahtani.html>.

51   See 'Cartoons are offensive, but reaction shows danger of extremists', *Austin American-Statesman*, 8 February 2006.

Observer produced the most degrading commentary examined in this study, depicting a battle between Western democracy and Islamic 'barbarism':

> Europe is turning into the battle ground of good versus evil; Western society versus a fundamentalist theocracy fuelled by the racist-themed manipulations of Islam. If Europe falls and doesn't stand up against these animals, it is only a matter of time before America finds itself in the same situation.[52]

See Table 10.3 (page 188) for more examples.

These actors dismissed the dominating ideals of the journalism field but their actions must still be examined within the objective structure of the field, and the habitus and practice they are opposing. For example, it is possible that many of these fringe agents derive their 'alternative' power within the field from their self-proclaimed deviation from the objective, newsworthy logic that defines the field: the *Oregon Commentator* is 'designed to provoke',[53] the *Harvard Salient* represents 'a few of Harvard's less worthy pursuits',[54] the *Tiger Town Observer* is 'Clemson's Conservative Journal of News and Opinion',[55] and the *Sacramento Valley Mirror* is 'an equal-opportunity offender'.[56]

Even so, the actions of these fringe agents probably contributed to the dominance that mainstream journalism agents have over the fringe players within the field. The mainstream agents avoided engaging the debate over clashing values and doctrines; they thereby avoided being associated with the 'extreme' or 'radical' perspectives which paraded the clash of civilizations rhetoric. Instead, the 'fringe' publications alone pursued the clash of civilizations thesis as an appropriate way of arguing and justifying their individual positions, the act of which confirmed the very logic the main agents sought to maintain. In other words, the case functioned as a way of maintaining an existing structure of power relations, that is, the 'pragmatic deal' between mainstream journalism and other mainstream agents to avoid conflicts over religious belief, a particularly sensitive area of US law and society. Furthermore, by this collective enactment of existing power relations, the attempts by 'alternative' players to challenge the status quo – the *doxa* – only exacerbated their status as alternatives, even making them into 'radicals' and 'extremes'.

The application of Bourdieu's conceptualization suggests that US news editors did not enter into the cartoon controversy debate with a neutral mind influenced only by their legal and moral values. Rather, they encountered this particular controversy as they are embedded in complex social mechanisms that objectively and subjectively define their 'rules of the game' and their positions of power within that game. The discussion takes into account each journalism agent's social capital and the correlating degree to which the agent subscribes to the logic of the modern US journalism field. The empirical evidence suggests that the decisions and explanations presented by these editors can best be understood in terms of their self-interested struggles for power, according to the rules and standards of journalism. By conceptualizing the case in this way, this examination avoids the bias that would be produced by an analysis that stays too close to the 'ideals', those abstract concepts of rights, freedoms, or responsibilities, as explanation for agents' commitments or priorities.

---

52   A Davis, 'A blood-drinking people', *The Tiger Town* (Clemson, SC), February 2006.
53   'Comics kill!' above, n. 48, at 4.
54   TR Kavulla (ed.), *Harvard Salient*, 8 February 2006, available at <http://www.hcs.harvard.edu/~salient/issues/060208/060208_index.html>.
55   Davis, above, n. 52.
56   T Crews, *The Valley Mirror*, email correspondence with author, 24 November 2006.

Table 10.3 Statements from news sources: The cartoons indicated a 'clash of civilizations'

Tiger Town Observer	Islam is a culture that thrives off of murder of the innocent, and extreme violence against the peaceful. Islam is a factory that pumps out terrorists brain-washed with lunatic ravings of mullahs in Madrassahs. Islam kills. This isn't some racist or bigoted charge. It is a very empirical, positive statement that any person with both eyes open … can see.[1]
Denver Rocky-Mountain News	Will the West stand up for its customs and mores, including freedom of speech, or will Muslims impose their way of life on the West? Ultimately there is no compromise; Westerners will either retain their civilisation, including the right to insult and blaspheme, or not.[2] 'Nothing could better illustrate the total lack of understanding of the foundations of a free society' [than the international Muslim reaction. Muslims have met the importance of free expression with] blank incomprehension.[3]
Stranger	There is no place for moral relativism when considering this group. Modern secular society is better than any ruled by religion, and if this truly is to be a war to the finish, as it appears to be, then I want secularism to win.[4]
Victorville Daily Press	The mindless violence by Islamic radicals is par for the course. But what is incredible is that the *Associated Press*, which distributes news stories and photos from across the globe, has decided that you shouldn't see it.[5] The fact that radical Muslims are going berserk over a cartoon says more about their mindset than it does about a cartoon … The sources of the riots and mayhem is not a cartoon. It is growing friction in a clash of cultures.[6]
Berkeley Beacon	This is an issue of freedom of speech, freedom of the press and the right to make political statements without fear of violent retribution. Declining to print these cartoons is handing a victory to a group that believes in precisely none of these values.[7] This issue indicated a clash between Western modern secular society heralding free speech and the 'primitive, barbaric thought' of Muslim 'reactionary extremists' who answer to ancient texts rather than liberal ideals.[8]
Syndicated Column Commentary	And unnaturally, much of the Western world has retreated into fetal repose. Only in Europe did a few newspapers republish the allegedly offensive cartoons, while most American papers have genuflected to the altar of multiculturalism.[9]
Chicago Tribune 'Letter to the Editor'	We are seeing an escalating clash of civilisations … But even more disturbing, the West is also increasingly unwilling to defend, or even articulate, its own unique values, in fear of seeming hurtful and judgmental. In this latest incident, Europeans are expected to show remorse – not so much for their bad taste as for their very way of life.[10]
USA Today 'Letter to the Editor'	I continue to be appalled by the reaction to the prophet Mohammed cartoons. To many in the US and world media, and certainly to a sizable part of the Muslim world, tolerance and cultural respect are a one-way street. Muslims literally demand it violently, yet they will not tolerate our cultural traditions … Our society thrives on political debate and discourse, but how can our society survive if the media selectively censor the information we receive in order to appease radical Islam?[11]
Harvard Salient	[We must] active[ly] assert … liberty in the face of a barbarian onslaught.[12]
Austin American-Statesman	I think it is becoming clearer and clearer that fundamentalism is a major problem in Islam. Much larger than the problem of fundamentalism in Christianity and other religions. As such, Islam must be destroyed as an ideology, much the same as we destroyed Nazism. We cannot discriminate between Islamic 'moderates' and 'extremists' at this point. The whole ideology must be destroyed.[13]

Note: [1] Davis, n. 52; [2] 'Europeans must stand up against intolerance: Cartoons that dare not show their face', *Denver Rocky Mountain News*, 7 February 2006, at 34A; [3] Ibid; [4] B Bawer, 'All the Rage: Islamic Fundamentalists Don't Just Have a Problem with Cartoons, They Have a Problem with Freedom', The Stranger, 9 February 2006, available at <http://www.thestranger.com/seattle/Content?oid=30432>; [5] D Holland, 'Our opinion: Censored image', *Victorville Daily Press*, 8 February 2006, available at <http://www.vvdailypress.com/2006/113940898034808.html>; [6] Ibid; [7] P Boyle, 'Mohammed cartoon creates controversy', The Berkeley Beacon, 16 February 2006, available at <http://www.berkeleybeacon.com/media/storage/paper169/news/2006/02/16/Opinion/Mohammed.Cartoon.Creates.Controversy-1617494.shtml?norewrite2 00701070630&so urcedomain=www.berkeleybeacon.com>; [8] Ibid; [9] Parker, note 6, Table 10.1; [10] VD Hanson, 'Connecting bad taste, freedom', *Chicago Tribune*, Commentary at 27, 10 February 2006, available at <http://uscpublicdiplomacy.com/index.php/newsroom/johnbrown_detail/060213_pdpr/>; [11] J Weaver, 'Cartoon furor points to clash of culture: Don't censor cartoons', *USA Today Final Edition* at 12A, 16 February 2006, available at <http://www.usatoday.com/news/opinion/editorials/2006-02-15-letters-cartoons_x.htm>; [12] Mahtani, n. 50; [13] 'Muhammad cartoon: Fundamentalism is a dangerous thing', Austin American-Statesman Online Statesman Blog, 3 February 2006, available at <http://cartoon.statesmanblogs.com/entry.aspx?q=956bbb1c-7456-4a68-98e2-975c017dda3a#comments>.

The Emerging Logic of the Terrorism Field

The previous section discusses the US journalism field's reaction to the Danish cartoon controversy; demonstrating that, on a micro-level, Bourdieu's trio concepts of habitus, practice and field provide a compelling explanation for journalists' perspectives and motivations, where even a field's norms of subjective morals have been structured by and have helped structure objective positions. An in-depth analysis of the international struggles that framed and moved this worldwide controversy and conflict extends far beyond this study. However, this final section applies Bourdieu's conceptualization to one troubling component of the international controversy – the concept of violent extremism – and suggests that modern-day terrorism can be understood as an emerging field of confrontation. This approach does two things. First, it provides a reasonable generalization as to why the Danish cartoon controversy erupted, within the context of broader international struggles rather than a clash of abstract rights. Second, it provides a context for assessing the deleterious effects that the divisive, militating 'clash of civilizations' rhetoric (as discussed in the previous section) has on the very threat of terrorism that these agents work to expose.

Many have speculated that some modern terrorism movements are, among other things, a product of transnational socio-political unrest and inequality.[57] Among them is social theorist Jürgen Habermas, who argued that fundamental extremist terrorism, including the attacks in the United States on 11 September 2001, reflects this current historical geopolitical condition of structural violence that spirals from distorted communication.[58] This distorted communication can be attributed to many factors, including cultural distance, societal socioeconomic disparities, or subordination owing to the 'unbounded capitalism' of the United States and its self-interested unilateral policies.[59]

Taking this thesis as a starting point, I suggest that the struggle amongst these 'terrorists' and the spectrum of agents who have responded to this emerging concept of terrorism have the qualities of an emerging field. This can be conceived as a new space of confrontation, in which violent, fundamentalist groups existing on the fringes of their religious field negotiate for a specific meaning of Islam and a specific position for Islam to hold, which would increase the power of selected individuals and increase their perceived 'right' to dominate. To be certain, the extremists that don themselves in the cloak of Islam are not a monolithic group but rather represent a myriad of cultures, beliefs, situations and demands. Nevertheless, these agents struggle at the periphery of the journalism, religion, government and economic fields to develop and carve out a space where the logic of religious-based violence is legitimate. They are struggling and negotiating at the periphery of those other fields to carve out a new space with a very specific *doxa*: the logic of religious extremism, where Islam is under attack and the integrity of the religion must be preserved at all costs – even holy war. This new field would strengthen the current and future objective positions of power enjoyed by these fringe agents if and as the logic of the new field emerges and gains legitimacy.

By naming terrorism as an emerging field, I do not implicate all agents within this field as terrorists. The epicentre of this emerging field of terrorism, I suggest, lies at the periphery of the

---

57   See, for example, J Esposito and D Mogahed, *Who Speaks for Islam? What a Billion Muslims Really Think* (New York: Gallup Press, 2007).

58   G Borradori, 'Reconstructing terrorism: Habermas', in G Borradori (ed.), *Philosophy in a Time of Terror: Dialogues with Jürgen Habermas and Jacques Derrida* (Chicago, IL: University of Chicago Press, 2003), at 64.

59   J Habermas, 'Fundamentalism and terror: A dialogue with Jürgen Habermas', in G Borradori (ed.), *Philosophy in a Time of Terror: Dialogues with Jürgen Habermas and Jacques Derrida* (Chicago, IL: University of Chicago Press, 2003), at 36.

religious field, where agents are struggling to establish an emerging logic which posits that terms of Islam – including *jihad* (holy struggle) – legitimately refer to terrorist acts including violence. Agents at the fringes of other fields (among them other religious or political fields) are exposed to, amenable to, influenced by, and potentially embody the logic of the terrorist field, based on their objective relations and habitus within those other fields and the power of the 'truth' of the specific logic of the emerging field.

A comprehensive social history of this emerging field of terrorism is beyond the purview of this study, but there is some evidence to suggest that this is an appropriate way to conceptualize terrorism. Agents around the world and from a variety of fields have engaged this struggle to promote or inhibit the emergence of this terrorism logic. For example, recent studies in Great Britain and the United States indicate a unique growing radicalization of Muslim populations (especially youth) who adopt the habitus of the terrorism field and consider violence and terrorism to be an appropriate expression of their religious identity.[60] Powerful agents in religious fields see the definition and legitimacy of Islam at stake amidst this emerging field of terrorism and have worked assiduously to maintain Islam's habitus as a religion of peace, contrary to the terrorists' claims. Powerful agents in the international fields, including the United Nations, the European Union, the United States and the OIC see the international stability at stake, and have asserted that terrorism is an ideological war that will only be won by divorcing Islam from violence. The US federal agencies[61] and US policy-makers[62] have spoken out arduously against the constant rhetorical association between Islam and violence, as an attempt to dismantle the habitus which the field of terrorism is attempting to claim and prevent the terrorism field from permeating, and amalgamating with, mainstream religious and political fields.

The original Danish cartoons pointed to the logic of terrorism and the ensuing controversy reflects the international struggles related to the emerging terrorism field at the periphery of other fields. In the journalism field, the original *Jyllands-Posten* publication identified and also strengthened the field of terrorism by framing the issue in terms of drastic stakes for Western journalism fields. It indicated that Islam, not terrorism, threatened the Western value of freedom of expression. In doing so, it framed high stakes for Western journalism (and democracy) but catered to the field of terrorism by inciting Muslims, demonstrating a preference for free expression above religious sensitivities, and failing to distinguish between terrorism and mainstream Islam.

In the government field, several Danish Muslims responded within the mainstream fields of governance in the Danish social and governmental system; the very rejection of their grievances provided support for the logic that Islam was somehow incompatible with secular governance. A few agents in Denmark then turned to external agents, those closer to the epicentre of the emerging

---

60   See, for example, *Muslim Americans: Middle Class and Mostly Mainstream* (Washington, DC: Pew Research Center, 2008). See also *Radicalization in the West: The Homegrown Threat* (New York: City of New York Police Department, 2007), available at <http://www.nypdshield.org/public/SiteFiles/documents/ NYPD_Report-Radicalization_in_the_West.pdf>.

61   The US State Department, Department of Homeland Security, and the National Counterterrorism Center; see '"Jihadist" booted from US government lexicon', *Associated Press*, 24 April 2008, available at <http://www.msnbc.msn.com/id/24297050/>.

62   See, for example, US Senator John Kerry (D-MA), speaking at the Center for American Progress Action Fund event, 'A New Approach to Fighting Terrorism', 31 July 2008 in Washington, DC, video available at <http://www.americanprogressaction.org/events/2008/07/senkerry.html>. See also US House of Representatives Congressmen Adam Smith (D-WA) and Mac Thornberry (R-TX), speaking at the Center for Strategic and International Studies event, 'Fighting Terrorism in the 21st Century: Sharpening the Tools of Strategic Communication and Public Diplomacy', 17 July 2008 in Washington, DC, video available at <http:// www.csis.org/component/option,com_csis_events/task,view/id,1743/>.

terrorism field, who intensified the case and delivered it to leaders of Muslim governments. It has been speculated that these leaders were losing grip of their peoples to Western democratic values. These Muslim government agents struggled to define the controversy as an indication that Europe did not respect Muslims, a logic which many, less powerful agents in the Muslim world adopted. Meanwhile, powerful religious and political leaders around the world struggled against this emerging logic, reasserting that Islam is not an inherently violent religion and therefore that the cartoons were both inaccurate and also dangerous.

When framed in terms of an emerging field of terrorism, it becomes clear that the cartoon controversy is fundamentally involved in the emerging negotiation for the power and legitimacy of terrorism. Taken from this lens, it is reasonable to speculate that those extreme, fringe newspaper agents discussed in the previous section whose text promoted the 'clash of civilizations' rhetoric and dehumanized Muslims were actually contributing to the strength of the emerging terrorism field. By implicating Islam as a whole, they reiterated and reasserted the logic that those at the epicentre of the terrorism field are struggling to establish: that liberal values militate against Islam.

Concluding Remarks

The Danish cartoons precipitated a controversy of startling and troubling proportions. It is likely to go down in history, along with the Rushdie affair, as a disturbing conflict that brings to bear several important and conflicting concepts. Among them are the right to free expression, the value of respecting religious sensitivities, the importance of not tolerating the intolerant and the issues of Islamophobia that colour our world. While these important topics are discussed, as they should be, they need to be considered at all levels within the context of power plays and social struggles.

This chapter intended to demonstrate that, while the cartoon controversy raised important questions about rights and responsibilities, these abstract concepts do little by way of explicating why the cartoon controversy imploded as it did. The controversy cannot be understood as one about free expression and civic responsibility, but rather one embedded in social and political contexts. The discourse about rights has a political context; it is not merely about abstract legal concepts but inevitably and inextricably linked to self-interest and objective power relations. This idea has important consequences. I suggested that even the concept of contemporary terrorism can be understood as an emerging field which is struggling for power against other, more mainstream religious and political logics; if this is the case, then the egregious statements made by agents in the fringes of the US journalism field not only represent negative conceptions of Islam that permeate and contaminate US conventional wisdom, but also have more widespread and deleterious effects on the strength and scope of terrorism. By reinforcing the erroneous and negative stereotypes against American Muslims, they ironically contribute to the purpose and agenda of terrorists and religious extremists.

Chapter 11

Pre-Empting Terrorism? Two Case Studies of the UK's Anti-Terrorism Legislation[1]

Reza Banakar

Introduction

Domestic and international terrorism, organized by groups and individuals who identify themselves with extreme interpretations of Islam, pose a serious threat to the security of Western democracies and the everyday safety of their citizens. Although the public generally supports special measures to prevent terrorism, a support which is partly a function of the official rhetoric on counter-terrorism, we find little consensus in legal and political circles on how these measures are to be planned and executed. The proponents of anti-terrorism policies argue that 'these are not "normal" times' and we live under extraordinary threats that can be met only by adopting exceptional (emergency) measures such as 'the suspension of normal rights and protections'.[2] The opponents, on the other hand, object to the excessive and draconian character of counter-terrorism measures, which in their opinion is leading to a gradual erosion of the fundamental rights underpinning the Western democratic systems.[3] Others argue that 'Western legal orders are not living in a time of emergency or terror', even though our leaders try very hard to convince us otherwise.[4]

Since the terrorist attacks of 9/11, much time and energy have been devoted to debating and devising ways of meeting the threat of terrorism without compromising democratic rights and civil liberties.[5] However, much of this debate is caught up in the ideological web of 'the clash of civilizations' manufactured by people such as Samuel Huntington in the 1990s.[6] Huntington views Islam from an essentialist standpoint as a monolithic cultural entity which is inherently despotic and oppressive and, subsequently, distinct from, and inevitably in confrontation with, the democratic Western civilization.[7] Those who knowingly or unwittingly share this monolithic

---

1   The editor acknowledges the kind permission of *Retfærd: The Nordic Journal of Law and Justice* to publish material from volume 3/122 (2008) in this chapter.

2   For a critical discussion see L Zedner, *Security* (London: Routledge, 2009), at 121–22.

3   C Walker, 'The treatment of foreign terror suspects', *Modern Law Review*, 70/3 (2007), 427–57.

4   D Dyzenhaus and R Thwaites, 'Legality and Emergency: The judiciary in a time of terror', in A Lynch et al. (eds), *Law and Liberty: In the War on Terror* (Leichhardt, NSW: Federation Press, 2007), at 9.

5   M Ignatieff, *The Lesser Evil: Political Ethics in an Age of Terror* (Edinburgh: Edinburgh University Press, 2005); WK Viscusi and RJ Zackhauser, 'Recollection bias and the combat of terrorism', *Journal of Legal Studies*, 34 (2004), 27–55; L Zedner, 'Security liberty in the face of terror: Reflections from criminal justice', *Journal of Law and Society*, 32 (2005), 507–33; L Lazarus and BJ Goold, 'Introduction: Security and human rights: The search for a language of reconciliation', in BJ Goold and L Lazarus (eds), *Security and Human Rights* (Oxford: Hart, 2007).

6   SP Huntington, *The Clash of Civilizations* (London: Simon and Schuster, 1997).

7   According to Abrahamian, after 9/11, 'the mainstream media in the USA, automatically, implicitly and unambiguously adopted Huntington's paradigm to explain September 11'. E Abrahamian, 'The US media, Huntington and September 11', *Third World Quarterly*, 24/3 (2003), at 529.

concept of Islam and believe in the inevitability of 'civilizational conflicts', understandably, treat domestic extremist groups and international terrorist networks as part of a homogeneous Islamic movement with the same anti-Western ideology and socio-political objective. Hence the tendency among many politicians, journalists, policy-makers and academics to privilege '"Islam" as an explanation for quite disparate phenomena, whether riots, disaffected inner-city youth, political radicalisation or violent extremism'.[8]

The basic assumption of this chapter is that versions of Islam operate as the medium through which loosely defined groups of people mobilise themselves around a religious banner in order to realize their political aims. Their chosen medium, that is, the various interpretations of Islam, admittedly becomes the message they communicate in respect to their identity and political and cultural aspirations, but this medium (like any other ideology) cannot act as a mobilizing force unless certain societal conditions are satisfied. These conditions, which ultimately shape the way Islamic movements manifest themselves, differ from society to society and over time. Thus, although militant networks and al-Qaeda groups operating in places such as Pakistan and home-grown Islamic terrorist groups in the UK might use the same type of anti-Western rhetoric, they represent different socio-political developments, address different audiences and serve different ends.[9] Violent resistance of the sort directed by 'nomadic insurgents'[10] against foreign troops in Afghanistan or Iraq, al-Qaeda's global war against infidels that is fuelled by a feeling of humiliation and resentment against the West, and the formation of Islamic militant groups in Britain are products of different social, cultural, economic and historical forces. Treating these as if they were the same political phenomenon provides for a fundamentally flawed conception of terrorism and the role of Islam in Western and Islamic countries.

Al-Qaeda, a shadowy network of Islamic militants and terrorists, which emerged out of the war against the Soviets in Afghanistan during the 1980s and the 1990s (in those days, they were supported and trained by the US, Pakistan and Saudi Arabia and celebrated in the West as freedom fighters), sees itself engaged in an epic battle for the re-establishment of the Islamic Caliphate.[11] Those engaged in Jihad against the foreign troops in Iraq and Afghanistan, misguided as their efforts might arguably be, justify their mission in terms of resistance to foreign occupation of their land. Finally, domestic terrorists and Islamic extremists, consisting mainly of British-born Muslims, are engaged in constructing an ethnic identity based on a common cause.[12] We shall not be able to grasp the aims and functions of their anti-Western sentiments and anti-democratic projects as long as we refuse to acknowledge their experience of political alienation and socio-

---

8   P Lewis, *Young, British and Muslim* (London: Continuum, 2007), at xiii.

9   For a historical analysis of the frustration and resentment that fuels Muslim extremist movements, see B Lewis, *The Crisis of Islam: Holy War and Unholy Terror* (London: Weidenfeld & Nicolson, 2003) and AS Ahmed, *Islam Under Siege* (Cambridge: Polity Press, 2003).

10   U Baxi, '"The war on terror" and the "war of terror": Nomadic multitudes, aggressive incumbents, and the new international law', *Osgood Hall Law Journal*, 43 (2005), 7–42.

11   This is, admittedly, an oversimplified description of al-Qaeda which is often employed by the media. Although al-Qaeda has a very small group of hardcore activists, it is not an organization but a world view; it is an idea, a style or a formula. As Jason Burke explains, many local groups, which are labelled as subsidiaries of al-Qaeda, have their own leaders and agendas and despite their 'supposed loyalty to al-Qaeda', do not 'recognize bin Laden as anything more than a fellow traveller'. J Burke, *Al-Qaeda* (London: Penguin, 2007), at 11.

12   I have discussed this issue at some length in R Banakar, 'The politics of legal cultures', *Retfærd: The Nordic Journal of Law and Justice*, 51/4 (2008), 69–90. Available at <http://papers.ssrn.com/sol3/papers.cfm?abstract_id=1323371>.

cultural marginalization in Britain.[13] Their resort to terrorism, which amounts to their rejection of democratic means for achieving political ends, is inseparable from their experience of exclusion from mainstream cultural and democratic processes.

UK law distinguishes between foreign nationals and British citizens suspected of terrorism. However, the political discourse that underpins the UK's anti-terrorism policy and justifies the draconian legal measure taken to pre-empt the threat of terrorism, treats national and international terrorism as having the same roots, that is, Islam. Thus, all Muslims – and the word 'Muslim' is used as a racial marker[14] – become potential suspects of terrorism.[15] Moreover, it is politically convenient to label various militant groups and individuals suspected of terrorism in Britain as agents of al-Qaeda, that is, as *alien* evil-doers. By regarding British-born Muslim extremists as alien elements controlled by an invisible evil hand from the mountain caves in Qandahar, one exonerates the British society and the UK Government of having any moral responsibility in respect of the radicalization of young British Muslims.

The focus of this study is on the measures adopted by the UK authorities to pre-empt the threat of Islamic terrorism in Britain. The impact of the UK's anti-terrorism policy and legislation on freedom of thought and expression, in general, and the socio-political and legal status of Muslim migrants living in Britain, in particular, provide the backdrop against which this study is conducted. *HMA v. Mohammed Atif Siddique* and *R v. Malik* provide our points of entry into the discourse on counter-terrorism. The remaining part of this chapter begins by briefly describing the Siddique case and the controversy that started with the statement made by his solicitor following the decision to sentence him to eight years on terrorism-related offences.[16] It then considers Malik's conviction at the Old Bailey and the decision of the Court of Appeal to quash her conviction on terrorism charges. Siddique's and Malik's cases will be examined in relation to the development of anti-terrorism legislation in the UK, arguing that the symbolic/ideological dimension of this body of legislation is realized within a neo-liberal paradigm of managerialism that has come to dominate the criminal justice system. Thus, this chapter will explore the anti-terrorism policy of the British Government in the light of what David Garland termed the 'culture of control', which marks the move from a criminal policy based on 'penal welfarism' to a governance of crime based on 'the management of risks'.[17] The chapter then goes on to discuss the identity politics of the 'war on terror' by examining the selective enforcement of anti-terrorism laws and asks if the modern liberal law can be a medium for dispensing justice in the 'war on terror' and safeguarding the rights of those who are affected by this 'war'. The chapter concludes by arguing that managerially inspired counter-terrorist measures aggravate the social conditions that give rise to terrorism.

---

13 According to Akhtar, the young Muslims' return to religion is not a revival of Islam as such – it does not necessarily mean 'an increased adherence to the Islamic code' – but 'instead refers more to individual empathy with a religious identity, an identity that provides group solidarity'. P Akhtar, 'Return to religion and radical Islam', in A Tahir (ed.), *Muslim Britain* (London: Zed Books, 2005), at 164.

14 K Goodall, 'Incitement to religious hatred: All talk and no substance?', *Modern Law Review*, 70 (2007), at 98.

15 See, for example, *Norwood v. DPP* [2003] EWHC 1 564 (Admin). In *Norwood*, the defendant was convicted under section 5 of the Public Order Act 1986 for displaying 'posters declaring "Islam out of Britain" and "Protect the British People"' following the events of 9/11. *The Law Gazette*, 'Silencing hatred', 7 June 2007, at <http://www.lawgazette.co.uk/print/2183>. Also see *Norwood v. United Kingdom* (Dec) (2004) 40 EHRR SE 11.1.

16 *HMA v. Mohammed Atif Siddique*, High Court of Justiciary, Glasgow, 14 September 2007.

17 D Garland, *The Culture of Control* (Oxford: Oxford University Press, 2001), at 18; also see Lazarus and Goold, above, n. 5, at 4–5.

The Terrorist from Alva

Mohammed Atif Siddique, a 21-year-old British-born Muslim student from Alva, a small town in Clackmannanshire, Scotland, was detained at Glasgow International Airport on 5 April 2006 as he was boarding a flight to Pakistan. He was released on the same day pending the examination of his laptop,[18] which later revealed to contain what the prosecution described as 'terrorist propaganda, partly emanating from al-Qaeda, glorifying terrorism […]'.[19] This material was purportedly to be used in the 'recruitment of English speakers, notably British nationals'.[20] A week later, Siddique's family home was raided at dawn by the police and security services who arrested and charged him under the Terrorism Acts 2000 and 2006. More than a year later, and after a trial lasting 19 days, he was found guilty of four terrorism-related offences[21] and, on 23 October 2007, sentenced to eight years' imprisonment.[22] When sentencing Siddique, Lord Carloway, the trial judge, explained that he was being convicted of a crime before he could actually commit it:

> The Terrorist Acts are designed by Parliament to stop, or at least reduce the risk of, terrorist outrages before that imminent stage is reached by creating a number of specific crimes, some of which you have been convicted of. These crimes enable a potential terrorist to be arrested, tried and ultimately convicted before actually committing whatever outrage he had in contemplation.[23]

On the day the jury delivered its verdict, Aamer Anwar, Siddique's lawyer, read a statement to journalists outside the courthouse criticizing the Scottish judiciary, the jury and the media reporting of the case. In this occasion, Anwar failed to explain if the statement he was reading represented his client's response to the court's decision, or his personal opinion of the outcome of the trial. He started by claiming that his client had been 'found guilty of doing what millions of young people do every day, looking for answers on the Internet', and went on to add that the verdict was a tragedy for justice and freedom of speech:

> It is farcical that part of the evidence against Atif was that he grew a beard, had documents in Arabic which he could not even read and downloaded material from a legitimate Israeli website […]. The sensational and biased reporting of this case breached the most important principle of justice – that people are innocent until proven guilty […]. Atif Siddique states that "he is not a terrorist and is innocent of the charges, that it is not a crime to be a young Muslim angry at global injustice". The prosecution was driven by the State, with no limit to the money and resources used

---

18   His laptop was seized by police officers who switched it on and opened the files against police protocol. *Stv. Tv News*. 'Terror trial told procedures were not followed', 28 August 2007. Posted at <http://www.stv.tv/content/news/main/display.html?id=opencms:/news/Terror_trial_told_procedures_were_not_fo>.

19   Lord Carloway's Statement on Sentencing Mohammed Atif Siddique, 23 October 2007.

20   Ibid.

21   Siddique was found guilty of the following four offences: 1) possession of articles which gave rise to a reasonable suspicion that they could be used 'for a purpose connected with the commission, preparation or instigation of an act of terrorism'; 2) breach of peace – he had shown images of suicide bombers and of the murder and beheading of persons by terrorists to various students; 3) provided 'instruction or training in the making or use of firearms and explosives' by means of the Internet; and 4) distributing or circulating 'terrorist publications by means of web sites'. See the Honourable Lord Carloway, High Court of Justiciary: Note at <http://www.scotcourts.gov.uk/opinions/CAR2510.html> [accessed 15 August 2008].

22   *HMA v. Mohammed Atif Siddique*, High Court of Justiciary, Glasgow, 14 September 2007. Also see <http://news.bbc.co.uk/1/shared/bsp/hi/pdfs/23_10_07_siddique.pdf>.

23   Honourable Lord Carloway, above, n. 19.

to secure a conviction in this case, carried out in an atmosphere of hostility after the Glasgow Airport attack and ending on the anniversary of 9/11. In the end Atif Siddique did not receive a fair trial and we will be considering an appeal.[24]

Lord Carloway described Anwar's statement as 'untrue or misleading' and referred it for contempt of court.[25] Thus, Anwar became the first lawyer in UK's legal history to be charged with contempt of court over a statement made after a trial and outside the courthouse. After considering all the relevant material in detail, a panel of three judges at the High Court of Justiciary in Edinburgh cleared Anwar of contempt of court, but criticized his conduct, reminding him that 'any solicitor practising in the High Court of Justiciary owes a duty to the court', which 'implies certain obligations upon such a solicitor' to ensure that his public utterances are accurate and not misleading.[26]

Although cases of Siddique and Anwar raise separate legal questions concerning terrorism offences and contempt of court, they are nonetheless parts of the same discursive process of negotiating Siddique's rights and duties. Inaccurate as Anwar's statement might have been from a legal standpoint, it constituted an attempt to *contextualize* Siddique's actions and intentions, the trial process leading to his conviction, and the eight-year sentence he was handed by the court, in the broader political setting of what it means to be a young Muslim living in post-9/11 and post-7/7 Britain. This broader *social context* can only be understood by taking into consideration the problematic relationship between mainstream British culture and politics, on the one hand, and the British Muslims, on the other. A recent study conducted by David Voas on behalf of the British Social Attitudes Survey shows, for example, that more than half of the British population have negative feelings towards Muslims and perceive them as a threat to their national identity and security (this point is further examined below under the section on Islamophobia).[27] The experience of living in a society, where more than half of the population considers one a threat to its national security and cultural identity, is an important part of the social context which is excluded from the judicial gaze. As we shall see in the final section of this chapter, the modern liberal law dislodges actions and intentions of the individuals brought before the law from their social contexts before legally examining them. In fact, abstracting actions and intentions from their socio-cultural setting is part of the methodology of modern law.

To form a better understanding of the forces that drive young British-born Muslim's towards extremism and the latent functions of the UK's anti-terrorism policy, we will consider Samina Malik's case in the next section. Malik's and Siddique's cases are similar in so far as they both concern young British-born Muslims convicted of possessing material downloaded from the Internet. However, the symbolic aspects of UK's counter-terrorism policy, that is, its potential to discipline young Muslims while pre-empting the risk they might pose to national security, are more evident in the Malik case.

---

24   The complete text of the statement can found in The Honourable Lord Carloway, 'High Court of Justiciary: Note' at <http://www.scotcourts.gov.uk/opinions/CAR2510.html> [accessed 15 August 2008].

25   *The Scotsman*, 'Lawyer faces jail for contempt', 30 April 2008, at <www.news.scotsman.com>.

26   *Aamer Anwar Case – Judgment Summary*, 1 July 2008, posted at <www.sacc.org.uk>.

27   The findings are to be published in 2010 in the British Social Attitudes Survey. See <http://www.telegraph.co.uk/news/newstopics/religion/6958571/Britons-are-suspicious-towards-Muslims-study-finds.html>.

The Lyrical Terrorist

Samina Malik, a 23-year-old British-born Muslim who worked as a shop assistant at Heathrow Airport, became the first woman convicted under the Terrorism Act 2000. The police arrested Malik at home, where she lived with her parents and siblings, in October 2006 after searching her room and finding her in possession of records likely to be used for terrorism purposes. This material, which included *The Al-Qaeda Manual*, *The Mujahidin Poison Handbook*, *Encyclopaedia Jihad* and *How to Make Bombs*, all downloaded from the Internet, became the basis for the prosecution's prima facie evidence. Some of these 'had been downloaded, opened, then deleted'.[28] On the basis of this evidence, Malik was charged with two counts of offences contrary to sections 57 and 58 of the Terrorism Act 2000:

> Count one alleged that the defendant had had "in her possession an article, namely, a computer hard drive with a collection of documents on it, in circumstances which gave rise to a reasonable suspicion that her possession of it was for a purpose connected with the commission, preparation or instigation of an act of terrorism", contrary to s 57 of the Act. Count two alleged that she had had "in her possession a record, namely, a computer hard drive with a collection of documents on it, which contained information that was likely to be useful to a person committing or preparing an act of terrorism", contrary to s 58 of the Act.[29]

At the Old Bailey, the court heard that Malik had posted poems on extremist websites under the screen name 'Lyrical Terrorist', 'praising Bin Laden, supporting martyrdom and discussing beheading'.[30] In addition, she had written on the back of a WHSmith receipt, 'The desire within me increases every day to go for martyrdom'.[31] She told the court that her poems were 'meaningless' and she had used the nickname 'Lyrical Terrorist' because she thought that it sounded 'cool'.[32] According to the Court of Appeal:

> Following her arrest, the defendant wrote several pages of notes in which she gave an account of how, two or three years earlier, she had been influenced by radical Islamic preachers and, as a result, had downloaded articles, books, talks and videos from the Internet and had started to write poetry about killings and beheadings. That was something she had come to regret and, for around two years, had had no further dealings with extremist material.[33]

In response, the prosecution argued that the records Malik had in her possession strongly indicated that she 'was deeply involved with terrorist related groups'.[34] The prosecution also argued that that 'she was an 'unlikely yet "committed" Islamic extremist, with a library of material which

---

28   *R v. Malik* [2008] All ER (D) 201 (Jun), Court of Appeal, Criminal Division, Lord Phillips of Worth Matravers CJ, Goldring and Plender JJ, 17 June 2008, <http://cyberlaw.org.uk/2008/06/18/r-v-malik-2008-all-er-d-201-jun/>.

29   *R v. Malik*, ibid.

30   *BBC News*, '"Lyrical Terrorist" found guilty', 8 November 2007, at <http://news.bbc.co.uk/2/hi/uk_news/7084801.stm>.

31   *The Sun*, 'Woman convicted over terror', 8 November 2007, at <http://www.thesun.co.uk>.

32   *The Independent*, 'UK woman found guilty of terror offences', 11 November 2007, at <http://news.independent.co.uk>.

33   *R v. Malik*, above, n. 28.

34   *BBC News*, above, n. 30.

she had collected for terrorist purposes'.[35] The head of the Metropolitan Police Counter Terrorism Command supported the prosecution by pointing out that:

> Malik held violent extremist views which she shared with other like-minded people over the Internet. She also tried to donate money to a terrorist group [...]. She had the ideology, ability and determination to access and download material, which could have been useful to terrorists. Merely possessing this material is a serious criminal offence.[36]

The jury deliberated for 19 hours before reaching its verdict. Malik was found not guilty of an offence under section 57 of the Terrorism Act 2000, which criminalizes the possession of an article for terrorist purposes, but guilty under section 58, according to which an offence is committed if a person (a) collects or makes a record of information of a kind likely to be useful to a person committing or preparing an act of terrorism; or (b) possesses a document or record containing information of that kind. The maximum sentence at Crown Court is 10 years.

The judge bailed Malik on 'house arrest' and ordered reports into her family background ahead of the sentencing on 6 December 2007. He told Malik that her 'crime was on the "margins" of the offence of which she was found guilty' and admitted that she 'was of "good character" and from a "supportive and law-abiding family who are appalled by the trouble that you are in"'.[37] The judge also admitted that Malik was in many ways 'a complete enigma' to him. Malik, who had already spent five months in custody, was sentenced to nine months' imprisonment, suspended for 18 months, under section 58 of the Terrorism Act 2000.

However, on 17 June 2008 the Court of Appeal quashed her conviction after the Crown conceded that it was unsafe. In his judgment, Lord Phillips explained:

> There had been a case to answer, based on the seven documents identified by the prosecution; however, the problem was that the case had been left to the jury on the basis that the other documents were also capable of forming the basis of the conviction. In relation to the issue of 'practical assistance' to a person committing or preparing an act of terrorism, the jury had not received a direction as to the issue of practical utility. There was not a great deal of difference in directing the jury that the document or record had to be likely to be useful, and directing them that it was likely to be of practical utility. In the right context, that direction might be unexceptionable. However, the primary problem in the instant case was that the jury had considered not merely documents which were capable of practical utility but also a large number which were not. There was scope in the instant case for the jury to have become confused. In all the circumstances, the conviction was unsafe.[38]

The 'other documents', which were presented to the jury as 'capable of forming a conviction', included Malik's poetry and other personal records.

Sue Hemming, Head of the Crown Prosecution Service's Counter Terrorism Division, responded by explaining that Malik had not been prosecuted for her poetry, but for possessing documents that could provide practical assistance to terrorists. In addition, while working at Heathrow Airport, she

---

35   *The Guardian*, '"Lyrical Terrorist" convicted over hate records', 9 November 2007, at <http://www.guardian.co.uk>.

36   *BBC News*, above, n. 30.

37   *The Guardian*, 'Lyrical Terrorist sentenced over extremist poetry', 6 November 2007, at <http://www.guardian.co.uk/uk/2007/dec/06/terrorism.books>.

38   *R v. Malik*, above, n. 28.

had supplied information about airport security procedures to Sohail Qureshi, who later pleaded guilty to a terrorist offence and, subsequently, was jailed for four and a half years for 'planning to travel to Afghanistan on a mission of "revenge" against British troops'.[39] Hemming also added that since Malik's conviction, the meaning of section 58 of the Terrorism Act 2000 had been clarified in a Court of Appeal decision.[40]

This case raises several interrelated questions. Firstly, it remains unclear whether Malik is a danger to national security. The Court of Appeal has clarified the law, but the prosecution and the Police Counter Terrorism Command remain adamant that it was right to prosecute Malik on terrorism charges. Why were Malik's terrorist connections not emphasized when she was prosecuted at the Old Bailey in 2006? Why does Hemming not explain the nature of Malik's involvement and the type of security information she passed on to the 29-year-old Qureshi who had been prosecuted for planning to travel to Afghanistan to fight the British troops? Is the CPS dropping Malik's case because there is no 'public interest' in pursuing a conviction? I am using the term 'public interest' in two senses here: (1) in the sense of public safety; and (2) in a broader sense of attracting the attention of the general public and the media. Secondly, there is more than a hint, in particular in the media, that Malik's poetry was sufficient grounds for her conviction. Notwithstanding Hemming's clarifications that Malik was not prosecuted for her poetry, her posting of poems on extremist websites was used by the prosecution to prove that she was 'deeply involved with terrorist related groups'.[41] It means that in anti-terrorism cases of this type, the rights of terrorism suspects can be obscured by a public discourse that combines official anti-terrorist rhetoric – anxious to talk and act tough – and Islamophobic sentiments. This was one of the controversial points in the statement made by Siddique's solicitor and the reason why he was charged with contempt of court after the trial and outside the court. Thirdly, why was Malik 'an enigma' to the judge? Had the court not been told that Malik was '20 years old when she "first started to consider Islam" and was "like most teenagers, somewhat rebellious"'?[42] Finally, what does this case and other similar cases such as Munshi's (discussed in Chapter 1) and Siddique's say about the relationship between law, justice and politics in today's Britain and in the wake of 9/11 and the 7 July bombings in London? Should we understand the actions of Malik, Munshi and Siddique in terms of how the British society views its Muslim communities, or should we attribute them to the influence of anti-Western terrorist networks external to Britain?

---

39   *The Telegraph*, '"Lyrical Terrorist" Samina Malik cleared on appeal', 17 June 2008, at <www.telegraph.co.uk>.

40   According to the Crown Prosecution Service (CPS), in *R v. K* in February 2008, the Court of Appeal 'ruled that an offence would be committed only if the document or record concerned was of a kind that was likely to provide practical assistance to a person committing or preparing an act of terrorism. A document that simply encouraged the commission of acts of terrorism was not sufficient'. *CPS response to Samina Malik appeal* at <http://www.cps.gov.uk/news/pressreleases/143_08.html>.

41   *BBC News*, above, n. 30.

42   *The Guardian*, 'Lyrical Terrorist sentenced over extremist poetry', 6 November 2006, at <http://www.guardian.co.uk/uk/2007/dec/06/terrorism.books>.

The Law

Anti-Terrorism Legislation

The first Prevention of Terrorism (Temporary Provisions) Act (PTA 1974) was introduced in 1974 as a response to Irish terrorism soon after the Birmingham pub bombings in which 21 people died and over 180 were injured.[43] This legislation, which was originally intended as a strictly 'temporary provision', was extended in 1984 to meet the rising incidents of international terrorism in the UK. Parliament enacted the Terrorism Act 2000 (TA 2000) following a review of terrorism legislation by Lord Lloyd. The British Government agreed with Lord Lloyd that 'there will be a continuing need for counter-terrorist legislation for the foreseeable future', and that there were sound reasons for replacing the temporary provisions of the PTA 1974 with a permanent legislation.[44] The TA 2000 introduced, for the first time, the main body of the anti-terrorism legislation in one code. It was further expanded a year later when, in a response to the 9/11 attacks, the Government rushed through emergency legislation to increase powers to deal with individuals suspected of planning or assisting terrorist attacks in the UK. The 9/11 attacks became a watershed for how the UK dealt with the issue of terrorism and shaped its counter-terrorist response.[45] The UK's new approach to terrorism is reflected in the controversial provisions of Part 4 of the Anti-Terrorism, Crime and Security Act 2001 (TCSA 2001), according to which:

> Firstly, the Act allows for indefinite detention without trial of certain suspected international terrorists. Secondly, it excludes the courts' customary powers of judicial review. Thirdly, in order to be compatible with the UK's international obligations under the European Convention of Human Rights (ECHR), the Government derogated from Article 5 which provides for an individual's right to liberty and security.[46]

The TCSA 2001 marked the UK's shift from a traditional, reactive counter-terrorism policy to 'intelligence-based proactive methods [with] the primary aim of preventing terrorist attacks'.[47] The new provisions enabled the authorities to 'target and control the activities of suspected terrorists' and more effectively manage the risk of terrorism and protect public safety by intervening earlier.[48] However, in *A and Others v. Secretary of State for the Home Dept*, the House of Lords declared the key provisions of Part 4, which allowed detention without trial, as incompatible with Articles 5 and 14 of the European Convention of Human Rights (ECHR).[49] To remedy this incompatibility,

---

43   See Legislation Against Terrorism: A consultation paper, December 1998, at <http://www.archive.official-documents.co.uk/>. Police arrested and charged six Irish Catholic men with 21 counts of murder for the Birmingham pub bombings. However, it transpired that police had beaten out the confessions that led to their conviction. They subsequently spent 16 years in jail before the Court of Appeal freed them in 1991.

44   HJ Bailey, *Civil Liberties Cases and Material* (London: Butterworths Lexis Nexis, 5th edn, 2001), at 567.

45   H Fenwick, *Civil Liberties and Human Rights* (London: Routledge/Cavendish, 4th edn, 2007), at 1329.

46   Detention of Suspected International Terrorists: Part 4 of The Anti-Terrorism, Crime and Security Act 2001. Research paper 02/52 (16 September 2002), at <http://www.parliament.uk/commons/lib/research/rp2002/rp02-052.pdf>.

47   N Whitty, T Murphy and S Livingstone, *Civil Liberties in Human Rights Era, 2001* (London: Butterworths, 2001), at 143.

48   Fenwick, above, n. 45, at 1332.

49   *A v. Secretary of State for the Home Department* [2004] UKHL 56; [2005] 2 AC 68; [2005] 2 WLR 87; [2005] 3 ALL ER 169.

the Government introduced the Prevention of Terrorism Act 2005 (PTA 2005), in which Parliament repealed the key provisions of Part 4 and, instead, gave the Home Secretary powers to impose the so-called 'control orders', restricting the freedom of terrorist suspects. The orders issued in 2005 often amounted to house arrests and 'several were subsequently struck down by the courts as incompatible with Article 5 of the ECHR'.[50] The Terrorism Act 2006 (TA 2006) did not introduce further proactive measures, but gave the police the powers to detain terrorist suspects up to 28 days without charge.

Symbolic Effects of the Anti-Terrorism Legislation

Fenwick points out that 'one of the most striking aspects of these provisions is their under-use'.[51] Although they apply to a wide variety of groups and individuals, from 'freedom fighters' to terrorists and to ordinary people who might unknowingly come into contact with terrorists, the executive applies these measures with discrimination. This is partly owing to difficulties that security services face in relation to producing evidence that can endanger, for example, their informants. However, Fenwick means that there are other reasons for the 'under-use' of these counter-terrorism sanctions:

> The counter-terrorism provisions [...] appear to be intended to have an effect that, to an extent, is more symbolic than actual. They are viewed by the government as playing an important role in signalling this society's rejection of the message of certain groups – to isolate and marginalise them, to deny them some legitimacy on the basis that they have refused to use democratic methods, restoring instead to an anti-democratic course of creating terror by using violence targeted at civilians.[52]

Fenwick's insight can be supported by numerous cases where British Muslims have been arrested and charged for terrorist offences with maximum publicity and under the media's watchful eye, but eventually found innocent. However, their acquittal as a rule fails to attract much media attention.[53] Fenwick's hypothesis also throws light on some of the unusual circumstances of the Malik case and provides tentative answers to some of the questions we raised earlier in the previous section. It explains, for example, why the Crown Prosecution Service (CPS) was not willing to pursue the case further; the CPS had succeeded in what it set out to do, namely to make an example of Malik. It also explains why there was so much emphasis on Malik's poetry by the prosecutor and the press; they represented the type of ideas and thoughts that 'this society' does not tolerate. In this sense, Malik, but also others such as the teenager Munshi (discussed in Chapter 1) and Siddique, were, arguably, prosecuted for 'thought crimes'. I should hasten to add that there is no conspiracy

---

50   C Walker, 'The United Kingdom's anti-terrorism laws: Lessons for Australia', in A Lynch et al. (eds), *Law and Liberty in the War on Terror* (Sydney: Federation Press, 2007), at 183.

51   Fenwick, above, n. 45, at 1333.

52   Fenwick, above, n. 45, at 1333.

53   The so-called 'ricin case' is a case in point. Police raided a flat in North London with maximum publicity, arrested several people and, on 6 January 2003, Scotland Yard issued a press release that ricin had been found. *The Daily Mail* carried the headline: POISON GANG ON LOOSE: huge hunt for terrorists armed with deadly ricin. Three years later, on 8 April 2005, the jury found those accused of the ricin plot innocent. Their acquittal, however, failed to make the headlines. In the meantime, Moulmoud Sihali, one of those arrested on suspicion of being involved in planning a ricin attack, spent two years and seven months in a high security prison. See C Atkins et al., *Taking Liberties* (London: Revolver Books, 2007), at 120–30.

between the Government, the courts, the law enforcing agencies and the press to depict the Muslim communities in a negative light in order to stigmatize them as terrorists. As we shall see in the next section, there is no need for such conspiracy; a large section of the public opinion already regards Muslims as a continuing threat to security and implicated in terrorism.

Zedner related this sense of continuing threat to the conflation of three meanings of the word 'security', as a 'condition of being without threat', a 'neutralisation of threats' and a 'form of avoidance of non-exposure to danger'.[54] The conflation of these three senses of security leads to a:

> [...] curious inversion of the usual logic of crime control. Instead of crime requiring crime control, we might say that crime control requires that there will be crime. The presumption of a continuing threat is an important factor in keeping crime high on a political agenda that has invested so much capital in its control.[55]

Muslims in general, and individuals such as Malik, Munshi and Siddique, are used in public political discourse to sustain and enhance this 'presumption of continuing threat'. How the symbolic effects of the anti-terrorism legislation translate into normative ordering of social relations and influence other areas of law and law enforcement can be seen, for example, in the discretionary enforcement of stop and search powers under the TA 2000.

Stop and Search Powers

The power to stop and search terror suspects under section 44 of the TA 2000 provides a senior police officer with the power to authorize blanket stop and search powers in a designated area if he or she considers it expedient for the prevention of acts of terrorism.[56] The 'law enforcement authorities enjoy extremely wide discretion in deciding how – and in particular against whom – to use these far reaching powers'.[57] Stop and search can also be authorized under the Police and Criminal Evidence Act 1984 (PACE). However, it is also an important part of the TA 2000; important in the sense that it demonstrates how the discretionary powers, which allow officers to stop and search persons or vehicles 'on reasonable grounds',[58] affect the individuals and communities that happen to find themselves at the receiving end of such policies. The official statistics collected by the police and the Home Office show that the uses of these powers have been disproportionately targeted on young black and British Asians, who 'are six times more likely to be stopped by the police than white people'.[59] The Home Office revealed in 2004 that the number of Asians being stopped and searched under the 2000 Terrorism Act had gone up by more than 300 per cent: from

---

54   L Zedner, 'The concept of security: An agenda for comparative analysis', *Legal Studies*, 23 (2003), 153–76, at 155.

55   Zedner ibid., at 155.

56   The power conferred under the TA 2000 allows an officer to search for articles of a kind that could be used in connection with terrorism, whether or not there are grounds for suspecting the presence of such articles (sections 45(1) and (2)). See Home Office, Circular HPAN-628GM4 at <http://www.knowledgenetwork.gov. uk/HO/circular.nsf> [accessed 28 January 2008].

57   D Moeckli, 'Stop and search under Terrorism Act 2000: A comment on R (Gillan) v. Commissioner of Police for the Metropolis', *Modern Law Review*, 70/4 (2007), 659–79, at 660.

58   Moeckli, ibid., at 669, argues that a stop and search under TA 2000 does not meet the proportionality requirement of Article 14 of the ECHR. Also see B Bowling and C Phillips, 'Disproportionate and discriminatory: Reviewing the evidence of stop and search', *Modern Law Review*, 70/6 (2007), at 936–37.

59   *The Guardian*, 'Stop and search', 31 January 2008.

744 to almost 3,000.[60] In practice, stop and search powers have come to rely on racial profiling to target primarily blacks and other ethnic minorities of colour in deprived areas of large cities.[61] As Bowling and Phillips point out, 'the concept of "reasonable suspicion" is frequently absent in many instances of the use of police stop/search powers', and instead are often based 'on generalisations and stereotypes, particularly where levels of discretion are highest'.[62]

The Culture of Control

Not only the application of stop and search powers, but also the enforcement of counter-terrorism legislation in general, as in Malik's conviction at the Old Bailey, should be studied against the background of the recent development of crime control strategies and the debate on the rise of punitiveness in contemporary Britain and other Western nations.[63] In the face of rising criminality and the failures of criminal policies of the 1960s and 1970s, which were based on rehabilitation and reform, penal-welfarism has been, according to Garland, replaced with a new form of repressive and managerial crime control strategy:

> The penal-welfare approach proceeded as if the interest of society and the interest of the offender could be made to coincide. Rehabilitating offenders, reforming prisons, dealing with the roots of crime – these were in the interest of everyone [...] today the interests of convicted offenders, in so far as they are considered at all, are viewed as fundamentally opposed to those of the public. If the choice is between subjecting offenders to greater restrictions or else exposing the public to increased risk, today's common sense recommends the safe choice every time. In consequence, and without much discussion, the interests of the offender, and even his or her rights, are routinely disregarded.[64]

The basic assumption of this new strategy is that significantly high levels of criminality should be regarded as permanent features of social life (similarly, the introduction of the TA 2000 was justified by arguing that 'there will be a continuing need for counter-terrorism legislation'). The question is no longer how the levels of criminality can be brought down, for all such attempts have failed, but how to manage the risks that criminality poses to the public (similarly, we are told that we must live with the continuing threat of terrorism). The general approach to criminality, whether it is the traditional forms of crime against person and property, or the more recent forms of terrorism, is to minimize its risk of happening. Judging from the evidence, this can also mean detaining those who, for whatever reason, have come under suspicion without charge. Admittedly, the detention of all those who fit the terrorist profile and/or draw suspicion of authorities might reduce the short-term risk of terrorism. It also sustains and enhances what Zedner meant by the 'presumption of

---

60   V Dodd, 'Asian men targeted in stop and search', *The Guardian* (17 August 2005), posted at <http://www.guardian.co.uk/> [accessed 28 January 2008].

61   For a discussion see R Banakar, 'Whose experience is the measure of justice?', *Legal Ethics*, 10 (2008), 209–22.

62   Bowling and Phillips, above, n. 58, at 936–37.

63   Nicola Lacey uses the idea of 'penal populism' to denote the same development within contemporary democracies. She writes: 'A substantial scaling down of levels of punishment and criminalisation is regarded as politically impossible, the optimism of welfarism a thing, decisively, of the past. The rehabilitative ideas [...] seem a distant echoes of a lost world [...]'. N Lacey, *The Prisoner's Dilemma: Political Economy and Punishment in Contemporary Democracies* (Cambridge: Cambridge University Press, 2008), at xv–xvi.

64   Garland, above, n. 17, at 180.

continuing threat'.[65] The problem with such a policy is that it concentrates on the symptoms rather than the causes of the problem, and it is nonchalant towards the rights of those who happen to fit the authorities' profile of a terrorist. In addition, as the incidents that led to Jean Charles de Menezes, a Brazilian immigrant living in South London, being gunned down mistakenly by the anti-terrorist police officers showed,[66] the police's profiling method is essentially based on ethnic categories.[67] Counter-terrorism policies, which fail to ensure that the state's response to terrorism is 'limited, well-defined and controlled', will pose 'greater threat to the political and civil traditions that are central to the liberal democratic way of life'.[68]

The text quoted above from Garland's *Culture of Control*, would give us a description of the UK's anti-terrorism policy if we replaced the word 'offender' with 'terrorist suspect'. There is, however, a significant difference between 'offender' and a 'terrorist suspect': the latter has neither been charged, nor tried, nor convicted of any crime. Yet, his/her rights are disregarded in the same way – a fact that has caused several clashes between the judiciary and the UK Government. The fact that the most draconian anti-terrorism measures, such as control orders[69] and stop and search powers, are imposed on ethnic minorities, and Muslims in particular, racializes the legislation as a whole.

The judicial system is often criticized for being oblivious to the racial aspects of law's internal operations.[70] This said, and in respect to issues rising out of the Government's anti-terrorism policy and legislation, the judiciary generally regards itself bound by the principles of human rights and the doctrine of the rule of law. The Government, on the other hand, publicly portrays the judiciary's emphasis on the rights of the suspects as an obstacle in the way of ensuring the safety of the public.

The Human Rights Act

Over the last few years, the Human Rights Act 1998 (HRA), which has enabled UK courts to adjudicate directly on the basis of the ECHR, has been a source of increased tension between Parliament and the judiciary. It has, at the same time, given rise to a growing public perception that the HRA 1998 'protects only the undeserving, such as criminals and terrorists, at the expense of the law abiding citizens'.[71] Subsequently, because of the HRA, which is also said to prevent the

---

65 Zedner, above, n. 54, at 155.

66 This event took place two weeks after the London bombings of 7 July 2005. Police shot Jean Charles de Menezes seven times in the head at the Stockwell Tube station after officers identified him by mistake as a terrorist. De Menezes just happened to live in an area under police surveillance and, being of dark complexion, fit police's terrorist 'profile', that is, he looked Middle Eastern.

67 O De Schutter and J Ringelheim, 'Ethnic profiling: A rising challenge for European human rights law', *The Modern Law Review*, 71/3 (2008), 358–84.

68 P Chalk, 'The response to terrorism as a threat to liberal democracy', *The Australian Journal of Politics and History*, 44 (1998), 373–88, at 373.

69 The Secretary of State needs only reasonable grounds to impose a control order, such as house arrest, on anyone who is suspected of, or has been involved in, terrorism-related activity. Control orders were created by PTA 2005 as a response to the House of Lords ruling against the detention powers in Part IV of the TCSA 2001. See *Explanatory Memorandum to the Prevention of Terrorism Act 2005) Continuance in Force of Section 1 to 9) Order 2008 No. 559*, at <http://www.opsi.gov.uk/si/si2008/em/uksiem_20080559_en.pdf>.

70 See, for example, P Tuitt, *Race, Law, Resistence* (London: GlassHouse, 2004) and S Shute et al., *A Fair Hearing? Ethnic Minorities in the Criminal Courts* (Cullompton: Willan Publishing, 2005).

71 Joint Committee on Human Rights, 'Thirty-Second Report', posted at <http://www.publications.parliament.uk/pa/jt200506/jtselect/jtrights/278/27811.htm>.

democratically elected Government of the UK 'from responding effectively to serious challenges that threaten the country', there have been recommendations that the Government withdraw the UK from the ECHR.[72] Public misgivings about the effects of the HRA, in turn, threaten the independence of the judiciary, which is blamed for the failure to deal effectively with problems related to organized crime and the threat of terrorism.

In 2006, a cross-party group of senior MPs and peers criticized Tony Blair and his senior ministers for using the HRA to conceal their own administrative failings.[73] According to this joint human rights committee, 'every senior minister' fuelled widespread public misunderstandings and myths about the HRA, which will persist as long as they fail to retract their 'unfortunate comments' and continue to use it to cover up administrative failings in their departments.[74] The committee looked into three high profile cases during 2006, which had triggered calls for the HRA to be repealed or amended and found that:

> In each case, senior ministers, from the Prime Minister down, made assertions that the Human Rights Act, or judges or officials interpreting it, were responsible for certain unpopular events when in each case those assertions were unfounded. Moreover, when those assertions were demonstrated, there was no acknowledgement of the error, or withdrawal of the comment or any other attempt to inform the public of the mistake.[75]

The Government, indeed, does make a point of clashing with the judiciary at every opportunity in order to demonstrate that it is constantly struggling to protect the public against the risk of crime and terrorism. To give two recent examples, the Government rushed through Parliament a new law allowing anonymous witnesses in criminal cases following a House of Lords ruling against anonymous evidence, which led to a murder trial collapsing. According to Jack Straw, then Justice Secretary, the Government had to act quickly to fill in the gap that was created by their Lordships' judgments: 'anonymous evidence is [...] fundamental to the successful prosecution of a significant number of cases, some of which involve murder, blackmail, violent disorder and terrorism'.[76] The second recent development concerns the Government's proposal to extend the period of pre-charge detention of terrorist suspects from 28 to 42 days, despite the lack of any evidence supporting that (1) the law enforcement agencies require such an extension; and (2) that such an extension will allow a more effective approach to combat the threat of terrorism. In addition, as the Joint Committee on Human Rights Counter-Terrorism Policy and Human Rights pointed out:

> [The] proposals are in breach of the right of a detained person to be informed 'promptly' of any charge against him; are an unnecessary and disproportionate means of achieving the aim of protecting the public; and fail to provide sufficient guarantees against arbitrariness. As such, they are incompatible with Articles 5(1), 5(2), 5(3) and 5(4) ECHR. (Paragraphs 10–21)[77]

---

72   Joint Committee on Human Rights, 'Thirty-Second Report', ibid.

73   See Joint Committee on Human Rights Act: the DCA and Hone Office Review, Thirty-Second Report of Session 2005–06. Posted at <http://www.publications.parliament.uk/pa/jt200506/jtselect/jtrights/278/278. pdf>.

74   *The Guardian*, 'Ministers accused of fuelling myths on human rights', 14 November 2006.

75   Joint Committee on Human Rights Act: the DCA and Hone Office Review.

76   *Metro*, 'Anonymity law to be rushed through', 27 June 2008.

77   Joint Committee on Human Rights Counter-Terrorism Policy and Human Rights (Eighth Report): Counter-Terrorism Bill, Ninth Report of Session 2007–08, at <http://www.publications.parliament.uk/pa/jt200708/jtselect/jtrights/50/50.pdf>.

The new Counter-Terrorism Bill, which allows terrorist suspects to be held for up to 42 days, scraped through the House of Commons by the small majority of nine votes. This again paves the way for a renewed clash with the judiciary, in which the Government will be portraying itself as the defender of public safety. In contrast, the judiciary will be depicted as disconnected from reality and unconcerned with the safety of ordinary law-abiding citizens.

Islamophobia

A Growing Culture of Hostility

'The post-9/11 climate', McGhee writes, 'is both a culture of fear and a culture of indignation in which established and asylum seeker migrant communities are viewed with suspicion'.[78] In this climate, complex historical and global conflicts are described in simplistic terms that fit into the ideological scheme of 'the clash of civilizations':[79] the terrorists belonging to the Islamic culture are on the one side and law-abiding citizens of Western democracies on the other. It is, thus, hardly surprising if we read in a report by the Muslim Council of Britain that 'Muslims in the United Kingdom feel particularly venerable, insecure, alienated, intimidated, marginalised, discriminated against and vilified since the 11 September tragedy'.[80] Since 9/11, 'attacks on Muslims, Sikhs and other Arab and Asian communities in the UK have increased four-fold in some areas'.[81] Shahid Malik, Britain's first Muslim minister, means that there is a growing culture of hostility against Muslims in the United Kingdom that allows them to be targeted in the media and political discourse in a way that would be unacceptable for any other minority. As a result, 'many British Muslims now feel like aliens in their own country'.[82] A poll accompanying a documentary in a Channel 4 *Dispatches* programme, made to coincide with the third anniversary of the London bombings of 7 July, highlights:

> [...] the growing polarisation of opinion among Britain's 1.6 million Muslims, who say they have suffered a marked increase in hostility since the London bombings. The ICM survey found that 51 per cent of Britons blame Islam to some degree for the 2005 attacks, while more than a quarter of Muslims now believe Islamic values are not compatible with British values. While 90 per cent of Muslims said they felt attached to Britain, eight out of 10 said they felt there was more religious prejudice against their faith since the July bombings.[83]

The word 'Islamophobia' has been coined to capture the new social reality that confronts the Muslim communities in Britain and elsewhere in the West. It consists of eight attributes:

---

78 D McGhee, *Intolerant Britain: Hate, Citizenship and Difference* (Maidenhead: Open University Press, 2005), at 100.

79 Huntington, above, n. 6.

80 The House of Lords -Select Committee on Religious Offences in England and Wales, 2003: para. 1.4. at <http://www.publications.parliament.uk/pa/ld/ldrelof.htm>.

81 McGhee, above, n. 78, at 102.

82 *The Independent*, 'Muslims feel like Jews in Europe', 4 July 2008, at <http://www.independent.co.uk/>.

83 *The Independent*, ibid.

1. Islam is seen as a monolithic block; static and unresponsive to change.
2. Islam is seen as separate and 'other'. It does not have values in common with other cultures, is not affected by them, and does not influence them.
3. Islam is seen as inferior to the West. It is seen as barbaric, irrational, primitive and sexist.
4. Islam is seen as violent, aggressive, threatening, supportive of terrorism and engaged in a clash of civilizations.
5. Islam is seen as a political ideology, used for political or military advantage.
6. Criticisms made of 'the West' by Islam are rejected out of hand.
7. Hostility towards Islam is used to justify discriminatory practices towards Muslims and the exclusion of Muslims from mainstream society.
8. Anti-Muslim hostility is seen as natural and normal.[84]

The post-9/11 approach adopted by Britain to meet the threat of terrorism strengthened existing ethno-cultural prejudice and legitimized racist violence against Britain's ethno-cultural groups. For many immigrants who are seen as Muslims (including Sikhs wearing turbans), Islamophobia is translated into daily violence, including murder, assaults, arson attacks and racist emails. Islamophobic violence is, admittedly, not new in Britain, but it has been on the rise since 9/11 and shows a significant increase after specific events, such as the 7 July bombing in London.[85] To quote Shahid Malik again: 'Somehow, there's a message out there that it's OK to target people as long as it's Muslims. And you don't have to worry about the facts, and people will turn a blind eye.'[86]

The social, and by implication also the legal, status of diverse groups of people, who in the eye of the majority culture in Britain are seen, classified and treated as Muslims, adds a social psychological dimension to the 'war on terror'. British society is organized in part using hierarchical racial categories (and the term 'Muslim', as mentioned before, is used in everyday discourse as a racial marker). These racial categories are, in turn, an essential part of the unarticulated, self-evident, commonplace assumptions and values that ultimately determine our conception of the social world and shape the relations of power.[87] In other words, we are dealing with those basic socio-cultural assumptions regarding the nature of social relations that are taken for granted and treated as patently true. As Bourdieu explains, 'the subjective and self-evidence of the commonplace world are validated by the objective consensus on the sense of the world, what is essential *goes without saying because it comes without saying*'.[88] This method of objectification of the assumptions renders the exercise of power through the force of law legitimate.[89] In the same way, the culturally embedded assumptions regarding Muslims as a racial category, justify Islamophobic sentiments, rationalize targeting them as a national security threat and legitimize the harsh treatment of Muslims suspected of acts of terrorism.

---

84   Quoted from *Muslims in the European Union: Discrimination and Islamophobia* (European Monitoring Centre on Racism and Xenophobia (EUMC), 2006), at 61.

85   A few weeks after the London bombings of 7/7, *The Times* reported that religious hate crimes had 'soared by 600 per cent in London as people attacked mosques and insulted Muslims'. See *Timesonline*, 'Religious hatred crimes shoot up', 3 August 2005, at <http://www.timesonline.co.uk/tol/news/uk/article550961.ece>. All large police forces in Britain reported significant increases in racial violence.

86   *The Independent*, ibid.

87   Bourdieu introduces the concept of *doxa* to explain this. P Bourdie, *Outline of a Theory of Practice* (Cambridge: Cambridge University Press, 1977).

88   Bourdieu, ibid., at 167.

89   P Bourdieu, 'The force of law: Towards a sociology of the judicial field', *Hasting Law Journal*, 38 (1987), 805–53, at 814.

Alarming Rhetoric

To clarify this point, we could compare the Malik case (but also Siddique's and Munshi's trials, which attracted a great deal of media attention) with the case of Martyn Gilleard, a 31-year-old Nazi, whose flat was raided by the police in search of child pornography. Besides some 39,000 indecent images of children, the officers found four homemade nail bombs, 'along with machetes, swords, bullets, gunpowder, balaclavas and racist literature'.[90] The bombs were intended to be used to attack Jewish and Asian targets. The Gilleard case is of interest for several reasons. Firstly, this case failed to attract the media's attention or cause public debate. *The Times* did not even carry a report of this case in its hard copy on 25 June 2008, which was the day after Gilleard was convicted.[91] Secondly, and more significantly, Gillard was not under police surveillance for his terrorist activities, but was caught accidentally when the police searched his flat for reasons not related to terrorism. Gilleard, a paid-up member of extreme right organizations such as the National Front and the White Nationalist Party, who had openly and publicly expressed violent racist views and his 'desire to act on them',[92] did not draw the authorities' suspicion upon himself and was not considered a threat to national security or the public safety.

In another case, police discovered 12 firearms, 54 improvised explosive devices including nail bombs, and a large collection of bomb-making manuals, books and magazines about guns and the military hidden at the Yorkshire home of Terrence Gavan, a bus driver and former soldier. Although Gavan was a member of the BNP and had expressed 'strong hostility' towards immigrants, according to the *Yorkshire Post* 'counter-terrorism experts could find no clear ideological purpose to his campaign and were surprised by the sheer volume of weapons that were hidden in [his] bedroom'.[93] Passing sentence at the Old Bailey, Mr Justice Calvert described Gavan as 'a lone operator with what amounts to almost an obsession with guns and explosives'.[94] This case too failed to attract much attention, but what makes it of particular interest in this connection is the language used by police and the court in regard to Gavan's intentions to commit acts of terrorism. Despite his right-wing connections and membership in the BNP, and the fact that he had 'planned to target an address [...] he believed was linked to the 7 July bomb attacks in London',[95] police regarded him as non-ideological. The judge, for his part, pointed out that although he had '"the potential to cause serious injury if activated" [...] there was no suggestion Gavan had tried to use them to injure people or passed on or sold them'.[96] Here we find none of the alarming rhetoric employed by the court in, for example, Siddique's case concerning the need 'to stop, or at least reduce the risk of, terrorist outrages before that imminent stage is reached'.[97] The language used by police and the court to describe Gavan is sober, recognizing him as a dangerous man, but

---

90   *Metro*, 'Nazi sympathiser is guilty of terrorism', 25 June 2008.

91   *Timesonline* did, however, carry a four-line notice a few days earlier announcing the trial of Gilleard. See *Timesonline*, 'In court today', 17 June 2008, at <http://business.timesonline.co.uk/tol/business/law/article4152235.ece>.

92   *Metro*, above, n. 90.

93   *Yorkshire Post*, 'Secret arsenal of the bus driver who harboured arms obsession', 15 January 2010, at <http://www.yorkshirepost.co.uk/news/The-BNP-man-who-hid.5986794.jp>.

94   *BBC News*, 'Bomb cache bus driver Gavan "obsessed with weapons"', 15 January 2010, at <http://news.bbc.co.uk/1/hi/uk/8462205.stm>.

95   Guardian.co.uk, 'BNP member given 11 years for making bombs and guns', 15 January 2010, at <http://www.guardian.co.uk/uk/2010/jan/15/bnp-member-jailed-guns-bombs>.

96   *Timesonline*, 'BNP member Terrance Gavan kept gun and bomb cache at home', 15 January 2010, at <http://www.timesonline.co.uk/tol/news/uk/crime/article6989752.ece>.

97   Honourable Lord Carloway, above, n. 19.

strikingly free from the *fear* of the imminent terrorist outrage that we find in the cases of British-born Muslims discussed above.

Cases such as Gillard's and Gavan's give further support to the thesis regarding the symbolic effects of the UK's anti-terrorism policy and legislation discussed above, but also suggest that anti-terrorism laws operate in a racially selective fashion.

Liberal Law

The social psychological aspect of the anti-terrorism cases discussed above – that those suspected of terrorism may be disadvantaged in their defence owing to what Siddique's solicitor called 'an atmosphere of hostility' – is enhanced by the way modern liberal law reconstructs the relationship between the individual and society. Liberal law's conception of justice involves, according to Alan Norrie, a process of forced abstraction that differentiates justice into parts that are in practice inseparable from each other.[98] Although liberal law remains institutionally tied up to socio-historically defined social relations, it nonetheless guides action by reference to abstract ahistorical criteria. The reason for this is that only by ignoring and denying the relevance of its socio-historical ties and forces can law appear as an internally coherent system of rules and doctrines, an autonomous normative system, and objective machinery for decision making. By overlooking the significance of the broader social and historical context out of which emerge not only legal practice but also institutions of law, law obscures and mystifies the relationship between legal practice and the societal context of law.[99] To unpack this, Norrie refers to the idea of 'legal subject as a responsible agent', which is represented by such doctrines as *mens rea* and *actus reus*. He argues that liberal theory, which underpins the subjective principles of criminal law, 'affirming the need for intention, foresight, knowledge and belief concerning actions and their consequences', is highly individualistic and atomistic.[100]

Malik's actions were abstracted from the socio-historical context of her life as a British-born Muslim. Her poetry was treated as a proof of her commitment to a form of Islamic extremism, but not as a fruit of her alienation in a society where she lived; a society that treated her as a terrorist by association. Similarly, Siddique's possession of material that could be used for terrorist purposes cannot be understood without considering what his solicitor called being 'angry at global injustice', an anger which is embedded in the specific situation of Siddique's life as a British-born Muslim. Liberal law abstracts Malik and Siddique from the context of the social conflict that generated their actions and excludes 'that context from the judicial gaze'.[101] Instead, it provides a partial and mystified image of the individual and society that allows it to justify an individualized relationship between legal and moral judgment. Hence, Malik became, as the judge admitted, an 'enigma' to the court because the social and historical relations, which had created her as a social agent, were excluded from the judicial gaze. The fact that liberal law is not the arena to counterbalance the effects of Islamophobia gives free reign to the managerial approach that has come to permeate the UK's counter-terrorism policy. While liberal law operates by abstracting actions from their socio-historical contexts, managerialism focuses on coping with risk in a cost-effective way. This, in turn, often requires disregarding the rights of the accused terrorists and omitting the causes of problems from the calculation.

---

98   A Norrie, *Law and the Beautiful Soul* (London: GlassHouse Press, 2005).
99   Norrie, ibid., at 28–31.
100   Norrie, ibid., at 53.
101   Norrie, ibid., at 30.

Conclusions: The War on Law

The 'war on law' started long before the atrocities of 9/11, writes Phillippe Sands, but 9/11 'added spur with the argument that international rules were somehow not up to the new challenge which the world now faced'.[102] The events of 9/11 constituted a decisive turning point not only in international politics, but also in international and national law. To borrow a phrase from John Strawson, 9/11 'turned law to Ground Zero', revealing 'international law as feeble, constitutional law as insecure', while transforming human rights law into something negotiable.[103] The conviction of Malik at the Old Bailey and the eight-year sentence meted out to Siddique, as well as incidents such as the execution of Jean Charles de Menezes[104] in the underground, exemplify what it means for national law to turn to Ground Zero. They show how the fundamental rights underpinning the rule of law may be set aside in dealing with terrorist suspects, how the burden of proof is reversed, and how the presumption of innocence gives way to the presumption of guilt. This is one aspect of the new reality of law. The other aspect is the emergence of the 'culture of control', which at the expense of disregarding the rights of offenders or those suspected of terrorism, 'manages' the risk of terrorism in what appears to be a cost-effective manner.[105] National and international terrorism, thus, are viewed as forms of individual or organized criminality existing independently of social, historical, political, cultural and economic developments or the interests of the UK and the US Governments.

To sum up, the UK's anti-terrorism legislation operates in a highly selective manner, targeting members of the minority groups whose religion, ethnicity and culture exclude them from mainstream culture and politics. The new paradigm of managerialism, which informs the UK's late modern penal policy, to a great extent also shapes its anti-terrorism legislation. This new form of 'penality' disregards the rights of the offenders (and subsequently also the rights of terrorist suspects) and focuses instead on minimizing the risks of crime at the expense of engaging with the causes of criminality. The judiciary, not known for its radical political views in times of emergency, clashes repeatedly with the Government on human rights issues, yet fails to counterbalance the negative side effects of the rise of punitiveness in contemporary Britain. This failure also has to do with the way modern liberal law operates by abstracting the individual from his/her socio-historical context before considering his/her actions and intentions. This new managerial criminal policy, together with the modus operandi of liberal law, perpetuates the Islamophobic sentiments shaping the UK's anti-terrorism policy and legislation. As a result, the UK's anti-terrorism legislation contains not only some of the most draconian provisions enacted over the last few decades, but also operates in a highly racialized fashion. It allows and legitimizes overt over-policing of Muslim communities while legalizing efforts to target and victimize Muslims.

These managerially inspired counter-terrorism measures are not part of the solution but part of the problem. They cannot ensure long-term national security or citizens' safety because they systematically aggravate the social conditions that give rise to terrorism. This will probably sound like a tune out of the 'discredited' criminal policy of the 1960s, but we shall succeed neither in managing nor in resolving the threat of domestic terrorism as long as we have not acknowledged and addressed the link between marginalization, racialization and victimization of British-born

---

102   P Sands, *Lawless World: America and the Making and Breaking of Global Rules* (London: Allen Lane, 2005), at xii.
103   J Strawson (ed.), *Law after Ground Zero* (London: GlassHouse, 2004), at xi.
104   See above, n. 66.
105   Garland, above, n. 17.

Muslims and their turn to Islamic extremism and anti-democratic methods. However, it is easier said than done.

PART III
The Strategies of Rights

Chapter 12

Human Rights Strategies in an
Age of Counter-Terrorism

Daniel Moeckli

The reaction to the events of 11 September 2001 and later terrorist attacks have posed a major challenge to the protection and, indeed, the very concept, of human rights. In the name of the 'war on terror', law enforcement agencies have been granted unprecedented powers,[1] people have been detained without charge or trial,[2] and the prohibition of torture has been questioned by academics[3] and systematically undermined by governments.[4] Whilst this shift away from liberty and towards more repressive criminal justice policies forms the backdrop to this chapter, it is not my aim to add to the burgeoning literature that explores whether or not the shift is justified by the necessities of the fight against terrorism.[5] This chapter starts from the premise that, even in an alleged 'age of terror',[6] human rights do deserve to be upheld. My intended readership consists of those who share this belief. I am interested not in *whether*, or to what extent, human rights should be protected, but instead in *how* this can be done effectively: what are promising strategies of challenging repressive counter-terrorism policies? This, it seems to me, is one of the key questions, if not *the* key question, facing 'the human rights movement' today.

Amongst those who are largely sympathetic to the idea of human rights, two main schools of thought have emerged on how to respond to the 'war on terror'. According to what is clearly the dominant position, human rights violations committed in the fight against terrorism are the consequence of an exceptional lack of legal regulation and must thus be addressed by insisting on the rule of law and turning to judicial mechanisms. This invocation of the rule of law and reliance on litigation has recently been increasingly subject to criticism from a number of authors who

---

1   For example, USA Patriot Act, Public Law No. 107–56, ss 201–25; Anti-Terrorism, Crime and Security Act (ATCSA) 2001; Prevention of Terrorism Act 2005; Terrorism Act 2006, ss 21–33.

2   For the United States, see USA Patriot Act, s 412; Disposition of Cases of Aliens Arrested Without Warrant, 8 CFR, s 287.3(d) (2001); Office of the Inspector General of the US Department of Justice (hereinafter OIG), *The September 11 Detainees: A Review of the Treatment of Aliens Held on Immigration Charges in Connection with the Investigation of the September 11 Attacks* (2003). For the United Kingdom, see ATCSA 2001, Part IV; *A v. Secretary of State for the Home Department* [2004] UKHL 56.

3   A Dershowitz, *Why Terrorism Works* (New Haven, CT: Yale University Press, 2002); M Bagaric and J Clarke, 'Not enough official torture in the world? The circumstances in which torture is morally justifiable', *University of San Francisco Law Review*, 39 (2005), 581.

4   See *Saadi v. Italy*, European Court of Human Rights, Judgment of 28 February 2008, Application No. 37201/06; KJ Greenberg and JL Dratel (eds), *The Torture Papers: The Road to Abu Ghraib* (New York: Cambridge University Press, 2005).

5   See, for example, RA Wilson (ed.), *Human Rights in the 'War on Terror'* (Cambridge: Cambridge University Press, 2005); RA Posner, *Not a Suicide Pact: The Constitution in a Time of National Emergency* (Oxford: Oxford University Press, 2006); M Ignatieff, *The Lesser Evil: Political Ethics in an Age of Terror* (Edinburgh: Edinburgh University Press, 2005).

6   Ignatieff, above, n. 5.

argue that the post-September 11 measures are not exceptional extra-legal phenomena, but in fact firmly rooted in the law. Therefore, these scholars, whom for want of a better term I will describe as 'critical', warn against an endorsement of the rule of law and instead call for a 'political response'. Their arguments made in the context of the 'war on terror', and especially Guantánamo Bay, reflect a wider scepticism in critical legal circles about the potential of the rule of law and legal procedures to prevent or rectify human rights abuses[7] and corresponding warnings against 'turn[ing] political conflict into technical litigation'.[8] I will argue that although the analysis of these critical scholars is largely correct, their suggested prescription of abandoning the rule of law should be rejected.

The first section provides an overview of the arguments advanced by the two schools of thought referred to above. The second section analyses the claim, central to the position of the first school, that the problem with counter-terrorism practices is their exceptional, extra-legal character. The third section examines the argument, made by the second school that it is futile to insist on the rule of law. The final section tries to draw some practical lessons for human rights activists from this rather theoretical discussion of the two opposed positions.

Two Views of the 'War on Terror'

There are, admittedly, myriad different analyses of the relationship between counter-terrorism and human rights. Nevertheless, two main sets of views can be distinguished that fundamentally differ in their diagnosis of 'the problem with' counter-terrorism practices and, accordingly, in their suggestions as to what should be done to protect human rights. Although this is a simplification, these sets of views will be described here as 'the liberal' and 'the critical' perspective.

The Dominant Liberal View

For the vast majority of commentators who are critical of the 'war on terror', the fundamental problem with contemporary counter-terrorism measures is their exceptional nature. Though often not expressly referring to the work of Carl Schmitt, they understand these measures as being based on his notion of the 'state of exception' as the realm where law is suspended and the sovereign exercises unfettered discretion.[9] According to this account, the emergency regimes established since September 11 are 'outside' the normally valid legal system – the exception to the rule – and it is this exceptional lack of legal regulation that carries with it the risk of human rights violations. The paradigmatic manifestation of this exceptionality is, of course, the US naval base at Guantánamo Bay, which has been characterized as a 'place [...] beyond the rule of law',[10] a 'legal black hole'[11] and a space of 'utter lawlessness',[12] where the detainees are left without 'any rights whatever'.[13] The fact that these are descriptions, not by human rights campaigners, but by English judges is

---

7   See, for example, C Douzinas, *The End of Human Rights* (Oxford: Hart, 2000), at 91.

8   Ibid., at 14.

9   C Schmitt, *Political Theology: Four Chapters on the Concept of Sovereignty* (translated by G Schwab) (Chicago, IL: University of Chicago Press, 2005), at 12.

10   D Hope, 'Torture', *International and Comparative Law Quarterly*, 53 (2004), 807, 830.

11   *R (on the application of Abbasi) v. Secretary of State for Foreign and Commonwealth Affairs* [2002] EWCA Civ 1598, para. 64.

12   J Steyn, 'Guantánamo Bay: The legal black hole', *International and Comparative Law Quarterly*, 53 (2004), 1, at 15.

13   Ibid., at 11.

an indication of the prevalence of this view. Even the then-British Prime Minister Tony Blair described Guantánamo as an 'anomaly'.[14] US commentators have used similar characterizations. Jordan Paust has described Guantánamo as a 'legal no man's land',[15] Gerald Neuman sees it as an 'anomalous zone'[16] and Harold Koh has maintained that the judgments of the military commissions convened at Guantánamo would be perceived as 'based on politics, not legal norms'.[17]

Also other counter-terrorism measures are typically described in terms that are meant to highlight their extraordinary, non- or quasi-legal nature. In the House of Lords decision on the detention of foreign terrorist suspects (the 'Belmarsh decision'), for example, Lord Nicholls stated that '[i]ndefinite imprisonment without charge or trial is anathema in any country which observes the rule of law'.[18] Therefore, '[w]holly exceptional circumstances must exist before this extreme step can be justified'.[19] Lord Hoffmann equally stressed the exceptional nature of the measure: 'The power which the Home Secretary seeks to uphold is a power to detain people indefinitely without charge or trial. Nothing could be more antithetical to the instincts and traditions of the people of the United Kingdom.'[20]

Counter-terrorism measures are thus understood as victories of the exception over the established rule (of law), and the human rights violations they entail are presented as the result of an extraordinary lack of law and legal protection. This understanding rests on a number of crucial binary distinctions: normalcy-emergency, norm-exception, inside-outside (the law), law-political power. This type of analysis leads its proponents to suggest a particular response to 'the problem' of counter-terrorism regimes. The key to the protection of human rights is, according to the predominant liberal view, to insist on the rule of law and to turn to legal institutions (domestic courts, international human rights bodies, etc.) to reclaim these extraordinary spaces of lawlessness.[21]

Although he would hardly describe himself as belonging to the liberal mainstream, Giorgio Agamben also highlights the exceptional character and lawlessness of Guantánamo and the 'war on terror' in general. He writes of the Guantánamo detainees that 'they are the object of a pure de facto rule, of a detention that is indefinite not only in the temporal sense but in its very nature as well, since it is entirely removed from the law and from judicial oversight'.[22] To Agamben, Guantánamo is the embodiment of the 'state of exception', which he characterizes as 'a space devoid of law, a zone of anomie in which all legal determinations [...] are deactivated'.[23] However, unlike the liberal commentators referred to above, Agamben sees this 'state of exception' not as 'outside' the legal order. Instead, it has a juridical form. In fact, '[t]his space devoid of law seems, for some reason, to be so essential to the juridical order that it must seek in every way to assure itself a relation with it, as if in order to ground itself the juridical order necessarily had to maintain

---

14 D Fickling, 'PM denies knowledge of "CIA torture"', *The Guardian*, 7 December 2005.
15 J Paust, 'Post-9/11 overreaction and fallacies regarding war and defense, Guantánamo, the status of persons, treatment, judicial review of detention, and due process in military commissions', *Notre Dame Law Review*, 79 (2004), 1335, at 1346.
16 G Neuman, 'Anomalous zones', *Stanford Law Review*, 48 (1996), 1197, at 1228.
17 H Koh, 'The case against military commissions', *American Journal of International Law*, 96 (2002), 337, at 341.
18 *A v. Secretary of State for the Home Department* [2004] UKHL 56, para. 74.
19 Ibid.
20 Ibid., para. 86.
21 See, generally, A Tsoukala, 'Democracy in the light of security: British and French political discourses on domestic counter-terrorism policies', *Political Studies*, 54 (2006), 607, especially 614–17 and 620–22.
22 G Agamben, *State of Exception* (trans. K Attell) (Chicago, IL: University of Chicago Press, 2005), 4.
23 Ibid., at 50.

itself in relation with an anomie'.[24] Not only is the state of exception 'the constitutive paradigm of the juridical order',[25] it also comprehensively subordinates the juridical order: 'the law employs the exception – that is the suspension of law itself – as its original means of referring to and encompassing life',[26] so that 'the exception everywhere becomes the rule'.[27]

The Critical View

This prevailing, mainly liberal, critical analysis of the 'war on terror' has itself recently been subject to criticism from 'critical' scholars. They argue that Guantánamo and other counter-terrorism measures are not exceptional at all. In fact, they contend, the very distinction between the norm and the exception, between law and lawlessness, is untenable.

Fleur Johns points out that the US Government has constructed an elaborate normative and institutional system at Guantánamo Bay (consisting of the military commissions, the Administrative Review Board, the Combatant Status Review Tribunal and other mechanisms) and concludes that Guantánamo, far from being a 'legal no man's land',[28] is 'a space filled to the brim with expertise, procedure, scrutiny and analysis'.[29] Johns adds that Guantánamo is in fact 'a profoundly anti-exceptional legal artefact'.[30] Claudia Aradau similarly argues that Guantánamo is 'not lawless or normless, but is filled with rules and regulations'[31] and that it is 'not [...] a singular and exceptional occurrence but [...] symptomatic of the transformation of law'.[32] Pointing to 'the sheer volume of [...] regulations and interpretations'[33] governing the 'war on terror', Nasser Hussain equally rejects the notion of exceptional lawlessness. In fact, he maintains that 'what one witnesses in contemporary emergency is a proliferation of new laws and regulations', almost to the point of 'hyperlegality'.[34] Thus, 'norm and exception have blurred severely'[35] and 'the exception as it has historically and theoretically been understood, as a suspension of regular law, even a space of nonlaw, no longer exists'.[36] In short, as Peter Fitzpatrick and Richard Joyce explain, 'the exception is not *to* but within law'.[37]

Accordingly, these authors have a radically different view than the liberal authors referred to above of how those concerned about human rights should respond to Guantánamo and other counter-terrorism practices. To them, the notion of lawlessness is misleading and dangerous because 'once such an idea of a space of nonlaw becomes commonplace the seemingly logical conclusion is to

---

24   Ibid., at 51.

25   Ibid., at 7.

26   Ibid., at 1.

27   G Agamben, *Homo Sacer: Sovereign Power and Bare Life* (trans. D Heller-Roazen) (Stanford, CA: Stanford University Press, 1998), at 9.

28   Paust, n. 15, at 1346.

29   F Johns, 'Guantánamo Bay and the annihilation of the exception', *European Journal of International Law*, 16 (2005), 613, at 618.

30   Ibid., 615.

31   C Aradau, 'Law transformed: Guantánamo and the "other" exception', *Third World Quarterly*, 28 (2007), 489, 495.

32   Ibid., at 489.

33   N Hussain, 'Beyond norm and exception: Guantánamo', *Critical Inquiry* (2007), 734, 742.

34   Ibid., at 741.

35   Ibid., at 750.

36   Ibid., at 735.

37   P Fitzpatrick and R Joyce, 'The normality of the exception in democracy's empire', *Journal of Law and Society*, 34 (2007), 65, at 76.

advocate the insertion of law, of more rules, regulations, conventions, and court cases'.[38] However, Johns contends, given the legal mechanisms in place, 'it is not upholding the rule of law that seems tricky'.[39] Aradau similarly warns against 'the endorsement of the "rule of law" by human rights lawyers, activists and even politicians against the exception of Guantánamo'[40] and the 'fortification of the legal space of the norm'.[41] Hussain, finally, points to 'the limits of the law as a response to an increasingly repressive and undemocratic sovereignty'.[42]

Instead, what is called for according to these scholars is 'a broader political and ethical response'.[43] This invocation of the need for politics reflects Schmitt's insistence on the pure politics of the decision on the exception.[44] For Schmitt, the decision on the exception is 'a decision in the true sense of the word' as the exception 'cannot be circumscribed factually and made to conform to a preformed law'.[45] Johns advocates a 're-invigoration of that sense of the exception that may be derived from the work of Carl Schmitt', that is, 'of operating under circumstances not pre-codified by pre-existing norms',[46] as a way of restoring appreciation of 'the scope for political action'[47] and 'decisional responsibility'.[48] 'Recognizing in herself or himself Schmitt's exceptional decision-maker,' she argues, 'the functionary implementing a programme [such as Guantánamo] might come to experience that programme as a field of decisional possibility and impossibility, with all the danger and difference that that implies'.[49] Hussain similarly invokes the political by again 'insisting on an awareness of the limits of law'[50] and repeating Schmitt's call 'for the pure politics of the decision on the exception, a decision that would break the "crust" of legal life'.[51] Aradau, finally, laments the fact that '[t]he law that governs Guantánamo functions through administrative practices from which decision has retreated [...] in a maze of institutions', whereas 'Schmitt's insight on the arbitrary decision at the heart of law could become a tool for critical thought inasmuch as it made norms contestable and exposed their reliance on an initial decision and foundational violence'.[52] In summary, the critical school of thought warns against appealing to the law, insisting on the rule of law and turning to the courts as a human rights strategy and instead advocates a 'political response' that would restore a sense of decisional responsibility.

Exceptionality

The second group of authors is, I believe, right to reject the prevailing characterization of Guantánamo and other counter-terrorism measures as exceptional phenomena that are somehow 'outside' the normal legal order. Not only does this kind of account draw on simplistic binary

---

38 Hussain, n. 33, at 751–52.
39 Johns, n. 29, at 618–19.
40 Aradau, n. 31, at 498.
41 Ibid., at 491.
42 Hussain, n. 33, at 735.
43 Ibid., at 752.
44 Schmitt, n. 9, at 15.
45 Ibid., at 6.
46 Johns, n. 29, at 615.
47 Ibid., at 635.
48 Ibid., at 615.
49 Ibid., at 635.
50 Hussain, n. 33, at 752.
51 Ibid., at 753.
52 Aradau, n. 31, at 491.

oppositions – between the norm and the exception, between law and lawlessness, between inside and outside – that do not stand up to scrutiny: it may also serve to legitimize questionable boundaries between what is accepted as 'normal' and rejected as 'exceptional'.

To describe Guantánamo as a 'legal black hole',[53] and thereby to imply that law is not implicated in the human rights abuses committed there, is clearly misleading. Both the detention and the trial systems in place at Guantánamo Bay have an explicit legal basis, originally in the Authorization for the Use of Military Force Joint Resolution[54] and a 2001 Presidential Military Order respectively,[55] and, since 2006, in the Military Commissions Act of 2006.[56] Furthermore, detention is subject to review by an elaborate system of different legal mechanisms.[57] As far as the military commissions are concerned, the 2006 Act is supplemented by the Manual for Military Commissions, which sets out the Rules for Military Commissions, the Military Commission Rules of Evidence, and the Crimes and Elements (setting out the crimes punishable by military commission).[58] Aradau's characterization of Guantánamo as a space 'filled with rules and regulations'[59] is thus apposite. Nor is there anything 'exceptional' about the US Government's use of the Guantánamo Bay naval base to detain people without charge. In the 1990s, the US authorities, in an attempt to block Haitian and Cuban refugees from entering the United States, used Guantánamo over several years as an offshore processing centre, detaining tens of thousands of people.[60]

The same could be said of pretty much any of the other repressive measures introduced after September 11: rather than being exceptional and unrelated to the 'normal legal system', their introduction was made possible by long-term structural conditions and they often build on previous laws. To again use the most prominent British example, detention of foreign terrorist suspects under the Anti-Terrorism, Crime and Security Act (ATCSA) 2001, it can hardly be argued, as Lord Hoffmann did in the Belmarsh case, that detention without charge or trial is 'antithetical to the instincts and traditions of the people of the United Kingdom'.[61] On the contrary, detention without trial of those thought to pose a national security risk has a long history in the United Kingdom. The first of a series of Habeas Corpus Suspension Acts, allowing the executive to hold individuals on treason charges without bringing them to trial, was introduced as early as 1688.[62] During the second part of the nineteenth century, Ireland was governed with the use of detention powers

53   *R (on the application of Abbasi) v. Secretary of State for Foreign and Commonwealth Affairs* [2002] EWCA Civ 1598, para. 64; Steyn, n. 12.

54   Authorization for the Use of Military Force, Public Law No. 107–40, 115 Stat 224 (2001).

55   Military Order of 13 November 2001: Detention, Treatment, and Trial of Certain Noncitizens in the War against Terrorism, 66 Fed Reg 57,833 (16 November 2001).

56   Military Commissions Act of 2006, Public Law No. 109–366, 120 Stat 2600 (codified at 10 USC sections 948a–950w and other sections of Titles 10, 18, 28, and 42).

57   See Department of Defense Order, 'Administrative Review Procedures for Enemy Combatants in the Custody of the Department of Defense at Guantánamo Bay Naval Base, Cuba', 11 May 2004; Deputy Secretary of Defense, 'Order Establishing Combatant Status Review Tribunal', 7 July 2004.

58   Manual for Military Commissions, 18 January 2007, available at <http://www.loc.gov/rr/frd/Military_Law/pdf/manual-mil-commissions.pdf>.

59   Aradau, n. 31, at 495.

60   HH Koh, 'America's offshore refugee camps', *University of Richmond Law Review*, 29 (1994), 139; A Kaplan, 'Where is Guantánamo?', *American Quarterly*, 57 (2005), 831.

61   *A v. Secretary of State for the Home Department* [2004] UKHL 56, para. 86.

62   RJ Sharpe, *The Law of Habeas Corpus* (Oxford: Clarendon Press, 2nd edn, 1989), 94.

that were shielded from any form of judicial supervision.[63] The British Government again relied upon preventive detention powers in both world wars to intern 30,000 and 28,000 'enemy aliens' respectively.[64] Furthermore, as Brian Simpson has pointed out, the power of executive detention was 'always valued in the colonies',[65] and, even in the waning years of the British Empire, used to incarcerate tens of thousands of troublesome political opponents.[66] As far as the specific context of terrorism is concerned, detention without trial was a regular feature of a series of anti-terrorism laws applicable in Northern Ireland throughout the last century.[67]

The constant invocations of the exceptional nature of the post-September 11 regimes not only obscure the fact that these repressive measures build on historical precedents and that they can, and have always been, accommodated by the 'normal' legal system. They also help to legitimize other sets of current repressive measures by letting them appear normal in comparison to the allegedly exceptional anti-terrorism regimes. Detention without charge or trial, for example, far from being limited to the counter-terrorism context, is a common feature of every state's legal system. Executive detention powers are employed against vagrants, the mentally ill, drug addicts, immigrants and other allegedly dangerous groups of people.[68] Especially immigration detention has become a widespread phenomenon throughout the Western world in recent years.[69] In the United Kingdom, for example, the immigration authorities detained approximately 35,000 foreign nationals in 2003.[70] Characterizations of detention without charge or trial as 'antithetical to our instincts and traditions' and as limited to the exceptional terrorism context thus distort the reality of mass incarceration at the executive's behest. And when European government leaders brand Guantánamo as 'anomaly', then this could also be read as a conscious rhetorical move to deflect attention away from the deprivations of liberty to which tens of thousands of immigrants are subjected to in Europe on a daily basis.

---

63   AWB Simpson, *In the Highest Degree Odious: Detention Without Trial in Wartime Britain* (Oxford: Clarendon Press, 1992), 3–4; AWB Simpson, *Human Rights and the End of Empire* (Oxford: Oxford University Press, 2001), at 79–80.

64   Simpson (1992), n. 63, at 163.

65   Simpson (2001), n. 63, at 876.

66   In 1954, for instance, 30,000 people were arrested in Kenya in an operation designed to identify Mau Mau supporters. Ibid., 879–80.

67   Civil Authorities (Special Powers) Act (Northern Ireland) 1922 and Northern Ireland (Emergency Provisions) Acts 1973–1998. See RJ Spjut, 'Internment and detention without trial in Northern Ireland 1971–1975: Ministerial policy and practice', *Modern Law Review*, 49 (1986), 712 and RJ Spjut, 'Executive detention in Northern Ireland: The Gardiner Report and the Northern Ireland (Emergency Provisions) (Amendment) Act 1975', *Irish Jurist*, 10 (1975), 272. For a historical account, see J McGuffin, *Internment* (Tralee: Anvil Books, 1973).

68   See European Convention on Human Rights, Art 5(1) (expressly authorizing the detention of all these categories of persons).

69   See J Hughes and O Field, 'Recent trends in the detention of asylum seekers in Western Europe', in Hughes and Liebaut (eds), *Detention of Asylum Seekers in Europe: Analysis and Perspectives* (The Hague: Kluwer Law International, 1998), at 5; P Morante, 'Detention of asylum seekers: The United States Perspective' in ibid., at 85; M Welch and L Schuster, 'Detention of asylum seekers in the US, UK, France, Germany, and Italy: A critical view of the globalizing culture of control', *Criminal Justice: The International Journal of Policy and Practice*, 5 (2005), 331. See also the Jesuit Refugee Service's website on detention in Europe <http://www.detention-in-europe.org/> and the website of the International Detention Coalition <http://www.idcoalition.org/portal/index.php>.

70   Amnesty International, *United Kingdom: Seeking Asylum is Not a Crime: Detention of People Who Have Sought Asylum*, 20 June 2005, at 43.

The Rule of Law

The conclusion that the post-9/11 measures are not exceptional, extra-legal phenomena, but firmly rooted in the legal system, leads the critical authors referred to above to argue that 'it is not upholding the rule of law that seems tricky'.[71] Thus, they warn against 'the endorsement of the "rule of law" by human rights lawyers'.[72]

Central to their argument in this respect is the quantity of legal regulations and mechanisms involved in contemporary anti-terrorism regimes. Hussain points to the 'sheer volume of these regulations', specifying that '[t]he well-known torture memoranda [...] run into hundreds of pages'.[73] Aradau highlights the 'detailed rules and norms' governing Guantánamo[74] and the 'maze of institutions' operating there.[75] Johns argues that there is 'a panoply of regulations' governing the handling of the Guantánamo detainees and that since 2004 'the normative and institutional network at Guantánamo Bay has become even denser', so that it is now 'a space filled to the brim with expertise, procedure, scrutiny and analysis'.[76] Today, one could add to this that the Military Commissions Act of 2006, supplemented by the 238-page-long Manual for Military Commissions issued in 2007, provides very detailed regulation of the commission trials.

Yet it is not clear how these repeated references to the sheer mass of regulations and procedures support the claim that it is futile to insist on the rule of law. Even a minimal, formal, conception of the rule of law requires more than just that the mere existence of law, that power must be exercised through detailed legal regulation.[77] According to Dicey's classic formulation, the rule of law means, first, 'the absolute supremacy or predominance of regular law as opposed to the influence of arbitrary power', excluding 'wide discretionary authority on the part of the government'.[78] Second, it requires 'equality before the law'.[79] Third, it implies that 'the rights of individuals' are protected by common law 'as defined and enforced by the courts'.[80]

Whether the Guantánamo system and the numerous other post-September 11 measures are compatible with a concept of the rule of law that builds on Dicey's three elements is, at the very least, highly doubtful. A detailed analysis of this issue is beyond the scope of this chapter, and so I will briefly list only a few concerns. First, the laws on which contemporary counter-terrorism measures are based are – even though, it is true, often very voluminous – typically not clear, stable and determinate as required by the 'regular law' element. Instead, they are vague and flexible, giving the executive wide scope of discretion. For example, terrorist offences are normally very broadly and vaguely drafted.[81] In addition, anti-terrorism laws grant law enforcement authorities wide discretionary powers to prevent terrorism, for instance to detain those who 'endanger national

---

71   Johns, n. 29, at 618–19.

72   Aradau, n. 31, at 498.

73   Hussain, n. 33, at 742.

74   Aradau, n. 31, at 491.

75   Ibid., at 496.

76   Johns, n. 29, at 618.

77   On the distinction between formal and substantive conceptions of the rule of law, see P Craig, 'Formal and substantive conceptions of the rule of law: An analytical framework', *Public Law* (1997), 467.

78   AV Dicey, *An Introduction to the Study of the Law of the Constitution* (Basingstoke: Macmillan, 10th edn, 1959), at 202.

79   Ibid.

80   Ibid., at 203.

81   See, for example, the offence of 'encouragement of terrorism' under section 1 of the British Terrorism Act 2006.

security',[82] or to stop and search people without having to show reasonable suspicion.[83] Second, counter-terrorism measures are typically based on distinctions between different categories of people ('unlawful enemy combatants' – 'other combatants', 'citizens' – 'foreign nationals', etc.) who are afforded different levels of legal protection or even subject, as in the case of the US military commissions, to trial before different types of tribunals. These categorizations undermine the principle of equality before the law. Since this issue is at the heart of the human rights violations committed in the 'war on terror', I will return to it in the following section. Third, post-September 11 laws tend to undermine the ability of courts to protect individual rights. Often these laws expressly exclude effective judicial review of the exercise of anti-terrorism powers[84] or they replace proper courts with quasi-judicial mechanisms that are not independent from the executive. Neither the US Combatant Status Review Tribunals nor the military commissions nor any of the other legal institutions at Guantánamo referred to by the critical scholars are truly independent decision-making bodies.[85]

In view of these different concerns, I find it difficult to understand how upholding the rule of law at Guantánamo and elsewhere in the 'war on terror' can be described as 'not tricky'. Upholding the rule of law is, in fact, not only very tricky, but also of crucial importance, as it is a highly effective means of protecting human rights in the 'war on terror'. For one of the features of even a Diceyan conception of the rule of law, which is only concerned with the formal structure of the law, is that it has a power-restraining effect. It requires that the law must be general, that is, that rules must be 'issued in advance to apply to all cases and all persons in the abstract'.[86] The rule of law forces those in power to articulate their claims in terms of rules that are equally applicable to everyone, both the powerful and the powerless, and, as EP Thompson understood, thus renders them 'prisoners of their own rhetoric'.[87] In this way, the very form of law functions as a crucial inhibition on state power. As the Frankfurt-school jurist Franz Neumann observed, '[t]he generality and the abstractness of law together with the independence of the judge guarantee a minimum of personal and political liberty'.[88] As such, these requirements of the rule of law have an ethical value.[89]

Of course, this is not to say that the rule of law is, as Thompson claimed, an '*unqualified* human good'.[90] Rather, it also has an ideological, disguising function. In a class society, the generality of the law conceals the realities of substantive inequality. In addition, as explained above, states that would claim to be based on the rule of law have not only always been able to accommodate repressive measures within their ordinary legal system but by grounding them therein may also let them appear as normal and acceptable. At the same time, however, the rule of law also 'has a socially and politically protective function. It is equalising'.[91] This is what Bob Fine has described as the 'contradictory character' of the rule of law: it may be part of the 'superstructure', masking

---

82   USA Patriot Act, s 412.

83   Terrorism Act 2000, s 44.

84   For example, USA Patriot Act, s 217.

85   See Report of the Special Rapporteur on the Promotion and Protection of Human Rights and Fundamental Freedoms While Countering Terrorism, Martin Scheinin: Addendum: Mission to the United States of America, 22 November 2007, UN Doc. A/HRC/6/17Add. 3.

86   F Neumann, *The Rule of Law: Political Theory and the Legal System in Modern Society* (Leamington Spa: Berg, 1986), at 213.

87   EP Thompson, *Whigs and Hunters: The Origin of the Black Act* (London: Penguin Books, 1990), at 263.

88   F Neumann, *Behemoth: The Structure and Practice of National Socialism* (London: Victor Gollancz, 1942), at 362–63.

89   Ibid., at 362. See also Neumann (1986), n. 86, at 213.

90   Thompson, n. 87, at 266 (emphasis added).

91   Neumann (1986), n. 86, at 213.

exploitation and oppression, but at the same time it is a crucial means of inhibiting the power of government and protecting the rights of the people.[92] Therefore, it should not be discarded. Also in this respect, I would hold with Neumann. If one replaces 'universalism' with 'the rule of law' in his following remark, then this is, I believe, a good summary of his view on the issue:

> To abandon universalism because of its failures is like rejecting civil rights because they help legitimize and veil class exploitation, or democracy because it conceals boss control, or Christianity because churches have corrupted Christian morals. Faced with a corrupt administration of justice, the reasonable person does not demand a return to the war of each against all, but fights for an honest system.[93]

The conclusion that it is futile to insist on the rule of law in the 'war on terror', because the post-September 11 measures involve detailed regulation and various legal mechanisms, rests on a misunderstanding of the functions of the rule of law and an underestimation of its potential to restrict state power. Of course, as argued above, Guantánamo Bay is not an exceptional lawless space and all the other post-September 11 measures are not extraordinary phenomena that are unrelated to the law. Yet just because law is implicated in the human rights violations committed in the 'war on terror' does not mean that there is no value in endorsing the rule of law. On the contrary, as I will try to show in the following section, rule-of-law arguments can be very effective tools to challenge what is arguably the root cause of these human rights abuses.

Lessons for Human Rights Campaigners and Lawyers

There are two main practical lessons for human rights campaigners and lawyers to be drawn from the above, largely theoretical, discussion. The first follows from my point about the (non-)exceptionality of counter-terrorism measures, the second from my point about the functions of the rule of law.

Reconsider Campaigning Focus

If one agrees that the post-September 11 measures are not as exceptional as they are commonly depicted, then some of the leading human rights organizations should clearly reconsider their campaigning focus. Since, as Johns has pointed out, 'it is the exception that rings liberal alarm bells',[94] most of the large human rights organizations have devoted a great – and, I would argue, disproportionate – share of their attention on counter-terrorism policies in recent years. Human Rights Watch, for example, set up a new programme devoted to terrorism and counter-terrorism, alongside its more established programmes on the different regions of the world and issues such as women's and children's rights. Since September 11, the organization has issued approximately 550 news releases, reports and other publications on the human rights impacts of counter-terrorism. In comparison, in the same time period, 51 of its publications dealt with 'health and human rights' and approximately 170 each with 'labor [sic] and human rights' and 'treatment of prisoners'.[95] In

---

92 B Fine, *Democracy and the Rule of Law: Liberal Ideals and Marxist Critiques* (London: Pluto Press, 1984).

93 Neumann (1942), n. 88, at 133.

94 Johns, n. 29, at 629.

95 See <www.hrw.org> [accessed 20 May 2008].

the United Kingdom, much of the energy of national human rights organizations such as Liberty and other critical commentators has been absorbed by the numerous counter-terrorism proposals put forward by the Government in recent years. Especially the proposed extension of pre-charge detention (14 days, 28 days, 42 days, 90 days, etc.) has provoked countless campaigns, policy papers, demonstrations and even international interventions by celebrities such as Desmond Tutu.[96] In contrast, Liberty's most recent press release on anti-social behaviour orders – an issue affecting the human rights of thousands of people in the United Kingdom – dates from March 2006.

But it is, above all, the degree of attention that Guantánamo Bay has attracted over the last few years that is, in my view, out of all proportions. All international (and countless national) human rights organizations have been running major campaigns against Guantánamo for several years. There have been films, demonstrations, readings of poems and even a 'virtual flotilla' to Guantánamo. The secretary general of Amnesty International justified the considerable resources and efforts invested by her organization by claiming that Guantánamo is 'the Gulag of our time'.[97] But if one was to make this kind of historical comparison (which I do not think one should), then surely 'the Gulag of our time' is not Guantánamo with its now approximately 270 detainees, but the worldwide web of immigration detention centres holding tens of thousands of people who have not committed any criminal offence.[98] From this perspective, it can be argued that most human rights organizations have fallen into the trap of blindly following the political agenda set by governments. Just like governments, they have made (counter-)terrorism their top priority, even though there are other human rights issues that are at least equally pressing.

My argument is not that Guantánamo and other instances of counter-terrorism detention do not deserve attention because they affect only a relatively small number of people. Nor is it to suggest that these battles against counter-terrorism policies do not deserve to be fought. Pre-charge detention of 42 days can, and should, be opposed even if one thinks that there are more pressing human rights issue. Therefore, following on from the above discussion of the role of the rule of law, the following section makes a few suggestions as to how human rights litigation and campaigning strategies can be designed effectively in the 'war on terror'. At the heart of these suggestions is my conviction that rule-of-law arguments should not be readily discarded. On the contrary, it is crucial to insist on the generality of the law.

Invoke the Rule of Law

A central aspect of the criticism of endorsements of the rule of law by the critical scholars is their warning against the common tendency to respond to governmental counter-terrorism measures by instigating litigation in national courts or international legal institutions.[99] I assume that this warning against turning to judicial fora is more intended to reflect a supposedly radical theoretical position than meant as a concrete practical recommendation. If it was the latter, then it could not be described otherwise than as cynical. Who would seriously suggest that, for example, terrorist suspects languishing in Guantánamo or elsewhere in indefinite detention should not exhaust every means available to them, whether legal or otherwise?

---

96   Liberty, 'The international perspective on pre-charge detention', available at <http://www.liberty-human-rights.org.uk/issues/2-terrorism/extension-of-pre-charge-detention/the-international-perspective.shtml>.

97   R Norton-Taylor, 'Guantánamo is Gulag of our time, says Amnesty', *The Guardian*, 26 May 2005.

98   See notes 69 and 70 above.

99   See Johns, n. 29, at 621; Hussain, n. 33, at 751; Aradau, n. 31, at 496–97.

A second aspect of the scepticism towards an insistence on the rule of law is the characterization of a strategy that relies on formal legal arguments as somehow 'too limited'. Instead, the critical school of thought calls for a 'broader political response' that would restore a sense of 'decisional responsibility'. Yet often formal legal, rule-of-law based, arguments are the most promising ones, both as far as litigation strategies and political processes are concerned. In the following, I point to two ways in which invocations of the rule of law can be used as effective argumentative tools to challenge counter-terrorism policies.

First, as explained above, a central element of the rule of law is the requirement of equality before the law or formal equality. Insisting on equality before the law is a particularly promising litigation strategy to challenge counter-terrorism policies. As Neal Katyal has pointed out, it will often be difficult for courts to decide whether counter-terrorism measures are *substantively* correct, that is, whether they strike the right balance between liberty and security or not.[100] Equality challenges do not require courts to make that decision: they are not about the *what* of anti-terrorism laws (that is, not about their substance), but about *who* is affected by them.[101] In this sense, they are just like separation-of-powers arguments (which are about *how* counter-terrorism measures are passed), formal or procedural. As such, they are more likely to be successful in court. The petitioner in *Hamdan v. Rumsfeld* won his case on the basis of a separation-of-powers argument.[102] In *A v. Secretary of State for the Home Department,* the Belmarsh prisoners prevailed because the House of Lords found that there was no justification for treating them differently from British terrorist suspects.[103] Since counter-terrorism policies typically involve distinctions between different categories of people, the same kind of equality challenges could be deployed to oppose numerous other government measures. Examples include the US military commissions, which only have jurisdiction to try foreign nationals,[104] or the widespread use of immigration restrictions as a means of countering terrorism.[105]

As the example of the Belmarsh case demonstrates, insisting on equality before the law is not only a promising litigation strategy: it may also have a profound impact on political processes. The original act providing for detention without trial, the ATCSA 2001, which was limited in scope to foreign nationals, had been passed with a comfortable majority and without attracting great public attention.[106] However, once the House of Lords had found that the ATCSA was incompatible with the prohibition of discrimination, the Government had to come up with legislation that was applicable to both foreign and British citizens. As a consequence, the proposed Prevention of Terrorism Act 2005 led to a major public debate on the relationship between liberty and security and to 'parliament's longest and sometimes rowdiest sitting for 99 years'.[107] The act was only passed after the Government had made substantial concessions, in particular by providing for

---

100   N Katyal, 'Equality in the war on terror', *Stanford Law Review*, 59 (2007), 1365.

101   Ibid., at 1368.

102   126 S Ct 2749 (2006) (holding that the US President did not have authority to establish the military commissions at Guantánamo Bay without congressional authorization).

103   *A v. Secretary of State for the Home Department* [2004] UKHL 56; [2005] 2 WLR 87 (holding that the detention of only foreign terrorist suspects violated the prohibition of discrimination of Article 14 of the European Convention on Human Rights).

104   10 USC ss 948a(3), 948c. See D Moeckli, *Human Rights and Non-Discrimination in the 'War on Terror'* (Oxford: Oxford University Press, 2008), at 140–62.

105   Ibid., 165–80; C Walker, 'The treatment of foreign terror suspects', *Modern Law Review*, 70 (2007), 427.

106   The vote was 341 to 77. *Hansard*, HC vol 375, col 404 (21 November 2001).

107   P Wintour and A Travis, 'The longest day', *The Guardian*, 12 March 2005.

greater involvement of the judiciary in the suggested control order process[108] and by making the act's key provisions subject to annual renewal by Parliament.[109] The extension of the scope of anti-terrorism powers to British citizens due to the House of Lords decision thus reshaped the debate in crucial ways. The discussants were forced to consider the possibility of the law being applied against themselves (or at least their constituents), and, as a consequence, the discussion now had to be articulated in terms of generally applicable rules and principles. This shift towards general rules resulted, as Thompson would have predicted, in a curtailment of the executive's powers: preventive detention was replaced with lesser forms of restrictions on liberty, which, in addition, are subject to greater judicial control. The import of insisting on equality should not be overestimated: generally applicable rules are not necessarily good rules. The control order system introduced by the Prevention of Terrorism Act 2005, authorising the Home Secretary to impose restrictions on terrorist suspects ranging from a ban on the use of the Internet to home arrest, still raises a number of important human rights issues.[110] Nevertheless, it would be absurd to claim that control orders are not an improvement on indefinite detention in a high-security prison.

A second, so far less explored, way in which invoking the rule of law can serve as an effective instrument of challenging counter-terrorism policies is by insisting on another, closely related, aspect of it, namely on the requirement that rules must be abstract and general rather than situation-specific. It is this requirement which, ultimately, secures equality before the law.[111] In recent years, the generality and abstractness of the law has come under increased pressure, including in the field of criminal justice. Following September 11, numerous states have adopted special anti-terrorism laws and created new specialized mechanisms and institutions, including ad hoc tribunals and special law enforcement agencies, to deal with terrorism.[112] A similar regime specifically designed to counter terrorism is emerging at the international level.[113] This special treatment approach is largely prompted by political pressures. Special laws are typically passed amidst great public outrage in the wake of terrorist attacks and designed to denounce terrorist acts, stigmatize the terrorists and reassure the public. As a consequence, those subject to these anti-terrorism regimes are inevitably singled out for particularly harsh treatment. To name just one example, the special terrorist sanctions regime imposed by the UN Security Council provides far less protection to those affected by the sanctions than is generally available under national and international law, in particular depriving them of the right to a fair hearing and the right to a judicial remedy.[114]

---

108   Prevention of Terrorism Act 2005, s 4.

109   Ibid., s 13.

110   See *Secretary of State for the Home Department v. JJ and others* [2007] UKHL 45; *Secretary of State for the Home Department v. MB* [2007] UKHL 46.

111   I Kant, *Groundwork of the Metaphysics of Morals* (Cambridge: Cambridge University Press, 1998); F Neumann, *The Democratic and the Authoritarian State: Essays in Political and Legal Theory* (New York: Free Press of Glencoe, 1957) at 42; Neumann (1986), n. 86, at 256–57.

112   Examples include the USA Patriot Act of 2001 and the Military Commissions Act of 2006; the British ATCSA 2001; the German *Gesetz zur Bekämpfung des internationalen Terrorismus*, 9 January 2002, BGBl. I, 361; and the Indian Prevention of Terrorism Act (POTA) of 26 March 2002. For a good overview, see VV Ramraj, M Hor and K Roach (eds), *Global Anti-Terrorism Law and Policy* (Cambridge: Cambridge University Press, 2005).

113   See, for instance, E Rosand, 'The UN-led multilateral institutional response to jihadist terrorism: Is a global counterterrorism body needed?', *Journal of Conflict & Security Law*, 11 (2006), 399.

114   See the contribution by Bill Bowring to this volume. See also 'Targeted Sanctions and Due Process', Study by Prof. B Fassbender commissioned by the UN Office of Legal Affairs, 20 March 2006; Council of Europe, 'The European Convention on Human Rights, Due Process and United Nations Security Council Counter-Terrorism Sanctions', Report prepared by Prof. I Cameron, 6 February 2006; A Bianchi,

This inferior level of due process protection has been judicially sanctioned on the basis that the Security Council's sanctions resolutions, by virtue of Article 103 of the UN Charter, prevail over every other obligation of states under domestic or international law, including obligations under human rights treaties.[115] In this sense, it is the notion that not all categories of people deserve the same level of legal protection and the corresponding fragmentation of the law at both the national and international level – the replacement of the general law by special, particularly restrictive, legal regimes – which is at the root of the human rights abuses committed in the 'war on terror'. Opposing this dangerous trend by insisting on the rule-of-law requirement that norms must be generally applicable must, therefore, be a central element of any effective strategy to protect human rights.

The relevance of the principle of the generality of law reaches far beyond the counter-terrorism context. The emergence of a specialized anti-terrorism regime is, arguably, part of a wider trend whereby criminal justice systems increasingly rely on special powers to deal with 'special' crimes and risks.[116] In the 'risk society',[117] government crime policies are concerned with categorizing people according to their dangerousness and subjecting these different subpopulations to different risk management models.[118] As also Hussain seems to acknowledge,[119] the emergence and proliferation of such specialized regulatory models of repression (immigration law, anti-social behaviour orders, sex offender orders, etc.) makes an insistence on the rule of law, on general rules, today more important than ever before.

Finally, it is important to stress that a strategy of insisting on the rule of law and turning to the courts is not only a potentially very effective 'tool' of challenging counter-terrorism policies, but instead constitutes an important 'resource' to mobilize wider political resistance and build up grassroots campaigns. This mobilizing, 'constitutive' function of law and legal claim-making has been explored and convincingly established by a number of authors,[120] including by Colm

---

'Assessing the effectiveness of the UN Security Council's anti-terrorism measures: The quest for legitimacy and cohesion', *European Journal of International Law*, 17 (2006), 881, 903–10; E de Wet and A Nollkaemper, 'Review of Security Council decisions by national courts', *German Yearbook of International Law*, 45 (2002), 166; E Miller, 'The use of targeted sanctions in the fight against terrorism – what about human rights?', *ASIL Proceedings*, 97 (2003), 46.

115   See European Court of First Instance, Case T-306/01, *Yusuf and Al Barakaat International Foundation v. Council of the European Union and the Commission of the European Communities* [2005] ECR II-3533; Case T-315/01, *Kadi v. Council of the European Union and the Commission of the European Communities* [2005] ECR II-3649.

116   C Walker, '50th anniversary article: Terrorism and criminal justice – past, present and future', *Criminal Law Review* (2004), 311, 325.

117   U Beck, *Risk Society: Towards a New Modernity* (London: Sage, 1992).

118   For its integration of insurance techniques into processes and practices of crime control, Feeley and Simon have termed this development 'actuarial justice'. M Feeley and J Simon, 'Actuarial justice: The emerging new criminal law', in D Nelken (ed.), *The Futures of Criminology* (London: Sage, 1994). See also S Cohen, *Visions of Social Control: Crime, Punishment and Classification* (Cambridge: Polity Press, 1985), ch. 4; N Reichman, 'Managing crime risks: Toward an insurance based model of social control', *Research in Law, Deviance and Social Control*, 8 (1986), 151; P O'Malley, 'Risk, power and crime prevention', *Economy and Society*, 21 (1992), 252.

119   Hussain, n. 33, at 752.

120   See, for example, M McCann, 'Reform litigation on trial', *Law and Social Inquiry*, 17 (1992), 715, esp. 735 ff.; M McCann and H Silverstein, 'Rethinking law's "allurements": A relational analysis of social movement lawyers in the United States', in A Sarat and S Scheingold (eds), *Cause Lawyering: Political Commitments and Professional Responsibilities* (New York: Oxford University Press, 1998), 261; C Coleman,

Campbell and Ita Connolly for the context of terrorism and counter-terrorism.[121] There is no need to review these arguments in detail here. It is sufficient to note that, in view of this additional function of appeals to the law and the instigation of court proceedings, a position that outright rejects these strategies as 'apolitical' appears all the more unconvincing. In fact, such a position is arguably itself based on an untenable binary distinction between law and politics.

Conclusion

The critical perspective adds an important dimension to the understanding of how, and how not, to protect human rights in the 'war on terror'. Critical scholars are right to point out that preventing human rights abuses is not simply a matter, as the dominant discourse would have it, of more regulation, legal mechanisms and judicial overview. Invocations of the lawlessness of anti-terrorism regimes only serve to obscure how the 'normal' legal system is implicated in, and may legitimize, human rights violations.

Yet it does not follow from this observation that the rule of law has no role to play in a response to repressive counter-terrorism policies. Rejection of an endorsement of the rule of law and calls for its replacement by a 'political response' are based on an equally untenable distinction between law and politics and an oversimplification of the choice at hand. In fact, perhaps the most striking feature of the critical analyses of the 'war on terror' described above is that, being framed in Schmitt's and Agamben's theoretical terms, they operate at an almost completely abstract level. None of the critical scholars referred to above explains what the suggested 'political response' might look like or what a 're-invigoration of that sense of the exception that may be derived from the work of Carl Schmitt'[122] might entail in practice.[123] What exactly is meant by restoring 'the experience of politics',[124] 'the space of political decision'[125] and 'decisional responsibility'?[126] Should unfettered discretion be given to decision-makers at Guantánamo Bay as 'the experience of deciding in circumstances where no person or rule offers assurance that the decision that one takes will be the right one'[127] automatically ensures that they will respect the human rights of the detainees? And who should these decision-makers be – some military officer, some political body? To take a parallel case, was the problem with Abu Ghraib that the interrogators lacked a sense of decisional responsibility and authority? Or was it not perhaps just the opposite? And does the call for deciding 'under circumstances not pre-codified by pre-existing norms'[128] imply that, for instance, the criteria for detention of terrorist suspects can be made up by whoever happens to be in charge of the decision?

LD Nee and LS Rubinowitz, 'Social movements and social-change litigation: Synergy in the Montgomery Bus Protest', *Law and Social Inquiry*, 30 (2005), 663.

121   C Campbell and I Connolly, 'A deadly complexity: Law, social movements and political violence'. *Minnesota Journal of International Law*, 16 (2007), 265.

122   Johns, n. 29, at 615.

123   For a similar criticism, see WE Scheuerman, *Between the Norm and the Exception: The Frankfurt School and the Rule of Law* (Cambridge, MA: MIT Press, 1994), at 247.

124   Johns, n. 29, at 634.

125   Aradau, n. 31, at 489.

126   Johns, n. 29, at 615.

127   Ibid., at 634.

128   Ibid., at 615.

Both the liberal and the critical schools of thought only obscure the issues at stake when they either reduce counter-terrorism practices to exceptional extra-legal phenomena or simply reject reliance on the rule of law as irrelevant and apolitical. Those concerned about human rights should neither pretend that Guantánamo Bay is some extraordinary lawless space, nor should they forgo rule-of-law arguments when opposing the US Government's practices there. They do not need to choose between law and politics. Instead, they should try to identify the most promising tools of challenging repressive counter-terrorism policies, one of which, as I have shown above, consists of insisting on the rule of law – especially on the requirement that laws must be generally applicable – and instigating court proceedings. Human rights activists should not be afraid to use these tools. Especially when they oppose the practices of a bureaucracy and a military machinery that see themselves as engaged in a war directed against particular groups of people, it is not enough to call for 'political agency under conditions of radical doubt' and to appeal to 'decisional responsibility'.[129] In a climate where the blame for terrorism is increasingly put on foreign nationals and particular ethnic groups, it is crucial to defend the few existing legal checks to protect those in the political minority from being subject to the unrestrained power of the state. Of course, legal checks are by no means sufficient to prevent human rights abuses and may lend the respective legal system a degree of legitimacy it does not deserve. However, at least to me, it seems equally clear that this is not a reason to reject them.

---

129   Ibid.

Chapter 13

'Terrorist Lists' and Procedural Human Rights: A Collision between UN Law, EU Law and Strasbourg Law?

Bill Bowring

Introduction

The designation of a person or an organization as 'terrorist' opens up a chasm in the rule of law, a space defined not by an absence of law, since there may well be a plethora of positive law, but by the absence of procedural rights. These are not only fundamental human rights in themselves, but crucially provide the best protection against torture and other forms of arbitrary state conduct. Drawing on my own previous work, this chapter engages with a number of issues arising from international and national responses to what is described as the 'war on terror'.[1] This chapter is therefore complementary to the chapter by Daniel Moeckli; my focus is on the issue of proscription and 'terrorist lists'.

I concur with Moeckli in observing that this space without rights was announced by none other than Carl Schmitt, as I show in my first section. Next, I suggest that the failure of the international community to work out an acceptable definition of 'terrorism' is closely linked to the construction of the 'terrorist' as an outlaw, a person outside the rule of law. Third, I outline the UN and EU law with regard to the drawing up of 'terrorist lists', and follow with the safeguards which the Council of Europe (CoE), and these bodies themselves, have endeavoured to put in place. Fourth, I analyse some case law. There have more recently been decisions that appear to show signs of a retreat from this hard line, in particular the astonishing about-turn in relation to the Peoples Mujaheddin of Iran (PMOI), and the *Yusuf* and *Kadi* decisions.[2] Fifth, I analyse three case studies of the effect on groups and individuals of placement on 'terrorist lists', and the very mixed results of legal action taken on their behalf.

However, my core argument and my conclusion are far from optimistic. I contend that a war against Afghanistan, Serbia or Iraq, or indeed a war against colonial occupation, can be analysed using existing resources, and we can discuss the legality or otherwise of such events. However, a

---

1   B Bowring and D Korff, 'Terrorist designation with regard to European and international law: The case of the PMOI', Joint Opinion (2003), at <http://www.statewatch.org/news/2005/feb/bb-dk-joint-paper.pdf>; and B Bowring (2007), 'The human rights implications of international listing mechanisms for "terrorist" organisations', background paper for OSCE/UN Expert Workshop on International Cooperation in Counter-terrorism, 15–17 November 2006 (final report published February 2007), 75–114, at <http://www.statewatch.org/terrorlists/OSCE-UN-feb-2007.pdf>.

2   *Ahmed Ali Yusuf and Al Barakaat International Foundation,* and *Yassin Abdullah Kadi v. Council of the European Union and Commission of the European Communities* (Case T-306/01 and Case T-315/01), Court of First Instance of the Court of Justice (CFI) 21 September 2005, and European Court of Justice (ECJ) 3 September 2008.

'war against terror' is a purported war against an abstraction, and can have no more legitimacy or limitation than a war against 'immorality' or even 'obscenity'. How can an abstraction be made to surrender? That is why the abstraction of 'terrorism' is transmuted, by force of law, into the individuals and organizations now placed on the 'terrorist lists', which form the subject-matter of my three case studies. And that is why those placed on the list find themselves in a void without rights.

Carl Schmitt, Terrorism and the Rule of Law

Unlike Moeckli, I do not start with Carl Schmitt's *Political Theology*,[3] but with one of his later works, his lectures delivered in 1962, and now published as *Theory of the Partisan*.[4] I do not wish to dissociate Schmitt from his role as the 'crown jurist of the Third Reich' and his later trajectory until his death in 1985 as an advocate of the New Right's concept of an 'integral Europe'.[5] His interest to me is as follows. In his usual robust manner, and without disguising his politics, Schmitt distinguished between the 'true partisan'[6] and the 'communist partisan'.

The 'true partisan' was for him the 'telluric' partisan, fighting on and for territory. This partisan has 'the tie to the soil, to the autochthonous population, and to the geographical particularity of the land',[7] and has a real but not an absolute enemy. The 'true' partisan's 'fundamental position' therefore remains 'defensive'. Schmitt cited Joan of Arc's answer when asked whether God hated the English: 'I do not know whether God loves or hates the English: I only know that they must be driven out of France.'

> Every normal partisan would have given this answer in defense of the national soil. Such a fundamentally defensive position also presupposes a fundamental limitation of enmity. The real enemy will not be declared to be an absolute enemy, also not the last enemy of mankind.[8]

Schmitt contrasted the 'true' partisan with the communist partisan, for whom the enemy is indeed 'the last enemy of mankind'. The communist partisan, for Schmitt, was the creation of Lenin, who turned the 'real' enemy, the object of defensive struggle, into an absolute enemy.[9]

Thus, Schmitt co-opted Lenin as a proto-Schmittean as well as a keen student of Clausewitz.[10] Lenin's insight was that '[...] the distinction of friend and enemy in the age of revolution is primary, and [...] it determines war as well as politics'.[11] Schmitt continued that 'for Lenin, only revolutionary war is absolute war, because it arises from absolute enmity'.[12] The concrete absolute

---

3   C Schmitt, *Political Theology: Four Chapters on the Concept of Sovereignty* (Chicago, IL: University of Chicago Press, 2005).

4   C Schmitt, *Theory of the Partisan: Intermediate Commentary on the Concept of the Political* (New York: Telos Press, 2007).

5   See J-W Müller, *A Dangerous Mind: Carl Schmitt in Post-War European Thought* (New Haven, CT: Yale University Press, 2003), at 207–9; the vision of an 'integral Europe' contains a belief in primordial, integral and homogenous ethnic groups.

6   Schmitt, above, n. 4, at 20.

7   Schmitt, above, n. 4, at 21.

8   Schmitt, above, n. 4, at 92.

9   Schmitt, above, n. 4, at 93.

10   As evidenced by his Notebooks on Clausewitz's *On War*, published in Berlin in 1957.

11   Schmitt, above, n. 4, at 51.

12   Schmitt, above, n. 4, at 52.

enemy was the class enemy – the bourgeois. Unlike Clausewitz, who could not conceive of a state becoming an instrument of a party, Lenin absolutized the party, so that the partisan 'also became absolute and a bearer of absolute enmity'.[13] Those who fight such an 'absolute' enemy 'feel morally compelled to destroy these other men [...]. They must declare their opponents to be totally criminal and inhuman, to be a total non-value.'

It can be no surprise that Schmitt paid close attention to the post Second World War period, and the fact the 'partisan warfare continued', as he put it, under the leadership of Mao Tse-Tung in China,[14] Ho Chi Minh in Vietnam, George Grivas in Cyprus, and Fidel Castro and Che Guevara in Cuba.[15] But nowhere did he give these struggles their proper name: anti-colonial struggles, the fight for national liberation. His Euro-centrism and nostalgia for the Congress of Vienna, in a word his deep conservatism, did not permit him to do so.

As William Scheuerman has pointed out, Schmitt's *partisan* 'occasionally appears to conflate partisan or guerrilla warfare with terrorism', when what is needed is to distinguish them.[16] For Scheuerman, guerrilla fighters *refigure* the traditional distinction between combatants and non-combatants, while terrorism simply condones indiscriminate violence against innocent civilians. Thus, he observed that Mao Tse-Tung and Che Guevara sharply criticized terrorism. As Scheuerman put it: 'In contrast to the potentially democratic or at least populist connotations of guerrilla warfare, terrorists *paternalistically* posit the existence of some (perhaps fictional) political entity which they hope to "awaken" or "unleash" by their acts of violence.'[17] He recounted Schmitt's views on the impossibility of codifying the laws of war for irregular fighters, and concluded that '[...] the Bush administration's legal arguments about the status of accused terrorists mirrors crucial facets of Schmitt's logic'.[18]

What Schmitt did, according to Scheuerman, was to surrender the rule of law. Scheuerman took as an example of the inevitable consequence the infamous 13 September 2003 report prepared by Major General Geoffrey Miller on the extension of Guantánamo interrogation techniques to Abu Ghraib.[19] In his view, Miller's justification '[...] eerily corroborates Schmitt's expectation that the dynamism of modern warfare potentially clashes with *any* attempt to develop a firm legal framework for the rules of war'.[20]

The use of violence for political or religious purposes by non-state entities is hardly new. In the twelfth and thirteenth centuries the Hashshashin or Assassins were ready to commit suicide in order to murder Arab rulers, and also European leaders of the Crusades.[21] The American and French Revolutions were far from peaceful.[22] In the late nineteenth century the Narodnaya Volya organization, active in the Russian Empire, carried out a campaign of murders that culminated in the assassination of Tsar Aleksandr II. Lenin's own brother Aleksandr was executed for his

---

13   Schmitt, above, n. 4, at 92–93.
14   Schmitt, above, n. 4, at 54–60.
15   Schmitt, above, n. 4, at 12–13.
16   W Scheuerman, 'Carl Schmitt and the road to Abu Ghraib', *Constellations*, 13/1 (2006), 108–24, at 112.
17   Scheuerman, ibid., 112.
18   Scheuerman, ibid.,118
19   M Danner, *Torture and Truth: Abu Ghraib and America in Iraq* (London: Granta Books, 2005).
20   Scheuerman, above, n. 16, at 121.
21   Hashshashin (which means 'those who take hashish') were members of the Persian Shiiate Ismaili movement led by Hassan Sabbah (a fellow student with Omar Khayyam). Ismailis used political assassination to undermine the security and stability of the Mongols who had invaded and ruled Persia at the time. See A Bausani, *The Persians* (London: Elek, 1975), at 97–98.
22   See T Eagleton, *Holy Terror* (Oxford: Oxford University Press, 2005).

involvement. Rulers all over Europe went in fear of their lives. In the Britain at the same time the Fenians carried out a campaign of bombings that culminated in the Clerkenwell Bombing of 1867, in which 12 people were killed and 126 injured. Ian Ward observes that '[t]here is nothing new in terrorist violence, just as there is nothing new in the violence of faith'.[23]

It now tends to be forgotten (and was ignored by Schmitt) that international law recognizes the legal right of peoples to self-determination; this applies especially to peoples resisting occupation and tyranny, and was recognized during the period from the 1960s until the end of the Cold War in the case of the National Liberation Movements. Thus, armed struggle was by no means prohibited by international law.[24] But under the proscription regimes adopted by the EU, UN, USA, UK and other states, armed struggle in self-defence has been criminalized as 'terrorism' and the solidarity of the so-called 'international community' lies increasingly with the oppressor.[25]

What is at stake in this chapter is whether the 'war on terror', inexorably institutes a rights-free zone; that is, the exclusion of one of the most fundamental human rights (indeed, civil liberties) – the procedural rights of due process. Of course, as Mark Neocleous reminds us, the 'war on terror', far from constituting a 'lawless world', or a 'legal black hole' or 'legal limbo', is underpinned by a plethora of law-making.[26] In this I entirely concur with the approach of Daniel Moeckli.

There is a further point, however. Scheuerman has noticed the conflation for Schmitt of the 'communist partisan' with 'terrorism'. I argue that 'terrorism' is an abstraction without substance; and that to provide a real, substantial target for attack, those in power need the 'terrorist lists'.

The Absence of a Definition of 'Terrorism'

It cannot be disputed that the international community has utterly failed so far to draw up an acceptable definition of 'terrorism', despite what Di Filippo describes as 'the uneasy search for a coherent framework'.[27] I strongly suspect that this is because the word 'terrorist' adds little to the identification of a particular action as a serious crime, save to express especially strong condemnation. Murder, after all, is murder. 'Terrorism', as already noted, is an abstraction.

It can therefore be no surprise that definitions of 'terrorism' in national legislation are notorious for spreading the net far too wide. John Dugard, the author of a seminal essay on the problems of the definition of terrorism,[28] hit the nail on the head in his Rhodes University Centenary Lecture delivered in 2004.[29] He pointed to the two UN Security Council resolutions adopted after 9/11, resolution 1368/2001 and resolution 1373/2001. These condemned terrorism in the strongest terms and directed states to act against it, but made no attempt to define it. He continued:

---

23   I Ward, 'God, terror and law', review essay, *Oxford Journal of Legal Studies*, 4 (2008), 783–96, at 796.

24   See H Wilson, *International Law and the Use of Force by National Liberation Movements* (Oxford: Clarendon Press, 1988).

25   See B Bowring, ch. 1, 'Self-determination – the revolutionary kernel of international law', in *The Degradation of the International Legal Order? The Rehabilitation of Law and the Possibility of Politics* (Abingdon: Routledge Cavendish, 2008), 9–38.

26   M Neocleous, 'The problem with normality: Taking exception to "permanent emergency"', *Alternatives*, 31 (2006), 191–213, especially at 205.

27   M Di Filippo, 'Terrorist crimes and international co-operation: Critical remarks on the definition and inclusion of terrorism in the category of international crimes', *European Journal of International Law*, 19/3 (2008), 533–70, at 536.

28   J Dugard, 'International terrorism: Problems of definition', *International Affairs*, 50/1 (1974), 67–81.

29   Text at <http://www.ru.ac.za/centenary/lectures/johndugardlecture.doc>.

Terrorism for the Security Council is what obscenity was for the American judge who remarked that he knew obscenity when he saw it! The danger of this approach is that it gives each State a wide discretion to define terrorism for itself, as it sees fit. It encourages States to define terrorism widely, to settle political scores by treating their political opponents as terrorists. It is a licence for oppression.

He went on to draw a chilling parallel with the EU's response, Council Framework Decision of 13 June 2002, which potentially includes protest action:

Of course, we in South Africa have experienced this before. Remember the Terrorism Act of 1967 which defined terrorism as any act, committed with the intent to endanger the maintenance of law and order? Such an intention was presumed if the act was likely to encourage hostility between whites and blacks or to embarrass the administration of the affairs of the State! ...

Colin Warbrick urged that:

[...] the insistence on the application and observance of international legal standards on human rights, even if they must be modified in extremis, should be an essential feature of any response to terrorism, even a war against terrorism, which is waged to protect the rule of law.[30]

The Powers of the UN Security Council

The events giving rise to the present UN anti-terror mechanisms were most certainly crimes. On 7 August 1998 the US embassies in Nairobi, Kenya and Dar es Salaam, Tanzania, were bombed, leaving 258 people dead and more than 5,000 injured. In response, the US launched cruise missiles on 20 August 1998, striking a 'terrorism training complex' in Afghanistan and destroying a pharmaceutical manufacturing facility in Khartoum, Sudan, that reportedly produced nerve gas. Both targets were believed to have been financed by the wealthy Islamist radical Osama bin Laden, whose organization al-Qaeda was allegedly behind the embassy bombings.[31] Acting under Chapter VII of the UN Charter, which gives it mandatory powers, the Security Council in UNSC Resolution 1267 (1999) of 15 October 1999 ordered states to:

freeze funds and other financial resources, including funds derived or generated from property owned or controlled directly or indirectly by the Taliban [...] as designated by the Committee established by paragraph 6 below, and ensure that neither they nor any other funds or financial resources so designated are made available [...] except as may be authorised by the Committee on a case-by-case basis on the ground of humanitarian need.[32]

By way of the same resolution, the Security Council established a 'Sanctions Committee' of all its members. This Committee, one of whose purposes is to 'freeze without delay the funds and other financial assets or economic resources of designated individuals and entities' has established and

---

30   C Warbrick, 'The European response to terrorism in an age of human rights', *European Journal of Human Rights*, 15/5 (2004), 989–1018, at 989.

31   See <http://www.infoplecase.com/spot/newsfacts-sudanstrikes.html>.

32   At <http://daccessdds.un.org/doc/UNDOC/GEN/N99/300/44/PDF/N9930044.pdf?OpenElement> [accessed 1 July 2009].

maintained 'The Consolidated List' 'with respect to al-Qaeda, Usama bin Laden [sic], and the Taliban and other individuals, groups, undertakings and entities associated with them', which are to be subjected to 'asset freezing'.[33]

This mechanism, already 10 years old, has been incrementally strengthened on many occasions, frequently in response to fresh events.

Thus, within days of 9/11, on 28 September 2001, the Security Council adopted Resolution 1373 (2001) (Terrorism),[34] which continues to be the focus of action by governments around the world 'for wide-ranging, comprehensive resolution with steps and strategies to combat international terrorism' including al-Qaeda. This Resolution makes the connection between terrorism and organized crime, drug trafficking, arms trafficking and the illegal movement of weapons of mass destruction.

Some scholars have expressed grave reservations as to whether, in adopting such resolutions under Chapter VII, the UN Security Council is engaging in unwarranted legislation. This is particularly the case with 1373. Clémentine Olivier commented: 'Allowing the Security Council to enjoy legislative power and modify States' obligations under international human rights law would not only be legally incorrect; it would also, from a political perspective, be unwise.'[35]

In the view of Matthew Happold,[36] by laying down a series of general and abstract rules binding on all UN member states, the UNSC in Resolution 1373, purported to legislate.[37] In doing so it acted ultra vires the UN Charter. He recognized that Security Council Resolutions are generally seen as being legal, at least prima facie.[38] He also noted that Resolution 1373 differed from all previous Security Council decisions in Chapter VII, in that 'the threat to the peace is identified is not any specific situation but rather a form of behaviour, "terrorist acts". Indeed, it is a form of behaviour that the resolution leaves undefined'.[39] That is my point once more: how can there be a war against an abstraction?

EU Powers

The EU acted promptly to put in place mandatory requirements to enforce the Security Council's measures. Thus, it adopted 'Common Positions' under Article 15 of the Treaty establishing the European Union. If a Common Position calls for Community action implementing some or all of the restrictive measures, the Commission will present to Council a proposal for a Council Regulation in accordance with Articles 60 and 301 of the Treaty establishing the European Community. It should be recalled that it is the member states acting in the Council that are ultimately responsible

---

33   See 'Security Council Committee established pursuant to resolution 1267 (1999) concerning Al-Qaida and the Taliban and Associated Individuals and Entities', at <http://www.un.org/sc/committees/1267/information.shtml>.

34   The text is set out in the press release at <http://www.un.org/News/Press/docs/2001/sc7158.doc.htm> [accessed 1 July 2001].

35   C Olivier, 'Human rights law and the international fight against terrorism: How do Security Council Resolutions impact on states' obligations under international human rights law? (Revisiting Security Council Resolution 1373)', *Nordic Journal of International Law*, 73 (2004), 399–419, at 419.

36   M Happold, 'Security Council Resolution 1373 and the Constitution of the United Nations', *Leiden Journal of International Law*, 16 (2003), 593–610.

37   See also P Szasz, 'The Security Council starts legislating', *American Journal of International Law*, 96 (2002), 901.

38   See *Certain Expenses of the United Nations* (Advisory Opinion) [1962] ICJ Rep. 151, at 168.

39   Happold, ibid., at 598.

for deciding who is included in the EU 'terrorist list', acting under the EU's Common Foreign and Security Policy. This is, of course, the context of unjust and arbitrary decision making.

It is no surprise that al-Qaeda is on the list, as is the PKK – although the PKK has recently had some considerable success in its legal fight for removal from the list. But a number of individuals also find themselves there.

Three questions arise. How did they get on to the list? What effects will it have on them? And how can they possibly get themselves removed? From the point of view of human rights and fundamental freedoms, the assessment by the international and national authorities of the need for an interference with a property right must be subject to procedural guarantees: there must be an avenue of appeal from the decision of a national authority to interfere with that right. Ben Hayes and Tony Bunyan of 'Statewatch' have created a splendid web resource, containing details on all the cases under consideration.[40]

The Judges Nullify the Right to Procedural Guarantees

There have been a number of judicial decisions which appear to nullify the right to procedural guarantees. The problem is as follows: Article 103 of the Charter provides that obligations under the Charter prevail over obligations under any other international agreement. There is no argument that resolutions and decisions of the Security Council are obligations under the Charter. Does this mean that a Security Council resolution can have the effect of 'trumping' treaty obligations under human rights treaties?

In a paper for the European Society of International Law, Noel Birkhäuser raised the following point:

> A more central question is whether the right to a fair trial and access to court prevails over Article 103 UNC. Affected individuals who are unable to challenge Security Council action against them, cannot assert the violation of other human rights. It is therefore essential for them to be able to obtain some kind of effective review of their situation. Since the Security Council action excludes all forms of challenging its measures before some form of independent tribunal that satisfies the standards of the ECHR and the ICCPR, "the very essence of the right of access to court is impaired". Even though Article 14 of the ICCPR is not included in the list of nonderogable rights of Article 4 paragraph 2 of the ICCPR, its core must remain untouchable even to the Security Council. Judicial guarantees relating to due process can even be counted to the *jus cogens*.[41]

The inviolability of the right to due process is not the position taken by the courts. On 21 September 2005 the Court of First Instance (CFI) of the EU's European Court of Justice (ECJ) decided the first two cases on 'acts adopted in the fight against terrorism', *Yusuf* and *Kadi*.[42]

The cases concerned the UN resolutions outlined above. The UN Sanctions Committee had the task of identifying the persons concerned and of considering requests for exemption. The judgments established a so-called 'rule of paramountcy', derived from Article 103 of the UN Charter:

---

40   Statewatch, 'Terrorist lists: Monitoring proscription, designation and asset-freezing', at <http://www.statewatch.org/terrorlists/terrorlists.html>.

41   N Birkhäuser, 'Sanctions of the Security Council against individuals – Some human rights problems', *European Society of International Law* (2005), at <http://www.esil-sedi.org/english/pdf/Birkhauser.pdf>.

42   See, above, n. 2.

> According to international law, the obligations of Member States of the UN under the Charter of the UN prevail over any other obligation, including their obligations under the ECHR and under the EC Treaty. This paramountcy extends to decisions of the Security Council.

The CFI drew a distinction between *jus cogens* rights, for example, the right not to be tortured or subjected to inhuman or degrading treatment, and other human rights, for example procedural rights, or other fundamental rights. However, they held that it is not for the Court to review indirectly whether the Security Council's resolutions in question are themselves compatible with fundamental rights as protected by the Community legal order.

This rule of paramountcy also, it was held, overrides the whole of the jurisprudence of the ECHR on procedural guarantees where property rights are concerned. There is no doubt that 'freezing orders' affect the property rights, and thus the civil rights, of the blacklisted organizations or individuals concerned. The ECHR's jurisprudence shows clearly that they must be able to challenge such orders in proper courts, in full and fair judicial proceedings in which the relevant matters can be argued in substance. Specifically, the courts must be regular courts, and the judges regular, independent and impartial; and the procedure must ensure 'equality of arms' to the parties.

To some commentators, the position of the CFI appeared unassailable. Rory Stephen Brown took the view that '[…] it is highly unlikely that even a national constitutional court would take it upon itself to overrule the Security Council resolution on the basis of (inter)national law standards […] the chance of any tribunal invalidating a determination of the Security Council are vanishingly small'.[43]

However, following very strongly worded opinions by the Advocate General in both *Kadi*[44] and *Yusuf*,[45] the European Court of Justice (ECJ) on 3 September 2008 astonished all observers by annulling the Council Regulation, on the ground that

> the Community courts must ensure the review, in principle the full review, of the lawfulness of all Community acts in the light of the fundamental rights forming an integral part of the general principles of Community law, including review of Community measures which, like the contested regulation, are designed to give effect to resolutions adopted by the Security Council.[46]

Thus, the ECJ affirmed the jurisdiction of the EU courts to examine the implementation of UN Security Council resolutions and ensure their compliance with human rights law. It held, forthrightly, that rights to due process had been violated: '[…] the rights of the defence, in particular the right to be heard, and the right to effective judicial review of those rights, were patently not respected'.

It also condemned the failure of the EC Regulation noted above to include any procedure for 'communicating the evidence justifying the inclusion of the names of the persons concerned in the list'. This too violated fundamental rights. The Court observed that: 'At no time did the Council inform Mr Kadi and Al Barakaat of the evidence adduced against them in order to justify the initial inclusion of their names in the list.' That violation of the right to defence also gave rise to a violation of the right to a legal remedy, since the appellants were prevented from defending their rights before the Community courts.

---

43   RS Brown, 'Case comment: *Kadi v. Council of the European Union and Commission of the European Communities*: Executive power and judicial supervision at European level', *European Human Rights Law Review*, 4 (2006), 456–69, at 468.

44   <http://www.statewatch.org/news/2008/jan/ecj-kadi-ag-opinion.pdf>.

45   <http://www.statewatch.org/terrorlists/docs/ECJalbarakaatopinion.pdf>.

46   <http://www.statewatch.org/news/2008/sep/02ECJ-UN-ruling.htm>.

The Court held that the EU Council was competent to adopt the freezing measures, and noted that there could be grounds where the restriction of the right to property could be justified, but ruled that 'the regulation in question was adopted without furnishing any guarantee enabling Mr Kadi to put his case to the competent authorities. Such a guarantee was, however, necessary in order to ensure respect for his right to property [...]'.

On 19 January 2009 the Chatham House International Law Discussion Group considered the effect of the case.[47] The issue was summarized as follows:

> The Kadi case could be presented as a conflict of obligations under different legal orders. On the one hand, there was a Security Council resolution, adopted under Chapter VII of the UN Charter and binding on all states, which obliged states to implement sanctions against listed individuals. On the other hand, the decision of the European Court of Justice (ECJ) required that in so far as EU member states were concerned, the Security Council sanctions could not be implemented because the persons challenging the EU regulation had not been given the opportunity to put their case.

Sir Michael Wood referred to the editorial written by Joseph Weiler for the *EJIL* immediately after the judgment,[48] in which Weiler argued that the *Kadi* decision is very similar to the decision of the Supreme Court of the US in the case of *Medellin*[49] and that the ECJ is really ignoring international law. It would not accept that member state courts could deal with European law in the same way as it had dealt with international law. Takis Tridimas on the other hand argued that the UN Security Council Resolutions bind the Community but only in international law; they do not in the view of the ECJ perforate the Community's own constitutional space. This means that the ECJ can review the validity of Community regulations which implement SCRs vis-à-vis fundamental rights as they are understood in Community law. He concluded that this was not the meeting of different legal orders as much as judicial pluralism. There have never been in the history of legal systems so many courts with overlapping jurisdictions at different levels.

In the most comprehensive analysis of the ECJ's judgment to date, De Sena and Vitucci comment on the undoubted peculiarity of the outcome:

> Checking the compatibility of these measures with the fundamental rights of the individuals or entities concerned would certainly be possible if they had been incorporated into EC regulations: should this be found to be the case – as it was in the *Kadi* decision – the CFI and the ECJ could in fact lawfully exercise their power of judicial review over these regulations, even if they amounted to nothing more than reproductions of SC resolutions. In this situation, the ECtHR could *not*, instead, check the lawfulness of the above measures under the terms of the ECHR, given that the

---

47   Summarized at <http://www.chathamhouse.org.uk/files/13293_il220109.pdf> [accessed 1 July 2009].
48   *European Journal of International Law*, 19 (2008), 895–96.
49   *Medellin v. Texas* 552 US (2008).

EC is not a party to the Convention. Furthermore, as a consequence of the *Behrami* and *Saramati* judgment,[50] the Court, in the absence of domestic acts of implementation by the states party to the Convention, could not even review the relevant SC resolutions.[51]

Dick Marty, the Council of Europe's rapporteur on UN Security Council and European Union blacklists observed that despite these recent judgments beginning to acknowledge the violations of fundamental fair trial rights in the current de-listing and review procedures, no court has yet addressed the unlawfulness of the underlying UNSC resolutions and EU regulations. As a result, the UNSC and the Council have little impetus to alter their procedures.[52]

The Case of Al-Jedda: The English Courts Confront UN and EU Law

To date, the UK courts have followed the line of the CFI in *Kadi*, as well as the ECHR's judgment in *Behrami* and *Saramati*. The judgment in *al-Jedda*, examined below, predated by a short period the ECJ's judgment in *Kadi*. It should be noted that in the Chatham House discussion reported above, Sir Michael Wood regarded the combined judgments of the CFI, the ECHR and the House of Lords as more 'mature' than that of the ECJ.

Hilal al-Jedda has British and Iraqi nationality. Whether he was ever involved in the insurgency, or resistance against the illegal invasion and occupation of Iraq by the UK and US, he became an exemplar of it.

In 2004 he was in Baghdad in order to obtain British visas for his two wives and to introduce his four British children by a former wife to their Iraqi relatives. The British military forces suspected him of involvement in terrorism (which he denied). On 10 October 2004 he was arrested and taken to a detention centre run by the British Forces in Basra. He was held in administrative detention without trial from that date until December 2007 (see below).[53]

On 29 March 2006 the Court of Appeal followed the CFI in holding that a UN Security Council Resolution,[54] in this case UNSCR 1546 (2004) of 8 June 2004, purporting both to end the occupation and to permit internment, trumped all human rights except *jus cogens*. The Court summarized the effect of the CFI judgment in the *Yusuf* and *Kadi* cases as follows:

> […] the court held (at paras 213–226) that the obligations of the members of the European Union
> to enforce sanctions required by a Chapter VII UN Security Council resolution prevailed over
> fundamental rights as protected by the Community legal order or by the principles of that legal

---

50   App. Nos 71412/01 and 78166/01 *Behrami and Behrami v. France* and *Saramati v. France, Germany and Norway*, ECHR judgment of 5 May 2007: these judgments, which concerned liability for actions of NATO forces in Kosovo, are highly controversial. See A Sari, 'Jurisdiction and international responsibility in peace support operations: The *Behrami* and *Saramati* cases', *Human Rights Law Review*, 8/1 (2008), 151–70.

51   P De Sena, Pasquale and MC Vitucci, 'The European courts and the Security Council: Between *dedoublement fonctionnel* and balancing of values', *European Journal of International Law*, 20/1 (2009), 193–228.

52   PACE Committee on Legal Affairs and Human Rights, Provisional draft report on UN Security Council and European Union blacklists, 12 November 2007 at <http://assembly.coe.int/ASP/APFeaturesManager/defaultArtSiteView.asp?ID=717>.

53   D Pannick, 'In Basra as in Basildon – subject to the rule of law', *The Times*, 30 October 2007, at <http://business.timesonline.co.uk/tol/business/law/columnists/david_pannick/article2763567.ece>.

54   C1/2005/2251 [2006] EWCA CIV 327.

order. The court also held that it had no jurisdiction to inquire into the lawfulness of a Security Council resolution other than to check, indirectly, whether it infringed *ius cogens*, understood as a body of higher rules of public international law binding on all subjects of international law, including the bodies of the United Nations, and from which no derogation is possible [… restricted to] aggression, genocide, slavery and racial discrimination, crimes against humanity and torture, and the right to self-determination.

Lord Justice Brooke concluded with a chilling addendum:

111. As an addendum to this judgment it is worth noting that in the last great emergency imperilling this nation's legislation was enacted to confer powers of internment similar to those that are in issue in the present case. Section 1 of the Emergency Powers (Defence) Act 1939 created the rule-making power and Regulation 18B(1) of the Defence (General) Regulations 1939, whose terms are set out in a footnote in *Liversidge v Anderson* [1942] AC 206, 207, created the power of detention. Lord Denning describes in *The Family Story* (Butterworths, 1981) at pp 129-130 how that power was exercised in practice in 1940 and 1941 when in the persona of Alfred Denning QC he was the legal adviser to the regional commissioner for the North-East Region:

"Most of my work in Leeds was to detain people under Regulation 18B. We detained people, without trial, on suspicion that they were a danger. The military authorities used to receive – or collect – information about any person who was suspected: and lay it before me. If it was proper for investigation I used to see the person – and ask him questions – so as to judge for myself if the suspicion was justified. He could not be represented by lawyers."

112. The equivalent arrangements, for the purposes of the emergency in Iraq, are described by General Rollo in his witness statement. Apart from the technical matters which the Divisional Court put right there is no challenge to the appropriateness of the procedures adopted for internment in accordance with the Security Council's mandate. The issue is rather that Mr Al-Jedda should be permitted access to a court of law where he could answer a charge against him and test the evidence against him before an independent judicial tribunal. I am satisfied that he has no such entitlement.

On 12 December 2007 the House of Lords unanimously dismissed al-Jedda's appeal. There is however a silver lining and he may win in the end, at the European Court of Human Rights.[55]

As noted by Lord Rodger, the House of Lords 'found itself deep inside the realm of international law'.[56] The judges were not as bold as the ECJ; they were unanimous that the United Nations Charter took priority over procedural rights. Lord Bingham stated:

39. Thus there is a clash between on the one hand a power or duty to detain exercisable on the express authority of the Security Council and, on the other, a fundamental human right which the UK has undertaken to secure to those (like the appellant) within its jurisdiction. How are these to be reconciled? There is in my opinion only one way in which they can be reconciled: by ruling that the UK may lawfully, where it is necessary for imperative reasons of security, exercise the power to detain authorised by UNSCR 1546 and successive resolutions, but must ensure that the

---

55   <http://www.parliament.the-stationery-office.co.uk/pa/ld200708/ldjudgmt/jd071212/jedda.pdf>.

56   J Harrison, 'House of Lords decides on detention without trial by UK forces in Iraq', 13 December 2007, at <http://internationallawobserver.eu/2007/12/13/house-of-lords-decides-on-detention-without-trial-by-uk-forces-in-iraq/>.

detainee's rights under article 5 are not infringed to any greater extent than is inherent in such detention. I would resolve the second issue in this sense.

However, the House of Lords rejected the UK Government's argument that it bears no legal responsibility for the acts of British soldiers in Iraq. The Government had argued that since the UN had in October 2003 sanctioned the multinational force in Iraq by UNSC resolution 1511, any legal responsibility for the acts of British soldiers in Iraq laid with the UN, not the UK. Thus, neither the European Court of Human Rights nor the House of Lords had jurisdiction to review the question of the legality of Mr Al-Jedda's detention, which was a matter for the UN alone. The Government also relied on the *Behrami* and *Saramati* judgments.

By a four to one majority the Lords rejected the Government's arguments, and held the UK fully to account for all the acts of its troops abroad. They distinguished the UK's role in Iraq from the position in Kosovo. The UN's role in Iraq had been secondary to that of the US and UK. The judges held that the UK could, however, lawfully intern suspected terrorists in Iraq on the authority of UNSC resolution 1546 (June 2004), but only if they complied with all the other requirements of due process. Keir Starmer QC[57] said:

> This is a crucial ruling. The idea that the UN was in control of British troops in Iraq as the Government argued is absurd. The decision to invade was made by the US and the UK, and they set up the administration in Iraq. Had the Government succeeded in its arguments, there would be no accountability for human rights abuses in Iraq. What happened in British detention facilities in Iraq needs to be explained by the troops that were there, not off-loaded to the UN.[58]

The Home Secretary sought to revoke Mr al-Jedda's British citizenship, without permitting his solicitors proper time to make representations on his behalf. However, on 7 December 2007 his lawyers made an urgent application for judicial review to challenge this potential decision and the court said that it would be 'in each party's interests to allow time for representations'.[59]

Finally, on 6 October 2008, the Defence Secretary, John Hutton, gave a written answer to a question from Harry Cohen MP, as follows: 'In December 2007, on the basis of the latest intelligence and security assessment, it was decided that it was no longer necessary to intern Mr Al-Jedda and he was released to a safe location in Iraq.'[60]

It is somewhat curious that Mr al-Jedda's release so closely followed the Lords' decision; and pre-empted a planned application for judicial review of his continued detention.[61]

Three Case Studies

I now turn to the manner in which the empty abstraction 'terrorism' has been transmuted into some very concrete individuals.

---

57   He represented the appellant; he is now the Director of Public Prosecutions.
58   <http://www.doughtystreet.co.uk/news/news_detail.cfm?iNewsID=233> [accessed 1 July 2009].
59   Reported at <http://www.cageprisoners.com/articles.php?id=22723> [accessed 1 July 2009].
60   <http://www.publications.parliament.uk/pa/cm200708/cmhansrd/cm081006/text/81006w0055.htm>.
61   See also C Walker, 'The treatment of foreign terror suspects', *Modern Law Review*, 70/3 (2007), 427–57.

The Case of Professor Sison

This is a particularly striking case of inclusion in the list, and asset-freezing, with respect to an individual. Jose Maria Sison, founding chairman of the Communist Party of the Philippines, has since 1987 resided in the Netherlands where he is seeking asylum as a political refugee.[62] Sison sees himself as engaged in a national liberation struggle against US imperialism in a country that was an American colony until 1946 and in which the US remains the dominant power.[63]

He was placed on 'terrorist lists' by the USA, by the Netherlands Government, and finally on 12 December 2002 by the European Union, by way of decision 2002/974/EC.[64]

On 6 February 2003 he applied to the CFI for the following remedy:

> Partial Annulment in regard to the inclusion of Professor Jose Maria Sison of Council Decision of 12 December 2002 (2002/974/EC) implementing Article 2(3) of Regulation (EC) No. 2580/2001 on specific restrictive measures directed against certain persons and entities with a view to combating terrorism [...].

His application listed the following consequences for him of inclusion in the list:

- imposing the loss of free disposition and a total dispossession of all the financial assets of the applicant – he can no longer make the least use of his assets;
- excluding him from all bank and financial services deprives him from the possibility to obtain effective compensation for the violation of his basic human rights by the Marcos-regime as granted to him by a US court as well as from the possibility to benefit from an income from lectures and publishing books and articles and from possible regular employment as a teacher;
- freezing his joint bank account with his wife and terminating his social benefits from the Dutch state agencies, depriving him of basic necessities and violating his basic human right to life.

On 11 July 2007 the CFI decided to annul the EU Council Decision to place Sison on the EU list of 'terrorists' for the purposes of asset-freezing. The Court held (para. 226):

> In conclusion, the Court finds that no statement of reasons has been given for the contested decision and that the latter was adopted in the course of a procedure during which the applicant's rights of the defence were not observed. What is more, the Court is not, even at this stage of the procedure, in a position to undertake the judicial review of the lawfulness of that decision in light of the other pleas in law, grounds of challenge and substantive arguments invoked in support of the application for annulment.[65]

However, the Court refused his claim for compensation.

Nevertheless, a few days before the Court's annulment, the EU Council included Sison in a new list. This obliged him to file a new application to the Court.

---

62   He is currently Chief Political Consultant of the National Democratic Front of the Philippines.
63   See <http://www.josemariasison.org/>.
64   See <http://www.defendsison.be/index.php?menu=1>.
65   <http://www.statewatch.org/news/2007/jul/eu-ecj-sison-judgment.pdf>.

Furthermore, the Dutch state moved swiftly following defeat in Court. On 28 August 2007 Sison was arrested on suspicion of having incited from The Netherlands two murders committed in the Philippines. It should be noted that Sison had been charged with the same offences in the Philippines. In a decision dated 2 July 2007 the Philippines Supreme Court dismissed all charges on the basis of:

> the obvious involvement of political considerations in the motivation of respondent Secretary of Justice and respondent prosecutors. [...] We cannot emphasize too strongly that prosecutors should not allow, and should avoid, giving the impression that their noble office is being used or prostituted, wittingly or unwittingly, for political ends, or other purposes alien to, or subversive of, the basic and fundamental objective of observing the interest of justice even-handedly [...].

These allegations were also used by the Council as a basis for keeping Sison on the list. These new decisions to include Sison in the list were based on a pro forma statement of reasons, including the assertion that the decision to include him in the list was based on two decisions taken in the 1990s by the Dutch State Council in the context of Sison's asylum application. The Council stated that these two decisions upheld the Dutch Minister of Justice in his decision to refuse asylum status to Sison, while in reality the State Council cancelled these ministerial decisions. The statement of reasons was therefore fundamentally flawed.

Sison was only released on 13 September 2007, after the Dutch court ordered his immediate release saying there was insufficient evidence to hold him on murder charges. The evidence was insufficient to show that Sison 'had a conscious and close cooperation with those in the Philippines who carried out the deed'.[66]

This was not the end of the persecution of Sison. After the decision of 13 September to release Sison, the investigating magistrate decided to put an end to the investigation. That decision was appealed by the prosecution, and on 5 June 2008 the District Court of The Hague decided in camera:

> that the Public Prosecution Service may continue the prosecution of Sison for involvement in, among other matters, a number of murders committed in the Philippines in 2003 and 2004; that while the prosecution's case file still held insufficient evidence, the investigation was ongoing and should be given time to unfold.[67]

Nearly 11 months later, on 31 March 2009, the Netherlands Prosecutor wrote to Sison to say that the case against him was closed, subject to any appeal, on the ground of 'insufficient legal and convincing evidence'.[68]

On 30 April 2009 the lawyers for Sison returned once again to the ECJ for an oral hearing, in their battle to seek his removal from the EU's 'terrorist list'. They argued that the list breaches the principle of proportionality (a fundamental principle of 'community law' that should limit action taken by the EU's institutions to that necessary to achieve the objectives of the Treaties – in this case a credible counter-terrorist financing policy) and constitutes an ongoing breach of the fundamental rights to due process in a fair trial (specifically the right to access an impartial

---

66   <http://www.live-pr.com/en/dutch-court-orders-release-of-philippine-r1048144631.htm>.

67   <http://www.bulatlat.com/2008/06/two-glaring-errors-5-june-2008-decision-hague-district-court-my-complaint>.

68   See <http://tonyocruz.com/?p=2013> [accessed 1 July 2009], which contains a copy of the prosecutor's letter with translation.

tribunal; violation of the principle of the presumption of innocence; and violation of the right to mount a defence).[69]

Ben Hayes, legal adviser to the European Centre for Constitutional and Human Rights (ECCHR), which supports Sison, said:

> The right to a fair trial is the heartbeat of the European justice system and must never be dispensed with on the say so of the executive. There is no evidence to justify the freezing of our client's assets or his ongoing designation as an international terrorist. The only place to deal with such serious allegations is a proper criminal proceeding in which full weight is given to the consideration of the facts and the pleas of both defence and prosecution. In the absence of such proceedings in the past seven years, the presumption of innocence must prevail and fundamental rights must be restored.[70]

The judgment of the Court is awaited. However, on 15 June 2009 the Council of the EU, in a new Common Position,[71] renewed the 'terrorist list'. Sison is still there.

The SEGI Cases

The fundamental right to judicial review, the procedural right referred to above, was considered by both the CFI in 2004[72] and by the European Court of Human Rights in 2002,[73] in the SEGI case. SEGI was a Basque youth movement, which requested the CFI to award damages for its allegedly illegitimate inclusion in the list. SEGI's policies included independence for the Basque Country in the context of socialism; it is supported by the youth movement of Sinn Fein.[74] It sees itself as a National Liberation Movement.

The Common Position in Article 1 provided for a definition of the term 'terrorist act', applicable across all three pillars.[75] It initiated concrete measures by the Community under the first pillar, such as the freezing of funds (Articles 2 and 3). Under the third pillar, it called upon member states to exchange information (Article 4). Its Annex set out a list of persons to whom the measures applied, including SEGI. A footnote to the list specified that SEGI, among others, should be the subject of Article 4 only. Article 4 was addressed to member states and called upon them to assist each other through police and judicial cooperation. Thus, Articles 2 and 3 did not apply to SEGI, and the Community was not required to freeze its funds.

The Second Chamber of the CFI rejected SEGI's action on competence grounds only, and did not consider the substance of its grievances. In brief, it had no remedy because it had not been

---

69   Press release at <http://www.statewatch.org/terrorlists/docs/Press%20release%20Sison%20-%20 April-2009.pdf> [accessed 1 July 2009].

70   Ibid.

71   Common Position 2009/468/CFSP of 15 June 2009, at <http://eur-lex.europa.eu/LexUriServ/ LexUriServ.do?uri=OJ:L:2009:151:0045:0050:EN:PDF> [accessed 1 July 2009].

72   T-338/02 Segi and others v. Council, order of 7 June 2004 [2004] ECR II-01647.

73   SEGI and others v. 15 Member States (SEGI and Gestoras Pro-Amnistia v. Germany and others) App. No. 6422/02, decision of inadmissibility of 23 May 2002.

74   See <http://ograshinnfein.blogspot.com/2007/02/segi-basque-youth-solidarity-protest.html>.

75   These were created by the Treaty of Maastricht. The first or 'Community' pillar concerns economic, social and environmental policies. The second or 'Common Foreign and Security Policy' (CFSP) pillar concerns foreign policy and military matters. The third or 'Police and Judicial Co-operation in Criminal Matters' (PJCC) pillar concerns cooperation in the fight against crime. This pillar was originally named 'Justice and Home Affairs'.

made subject to a Community measure, that is, asset freezing. As Christina Eckes comments: 'SEGI was left without any legal protection [...] the [...] case demonstrates forcefully that being listed as someone supporting terrorism will not in itself open the way to the Courts'.[76] She disagrees strongly with the Court's rejection of the argument that the rule of law and fundamental rights, in particular the rights to access justice enshrined in Articles 6 and 13 of the ECHR, require the exercise of judicial control – 'even in the absence of a specific competence norm'.[77] She points out that '[a] listing in an anti-terrorist measure constitutes a considerable impairment of the target's right to reputation,[78] as well as her property rights'.[79]

The European Court of Human Rights also refused to consider the substance of the applications, but dealt with them on the issue of standing. It stated:

> Moreover, the applicants have not adduced any evidence to show that any particular measures have been taken against them pursuant to Common Position 2001/931/CFSP. The mere fact that the names of two of the applicants (Segi and Gestoras Pro-Amnistía) appear in the list referred to in that provision as "groups or entities involved in terrorist acts" may be embarrassing, but the link is much too tenuous to justify application of the Convention.[80]

Eckes comments that 'the Court's conclusions that the listing "may be embarrassing – *peut être gênant*" amounts to an ironic comment, in the light of its effects on the situation, or even the existence, of the applicants'.[81] She concludes:

> The CFI [...] did not satisfy the fundamental principles upon which the Union is built and which the Courts have upheld in the past. This is deplorable. It not only infringes fundamental rights in the individual case, but it also harms the objective of promoting fundamental rights as such. Additionally, the doubtful factual basis on which the European blacklists are drawn up and the fact that the ECtHR did not show itself ready to grant protection of last resort, render the situation even more alarming.[82]

In its latest decision, on 27 February 2007, the Grand Chamber of the ECJ dismissed, with costs, the appeal of *SEGI* and the Basque human rights organization 'Gestoras Pro Amnistia' against the dismissal by the CFI of its claim for damages suffered as a result of inclusion in the 'terrorist list'. Once again the UK intervened, with Spain, on behalf of the Council – the only other EU state to do so.[83]

---

76 C Eckes, 'How not being sanctioned by a Community instrument infringes a person's fundamental rights: The case of SEGI', *Kings College Law Journal*, 17/1 (2006), 144–54.

77 Eckes, ibid., at 148.

78 As in *Bladet Tromso and Stensaas v. Norway*, Application no. 21980/93, judgment of 20 May 1999

79 Eckes, above, n. 76, at 149.

80 Decision of inadmissibility of 23 May 2002, at 9.

81 Eckes, above, n. 76, at 152.

82 Eckes, above, n. 76, at 154.

83 Case C-354/04 P, <http://www.statewatch.org/news/2007/mar/ecj-feb.pdf>; see <http://www.liberty security.org/article1386.html>.

The UK's 'Financial Guantánamo'

The UK also sought to implement the UN Security Council Resolutions 1373/2001 and 1452/2002 through Orders in Council made under the United Nations Act 1946. These were the Terrorism (United Nations Measures) Order 2006 and the Al-Qaida and Taliban (United Nations Measures) Order 2006, designed to strengthen domestic controls on the financing of terrorism and to comply with the British Government's international obligations to enforce UN Resolutions requiring such controls. They were not scrutinized, debated or approved by Parliament.

These orders were challenged by five British citizens who were designated under the Orders, and, as a result, had their assets frozen, were only allowed to access enough money to meet basic expenses, and were compelled to account to a civil servant for every penny they spent. They were subject to unprecedented levels of intrusion and control. They required permission for all economic activity, however modest. The complex regime governed by permissions and licences was not merely harsh but at points absurd. Their solicitors pointed to 'the madness of civil servants checking Tesco receipts, a child having to ask for a receipt every time it does a chore by running to the shops for a pint of milk and a neighbour possibly committing a criminal offence by lending a lawnmower'.[84]

On 24 April 2008 Mr Justice Collins delivered judgment on their applications. He was clearly concerned at the need to obtain licences for all kinds of activities, and pointed, at para. 42, to the fact that those in the Treasury who have to deal with those matters have had to consider whether licences should be granted on more than 50 occasions.

> A specific query arose, and it is a good illustration of the absurdity which can result, in relation to the loan of a car to an applicant to enable him to go to the supermarket to get the family's groceries. After some delay, the Treasury (in my view wrongly) decided that a licence was needed. The car was an economic resource and could be used to obtain or deliver goods or services. This was only resolved by the Treasury after seeking ministerial consideration. Similar concerns have been raised in relation to an Oyster card to enable the applicant to travel and any borrowing of items for any purpose. Since the possible penalty on conviction is severe, the concerns are understandable and the effect on the applicant and his family, whose human rights are also in issue, is serious.

Following the CFI cases noted above, and *Al-Jedda*, he made the following finding:

> Governments may have their own reasons to want to ensure that [an applicant] remains on the list and there is no procedure which enables him to know the case he has to meet so that he can make meaningful representations. Nevertheless, that is what the Security Council has approved and the Resolution, which Member States are obliged to put into effect, requires the freezing of the assets of those listed. Article 103 of the Charter makes clear that the obligations under the Charter take precedence over any other international agreements. Thus human rights under the ECHR cannot prevail over the obligations set out in the Resolutions.

He did, however, quash both Orders on the ground that they had not been considered by Parliament.[85] Nevertheless, although he expressed sympathy for the Advocate General's opinion in the *Yusuf* and

---

84   <http://www.statewatch.org/terrorlists/docs/A-K-M-Q-G-press-release.pdf>.

85   See B Hayes, 'Britain's financial Guantánamo' at <http://www.statewatch.org/news/2008/apr/04 financial-guantanamo.htm>.

Kadi and other appeals, he found himself unable to follow that lead. The Government will be able to lay the same or similar measures before Parliament.

The PMOI

There has recently been another positive – though limited – development. The People's Mojahedin of Iran (PMOI) was the armed wing of the 'National Council for Resistance in Iran', and represents itself as an important or even the most important movement in opposition to the present regime in Iran – a National Liberation Movement.[86] On 12 December 2006 the CFI ruled in favour of an appeal by the PMOI against asset-freezing as a result of their inclusion in the EU 'terrorist list'.[87] The Court's ruling represented the first successful legal challenge, but left undisturbed the EU legislation on 'terrorist lists'. The ruling was limited to the decision to freeze the PMOI's assets, rather than the broader issue of its designation as 'terrorist'. The Court made a further distinction between organizations proscribed by the EU member states, and organizations proscribed the UN Security Council. Further challenges by some of these are on the way.

It is significant that PMOI was originally listed as a terrorist organization by the UK under the Terrorism Act 2000. Accordingly, the UK supported the European Council in opposing PMOI's appeal. The CFI's judgment contains an extraordinary rebuke to the Council and the UK.

> 170. […] it is not possible simply to accept the United Kingdom's position at face value. At the hearing, moreover, the applicant reiterated its position that it did not know which competent authority had adopted the national decision in respect of it, nor on the basis of what material and specific information that decision had been taken.

> 171. Furthermore, at the hearing, *in response to the questions put by the Court, the Council and the United Kingdom were not even able to give a coherent answer to the question of what was the national decision on the basis of which the contested decision was adopted.* According to the Council, it was only the Home Secretary's decision, as confirmed by the POAC (see paragraph 169 above). According to the United Kingdom, the contested decision is based not only on that decision, but also on other national decisions, not otherwise specified, adopted by competent authorities in other Member States. (My emphasis)

In its statement made on the day of the ruling, the Council gave the following rather vague assurance:

> The Council intends to provide a statement of reasons to each person and entity subject to the asset freeze, wherever that is feasible, and to establish a clearer and more transparent procedure for allowing listed persons and entities to request that their case be re-considered.

It remains very unclear exactly how this promise will be put into effect.

On 4 April 2008 the CFI quashed decisions by the EU Council to include the Kurdish organizations PKK and Kongra Gel on the EU 'terrorist list'. In Case T-253/04,[88] brought on behalf of Kongra

---

86   See the NCRI website at <http://www.ncr-iran.org/> [accessed 1 July 2009].

87   Case T-228/02, <http://www.statewatch.org/terrorlists/docs/CFI-PMOI-judgment.pdf>.

88   <http://curia.europa.eu/jurisp/cgi-bin/form.pl?lang=en&Submit=Rechercher&alldocs=alldocs&doc
j=docj&docop=docop&docor=docor&docjo=docjo&numaff=t-253/04&datefs=&datefe=&nomusuel=&dom
aine=&mots=&resmax=100>.

Gel and 10 other individuals, the EU court ruled that the organization was not in a position 'to understand, clearly and unequivocally, the reasoning' that led the member states' governments to include them. It reached the same conclusion in Case T-229/02,[89] brought by Osman Öcalan on behalf of Kurdistan Workers Party (PKK).

These judgments followed the ruling in favour of Sison in July 2007 and the precedent set in the PMOI ruling in December 2006.[90]

In response to the PMOI ruling, the EU 'reformed' its procedures for listing and de-listing. Whereas prior to the PMOI judgment no mechanism existed for those proscribed to either receive an explanation for their inclusion or to challenge that explanation, the EU now provides affected parties with a 'statement of reasons'. In turn, those parties may then write back to the secret EU group responsible for the decision to contest the statement and request de-listing.

In fact, the EU has maintained in the 'terrorist list' the groups and individuals who have already successfully challenged their proscription at the EU Courts on the grounds that its 'reforms' remedy the fair trial breaches that the Court has identified. This issue will not be resolved until the PMOI's new challenge to the EU's decision to maintain them in the list (case T-157/07[91]) returns to the Court, which may take several years.

However, the UK Government suffered a dramatic reversal in the UK courts.

On 30 November 2007 the UK's Proscribed Organisations Appeal Commission (POAC) ruled that the Home Secretary had acted illegally in refusing to remove the PMOI from its proscribed list of 'terrorist' organizations.[92] The case was brought by more than 30 Members of Parliament and the House of Lords. POAC held first, that in concluding that the PMOI was an organization concerned in terrorism, the Secretary of State had misconstrued the provisions of section 3(5) of the 2000 Act and failed to direct himself properly as to those provisions; secondly that in concluding that the PMOI was an organization concerned in terrorism, the Secretary of State had failed to have regard to relevant considerations; and thirdly, that the conclusion reached by the Secretary of State that the PMOI was an organization concerned in terrorism was perverse. As Clare Dyer pointed out in *The Guardian*:

> Courts rarely call government decisions perverse, and the panel, chaired by former high court judge Sir Harry Ognall and cleared to see secret material, said: "We recognise that a finding of perversity is uncommon." It added: "We believe, however, that this commission is in the (perhaps unusual) position of having before it all of the material that is relevant to this decision."[93]

On 7 May 2008 the Court of Appeal refused to permit an appeal against the POAC decision, ruling that there were 'no valid grounds' to contend that it made legal errors when it ordered the PMOI to be removed from the list.[94] Finally, on 24 June 2008 the UK Parliament withdrew PMOI from the 'terrorist list'. The late Lord Slynn of Hadley, former Judge of the European Court of Justice and the UK's House of Lords, said: 'The very strong judgments of the POAC, the Court of Appeal and

---

89   Ibid.

90   In this case the Court found that the EU's proscription regime had denied the PMOI the right to a fair hearing in which it could challenge its designation as 'terrorist' in accordance with its fundamental right to a fair trial (see analysis of PMOI judgment). This paved the way for other proscribed groups and individuals to challenge their inclusion in the list.

91   See, above, n. 88.

92   <http://www.statewatch.org/terrorlists/PC022006%20PMOI%20FINAL%20JUDGMENT.pdf>.

93   <http://politics.guardian.co.uk/print/0%2C%2C331424166-116499%2C00.html>.

94   <http://www.bailii.org/ew/cases/EWCA/Civ/2008/443.html>.

indeed the CFI made it utterly plain that justice required the PMOI to be taken off the list. There can be no doubt about that. [Removal from the list] will do a great deal to establish and underline the concept of the rule of law.'[95]

The Council has continued to refuse to remove PMOI from the EU's list, despite the fact that inclusion in the first place was justified solely by the UK's list – and that the POAC had by then ordered their removal from the UK list. On 4 December 2008 the CFI rendered yet another judgment annulling, for the third time, the Council's decision of 15 July 2008 to keep PMOI on the list.[96] The first two judgments were delivered on 12 December 2006 and 23 October 2008. The CFI stated that the PMOI was not in a position effectively to make known its view of the matter, prior to the adoption of the contested decision, and found that the contested decision was adopted in breach of the PMOI's rights of defence. The Court considered that, contrary to what the Council suggested, nothing prevented it from adopting the decision in accordance with a procedure in which the PMOI's rights of defence were respected. In particular, the Court rejected the Council's argument that it was necessary to adopt a new funds-freezing decision so urgently that it was not possible to respect PMOI's rights of defence, as laid down in the OMPI judgment. The Court further held that neither the information contained in the contested decision, its statement of reasons and the letter of notification, nor even those contained in the Council's answers to the Court's request for information, establish to the requisite legal standard that the judicial inquiry opened in France in 2001 and the supplementary charges brought in 2007 constitute a decision by a competent judicial authority, in respect of the PMOI itself. In particular, the Council had failed to explain the specific reasons as to why the acts ascribed to the persons alleged to be members of the PMOI should be attributed to the PMOI.

Finally, the Court noted that at the request of the French authorities the Council refused to communicate to the Court certain extracts of a document containing a 'summary of the main points which justify the keeping of [the PMOI] on the EU list', even though this information had been communicated to the Council and subsequently to the 26 other member states. The Court considered that the Council was not entitled to base its funds-freezing decision on information or material in the file communicated by a member state, if that member state was not willing to authorize its communication to the Court whose task is to review the lawfulness of that decision. The refusal by the Council and the French authorities to communicate, even to the Court alone, the information contained in this document had the consequence that the Court is unable to review the lawfulness of the contested decision, which infringed the PMOI's fundamental right to an effective judicial review.

Continued inclusion of PMOI on the EU list, even after the Court of Appeal judgment, has been based on 'judicial inquiries' opened by the Paris Prosecutor's Office (not a 'judicial body' as required by EU law) in 2001 and then in March and November 2007, when 'the Paris anti-terrorist prosecutor's office brought supplementary charges against alleged members of the PMOI'. In a stinging critique of the Council's decision of 15 July 2008, Professor Antonio Cassese,[97] described reliance on this action as a serious violation of EU law and French law, and concluded that the Council had engaged in serious misuse of powers.[98]

---

95   <http://www.publications.parliament.uk/pa/ld200708/ldhansrd/text/80623-0013.htm>.

96   <http://www.statewatch.org/news/2008/dec/ecj-pmoi-judgment-prel.pdf>.

97   President of the International Criminal Tribunal for the Former Yugoslavia in the Hague from 1993 to 1997, and more recently chairman of the UN's commission to investigate genocide in Darfur.

98   <http://www.scribd.com/doc/6156445/Antonio-Cassese-The-Illegality-of-the-EUCouncil-Decision-2008583EC-concerning-PMOI>.

In the words of Professor Steve Peers of Essex University '[...] the fact that the PMOI remains on the list today [...] simply beggars belief'.[99]

Conclusion

Professor Christian Tomuschat has commented:

> In the long run, such a denial of legal remedies is untenable. To be sure, no one wishes to protect Al-Qaeda or the Taliban. But the freezing of assets is directed against persons alleged to have close ties to these two organisations. Everyone must be free to show that he/she has been unjustifiably placed under suspicion and that therefore the freezing of his/her assets has no valid foundation.[100]

On 23 January 2008 the Parliamentary Assembly of the Council of Europe (PACE) resolved that the procedures used by the UN Security Council and the EU to blacklist individuals and groups suspected of having connections with terrorism violate basic rights and are 'completely arbitrary'.[101] It insisted that they must be reviewed 'to preserve the credibility of the international fight against terrorism', and added that '[i]njustice is terrorism's best ally – and we must fight it too'.[102] Dick Marty said:

> Even the members of the committee which decides on blacklisting are not given all the reasons for blacklisting particular persons or groups. Usually, those persons or groups are not told that blacklisting has been requested, given a hearing or even, in some cases, informed of the decision – until they try to cross a frontier or use a bank account. There is no provision for independent review of these decisions.[103]

His report pointed out that there were currently some 370 people worldwide whose assets had been frozen, and who could not travel, because the UN had put them on a blacklist.[104] Some 60 groups and bodies were on the other blacklist kept by the EU. 'Mere suspicion' is ground enough for these sanctions. This situation 'is deplorable and a violation of human rights and fundamental freedoms'.[105]

PACE insisted that this kind of procedure is 'unworthy' of international institutions like the UN and EU, and undermines the legitimacy of using 'targeted sanctions' against terrorists.

---

99   Communication to the author.

100   C Tomuschat, *Human Rights: Between Idealism and Realism* (Oxford: Oxford University Press, 2003), at 90.

101   Press release 23 January 2008, 045(2008), 'PACE demands review of UN and EU blacklisting procedures for terrorist suspects, which "violate human rights"', at <https://wcd.coe.int/ViewDoc.jsp?id=1 237597&Site=DC&BackColorInternet=F5CA75&BackColorIntranet=F5CA75&BackColorLogged=A9BA CE>.

102   Ibid.

103   Ibid.

104   <http://www.assembly.coe.int/Mainf.asp?link=/Documents/WorkingDocs/Doc07/eDOC11454. htm>; addendum at <http://assembly.coe.int/Mainf.asp?link=http://assembly.coe.int/Documents/Working Docs/doc07/edoc11454add.htm>.

105   Press release (23 January 2008), ibid.

States required to enforce these sanctions may well violate their obligations under the European Convention on Human Rights.

What I have sought to show in this chapter is that such gross violations of fundamental human rights are the direct consequence of the operation of the 'terrorist lists'.

I have also argued that the real problem of the 'terrorist lists' is to be found at a much more fundamental level. I have shown that, as Moeckli argues in his chapter in this collection, the 'war against terror' is far from being a void without law. The dense web of UN Security Council Resolutions, EU Common Positions and Regulations, and UK Orders in Council is designed to fill the space within which the 'war on terror' is fought so that there can be no escape. The very perfection of the closure of this space is the reason why there can be no room for procedural human rights. In order to give substance and form to the abstraction 'terrorism', law requires the creation of the list, and those who inhabit the list. The inhabitants of the list are those who are identified, in the manner adopted by Carl Schmitt, as partisans without legitimacy, as persons who having taken up arms against an absolute enemy, become the exemplars of an absolute enemy. As we have noted, for Professor Sison and for many others this is a list from which he cannot escape, and which deprives him of many of the most essential characteristics of personhood.

Chapter 14

Human Security and International Law: Much Ado about Nothing?

Emma McClean

Introduction

When the United Nations (UN) declared the entitlement of all individuals to freedom from fear and want and, to this end, pledged to discuss and define the notion of human security at the 2005 World Summit,[1] human security was firmly placed on the UN policy agenda and entered 'our common international discourse',[2] especially in the context of international relations analysis. Yet consideration of human security is largely absent from international legal scholarship. This is somewhat surprising as incidents of human insecurity – the ongoing crisis in Darfur for example – bring into sharp relief a number of key issues currently besieging international law such as the place of non-state actors in international law and the question of humanitarian intervention. Indeed the emergence of human security on to the UN policy agenda is underpinned by fundamental questions as to the role of international law in the international landscape. It is in this sense that the chapter explores the relevance of human security to international law by way of evaluating the implications and consequences for international law of human security as a UN policy agenda. By doing so, the chapter advances the argument that human security, particularly as a UN policy agenda, offers a 'versatile, penetrating and useful approach to the study' of international law.[3]

The chapter consists of three parts, the first of which charts the emergence of human security on to the international stage as a policy agenda to address issues as diverse as child soldiers and HIV/AIDS, along with sketching the normative heritage of human security. The second part engages with human security at the UN and in doing so discusses the translation of human security into UN practice, with a focus on the practice of the UN Security Council (SC) in relation to human rights issues. Against this background, the chapter concludes with the implications and consequences of a UN human security policy agenda for international law, with a focus on the responsibility to protect and international human rights law, which serves to demonstrate the value-added of a human security approach to the study of international law.

---

1   UN GA Res 60/1, '2005 World Summit Outcome Document' (16 September 2005) UN Doc A/RES/60/1, para. 143

2   K Krause, 'Is human security more than just a good idea?', in M Brzoska and PJ Croll (eds), *Promoting Security: But How and For Whom?* (Bonn: Bonn International Center for Conversion, 2004), at 43.

3   B Buzan, *People, States and Fear: An Agenda for International Security Studies in the Post-Cold War Era* (Boulder, CO: Lynne Rienner, 1991), at 3.

What is Human Security? Emergence and Context

Human security claims ancestry in key evolutions in the understandings of 'development' and 'security' at the international level.[4] It emerged at the confluence of efforts to 'broaden and deepen' the legitimate remit of security and to 'humanize' development.[5] The broadening of security to include, for example, non-military threats such as environmental degradation, HIV/AIDS and terrorism and the corresponding 'deepening' to consider the security of individuals and groups[6] may be attributed in part to a series of reports by blue-ribbon commissions in the 1980s and 1990s, namely, the Independent Commission on International Development Issues (the Brandt Commission), the Independent Commission on Disarmament and Security (the Palme Commission), the Stockholm Initiative on Global Security and Governance and the Commission on Global Governance.[7]

The Brandt Commission presented a persuasive argument for a new concept of security based on the idea of mutual interest in the early 1980s. The Commission explained mutual interest as 'mankind wants to survive, and one might even add has the moral obligation to survive'.[8] This in turn raised questions of peace and war along side issues of 'world hunger, mass misery and alarming disparities between the living conditions of rich and poor'.[9] This led to the observation that there is a 'growing awareness' that chaos and insecurity stemming from 'mass hunger, economic

---

4 For an assessment of the heritage of human security in development see G King and C Murray, 'Rethinking human security', *Political Science Quarterly*, 116 (2001), 585. For a genealogy of human security within security studies, see See K Bajpai, 'Human Security: Concept and Measurement' (Kroc Institute Occasional Paper #19:OP:1, August 2000) <http://kroc.nd.edu/ocpapers/op_19_1.PDF> [accessed 22 September 2008]; more generally, see SN MacFarlane and Y Foong Khong, *Human Security and the UN: A Critical History* (Bloomington and Indianapolis, IN: Indiana University Press, 2006).

5 Simon Chesterman has remarked in the context of the evolution of peacebuilding missions of the UN that practice led policy development and often academic commentary had to catch up on practical developments. See S Chesterman, *You the People: The United Nations, Transitional Administration and State-Building* (Oxford: Oxford University Press, 2004), at 7. A similar observation may be made in respect of the evolution, emergence and consolidation of human security on to the international agenda as states such as Canada and Japan led the field in terms of policy development, while academia struggled to maintain apace of such developments. Keith Krause has remarked that '[t]he most striking thing about the concept of human security is that it was born in the policy world and did not spring forth from academics or analysts'. Krause, above, n. 2, at 43.

6 See R Paris, 'Human security: Paradigm shift or hot air?', *International Security*, 26 (2001), 87–88.

7 The Brandt Commission issued two reports, the first in 1981 and the second in 1983. Independent Commission on International Development Issues, *North-South: A Programme for Survival* (London and Sydney: Pan Books, 1981) and Independent Commission on International Development Issues, *Common Crisis: North-South: Co-operation for World Survival* (Massachusetts: MIT Press, 1983). In the interim the Palme Commission had published its report, *Common Security*, in 1982. Independent Commission on Disarmament and Security, *Common Security: A Programme for Disarmament* (London: Pan Books, 1982). In 1991 the report of the Stockholm Initiative recommended the establishment of the Commission on Global Governance, which duly delivered its report in 1995. The Stockholm Initiative on Global Security and Governance, *Common Responsibility in the 1990s* (Stockholm: Prime Minister's Office, 1991); Commission on Global Governance, *Our Global Neighbourhood* (Oxford: Oxford University Press, 1995).

8 Brandt Commission, *North-South*, above, n. 7, at 13.

9 Ibid.

disaster, environmental catastrophes, and terrorism' may pose an equal danger to peace on a par with military conflict.[10] The Commission thus stated:

> true security cannot be achieved by a mounting build-up of weapons – defence in the narrow sense – but only by providing basic conditions for peaceful relations between nations, and solving not only the military but also the non-military problems which threaten them.[11]

By advocating an expansion of security threats beyond the military, the reports of the Brandt Commission epitomize what has become known as the notion of *comprehensive security,* while in 1982 the Palme Commission put forward the notion of *common security*.[12] Common security, like comprehensive security, stressed that 'international peace must rest on a commitment to joint survival rather than a threat of mutual destruction',[13] which also depends on addressing the discrepancies in the 'basic conditions of life in the different parts of the world'.[14] The Palme Commission argued that it was only on the basis of 'cooperative efforts and policies' that 'all the world's citizens' would be 'able to live without fear of war and devastation, and with the hope of a secure and prosperous future for their children and later generations'.[15] The reports of the Brandt and Palme Commissions in the early 1980s, concerned with traditional military threats to security and the impact of an increasing gap in the economic development of the global North in comparison to the global South,[16] broadened the legitimate reach of security. At the same time, academic literature on the notion of security was becoming increasingly critical of narrow understandings tied to the territorial integrity and political independence of states and argued that 'a notion of security bound to the level of individual states and military issues is inherently inadequate'.[17]

The 1991 Report of the Stockholm Initiative stressed the importance of a wider concept of security which includes 'threats that stem from failures in development, environmental degradation, excessive population growth and movement, and lack of progress towards democracy'.[18] The assessment of developmental and environmental threats to security and the role of democracy and human rights carried out by the Stockholm Initiative provided the foundation and the impetus for the report of the Commission on Global Governance. The 1995 Report advocated a concept of *global security* that is broader than the 'traditional focus on the security of states' and encompasses

---

10   Ibid.

11   Ibid., at 124.

12   Palme Commission, above, n. 7, at 6–11. In explaining 'common security' the Palme Commission proceeded from the assertion that a secure state is one which is free from external military threat and 'preserves the health and safety of its citizens'. Ibid., at 4.

13   Ibid., at 139.

14   Ibid., at 7.

15   Ibid., at 8. In a similar vein the Palme Commission explained one of the four principles of common security – all nations have a legitimate right to security – in the following terms: 'A secure existence, free from physical and psychological threats to life and limb, is one of the most elementary desires of humanity. It is the reason why human beings choose to organise nation states, sacrificing certain individual freedoms for the common good – security. It is a right shared by all – regardless of where they live, regardless of their ideological or political belief.' Ibid.

16   For example, the second report of the Brandt Commission was prompted by '[d]eteriorating economic conditions [that] already threaten the political stability of developing countries'. Brandt Commission, *Common Crisis*, above, n. 7, at 1.

17   Buzan, above, n. 3, at 6. Buzan noted the substantial contributions of Ken Booth, Hedley Bull and others to conceptualizing security.

18   The Stockholm Initiative, above, n. 7, at 17–18.

'the security of people and the planet'.[19] This latter aspect broadens the range of threats falling within the global security agenda beyond military threats to include 'pressing post cold-war humanitarian concerns' such as famine and ethnic conflict.[20] This expansion is important as 'states cannot be secure for long unless their *citizens* are secure'[21] and in this way, by shifting the focus of security to people, the Commission on Global Governance deepens the reach of the notion of security. Indeed the Commission postulates that the 'security of people' must be placed on an equal footing to security of states on the global security agenda.[22]

The lineage of human security in concepts such as comprehensive security, common security and global security reflects the growing concern, evident in UN policy documents such as the 2003 Report of the High-Level Panel on Threats, Challenges and Change (HLP) and the 2000 and 2005 Reports of the UN Secretary-General (SG),[23] as to the changing nature and type of threats, such as terrorism, and the inadequacy of existing institutional structures and mechanisms to address the new security threats.[24] This trilogy of documents, which also forms part of the key policy documents on UN reform, speaks of the need for a more human-centred approach to security. In particular the SG advocated a 'human-centred approach to security' in the Millennium Report,[25] while the HLP, in counting poverty, infectious disease, environmental degradation and terrorism as amongst the biggest security threats today, observed that '[t]he threats are from non-State actors as well as States, and to human security as well as State security',[26] and thus fashioned a broader notion of security which the SG welcomed in his 2005 Report, *In Larger Freedom*.[27]

The understanding of 'development' at the international level has similarly 'shifted over time'.[28] According to Keon de Feyter, when the UN was established development was equated with economic development as the dominant theory in 1945 'on international economic and social co-operation [...] was functionalism'.[29] However, the UN abandoned this approach to development as early as 1970 when a report documenting the first UN Development Decade warned of the implications of an undue emphasis on economic growth, particularly for the realization of human rights.[30] As de Feyter observes, the biggest change in the understanding of development, particularly for the UN, came with the broadening of the concept of development 'beyond its purely economic

---

19   Commission on Global Governance, above, n. 7, at 78.

20   Ibid., at 81.

21   Ibid. (emphasis added).

22   Ibid., at 82.

23   The High-Level Panel on Threats, Challenges and Change (HLP), *A More Secure World: Our Shared Responsibility* (New York: UN Dept of Public Information, 2004); UN SG, *We the Peoples: The Role of the United Nations in the 21st Century* (New York: UN Dept of Public Information, 2000) [hereinafter referred to as the Millennium Report]; and UN SG, *In Larger Freedom: Towards Security, Development and Human Rights for All* (New York: UN Dept of Public Information, 2005).

24   For example, the SG acknowledges the 'changed nature of threats to peace and security faced by the world's people today' and the inadequacy of the Charter provisions on collective security and concludes 'we have not yet adapted our institutions to this new reality'. UN SG, *We the Peoples*, above, n. 23, at 11.

25   Ibid.

26   HLP, above, n. 23, at 1.

27   UN SG, *In Larger Freedom*, above, n. 23, para. 17.

28   K de Feyter, *World Development Law: Sharing Responsibility for Development* (Antwerpen: Intersentia, 2001), at 2.

29   Ibid.

30   T van Boven, 'Human rights and development: The UN experience', in DP Forsythe (ed.), *Human Rights and Development: International Views* (London: Macmillan, 1989), at 126.

dimension'.[31] De Feyter places this 'major breakthrough' as occurring in the 1990s, which, unsurprisingly, coincides with the work of the United Nations Development Programme (UNDP) in respect of the notion of *human* development.[32]

The UNDP championed the notion of human development in direct response to the deficiencies involved in equating development with economic growth as measured through GNP, savings, investments and other 'national aggregates',[33] which also, as documented by Jack Donnelly, involved the suspension of human rights as a necessary precondition to economic development.[34] According to the UNDP, human development is 'a process of enlarging people's choices',[35] the 'most critical' of which pertain to leading a long and healthy life, to being educated and to enjoying a decent standard of living.[36] This 'humanizing of development' is also apparent in Amaryta Sen's notion of development *as* freedom, that is, 'development as a process of expanding the real freedoms that people enjoy',[37] which Mahbub ul Haq as Special Advisor to the UNDP, relied upon in formulating the notion of human development. The process of humanizing development has produced an understanding of development that has the human being at the heart and, as such, development 'aims at enlarging the opportunities people have in their lives' and emphasizes environmental, social and political aspects alongside 'the goals of increasing productivity and income'.[38] Hence, the UN General Assembly (GA), in declaring the 'inalienable human right' to development,[39] stated that 'the human person is the central subject of development',[40] which, as 'a comprehensive economic, social, cultural and political process', has the 'constant improvement of the well-being of the entire population and of all individuals' as its aim.[41]

The UNDP and the Human Development Reports (HDR) provided the platform from which to launch human security on to the international stage. In the 1994 HDR the UNDP advocated a realignment of security from states to people, and, in doing so, recognized the multifaceted sources of insecurity, such as famine and disease alongside conflict and war, as part of the new design for development cooperation in the post Cold War era. As noted above, the SG subsequently spoke of a similarly 'human-centred' understanding of security in the 2000 Millennium Report and again in the 2005 Report, *In Larger Freedom*. These reports, along with the 2003 Report of the HLP, helped to ensure that human security was sufficiently embedded in UN policy and discourse to be included in the Outcome Document of the 2005 World Summit when the UN declared the entitlement of all individuals to freedom from fear and want.[42]

Human security is also evident in the policies of the African Union (AU) and the European Union (EU). For instance, the AU firmly places human security within regional security matrices

---

31   De Feyter, above, n. 28, at 32.

32   Ibid., at 32.

33   MacFarlane and Foong Khong, above, n. 4, at 161.

34   J Donnelly, 'Human rights and development: Complementary or competing concerns?', *World Politics*, 36 (1984), 255. See also J Donnelly, 'Human rights, democracy and development', *Human Rights Quarterly* 21 (1999), 608.

35   UNDP, *Human Development Report 1990* (Oxford: Oxford University Press, 1990), at 9.

36   The Report did add a further three choices of relevance to the concept of human development, that of political freedom, guaranteed human rights and self-respect. Ibid., at 10.

37   A Sen, *Development as Freedom* (Oxford: Oxford University Press, 1999), at 1.

38   de Feyter, above, n. 28, at 32.

39   UN GA Res 41/128, 'Declaration on the Right to Development' (4 December 1986) UN Doc A/RES/41/128, article 1.

40   Ibid., article 2.

41   Ibid., preamublar para. 2.

42   UN GA Res 60/1, 'Outcome Document', above, n. 1, para. 143.

which emphasize, amongst others, human rights and good governance,[43] while the EU is somewhat cautiously exploring a human security approach to foreign policy that also stresses the importance, if not the primacy, of human rights along with multilateralism, and advocates the use of legal instruments, especially international law and drawing up guidelines for the use of force in instances of human insecurity.[44] Governments have similarly recognized the potential of human security as a policy agenda with the governments of Canada, Japan, Norway and Switzerland for example, adopting human security approaches to foreign policy to better reflect the multifaceted sources of insecurity from child soldiers to AIDS.[45] In 1999, the Governments of Canada and Norway established the Human Security Network which, with a total of 13 members, undertakes activities in relation to small arms alongside considering issues such as environmental degradation in furtherance of the vision of:

> [a] humane world where people can live in security and dignity, free from poverty and despair [...].
> In such a world, every individual would be guaranteed freedom from fear and freedom from want,
> with an equal opportunity to fully develop their potential.[46]

It is unsurprising that human security emerged as a policy agenda for various members of the international community in the 1990s, as this decade bears witness to what one commentator has vividly described as a 'tsunami of ethnic and nationalist conflict',[47] which organizations such as the UN, the AU (then the OAU) and the EU, struggled to address, compounded by legal difficulties such as the position of non-state actors in international law. Indeed, the Human Security Report Project records intra-state conflict, of which ethnic conflict is a subset, as the predominant form of conflict within the international system today,[48] which for the AU, for example, demands 'a new emphasis on human security'.[49] Thus, notwithstanding that the tidal wave of intra-state conflict has

---

43   See for example, Peace and Security Council, 'Statement of Commitment to Peace and Security in Africa' 25 May 2004, available at <http://www.africa-union.org/News_Events/Calendar_of_%20Events/Lancement%20PSC/Statement.pdf> [accessed 22 September 2008].

44   See for example, The Study Group on Europe's Security Capabilities, 'A Human Security Doctrine for Europe, 15 September 2004, available at <http://www.lse.ac.uk/Depts/global/Publications/HumanSecurityDoctrine.pdf> [accessed 22 September 2008] and Human Security Study Group, 'A European Way of Security', 8 November 2007, available at <http://www.lse.ac.uk/Depts/global/PDFs/Madrid%20Report%20Final%20for%20distribution.pdf> [accessed 22 September 2008].

45   See Canada's human security website <http://geo.international.gc.ca/cip-pic/cip-pic/humansecurity-en.aspx>; Japan's Ministry of Foreign Affairs website <http://www.mofa.go.jp/policy/oda/sector/security/action.html>; also Switzerland's foreign policy website <http://www.eda.admin.ch/eda/en/home/topics/peasec/sec/humsec.html>.

46   Human Security Network, 'The Vision of the Human Security Network' <http://www.humansecuritynetwork.org/menu-e.php> [accessed 22 September 2008].

47   TR Gurr, *People Versus States: Minorities at Risk in the New Century* (Washington, DC: United States Institute of Peace, 2000), at xiii.

48   Human Security Report Project, *Human Security Report 2006* (Oxford: Oxford University Press, 2006). See also P Wallensteen, *Understanding Conflict Resolution: War, Peace, and the Global System* (London: Sage, 2002). The UN has acknowledged this – UN SG, *We the Peoples*, above, n. 23, at 17.

49   See African Union, 'Draft African Non-Aggression and Common Defence Pact' <http://www.africa-union.org/News_Events/Calendar_of_%20Events/Pacte%20de%20non-agression/Aggression%20Pact%20amendment%20by%20the%20Libyan.pdf> [accessed 22 September 2008]. In respect of human security in Africa see, generally, the African Human Security Initiative <http://www.africanreview.org> Jakkie Cilliers, 'Human Security in Africa: A conceptual framework for review' <http://www.africanreview.org/docs/humsecjun04.pdf> [accessed 22 September 2008].

receded in recent years,[50] it remains a constant and steadfast feature of the international landscape of concern to the main international and regional organizations. Terrorism as 'the most recent avatar in the genealogy of global risks'[51] has exposed similar deficiencies in international law.[52] In short, the changing nature and type of threats coupled with the inadequacy of the existing tools and mechanisms, including international law, at the disposal of the main international and regional organizations, have provided the practical impetus for the emergence of human security as a policy agenda, while the creation of the International Criminal Court and the ban on anti-personnel landmines are testimony to human security as a galvanizing policy agenda that contributes to the development of international law.

The Challenge of Human Security

In a broad stroke human security is the entitlement of all individuals to freedom from fear and want and 'freedom from fear' and 'freedom from want' may be properly considered the 'common core' of human security.[53] The central debate eddying around human security, particularly in international relations discourse, is between broad and narrow understandings of human security – those founded on freedom from fear *and* want as opposed to freedom from fear – in essence the broadening of security to include 'death by economics'.[54] This is somewhat exemplified by the definition of human security offered by the UNDP – perhaps the most cited and arguably the most authoritative definition – which is founded on the twin aims of freedom from fear and freedom from want.[55] However, in acknowledging that 'human security is more easily identified through absence than its presence' and merely listing seven human security threats,[56] the definition has been criticized as being excessively vague and, more specifically, as an 'unwieldy policy instrument'.[57] In contrast, definitions based on freedom from fear, such as that adopted by the Human Security Report Project, are lamented as robbing human security of its holistic and integrated promise. As such, S Neil MacFarlane suggests judging broad and narrow conceptions of human security 'in terms of conceptual value added and policy consequences'.[58] For instance Andrew Mack, Director of the Human Security Report Project, argues that while broad conceptions of human security may have 'political/advocacy benefits', the practical utility of such conceptions is undermined as re-labelling issues, such as epidemics and environmental degradation, to fall within human security, adds little analytical value as a 'concept that explains everything in reality explains nothing'. Moreover, including such concerns within the human security rubric renders 'causal analysis virtually impossible'.[59] In this light it is unsurprising that MacFarlane concluded in favour for

50   Human Security Report Project, above, n. 48. See also Gurr, above, n. 47.

51   U Beck, *Cosmopolitan Vision* (Cambridge: Polity Press, 2006), at 2.

52   See, generally, A Cassese, 'Terrorism is also disrupting some crucial legal categories of international law', *European Journal of International Law*, 12 (2001), 993.

53   J Rawls, *A Theory of Justice* (Oxford: Oxford University Press, 2nd edn, 1999), at 5.

54   AJ Bellamy and M McDonald, '"The utility of human security": Which humans? What security? A reply to Thomas and Tow', *Security Dialogue*, 35 (2002), 373, at 374.

55   UNDP, *Human Development Report 1994* (Oxford: Oxford University Press, 1994), at 24.

56   Ibid., at 23. The human security threats are: economic security, food security, health security, environmental security, personal security, community security and political security.

57   Department of Foreign Affairs and International Trade (DFAIT), *Human Security: Safety for People in a Changing World* (Ottawa: Department of Foreign Affairs and International Trade, 1999), 3.

58   SN MacFarlane, 'A useful concept that risks losing its political salience', *Security Dialogue*, 35 (2004), 368, at 369.

59   A Mack, 'The concept of human security', in Brzoska and Croll (eds), above, n. 2, at 49.

narrow conceptions as founded on freedom from fear. However, in doing so, he acknowledged that '[t]here is no intrinsic reason to favour narrow over broad conceptions of human security',[60] and Mack similarly recognized that 'it is quite possible to share the values that underpin the "broad" conception of human security while still rejecting its analytical utility'.[61] In the last analysis, therefore, '[a]ll approaches to human security focus on the security and development nexus, and all see improvements in socio-economic conditions as crucial for the prevention of conflict; the differences are not of substance, but of packaging'.[62]

Nonetheless it is the deepening of security to include the security of individuals that exposes a more fundamental challenge, even paradox, of human security. Human security advocates a recalibration of security concerns towards the individual as the 'referent object'[63] or the 'normative unit'[64] of security and thus, as Edward Newman asserts, 'stands apart from the prevailing order of the world and asks how that order came about'.[65] However, with its firm roots in policy, traditional notions of security tend to be included within the human security rubric and hence the SG spoke of human security complementing state security.[66] While recent events in Georgia and the 1990 Iraqi invasion of Kuwait testify to the continued significance of an understanding of security that includes territorial integrity and political independence, according such a role or position to the state in human security policies has been vigorously criticized as inimical to human security. As Alex J Bellamy and Matt MacDonald argue such understandings of human security should be resisted for states, as agents of human insecurity, are reinforced and even legitimized.[67] Thus human security in grappling with the age-old conundrum of the relationship between the individual and state simultaneously seeks to challenge the assumptions of the state-centric system of the international landscape and to reinforce such assumptions.

The United Nations and Human Security

With the end of the Cold War, faced with new challenges and exposed to new vulnerabilities to old threats, the UN began to speak of human security as part of a wider policy agenda of putting 'people at the centre of everything we do'.[68] The UN first alluded to the term human security in the 1992 document 'An Agenda for Peace'. Buried amongst expressions of renewed opportunity to build peace, stability and security in the aftermath of the Cold War, the SG proclaimed that each organ of the UN has a 'special and indispensable role to play in an integrated approach to human security'.[69] A similar reference is found in the 1994 document 'An Agenda for Development', where the SG spoke of human security as being intimately tied to a revitalized concept of development.[70]

---

60   MacFarlane, above, n. 58, at 369.

61   Mack, above, n. 59, at 49.

62   D Hubert, 'An idea that works in practice', *Security Dialogue*, 35 (2004), 351, at 351.

63   Buzan, above, n. 3, at 106.

64   See generally F Tesón, *A Philosophy of International Law* (Oxford: Oxford University Press, 1998) and also, 'The Kantian theory of international law', *Columbia Law Review* (1992), 53.

65   E Newman, 'Human Security and the Future of International Public Policy', paper delivered at an International Symposium at the Osaka School of International Public Policy, 11 February 2008, at 6.

66   UN SG, *We the Peoples,* above, n. 23, at 43.

67   Bellamy and MacDonald, above, n. 54, at 374.

68   UN SG, *We the Peoples*, above, n. 23, at 7.

69   UN SG, 'An Agenda for Peace: Preventive diplomacy, peacemaking and peacekeeping' (17 June 1992) UN DOC A/47/277-S/2411, para. 16

70   UN SG, 'An Agenda for Development' (6 May 1994) UN DOC A/48/938, paras 16–20.

Subsequent policy documentation such as the Millennium Report and *In Larger Freedom*, which equated freedom from fear with the UN security agenda and freedom from want with the UN development agenda, spoke of the interdependence of the three great purposes of the UN – human rights, development and security.[71] The mantra of 'we will not enjoy security without development, development without security and neither without human rights'[72] permeates these documents and is echoed in the Outcome Document of the 2005 World Summit. Here the UN recognized that 'development, peace and security and human rights are interlinked and mutually reinforcing' and declared the entitlement of all *individuals* to freedom from fear and freedom from want.[73] In doing so the UN seeks to realign the UN security and development agendas towards the individual. As noted above the process of injecting the idea that people matter into UN development policy and practice began with the articulation of human development. Thus, human security for the UN is about injecting the idea that people matter into UN security policy and practice. This part explores the UN development and security agendas in terms of the idea that people matter which, especially in relation to development, exposes a role for human rights.

Freedom from Want: The UN Development Agenda

The idea that people matter is particularly evident in the UN development agenda. Indeed the lodestar of the UN development agenda – the Millennium Development Goals (MDGs) – translates the idea that people matter into concrete terms whereby UN member states are committed to achieving the eight goals, namely; the eradication of extreme poverty and hunger; the achievement of universal primary education; the promotion of gender equality and the empowerment of women; the reduction of child mortality; the improvement of maternal health; the combating of HIV/AIDS, malaria and other diseases; the ensuring of environmental sustainability; and the creation of a global partnership for development.[74] The MDGs may be seen as a product of the humanizing forces brought to bear on development policies and practices that culminated with the UNDP championing the notion of human development in 1990 and that has subsequently provided the basis for the work of the UNDP. Nevertheless, it is the connections drawn with human rights in the UN development agenda that has consolidated the realignment of development towards the individual. Although initially sceptical as to the relevancy of human rights to development the UNDP, spurred by the inaugural promise of SG Annan to mainstream human rights, produced the policy document 'Integrating Human Rights with Sustainable Human Development', which recognized the relationship between human rights and development as one of interdependence and mutual reinforcement. By 2000 the UNDP had sufficiently elucidated its position with respect to human rights to state: 'Human development and human rights are close enough in motivation and concern to be compatible and congruous, and they are different enough in strategy to supplement each other fruitfully.'[75]

---

71   UN SG, *We the Peoples,* above, n. 23, at 11. See also UN SG, 'The Secretary-General Statement to the General Assembly' (New York, Speech delivered to the UN General Assembly, 21 March 2005) <http://www.un.org/largerfreedom/sg-statement.html> [accessed 22 September 2008].

72   UN SG, *In Larger Freedom*, above, n. 23, para. 17.

73   UN GA Res 60/1, 'Outcome Document', above, n. 1, para. 143.

74   For definitions and explanations as regards these MDGs and the targets and indicators see <http://unstats.un.org/unsd/mi/mi_goals.asp> [accessed 20 August 2008]. See also, more generally, UN Millennium Project, *Investing in Development* (New York: United Nations, 2005). For more information on the Millennium Project see <http://www.unmillenniumproject.org>.

75   UNDP, *HDR 2000* (Oxford: Oxford University Press, 2000), at 19.

These points of correlation provided the basis for the identification in 2005 of three strategies by which to inject human rights into the development policies and practices of the UNDP. One such strategy is the promotion of the application of human rights-based approaches to development programming. This involves capacity building and training UNDP staff to understand and apply human rights-based approaches, alongside human rights-based assessments and analyses of development situations and the integration of human rights into country programmes.[76] In short, human rights-based approaches inject international human rights *law* into development programming. Indeed one of the distinctive features of human rights-based approaches – as opposed to rights-based approaches – is the emphasis on the 'legal codification and normative universality of rights' as embodied in international human rights law.[77] As such, international human rights law provides the legal and normative framework for UNDP development programming, including the MDGs. In addition the UNDP identified supporting national systems for the promotion and protection of human rights as one of its strategies to inject human rights into development and, to this end, produces the Human Rights World Map, which collates country-specific human rights information to aid UNDP staff. The final strategy is strengthening engagement with the UN human rights machinery that saw the establishment of HURIST (Human Rights Strengthening Initiative). HURIST is a joint programme with the Office of the High Commissioner for Human Rights, the primary purpose of which is to identify best practices and learning opportunities to develop national capacities for promoting and protecting human rights and applying a human rights-based approach to development.[78]

Freedom from Fear: The UN Security Agenda

The UN security agenda has not been as receptive to either the idea that people matter or the insertion of human rights concerns into security policy or practice. For instance, the 'more comprehensive concept of collective security' advanced by the HLP in response to the 'unwillingness to get serious about preventing deadly violence' on the part of the Security Council (SC) and the UN more generally,[79] failed to garner the support necessary at the 2005 World Summit. UN member states gathered at the Summit could only muster a reaffirmation of the 'commitment to work towards a security consensus',[80] despite the endorsement by the SG of the more comprehensive notion as bridging the 'gap between divergent views of security' in his 2005 Report, *In Larger Freedom*.[81] Notwithstanding, the Outcome Document did continue to record the recognition of UN member states that:

---

76   UNDP, 'Human Rights in UNDP' (Practice Note 2005) at 4 <http://www.undp.org/governance/docs/HRPN_English.pdf> [accessed 22 September 2008].

77   C Nyamu-Musembi and A Cornwall, 'What is the 'rights-based approach' all about? Perspectives from international development agencies' (IDS Working Paper 234, 2004) <http://www.ids.ac.uk/ids/bookshop/wp/wp234.pdf> [accessed 19 July 2005], 14. The UN OHCHR has stated that the legal character of international human rights law lies at the heart of the human rights based approach to development See UN High Commissioner for Human Rights, 'Bridging the gap between human rights and development: From normative principles to operational relevance' (Presidential Address to the World Bank, 3 December 2001) <http://www.unhchr.ch/huricane/huricane.nsf/view01/2DA59CD3FFC033DCC1256B1A0033F7C3?opendocument> [accessed 11 August 2006].

78   <www.unhchr.ch/development/huristproject.doc> [accessed 11 August 2006].

79   HLP, above, n. 23, para. 39.

80   UN GA Res 60/1, 'Outcome Document', above, n. 1, para. 72.

81   UN SG, *In Larger Freedom*, above, n. 23, para. 77.

[M]any threats are interlinked, that development, peace, security and human rights are mutually reinforcing, that no State can best protect itself by acting entirely alone and that all States need an effective and efficient collective security system pursuant to the purposes and principles of the Charter.[82]

Further, and importantly for present purposes, UN member states recognized 'a whole range of threats'[83] that know 'no national boundaries',[84] and thus acknowledged a wider conception of security beyond the confines of the traditional or classical understanding, whereby security pertains to the protection of the political integrity and territorial independence of a state from external aggression of another state.[85]

This broader understanding of security is somewhat born out in the practice of the UN SC, the body with primary responsibility for the maintenance of international peace and security, in relation to human rights concerns. Indeed, it is clear that 'threat to the peace' as the jurisdictional trigger under Article 39 of the Charter for SC enforcement action has evolved to include human rights issues. However, this was not always the case, as the SC was reluctant to account for human rights concerns during the Cold War, seeing such issues within the realm of domestic jurisdiction. That said a series of resolutions in the 1960s and 1970s saw the SC condemn the apartheid and racially discriminatory regimes in South Africa and Southern Rhodesia as threats to the peace.[86] While these resolutions pierced the veil of sovereignty embodied in the principle of non-interference found in Article 2 (7) of the UN Charter, the consideration of human rights issues by the SC in determining a threat to the peace under Article 39 is by no means a settled matter of principle or doctrine. Indeed, a closer inspection of relevant SC practice reveals the need for an 'international dimension', as was evident in the South Africa resolutions which stressed the de-stablizing effect of South African policies in the region and permeates subsequent SC practice in relation to human rights issues. Indeed Karel Wellens concludes his detailed survey of SC practice in relation to human rights issues between 1990 and 2003 with the forceful observation that '[n]o situations have arisen where such violations of human rights provided the exclusive underpinning of a pronouncement or determination of a threat [to the peace]'.[87]

In brief, while human rights issues are considered by the SC when making an Article 39 determination which triggers enforcement action under Chapter VII of the Charter, such issues are not determinative of a situation constituting a threat to the peace. In addition the SC is also

---

82   Ibid. Peggy Hicks remarked that the Report of the HLP 'takes an important step by recognising that security, development, and human rights are intertwined, and that all three prongs need to be addressed to create a more secure world'. See P Hicks, 'Correct diagnosis, wrong prescription: The human rights component of security', *Security Dialogue*, 36 (2005), 380, at 380. Chris Landsberg was more forthright in his observation in respect of the refrain of the Secretary-General in the Report *In Larger Freedom* that 'there can be no development without security, no security without development, and neither without human rights, is an important new paradigm'. C Landsberg, 'The UN high-level reports and implications for Africa', *Security Dialogue*, 36 (2005), 388, at 389.

83   UN GA Res 60/1, 'Outcome Document', above, n. 1, para. 69.

84   Ibid., para. 71.

85   Barry Buzan has described national security as 'the ability of states to maintain their independent identity and their functional integrity'. Buzan, above, n. 3, at 116.

86   See, for example, UN SC Res 217 (20 November 1965) UN Doc S/RES/217 (Southern Rhodesia) and UN SC Res 181 (7 August 1963) UN Doc S/RES/181 (South Africa).

87   K Wellens, 'The UN Security Council and new threats to the peace: Back to the future', *Journal of Conflict and Security Law*, 8/1 (2003), 15, at 44.

circumspect to guard against bestowing precedential value on such resolutions.[88] To this end, the SC adopts 'case-by-case authoritative decisions'[89] in discharging its Charter mandate to maintain international peace and security which serves to underscore the well-documented challenges and obstacles facing the SC.[90] Indeed, the HLP noted with disdain the 'glacial speed' at which the SC responded to the crisis situation in Darfur.[91] For instance, the SC made an Article 39 determination which noted, amongst others, 'grave concern at the ongoing humanitarian crisis and widespread human rights violations' and condemned 'all acts and violence and violations of human rights and international humanitarian law',[92] more than two years after the outbreak of the current hostilities, with UNMIS – the UN mission in Darfur – created a year later.[93] The hesitancy of the SC to act in this instance has been attributed to a lack of political will along with reduced operational capacity owing to the military commitments of UN member states in the war on terror.[94] In addition to exacerbating the existing institutional and operational challenges facing the SC, the tenor of the war on terror whereby 'human rights are subordinate to security concerns, even antithetical'[95] appears to have permeated SC deliberations. For example, in January 2007 Russia and China vetoed a SC resolution tabled in respect of the political unrest in Myanmar which called for the release of political prisoners and the cessation of military attacks on ethnic minorities and associated human rights violations.[96] China rejected the resolution on the basis that the situation fell within the domestic jurisdiction of Myanmar while Russia cautioned against using the SC 'to discuss issues outside its purview'.[97] This is the first use of the double veto since the end of the Cold War and coupled with recourse to arguments based on domestic jurisdiction, suggests an imperceptible shift away from human rights in favour of state security – a dynamic that characterized SC practice during the Cold War.

---

88   For example, Rob Cryer notes the limited precedential value of the resolutions on the situation in Southern Rhodesia and South Africa in terms of proposition that gross violations of human rights can constitute a threat. See R Cryer, 'The Security Council and Article 39: A threat to coherence?', *Journal of Armed Conflict Law*, 1 (1996), 161, at 178–80.

89   MJ Aznar-Gomez, 'A decade of human rights protection by the UN Security Council: A sketch of deregulation?', *European Journal of International Law*, 13 (2002), 221, at 224.

90   For concise reviews of the calls to reform the SC from different perspectives, see for example, TG Weiss and KE Young, 'Compromise and credibility: Security Council reform?', *Security Dialogue*, 36 (2005), 131; J Morris, 'UN Security Council reform: A council for the 21st century', *Security Dialogue*, 31 (2000), 265; and YZ Blum, 'Proposals for UN Security Council reform', *American Journal of International Law*, 99 (2005), 632. For a succinct presentation of the 'generic' issues see FL Kirgis Jr, 'The United Nations at fifty: The Security Council's first fifty years', *American Journal of International Law*, 89 (1995), 506. See also DD Caron, 'The legitimacy of the collective authority of the security', *American Journal of International Law*, 87 (1993), 552 and M Glennon, 'Why the Security Council failed', *Foreign Affairs*, 82 (2003), 16.

91   HLP, above, n. 23, at 42.

92   UN SC Res 1556 (30 July 2004) UN S/RES/1556, preamublar paras 7 and 8.

93   UN SC Res 1590 (24 March 2005) UN S/RES/1590. A hybrid UN and AU peacekeeping force is now in place.

94   TG Weiss, *Humanitarian Intervention: Ideas in Action* (Cambridge: Polity Press, 2007), at 122–36.

95   MR Ishay, *The History of Human Rights: From Ancient Times to the Globalisation Era* (Berkeley, CA: University of California Press, 2004), at 279.

96   For the text of the draft resolution see, 'Security Council Fails to Adopt Draft Resolution on Myanmar, Owing to Negative Votes by China, Russian Federation' (12 January 2007) SC/8939 <http://www.un.org/News/Press/docs/2007/sc8939.doc.htm> [accessed 19 July 2010].

97   Ibid. See also UN News Centre, 'China and Russia veto US/UK-backed Security Council draft resolution on Myanmar', <http://www.un.org/apps/news/story.asp?NewsID=21228&Cr=myanmar&Cr1#> [accessed 19 July 2010].

The UN has engaged with the underlying concern of human security – freedom from fear and want – since its inception. The realignment of the UN development agenda towards the individual – which began with human development and facilitated the emergence of human security – ossified with the UNDP integrating human rights into development policies and practices, largely through human rights-based approaches to development. However, the prospects for recalibrating the UN security agenda towards the individual and embedding human security are less certain, particularly as the above brief survey of SC practice reveals a SC resistant to the idea that people matter. This is unsurprising for, notwithstanding the 'humanitarian impulse'[98] of the 1990s, which saw the evolution of 'threat to the peace' rubric to include human rights concerns, the collective security system envisaged by the UN Charter for which the SC is responsible for, is founded on the primacy of the state as buttressed by legal principles such as the non-interference in the domestic affairs of states. The challenge of human security to fundamental precepts of international law and the UN is clear. Moreover, in the sense that human security is presented in UN policy documentation as reinvigorating the UN as an international organization that 'exists for, and must serve, the needs and hopes of peoples everywhere',[99] human security challenges international law and the UN to better reflect the realities of today's world.

International Law and Human Security

That human security challenges international law to do better along with challenging fundamental principles of international law, such as the principle of non-intervention, is readily apparent in the responsibility to protect. As is explored below, the responsibility to protect as a response to genocide, war crimes, ethnic cleansing and crimes against humanity, illustrates Gerd Oberleitner's assertion that 'a human security approach to international *can* reinforce and strengthen attempts to bring international law into line with the requirements of today's world'.[100] However, as a UN human security initiative, the responsibility to protect embodies the paradox of human security noted above, namely that while the responsibility to protect challenges basal precepts of international law such as its state-centric character, it simultaneously operates to reinforce such precepts. The resultant dilution of the potency of the responsibility to protect as a human security initiative prompts the investigation of the nexus between human rights and human security, specifically the contribution of international human rights law, undertaken in the second section of this part.

The Responsibility to Protect: A Human Security Challenge to International Law

The responsibility to protect was articulated by the International Commission on Intervention and State Sovereignty (ICISS) in 2001 with the underlying thesis that:

---

98   TG Weiss, 'Humanitarian impulse', in D Malone (ed.), *The UN Security Council: From the Cold War to the 21st Century* (Boulder, CO: Lynne Rienner Publishers, 2004), at 37.

99   UN SG, *We the Peoples*, above, n. 23, at 6.

100   G Oberleitner, 'Human security: A challenge to international law', *Global Governance*, 11 (2005), 185, at 186 (emphasis added).

[S]overeign states have a responsibility to protect their own citizens from avoidable catastrophe – from mass murder and rape, from starvation – but that when they are unwilling or unable to do so, that responsibility must be borne by the broader community of states.[101]

Thus, for the ICISS the responsibility to protect lies first and foremost with the state and a secondary or surrogate responsibility to protect falls to the international community when the state is unable or unwilling to halt or avert a population suffering serious harm, whether resulting from internal war, insurgency, repression or state failure. Alongside human security, the ICISS grounds the responsibility to protect, especially the secondary or what may be termed the international responsibility to protect, on a re-fashioned notion of sovereignty as responsibility, the impact of human rights 'in establishing new standards of behaviour and new means of enforcing those standards', international criminal law and humanitarian law, in addition to the practice of the SC and organizations such as ECOWAS and NATO to garner support for the emergence of a norm of intervention for human protection purposes in extreme cases of major harm to civilians.[102] That said, the ICISS was not, in the words of co-chair Gareth Evans, solely concerned with producing an 'intellectually credible' report, but also with 'motivating action and mobilising support',[103] and, to this end, put forward the responsibility to protect framework consisting of three dimensions: the responsibility to *prevent*, the responsibility to *react* and the responsibility to *rebuild*. These dimensions exist along what Evans has called a 'continuum of obligations'.[104] The responsibility to prevent is the most important dimension and is directed towards the prevention of deadly conflict and other man-made catastrophes that put populations at risk. It involves, for example, establishing early warning systems, addressing root causes of conflict such as economic deprivation and the lack of economic opportunities by using a 'toolbox' of political, economic, legal and military measures. The responsibility to rebuild sits at other end of the continuum and involves aspects of peace-building, reconstruction and reconciliation, and issues of territorial administration, especially by the UN in post-conflict situations. Indeed, Siobhán Wills sees the responsibility to rebuild as particularly relevant in aiding the clarification of the legal responsibilities of UN peacekeepers, especially in respect of human rights obligations.[105] However, the responsibility to react has been the focus of academic attention and commentary,[106] in part owing to the formulation of guidelines

101   ICISS, *The Responsibility to Protect* (Ottawa: International Development Research Centre, 2001), at viii.

102   Ibid., at 14–16.

103   G Evans, 'The responsibility to protect: Humanitarian intervention in the 21st century' (Wesson Lecture in International Relations Theory and Practice, 2002) <http://www.crisisgroup.org/home/index.cfm?id=2288&l=1> [accessed 28 August 2007].

104   G Evans, 'From humanitarian intervention to the responsibility to protect', *Wisconsin International Law Journal*, 24 (2006), 703, at 708.

105   S Wills, 'Military interventions on behalf of vulnerable populations: The legal responsibilities of states and international organisations engaged in peace support operations', *Journal of Conflict and Security Law*, 9 (2004), 387. See also S Wills, *Protecting Civilians: The Obligations of Peacekeepers* (Oxford: Oxford, 2009), chs 2–4.

106   See for example C Stahn, 'Responsibility to protect: Political rhetoric or emerging legal norm', *American Journal of International Law*, 101 (2007), 99; RJ Hamilton, 'The responsibility to protect: From document to doctrine – but what of implementation?', *Harvard Human Rights Journal*, 19 (2006), 289; G Day and C Freeman, 'Operationalising the responsibility to protect – the policekeeping approach', *Global Governance*, 11 (2005), 139; AJ Bellamy, 'Whither the responsibility to protect? humanitarian intervention and the 2005 World Summit', *Ethics and International Affairs*, 20 (2006), 144; AJ Bellamy, 'Responsibility to protect or Trojan horse? The crisis in Darfur and humanitarian intervention after Iraq', *Ethics and*

for the use of SC enforcement mechanisms for human protection purposes. Thus, the responsibility to react stipulates a response to 'situations of compelling human need with appropriate measures', which span the spectrum from sanctions to military intervention.[107] In respect of the latter, the Report sets down six criteria – right authority, just cause, right intention, last resort, proportional means and reasonable prospects – by which to determine when, how and by whom the international responsibility to react should be exercised.

The just cause criterion establishes a threshold broadly conceived of as large-scale loss of life and large-scale ethnic cleansing which triggers the responsibility to react in order to halt or avert such loss of life or ethnic cleansing. The requirement that intervention is a last resort in order to halt or avert human suffering, along with the stipulations that the intervention has a reasonable chance of success and that proportionate measures are used to this end, are precautionary criteria which 'strictly limit the use of coercive military force for human protection purposes'.[108] The issue of ensuring that the 'right authority' determines whether the responsibility to react should be exercised by way of military intervention was resolved by the ICISS in terms of etching out a role for the SC as the sole arbiter of military interventions for human protection purposes.[109] Yet, the ICISS is not alone in putting forward criteria for military intervention for human protection purposes. For instance the Independent International Commission on Kosovo, established by the Swedish Government to assess, amongst others, 'the adequacy of present norms and institutions in preventing and responding' to ethnic conflict as seen in Kosovo,[110] laid down a similar list of criteria. Academics have also offered guidelines for military intervention, such as those offered by Ian Johnstone who was motivated by a desire to inject the 'power of the better argument' into SC deliberations and 'enhance the power of persuasion based on law'.[111]

Nevertheless, it is the responsibility to protect as articulated by the ICISS that has been proclaimed as 'the most sophisticated attempt at establishing a moral guideline for international action in the face of humanitarian emergency'[112] as 'the most influential intellectual contribution' to the contemporary debate on the dilemma of intervention,[113] and as 'a watershed even in

---

International Affairs, 20 (2005), 31, at 42–50; PD Williams and AJ Bellamy, 'The responsibility to protect and the crisis in Darfur', *Security Dialogue*, 36 (2005), 27; TG Weiss, 'The sunset of humanitarian intervention? The responsibility to protect in a unipolar era', *Security Dialogue*, 35 (2004), 135; R Thakur, 'Intervention, sovereignty and the responsibility to protect: Experiences from ICISS', *Security Dialogue*, 33 (2002), 323.

107   ICISS, above, n. 101, at xi.

108   Ibid., at 35.

109   This is made explicitly clear: 'Security Council authorisation must in all cases be sought prior to any military intervention action being carried out'. Ibid., at 50. However, the ICISS does consider the situation of a deadlocked SC and sources of alternative authority. In this respect, cf. HLP, above, n. 23, at 199–203.

110   The Independent International Commission on Kosovo, *The Kosovo Report: Conflict, International Response, Lessons Learned* (Oxford: Oxford University Press, 2000), at 25, citing the Mission Statement of the Commission. The Commission proposed a principled framework of three thresholds to be satisfied for any claim to humanitarian intervention to be considered legitimate. These are: 'the suffering of civilians owing to severe patterns of human rights violations or the breakdown of government, the overriding commitment to the direct protection of the civilian population, and the calculation that the intervention has a reasonable chance of ending the humanitarian catastrophe'. Ibid.

111   I Johnstone, 'Security Council deliberations: The power of the better argument', *European Journal of International Law*, 14 (2003), 437, at 480. Ryan Goodman has advanced a similar argument, although in respect of unilateral humanitarian intervention. R Goodman, 'Humanitarian intervention and pretexts for war', *American Journal of International Law*, 100 (2006), 107.

112   Day and Freeman, above, n. 106, at 139.

113   Wills, 'Military interventions', above n. 105, at 388.

international discussions of humanitarian intervention'.[114] As Ulrich Beck observes, the *obligation* to intervene is a 'revolutionary development' as it means that 'international law is now addressed directly to individuals over the heads of states'.[115] Furthermore, UN member states endorsed the responsibility to protect in the Outcome Document, declaring that while '[e]ach individual state has the responsibility to protect its populations from genocide, war crimes, ethnic cleansing and crimes against humanity', a residual responsibility to protect falls to the international community, acting through the UN. The Outcome Document proclaims:

> We are prepared to take collective action [...] through the Security Council, in accordance with the Charter, including Chapter VII, on a case-by-case basis [...] should peaceful means be inadequate and national authorities are manifestly failing to protect their populations from genocide, war crimes, ethnic cleansing and crimes against humanity.[116]

A year later the SC endorsed 'the responsibility to protect populations from genocide, war crimes, ethnic cleansing and crimes against humanity',[117] while the new SG, Ban Ki-moon, demonstrated his commitment to 'translate the concept of the responsibility to protect from word to deed'[118] by creating the post of Special Advisor on the Responsibility to Protect in 2008. Moreover, the International Court of Justice (ICJ) recently found that Serbia had a responsibility to prevent the genocide at Srebrenica in the *Bosnian Genocide Case*.[119] Notwithstanding the endorsement of UN member states and three principal organs of the UN, the responsibility to protect does not quite meet the challenge of human security for international law to better reflect the 'requirements of today's world'[120] which tempers Beck's claim that the responsibility to protect is a 'revolutionary development'. The guidelines for military intervention for human protection purposes are conspicuously absent from the above endorsements of the responsibility to protect. Indeed they were jettisoned from the Outcome Document as a result of a pincer movement by the US on the one hand, which was concerned about fettering the discretion of the SC, and Third World countries on the other, which saw the responsibility to protect as a 'Trojan horse' for other kinds of interventions in the domestic affairs of states.[121] In short, the responsibility to protect was diluted in the transition from 'document to doctrine',[122] which underscores the absence of political will to galvanize the SC to respond to mass human rights violations on a principled and coherent basis. Notwithstanding the commitment of the SC to the responsibility to protect, it is not a policy option exercised by the SC. For instance, the crisis situation in Darfur, often regarded as the litmus test for the responsibility to protect, saw the SC equivocate over the consent of Sudan to the proposed UN peacekeeping

---

114   J Donnelly, *Universal Human Rights in Theory and Practice* (London: Cornell University Press, 2003), at 251.

115   Beck, above, n. 51, at 122

116   UN GA Res 60/1, Outcome Document, above, n. 1, para. 139.

117   UN SC Res 1674 (2006) (28 April 2006) UN S/RES/1674, para. 4.

118   UN SG, 'Secretary-General Expresses Determination to ensure we make progress on pressing issues of our time, step by step', in message for United Nations Day, 24 October available at <http://www.un.org/News/Press/docs/2007/sgsm11203.doc.htm> [accessed 19 July 2010].

119   *Application of the Convention on the Prevention and Punishment of the Crime of Genocide (Bosnia and Herzegovina v. Serbia and Montenegro)* [2007] ICJ Reports [hereinafter referred to as the *Bosnian Genocide Case*]. See, generally, Mark Gibney, 'Genocide and state responsibility', *Human Rights Law Review*, 7 (2007), 760.

120   Oberleitner, 'Challenge to international law', above, n. 100, at 186.

121   Bellamy, 'The responsibility to protect or Trojan horse?', above, n. 106.

122   This phrase is borrowed from Rebecca J Hamilton. Hamilton above, n. 106.

mission. The SC ultimately 'invited' the Sudanese government to 'approve of the mission',[123] thereby consigning Beck's claim that the responsibility to protect means that 'international law is now addressed directly to individuals over the heads of states' to the realms of wishful thinking.

It is important at this juncture to acknowledge that the responsibility to protect, in particular the international responsibility to react, as a human security initiative is not a legal norm. The pillars, upon which the ICISS rest the emerging norm of intervention for human protection purposes in extreme cases of major harm to civilians, are problematic. The reliance on SC practice is particularly dubious for, as discussed above, human rights concerns are not determinative of an Article 39 determination that a threat to the peace exists and indeed the SC has been careful not to bequeath precedential value on resolutions dealing with human rights concerns. The concern with preserving the discretion of the SC permeated the Outcome Document which speaks of the international responsibility to react exercisable on 'a case-by-case basis'. Further, the re-casting of sovereignty as responsibility by the ICISS, which, in essence, means that states are internally responsible to citizens and, through the UN, externally responsible to the international community,[124] was based on the assertion that 'the exercise of state sovereignty has always been more constrained and porous' than the legal principle of non-intervention would suggest.[125] This assertion does not stand upon closer scrutiny as the response of the SC to the crisis situation in Darfur noted above readily testifies and thus the *legal* barrier of Article 2 (7) remains intact. For instance, the recent recourse to arguments premised on Article 2 (7) by Russia and China intimate the enduring impermeability of the principle of non-intervention and the supremacy of the state. Finally, the recognition of the responsibility to prevent genocide as found in the Genocide Convention by the ICJ in the *Bosnian Genocide Case* is qualified by the explicit caveat that the decision does not 'purport to establish a general jurisprudence applicable to all cases where a treaty instrument or other binding legal norm, includes an obligation for States to prevent certain acts'.[126]

The auguries for the responsibility to protect to alleviate human insecurity stemming from genocide, ethnic cleansing, war crimes and crimes against humanity are not promising. Indeed the Achilles heel of the responsibility to protect in preventing 'future Rwandas and Kosovos',[127] aside from the questionable legal status, is that the legal principle of non-intervention as an expression of sovereignty – however understood – remains intact. Thus the responsibility to protect as a human security initiative attempts to 'fundamentally question existing structures and institutions'[128] by refashioning sovereignty as responsibility while remaining within 'the sovereignty discourse'.[129] This raises the possibility of a role for international human rights law to strengthen UN human security initiatives – comparable to that seen in respect of the UN development agenda – for, as Henry Steiner and Philip Alston observe, the proliferation of UN human rights treaties speaks to the 'waning obstacle of domestic jurisdiction'.[130]

---

123   Weiss, *Humanitarian Intervention*, above, n. 94, at 56.

124   ICISS, above, n. 101, at 13.

125   Ibid., *Research Essays*, 3.

126   *Bosnian Genocide Case*, above, n. 119, para. 432.

127   Bellamy, 'Wither the responsibility to protect?', above, n. 106, at 166.

128   Newman, above, n. 65, at 6.

129   J Tanguy, 'Redefining sovereignty and intervention', *Ethics and International Affairs*, 17 (2003), 141, at 144.

130   HJ Steiner and P Alston, *International Human Rights in Context: Law, Politics and Morals* (Oxford: Clarendon Press, 1996), at 364

Human Security and Human Rights: A Tangled Web

There is an 'intricate convergence' between human security and human rights, especially the international law of human rights.[131] This is unsurprising, as human rights and human security share the core motivational underpinning that people matter. Certainly, international human rights law, international humanitarian law and refugee law are clear examples of the translation of the idea that people matter into international law, with the development of the international law of human rights being hailed as the 'humanisation of international law'.[132] Thus, it is understandable that, at first glance, a UN human security policy agenda has direct and immediate bearing on international human rights law. Indeed, there are significant points of correlation between such a policy agenda – the entitlement of all individuals to freedom from fear and want – and international human rights law, not in the last the focus on the individual as the 'referent object'[133] or 'normative unit'.[134] The 'individualistic perspective'[135] dominates international human rights law with, and notwithstanding the rights of minorities and the right to self-determination which are interpreted in a manner that reinforces this individualistic perspective, individuals as the right holders under international human rights law. The international law of human rights also gives voice to freedom from fear and freedom from want with freedom from fear relating to civil and political rights, epitomized by the International Covenant on Civil and Political Rights and freedom from want pertaining to socio-economic rights, exemplified by the International Covenant on Economic, Social and Cultural Rights.[136]

In light of these 'important parallels', the recurrent assertion in human security discourse and practice that human rights, especially international human rights law, defines human security appears relatively innocuous. As Barbara von Tigerstrom observes the assertion is based on a desire to lend human security 'greater force or legitimacy, as well as providing a legal framework and conceptual point of reference from which it can develop'.[137] However, this proposition is not only under-explored in human security discourse, but a closer examination reveals it to be deeply problematic. For instance, issues that may be considered human security issues such as 'death by economics'[138] are not human rights issues and are thus absent from human security when defined in terms of human rights. On the other side of the coin, the logical conclusion of the assertion that human rights, particularly international human rights law, defines human security, as Gerd Oberleitner has correctly observed, is to render human security 'superfluous because all its concerns are covered by the human rights system'.[139] Moreover, Oberleitner also pointed out that defining human security in terms of international human rights law may have the detrimental effect of detracting from the legal character of human rights and, further, presents governments with the

---

131   G Oberletiner, 'Porcupines in love: The intricate convergence of human rights and human security', *European Human Rights Law Review*, 6 (2005), 588, at 588.

132   T Buergenthal, 'The normative and institutional evolution of international human rights', *Human Rights Quarterly*, 19 (1997), 703.

133   Buzan, above, n. 3, at 106.

134   See generally Tesón, above, n. 64.

135   L Henkin citing A Addis, 'Individualism, communitarism, and the rights of ethnic minorities', *Notre Dame Law Review*, 66 (1991), 1219 in L Henkin et al., *Human Rights* (New York: Foundation Press, 1999), at 429.

136   L Sohn, 'The United Nations at fifty: How American international lawyers prepared for the San Francisco Bill of Rights', *American Journal of International Law*, 89 (1995), 540, at 540–1.

137   B von Tigerstrom, *Human Security and International Law* (Oxford: Hart, 2007), at 65.

138   Bellamy and MacDonald, above, n. 54, at 374.

139   Oberleitner, 'Porcupines in love', above, n. 131, at 596.

'tempting policy option' of choosing the 'more palatable dish' of human security in preference to obligations under the international law of human rights.[140]

However, such an analysis is somewhat simplistic as it suggests the exclusion of human rights from human security policies and analytical frameworks. This is unwarranted in light of the significant points of correlation between human security and human rights, especially the international law of human rights, which demands an assessment of the contribution of international human rights law to human security and specifically a UN human security policy agenda. Central to such an assessment is the question of the *capacity* of international human rights law to protect the rights – civil, political and socio-economic – of individuals. While the ills and shortcomings of situating such protection within international law are well documented, an awareness that international human rights law does not always 'operate in ways that are beneficial from a human security perspective' is required.[141] For instance, one commentator has described the indeterminate language adopted in the relevant UN human rights treaties as a 'fundamental weakness',[142] while the weak supervisory mechanisms therein prompted another commentator to remark that 'states give up their sovereignty only insofar as they are obliged to submit a report'.[143] However, it is the application of the law of reservations, enunciated in the Vienna Convention on the Law of Treaties, to UN human rights treaties that is the example par excellence of the ability of states to retain control of their legal obligations as the effect of a reservation to a provision of a UN human rights treaty is to 'exclude or modify the legal effect' of the provision in question. Indeed an understanding of these 'limits and ambiguities' of international human rights law is crucial to an appreciation of human security in UN policy.[144] Human security refocuses our attention on the why of international human rights law – that people matter – and in doing so illuminates the 'recurring dissonance between self-satisfied rhetoric and social reality' permeating international human rights law'.[145] This disjuncture has been eloquently described by Upendra Baxi in the following terms: 'The more people stand endowed with normative human rights by international and constitutional instruments, the greater and keener emerges the suffering of people existentially deprived of realisation and enjoyment of human rights.'[146]

Observations such as these raise the spectre of sovereignty and more generally question the effectiveness of the international law of human rights to protect the rights of individuals. While the empirical measurement of human rights protection is outside the scope of the present chapter, suffice it to say that the legal tools noted above, such as reservations, employed by states can undermine the effectiveness of international human rights law to protect individual civil, cultural, economic, political and social rights.

---

140   Ibid.

141   von Tigerstrom, above, n. 137, at 90.

142   DL Donoho, 'The role of human rights in global security issues', *Michigan Journal of International Law*, 14 (1993), 827.

143   C Schreuer, 'The waning of the sovereign state: Towards a new paradigm for international law?', *European Journal of International Law*, 4 (1993), 448, at 448.

144   Ibid.

145   Ishay, above, n. 95, at 2.

146   U Baxi, *The Future of Human Rights* (Oxford: Oxford University Press, 2002), at viii. Michael Ignatieff expresses a similar sentiment when he observes that 'juridical, advocacy and enforcement revolutions have dramatically raised expectations'. M Ignatieff, *Human Rights as Politics and Idolatry* (Princeton, NJ: Princeton University Press, 2003), at 17.

Concluding Remarks

In May 2008 the GA, in furtherance of the 2005 commitment to discuss and define 'the notion of human security',[147] held a thematic debate which reflected on the scope of human security along with the significance of human security in facing the challenges of today's world.[148] Central to the debate was the acknowledgement that 'human security can be a useful vehicle' to pursue integrated responses – spanning human rights, development and security – to the 'challenges facing all of us in the international community'.[149] This acknowledgement is underscored by the practical imperative to alleviate human insecurity, as readily attested to by the continued crisis situation in Darfur. Indeed, such incidents of human insecurity which 'dominate today's headlines',[150] including the civilian death-toll in Iraq and the humanitarian situation in Myanmar, expose the deficiencies of the international legal framework and highlight seemingly intractable issues such as that of 'humanitarian intervention'. It is in challenging international law to better reflect the realities and requirements of today's world that human security holds direct relevance for international law. For instance the articulation and subsequent endorsement of the responsibility to protect as a response to genocide amongst others by the UN, speaks to the potential of human security to meaningfully contribute to the normative development of international law. Notwithstanding the dilution from 'document to doctrine', the recognition of the need for the SC to unite 'around the aim of confronting massive human rights violations and crimes against humanity'[151] stands as a significant shift towards the 'power of the better argument' and the rule of law[152] and thus acts as a counterweight to the 'broader attack on international law' which, according to Simon Chesterman 'proposes to order the world not around norms and institutions but the benevolent goodwill of the US' as evidenced by war in Iraq.[153] Indeed the Iraq war provides 'the starkest example of the tension between the rhetorical commitment to human security and the imperatives of state security'[154] which raises the question of the prospects of translating human security into UN practice.

For the UN, human security is the entitlement of all individuals to freedom from fear and want and thus is about realigning the UN security agenda towards the individual. However, as was evident from the above discussion, UN practice in the field of security has not been particularly receptive to the idea that people matter. Yet SC practice has evolved sufficiently for the responsibility to protect to emerge as a policy option to respond to genocide, war crimes, ethnic cleansing and crimes against humanity. In doing so, the responsibility to protect provides a concrete example of the challenge which human security poses to international law to better reflect the realities and requirements of today's world and the challenge to basal principles of international law, such as the principle of non-intervention. However, the insistence by the fledging UN human security policy

---

147   UN GA Res 60/1, 'Outcome Document', above, n, 1, para. 143.

148   See generally <http://www.un.org/ga/president/62/ThematicDebates/humansecurity.shtml> [accessed 22 September 2008].

149   President of the General Assembly, HE Srgjan Kermin, 'Concluding Remarks at the Thematic Debate on Human Security', 22 May 2008, available at <http://www.un.org/ga/president/62/statements/crhumansecurity220508.shtml> [accessed 22 September 2008].

150   S Ogata and J Cels, 'Human security: Protecting and empowering the people', *Global Governance*, 9 (2003), 273, at 273.

151   UN SG, 'Unifying the Security Council in Defence of Human Rights' (Address delivered at the centennial of the first International Peace Conference, 18 May 1999) reprinted in SG, *The Question of Intervention: Statements by the Secretary-General* (New York: UN Dept of Public Information, 1999), at 33.

152   Johnstone, above, n. 111, at 480.

153   S Chesterman, 'Bush, the United Nations and Nation-Building', *Survival* (49) 1 (2005) 101, at 101.

154   Ogata and Cels, above, n. 150, at 273.

agenda that 'the security of the state has to be seen alongside the security of the individual'[155] seems to limit '[t]he commitment of the UN to human security [...] in fundamental ways'.[156] For instance, human security initiatives such as the responsibility to protect, although premised on a refashioned notion of sovereignty as responsibility, remains within the 'sovereignty discourse' as the legal principle of non-intervention remains intact.

The connections between human security and human rights, especially international human rights law, help to situate human security with respect to international law insofar as the correlations show that human security is 'not entirely alien to international law'.[157] Nonetheless, bringing a human security perspective to bear on international human rights law highlights the disjuncture in international human rights law, namely that as 'the number of *rightless* people grows [...] human rights norms and standards proliferate'.[158] In this light human security operates 'less as a policy agenda', as is evident with the responsibility to protect and more as a 'critique' of international law,[159] and speaks to the oscillation between conformity and critique apparent in most approaches to human security. Hence, a UN human security policy agenda demands increased scrutiny, not only of the founding principles of international law, but also of the 'assumptions and commitments' of international legal scholarship.[160] In this way, human security has the potential to offer a 'versatile, penetrating and useful approach to the study' of international law.[161]

That said, in challenging international law to do better a UN human security policy agenda affords the opportunity to 'interrogate, evaluate and criticise the practices that make people insecure in the first place'.[162] Moreover, while the implications of a UN human security policy agenda for international law lie in the potential contribution to the normative development of international law, the translation of human security – in essence injecting the idea that people matter into UN practice – also demands the strengthening of the UN to better face the challenges of today's world and thus is intimately tied to UN reform processes which, for example, led to the creation of the Human Rights Council and the Peacebuilding Commission.[163] It is in this sense that human security, as the entitlement of all individuals to freedom from fear and want, is a welcome step forwards in the quest that began at San Francisco in 1945 for a 'life in larger freedom'.[164]

---

155   Oberleitner, 'Challenge to international law', above, n. 100, at 186.
156   Newman, above, n. 65, at 1.
157   Von Tigerstrom, above, n. 137, at 90.
158   Baxi, above, n. 146, at viii (italics in original).
159   Bellamy and MacDonald, above, n. 54, at 376.
160   H Charlesworth and C Chinkin, *Boundaries of International: A Feminist Analysis* (Manchester: Manchester University Press, 2000), at 25.
161   Buzan, above, n. 3, at 3.
162   Bellamy and MacDonald, above, n. 54, at 376.
163   UN GA Res 60/1, 'Outcome Document', above, n. 1, paras 157–160 (Human Rights Council) and paras 97–105 (Peacebuilding Commission).
164   UN Charter, Preamble.

PART IV
The Reconstruction of Rights

Chapter 15

Rights and Diverse Effects in EU Law: A Hohfeldian Approach to the Doctrine of Direct Effect of Directives

Joxerramon Bengoetxea and Niilo Jääskinen

Introduction

Directives are the most intriguing and challenging type of legal instrument used in European law. Binding as regards results, directives are open-ended as regards formalities. Law-making in the legal system of the EC thus largely depends on the effectiveness of results and the doctrine of direct effect ensures, under certain conditions, the possibility of safeguarding the results, that is, the rights recognized and the obligations imposed, in the directives. This doctrine implies that all EU jurists should engage in a certain type of interpretative technique committed to maximizing the effectiveness of the said results, which makes direct effect of directives the most important legal technique in Community law and a central element of contemporary European legal culture. This chapter explains how this process operates.

Ensuring maximum useful effect of rights contained in directives requires a strategy that reaffirms this special understanding of directives, while at the same time keeping a sound theory of the legal positions of individuals, as determined by the interplay of different legal orders. As Neil MacCormick writes, 'there has been a lot of recent and current writing about rights and related concepts, but surprisingly little that seeks to integrate this with a sustained theoretical account of the law that gives rise to them'.[1] In our opinion, WN Hohfeld's analysis of rights provides a basis for developing such a theory. Thus, the first section of this chapter presents the doctrine of direct effect in the context of directives; the second section considers the diversity of effects that can be produced by the norms contained in directives and discusses policy factors that explain these effects, together with the *structural connections between the legal orders* involved – EC or EU law and domestic laws of the member states; and the final section explores *the legal positions of individuals* as a result of the interplay of those legal orders. The approach is analytical but still aware of the many sociological and political implications behind the doctrine of direct effect and the analysis of rights.

---

1   N MacCormick, *Institutions of Law* (Oxford: Oxford University Press, 2007), at 3.

Rights in Directives and the Doctrine of Direct Effect

Rights and EC Legal Instruments

This chapter deals with 'rights' in a very particular and specific context. It analyses the legal positions of individuals – including their rights – as regulated by a particular instrument of the legal order of the European Union, the directive. In contrast to regulations, directives are not directly applicable: they do not, as such, penetrate the legal order of the member states. Directives are not addressed to individuals but to the member states. In order to function adequately and effectively, directives require the combined and coordinated application of the supranational European Union legal order where the instrument is adopted and the national laws, the legal orders of the member states where the directive is transposed or transformed into legislative instruments typical of those legal orders.

This coordination between legislators or regulators is necessary if the ultimate addressees of the norms contained therein are to enjoy their rights in a uniform way across the EU and govern their behaviour according to the common harmonized standards. The essence of such coordination consists in reaching a common view on harmonization through 'the Community method' at the supranational level, by adopting uniform norms and requiring the member states to make sure that their legal orders include those norms. Those norms will create or regulate new duties, claims, empowerments or abilities, and so on.

Transposition Problems and Direct Effect

Difficult questions arise when the member states fail to transpose the norms contained in the directive: in principle individuals are left with no harmonized regulation and continue to govern their affairs according to the laws of the member state concerned. The legal regulation for a given good or service or situation might, as a result, be different in the different member states, to the detriment of the idea of a single market: uniform and 'common' law. However, a number of legal techniques or doctrines have been developed by the combined efforts and approaches of member state jurisdictions and the European Court of Justice (ECJ) that contribute to minimizing the consequences of non-transposition or incorrect transposition.

The most significant development has taken place with the so-called doctrine or principle of direct effect, which will be analysed in this chapter. Direct effect and other techniques make it possible for individuals to benefit, in certain circumstances, from the rights contemplated in non-transposed directives. Member states' jurisdictions can thus enforce those rights under certain circumstances, in spite of the legislative inaction of their state. The empowerment of domestic jurisdictions is quite noteworthy. The analysis and the approach will therefore be rather technical, looking at legal reasoning rather than uncovering the wider and deeper political and constitutional issues involved, which are at least worth mentioning from the outset. These wider and deeper implications concern the separation of powers, the federal distribution of competences, the powers recognized to judges.

The starting point is the Community method. The EC can make law in areas where it has been attributed competence by the member states in the Treaty. In areas of exclusive competence, there are very few limits to what it can legislate, besides having to respect the limits imposed by fundamental rights protection and valid EC law, which includes *ius cogens* and general principles of law, but the operation of these limits is obviously contentious in hard cases. In areas of shared competence, there are further criteria of subsidiarity and proportionality that need to be respected.

Thus, when adopting harmonizing directives, the EC must strike a balance between the need for common norms and the legitimate claim of national or regional legislators to cater for local solutions. Since the legislator at all levels – European, member state, regional – can foresee the adoption of certain rules by the stakeholders concerned, issues of self-regulation also need to be taken into consideration. In addition, one needs to consider the role of pressure groups and lobbies, which can also be involved throughout all stages of law-making, whether the concrete legislative procedures contemplate the need of consultation or not.

However, the implementation (or transposition) of directives by the member states raises yet further questions also related to federalism and the *trias politica*. To begin with, the directive will need to be incorporated through legislative acts and there might be debates in the member states as to whether it is the federation or the federated entities, or all of them, who are competent to act. Of course, the question whether Parliament or the Government will adopt the instruments depends as much on constitutional division of powers and sources of law as it does on practice and convention. A balance between efficiency in the correct transposition within often rather stringent deadlines and legitimacy of representative democracy needs to be struck. This balance is difficult to achieve.

The analysis of the legal relation involved in direct effect should always start with the obligation foreseen in the directive, that is, an obligation on someone to do or secure something to somebody in some given circumstances and within a given time frame. The intensity of the obligation, its deontic indicator, also becomes crucial. But the questions to be solved are not the same in each situation. In some cases the question is, does the directive recognize the individual a right – a claim – to seek legal protection for performance of the obligation or a duty? In other cases the question is, does the Community have the right – the power – to enforce the obligation? And there may be a series of different problems and positions to which the same apparent reasoning is applied.

To equate the concept of direct effect with the creation of claim-rights, neglecting elements or, to use Hohfeldian terms, incidents like powers, immunities and privileges, or even interests, unnecessarily restricts the spectrum of effects produced by legal norms. Put this way, the questions at issue are not materially so different from questions that arise in any law: there is a diversity of effects produced by legal norms, and some of these effects are formal or procedural. 'Direct effect' (using that expression in a broad way) provides us with criteria for selecting or rejecting the norms to be applied and judicially enforced and for clarifying the scope of judicial competence, and this, again, is an issue of constitutional importance concerning the powers of the judiciary. The degrees or intensities of effects of a norm might depend on the question whether such norm was meant to be invoked by individuals before domestic courts and enforced by these courts without the need for further intervention by the domestic legislator. Thus, Lenaerts and Corthaut advocate a more nuanced approach to invocability which consistently aims to give full effect to EU legal instruments – even framework decisions which are expressly deprived of direct effect – as far as their status as legally binding norms allows.[2] Let us therefore explain the diversity of effects of the norms contained in directives.

---

2   K Lenaerts and T Corthaut, 'Towards an internally consistent doctrine on invoking norms of EU law', in S Prechal and B van Roermund (eds), *The Coherence of EU Law* (Oxford: Oxford University Press, 2008), at 495–515.

Diverse Effects of Norms Contained in Directives

Varieties of Direct Effect

Classical works in this area essentially distinguish two varieties of direct effect. Vertical direct effect occurs when the norms of EC law are invoked in legal relations between individuals and the state, understood in a wide sense – as covering any of its organs or emanations exerting authority or functions attributed to the state as in services of general public interest. Horizontal direct effect occurs when the norms of EC law are invoked before and enforceable upon other individuals. Horizontal direct effects of norms occur when these norms are contained in instruments that can be invoked by private parties as against other individuals. Such is the case for norms contained in Treaty provisions, or in regulations, but not in directives.

In vertical relations, a nuance can next be introduced depending on whether the norm is invoked upwardly by an individual against the state or downwardly by the state as against any individual. The state is treated as an institutional unity for the purposes of EC law, which in this respect follows a principle of single personality of the state, as in public international law. Vertical upward effects presuppose the existence of a precise, clear, unconditional obligation imposed on the state, which leaves no scope for discretion regarding the scope, the addressee and the extent of the obligation. Effects are here understood as enforceable claims invoked before the courts on the basis of an obligation binding the state, either to the individuals directly, as would be the case for norms contained in instruments or sources that are directly applicable, like Treaties, regulations and decisions, or to other member states and to the EU, as would be the case for norms contained in instruments or sources that are not directly applicable, that is, directives. The main normative relationship governed by the directive has the member states as its addressees. Therefore, any claim made by an individual to derive a right from such a normative relation will be a claim on an implied or 'logical' consequence of the primary norm addressed to the member state; it would be a claim based upon a derived norm, as a result of an interpretation of the primary normative relationship. These kinds of legal implication have been motivated and justified with reference to the special nature of Community law as a new autonomous supranational legal order with uniform effects in all the member states.

Vertical downward effects operate in a different manner. There are instruments or official sources of law that are capable of imposing obligations, duties or prohibitions on individuals. Statutes and Acts of Parliament are the classical example in state legal systems. In EU law, these instruments are the Treaties themselves, and regulations and decisions, because they are directly applicable, that is, they enter the law of the member states directly and without further need for incorporation. Therefore the obligations they might contain are immediately applicable and enforceable upon their addressees, including any individuals to whom they might be addressed.

On the other hand, directives are sources that do not immediately or directly penetrate the legal orders of the member states; they are addressed to the member states and they need incorporation into their laws, in order for the norms contained therein and creating possible duties, obligations, and prohibitions upon individuals to become enforceable upon them.

Indirect Effects

Estoppel effects derive precisely from the non-applicability of directives.[3] An individual who is summoned before national authorities or the courts in order to execute an obligation allegedly concerning this individual derived from a norm contained in a directive can invoke an immunity producing estoppel effects: a directive has to be duly implemented in the law of the member state; otherwise it cannot bind the individual.

From the perspective of the state, it is prevented from relying against an individual upon a directive that it ought to have implemented; the state cannot invoke its own wrong (*nemo auditur* or even *venire contra factum propium*). From the perspective of the individuals, they have a legitimate expectation that all obligations imposed against them are contained in instruments that directly apply. The principle of legality applies, *nulla poena sine lege*, and since there is no *lege*, no law proper, there can be no *poena*, no obligation. This principle of responsibility is linked to the principle of liberty in theories of justice, such as that of Rawls:

> [U]nless citizens are able to know what the law is and are given a fair opportunity to take its directives [meaning precepts] into account, penal sanctions should not apply to them. This principle is simply the consequence of regarding a legal system as an order of public rules addressed to rational persons in order to regulate their cooperation, and of giving the appropriate weight to liberty.[4]

The effectiveness of the directive is checked by the rule of law principle of legal certainty, which would be jeopardized if obligations were imposed on individuals through instruments that, although legally valid, are not addressed to them. However, individuals cannot safely ignore EU legal instruments that are not addressed to them but only to member states, because these instruments may have an effect on the interpretation of national law that is detrimental for their interests.

A similar logic applies to the situation concerning the absence of direct horizontal effect of norms contained in unimplemented directives: they cannot produce obligations directly on individuals and therefore an individual cannot invoke (the claims deriving from) those obligations directly against another individual.[5] This leaves the potential holder of the claim in a prejudicial situation, which is provoked by, but still depends on the behaviour of the defaulting member state. If it does not implement the directive in its legal order, individuals will not be able to rely on whatever rights the directive's norms might contain, at least as regards horizontal relations. Individuals are thus deprived of potential claims. As a result of the member state's failure to implement, the individual is left without the right contained in the directive's norms. The effectiveness of this right is dependent on member state positive action of transposition of the norm into its own law. The member state is given a deadline to adopt such action and if it does not respect the deadline, it can be found to be in breach of its Community law obligations.

---

3   *Oficier van Justitie v. Kolpinghuis Nijmegen*, Case 80/86 [1987] ERC 3969.
4   J Rawls, *A Theory of Justice* (Oxford: Oxford University Press, 1972), at 241.
5   *Marshall v. Southampton Area Health Authority*, Case 152/84 [1986] ECR 723.

The Principle of Member state Liability and Conform Interpretation

It seems rather coherent therefore that the Court should have developed the doctrine of member state liability in these situations.[6] The rationale behind this development is therefore to maximize the effects of unimplemented norms of the EC legal system existing only in directives addressed to member states that would otherwise be 'handicapped' norms, producing no effects until such time as they were completely and perfectly incorporated, almost resuscitated, into the internal legal system. A new type of effect follows therefore from the unimplemented norm of the directive, a reparation effect that can be invoked before the defaulting member state. This reparation or correction effect will later spread into other situations of breach of EC law, giving rise to the general principle of member state liability for breaches of EC law.

Also coherent with the rationale of giving maximum possible effect to norms of EC law contained in directives is the doctrine of conform interpretation developed by the Court, which leads to a situation close to horizontal direct effects.[7] In principle, the norm contained in the directive foresees a legal relation, as a result to be achieved. In the normal situations, the legislator of a member state will adopt new instruments to adapt its law to make sure that it regulates the legal relation in the same manner as the directive. But it might be the case that the internal law of the member state already regulates the legal relation in the same manner as the directive, in which case this member state will have been in compliance with the directive since its adoption. It might, however, be the case that the member state adopts no measures to transpose the directive and its internal law does not regulate the legal relation in a way that matches the directive's norm exactly.

The question can then be asked whether its internal law can, nevertheless, be interpreted in a manner compatible with the legal relation regulated by the directive. If provisions of internal law are susceptible of more than one interpretation, which is not something exceptional, and if one of the possible interpretations of those provisions renders a result, that is, a norm, which is closer or even equivalent to the legal relation that it is the object of the directive to bring about, then this interpretation should be preferred over others because it manages to give effect to the directive without straining internal law in a manner contrary to the principle of legal certainty. This principle of conform interpretation also pays tribute to the rationale of maximizing the effects of EC law, but it is clearly limited by other general principles like that of legal certainty: a provision of internal law P cannot be strained to convey a norm N, which is in conformity with the norm of the directive N', but which cannot be considered as an acceptable interpretation of the provision P. This takes us to a background theory and doctrine of interpretation, which is, in turn, related to the issues of discretion, activism and restraint and of legal culture.

Effect of Time on an EC Norm's Operation

The effect of time on the norm's operation is another interesting possibility in the spectrum of effects of norms of EC law contained in directives. There are other, interesting effects that can be produced by norms contained in directives that have not been implemented, or that have been incorrectly implemented, or even those that have been implemented. Even after implementation has occurred, the directive still is binding upon its addressees, the member states, and, as a result,

---

6 *Francovich and Bonifaci v. Italy*, joined cases C-6/90 and C-9/90 [1991] ECR I-5357 and *Faccini Dori v. Recreb Srl*, Case C-91/92 [1994] ECR I-3325.

7 *Von Colson and Kamann v. Land Nordrheinland-Westfalen*, Case 14/83 [1984] ECR 1891 and *Marleasing*, Case C-106/89 [1990] ECR I-4235.

any norm contained in the directive maintains its legal existence, its validity. The norm does not disappear simply because it will have been transposed or incorporated into internal, domestic law. Thus, a member state introducing a new rule into its legal order will have to ensure that it respects the norms contained in EC law, including, of course, the directives that have not been explicitly or implicitly derogated. Likewise, conform interpretation will always hold in these situations, and judicial review of internal law by reference to its conformity to EC law, including transposed directives, might be an available option to control the validity of a norm of internal law, which can still be defeated by the norm contained in the directive.

A related issue is that of the effects of the norms contained in directives that are not yet implemented but the transposition deadlines of which have not yet expired. The question is: exactly when are the norms contained in the directive to be considered to have entered into existence so that they produce some effects? The issue was raised in *Inter-environnement Wallonie*,[8] a case that involved a regulation adopted by the Walloon region in direct contradiction with a directive during the period for transposition foreseen in the directive. The question was whether member states have an obligation to refrain from adopting legislation that contradicts a directive that has been adopted and published in the Official Journal and thus addressed to the member states, but where the deadline for transposition has not yet been reached. The answer by the ECJ was consistent with the concept of diverse effects of norms of EC law and with the underlying rationale of effectiveness. The norms contained in the directive exist and are valid from the moment of their adoption and as such they produce *some* effects like precluding the adoption of contrary norms, or defeating them or allowing for conform interpretation. They do not create enforceable obligations as against the member states until the deadline for transposition has expired, but they can be used in the control of validity of acts adopted by the state organs.

Similarly, the obligations which directives impose on member states can give rise to diverse situations which some authors call substitution effects, *invocabilité de substitution*, *alternative Normierung*, or exclusion effects, *invocabilité d'exclusion*, or even incidental or triangular effects,[9] and which involve the possibility of invoking the norms of a directive with effects upon other individuals. These concepts refer to the consequences in the legal relationships prevailing in the internal legal order when, as a result of the operation of a norm contained in a directive, internal norms contained in primary or secondary legislation or in administrative acts or decisions are struck down, thereby affecting the interests of those individuals concerned by the said acts. Sometimes the situation is such that a different universal or individual norm of the internal legal order is activated (substitution effects), but other times there is no possible replacement since no other internal norm regulates the relationships and the one that does exist is defeated by the norm of the directive (exclusion effects).

The effects of these situations on individuals are incidental, tangential or co-lateral, and this is why they can also be referred to as inverse or 'indirect' direct effect. The definition or the concept of direct effect would need to account for these situations. Thus Sacha Prechal defines

---

8   C-129/96 [1997] ECR I-7411.

9   Referring to cases like *Smith & Nephew and Primecrown*, C-201/94 [1996] ECR I-5819; *CIA Security v. Signalson and Securitel* C-194/94 [1996] ECR I-2201; *Luxembourg v. Berthe Linster e.a.* [2000] ECR I-6917; *Lemmens* C-226/97 [1998] ECR I- 3711; *Unilever Italia SpA v. Central Food SpA* [2000] ECR I- 7535; *Wells* C-201/02, judgment of 7 January 2004 – some of them involving contractual relations, others not, but all of them concerning the intervention of administrative authorities in the exercise of economic activites by private parties, licences, authorizations, of different sorts. Authors like A Arnull, *The European Union and its Court of Justice* (Oxford: Oxford University Press, 2006) or S Weatherill, *Cases and Materials on EU Law* (Oxford: Oxford University Press, 2006) use such terms.

direct effect as 'the obligation of a court or another public authority to apply the relevant provision of Community law either as a norm which governs the case or as a standard for legal review'.[10] The effects of the norm (N1) contained in the directive are, in all these cases, to defeat the operation or the existence-validity of some norm of the domestic legal order (N2) with the result that the legal relation governed by N2 is altered or transformed. Whether this might lead as far as, for example, to annul a theretofore valid contract is something for internal law to determine according to its law on contracts, but from the point of view of the EU legal system what obtains is merely the operation and effectiveness of its own norms. Certainly all provisions but also, and this is the strong claim from the general theory of legal norms, legal norms of the legal system would then be only prima facie norms, they would be presumed to have a certain extent, normative meaning, validity and effect until such time as some other norm would defeat their operation, or restrict their scope in a specific case of application and (re)interpretation. As a result of a norm of internal, domestic law being defeated it might be that a gap obtains and that no normative solution is found, but it might also be the case that other existing norms, including principles, cover the situation or happen to be interpreted in accordance with the directive.

Interesting consequences follow for the existence of norms. The type of defeasibility we are dealing with is not one of hierarchy between the legal orders, but rather one of effects; it is based on application more so than on hierarchical superiority or primacy, a term the ECJ has positively avoided in favour of effectiveness. Thus, the normative consequence that obtains from the operation of norms of EU law (including, of course, norms contained in directives) as regards incompatible, inconsistent, contrary or contradictory norms of the domestic law of the member states is only the non-application of the domestic norm: this incompatible norm is left unapplied, as a result of the effectiveness of the norms of EU law (and the principles of primacy and uniformity) and the defeasibility of domestic norms.

Rights and Legal Positions

Rights and Effects in EU Law

We have seen the concept of right appear once and again in the context of direct effect of directives. In EU law, the concept of fundamental rights or even human rights can be distinguishable from the more classical European Community, free movement rights, often referred to as common market liberties or freedoms; but they can arguably be distinguished even from the more modern citizenship rights, which are not fundamental or universal strictly speaking. But rights in EU law can also be divided into different categories: economic rights, environmental rights, social rights and political rights.

Freedoms and rights are furthermore resorted to in many different contexts and with possibly different meanings and implications. As a result there is great confusion on the notion and concept, which potentially provokes many misunderstandings. This situation, however, has not led to any serious and certainly not to any successful attempt to do away with the term altogether, perhaps because a special magnetism, a definitely positive charge is a major feature of the term *rights*, like *democracy*. Even those currents of legal theory, such as Scandinavian realism, that take a sceptical attitude towards rights as entities or as conceptual constructs applied in legal reasoning, admit their usefulness in the exposition of law for systematizing and pedagogical purposes.

---

10   S Prechal, *Directives in EC Law* (Oxford: Oxford University Press, 2nd edn, 2005), at 241.

The very notions of 'rights' and 'effects' we resort to when analysing EC law need closer analytical scrutiny. 'The ECJ emphasizes EU rights especially in three contexts: judicial enforceability, the liability of the Member States and the Union, and finally regarding the requirements for the implementation of directives.'[11] We join Hilson and Downes in their contention that the ECJ has abandoned a simple approach to Community law rights in favour of a more complex and multi-tiered taxonomy of juridical effects, and we have just analysed these effects as regards the norms contained in directives. Indeed the 'rights/interests framework may make a significant contribution to understanding the concepts of direct and indirect effect'.[12]

Rights, as positions of benefit or advantage recognized by institutional normative order and developed through legal reasoning, ultimately concern the inter-subjective positions of persons. The legal positions of individuals and the legal reasoning involved in the discourse about them need some clarification. There are many possible approaches to rights, and the current one aims to provide some light by focusing on technical analytical aspects. The type of analysis carried out almost a century ago by WN Hohfeld can still be considered as illuminating. Hence, we agree with Carl Wellman that '[a]ny adequate theory of legal rights must begin with Wesley Hohfeld's fundamental legal conceptions'.[13]

The previous section has provided an account of the law (the interaction of domestic and supranational legal orders taking place through harmonizing directives) giving rise to the rights; and the next section now examines the legal positions involved in what we tend to group under the term 'rights'.

Rights are thus to be understood as relations or positions arising within institutional normative order, and appreciated by an interpretation of specific situations read against general rules and principles. According to MacCormick, 'it is by an interpretation of our given situation against an assumed background of institutional normative order that we can consider ourselves to have various particular rights'.[14] This makes 'right' a very markedly relational or system-relative notion, to the extent that rights are meaningless deprived of the social normative networks and relationships in which they occur. Thus, the necessary analysis of the techniques and analytical tools developed in law in order to formalize such relationships should not blind the scholar to the social background of rights: relations of power, allocations of power in society, distribution of goods in a society, theories of fairness in such distribution. Hopefully, these will enable a further and deeper understanding of social, constitutional, economic, institutional and political contexts in which reference to rights take prominence, all of which are necessary to understand rights discourses.

Structural Analysis and Justification of Rights

But our analysis is theoretical, systemic and analytical because rights do not exist in isolation; rather they belong to different normative systems, be they moral-ethical, political or legal and

---

11   S Beljin, 'Rights in EU law', in S Prechal and B van Roermund, *The Coherence of EU Law* (Oxford: Oxford University Press, 2008). Beljin follows in this classification Sacha Prechal, *Directives in European Community Law*, above, n. 10, at 117.

12   C Hilson, and T Downes, 'Making sense of rights: Community rights in EC law', *European Law Review*, 24 (1999), 121–138.

13   C Wellman, *An Approach to Rights: Studies in the Philosophy of Law and Morals* (Dordrecht: Kluwer, 1997), at 63. Two recent studies profoundly discussing the problems of Hohfeld's system are A Halpin, *Rights and Law: Analysis and Theory* (Oxford: Hart, 1997) and GW Rainbolt, *The Concept of Rights* (Dordrecht: Springer, 2006).

14   MacCormick, above, n, 1, at 163.

then again they will pertain to the different legal systems. Within the same social system, different actors may claim rights allegedly based upon or derived from different normative systems all potentially identifiable in the cultural system of society, especially of pluralist society. Some of these contending rights are simply not solved, but when the conflict reaches a court of final instance, for example, the European Court of Human Rights in Strasbourg, a final interpretation is made as to the extent of the right and the positions of the relevant actors and the level of protection afforded by the Convention.

Incidents or positions thus become crucial: the theoretical holder of the right (not in isolation, also in relation to other persons, or society at large) and in relation to this same person in different circumstances; scope of the rights (the theoretical object and extent); the justification for the right and the intension and function of the right (its consequences). The analysis carried out by Hohfeld is still valid.

A distinction between negative and positive rights is popular among some normative theorists, especially those with a bent toward libertarianism. The holder of a negative right is entitled to non-interference, while the holder of a positive right is entitled to provision of some good or service. A right to physical integrity (for example, against torture) is a classic example of a negative right, while a right to welfare assistance is a prototypical positive right. But the allegations that the right against torture has been violated will require very complex and active fact-finding investigations, reports, qualification of evidence and interpretation that would again mobilize important resources. Likewise, adequate protection against torture requires preventive and supervisory measures to be adopted at different levels. As a result, active and negative rights tend to interact.

Then there are different theories as regards the ultimate function or justification of rights: *will* or control theorists, insisting on the exercise of a power by the right holder, and *interest* theorists, stressing the fact that holders have rights not because they are actively asserted but because it is in their interest, which makes some rights inalienable and *unwaivable*. These debates are not concluded.[15] We might be accused of eclecticism, but perhaps we can find a compromise in the awareness that each theory has a point: as regards fundamental rights, interest theories can probably explain and justify legal claims more accurately, especially when debating the rights of persons whose abilities and powers to invoke them are seriously damaged or maimed, but as regards less fundamental, more technical positions and certainly the possibility to invoke rights derived from norms contained in directives will theorists carry the day because invocability is so close to normative control or 'transactional capacity' by the holder. 'That rights would be practically useless without remedies does not make remedies constitutive of rights'.[16] Control theorists might very well be confusing the right with its enforcement, true; but without access to 'receptive' courts as relevant enforcers to protect one's interest it would have been impossible to develop the diverse effects of norms of Community law contained in directives that were not transposed. The rights were potentially contained in the directives, or in the very system of Community law, using the idea of system as a regulative ideal, but it is the interpretation by the ECJ and their enforcement by national courts that deployed their effects. But again, one can note that the will of individuals has been protected in order to safeguard the effectiveness of the Community legal order, and this is a legal policy interest of European integration.

---

15   GW Rainbolt's 'neo-Hohfeldian' theory of rights as justified normative constraints presents a third alternative to the discussion. See Rainbolt, above, n. 13, at 117–56.

16   MacCormick, above, n. 1, at 120.

It is important to remember that the positions of actors in the diverse effects of norms contained in non-transposed directives concern two legal systems, if not more: that of EU law and that of the member state, and that shifts in legal positions may take place between these systems.[17]

WN Hohfeld's System of Fundamental Legal Conceptions[18]

Wesley Newcomb Hohfeld (1879–1918) published his famous article 'Some fundamental legal conceptions as applied in judicial reasoning' in *Yale Law Journal* in 1913.[19] There he introduced eight fundamental legal conceptions or notions that allowed a more accurate presentation of the legal relations between subjects than the traditional notions of rights and duties.[20] According to Hohfeld, the term *right* has in legal language four basic meanings. These meanings are a 'right': (1) as a simple right or a claim(-right); (2) as a privilege or a liberty; (3) as a power or a competence; and (4) as an immunity.[21] In the following, these four meanings are referred to as Hohfeldian entitlements. Their jural opposites, that is, duties, 'no-rights' (or no-claims), liabilities and disabilities are referred to as Hohfeldian burdens. We use the term 'Hohfeldian element' to refer to both entitlements and burdens.

In Hohfeld's system, the concepts form pairs of correlates when they are juxtaposed within the context of a legal relation between two subjects (parties A and B). These correlates are:

A: claim	B: duty
A: liberty	B: 'no-claim'
A: power	B: liability
A: immunity	B: disability

The correlate relations between the concepts mean that:

- if A has a claim that B shall do Φ, then B has a duty to do Φ;
- if A has a liberty against B that Φ, then B has a no-claim (that is, no right to claim that) A Φ;

---

17   On the idea of shifts see MacCormick, above, n. 1, at 143: 'Real rights are grounds for a variable and shifting set of consequential rights, powers, duties, liabilities, and disabilities, the rights being at least in reasonable measure hedged around with immunities against unilateral divesting.'

18   The remaining part of this chapter is based on N Jääskinen, 'EU ja Hohfeld', in H Kanninen, H Koskinen, A Rosas, M Sakslin and K Tuori (eds), *Puhuri käy. Muuttuva suomalainen ja eurooppalainen valtiosääntömme, Heikki Karapuu 30.12.1944–15.6.2006* (Helsinki: Edita, 2008). Hohfeld's system, especially its logical and semantic problems, has been met with both wide support and severe opposition. We shall not enter here into a deeper discussion of these matters.

19   WN Hohfeld, *Fundamental Legal Conceptions* (New Haven, CT: Yale University Press, 1964, 4th edn, 1966).

20   According to Hohfeld, one of the greatest obstacles to a clear understanding of legal problems frequently arises from the express or tacit assumption that all legal relations may be reduced to 'rights' and 'duties'. Ibid., at 35.

21   The terminology of Hohfeld's system is not uniform. Different writers use different synonymous terms as follows: (a right = a simple right = a claim-right = a claim); (no-right = no-claim); (a privilege = a liberty = a freedom); (a power = a competence = an ability); (a disability = no-power). It should be noted that Hohfeld's intention was to purify legal language at the conceptual level, not to change current linguistic usages of legal English.

- if A has a power with respect to B concerning Ψ, then B has a liability with respect to A concerning Ψ;
- If A has an immunity against B concerning Ψ, then B has disability (no power) with respect to A concerning Ψ[22]

The corresponding relations between the jural opposites are:

- A: claim that Φ   ¬ (A: no-claim that Φ)
- A: liberty that Φ   ¬ (A: duty to ¬Φ)
- A: power Ψ   ¬ (A: disability Ψ)
- A: immunity Ψ   ¬ (A: liability Ψ)[23]

Hohfeld's fundamental conceptions are not logically independent but they are reducible in terms to the concept of a duty (and/or a claim-right).[24]

In Hohfeld's system, 'power' and 'immunity' are second-order concepts in relation to 'claims' and 'liberties'. The latter mentioned have acts/omissions as their objects. On the other hand, powers and immunities concern changes of claims or liberties. Hence, A has a power with respect to B if A can change the Hohfeldian elements pertaining to B's position and correspondingly B has a liability with respect to A. Similarly A has an immunity against B if B does not have a power to change the Hohfeldian elements pertaining to A's position, that is, B has a disability with respect to A.

In Hohfeldian terms, the parties can, in addition to individuals, be legal persons, authorities and institutions etc. It should be recalled that individual (subjective) legal rights cannot be identified with single Hohfeldian entitlements. For example, the right of property ownership is a complex whole that includes all four types of Hohfeldian entitlements. From this perspective Hohfeldian elements can be regarded as elementary particles of legal thinking that are combined as atoms and molecules in the various 'rights' and 'obligations' present at different legal relationships.

A Hohfeldian Framework for the Analysis of Direct Effect

The notion of direct effect has from the very beginning been linked to situations where Community law has been studied from the point of view of private litigants in national administrative or judicial proceedings. This notion, echoing the vocabulary used by the ECJ in the *Van Gend en Loos* case, was for a long time understood as the capacity of Community law to create subjective rights (Community rights, individual rights) that must be afforded legal protection in the national courts. However, it is maintained in the newer doctrine that the notion of direct effect is no longer linked to the subjective Community rights of the individuals.[25] The notion is seen as expanding to a more

---

22   The variable Φ refers to acts (or omissions) whereas the variable Ψ refers to changes pertaining to the Hohfeldian elements of the parties.

23   The relation of an opposite cannot be interpreted as a similar binary notion like the correlate. For example, the opposite of A's claim is A's no-claim, not B's no-claim or B's duty, of which the last one correlates with A's claim. See MI Niemi, 'Hohfeld ja oikeuksien analyysit' (Rovaniemi: Lapin yliopisto, 1996), at 45–46.

24   See, for example, J Finnis, *Natural Law and Natural Rights* (Oxford: Clarendon Law Series, 1980, reprinted with corrections 1986), at 199–200, and Halpin, above, n. 13, at 47.

25   Sacha Prechal concludes (at 305) that '[o]ne should not equate, on the one hand, the concept of direct effect and, on the other hand, the creation of rights'. S Prechal, 'Member state liability and direct effect', *European Business Law Review* 17 (2006), 299–316.

general entitlement to initiate judicial review concerning the compatibility of national legislation or national administrative practices with the EU law obligations of the member states.

We have found it interesting to conceptualize direct effect of EU law in different legal relations by using Hohfeldian concepts.[26] This is based on the assumption that direct effect expresses itself as a legal shift or transition where the original Hohfeldian elements pertaining to the position of the parties according to national law are changed because of EC law.

We shall use the following symbols in the presentation:

EU =	European Union
MS =	Member state
PP =	private party (= $\neg$ MS according to the wide definition adopted by the ECJ)[27]
Φ =	act variable
Ψ =	variable referring to a change of Hohfeldian elements
$\neg$ =	negation

As we have explained earlier, direct effect of directives concerns how the EU law obligations of the member states are reflected in the legal position of private parties. EU law creates obligations to member states either directly, as legal consequences of the provisions the Treaties, or indirectly, on the basis of the legal acts that the EU institutions have adopted using their powers pursuant to the Treaties.

We can thus separate between two situations:

An EU obligation directly stemming from the Treaties
1.   EU: claim that MS Φ
        MS: duty to Φ
2.   EU: claim that PP Φ (for example, Articles 81 and 82)
        PP: duty to Φ

However, more often the Treaties create powers to the EU and its institutions, and a pattern of conduct, that is, a norm, is prescribed to the member states by using this competence. The prescribed patterns of conduct in conjunction with the general provisions of the Treaties on the obligations of the member states create a concrete EU obligation. Hence, disregard by a member state of its obligations provided in the secondary EU legislation entails a Treaty infringement:

An EU obligation stemming from the excercise of an EU competence
EU: competence to Ψ + exercice of the competence $\Psi \rightarrow$ EU: claim that Φ
MS: liability that Ψ
MS: duty to Φ

The purpose of the Hohfeldian reconstruction of the notion of direct effect as it has been expressed in the jurisprudence of the EJC is to demonstrate that in the situations of direct effect the membership obligations of member states, which are Hohfeldian burdens, are transformed into Hohfeldian entitlements of individuals. In principle, a EU obligation of a member state cannot be transformed

---

26   Hilson and Downes, above, n. 12, also present a Hohfeldian analysis of Community rights. However, they limit their discussion to claims and immunities disregarding liberties and powers. Their perpective is more doctrinal and less legal-theoretical than ours.

27   Non-member states and international organizations are not taken into account in this definition.

to a duty of a private party. (However, as described earlier, directly applicable EU law may create Hohfeldian duties to private parties, as in the law of undistorted competition.)

Direct effect is not a logical deduction derived from EU law, neither does it follow from a rule of general international law or from a principle belonging to the common constitutional traditions of the member states. Rather it is something that Alexander Peczenik has described as non-logical transformations in law. These non-logical 'jumps' in legal reasoning are based on substantive legal arguments, in EU law mostly on the principle of effectiveness (so-called *effet utile*).[28] It is essential to note that we are speaking of a choice made in the jurisprudence, not of a logical necessity.

Direct Effect as a Hohfeldian Liberty

Typical cases of direct effect are those where private parties invoke EU law rules in order to prevent the application of a duty-imposing national rule to them. Already the *Van Gend en Loos* case concerned the possibility for a private party to invoke standstill provisions of the EEC Treaty in order to escape the application of raised customs duties. In the *Becker* case a German undertaking invoked a tax exemption stipulated in the sixth VAT directive.[29] Whereas the directive had not yet been duly implemented in Germany, Mrs Becker had been imposed VAT according to the national rules. ECJ declared that in such situations individuals could invoke the sufficiently clear and unconditional provisions of the directive aiming at the creation of individual rights.

In situations like the *Becker* case the normative starting point is national law. The original relationship between the member state and the private party can be described in Hohfeldian terms as follows:

> *The national situation*
> MS: claim that PP do Φ
> PP: duty to Φ

The value of act variable Φ can be defined as 'pay the tax f'. Pursuant to national law the member state has the right to claim the tax f and correspondingly the private party has a duty to pay the tax f.

A prohibition or an obligation prescribed by an EC norm transforms the claim of the member state to its opposite, that is, to a no-right (no-claim) that in Hohfeld's system is the opposite of a claim. However, translation of the effects of an EC rule into Hohfeldian terms is not unproblematic because of the ambiguities inherent in Hohfeld's concept of an opposite. The opposite of the Hohfeldian position of the member state is 'MS: no-claim that PP Φ', that is, that the member state lacks a claim against PP to require that she does act Φ, that is, pays the tax f. However, the Hohfeldian opposite of the position of the private party according to national law is not 'PP: liberty that Φ', viz. PP's liberty to pay the tax f, but PP's liberty that $\neg\Phi$, that is, her liberty not to pay the tax f. This follows from the fact that the Hohfeldian entitlement corresponding with a no-claim is a liberty and the opposite of a liberty is a duty concerning the contrary act. By definition a liberty is the absence of a duty concerning the contrary act. Similarly the correlate of A's liberty to do Φ is B's no-claim concerning the contrary act $\neg\Phi$.

---

28   Hilson and Downes, above, n. 12, at 133 refer to the principle of effectiveness as an explanation to the ECJ jurisprudence on direct effect. See also J Bengoetxea, 'Is direct effect a general principle of European law?', in U Bernitz et al. (eds), *General Principles of European Community Law in a Process of Development* (The Hague: Kluwer Law International, 2008), at 3–24.

29   Case 8/81, Becker [1982] ECR 53.

Direct effect of EC law in situations like the *Becker* case can be expressed as follows:

EU law situation
PP: privilege that ¬Φ ↔ no-duty that Φ
MS: no-right that PP Φ

Following the definition presented above the position of the private party (liberty that ¬Φ) is equivalent with the absence of her duty that Φ, or concretely, with the absence of PP's duty to pay the tax f. Correspondingly the 'no-claim' of the ember state means that it cannot require the private party to perform act Φ. Thus the member state lacks the right to claim Φ, that is, to impose the tax f on PP. However, the discussion on Hohfeldian privileges or liberties usually concerns the right of the holder of the liberty to do something, that is, the absence of a duty concerning a contrary act which is the omission of the positive act in question. In those cases the no-claim that is the correlate of A's liberty in question can plausibly be interpreted as an absence of B's right to prohibit the act, that is, to impose a negative obligation of conduct regarding the act in question.[30]

Direct effect of EU law appears very often in situations of the last mentioned kind, especially as far as the four freedoms of the internal market are concerned. In these situations a liberty or an internal market freedom based on EU law sets aside a prohibition based on national law.[31] This shift can be expressed as follows:

The national situation
MS: claim that PP ¬Φ
PP: duty that ¬Φ

Direct effect of EU law leads to a reversed situation:

EU law situation
PP: privilege that Φ ↔ no duty that ¬Φ
MS: no-right that PP ¬Φ

As the value of the act variable Φ can be ascribed, for example, carrying on of professional activities without a required national diploma if a member state is pursuant to EU law obliged to recognize the relevant diplomas issued by the other member states. However, as demonstrated by the *Becker* case, in tax law contexts the direct effect of EU law appears as an absence of fiscal obligations based on national law, that is, as liberty to refrain from acts prescribed by national law.

The member states owe their EU law obligations to other member states as contracting parties to the Treaties or to the Union as a whole. In situations like the *Becker* case, the member states do not have Hohfeldian duties to private parties, neither do private parties have against them Hohfeldian claims stemming from EC rules with direct effect. If we, as WN Hohfeld himself did,[32] accepted as rights in the strict sense only claim-rights, we could not speak of Community rights of the individuals in the context of the internal market freedoms. However, it seems plausible to describe as a right the legal position of a private party where unconditional and sufficiently precise EU law obligations of member states are reflected as liberties of private parties. In those situations

---

30   See Niemi, above, n. 23, at 35.
31   This is then extended in the jurisprudence of the ECJ from straightforward prohibitions to the removal of obstacles to free movement.
32   See Hohfeld, above, n. 19, at 38.

we could, following Carl Wellman's vocabulary, speak of an EU law core, constituted by a liberty stemming from directly effective EU rules, and surrounded by protective parameters provided by the national systems of legal protection, especially by the administrative law and/or criminal law remedies against unlawful exercise of public authority. It follows from the general principles of EU law that the member states have an obligation to uphold an effective system of legal protection to ensure that the public authorities do not infringe the EU law based entitlements of the private parties.[33]

Thus, the EU law based liberties of private parties have as their correlates no-rights (no-claims) of member states. The member states may not prohibit the private parties from doing the acts covered by the EU law liberties or to prescribe something that the private party according to EU law may refuse to do. Conceptually a no-right (no-claim) is weaker than a duty as the liberties of the private parties do not imply corresponding duties of the member states. In this respect the duties of the member states must be derived from other Treaty provisions like the legal bases concerning harmonization of laws, and from the general principles of EU law such as the principles of loyal cooperation and effectiveness of EU law.[34]

Direct Effect as a Claim-Right

EU law contains innumerable provisions that create member states' duties towards private parties and correspondingly claims of private parties against member states. Typical cases are claim-rights based on directly applicable EU provisions to receive agricultural subsidies, to belong to a national system of social security or to enjoy legal protection in competition law proceedings.[35] Usually it is not necessary to raise the issue of direct effect separately in these cases, because the *ratio legis* of these EU provisions is to create rights for individuals. Treaty provisions and directly applicable EU legal acts may create claim-rights and corresponding duties also in horizontal relationships between private parties. According to the jurisprudence of the ECJ, this is not possible in so far as directives are concerned.

Claim-rights based on direct effect of directives are not usual but it is clear that a directive can create private claims against member states if the conditions of direct effect are fulfilled. According to newer jurisprudence, claim-rights may even follow from directives, the purpose of which is not to create individual rights. The *Wells* case concerned an obligation to carry out an environmental impact assessment pursuant to Directive 85/337/EEC prior to reactivating a mine that had remained unused for several decades.[36] EC provisions on environmental impact assessment (EIA) do not intend to create rights to private parties. On the other hand, an obligation to carry out EIA may impose burdens on the economic operators concerned. Despite this the ECJ found that Mrs

---

33   See A Rosas, 'Oikeus kansalliseen oikeudenkäyntiin EU-oikeuden mukaan', in *Juhlajulkaisu Pekka Hallberg 1944-12/6-2004* (Helsinki: Suomalainen Lakimiesyhdistys, 2004), 361, at 365–66. See also Bengoetxea, above, n. 28.

34   The weakness of the Hohfeldian liberties compared to claims relates to the fact that they do not correlate with duties. Neither are liberties mutually exclusive. See N Lazarev, 'Hohfeld's analysis of rights: An essential approach to a conceptual and practical understanding of the nature of rights', *Murdoch University Electronic Journal of Law*, 12 (2005), <http://www.austlii.edu.au/au/journals/MurUEJL/2005/9.html>.

35   Less typically, or rather exceptionally, indirect creation of obligations on member statesmember states with possible duties (on operators) and rights (on individuals) can obtain in other areas like consumer protection, which is otherwise a field for harmonization through directives. See Regulation (EC) No. 2006/2004 on consumer protection cooperation.

36   Case C-201/02, Wells [2004] ECR I-723.

Wells could invoke the precise and unconditional provisions of the EIA directive and claim that an environmental impact assessment be carried out before a permission was issued for reopening of the mine.

The original situation according to national law can be presented in Hohfeldian terms as follows when Φ refers to carrying out EIA:

> *The national situation*
> MS: liberty against PP that $\neg \Phi \leftrightarrow \neg$ duty that Φ
> PP: no-right that Φ

According to national law, in the *Wells* case the member state did not have a duty to carry out an environmental impact assessment and, consequently, private parties concerned could not claim it. On the other hand, the member state may have had a liberty, that is, an option, to carry out an EIA; this depends on the content of national legislation. As a consequence of direct effect of EC law, the legal position of the member state is reversed to the contrary. Now it has a duty to Φ with a corresponding claim of the private party.

> *EU law situation*
> PP: claim to MS that Φ
> MS: duty to Φ

In the *Wells* case, the private party could invoke a directly effective EC rule even if the rule did not intend to protect her interests or to create rights to her.

Direct Effect as a Power

The second-order Hohfeldian entitlements, that is, powers and immunities, have been defined above so that A has a power with respect to B if A can change the Hohfeldian elements pertaining to B's position. Then B has, as a correlate of A's power, a liability with respect to A. Correspondingly A has an immunity against B if B lacks a power to change the Hohfeldian elements pertaining to A's position, that is, when B has a disability with respect to A. In the following we shall discuss two situations where direct effect of EU law appears as a power or as an immunity of a private party.

The first situation concerns direct effect as private party's power to require that a national court reviews the discretion exercised by the member state concerned in the transposition of a directive, that is, the power to initiate legality review or judicial review of transposition. We use as an example the *Kraaijeveld* judgment of the ECJ.[37] Also this case concerned the EIA directive. In situations covered by Annex II to the directive, the member states have certain discretion as to whether an EIA is required or not. Because of this discretion the Dutch Supreme Administrative Court (*Raad van State*) had in another case found that Annex II of the directive had not direct effect and that an individual could not rely on it. The ECJ found, however, that despite the discretion that Annex II left to the member states of EIA, this discretion was limited by the general rules provided in Article 2 of the directive. It was up to the national courts to review that national implementation took place within the margins of discretion pursuant to the directive.

In Hohfeldian terms, the *Kraaijeveld* judgment recognizes that private parties have an EU law-based power to change the legal position of member states. According to national law, the legal

---

37   Case C-72/1995, Kraaijeveld [1996] ECR I-5403.

position of the member state was 'no duty to Φ' as it was not obligatory to carry out an EIA under the prevailing circumstances. According to the ECJ the legal position of the member state was $\neg\Phi$ or Φ depending on whether the national court found that the solution $\neg\Phi$ adopted during the transposition of the directive fell within the margin of discretion allowed by the directive. Thus the dynamics of the legal position of the member state can be described as the following path:

$$\text{Raad van State: } \neg\Phi \;\rightarrow_1\; \text{ECJ: } \neg\Phi \text{ or } \Phi \;\rightarrow_2\; \text{Raad van State: } [\Phi?]$$

This means a shift from the absence of a duty to its possible existence and to the final outcome of the case (that remains unknown to us).

Pursuant to the earlier decision of the *Raad van State*, the EIA directive did not have direct effect concerning the relevant issue, and, consequently, an individual could not rely on it. The private party could not invoke the directive in order to find out whether it was correctly transposed, which also determined the answer as to the existence of an obligation to carry out an EIA in the case. When we define Ψ as a power to call for judicial review, the original situation pursuant to national law is as follows:

> *The national situation*
> MS: immunity with respect to PP concerning Ψ
> PP: disability, that is, absence of power, concerning Ψ

According to national law the private party did not have the power Ψ to initiate judicial review concerning the correctness of the transposition of the directive. Hence he has the opposite of a power, that is, a disability with respect to the member state concerning Ψ. The correlate of the private party's disability is the member state's immunity which means that the private party cannot change the first order Hohfeldian elements (in this case $\neg\Phi$) of the member state's position.

The judgment of the ECJ recognizes the power of the private party to invoke the directive, or, in other words, to have the correctness of the transposition reviewed by a court. This changes the legal position of the member state at the level of primary Hohfeldian entitlements as it causes a transition from the absence of a duty to a situation where the existence of the duty becomes unclear. Hence, the private party has a second-order Hohfeldian entitlement, that is, the power Ψ with respect to the member state. This power has as a correlate the member state's liability because it cannot prevent this transition. (It should be noted that it is up to the national court to rule on whether an EIA is to be carried out or not. In the path presented above the power of the private party concerns step $\rightarrow_1$ but not step $\rightarrow_2$.)

The EU law situation is as follows:

> *EU law situation*
> PP: power Ψ
> MS: liability with respect to PP that Ψ

Hilson and Downes discuss extensively situations where direct effect of EU law materializes as procedural rights of individuals.[38] For some reason they do not apply Hohfeld's concept of a power in this context. In our opinion they also fail to make the necessary distinction between the grounds

---

38   Hilson and Downes, above, n. 12, at 131–37.

or justifications of rights or entitlements and the question how they appear in a certain relationship between subjects.

Hohfeld's system takes the parties to a relation (A and B) as given. This is problematic regarding agreements that create rights for third parties C, as in those cases in which it is not possible to determine who is the holder C of a claim corresponding to a duty in the relation between A and B.[39] Thus, in the study of EU law, an answer to the question of whether a member state's (Treaty based) duty creates a corresponding right to a private party cannot be deduced from Hohfeld's system. On the other hand, using Hohfeldian concepts, we can describe analytically the jurisprudence of the ECJ where this kind of reasoning has been approved.

Direct Effect as Immunity

The fourth Hohfeldian entitlement, immunity, means absence of a liability and corresponds with a disability. If B lacks a power with respect to A, then A has no liability with respect to B, or B cannot change the Hohfeldian elements pertaining to A's position and A has an immunity against B.

The *CIA Security* case concerned legal consequences of the non-notification to the Commission of the Belgian technical regulations on alarm systems in a dispute between two undertakings relating to alleged disloyal competition. The relevant national regulations had not been notified to the Commission before their adoption as required by Directive 83/189/EEC. In its judgment the ECJ found that the directive also had legal effects in a horizontal relationship. The national regulations adopted in infringement of the directive were further considered as *non-scriptum* between the private parties (*invocabilité d'exclusion*). This means that not even private law claims can be based on such national regulations.

The legal position of the undertaking (CIA Security) with respect to the authorities could be interpreted as a Hohfeldian liberty. Because the undertaking lacks a duty to not use equipment that does not conform to the national regulations, it has a Hohfeldian liberty to use it. Correspondingly, the Hohfeldian element of the position of the competitors and/or authorities with respect to CIA Security is a no-claim. The reasoning of the ECJ is not limited to rebut an individual claim but it emphasizes that no claims whatsoever against CIA Security can be derived from national regulations that have been adopted in conflict with the procedural requirements stemming from the directive. From this perspective, the CIA Security judgment raises the need of a more comprehensive and dynamic Hohfeldian analysis of the legal relations. It allows us to describe a situation where a member state may neither afford legal protection to any private claims nor raise itself any administrative or penal charges on the basis of national regulations that have not been duly notified prior to their adoption.

Thus, the starting point according to national law is a member state's power Ψ, without a prior notification to the Commission, to adopt and apply regulations on product requirements and to change the Hohfeldian elements pertaining to the legal position of undertakings in that context:

The national situation
MS: power Ψ
PP: liability with respect to MS concerning Ψ

---

39   Finnis, above, n. 24, at 202–5.

Also, in this situation, direct effect of EU law reverses the legal position. The opposite of the member state's power is disability, and the Hohfeldian entitlement of the other party correlating with a disability is immunity. Hence, the EU law situation can be presented as follows:

> *EU law situation*
> PP: immunity against MS concerning Ψ
> MS: disability with respect to PP concerning Ψ

It should be noted that the EU law situation has the same structure with respect to the legal relationship between the two private parties to the dispute too:

> *EU law situation*
> PP_1: immunity against PP_2 concerning Ψ'
> PP_2: disability with respect to PP_1 concerning Ψ'

Of course, in the context of the legal relation between the private parties we cannot speak about the member state power Ψ but we have to refer to the normative effects of the exercise of that power Ψ' instead. The disability of PP_2, although it is a legal burden when compared to the national law situation, does not mean that the directive would create a Hohfeldian duty to this private party.[40]

Vertical Burdens and Horizontal Duties

As we have mentioned, EC law may have direct effect in horizontal legal relations between individuals. For example, according to the so-called *Defrenne* jurisprudence of the ECJ, the provision on equal pay in Article 141(1) EC is directly effective concerning the relationship between employers and workers. A female worker may base her claim for equal pay with male workers directly on that provision. In Hohfeldian terms, the relationship between a worker (PP_w) and an employer (PP_e) can be given the following description when Φ means 'to pay/receive equal pay for equal work':[41]

> PP_w: a claim against PP_e that Φ
> PP_e: duty that Φ

Similarly, the EC Treaty or a directly applicable EC legal act may create a Hohfeldian liberty (privilege) with a corresponding no-claim in a legal relation between individuals. For example, restrictions of competition that are prohibited in Article 81(1) EC are 'automatically void' according to Article 81(2) EC. This equals with the absence of any contractual obligations to restrict competition (Φ = 'to restrict competition according to the terms of agreement'), or in other words, legal liberty to not follow the agreement. The legal relation between the parties is as follows:

---

40   Hilson and Downes, above, n. 12, at 125–27. See the CIA Security judgment as an example of a Hohfeldian correlate pair of an immunity and a disability.

41   Formally, however, the obligation is imposed on member statesmember states: EU has a claim against MS that Φ (is ensured) and MS has a duty to (ensure) that Φ.

PP_1: a liberty that $\neg\Phi$
PP_2: no-claim against PP_1 that Φ

However, from the public law perspective, the parties have a duty to $\neg\Phi$ because the prohibition set out in Article 81(1) EC is based on public interest and sanctioned with administrative penalties.

Directives bind only their addressees, usually all the member states. The jurisprudence of the ECJ has consistently rejected the idea that a directive could directly create duties to individuals. This means that directives do not have so-called horizontal direct effect. The ECJ has recently confirmed the absence of horizontal direct effect of directives in its judgment in *Pfeiffer*.[42] The case concerned applicability of the Directive 93/104/ EC concerning certain aspects of the organization of working time (OJ 1993 L 307, p. 18) to the ambulance personnel of the German Red Cross. The Court concluded that 'even a clear, precise and unconditional provision of a directive seeking to confer rights or impose obligations on individuals cannot of itself apply in proceedings exclusively between private parties'.[43]

The structure of the legal relation between two private parties (PP_1 and PP_2) can be described as follows. A member state's duty Φ means in this context a duty to prescribe/prohibit a generic act. Correspondingly, Φ_i is an instance of Φ, that is, some singular act belonging to its semantic reference.

Absence of horizontal direct effect

EU: claim against MS that Φ PP_1: $\leftrightarrow$ no-claim against PP_2 that Φi
MS: duty that Φ PP_2:$\leftrightarrow$ liberty that $\neg\Phi_i$

Because one cannot derive duties of private parties from the obligations of the member states, a member state obligation Φ does not create to PP_1 a claim against PP_2 that Φ_i. Hence, PP_2 does not owe the duty Φ_i to PP_1. The position of PP_2 can be described as a liberty that $\neg\Phi_i$ which correlates with PP_1's position of a no-claim that Φ_i.

The principle that a directive cannot impose obligations on individuals also applies to relations between the public authorities and individuals. That EC law excludes the so-called inverse direct effect of directives was expressed, for example, in the *Kolpinghuis* judgment of the ECJ.[44] The Dutch authorities invoked the criminal law liability of an individual on the basis of a directive that had not been transposed in national law. The ECJ ruled that 'a directive cannot, of itself and independently of a law adopted for its implementation, have the effect of determining or aggravating the liability in criminal law of persons who act in contravention of the provisions of that directive'.

Hence, a directive cannot have as its effect the following transition:

The national situation	The situation prescribed by the directive
PP: liberty Φ	MS: claim against PP that $\neg\Phi$
MS: no-claim against PP that $\neg\Phi$	PP: duty that $\neg\Phi$

---

42   Joined Cases C-397/01 – C 403/01, Pfeiffer etc. [2004] ECR I-8835.
43   Ibid.
44   Case 80/86, Kolpinghuis [1987] ECR 3969.

However, the ECJ has ruled that the principle of conform interpretation may require that national law is given an interpretation that runs counter to the interests of an individual in order to make it consistent with the requirements of EC law. The ECJ confirmed this view in its recent *Kofoed* judgment, where it stated that 'although it is true that the requirement of a directive-compliant interpretation cannot reach the point where a directive, by itself and without national implementing legislation, may create obligations for individuals or determine or aggravate the liability in criminal law of persons who act in contravention of its provisions, a Member state may nevertheless, in principle, impose a directive-compliant interpretation of national law on individuals'.[45]

The ECJ has approved that both the indirect interpretative effect of directives as well as the so-called horizontal side effects of direct effect may cause negative consequences for individuals, if these consequences cannot be regarded as obligations or duties. Hence, directives may create situations where a Hohfeldian entitlement afforded to a private party by national law is transformed to a Hohfeldian burden other than a duty because of the direct effect of a directive. For example, in *Wells* the mine owner lost his possibility to restart the activity without carrying out an EIA and in *CIA Security* the competitor could not invoke the fact that the equipment of CIA Security did not conform to the national regulations.

There are, in the jurisprudence of the ECJ, some individual cases where the Court seems to have approved that a directive imposes on an individual obligations affecting another individual.[46] In Hohfeldian terms, we speak about situations where a private party has a liberty pursuant to national law but, according to the Court, the national law has to be interpreted so that the legal position of the party concerned is reversed to a duty. At the same time the position of the other party becomes a claim instead of a no-claim according to national law. The cases have concerned mandatory traffic insurance[47] and company law.[48]

There have been given various explanations to these judgments.[49] For our purposes it is sufficient to discuss the explanation according to which the duties imposed on the individual concerned were not derived from the directive but from national legislation. That, however, was because of the directive, interpreted differently than would have been the case on a purely national basis. At the level of the doctrine this explanation may be justified. If a national provision has three alternatives of interpretation (I_1–I_3) but alternatives I_1 and I_2 are not consistent with the directive, it is possible to claim that a duty imposed by the remaining alternative I_3 is not a consequence of the directive but of the national provision. However, it is also possible to argue that the duty or obligation is an effect of the directive if without it one would have chosen either of the alternatives I_1 and I_2 and excluded alternative I_3.[50]

---

45   C-321/05, *Kofoed v. Skatteministeriet*, 5.7.2007. [nyr] In this judgment, the Court referred, in addition to Kolpinghuis, also to its judgment in Arcaro (C-168/95).

46   See Hilson and Downes, above, n. 12, at 126–27.

47   C-129/94, *Rafael Ruiz Bernáldez* [1996] ECR I-1829 C-537/03, *Candolin etc v. Vahinkovakuutusosakeyhtiö Pohjola and Ruokoranta* [2005] ECR I-5745.

48   C-441/93, Panagis Pafitis [1996] ECR I-1347.

49   About the explanations see Hilson and Downes, above, n. 12, at 127–28, JH Jans et al., *Europeanisation of Public Law* (Groningen: Europa Law Publishing, 2007), at 79 and M Dougan, 'When worlds collide! Competing visions of the relationship between direct effect and supremacy', *Common Market Law Review* (2007), 931–63.

50   The official position of the ECJ has been expressed its president Vassilios Skouris as follows: 'Contrary to suggestions to the opposite, the Court never overruled the general rule that directives can not produce horizontal direct effect. Rather, it promoted the *effet utile* of Community law by imposing on the national judge the obligation to construe national law in conformity with the directive in question.' V Skouris,

Conclusion

Our discussion shows that direct effect of EU directives can be described as a situation where the legal position of the parties pursuant to national law and expressed in Hohfeldian terms is reversed to its mirror image. The private party who has a Hohfeldian burden according to national law receives, as an effect of EU law, against the member state an entitlement or 'Community right' corresponding to the burden and vice versa. The concepts of a power and an immunity enable a description of situations where the effect of a EU rule is not the creation of a material substantive right on an individual but a dynamic competence of an individual to initiate judicial proceedings concerning application of EU law or non-application of national law. The empowerment of individuals on the basis of claims based on EU law and the institutional behaviour of courts favouring the admissibility of such claims and sometimes enforcing them are crucial to these developments.

There are some judgments of the ECJ that can be seen as imposing duties on individuals on the basis of directives. This is a consequence of the operation of the doctrine of direct effect, and effectiveness as a general principle of European law. Doctrinally the ECJ does not consider them cases of horizontal direct effect and from a legal-theoretical point of view the burdens on individuals following from such judgments can be said to have their source in national law, not in the directives. The Court is keen to be seen as respecting the limits of 'permissible interpretation'; but the meaning of this expression cannot be determined in advance; it is a function of the dominant legal culture.

The application of Hohfeld's categories, in the context of interacting legal orders, gives rise to quasi-pluralist situations or positions that can be approached from different legal and ideological standpoints, either privileging national law or making it yield to the directive. But, at any rate, Hohfeld's analysis provides the necessary theoretical support for the type of constitutionally meaningful social action the ECJ and many domestic jurisdictions are engaging in: opting for an interpretative strategy that maximizes the (effects of the) results intended by unimplemented directives while at the same time safeguarding the limits of legal certainty in interpretation, the federal distribution of competences between legal orders and the separation of powers between judge and legislator.

'*Effet utile* versus legal certainty: The case-law of the Court of Justice on the direct effect of directives', *European Business Law Review* (2006), 241–55, at 254–55.

Chapter 16

Investor's Rights to Disclosure of Complex Financial Instruments: A Risk Symmetric Analysis

Joseph Tanega

In this chapter, we compare investors' rights to ever-increasingly complex financial instruments under US and EU securities law, and explore the various differences through the lens of a risk symmetries theory.[1] Complex financial instruments are principally any sort of financial contracts that are usually in form of a debt or a note manufactured by financial institutions such as investment banks and sold to a variety of market participants, such as commercial banks, central banks, pension funds and insurance companies. These instruments are bought and sold like commodities and form the fabric of financial trading around the world. It is a fabric that interlinks parties throughout the world by the very terms and conditions of the contracts, which refer to indices such as stock prices or commodities prices, and by referring to the performance of each other.

In this densely complex market space, we ask 'Why is it so complex?' In order to answer this question, we limit the scope of our enquiry to identify a set of high-level principles relating to investors' disclosure rights to ever-increasingly complex financial instruments and to focus on the features of disclosure requirements of a particular complex financial instrument in its generic form, namely, the asset-backed security and the legal-financial technique, more generally called, securitization. The concept of disclosure underlies all securities regulations and simply means that the party issuing the complex financial instrument must reveal in writing certain types of information required by securities regulations that will better inform the potential buyers about the party who is selling the instrument, how the instrument will pay the buyer and what are the events and risks that may occur to disrupt payment to the buyer. The concept of securitization, which is defined more specifically in the following section, is simply the financial-legal technique whereby the contractual promises to pay a certain amount by a large group of promissors (called 'receivables') are transferred to a legal entity such as a corporation or a trust (the so-called 'special purpose vehicle' or SPV) and the SPV then sells said receivables to investors in the form of promissory notes. The first part of the securitization process where the receivables are created between the obligors (for example, mortgagor-borrowers) and the originators (that is, retail banks or savings and loans companies) is called 'origination'. The second part of the securitization process whereby the notes issued by the SPV are sold in various classes of notes or 'tranches' to investors is called 'distribution'.

Our focus on asset-backed securities and securitization is not entirely arbitrary, since these instruments and their implied originate-to-distribute business model are generally considered to be the catastrophic epicentre of the global credit crisis.[2] In many minds, asset-backed securities,

---

1 See J Tanega, 'Securitisation disclosures under Basel II: Part II-Applications of the risk symmetry principle to economic substance over legal form', *Journal of International Banking Law*, 21/1 (2006), at 7–11.

2 See M Crouhy and S Turnbull, 'The Subprime Credit Crisis of 07', 5 March 2008, at 3, available at SSRN <http://ssrn.com/abstract=1112467>.

especially residential mortgage-backed securities (RMBS) linked to subprime mortgages, and securitization, need to be understood before we can comprehend the etiology[3] and continuing illiquidity[4] of the credit crisis. Illiquidity simply means the state of market trading failure, that is, the state of the market where there is no buyer for sellers or no seller for buyers and, thus, no market price for the item in question. Although there is no single regulatory definition of subprime mortgages, in general, we mean the type of mortgages that are the product of defective origination processes, whereby the credit history and character of the mortgagor were not screened prior to loan approval and the basis of mortgage approval was simply on the assumption that the value of the residences would go up forever. This faulty origination process contributed to the growth of securitization which in turn inflated the prices of houses, and together securitization and house price inflation created a massively expanded financial bubble. Our purpose, however, is not to provide a detailed history of the credit crisis but rather to examine the logic of investors' rights to disclosure as found in US and EU securities regulations in terms of a risk symmetries analysis and which rights are now being asserted in the form of a giant wave of litigation[5] and politicized calls for increased government aid to the foreclosures and delinquency problems in the housing market.[6] In fact, the problem has escalated to a level of global systemic risk or the fear of global financial chaos, for as of 20 September 2008, the US Secretary of the Treasury, Hank Paulson, has proposed new legislation for the establishment of a $700 billion fund to buy up the illiquid mortgage-backed securities.[7] From the perspective of market participants, the problem in the short term is how to kick-start the asset-backed securities market, which has been on strike since August 2007,[8] and in the long term how to fashion financial regulations that aim to eradicate or at least reduce future bubbles and ameliorate systemic risk.[9] We ask: (1) what are the genuine rights of investors to asset-backed securities in the worlds pre-default and post-default of the credit crisis; and (2) how might we wish to design investor rights that are fair given the complex nature of the financial instruments? It is our hypothesis that if complex financial instruments were designed with the specific objective of social fairness, they would have the catalytic power to kick-start the asset-backed securities market and require only little more regulation to clarify or enhance the disclosure requirements of already existing disclosure regimes.

---

3   Ibid., at 4–8. See also Y Demyanyk and O van Hermert, 'Understanding the Subprime Mortgage Crisis', 5 March 2008, at 1, available at SSRN <http://ssrn.com/abstract=1020396> claiming that the 2007 credit crisis was detectable in 2003. Ibid., at 1–2.

4   See M Wolf, 'Why Britain's economy will change', 2 May 2008, *Financial Times*, at 13 and J Mackintosh, 'Government bond traders pulled into deleveraging vortex', 2 May 2008, *Financial Times*, at 39.

5   R Evans, 'It will be hard to prove issuer fraud', *International Financial Law Review* (2008), available at <http://www.iflr.com/default.asp?Page=9&PUBID=263&ISS=24675&SID=705703&LS=EMS176061>, stating '[...] more than 280 class actions were filed with federal courts in 2007 that relate to sub-prime'.

6   See B Frank, 'FHA Housing Stabilization & Homeownership Retention Act', 13 March 2008, available at <http://www.house.gov/frank/fha0308.html>.

7   See Anonymous, 'Text of Draft Proposal of Bailout Plan', setting out the 'Legislative Proposal for Treasury Authority to Purchase Mortgage-Related Assets', 20 September 2008, available at <http://www.nytimes.com/2008/09/21/business/21draftcnd.html>.

8   For an explanation of the continuing illiquidity of triple-A CDO bonds despite their historical cheapness, see G Tett, 'Why triple A prices are out of sync with fundamentals', 2 May 2008, *Financial Times*, at 38.

9   J Eatwell, 'The challenges facing international financial regulation', in AK Dutt and J Ros (eds), *Development Economics and Structuralist Macroeconomics* (Cheltenham: Edward Elgar, 2003), at 354.

This chapter is divided into three sections. In the first section, we define asset-backed securities operationally and in terms of the disclosures regimes of the US and EU. In the second section, we re-examine the theory of disclosures à la Akerloff's classic Nobel Prize winning 1970 paper on lemons and find an ironic twist to the theoretical tale. In the third section, we present investor rights to disclosure in the context of pre-default and post-default states of asset-backed securities world, and ask ourselves, can we not innovate better? As a necessary preliminary, we provide operational and regulatory definitions of asset-backed securities and the rights of investors to disclosure therein.

Operational and Regulatory Definitions of Asset-Backed Securities

Operational Definition

In general, asset-backed securities finance or securitization may be defined as the set of legal and financial techniques that transforms illiquid assets into tradable financial instruments. The practice of securitization throughout the world, whether or not there are securities regulations governing their special purpose nature, is a multi-step procedure which requires: (1) the recognition of the legal rights to assets that are, in effect, obligations of payment to an originator; (2) the transfer of these legal rights to a clean unencumbered legal vehicle in the form of either a trust or special purpose corporate vehicle (SPV) which transfer achieves the legal effect of 'bankruptcy remoteness' from the credit risk of the originator; and (3) the sale of the rights to the cash flows of the assets in the SPV to investors.

The underlying assets that provide the basis for the cash flow to the asset-backed securities, can be anything that can have legal title or be legitimately owned; but are usually of a homogenous character formed by standard contracts, such as mortgages, credit card receivables, car loans, student loans and so on.[10] In its simplest diagrammatic form (see Figure 16.1), securitization is typically portrayed in terms of the obligors forming the underlying assets to an originator, which in turn transfers the title or assigns the rights to the cash flows of the underlying assets to an SPV. The SPV, being bankruptcy remote from the originator, then issues tranches of securities that are bought by investors. The proceeds from the securities sales are then used to purchase the title or rights to the cash flows of the underlying assets.

Under US Regulation AB,[11] which governs all asset-backed securities disclosures in the US from 1 January 2006, all underlying assets to an asset-backed securities transaction must have a 'self-liquidating' character,[12] meaning that the underlying receivables convert into cash within a finite period of time,[13] and the definition does not include synthetic securitizations.[14] In sharp contrast, under EU law, asset-backed securities are not limited to self-liquidating assets and may even include open investment type funds with managers having discretion to select any type of

---

10   See JD Finnerty and DR Emergy (2001) *Debt Management, A Practitioner's Guide, Chapter 8: Debt Innovations*, at 165–97; A Davidson et al., 'Securitization structuring and investment analysis' (2008) *passim* (various types of asset-backed securities).

11   17 C.F.R. §229.1100–1123.

12   See US Regulation AB, §1101(c)(1).

13   Ibid.

14   *Final Rule*, below, n. 29, at 1514.

asset,[15] and by regulatory definition, includes derivative and synthetic type of transactions.[16] Since the underlying assets are bundled together and their payment streams are assessed in a statistical manner, almost all securitization transactions rely on the relative certainty of payment of a large group of obligors.

Although there are large differences in disclosure between EU and US law, the common principle underlying both is that parties who have a significant interest in the transaction should be made to disclose their identity and their interests in the transaction in order to avoid any conflict of interest. This disclosure principle is also consistent with the principle of overcoming the information asymmetry that favours the seller.

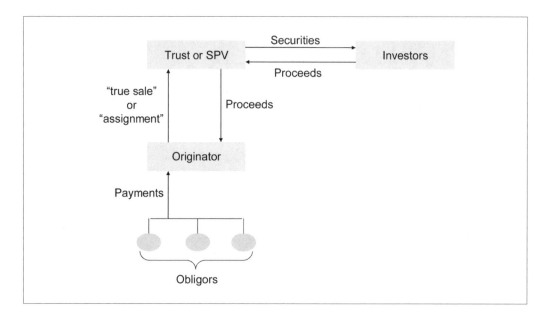

Figure 16.1 Simplified asset-backed securities transaction

Parties Responsible to Disclose or be Disclosed under EU Prospectus Regulation

Under EU law, the investor's rights to disclosure not only obligate the issuer-SPV to provide disclosures,[17] but also requires disclosures of all parties that have contributed any information to the prospectus,[18] including statutory auditors,[19] persons having direct or indirect ownerships or control between the parties in the securitization programme,[20] persons working within the issuer having

---

15   See Commission Regulation (EC) No. 809/2004 Annex VIII, Item 2.3; and Regulation AB, §1101(c)(2)(i).

16   See PR Article 2(5)(a) and (b); and J Tanega, 'Some principles of disclosure for asset-backed securities under EU law', *Journal of International Banking Law and Regulation*, 6 (2008).

17   See Prospectus Regulation, Annex VII, Item 4 *et seq* and Regulation AB §1101(f).

18   PR Annex VII items 1.1 and 1.2.

19   Ibid., 2.1.

20   Ibid., 5.2.

duties outside of the issuer in administrative, management and supervisory bodies,[21] partners with unlimited liability,[22] major shareholders of the issuer,[23] names of governmental, legal or arbitration proceedings that may have a significant effect on the issuer,[24] third party experts identified in the registration document[25] and providers of undertakings or obligors.[26] This list appears merely to require the identification of potential parties to the transaction. However, from a risk symmetric analysis the list tells us which parties the regulators think are those that pose an expected risk to the investor and therefore should be disclosed. It is important to note the obligor is excluded from any benefits in the transaction. This fact forces us to re-evaluate the risk symmetric fairness of securitization transactions.

Parties Responsible to Disclose or be Disclosed under US Regulation AB

Under section 11(a) of the Securities Act of 1933, the person having the direct and primary liability to the investor for false disclosure or omission for a false registration statement is the issuer who signs the registration statement.[27] This general rule is further limited and specified by Regulation AB to include primarily the depositor[28] deemed as the 'issuer' and therefore, primarily liable for any material misstatements or omissions.[29] Similar to the PR, Regulation AB requires that a number of 'transaction parties' be identified in the prospectus and may have indirect liability if the information that they provide is inaccurate or misleading. These parties include: the sponsor,[30] issuing entity,[31] trustee,[32] servicers and back-up servicers,[33] originator,[34] significant obligor,[35] providers of credit enhancement,[36] counter-parties to derivative instruments,[37] parties in legal proceedings against the sponsor, depositor, trustee, issuing entity or servicers,[38] parties representing other asset pools,[39] parties who prepared or provided reports,[40] affiliates or parties to related transactions,[41] and credit rating agencies.[42] While the number of transaction parties required to be disclosed under Regulation AB is larger than that required under the EU PR, the PR offers discretion to disclose a group of

---

21 Ibid., 6.1(a).
22 Ibid., 6.1(b).
23 Ibid., 7.1.
24 Ibid., 8.3.
25 Ibid., 1 and 9.2.
26 See Annex VIII items 1.2, 2.2 and 2.2.11.
27 See Securities Act of 1933 section 11(a) for persons liable for a false registration statement.
28 Regulation AB §1106.
29 See Final Rule, VI. Offerings of Asset-backed Securities, C. signatures, at 1618.
30 Regulation AB §1104.
31 Ibid., §1107.
32 Ibid., §1109.
33 Ibid., §1108(a)(1) and (2).
34 Ibid., §1110.
35 Ibid., §1112(a).
36 Ibid., §1114(b)(1).
37 Ibid., AB §1115.
38 Ibid., §1117.
39 Ibid., §1100(d)(1).
40 Ibid., §1118.
41 Ibid., §1119.
42 Ibid., §1101(h).

transaction parties larger than that found under Regulation AB. In the language of the PR, the issuer is 'entitled' to provide the appropriate set of disclosures.[43]

Other Meaningful Differences in Disclosure Requirements

Although the EU entitles the issuer to use his discretion to ferret out disclosures that are relevant to the investor's ability to make an informed assessment,[44] there are simply so many categories of disclosure which are not well-enough defined in comparison to US Regulation AB. For example, under the PR, the disclosure requirements for the structure of the asset-backed securities transaction is stated in just 13 words,[45] while under Regulation AB the disclosure requirements for the transaction structure[46] is stated in 1,551 words! This difference is so staggering for such an essential disclosure that one can only wonder whether the entire system of disclosures is being called into question. This difference *cannot* be plausibly explained in terms of a difference between principles-based versus rules-based approaches, because both disclosure systems require disclosures to factual levels of specificity for sake of investor protection. Ironically, Regulation AB is essentially by self-declaration[47] and by its own internal logic, much more principles-based than the PR, since it has a tightly defined legal concept of asset-backed securities with all the other requirements logically connected to the principled definition while the PR has an extraordinarily broad definition of asset-backed securities for which there are lacunae of required expected risks.

One giant gap that can only be interpreted as a win for the powerful pro-issuers' lobby composed of European financial institutions to the detriment of the investors is the lack of any mandatory disclosures by the servicer. Although the definition of asset-backed securities includes the bare mention of the word 'servicing',[48] there is no explicit requirement of disclosures relating to the servicer, leaving the matter to the discretion and morals, one supposes, of the enlightened issuer.

Information Asymmetry Leads to Degrees of Emptiness

Akerloff's 1970 information asymmetry theory sets out a symmetric argument for the justification of disclosures based on a world where individuals are Machiavellian, and can be used as a means for explaining why disclosures are required for securities transactions.[49] We will, however, use it to explore the limits of investor rights to complex financial instruments and show how it gives rise to both ever-increasing complexity of financial instruments and, ultimately, market failure. Akerloff's argument about lemons comes in two parts. The first part has been woven into the fabric of information asymmetry analysis like a magical origination myth, while the second part is much ignored. Both parts sound too simple to be true, but, as we shall see, together they form what might

---

43   See PR recital (5).
44   Article 5(1) of Directive 2003/71/EC.
45   PR Annex VIII, item 3.1.
46   Regulation AB §1113.
47   Final Rule, above, n. 29, at 1508, stating: 'We are adopting a principles-based definition of asset-backed security [...].'
48   See EU PR Article 2(5)(a) and (b) for the definition of asset-backed security.
49   See G Akerloff, 'The market for lemons: Quality uncertainty and the market mechanism', *Quarterly Journal of Economics* (August 1970).

be called 'logically complete and symmetric arguments' that are disturbingly persuasive if the premises are accepted.[50]

Since disclosures are at the heart of securities regulations[51] and are intended to influence behaviour,[52] the purpose of disclosures in securities regulations at least at the level of the initial public offering is to mitigate the information advantage which issuer-sellers have over investor-buyers. As Akerloff (1970) famously argued,[53] markets in which the sellers have an information advantage have a temptation to sell and represent lower quality items as higher quality items to less informed buyers. Let us call this form of information asymmetry 'dysfunctional asymmetry'. As a consequence of this dysfunctional asymmetry, the lower quality goods will tend to drive out higher quality goods from the market, which if iterated over time, will lead to an equilibrium where there is no trading at all or market failure where it becomes impossible for the participants to calculate the market value of the goods in question. Ironically, there is less chance of market collapse where the information advantage favours the buyer. Let us call this form of information asymmetry 'functional asymmetry'. Since the buyer will be able more accurately to assess the quality of the goods, the forces of supply and demand will prevail, and bad quality items will be seen for what they are and more accurate pricing will occur. That is, transactions will occur at prices distinguishing between lower level and higher quality goods.[54] Although scholars have called this latter situation information asymmetry in favour of the buyer, it would be more precise to say that the situation in which buyers and sellers transact is when they are in a state of risk symmetry.[55] That is, when their subjective perception of the risk for a given level of information is equivalent. Schwarz, in summarizing the Akerlof solution to the 'lemons problem' states that it is 'it is up to the seller to achieve a solution to this problem of quality uncertainty' and 'one obvious solution is guarantees, such as warranties on the sale of goods, in order to shift the risk from the buyer to the seller'.[56] However, the lesson to be learned for the asset-backed securities markets is that mandatory disclosures by the seller help overcome dysfunctional asymmetry so long as such information is pertinent to the investor understanding the quality of the investment. A well-structured disclosure regime that aims at functional asymmetry therefore should reduce the risk of market failure since more accurately informed investors will be able to distinguish between lower and higher quality issues, encouraging market expansion.

It is important to note that Akerloff's information asymmetry idea was further developed by Stiglitz and Weiss in their pivotal paper focusing on the credit rationing behaviour of financial

---

50   J Tanega et al., 'Codeword STRIDE: Standard Risk Disclosure Environment' in (Nov 2007) IFC, World Bank Group, forthcoming publication of IFC available from Andrey Milyutin, IFC, at <amilyutin@ifc.org>.

51   See TL Hazen, *Securities Regulations* (St Paul: West Group, 4th edn, 2002), where he states that 'federal securities law's exclusive focus is on full disclosure'. Ibid., at 740.

52   See JR Brown, Jr, 'Corporate Governance, the Securities Exchange Commission and the Limits of Disclosure' in (April 23, 2007) University Denver Legal Studies Research Paper No. 07-27, at 48 *et passim*, available at SSRN <http://ssrn.com/abstract=982444>.

53   See G Akerloff, 'The market for lemons: Quality uncertainty and the market mechanism', *Quarterly Journal of Economics* (1970).

54   See J Tanega, 'Securitization framework under Basel II: A risk based approach to substance over form', *Journal of International Banking Law and Regulation*, 12 (2005), 623–25.

55   Ibid.

56   SL Schwarz, 'Rethinking the disclosure paradigm in a world of complexity', *University of Illinois Law Review* (2004), at 25.

institutions in relation to risk-seeking and risk-averse borrowers.[57] And some researchers such as Zywicki and Adamson, have used Stiglitz and Weiss to argue that financial innovations 'have ameliorated and in many cases even reversed the traditional information asymmetry to the point where today *lenders* have more information than borrowers about the borrower's ability to repay loans or the suitability of certain terms for certain borrowers'.[58]

We might translate the Akerloffian argument into three different states. In state (1) the information asymmetry favours the seller and if the buyer and seller iterate the trade, then the market price falls to zero and the market collapses. In state (2) the information asymmetry favours the seller but there is a guarantee that the buyer accepts and pays for, which completely covers any risk to the buyer. And in state (3) the information asymmetry favours the buyer, which is the situation alluded to above by Zywicki and Adamson above, and where the trade if iterated establishes a sustainable market price, never falling to zero. State (1) would appear to be the normal state of affairs and, if nothing more, then it predicts an inevitable market collapse. State (2) draws a picture of the world where the market continues *so long as* the guarantees are credible to the buyer. And state (3) is relatively rare, where the expertise, experience, competence and inside knowledge of the buyer is superior to the seller. State (2) of Akerloff's argument may help explain the 'market expansion' of the ever-increasing complexity of financial instruments towards market collapse and, if not, extinction. This is not an empirical argument so much as a logical one.

Consider dysfunctional asymmetry in relation to asset-backed securities. The underlying policies of securities regulations in both the US and the EU emphasize both 'investor protection'[59] and 'market confidence',[60] as well as 'financial innovation'.[61] There is no inherent limit to financial innovation. If we allow financial innovation to continue because of dysfunctional asymmetry, we are merely transferring the uncertainty from one party to another, and asking for a guarantee. But then what is the nature of a financial instrument? Essentially, a financial instrument is an unfulfilled promise and here is the fault of the Akerloffian analysis. Whilst we may swap real goods for money, if we swap what should be a payment for a financial instrument, all we are doing is emphasizing the character of the unfulfilled promise. In somewhat metaphysical sounding terms, we are merely swapping the empty promise for another empty promise. If we allow 'guarantees' such as those which are so elegantly allowed under Regulation AB and the PR in the form of credit enhancement, liquidity support, swaps and other derivatives, we are actually allowing further and further degrees of emptiness.

Under the Akerloffian analysis of dysfunctional asymmetry, the credit substitution function is sufficient to stave off market collapse. But this is simply not true. The substitution function allows greater and greater pressure of performance risks to build up since the reputational risk of each party can only be substituted for by the performance risk of another. As more transaction parties are required to fulfil the essential epistemological gap, 'guaranteeing the future' so to speak, the performance risk of the legally dependent financial instruments increases. If any of the parties in

57   JE Stiglitz and A Weiss, 'Credit rationing in markets with imperfect information', *Amer. Econ. Rev.*, 71 (1981), 393.

58   Where TJ Zywicki and JD Adamson, 'The law and economics of subprime lending', *George Mason Law & Economics Research Paper*, 8/17 (2008), at 73, available at SSRN <http://ssrn.com/abstract=1106907>, set out the arguments made by Engel and McCoy in KC Engel and PD McCoy, 'A tale of three markets: The law and economics of remedies for predatory lending', TEX. L. REV., 80 (2002) (separating mortgage markets into prime, legitimate subprime, and predatory segments).

59   See EU PD recital (41) and US Final Rule on Asset-backed Securities at 1515.

60   PD recital (41) and US Final Rule Asset-backed Securities at 1590–1591.

61   See PD recital (41); and US Final Rule on 'capital formation' at 1557 and 1591.

the credit substitution game have even a whiff of discredit, then the house of promises will fall precipitously, because, after all, they are all just paper, and not goods. At the same time, the very complex financial instruments are hit the hardest because it was through the credit substitution mechanism that the financial instruments grew ever-increasingly complex. The ever-increasing complexity justified in the name of financial innovation was also justified under the pretext of meeting market demand. The just-so story told by the investment banking tribe is this: ever-increasingly complex financial instruments were necessary because there was huge market demand for them, otherwise they would not have grown. Yes, market demand for instruments that linked and depended on the worth of other instruments so that their 'inherent risks' could be sliced, diced and distributed to others who believed that they would act like primary level stable financial instruments (triple-A) used to purchase goods. In the period September 2007 to April 2008 triple-A simply descended into untradable paper.[62] Pre-credit crisis, this type of ontological essentialist argument against the nominative nature of money and the essential emptiness of financial instruments would have been laughed out of court. But, of course, the world is different now. Faith in the signs, symbols, rites and rituals of the investment banking tribe have been shaken and stirred.

A Social Reality of Disclosures Increases Noisy Complexity

Given the wide array of disclosures for asset-backed securities under EU and US securities regulations, it is important to keep in mind the reality amongst practitioners. The widely practised disclosure game is that so long as the issuer discloses material facts that are not misleading or inaccurate, he is most likely absolved of any harm to the investor caused by the item so disclosed. Thus, the informal rule among the lawyers who intend to reduce their client's risk of liability for false disclosure is 'disclose if in doubt'. This means that in the US the issuing entity of any security has a strong incentive to disclose any material fact that verges on being relevant to the decision making of the investor. In the EU, the rule is similarly broad ranging, requiring the issuer to disclose any fact or any risk that impact the investor's ability to make an informed assessment of the investment.[63] Although the US Final Rule on Asset-backed Securities repeatedly cautions against the urge to repeat the legal babble of boiler plate provisions,[64] lawyers have no incentive but to do otherwise in order to protect their client-issuers from the potential claims by investors that the disclosures were legally indefensible, that is, that the client-issuer had the chance to disclose, but did not do so.

Although the disclosure regime for asset-backed securities is very complex, there is a large body of literature defining and tracing the history of asset-backed securities as part of US legal practice, mostly on the 'cheerleading' side as Professor Kettering says,[65] but surprisingly little academic scrutiny of what the assumptions of securitization mean to society. In order to partially redress the balance, consider Figure 16.2.

---

62   See M Mackenzie, '"Super-senior" CDO investors begin to flex their muscles', 15 April 2008, *Financial Times*, at 15.

63   See PD Article 5(1).

64   *Final Rule,* above, n. 29, at 1509.

65   KC Kettering, 'Securitization and its discontents: The dynamics of financial product development' (draft as of 12 September 2007), available at <http://ssrn.com/abstract=1012937>, at 5.

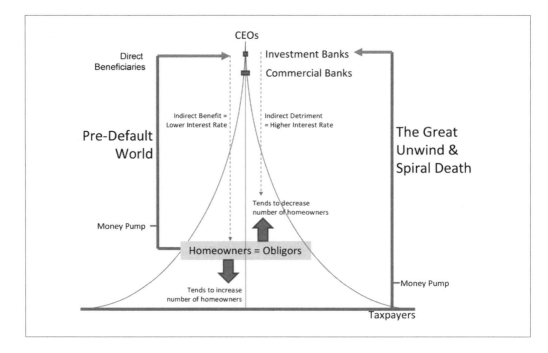

Figure 16.2 The logic of the pre-default versus post-default world

In the figure above, we have two states of the world consisting of pre-default on the left-hand side and post-default on the right-hand side, and a population pyramid with taxpayers representing the base of the population and homeowners who have mortgages as obligors, representing a smaller part of the taxpaying population. At the top of the triangle are CEOs, investment banks and commercial banks representing a tiny fraction of the population who thrive on the trading of complex financial instruments. The list of transaction parties under Regulation AB outlined above roughly corresponds to the main functional parties involved in the primary production of asset-backed securities. Identifying all the characters is not important for our purposes. The important point of the figure is that it shows how the money pumped from the homeowners up to the banks allowed banks to have an *accelerated replenishable* supply of cash to lend, with fees earned by all the various parties involved in the transaction.

In brief, from the early 1980s with a surge in growth in the late 1990s and again from 2002 to 2007, many trillions of dollars worth of asset-backed securities were manufactured with many thousands of bankers or financiers making many tens of billions in fees. Kettering quotes a figure of $3.6 trillion as the aggregate outstanding value of securitization in the US for 2006.[66] With so much cash available, this provided an indirect benefit to homeowners by increasing the amount of funds available for lending and thus, contributing to the lowering of interest rates to homeowners. In this virtuous pre-default world, securitization allows more money to circulate, significantly

---

66   Kettering, above, n. 65, at 4–5 citing Board of Governors of the Federal Reserve System, Federal Reserve Statistical Release Z.1: Flow of Funds Accounts of the United States, Flows and Outstandings, Fourth Quarter 2006, at 79 (8 March 2007) (table L.126). Available at <http://www.federalreserve.gov/releases/z1/>.

increasing the prospect of homeownership via mortgages to millions of people in the US and other jurisdictions where RMBS took hold.

When securitization fails this virtuous circulation judders to a dead stop. Where before, hundreds of billions of dollars worth of asset-backed securities per year were being pumped out, as of late August 2008 there are hardly any issues in private label residential mortgage backed securities, while government-chartered mortgage finance in the US accounted for about 90 per cent of the market by the end of 2007.[67] Structured finance products, especially collateralized debt obligations (CDOs), which were created with mortgage backed securities as their underlyings, have seen massive losses with Standard & Poor's announcing more than 4,000 downgrades in 2008, or '90 per cent of all downgrades issued to CDOs', with recovery rates for single-A or lower likely to be zero, for double-A at best 5 per cent.[68] Although many of the top banks have reported billions or tens of billions of dollars worth of loss,[69] the reported figures themselves are susceptible to miscomprehension, confusion and incredulity because the standard accounting principles for the determination of fair value of complex financial instruments appear to be unable to provide a reasonable rule for the determination of the their value.[70] The headline numbers by the 'authorities' include the OECD estimated the subprime debacle will cost approximately $420 billion,[71] the IMF estimated the fallout from the subprime mortgage crisis at $945 billion,[72] and one of the gloomiest predictions coming from Professor Roubini, not to be outdone, estimates the loss at about $3 trillion, roughly 20 per cent of the US' GDP.[73]

Returning to Figure 16.1, the arrow labelled 'The Great Unwind and Spiral Death' represents the taxpayer's money through government intervention that is being used to help stem the losses. There are a number of new policy mechanisms that the central banks and, especially, the US Fed, have used to try to kick-start the asset-backed securities market, especially the RMBS market such as allowing investment banks to put up AAA-rated mortgage-backed securities as collateral for three-month US treasury paper to the Fed. Similarly, in the UK, £50 billion of UK gilts are borrowable with AAA-rated RMBS as collateral. Howard Davies, former chairman of the Financial Services Authority, likens this game to that of putting 'dead mice' at the central bank's counter and getting 'hard cash'.[74] As the taxpayers money is put at risk to support and give confidence to the market so that major financial institutions will not fall, other areas of the financial system are put at risk. For example, with the continued stagnation of the money market, institutions are wary of counter-party credit risk, the risk of insolvency and the reputational risk of banks or funds being trapped without sufficient liquidity to meet their obligations when due. In this rumbling mess, a few traders and funds speculating on the failure of financial institutions and the market have made fortunes in short-selling.[75] The appreciable asymmetry between the pre-default world and the Great

---

67 S Scholtes, 'Fannie and Freddie drive home loans', 2 April 2008, available at <www.ft.com>.

68 PJ Davies, 'S&P delivers blow to CDOs', 29 April 2008, *Financial Times*, at 39.

69 K Guha, 'IMF points to high cost of global credit crisis', 8 April 2008, available at <www.ft.com>.

70 See International Accounting Standards Board (March 2008) Discussion Paper Reducing Complexity in Financial Reporting, available at <http://www.iasb.org/NR/rdonlyres/A2534626-8D62-4B42-BE12-E3D14C15AD29/0/DPReducingComplexity_ReportingFinancialInstruments.pdf>.

71 D Strauss, 'OECD predicts subprime loss of £450bn', 16 April 2008, available at <www.ft.com>.

72 Guha, above, n. 69.

73 M Wolf, 'A rising auction of scary scenarios', 11 March 2008, available at <www.ft.com>.

74 H Davies, 'Sharks circle Paulson's Aussie plan', 1 April 2008, available at <www.ft.com>.

75 G Soros, 'The game changer', 29 January 2009, available at <www.ft.com> and <http://www.ft.com/cms/s/0/09b68a14-eda7-11dd-bd60-0000779fd2ac.html>.

Unwind is that homeowners as the long-suffering obligors have lost because of higher lending rates and higher foreclosure rates.

To put the matter in risk symmetries terms, the pattern of trades and the flow of risks from one segment of society to another is asymmetric between the pre-default and post-default world states. The essential pattern in risk symmetric terms for Figure 16.1 is symbolized as follows, in Figure 16.3.

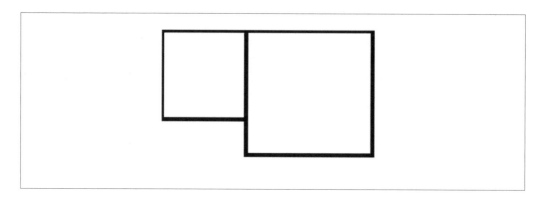

Figure 16.3 Asymmetry between pre-default and post-default world states

This childish picture serves to remind us that the flow of funds, the actual trades concerning a complex financial instrument, such as an asset-backed security, are limited to transaction parties and the expected risks of the transaction are not captured symmetrically in the post-default state since the taxpayer's funds are implicated in the post-default state of the world. In the post-default state, where the transactions are 'un-winding' and where there are insufficient cash flows to make good the promises made on the contracts, more parties are involved than those explicitly stated in the prospectus or transaction documents. This is symbolized by the larger square on the right. In a strong sense, financial instruments that pose this sort of risk asymmetry are unfair to societies in which they are unfair to the investors since (1) the parties to the original transaction and especially, the investors are not apprised of the specific extreme tail-end risks;[76] and (2) the external or social parties, that is, the taxpayers are not beneficiaries to the risk taking generated by the original transaction. Kettering, after reviewing the major scholarship critiquing securitization in the pre-default era, has argued persuasively that the '[…] prototypical securitization structure has no purpose, and no significant effect, other than to circumvent the burdens that the Bankruptcy Code places on the lender of a simple secured loan to an Originator who has gone bankrupt'.[77]

Kettering's argument is about how the securitization structure is against the fundamental rights to reapportion debt that is regulated by the Federal Government and, therefore, by society in general. This is a normative legal argument pre-credit crisis. However, post-credit crisis, Kettering's

---

76   It is arguable that they are 'apprised' in the sense that the documentation defines various types of catastrophic risks and default. However, prior to the credit crisis it would be very difficult to *comprehend let alone believe* that triple-A asset-backed securities would become illiquid. Anecdotal evidence suggests that fund managers who called the market correctly during the credit crisis failed to make the appropriate hedges by *buying* triple-A paper.

77   Kettering, above, n. 65, at 8.

argument does not go far enough, because securitization does not merely deny 'bankruptcy tax', but, in crisis, when the conditions of the securitization are required to be read and used to distribute allocations of cash flow, the parties required ultimately to foot the bill are the taxpayers. The asset-backed securities are sufficiently complex so as to require the entire society in the jurisdiction where the issuer has failed to provide sufficient cash flow to fill the shortfall, which is arguably 100 per cent of the transaction value if the securitization business model ultimately fails.

The question arises, is it possible to design complex financial instruments that are, in a word, more socially fair and, in our terms, more risk symmetric? Before answering this question, let us dip once again into the deep theory of financial innovation.

A Digression into the Nuclear Financial Economics of Financial Alchemy

Sharpe, in a pivotal article entitled 'Nuclear financial economics' (1995),[78] somewhat jokingly describes the nuclear foundations of financial economics alluding to Arrow[79] and Debreu.[80] He shows how financial engineering is based implicitly on Arrow's and Debreu's fundamental idea of an infinitely divisible contingent world, with the financial economic definition of a financial instrument, as being the set of all conditions of the world at time 1 being the same at time 2 except for the one condition of payment, meaning that any and all financial instruments can describe any and all states of the world. The fascinating theoretical assertion is that between time 1 and time 2 the only other condition of this model is that the world be absolutely unchanged. Thus, simply because we can describe a particular state of the world at time 1 as having a particular set of rights over the world embedded within a particular financial contract, it means that so long as there are no 'discontinuities', financial contracts can well define the state of the world from time 1 to time 2. The consequence of these deep ideas is that financial innovation (that is, the construction of new financial instruments) moves irrevocably towards an ever more complete coverage of the infinite contingent states of the world – the movement of which is called 'market completion'.[81]

Against this theoretical background of an infinitely dynamic growth towards market completion with ever-increasing complexity of financial instruments to meet particularly unique conditions of the contingent world, we have the counter-fact of the failure of complex financial instruments in the time of the Great Unwind.[82] We can think of the premises of the Arrow and Debreu model as being either true or false in relation to the post-credit crisis world. If the Arrow and Debreu model is incorrect then we would not have a movement towards complete markets. But this is contradicted by the facts in the Great Unwind because there were short-sellers in the derivative markets that allowed individuals to take positions on credit collapse. Assuming that the Arrow and Debreu model is fundamentally correct, how was it possible for the Great Unwind to occur? And is there a way for us to remove the bind of Akerloff's dysfunctional asymmetry that results in

---

78   WF Sharpe, 'Nuclear financial economics', in WH Beaver and G Parker (eds), *Risk management Problems and Solutions* (New York: McGraw-Hill, 1995), 17–35, at 17.

79   KJ Arrow, 'The role of securities in the optimal allocation of risk-bearing', *The Review of Economic Studies*, 31/2 (1964), at 91–96.

80   G Debreu, *Theory of Value* (The Cowles Foundation Monograph 17, 1959).

81   Sharpe, above, n. 78, at 18–19.

82   See J Plender, 'The return of the state: How government is back at the heart of economic life', 21 August 2008, available at <www.ft.com> and <http://www.ft.com/cms/s/0/73dfc892-6fb2-11dd-986f-0000779fd18c.html>.

the accumulation of worthless paper? In a word, is there a way of formulating complex financial instruments that can avoid the asymmetry of the pre-default and post-default worlds?

Constructing Socially Just Complex Financial Instruments

Taking account of the above, that is, the disclosure requirements for asset-backed securities, the investor rights to these disclosures, the dangers of information asymmetry of Akerloff, the potential to capture any particular condition of the world through complex financial instruments based on the nuclear financial economics of Sharpe, Arrow and Debreu, is it possible to design a socially fair complex financial instrument? For our purposes, a socially fair transaction is one having two conditions fulfilled: (1) that the parties to the original transaction anticipate the expected risks to the transaction and agree to share the risks and rewards of such a transaction; and (2) that exogenous parties, such as the taxpayers through government agents, are not required to re-jig the risks allocated by the parties. Although this sounds like an extraordinarily complex problem, according to a risk symmetries approach, the range of solutions to this problem would simply be something requiring the following shape, in Figure 16.4, as per the symbolism of Figure 16.3 above.

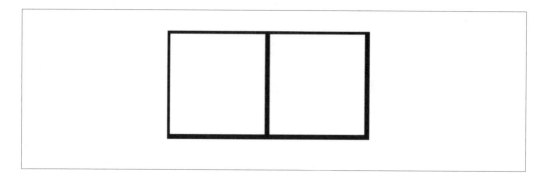

Figure 16.4 Risk symmetric transaction

Again, as before in explaining Figure 16.3, this looks like a childish and inane picture of possibly exceedingly complex financial instruments and their markets across two periods of time, pre-default and post-default. In Figure 16.4 the two boxes are indicative of the circulation of cash flows and the risks, coming and going to the same parties as set out in the original transaction. Nirvana would be to not have the taxpayer burdened with any residual risk in the post-default period. There is a strange message from this picture about the securitization states of the world, because the right-hand box should represent the post-default world as *not asymmetric* to the pre-default world. How is this possible?

   It is possible because the cash flows (rewards) and the entirety of the risks are shared by all the parties to the transaction. Recall, one of the odd asymmetries of the prototypical mortgage-backed securitization structure is that the obligors are long suffering and continue to pay for their mortgages until a long-dated maturity of 20 or 25 years. They receive only an indirect benefit in the pre-default world of generally lower market interest rates, but no explicit direct benefits from the securitization transaction. This is despite the fact that all the other parties to the transaction are expected to make profits from the collective payments of the obligors through time.

A fairer securitization programme, and therefore a more risk symmetric one, would be for the obligors to be given a tranche in their favour. The author, together with a few colleagues who prefer to remain anonymous but may be said to be highly experienced professionals in structuring mortgage-backed securities,[83] has generated a simple model of a four tranche RMBS, where one of the tranches is an obligor's free tranche. Tranches are the notes that are normally structured for the purpose of satisfying the particular interests of particular institutional investor's demands. The major benefits of this structure include: (1) the obligors would benefit from pre-payment risk; (2) the obligors would have an incentive to remain good payors and be given an incentive to pay down their principal balance; and (3) investors would objectively have less risk of obligors defaulting. Our stress-testing shows that there is now a theoretical possibility for achieving an approximation of the risk symmetry symbolized in Figure 16.4.

Figure 16.4 and its risk symmetric implications should be taken rather seriously since there are now a number of proposals by well-intentioned regulators and fervent politicians who believe that some kind of new regulations in the area of mortgage origination and government sponsored programmes are required. According to the risk symmetric analysis, these new proposals should be measured against risk symmetric principles and outcomes.

For example, on 30 April 2008, Sheila Blair, Chairman of the US Federal Deposit Insurance Corporation, set out a proposal to unlock the desperate 'growing tide of foreclosures' and 'delinquency rates for subprime mortgages' in the US. As she says:

> The question is how to restructure unaffordable mortgages on a sufficient scale to stabilize home values and contain the broader economic damage. Solutions must be practical and administratively quick and simple to implement. We must also minimize any burden on taxpayers by keeping the risk of mortgage defaults in private hands.[84]

Her proposal is for Congress to create a publicly funded borrow loan programme, where the Treasury, authorized by Congress, would make loans to borrowers with unaffordable mortgages to pay down as much as 20 per cent of their outstanding principal balance.

How would Chairman Blair's proposal work with a risk symmetric analysis? On the plus side, the amount of taxpayers' money at risk the post-default world would be less than if the Government were to support all mortgage-backed securitization programmes that failed. She is hoping that offering to cut 20 per cent of the principal on 'unaffordable mortgages', as defined by the debt to income ratio at time of origination, would be sufficient to stem the tide of foreclosures and defaults. However, on the negative side, allowing 20 per cent to be paid in effect by the taxpayer means that the Government is subsidizing bad mortgage lending practices, and would contribute to the perception of the Government supporting options of moral hazard. Is the proposal risk symmetric? Unquestionably, no. But its degree of risk asymmetry is certainly much less than making the Government take over the entirety of the 'bad mortgages'.

---

83   See blog on 'New Plain Vanilla'; for access contact the author at joetanega@gmail.com.
84   S Blair, 'How the state can stabilise the housing market', 30 April 2008, *Financial Times*, at 13.

Conclusion

It is curious that compared to the scientific disciplines of the twentieth and twenty-first centuries where symmetry arguments pervade, the social sciences and, especially, the law have almost nothing to say about the theoretical implications of symmetry, let alone risk symmetries. As Van Frassen, the philosopher of science elegantly puts it, symmetry arguments '[...] carry us forward from an initial position of empirical risk, to a final point with still exactly the same risk [where] the degree of empirical fallibility remains invariant'.[85] In this chapter, we have shown how investor rights to asset-backed securities appear in a set of rather complex securities regulations in the US (Regulation AB) and the EU (the Prospectus Regulation) and how the theories of information asymmetry of Akerloff have encouraged the production of ever-increasingly complex financial instruments. With the unfolding phenomenon of the credit crisis, these complex financial transactions show an asymmetry at a social level that threatens to undermine social cohesion by discrediting the financial system. While the fundamental premises of financial instruments and financial engineering tell us that complex financial instruments may be used to mimic any and all conditions of the real world, the world created by complex financial instruments has not protected all the parties to such instruments. The solutions to the credit crisis are inherent within the financial system if the instruments, whether public or private, are designed consciously to meet risk symmetric criteria. Socially just complex financial instruments are not just a possibility, but, more than ever, a requirement in a world filled with continuous risk and uncertainty.

---

85   BC Van Frassen, *Laws and Symmetry* (Oxford: Oxford University Press, 1980), at 261.

Chapter 17

Women, Culture and Human Rights: Feminist Interventions in Human Rights Law?

Harriet Samuels

Introduction

Feminism, culture and human rights have always been a controversial mix. In recent years, tensions have intensified. The popular press and politicians have appropriated feminist concerns about religious and cultural harms in a way that feeds into racist discourses in the post-9/11 environment. This presents a dilemma for feminist lawyers and activists committed to using legal and, more specifically, rights-based strategies. Two House of Lords cases decided in 2006, in different areas of the law, illustrate the way in which the courts can use rights and equality-based approaches to negotiate some of these sensitive conflicts. Both cases concern issues that have, perhaps disproportionately, occupied the attention of feminist scholars and activists, namely the practice of female genital mutilation (FGM) (*Fornah*)[1] and religious dress (*Begum*).[2] Both practices have contested cultural, social and religious meanings, and raise questions of autonomy. The intention is to situate the analysis of these cases within the context of the debate by feminists on the utility of human rights law. It is argued that the potential of human rights law should not be underestimated. The analyis draws on the concept of democratic iteration posited by Benhabib to demonstrate the way universal norms are absorbed into the domestic legal setting. By democratic iterations Benhabib means the '[...] complex processes of public argument, deliberation, and exchange-through which universal rights claims are contested and contextualised, invoked and revoked, posited and positioned-throughout legal and political institutions as well as in the associations of civil society'.[3]

The use of international instruments, ideas of universality and equality and the concept of proportionality are examples of democratic iterations that lend themselves towards the development of a more flexible and gendered human rights jurisprudence. In particular, concepts such as proportionality have the potential to provide a legal mechanism to mediate between the individual, public interest and the community.

The aim here is to engage with some feminist critiques of human rights law in an attempt to re-emphasize the centrality of human rights in any progressive feminist strategy. This effort is located within a loose tradition of what Naffine calls legal feminism. The purpose of legal feminism is to '[...] make sense of the many ways gender shapes law, to reveal the many ways that law, as a consequence harms women, and to try to change law so that women are helped'.[4]

---

1   *Secretary of State for the Home Department (Respondent) v. K (FC) (Appellant) Fornah (FC) (Appellant) v. Secretary of State for the Home Department (Respondent)* [2006] UKHL 46 [hereafter Fornah].

2   *R (on the application of Begum (by her litigation friend, Rahman)) (Respondent) v. Headteacher and Governors of Begum School (Appellants)* [2006] UKHL 15 [hereafter Begum].

3   S Benhabib, 'The legitimacy of human rights', *Daedalus* (Summer 2008), 94, at 98.

4   N Naffine, 'In praise of legal feminism', *Legal Studies*, 22 (2002), 71, at 72.

This stress on changing the law seems particularly pertinent to human rights law where Mullally observes that feminist human rights activists are appealing to universal norms but academic feminism risks becoming irrelevant. She reasons that '[t]he discourse of human rights is an open and dynamic one. The challenge for feminism is to transform that discourse rather than to abandon it.'[5] The multiplicity of feminist positions on many human rights issues and the complications involved in transposing feminist ideas into a legal frame are not to be underestimated. But, as Gotell proposes in her discussion of feminist approaches to the Canadian Charter of Rights, '[p]erhaps […] feminist legal argument should attempt to reflect complexity, contingency and contending feminist positions. Perhaps it also means we should encourage multiple and sometimes competing feminist interventions in law'.[6] There is already a considerable literature analysing feminism and human rights much, although not all of it, is engaged in critiques of human rights that query its value. Postmodern feminism, in particular, has called into question many of the foundations on which human rights law and practice are built.[7] As Dembour states:

> Postmodernists typically explore rather than explain, as their theoretical perspective makes them wary of conceptual generalisation. As a result, they avoid suggesting how the world could be put right. They do not have an agenda as such. Rather they offer a critique which does not take one definite direction.[8]

Postmodern methods challenge, inter alia, the universality of rights, the nature of the subject and the supposed progressive enlightenment narrative that underlies this ideology.[9] This analysis of human rights law, drawn on by postcolonial scholars, has been particularly critical where issues of gender, religion and culture are in dispute as exemplified by many of the critiques, of the decision in *Begum*.[10]

It is argued that human rights are too dominant and meaningful an ideology to escape feminist influence. They are both prevalent in international law and of growing significance in domestic law, particularly since the enactment of the Human Rights Act 1998 in the United Kingdom. There has been a significant investment of energy in international human rights law by feminists.[11] This followed the acknowledgement that human rights law ignored women's interests. Subsequently,

---

5   S Mullally, *Gender, Culture and Human Rights: Reclaiming Universalism* (Oxford: Hart, 2006), at 25.

6   L Gotell, 'LEAF's changing approach to charter equality', in R Jhappan (ed.), *Women's Legal Strategies in Canada* (Toronto: University of Toronto Press, 2002), 135, at 165.

7   Postmodern feminism is used in a broad sense here to refer to those feminists who have '[…] mobilised the postmodern critique of the authority and status of science, truth, history, power, knowledge, and subjectivity, bringing a transformative gender to postmodern theory and developing new conceptions of sexual difference'. C Weedon, 'Postmodernism', in AM Jaggar and I Young (eds), *A Companion to Feminist Philosophy* (Oxford: Blackwell, 1998) at 75.

8   MB Dembour, *Who Believes in Human Rights?: Reflections on the European Convention* (Cambridge: Cambridge University Press, 2006), at 211.

9   On the relationship between postmodernism and feminism see S Benhabib et al., *Feminist Contentions: A Philosophical Exchange* (London and New York: Routledge, 1995) and V Munro, *Law and Politics at the Perimeter: Re-Evaluating Key Debates in Feminist Theory* (Oxford: Hart, 2007).

10   S Motha, 'Veiled women and the affect of religion in democracy', *Journal of Law and Society*, 34 (2007), 139; L Gies, 'What not to wear: Islamic dress and school uniforms', *Feminist Legal Studies*, 14 (2006), 377; and A Vakulenko, 'Islamic dress in human rights jurisprudence: A critique of current trends', *Human Rights Law Review*, 7 (2007), 717.

11   R Cook (ed.), *Human Rights of Women* (Philadelphia: University of Pennsylvania Press, 1994); H Charlesworth and C Chinkin, *The Boundaries of International Law: A Feminist Analysis* (Manchester:

judicial and political institutions began to recognize and apply women's rights in their work.[12] Reflecting on the impact of feminism on human rights and international law Charlesworth, Chinkin and Wright comment on the opportunities that human rights, with their emphasis on dignity and equality provided for women.[13]

Within the domestic legal sphere, there has been much debate about the utility of using the human rights frame to shape issues of feminist politics. The introduction of the Human Rights Act 1998 based on the mainly civil and political rights of the European Convention on Human Rights (ECHR) intensified the discussion of the gains and losses for women.[14] The European Court of Human Rights has acknowledged that rape can be a form of torture and the failure to prosecute rape can, in some circumstances, be a breach of Articles 3 and 8.[15] Positive rights have been important in challenging government attitudes towards domestic violence.[16] Domestic women's organizations have also adopted a rights-rhetoric and promoted the use of human rights.[17] Human rights law is embedded in the legal and political system. The creation of the Commission for Equality and Human Rights confirms this.[18]

Feminist critiques of human rights provide valuable insights. But given that law is a site of power and resistance it remains politic for legal feminists to retain a keen interest in the possibilities of gendering rights-based processes. As Munro observes, relying on rights-based analysis to effect change is a high risk strategy but 'that it would be riskier still to abandon it to those unconcerned with, or opposed to, the goal of gender equality'.[19]

This chapter will consider the critiques of the use of human rights to resolve disputes concerned with gender, culture and religion and, in particular, focus on the troubling postcolonial feminist concerns that human rights frames produce victim subjects without agency.[20] According to this critique women are perceived as victims of their primitive cultures in need of rescue. As Kapur states, '… the veil is assumed to be an oppressive and subordinating practice that typifies Islam …' and 'Female circumcision … has been represented as a brutal procedure that is practised by all Africans'.[21]

Manchester University Press, 2000); K Knop (ed.), *Gender and Human Rights* (Oxford: Oxford University Press, 2004).

12   H Charlesworth, C Chinkin and S Wright, 'Feminist approaches to international law: Reflections from another century', in D Buss and A Manji (eds), *International Law: Modern Feminist Approaches* (Oxford: Hart, 2005), at 21.

13   Ibid., Charlesworth and Chinkin (2005), at 25.

14   A McColgan, *Women under the Law: The False Promise of Human Rights* (London: Longman, 2000) and E Grabham and R Hunter, 'Special Issue: Encountering human rights: Gender/sexuality, activism and the promise of law', *Feminist Legal Studies*, 16 (2008), 1.

15   I Radacic, 'Rape cases in the jurisprudence of the European Court of Human Rights: Defining rape and determining the scope of the state's obligations', *European Human Rights Law Review* (2008), 358.

16   S Choudhry, and J Herring, 'Domestic violence and the Human Rights Act 1998: A new means of legal intervention', Winter *Public Law* (2006), 752.

17   See, for example, Rights of Women <http://www.rightsofwomen.org.uk/>.

18   See the Equalities Act 2006 <http://www.equalityhumanrights.com/en/Pages/default.aspx> and Lord Lester and K Beattie, 'The New Commission for Equality and Human Rights', *Public Law* (Summer 2006), 197.

19   See Munro, above, n. 9, at 85.

20   R Kapur, *Erotic Justice: Law and the New Politics of Postcolonialism* (London: GlassHouse Press, 2005) and D Otto, '"Disconcerting "masculinities": Reinventing the gendered subject(s) of international human rights law', in D Buss and A Manji (eds), *International Law: Modern Feminist Approaches* (Oxford: Hart, 2005).

21   Ibid., Kapur at 107.

These concerns will be examined through the lens of the House of Lords decisions in *Fornah* and *Begum*. These cases take place in different legal contexts but raise common issues that are central to the debates on feminism, rights and culture. The women in both cases can be seen as the 'exotic other' who are bearers of their culture or religion. The cases also reflect many of the difficulties of operating within the human rights paradigm. However, the judgments, particularly those of Baroness Hale, reveal the gains of working with human rights. *Fornah* demonstrates the advantages of universalism in allowing the translation of international norms into national settings for the benefit of the individual concerned. The *Begum* case indicates how the doctrine of proportionality could be reformulated to balance the claims of community and individual without producing a victim subject without agency.

Cultural and Religious Conundrums: *Fornah* and *Begum*

Fornah illustrates the deployment of universal human rights norms to advance a more gender-sensitive jurisprudence.[22] It is a landmark case because it recognizes that women who leave their country of residence because they fear FGM can be considered to be refugees.[23] Fornah fled Sierra Leone because she feared that she would be subject to FGM.[24] Her claim for refugee status was rejected because it did not fall within one of the grounds in the Refugee Convention. This defines a refugee as someone who 'owing to well-founded fear of being persecuted for reasons of race, religion, nationality, membership of a particular social group or political opinion, is outside the country of his nationality and is unable or, owing to such fear, is unwilling to avail himself of the protection of that country […]'.[25] The Refugee Convention does not include sex as one of the grounds of persecution. Feminist activism has centred on persuading domestic and international institutions, including the courts, to interpret the Convention to take account of the gender persecution suffered by women.[26] The tactic most often used to bring women within the refugee definition was to establish that women were a 'particular social group'.[27]

According to the Home Secretary Fornah's claim failed as it was not possible to identify the particular social group to which she belonged. If the group was defined in such a way as to include

---

22   The case was reported in the press. N Walter, 'Flight from the knife,' *The Guardian*, 18 October 2006, G2, at 12.

23   An earlier House of Lords decision held that two Pakistani women accused of adultery and fleeing domestic violence were members of a social group. See *R v. IAT ex parte Shah* [1999] 2 A.C. 629.

24   For a description of the practice of FGM see Baroness Hale in *Fornah* para. 91. See also UNICEF, *Female Genital Mutilation/Cutting: A Statistical Exploration* (Geneva, UNICEF 2005). There is considerable feminist literature on FGM. On Africa see F Banda, *Women, Law and Human Rights: An African Perspective* (Oxford: Hart, 2005) and more generally I Gunning, 'Arrogant perception, world travelling and multicultural feminism: the case of female genital surgeries', *Columbia Human Rights Law Review*, 23 (1991–92), 189.

25   Article 1A(2) of the Refugee Convention 1951 as amended by the 1967 Protocol United Nations, *Treaty Series*, vol. 189, p. 137 and 606 UNTS 267, *entered into force* 4 October 1967.

26   See A Macklin, 'Refugee women and the imperative of categories', *Human Rights Quarterly* (1995), 213 and N Kelley, 'The Convention refugee definition and gender based persecution: A decade's progress', *International Journal of Refugee Law*, 13 (2001), 559.

27   When the Convention was drafted in 1951 this was probably intended to cover former members of the landowning, capitalist or bourgeois classes. This category was expanded so women and homosexuals were held to be members of a particular social group. The 2002 San Remo Expert Roundtable Guidelines go on to confirm this definition. See G Goodwin-Gill and J McAdam, *The Refugee in International Law* (Oxford: Oxford University Press, 2007), at 74–75.

females in Sierra Leone it would be too wide, as it would include many members who did not fear persecution because they had already been subject to FGM. If the group was narrowly defined to include only those women who are at risk, the group would be defined by the persecution they suffered. As a matter of principle, this was not permitted.[28] Fornah's initial appeal to an adjudicator was successful, but reversed by the Immigration Appeal Tribunal on the basis that no social group to which Fornah belonged could be identified; and this was upheld by a majority of the Court of Appeal.[29] In the Court of Appeal Auld LJ made some rather dubious claims about the relationship between women and harmful cultural practices. He opined that women who had undergone FGM were not discriminated against by society at large: 'Although FGM may be repulsive to those outside Sierra Leone it was widely accepted in that country by men and women as traditional and part of the cultural life of its society as a whole.'[30] The Court also held that not all women could be considered part of the social group, as after the FGM they were no longer in fear of persecution and also because the practice of FGM was mainly carried out by women.[31]

The House of Lords overturned the decision of the Court of Appeal and held that Fornah was a refugee, because she was persecuted as part of a 'particular social group'. The majority of their Lordships held that this social group was composed of uninitiated indigenous females in Sierra Leone. This narrow definition excluded those who had already undergone FGM as they were no longer at risk.[32] However, Lord Bingham and Baroness Hale preferred a wider test that included all women from Sierra Leone on the basis that all women are discriminated against, and it was irrelevant that not all women in the group were persecuted.[33]

Fornah concerned a challenge to a cultural practice that the claimant did not wish to experience. This contrasts with *Begum* where the claimant, Shabina Begum was a British Muslim schoolgirl who attended a secular comprehensive school in Luton where over 80 per cent of the pupils were Muslim. She argued that the school's refusal to allow her to wear the jilbab was a breach of her right to manifest her religion contrary to Article 9 of the ECHR and of her right to education under Article 2 of the First Protocol to the ECHR. The school allowed headscarves and students who were Muslim, who wished, could wear the shalwar kameeze as an alternative to the standard school uniform.[34] Shabina Begum attended the school for two years and wore the shalwar kameeze. But over the summer holidays she decided she wanted to wear a jilbab, which is a long shapeless dress that does not show the contours of the leg as does the shalwar kameeze. When she attended school in the jilbab, accompanied by her brother and his friend, on the first day of term she was told to go home and return in school uniform, which she declined to do. The school's justification for this refusal was that some girls feared being pressured into wearing the jilbab if it was permitted. There were demonstrations outside the school by an extreme Muslim group unconnected with the claimant's family, protesting against the secular education of Muslim children, and some pupils

---

28 See, above, n. 1, para. 38.
29 [2005] 1 W.L.R. 3773
30 Ibid., para 44.
31 Chadwick LJ, ibid., para. 52
32 See Lord Hope para. 35 for the majority view.
33 Baroness Hale at para. 114 and Lord Bingham at paras 31–32.
34 There is an extensive literature on veiling. This includes D McGoldrick, *Human Rights and Religion: The Islamic Headscarf Debate in Europe* (Oxford: Hart, 2006), NJ Hirschmann, 'Western feminism, eastern veiling, and the question of free agency', *Constellations*, 5 (1998), 345, D Lyon, and D Spini, 'Unveiling the headscarf debate', *Feminist Legal Studies*, 12 (2004), 333–45; C Laborde, 'Female autonomy, education and the *hijab*', *Critical Review of International Social and Political Philosophy*, 9 (2006), 351–76.

complained about harassment. There were concerns that if the jilbab was allowed it would lead to conflict, as had occurred in the past, between groups of Muslim pupils according to the strictness of their beliefs.[35]

The House of Lords decided by a majority that there had been no interference in the claimant's right to manifest her religion. She could have chosen to attend another school where she could have worn her jilbab.[36] However, the court was unanimous that even if there had been an interference with her right to manifest her religion, this was justified on the basis that it was necessary to protect the rights of others. The court accepted the school's reasons for refusal, impressed by the trouble the school had taken to consult with the local community to find a uniform that complied with Muslim requirements. Furthermore, the school's discretion was deemed worthy of respect as it was in the best position to make a judgment.[37]

Producing Victim Subjects

The cases of *Fornah* and *Begum* are rooted in the language of rights much criticized by postcolonial feminists as producing victim subjects without agency.[38] The identification of the victim subject by postcolonial feminists is part of a wider critique by postmodern feminist scholars, amongst others, that perceives liberal and radical feminism as 'essentializing' women.[39] For example, Brown, in her critique of MacKinnon's well known attempts at law reform, asks '[...] precisely which women's experience drawn from which historical moments, and which culture, racial and class strata, is MacKinnon writing?'[40] In a continuation of this theme postcolonial feminists such as Kapur have argued that human rights campaigns on violence against women create a victim subject based on stereotypes of Third World women.[41] Otto also warns that 'feminist human rights advocates need to be wary of legal constructions that cast, women as victims, in need of protection [...]'.[42]

---

35   See, above, n. 2, per Lord Bingham para. 18.

36   See Lord Bingham's reasoning on this point, above, n. 2, para. 25. Baroness Hale and Lord Nicholls dissented on this point but agreed that the interference with the right was justified to protect the right of others.

37   Lord Bingham, above, n. 2 para. 28. The decision was followed in *R. (on the application of X) v. Headteachers and Governors of Y School* [2008] 1 All ER 249 (school's decision to prohibit a Muslim student wearing a face veil or niqab was not contrary to Article 9). Similarly in *R. (on the application of Playfoot) v. Millais School Governing Body* a school's decision to prohibit a student wearing a chastity ring in accordance with her Christian belief was not in conflict with Article 9 [2007] EWHC 1698 (Admin).

38   See, for example, Kapur and Otto, above, n. 20.

39   Essentialism refers to the assumption that women have a shared experience or a common identity based on their gender. The accusation is that the experience of some women is privileged as the experience of all women. For a discussion of essentialism see J Conaghan, 'Reassessing the feminist theoretical project in law', *Journal of Law and Society*, 27 (2000), 351–85, at 375.

40   See CA MacKinnon, *Feminism Unmodified: Discourses on Life and Law* (Cambridge, MA: Harvard University Press, 1987) and *Toward a Feminist Theory of the State* (Cambridge, MA: Harvard University Press, 1989). W Brown, *States of Injury: Power and Freedom in Late Modernity* (Princeton, NJ: Princeton University Press, 1995), at 131.

41   For a description of the Violence Against Women campaign see Report of the Secretary-General, *Advancement of Women: In-depth Study on all Forms of Violence against Women*, United Nations A/61/122/ Add.1, July 2006. See also J Fitzpatrick, 'The use of international human rights norms to combat violence against women', in R Cook (ed.), *Human Rights of Women: National and International Perspectives* (Philadelphia: University of Pennsylvania Press, 1994), 532, U O'Hare, 'Realising human rights for women', *Human Rights Quarterly*, 21 (1999), 364.

42   Otto, above, n. 20, at 122.

Kapur, influenced by the work of Mohanty presents a compelling critique of the Violence Against Women campaign.[43] Although Kapur's work is set in the context of India she sees the victim subject as a 'transnational phenomenon'. She appears within legal discourse in the West and postcolonial states. Her main criticism is that this discourse produces an essentialized, gendered and cultured subject. This underestimates the differences between women based on race, class, religion and other categories. It encourages legal interventions that belie progressive politics and that call for regulation of the subaltern woman. For example, in her discussion of the UK Government's White Paper *Secure Borders, Safe Haven: Integration with Diversity in Modern Britain,* Kapur discusses the United Kingdom Government's attempt to prevent sham marriages being used to avoid immigration controls.[44] Arranged marriages by members of minority communities from the Indian sub-continent are portrayed as problematic where the spouse comes from abroad to marry a UK citizen: 'Women in these communities are further cast as victims of their culture, which is regarded as backward and uncivilised [...]. Championing of women's rights in the subaltern community and family also becomes a way of delegitimising the community and its family structures.'[45]

The application of a human rights frame in cases such as *Fornah* and *Begum* is problematic for postcolonial feminists such as Razak and Kapur. This is because they appear to focus unduly on issues of gender and culture and ignore the larger realities of cultural racism and colonialism. Razak, in her work on refugees, explores how 'gender persecution, as it is deployed in refugee discourse, can function as a deeply racialized concept in that it requires third world women to speak of their realities of sexual violence at the expense of their realities as colonized peoples'.[46]

Fornah can be viewed as the 'exotic other' who comes to British shores seeking asylum from a brutal custom. She is literally rescued from the 'barbarities' of her own culture. Ironically, the most emotive language used is by Auld LJ in the Court of Appeal, who held that Fornah was not entitled to refugee status. He describes FGM as an 'evil practice' but fails to locate the custom in the context of the wider social relationships and inequalities, and mistakenly concludes that FGM is not discriminatory.[47] The House of Lords rejects the analysis of the lower court, and, on the whole, the language describing FGM is a little more muted than in the Court of Appeal. Several members of the House of Lords note that women in the UK are protected against FGM by legislation which prohibits the practice.[48] They compare the 'bad' laws of Sierra Leone with the 'good' laws of the UK, thus reproducing the colonial native fleeing from her culture.[49] None of the judges specifically address the issues of cultural racism or discuss the problem of vilification of Sierra Leonean culture. This is not surprising given that the court was not engaging in an academic debate. But Baroness Hale does at least refer to some of the controversies surrounding FGM, and that campaigns against it may be seen as an attack on culture or tradition. She notes the attempts to

---

43   C Mohanty, 'Under Western eyes: Feminist scholarship and colonial discourses', in C Mohanty et al. (eds), *Third World Women and the Politics of Feminism* (Bloomington and Indianapolis: Indiana University Press, 1991), at 51.

44   HMSO, Cm 5387 February 2002.

45   Kapur, above, n. 20, at 156. See also S Razak, 'Imperilled Muslim women, dangerous Muslim men and civilized Europeans: Legal and social responses to forced marriages', *Feminist Legal Studies*, 12 (2004), 129.

46   S Razak, 'Domestic violence as gender persecution: Policing the borders of nation, race and gender', *Canadian Journal of Women and Law*, 8 (1995), 45.

47   See, above, n. 29, at para. 44.

48   Lord Hope, above n. 1, para. 54.

49   The Sierra Leone Government reportedly saw the decision as an attack on its culture. See 'Sierra Leone anger at FGM asylum in UK', *The Guardian*, 19 October 2006.

use neutral terms such as genital cutting rather than genital mutilation in order to 'avoid alienating the communities which practise it. The common aim, however, is to persuade them that it is a harmful and degrading practice which can be stopped without giving up meaningful aspects of their culture'.[50] She also tries to contextualise FGM and explains its prevalence as a consequence of the civil war and the attempt to reassert traditional cultural practices.[51]

The *Begum* case also juxtaposes the Muslim girls in question against a potentially 'illiberal' and 'menacing religion', producing a 'victim subject'. This happens on several levels. First, there is the image of the claimant in the case. She can be construed as the 'other' or as a 'victim subject'. She is in need of protection from 'dangerous fundamentalists' who have imposed their views on her.[52] Shabina Begum's brother and his friend represent the 'dangerous fundamentalists' in this case. The Law Lords imply that the way the complaint was made by the claimant's brother and friend was menacing. Several of the Law Lords refer to the 'unnecessarily confrontational approach' and the fact that the men 'talked of human rights and threatened to sue the school'.[53] The assistant headteacher who spoke to the claimant and the men who accompanied her felt 'that their approach was unreasonable and he felt threatened'. There is also some suggestion in the press that her family is associated with Hizb-ut-Tahrir and by bringing the case there is an intention to advance the agenda of that group.[54] The Muslim fundamentalists who demonstrated outside the school are also discussed. The immigrant status of the family is emphasized as we are told her mother did not speak English.[55] In contrast to this the headteacher provides another image of a Muslim woman. She is described by Lord Bingham as being a successful head:

> born into a Bengali Muslim family and grew up in India, Pakistan and Bangladesh before coming to this country. She has had much involvement with Bengali Muslim communities here and abroad, and is familiar with the codes and practices governing the dress of Muslim women.[56]

She is presented as a more secularized version of Islamic womanhood striving to improve the education at a challenging school. Her contribution to the debate is lost in most commentaries on the case because the focus is on Shabina Begum as the 'victim subject'.[57]

There are many different images of the Muslim community and Muslim women being put forward here. At one level Shabina Begum can be seen simply as a 'victim subject' of a religion that wants to impose a restrictive form of dress. She is a victim as she loses two years of her education. She is a victim of the intransigence of her family and of the school. But, in general, the judges assume her decision to be genuine and those of a young woman making choices for herself about the appropriate form of dress for a Muslim girl who has reached puberty.[58] Yet the case is

---

50　Above, n. 1, para. 90.

51　Above, n. 1, para. 95.

52　See A Scolnicov, 'A dedicated follower of (religious) fashion?', *Cambridge Law Journal*, 64 (2005), 527. In her discussion of the Court of Appeal decision she suggests the claimant may have been pressured by her family to wear the jilbab.

53　See, above, n. 2, para. 80.

54　D Kennedy, 'Teenagers fight was inflamed by radicals', *The Times*, 23 March 2006.

55　Above, n. 2, para. 78.

56　Above, n. 2, para. 5.

57　But see G Davies, 'The House of Lords and religious clothing in *Begum v. Head Teacher and Governors of Denbigh High School*', *European Public Law*, 13 (2007), 423.

58　Only Baroness Hale discusses the claimant's age. She notes that it is likely that her parent or guardian chose her school. See also S Edwards, 'Imagining Islam … of meaning and metaphor symbolising the jilbab

permeated by another image, and that is the one of an individual who has decided to 'fight' her case all the way to the House of Lords. She can be regarded as someone who is using egalitarian and rights-based norms to advance her case.[59] Of course, there is a degree of speculation in this interpretation of the facts. But the point is that it is unsatisfactory to dismiss the use of human rights here as simply producing a victim subject without agency. It is one perspective, but it is incomplete and disrupted by looking at the facts in a different light.

The other possible 'victim subjects' in the case are the Muslim girls in the school who need 'protection from fundamentalists' who might pressure them into wearing the jilbab. Gies argues that this protective stance is similar to the French headscarf affair 'in which state schools have been thrust in the role of counterbalance to the oppression which young Muslim women are thought to suffer routinely in their own communities'.[60] However, this group of 'victim subjects' can be construed in a less passive light. The judgments note that they have approached the school to indicate their disquiet about the jilbab becoming part of the school uniform. As the subjects of the ban their participation in the dialogue is important. The girls can be seen as welcoming the school's uniform policy and participating in a conversation about the way the school deals with intra-religious issues between Muslim groups, and also the wider community.[61]

Human Rights Approach

These cases produce a much more complex subject than the 'victim subject' of postcolonial theory. But how do they begin to make the case for retaining the human rights framework and actively engaging in the ongoing debate on human rights? In *Fornah* the House of Lords drew heavily on international law and practice that was largely the result of feminist activism, and in *Begum* Baroness Hale's approach to the question of proportionality shows how that doctrine might be refashioned to respond to feminist concerns.

Fornah: Human Rights and FGM

The legal mechanisms that Baroness Hale draws on in the *Fornah* case are those of international human rights law. It may appear to be a simplistic point but it is worth noting that in 2006 it was not settled law in the United Kingdom that a woman could claim asylum based on her fear of FGM. Fornah's lawyers had to find a legal mechanism and they used the language of human rights. The judgments refer to the international law and norms, much of it campaigned for by feminists in order to develop the law.

R (Begum) v Headteacher and Governors of the Denbigh High School', *Child and Family Law Quarterly*, 19 (2007), 247.

59 Benhabib makes the same point in relation to *l'affaire foulard* (the headscarf controversy that broke out over French schools). She argues it was the egalitarian norms of the French education system that 'brought these girls out of the patriarchal structures of the home and into the French public sphere'. See below, n. 62, at 56.

60 L Gies, 'What not to wear: Islamic dress and school uniforms', *Feminist Legal Studies*, 14 (2006), 377–89.

61 For further discussion of this aspect of the case see P Patel, 'Faith in the state?: Asian women's struggle for human rights in the UK', *Feminist Legal Studies*, 16 (2008), 9, at 20

The adoption and adaptation of human rights norms are part of a process of what Benhabib calls democratic iteration.[62] She sees democratic iteration as a method whereby people bound together by 'certain guiding norms and principles re-appropriate and reinterpret these [...] and in doing so become authors rather than just subjects'.[63] This is part of the dialogic process through which fundamental norms are negotiated from the international to the national setting and are part of Benhabib's attempt to explain how democracies engage with the universal norms of human rights. In *Fornah* it is clear that the court is looking to the gendered universalized interpretations of international law to progress refugee law in its domestic setting.

Baroness Hale, for example, states that FGM is a human rights issue, as FGM will almost always amount to torture under various international human rights treaties. She also refers to the Programme for Action for the International Conference on Population and Development in Cairo in 1994, and the Declaration and Platform for Action of the Fourth World Conference on Women in Beijing, 1985, both of which called for an end to FGM.[64] This use of human rights reflects the benefits of reconceptualizing human rights as women's rights. This is because conceiving of FGM as torture speaks of it in a language the court is able to understand and allows the court confidently to identify a specific legal wrong. The use of human rights makes the comments less judgmental and parochial than a simple comparison with national UK standards.

This reference to international developments in *Fornah* is significant in underlining the influence of international human rights law and practice in contributing towards the development of domestic legal norms. Feminist activism in international and transnational non-governmental organizations (NGOs) have contributed to the 'overlapping communities of conversation' that help to form these norms and to spread what Benhabib refers to as 'legal cosmopolitanism'.[65]

The court's analysis of discrimination and equality is reflective of a human rights methodology. The House of Lords rejects the formal equality of Auld LJ in the Court of Appeal that as women would benefit in societal terms if they undergo FGM they are not discriminated against.[66] Lord Bingham adopts a substantive approach to the issue of equality. He locates FGM in the context of the discrimination that women in Sierra Leone suffer, noting that despite constitutional guarantees against discrimination women have limited rights. Women in Sierra Leone would still be in a position of social inferiority even if FGM was not practiced, although FGM is said to be '[...] an extreme and very cruel expression of male dominance'.[67]

Yet the image of Sierra Leonean women presented is that they are enmeshed in their culture and unable to exercise a free choice. One possible explanation is that those involved in FGM are suffering from a 'false consciousness'. Malik has acknowledged that '[w]e owe feminist theory a great debt for this particular insight: that women can develop a false understanding of their own best interests [...]'.[68] Liberal feminist theorists such as Nussbaum stress the nature of the social

---

62   See S Benhabib in R Post (ed.), *Another Cosmopolitanism* (Oxford: Oxford University Press, 2006).

63   Ibid., at 99. For a critique of the universality and state centric views of Benhabib see J Waldron, 'Cosmopolitan norms', in R Post (ed.), *Another Cosmopolitanism* (Oxford: Oxford University Press, 2006), at 84 and B Honig, 'Law and politics in the new Europe', in R Post (ed.), *Another Cosmopolitanism* (Oxford: Oxford University Press, 2006), at 102.

64   Above, n. 1, para. 94.

65   Benhabib, above, n. 3, at 97.

66   Above, n. 1, para. 44.

67   Above, n. 1, para. 31.

68   M Malik, '"The branch on which we sit": Multiculturalism, minority women and family law', in A Diduck and K O'Donovan (eds), *Feminist Perspectives on Family Law* (London: Cavendish, 2005). Baroness Hale refers to the novel *Tom Brown's School Days* to illustrate that those who appear to participate willingly

pressures underlying the choice to undergo FGM.[69] Nussbaum refers to the loss of capacity, the link with sexual oppression and customs of male domination. She argues, in accordance with her capability theory, that apart from the health problems, FGM leads to the loss of sexual functioning at an age when women are usually too young to appreciate its significance. She questions whether the mothers of girls who lack literacy and are immersed in traditional beliefs about sex can really make an informed choice about FGM.[70]

Accusations of false consciousness come perilously close to the patronizing, racist and imperialist 'othering' warned of by postcolonial scholars. Saharso objects that prohibitions on cultural rules that appear to undermine equality norms assume that '[…] Western women are fully autonomous in their decision making, while women from non Western cultures, as victims of their culture are not'.[71] Chambers, in response to accusations of cultural imperialism, claims that some Western women also engage in harmful practices such as undergoing surgery for breast enlargements. They feel compelled by social norms to conform to a particular body shape to succeed in their career or have a sense of self-worth.[72]

It is not possible here to do justice to the many and complex theories that attempt to reconcile autonomy with cultural and religious practices. In *Fornah* the court is not asked to compare FGM with other possible harmful procedures practised by the beauty industry in the West. But what is of interest in the case is the way that equality norms are used to de-exoticise FGM. It is seen as part of a global pattern of violence against women, and this makes it seem less extraordinary. Human rights norms developed to perceive of violence against women as a human rights violation are deployed to explain the nature of the practice. Considering FGM from a substantive equality and a human rights perspective enabled the court to understand why women participate in FGM, and to discuss why some women willingly undergo the procedure or perform it on others. Ultimately, the decision in *Fornah* was easier for the House of Lords because the claimant did not want to undergo the procedure. The nature of the harm caused meant that even if other women did consent because of cultural norms the practice was seen as discriminatory.

Begum, Religious Dress and Human Rights

The *Begum* case illustrates the potential of the principle of proportionality. There are different legal formulations of this test. The European Court of Human Rights approach and that of the United Kingdom courts has been intensely scrutinized by academic commentators.[73] The House of Lords discussed the application of the proportionality test in *Huang* and affirmed that the test, as laid down in the case of *de Freitas*, applied. The test is:

---

in a harmful practice might also be victims. 'It cannot make any difference that it is practised by women upon women and girls. Those who have already been persecuted are often expected to perpetuate the persecution of succeeding generations, as any reader of *Tom Brown's Schooldays* knows.' Above, n. 1, para. 110.

69   M Nussbaum, *Sex and Social Justice* (Oxford: Oxford University Press, 1999).

70   Ibid., at 127.

71   S Saharso, 'Feminist ethics, autonomy and the politics of multiculturalism', *Feminist Theory*, 4 (2003), 199.

72   See C Chambers, 'Autonomy and equality in cultural perspective: Response to Sawitri Saharso', *Feminist Theory*, 5 (2004), 329.

73   For an analysis of the proportionality test see, for example, J Rivers, 'Proportionality and variable intensity of review', *Cambridge Law Journal*, 65 (2006), 174–207, P Craig, 'The courts, the Human Rights Act and judicial review', *Law Quarterly Review*, 117 (2000), 588; I Leigh, 'Taking rights proportionately: Judicial review, human rights and Strasbourg', *Public Law* (Summer 1997), 265.

whether: (i) the legislative objective is sufficiently important to justify limiting a fundamental right; (ii) the measures designed to meet the legislative objective are rationally connected to it; and (iii) the means used to impair the right or freedom are no more than is necessary to accomplish the objective.[74]

In *Huang* the House of Lords went on to stress that proportionality is about the 'the need to balance the interests of society with those of individuals and groups'.[75] The proportionality test is malleable because the court has to decide how intensively the criteria should be applied, and whether alternative strategies should have been used to achieve the desired objective.[76] This balancing of competing interests provides an opportunity for various standpoints, including feminist ones, to be weighed in the balance. Feminist legal actors need to consider how the application and formulation of the proportionality principle might be fashioned to achieve a more egalitarian and less culturally reductive outcome. The redevelopment of the doctrine of proportionality would be a major, but productive project for feminists. It is consistent with a dialogic approach to human rights that sees the evolution of the values that underpin human rights as an ongoing conversation.[77] This conversation is also one that is taking place between the courts, the executive and Parliament.[78] Feminist theories have much to contribute to such a debate. Conceiving of proportionality as a dialogue fits within the paradigm of democratic iterations. Benhabib explains that when an original norm or meaning is repeated then it involves:

> making sense of an authoritative original in a new and different context. The antecedent thereby is reposited and resignified via subsequent usages and references. Meaning is enhanced and transformed; conversely, when the creative appropriation of that authoritative original ceases or stops making sense, then the original loses its authority on us as well. Iteration is the re-appropriation of the "origin" ; it is at the same time its dissolution as the original and its preservation through its continuous deployment.[79]

When the court applies the proportionality test it is a reaffirmation of the rights in question. But through its application of the right it develops new principles and modifies its application dependent on the context. This provides opportunities for feminist interventions in the development and refinement of the case law. Additionally, the role of civil society has become more important under the Human Rights Act in helping the courts to formulate legal principles. The use of third party interventions means that NGOs have briefed the courts and presented perspectives of marginalized

---

74   *Huang v. Secretary of State for the Home Department* [2007] UKHL 11, at para. 19. See also *de Freitas v. Permanent Secretary of Ministry of Agriculture, Fisheries, Lands and Housing* [1999] 1 AC 69 and *R (Farrakhan) v. Secretary of State for the Home Department* [2002] QB 1391, *R v. Secretary of State for the Home Department ex parte Daly* [2001] UKHL 26.

75   Huang, at para. 19.

76   P Craig, *Administrative Law* (London: Sweet and Maxwell, 2008), 628.

77   S Palmer, 'Feminism and the promise of human rights: Possibilities and paradoxes', in S James and S Palmer (eds), *Visible Women: Essays on Feminist Legal Theory and Political Philosophy* (Oxford: Hart, 2002), at 91–116; S Mullally, above, n. 5, and Benhabib, above, n. 62.

78   See D Nicol, 'Law and politics after the Human Rights Act', *Public Law* (Winter 2006), 722.

79   Benhabib, above, n. 62, at 48.

groups.[80] Although this development is not welcomed by all it does provide opportunities for greater dialogue between the courts and outside interests.[81]

The potential use of a feminist perspective is indicated in Baroness Hale's more rigorous application of the proportionality test in *Begum*. It suggests how proportionality can provide a framework for a more nuanced, less essentialist and culturally sensitive way to balancing conflict. First, Baroness Hale only agreed to defer to the school's judgment after being satisfied that there was evidence of harm. One might dispute the nature of the evidence she accepts or where she draws the line but the principles that she relies on are vital. They will at least make explicit the assumptions behind any limitation on rights. Secondly, Baroness Hale emphasizes the importance of listening to those who are the subject of the prohibition. This is significant given that one of the strongest criticisms of the headscarf ban in French schools was that the girls' voices were rarely heard.[82] Taking the motives and views of the relevant subjects in the case into account will go some way towards eliminating misunderstanding and avoid creating victim subjects.

Baroness Hale provides that some feminists might see the veil as oppressive but that this cannot provide a justification for a prohibition. Drawing on the feminist literature she states that women may be seen as 'bearers of culture' and that dress codes may require women to dress modestly but not men.[83] Religious dress may be associated with a confinement of women to the private sphere. But she recognizes the centrality of agency when she observes that men who wear religious dress such as a turban or yarmulke are presumed to have acted from choice and therefore the same assumption should be made about adult Muslim women.[84] She tries not to fall back on stereotypical tropes of Muslim women and to understand the complex choices that are being made. In order to justify her decision to support the ban she refers briefly to Judge Tulkens' dissent in *Sahin v. Turkey*.[85]

In *Sahin* the majority of the Grand Chamber of the European Court of Human Rights rejected a challenge by a Turkish medical student to a ban on headscarves in universities.[86] Applying the margin of appreciation the court accepted the Turkish Government's argument that the interference with the freedom to manifest her religion under Article 9 was justified on the grounds of protecting the principles of secularism and upholding equality between the sexes. Judge Tulkens dissented on the basis that wearing the headscarf did not infringe the rights of others. Disputing the assumption of the majority that wearing a headscarf was associated with fundamentalism she noted that there was

---

80   M Arshi and C O'Cinneide, 'Third party intervention: The public interest reaffirmed', *Public Law* (Spring 2004), 69 and H. Samuels, 'Feminist activism, third party interventions and the courts', *Feminist Legal Studies*, 13 (2005), 15.

81   S Hannett, 'Third party interventions: In the public interest?', *Public Law* (Spring 2003), 128–50 and C Harlow, 'Public law and popular justice', *Modern Law Review*, 65/1 (2002), 1–18.

82   J Scott, *The Politics of the Veil* (Princeton, NJ: University of Princeton Press, 2007), 141.

83   Baroness Hale refers to the work of G Sahgal and N Yuval-Davis, 'Fundamentalism, multiculturalism and women in Britain', in G Sahgal and N Yuval-Davis (eds), *Refusing Holy Orders: Women and Fundamentalism in Britain* (2000), at 14 and F Radnay, 'Culture, religion and gender', *International Journal of Constitutional Law*, 1 (2003), 663.

84   Above, n. 2, para. 94.

85   (2005) 44 EHRR 5. The court also rejected the argument that there was a breach of the right to education contrary to Article 2 of Protocol No. 1. For an analysis of the decision see J Marshall, 'Freedom of religious expression and gender equality: *Sahin v. Turkey*', *Modern Law Review*, 69 (2006), 452–61.

86   For earlier decisions upholding prohibitions on headscarves as consistent with Article 9 see *Karaduman v. Turkey* (1993) 74 DR 93 and *Dahlab v. Switzerland* (Application 42393/98) decision of 15 February 2001.

no evidence that the claimant had acted aggressively, was trying to provoke others or proselytize.[87] She questioned the paternalism of the court and noted that it was contrary to the principles of autonomy developed in other case law to hold that '[…] the principle of sexual equality can justify prohibiting a woman from following a practice which, in the absence of proof to the contrary she must be taken to have freely adopted'.[88]

Judge Tulkens' dissent in *Sahin* is important to Baroness Hale in *Begum*. Her engagement with the judgment forces her to consider as problematic the assumption that the veil is not freely adopted or that it conflicts with principles of equality. However, she distinguishes *Sahin* on the grounds that there is evidence of interference with the rights of others. This is because some girls at Denbigh High school had expressed concern that if the jilbab was introduced that they would be pressured into adopting it.[89] Baroness Hale then states: 'Here is the evidence to support the justification which Judge Tulkens found lacking in the *Sahin* case.'[90]

The judgments of Judge Tulkens in *Sahin* and Baroness Hale in *Begum* provide some justification for arguing that the proportionality test could be used to introduce feminist notions of autonomy that provide a more complicated view of the subject than those of the majority judgments. Both judges are attempting to understand the claimant through the lens of culture without producing subjects that are as Phillips states, 'captives of their cultures or robots programmed by cultural rules' whose choices are regarded as being inauthentic because they are made 'under conditions of social pressure'.[91]

The development of a notion of harm in gendered conflicts with religion and culture is vital if general and unsubstantiated claims about the nature of such practices are to be avoided. If individual choice to engage in a religious or cultural practice is overridden there must be evidence of harm.[92] A wide notion of harm would have the potential to prohibit significantly harmful conduct that conflicted with norms of gendered equality.[93] A narrow definition of harm might be restricted to physical harm to self or others. Phillips argues that '[…] a defensible multiculturalism has to put agency at its core, and that limits the kind of protections that can be offered to individuals choosing what others may consider self-denying or self-destructive behaviour'. But she also accepts that there are occasions when public agencies have a responsibility to intervene. So the right to follow religious and cultural beliefs is not unconditional, as rights 'depend on context and may need to be balanced against other rights'.[94] A narrow conception of harm or at least one based on firm evidence would be consistent with Phillip's theory.

The case law under Article 8 of the Convention may be of use here. Vakulenko has noted that, in Article 8 cases, the court has been unwilling to accept unsubstantiated assertions based on prejudice as evidence of harm to others.[95] So in *Smith and Grady v. United Kingdom* the European Court of Human Rights rejected the Government's unsubstantiated assertion that the presence of

---

87   Above, n. 85, para. 143.

88   Above, n. 85, paras 143–44.

89   Above, n. 2, para. 98.

90   Above, n. 2, para. 98.

91   A Phillips, *Multiculturalism without Culture* (Princeton, NJ: Princeton University Press, 2007), at 176.

92   See S Knights, 'Religious symbols in school: Freedom of religion, minorities and education', *European Human Rights Law Review*, 5 (2005), 499, at 514.

93   C Chambers, *Sex, Culture and Justice: The Limits of Choice* (Pennsylvania: Pennsylvania State University Press 2007) at 201

94   Above n. 91 Phillips 2007, at 176 and 165.

95   See A Vakulenko, 'Islamic dress in human rights jurisprudence: A critique of current trends', *Human Rights Law Review*, 7 (2007), 217, at 723.

homosexuals in the armed services would hinder its operations.[96] The hostility of some members of the armed forces towards homosexuals was not a legitimate justification for restricting the right of the claimants. However, the Article 8 case law also shows that consent to physical harm is treated with greater suspicion by the courts and that it is easier for public authorities to justify such prohibitions as proportional.[97] So prohibitions on FGM should be much easier to justify than restrictions on religious attire. Assertions about the nature of religious dress should be subject to strict scrutiny by the courts and assertions of harm should be substantiated with evidence.

The case law on Article 9 does refer to the importance of harm. For example in *Williamson* the House of Lords accepted that the ban on corporal punishment in schools did interfere with the claimants' right to manifest their Christian belief under Article 9, but it was justified in order to prevent harm to vulnerable children.[98] In his judgment Lord Walker referred to the importance of a nuanced and contextual approach in deciding how far democracies should go in allowing members of religious communities to decide what laws they will obey.[99] It was acknowledged that on a moral issue such as corporal punishment there would be evidence on both sides of the debate. But the court did take into account the various reports and recommendations that Parliament had considered when deciding to legislate against corporal punishment. Baroness Hale referred to the 'large body of professional educational and child care opinion in support of the ban'.[100] Even if it could be shown that an individual child might benefit from corporal punishment the ban was justified in order to protect a vulnerable class of persons such as children.[101]

The reasoning in *Williamson* works best where there is evidence of a risk of physical harm, such as in cases involving FGM. But a greater interrogation of assertions of harm is also possible in other cases as well. For example, the Supreme Court of Canada case of *Multani v. Attorney General of Quebec* illustrates how the court might look at the evidential base behind an assertion of harm.[102] The Supreme Court held that it was a breach of the right to religious freedom under the Canadian Charter for a school to prohibit a Sikh pupil from wearing a kirpan. This is a dagger-like religious object that orthodox Sikhs believe they are required to wear. The argument that the kirpan was a symbol of violence and might be used in disputes between pupils was rejected. There was no evidence of a kirpan being used inappropriately and knowledge of Sikhism showed that the kirpan was not a symbol of violence. The court commented that '[…] it is not necessary to wait for harm to be done before acting, but the existence of concerns relating to safety must be unequivocally established for the infringement of a constitutional right to be justified'.[103] It also gave short shrift to the school's fear that if the kirpan was allowed it might lead to a feeling of unfairness among some students who would perceive it as special treatment. The importance of religious tolerance

---

96   (2000) 29 EHRR 493.

97   *Brown* [1993] 2 WLR 556, *Laskey, Jaggard and Brown v. UK* (1997) 24 EHRR 39, *ADT v. UK* [2002] 2 FLR 697. For further discussion of the issues raised see P Roberts 'The philosophical foundations of consent in the criminal law', *Oxford Journal of Legal Studies*, 17 (1997), 38.

98   *R v. Secretary of State for Education and Employment ex parte Williamson* (2005) UKHL 15.

99   Ibid., para. 67.

100   Ibid., para. 85.

101   Baroness Hale cited the case of *R (Pretty) v. DPP* [2001] UKHL 61 where the court upheld a ban on assisted suicide. Noting that although Mrs Pretty was not at risk it was the vulnerability of the class that justified the ban. Ibid., para. 80.

102   [2006] 1 SCR 256.

103   Para. 66

was underlined and the Supreme Court suggested that the school had an obligation to instil such tolerance in its students.[104]

The concentration on harm in cases involving gender, culture and religion would force the court to examine the evidential base for its assumptions more carefully. Although harm is not an uncomplicated idea it does demand a greater investigation of the reasons for the restriction. The level of harm that would justify an interference with a religious or cultural right would have to be worked out through the case law.

Conclusion

Benhabib describes human rights as one of the most significant legal discourses of the post Second World War era and she argues it has become 'an almost universally accepted mode of moral communication'.[105] It is the pervasive nature of rights that makes it impossible for legal feminists, even if it were desirable to step away from them. Feminists, particularly postcolonial feminists, have expressed scepticism of the human rights project for constantly recreating the victim subject. This once again underscores the need for vigilance in rooting human rights in the reality of women's lives. It also calls for close examination of racist and cultural tropes. But it does not make the case for undermining the human rights project per se. If legal feminism is to retain a connection with law and activism it must rework and revise the ideology and practice of human rights. The cases of *Fornah* and *Begum* both show the complexities of applying human rights. But they also demonstrate the potential of using the tools of positive legal reasoning to expose the law to alternative perspectives, including feminist ones. During the process of democratic iteration, when legal norms make their way from the international to the national setting, feminisms' contributions can open up the process. Legal tools such as proportionality are not impervious to feminists' interventions. An emphasis on autonomy and harm may dispel images of minority women as captured by their culture and religion. It would demand greater emphasis on listening to women and understanding the experiences of minority women's lives. As Benhabib observes through these processes '[…] both the identities involved and the very meaning of rights claims are reappropriated, resignified and imbued with new and different meanings'.[106]

---

104   In *R. (on the application of Watkins-Singh) v. Aberdare Girls' High School Governors* [2008] EWHC 1865 the Administrative Court held it was indirect race and religious discrimination under section 1(1A) of the Race Relations Act 1976, the Equalities Act section 49(1) and contrary to the school's obligations under s 71 Race Relations Act 1976 s 71(1) for a school to prohibit a Sikh pupil from wearing a religious bangle to school. The court distinguished the bangle from the jilbab in *Begum* on the grounds that the bangle was unobtrusive. It rejected the school's argument that if the bangle was allowed other students might think it unfair that other kinds of jewellery was prohibited. The court stressed that the school had a duty to foster respect for different cultures and to educate against racism.

105   S Benhabib, 'Response by Seyla Benhabib' to B Parekh, 'Finding a proper place for human rights', in KE Tunstall (ed.), *Displacement, Asylum, Migration: The Oxford Amnesty Lectures 2004* (Oxford: Oxford University Press, 2006), at 44.

106   Above Benhabib 2006, n. 62, at 67.

Chapter 18
Rights and Responsibilities[1]

Hanne Petersen

Figure 18.1 Poul Anker Bech: Det tabte land [The Lost Land], 2001 © DACS

[The project is] my ultimate answer to that great Nordic enigma of the lost land – the lost time, first and foremost. The fact that we have lived and things disappear through our hands. We as Nordic people are prone to going around pondering and dreaming and thinking – about the future, too – and we are not so good at living in the moment, as we are, by nature, dreamers. The Nordic myth, which there are so many answers to, primarily in Johannes V. Jensen but also in Scandinavian literature in general with, for instance, Niels Lyhne, Lykkeper, Jørgen Stein, Per Gynt, Hamsun's Pan, and innumerable others, has dealt with the almost tragically unhappy Nordic people who cannot live in the moment but have to get out in to time.[2]

---

1   I would like to thank my colleagues Annette Kronborg and Michael Gøtze for comments on earlier versions of this chapter. Written in 2008, it has not followed up on later discussions of the 2009 legal changes.
2   B Raben-Skov, 'This yearning and longing for infinite space' – *interview with Poul Anker Bech*. Extract from a taped conversation with Poul Anker Bech in his studio at Bastholm on 10 July 2005, <http://www.poulankerbech.dk/Litteratur/Index_skrevet_om_UK.htm> [accessed 8 May 2006].

'The Lost Land' of Modern Rights?

In Poul Anker Bech's painting 'The Lost Land', the sunny fields of wheat – or is it wool? – are floating in the air. This may reflect the loss of the countryside by the many people in Denmark and the Nordic countries who have migrated to urban spaces over the last century in order to improve their living conditions. It may also relate to the loss of the land of childhood, or to the loss of a myth – an important story of times and places.[3] I think, however, that the painting might also be interpreted as an illustration of the loss of the nation state (of Denmark) – of the Nordic land, which was also the land of welfare and rights – a land which is now portrayed nostalgically and perhaps also enigmatically not only as one of harmonious and mutually beneficial relations between states and individuals, but also as a land which is vanishing. I will claim that the sense of a loss of land might be linked to a sense of a loss of rights – and of rights as a source of security.

Rights have often been understood as legally enforceable within the boundaries of national political jurisdictions. When we speak of rights, we tend primarily to think of the rights of citizens towards the state. In Nordic and many Western countries, the peak of rights thinking was reached in the period after the Second World War, when welfare states granted, guaranteed and secured rights for primarily large urban groups of people and workers. This development was strengthened in 1948 by the UN Declaration of Human Rights, leading to the two Cold War conventions on human rights, as well as by the European Convention on Human Rights from 1950 and the European Court of Human Rights established in 1959. The second half of the twentieth century may be called the era of rights. In this heyday of the democratic welfare state, the demand for rights and security – in education, health, child care, and old age – grew strong. Seen from the contemporary position, the demand was felt to be fulfilled by a strong state; a state capable of providing security. This is the era that now seems lost, together with the land.

This era of an omnipotent state leads on to an era of globalization, which weakens the state and, thus, undermines the idea of rights. This shift also shows the way towards an increased importance of ethics, as well as of duties and responsibilities, which belong to the realm of morality and increasingly spread out beyond the traditional boundaries of local and national spaces. *Duties* or *responsibilities* – terms which have a somewhat unclear definition – relate to a wider plurality of relations than those between the state and the individual. They may refer to relations within the family, educational institutions such as schools, in hospitals and homes for the elderly, in religious communities, in business or workplaces. They may also consist of relations towards nature and future generations, and towards those who manufacture the goods and provide the services we enjoy as consumers. Duties – but also responsibilities in the broader sense of the word – have especially been underlined by religious normative traditions, whereas rights, especially individual rights against the state, have been underlined in modern state and international regimes.

Bart Landheer, one of the few sociologists of international law, and former director of the Library at the Peace Institute in the Hague, wrote about the need for 'the feeling of global social responsibility of the scientist' in 1974. He claimed that the knowledge the world-system needs most is a critical form of knowledge that analyses reality and formulates its implications and possibilities.[4] A world-system is, writes Landheer, in a sense something spiritual, 'because it

---

3   I have discussed Poul Anker Bech's work in another article '"Væltede horisonter" – Globalisering, fortidsopgør og nye juridiske landskaber' in *Liber Amicorum Kjell Åke Modéer* (Lund: Juristforlaget, 2007), at 553–68.

4   B Landheer, *The Role of Knowledge in the Worldsystem* (The Netherlands: Van Gorcum & Comp. B.V. – Assen, 1974), at 7 (emphasis added). Bart Landheer (1904–1989) was educated in law and sociology,

transcends national and regional interests while it symbolizes Man's desire for continuity and, above all, for awareness of his role in the universe'.[5]

Will globalization undermine the rights that were secured within a national context? Will more attention be drawn to responsibilities in contrast to rights? And, if so, what will be the consequences of this change of focus?

Expanding Contexts, Plural Relations and Global Responsibility

Today, there is no alternative to an ethics of global responsibility, for we are entering an era of consequences.[6]

The move – back and forth – from rights to responsibilities is linked to a changing perception of time and space, a much longer time perspective and an expansion from the national context to the world or global context: 'For a world system there is time: the many centuries to come!'[7]

According to the geographer E Jeffrey Popke, responsibility can be linked to a notion of 'radical interdependence'. 'The ethical relationship [...] is not diminished by the contingencies of geographical location. Our responsibility is unconditional, and holds equally to those who are 'distant' as those who are near.'[8] As Popke sees it, space is 'far from a passive stage or container, but is radically open, constituted through perturbation, oscillation and movement [...]'. He describes a movement towards 'a spatial imaginary grounded in intersubjectivity, responsibility and community',[9] a move beyond the territory of the nation-state as a central space. Popke refers to Nancy, for whom freedom and autonomy 'are not the properties of a bounded subject existing in Cartesian space, but instead the opening of space itself as a form of community or sharing'.[10]

To a certain extent, the development witnessed after the turn of the millennium has been one of the now 'old modern state' closing in on itself and denying and rejecting this interdependence. Especially after September 11, the politics of fear has been an important instrument for many weakened Western (and non-Western) states to uphold and secure some of their watered down legitimacy. They have claimed to protect citizens against non-state terrorist violence in a period where it becomes ever clearer that they are hardly able, or willing, to protect citizens against market forces, not to mention death and injury in traffic,[11] and it is increasingly suspected that 'the war against terror' may produce more terrorism and terrorists. This move from a politics of rights to a politics of fear has not been spelled out clearly, nor are the consequences fully understood.

---

director for the library of the Peace Palace in The Hague (1952–1969) and later professor. He also published *On the Sociology of International Law and International Society* (The Hague: Martinus Nijhoff, 1967).

5   Ibid., at 70

6   The Hamburg Call to Action by the World Future Council, Founding Congress, Hamburg, 9–13 May 2007. <http://www.worldfuturecouncil.org/fileadmin/user_upload/Rob/Hamburg_Call_to_Action-engl_01.pdf> [accessed 6 May 2008].

7   Landheer, above, n. 4, ibid., at 17.

8   EJ Popke, 'Poststructuralist ethics: Subjectivity, responsibility and the space of community', *Progress in Human Geography* (2003), at 303–4.

9   Ibid., at 309.

10   Ibid., at 310.

11   In a recent Swedish doctoral thesis, Måns Svensson writes that on a global scale about 1.2 million people are killed and about 50 million are injured annually in traffic accidents at great individual and societal cost. M Svensson, *Sociala normer och regelefterlevnad – Trafiksäkerhetsfrågor ur ett rättssociologiskt perspektiv* (Lund Studies in Sociology of Law, Media-Tryck, Sociologen, Lund, 2008), at 15.

To Landheer, this move *could* be seen as a positive one, since 'the decrease of the dynamism of a subsystem of world society reflects a decrease in expansionism, and as such it is positive in terms of a worldsystem'.[12]

During and since the first Cartoon Crisis in February 2006, Denmark has had a crash course in the consequences of globalization and experiences of what might perhaps be called 'radical interdependence'; rights that were traditionally exercised within, and limited to, the local national space – such as freedom of expression – turned out to have global consequences, which may have made individuals and institutions rethink the relationship between rights and responsibilities, even if this may not be explicitly expressed. Some of the different and confused reactions to these events – as well as to the war in Iraq – have probably been feelings of disorientation, frustration, anger and more fear, as well as feelings of powerlessness and shame on behalf of a fragmented population.

In an article from 2003, where Leonard Kaplan analyses *Shame*, one of Bergman's movies from 1968, he writes that Bergman makes the case that 'shame reveals more about social and individual denial, or even more significantly a failure of a social imperative of responsibility to the other'.[13] I think that many Danes have felt both sad and ashamed of being Danes in the world following the Cartoon crises, as there has been both social and individual denial and great difficulty in identifying responsibility. Leonard Kaplan asks: 'What is the responsibility of the citizen as citizen rather than as merely a human, in a world where state sovereignty seems precarious in a globalized economy and where the complexity of the liberal state seems to alienate more and more of the populace, who have become more or less disaffected consumers and not citizen actors?'[14]

Frustration and anger have probably been felt mainly by socially excluded immigrants and by young people, who have been subjected to conformity, whereas fear and insecurity may have been felt more by the old and those with limited or meagre resources. Failure, impotence and shame may have been felt more by relatively privileged, but not necessarily influential, groups. Could it be that all these groups are – in spite of, or even because of, shame and frustration – gradually beginning to participate in the process that changes their mentality from one based on a national, law-abiding and rights-oriented frame of mind to one that is globally responsible?

Weakened Rights and Strengthened Responsibilities?

On 22 April 2008 the Danish Administration of the Courts of Justice (*Domstolsstyrelsen, Danmarks Domstole*) issued a 'Memorandum on Behaviour and Personal Appearance', which gave rise to some local political and media attention. The administration laid down that no specific dress code existed for Denmark's Courts. It was thus local management that had to ensure that those employed at Danish Courts generally and at the local court were informed of what was required and expected of them in terms of personal appearance. The controversial part of the memorandum declared that, according to common procedure, 'there is nothing to hinder an employee of Danish Courts who wishes to wear a scarf, turban or similar religious or cultural headdress to do so, as long as his/her face is not covered'.[15] The requirement not to cover one's face would enable the users of the court to identify who was responsible for processing their case.

---

12   Landheer, above, n. 4, at 29.
13   LV Kaplan, 'Shame: Bergman on responsibility and blame', *Brooklyn Law Review* 4 (2003), at 1185.
14   Kaplan, ibid., at 1166.
15   Domstolsstyrelsen, Danmarks Domstole, Notat om adfærd og personlig fremtræden ved Danmarks Domstole, 22 April 2008 <http://www.domstol.dk/om/Nyheder/ovrigenyheder/Documents/Notat%20om%20

The draft proposal for this memorandum was drawn up at a meeting of the board of the Danish Administration of the Courts of Justice on 18 December 2007. The board consisted of one Supreme Court judge, two High Court judges, two magistrate judges, one representative for the other judicial staff at the courts, two representatives for the administrative staff at the courts, one practising lawyer, and two members with specific management and societal knowledge. The Administration claimed that this proposal was, in their opinion, in agreement with the existing legal situation.

They further explained that the guideline required of the administration of the courts to ensure that employees at the courts 'signal respect for the legal system and the values which are of superior authority for Denmark's courts. These values encompass *openness, dialogue and cooperation*'.[16] One might perhaps interpret this decision as a reaction to a global experience of interconnectedness and an emerging acknowledgment of a need to show openness, dialogue and cooperation in a broader spatial community by a very symbolic local working community such as the Danish courts.

A colleague who has worked as a judge in one of the two Danish High Courts agrees with my interpretations that an otherwise very conservative institution influenced by patriarchal norms is depicting itself in a very positive light in this context.[17] Nonetheless, it is also an institution that has undergone significant reforms over the last few years, and has further become strongly feminized, especially on the lowest levels. Of all of the 2,226 employees in the Danish courts, 84 per cent are women and 16 per cent men. Among the judges on different levels, women have constituted about 50 per cent, while on the lowest level – deputy judges – this has risen to about 70 per cent over the last five years. Among university candidates with a law degree, women have made up more than the majority since 1987. Since 2007, 47 per cent of magistrate judges, 35 per cent of High Court judges and 22 per cent of Supreme Court judges have been women.[18] Judges have a privileged employment status as civil servants and cannot be dismissed easily – similar to priests, who have also expressed criticism of Danish immigration policy and legislation.

The court administration must have been well aware that this decision would lead to critique and provoke reaction. On 1 May 2008, about a week after the publication of the dress code memorandum was issued, the populist and nationalistic Danish People's Party started an advertisement campaign against this decision in major (conservative) Danish newspapers. The first advertisement (of the three they had planned) showed a woman – a female judge – wearing a black burkha covering all but her eyes (but wearing nail varnish, handcuffs and, on close inspection, also a wedding ring) and holding the wooden hammer often associated with a court – but never used in practice in Denmark – in her hand. The title on top of the image is 'THI KENDES FOR RET' – the traditional and formulaic way to start a judgment, meaning 'Be it considered right'. The title below the image is the same in all three advertisements and runs as follows:

---

adf%C3%A6rd%20og%20personlig%20fremtraeden%20ved%20Danmarks%20Domstole.pdf> [accessed 6 May 2008 (my translation)].

16   Emphasis added.

17   M Gøtze, 'Operation morgenluft i dommerstanden har åndenød' [Operation Morning Air in the Judiciary Short of Breath] (2008) 4 *Advokaten*, at 8–10.

18   Danmarks Domstoles LIGESTILLINGSRAPPORT 2007 <http://www.domstol.dk/om/publikationer/ Publikationer/Ligestillingsrapport%202007.pdf> [accessed 8 June 2008].

SUBMISSION

The Islamic headscarf is a symbol of the submission of woman. Islamists use it as a strong and clear sign of the dominance of faith over both man and woman, Muslim and non-Muslim. This is not simply about "30 grams of cloth"![19] It is tyranny and submission. A majority in Parliament (*Folketinget*) wants to accept it in the House. And the Administration of Courts of Justice has decided that you as a citizen must in future accept meeting a judge wrapped up in the scarf of tyranny.

Stop it. Now!

Give us Denmark back

This brings us back to the lost land. The advertisement attracted a great deal of media attention, which was undoubtedly one of its major aims. Most of this issue has been once again about headscarves, the subjection of Muslim women and the divisive style of the DPP. The text of the advertisement of the DPP, as well as of two other planned advertisements with identical texts, ends with a demand, or perhaps an appeal, to '*Give us Denmark back*' – in handwriting and without an exclamation mark. It is unclear to whom this demand is directed. Who would be able to guarantee such a right? It is neither clear what this 'Denmark' is that the DPP wishes to have back, nor is it apparent who is making this demand and to whom it is addressed.

The state of Denmark has become fragmented over the last generations. A generation ago, it became a member of the European Union, which has had great difficulties developing and securing legitimacy amongst the populations of Europe. 'Denmark' is no longer what it 'used to be' – not that it is clear what it used to be.[20] The DPP might be begging to return to the vanished post Second World War 'sovereign modern democracy/welfare-state' – or to get back some immutable imagined traditional and pure community where people would take care of each other (to the Danish version of the Paradise Lost). This lost or disappeared Denmark might be something that always was in the imagination, or that has become an illusion. Or it might be something 'real' that had died, the loss of which was now being mourned.

Who was asked to give the lost land back? It was unclear whether the claim was directed at the Government, at the politically correct elites – sometimes also called 'Upper Denmark' by the DPP – or at the courts and Parliament, which were seen to behave irresponsibly by taking or giving away 'Denmark'. Was it directed at (fundamentalist) Muslim immigrants, who have taken away 'Denmark' as 'we' knew it? Was it the majority of the Danish population that was addressed in the advertisement to give back Denmark? Who was/is ultimately responsible for the disappearance of 'Denmark'?

---

19   This quote refers to comments (on wearing headscarf) made by Asmaa Abdol-Hamid, who ran as a candidate for the left-wing Unity List (Enhedslisten) for elections in 2007 and who might at that time have been expected to become a Member of Parliament. She described the headscarf as '30 grams of cloth'.

20   The Faroe Islands never became a member of the European Community, as they received Home Rule already in 1948 and Greenland left the EEC in 1985, after having received Home Rule in 1979.

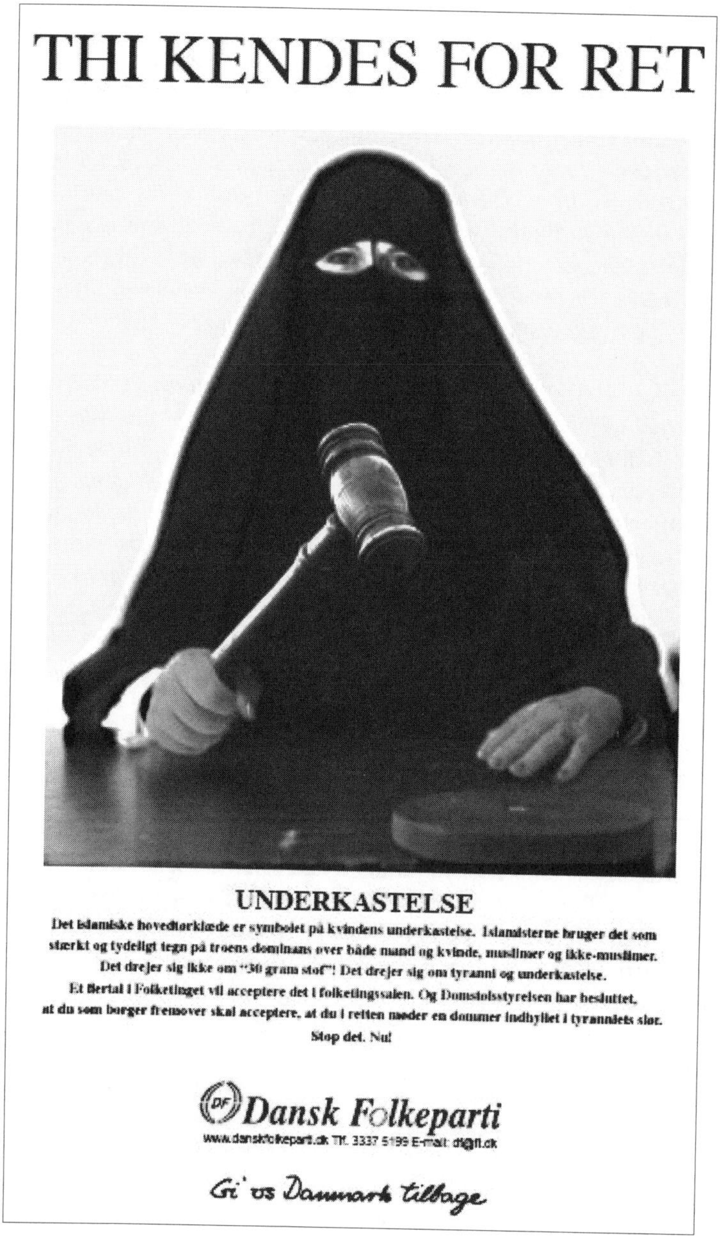

Figure 18.2 Advertisement by the Danish People's Party shown in a number of Danish newspapers in the beginning of May 2008

Note: The last line reads: Give us Denmark back.

In her weekly comments on the decision by the Administration of the Courts, the female party leader, Pia Kjærsgaard, wrote that when the new (neo-liberal) Government took power in 2001, they declared that the so-called 'judges of taste' or experts (*smagsdommere*) should be done away with. 'The everyday life of Danes should no longer be governed by a group of arbitrarily appointed civil servants with long academic titles and politically correct attitudes to everything between heaven and earth.'[21] They had still not been done away with and the Administration of Courts belonged to them, she claimed. She described this administration as dragging on its anonymous existence, and now even accepting the Islamist symbol of the headscarf. In this way, it was 'disregarding the traditions of the Danish people and their respect for courts as an unbiased and highly esteemed founding institution in Danish society'.[22] These judges were described as having a limited knowledge of the world outside the thick walls of Danish court rooms.

This indicates that it was Muslims and parts of the 'Upper Denmark' elite who had caused the loss of 'Denmark', but it was and is unclear who may bring it back – unless it might be the Danish People's Party.

And who were and are the 'us' requesting the return of 'Denmark'? Is it also the DDP, the members or supporters of this party, or is it non-Muslims generally? In the first case, 'us' constitutes a part of the Danish population, which probably feels most lost and insecure because of global developments. This insecurity is linked to a fear of loss of a feeling of unity, social coherence and welfare in a social democratic welfare state, which has been strongly dominated by Protestant values and, until a generation ago, was also a very homogenous population. Arjun Appadurai speaks of the 'anxiety of incompleteness' that may drive majorities into 'paroxysms of violence against minorities', as well as of 'the link between minorities *within* the modern nation state and the marginalization of the nation state by the forces of globalization'.[23]

Perhaps this is also a fear of the disappearance of a space and a community strongly dominated by *a culture of rights*. Until now, these rights have been secured by the state, which may, however, no longer be fully trusted. The culture of rights is changing owing to the move from welfare state to market state and from industrial economy to an information and service economy. It is probably also weakening owing to the demographic and ethnic reconstitutions of the populations. A population dominated by old and weak may not on its own be able to uphold a regime that requires many more 'hands' than are currently available, as the strikes by the Danish social workers and nurses revealed in April and May 2008. The discourse on the lack of 'hands' in the welfare sector dominated the debate up to the financial crisis in late 2008. The overheated Danish economy had experienced labour shortage, especially in the low-paid, female-dominated public welfare sector. What seemed to become clearer was that without 'hands' there might be no welfare rights. The discourse on hands was seemingly both gender-neutral and ethnically neutral. Nevertheless, maybe the message was that there are not enough women around to take care of the children, the sick and the elderly. Will society have to return to the female informal duty of care to secure rights? Does the survival of this (female) sense of responsibility have to be secured by immigrant women, who have been brought up in a culture of family and caring responsibility? Is there also a general fear of strong (local and non-indigenous) women in positions of *state* authority in Western modern states with a Christian cultural background, be it as presidents, prime ministers or judges.

The faith in rights that has been very strong among the social democratic-leaning members of the DPP is losing power in a very painful and perhaps paradoxical process. Rights no longer seem to be able to give a sense of security to national populations, who may now perceive themselves

---

21   Pia Kjærsgaards ugebrev, Monday April 28, 2008 Domstolene skal holdes fri fra politik og religion [The courts must be kept free of politics and religion] <http://www.danskfolkeparti.dk/Domstolene_skal_holdes_fri_fra_politik_og_religion.asp>.

22   Ibid.

23   A Appadurai, *Fear of Small Numbers: An Essay on the Geography of Anger* (Durham and London: Duke University Press, 2006), at 8 and 33.

as victims. There seems to be diminishing trust that there will be anybody around to perform the duties, which may secure a fulfilment of the rights of the weak in the future; it is not only the so-called failed and collapsed states that are losing trust among their weak citizens.[24] The sense of loss probably goes far beyond that. The DPP has been thriving on this fear and insecurity since its establishment in 1995. The party's de facto membership of the Government since 2001 has not relieved the population of this insecurity, in spite of its considerable influence on law-making. Perhaps the contrary might be closer to the truth. The need for security – perhaps of a realist and responsible understanding of security – is being strengthened, in a period characterized by confusion in all walks of political and social life. It seems that what is emerging is a local underclass, which feels vulnerable and perhaps even unprotected in terms of rights and welfare, and thus becomes exclusivist and xenophobic, and a globalized upper class, which does not (yet?) feel responsible for much more than its own well-being.

In his book *Facing a World in Crisis: What Life Teaches us in Challenging Times*, the Indian spiritual teacher Jiddu Krishnamurti writes:

> We don't know what to do, we don't know what to think, we have put our faith in something, and that has failed; we have believed in something, and that has failed. We have relied on tradition, and that has gone. We have relied on friends, relationships, family, and everything has broken down. So the mind is utterly confused, uncertain, seeking, asking. Isn't that true of most of us?

> And so what shall a mind that is confused do? A confused mind mustn't do a thing. Because whatever it does out of that confusion will be confused. Whatever choice it makes must be confused. It will be confused following any leader. The leader must be confused too, otherwise you wouldn't accept him.[25]

The reaction to the decision of the Administration of Courts demonstrates much confusion not only amongst the DPP, but also perhaps even more among the Social Democratic Party, which came up with several different public statements on the headscarf issue in courts within a day of the DPP advertisements being published. A number of public figures, artists, present and former politicians, businessmen, intellectuals and professors, authors, the former President of the Supreme Court, and the former Director of the National Bank wrote an 'Open letter against hostility', published in several newspapers.[26] The female Minister of Immigration and Ecclesiastical Affairs, Birthe Rønn Hornbech, who is both a lawyer and a believing Christian, published a much-discussed feature article, where she criticised the DPP for being 'anti-Muslim'.[27] This led to severe criticism of her in both government and some media. An announced draft legislation disallowing headscarves in courts led to considerable bewilderment about how individual members of the parties constituting the formal government may vote, but it was finally adopted – leading to more discussion and commissions.

I think we are seeing an increasing number of confused individuals, populations and leaders in and around Europe and the world today. We are ourselves experiencing increasing confusion as individuals as well as professionals. Fear of terrorism may sidetrack the fear of loss of protection

---

24 It remains to be seen how the financial crisis will influence the trust in the state in a longer time perspective.

25 J Krishnamurti, *Facing a World in Crisis: What Life Teaches us in Challenging Times*, ed. by David Skitt (Boston and London: Shambala, 2005), at 69.

26 'Åbent brev imod fjendtligheden', *Information*, 8 May 2008.

27 BR Hornhech, 'Dommertørklædet og de to regimenter', *Politiken*, 14 May 2008.

by states, rights and local communities for some time, but it does not disappear. And it may produce unexpressed generational conflicts of a more general kind in Western democracies, where demography indicates serious difficulties for young people of local origin to find a voice for their needs and wishes.

**Figure 18.3 Natasja Saad (1974–2007), musician and author of
the song 'Give me my Denmark back', 2007**

Natasja Saad – on the image above – was a reggae, rap and hip-hop singer born in 1974 of a Danish mother and a Sudanese father. In the summer of 2007 she died tragically in a traffic accident in Jamaica, where she had earlier been visiting, giving concerts and winning prizes. Before her death she produced a song she had written and called 'Give me my Denmark back', and Danish-Egyptian stand-up comedian Omar Mazouk produced a video, in which she sings the song.[28] In 2007 Natasja received the Zulu award – an award given by listeners – as the best Danish female singer. In February 2008 she was posthumously awarded both the prize for the best Danish female singer, the prize for the best Danish hit – 'Give me my Denmark back' and the prize for the best Danish album *In Denmark I am Born*. The first part of 'Give me my Denmark back' reflects a longing for a Denmark that has disappeared. It asks what happened to the old Denmark where a 'free bird was

---

28   <http://www.youtube.com/watch?v=ECPaINIYTGY&feature=related> – interview with Natasja from May 2007 about the production of the video. <http://www.youtube.com/watch?v=NONnUBKcNZI> (video "Giv mig Danmark tilbage"). Posthumous album "I danmark er jeg født" (*In Denmark I am Born* – original lyrics by Hans Christian Andersen) Playground Music. Thanks to Kristine E. Raunkjær for drawing my attention to the relation between this song and the DPP media campaign.

free' and 'people meant what they said'. However, this Denmark is also a source of fear – it 'scares me' sings Natasja Saad, and yet she adds: 'I want you back because I'm grieving.'

The song includes an indirect criticism of both the DPP, of the (government) plans of closing down Christiania – the so-called free city in Copenhagen, and the closing down in March 2007 of the youth house – *ungeren* – in social-democratically governed Copenhagen.

On YouTube[29] it is still possible to view Natasja singing this song as well a a number of video clips and 'memorials' relating to her untimely death. On 3 May 2008 the liberal newspaper *Politiken* carried a story indicating that the DPP slogan was an imitation of Natasja's popular song.[30] A few days later the Nordic music publisher, Edition Wilhelm Hansen, which holds the rights to the song, sued the DPP, which denied any responsibility and claimed that the words were far too general.[31] The views on this case have been ambivalent – it has been seen as a way of using intellectual property rights that may threaten to limit creativity.

The overlap or identity between the title of a very popular hit by a young female artist with a multicultural background and the slogan of a female-led party for older ethnically Danish (male) voters indicates both similarities and differences in what might perhaps be called an undecided 'cultural war' between generations about the expansion or limitation of local/global identity. These generations – not only in Denmark – have different experiences, different demographic, electoral and legal as well as economic power. These asymmetries may lead to important differences in the evaluation of symbolic identity issues and perhaps 'identity rights'. The use of dress – and especially the headdress – which has been interpreted symbolically has been an issue of both local and European concern. A Danish legal academic, Pernille Boye Koch claims in her article on the case of *Leyla Sahin v. Turkey*, about a female medical student who wanted to be able to wear the headscarf at her university, that the European Court of Human Rights is developing a paternalistic interpretation that is hostile to religious rights and in actual fact favours mainstream Christianity, without taking concrete conditions into consideration. 'The underlying message seems to be that even if the concrete individual does not understand the scarf as gender oppressive, proselytising or as an attack on the democratic, secular state, the court knows better.'[32]

The contest over representation and voice may, however, also lead to innovations and expressions of new ways of conviviality and dress statements – as in the fashion competition on the most beautiful scarf, '*Miss Tørklæde 2008*', taking place at the beginning of June 2008 and organized by the youth programme SKUM on Danish broadcasting.[33]

---

29   YouTube is a video sharing website where users can upload, view and share video clips. YouTube was created in February 2005. <http://en.wikipedia.org/wiki/YouTube>.

30   <http://politiken.dk/kultur/article503285.ece> 'DF's brug af Natasja forarger', 3 May [accessed 8 June 2008].

31   <http://www.dr.dk/Nyheder/Indland/2008/05/07/203226.htm> 'Natasjas forlag kræver erstatning af DF' [accessed 8 June 2008].

32   PB Koch, 'Religiøse symboler i skolerne: et kritisk perspektiv på Den Europæiske Menneskerettighedsdomstols dom i Leyla Sahin v. Turkey' in (2008)1 *Retfærd* at 67.

33   'Miss Tørklæde [Scarf] 2008' posted at <http://community.dr.dk/default.ns?lngItemID=1399> [accessed 8 June 2008].

Changing Mentalities and Developing Responsibilities?

> *Too much legislation numbs the sense of individual responsibility. Too little legislation leads*
> *to anarchy and disorder. Legislation is best when it is conducive to the promotion of individual*
> *responsibility.*[34]

Do local space and its political and normative orders need to be reconstructed as orders that are also carrying responsibilities beyond the local for something like 'Denmark' to reappear as a community that may produce trust and security for the many insecure and confused 'us' who have been around for shorter and longer periods and many or few generations, or perhaps for a more individualistic, but also more multicultural, 'I'? Is a stronger culture of responsibilities needed in order to regain or reconstruct feelings of security? Or is there a development towards a culture of responsibilities because of a gradual collapse of the culture of rights? Who is initiating such developments?

In their New Year's speeches at the beginning of 2008, the Danish Prime Minister, as well as the Queen, emphasized issues of responsibility. The topic of corporate social responsibility has been on the agenda for decades and is gaining ground in some corporate mentalities. A shift from rights to responsibilities is, as already mentioned, a shift towards ethics in plural relations inasmuch that individual and group responsibilities may be experienced as a burden, but may perhaps also contribute to a revitalized sense of belonging and of feeling protected through participation.

The Danish Government demanded increased parental responsibility after the youth riots in Copenhagen in February 2008, which were related to youth claims for a youth centre after the house that served as their centre was demolished by public authorities in March 2007. There is an increased demand for personal and individual responsibility by a weakened government in relation to health, especially obesity, and smoking. There is a demand in relation to climate change, child labour, fair trade and global justice, much of which is government demand for what might perhaps be described as a privatization of moral responsibility.

However, there is also a question of responsibility beyond the demand made by the state. Kaplan asks: 'How do we define or account for individual responsibility to others or the society outside of dispute resolution or other formalized state institutions?'[35] According to Kaplan, Bergman's film *Shame* 'portrays the consequences of self-defence and the avoidance of responsibility in the face of ambiguity, contingency and horror'.[36]

> The film ends with the survivors at sea, rudderless, with a watery horizon, seemingly out of food
> and water. Where horizon can mean openness, freedom, here the implication is a desert of inhuman,
> endless despair. Where water symbolizes life in Bergman's Virgin Spring, here it represents a
> meaningless, inescapable death.[37]

Levinas, according to Kaplan, maintains that everyone owes 'an asymptotic responsibility to the other, stranger or intimate'.[38] To Levinas, responsiveness to the other must occur at a certain level of human development; understanding, and responding to the other becomes meaningful only when

---

34 'A common framework for the ethics of the 21st century', in Y Kim, *Division of Philosophy and Ethics. UNESCO*, September 1999, Paris, <http://www.unesco.or.kr/ethics/yersu_kim.htm> [accessed 6 May 2008].

35 Kaplan, above, n. 13, at 1169.

36 Ibid., at 1170.

37 Ibid., at 1177.

38 Ibid., at 1181.

a certain security in the self is achieved, a certain level of narcissism. Perhaps this is particularly difficult in times of confusion: 'For Levinas, one must reach a certain level of autonomy to appreciate that an autonomous state is insufficient for psychological development and recognition of the obligation of responsibility of the other.'[39]

However, there is also an increased call for global responsibility. In relation to the 50th anniversary of the Declaration of Human Rights, the UN General Assembly in 1999 decided on a new declaration on responsibility.[40] The German Catholic theologian, Hans Küng, who was a member of the InterAction Group of high-profile, globally concerned 'world citizens' who took the original initiative to the declaration writes:

> Like the Declaration of Human Rights, the Declaration of Human Responsibilities is indeed primarily a *moral appeal*. As such it does not have the direct binding character of international law, but it proclaims to the world public some basic norms for collective and individual behaviour which should apply to everyone. This appeal is, of course, also meant to have an effect on legal and political practice. However, it does not aim at any legalistic morality. A key feature of the Declaration of Human Responsibilities is that it precisely *does not aim at legal codification*, which is impossible anyway in the case of moral attitudes like truthfulness or fairness. It aims at *voluntarily taking responsibility*. The Declaration of Human Responsibilities should therefore be considered as *morally* rather than *legally* binding.[41]

In 2008 UNICEF UK published a report called 'Our climate, our children, our responsibility', wherein the chapter on responsibility indirectly links to the issue of sustainability:

> Tackling the drivers and impacts of climate change is a collective responsibility. We all have a responsibility to ensure that each person across the world is protected from the impacts of climate change, wherever they live, and that our children – and their children in due course – are not asked to bear the brunt of the consequences stemming from today's unsustainable patterns of production and consumption.[42]

The moral responsibilities of individuals and collectives seem to be emphasized in a situation where rights may no longer secure the survival or welfare of individuals and groups. What may be the consequences of that?

---

39 Kaplan, above, n. 13, at 1181–82.

40 Declaration on the Right and Responsibility of Individuals, Groups and Organs of Society to Promote and Protect Universally Recognized Human Rights and Fundamental Freedoms, General Assembly resolution 53/144, /RES/53/144 8 March 1999.

41 H Küng, 'Global Ethic and Human Responsibilities', posted at <http://www.scu.edu/ethics/practicing/focusareas/global_ethics/laughlin-lectures/global-ethic-human-responsibility.html> [accessed 6 May 2008 (emphasis in the original)].

42 Our climate, our children our responsibility. The implication of climate change for the world's children. UNICEF UK Climate Change Report 2008 posted at <http://www.unicef.org.uk/campaigns/publications/pdf/climate-change.pdf>. This issue of general responsibility of individuals and populations was hardly discussed openly among the rich nations at the UN COP 15 meeting in Copenhagen in December 2009, but it will probably become more pertinent in future meetings.

'The Gift of Death' and the 'Secrets of European Responsibility'

> *It is a religious act to clean out a gutter and to prevent cholera, and it is not a religious act to pray*
> *[in the sense of asking]. Real value is in giving, and doing what is necessary for the welfare of*
> *others, not in asking and taking.*[43]

In his chapter on 'Secrets of European responsibility' in the book *The Gift of Death*, Derrida discusses the Czech philosopher, Jan Patocka, whom Kaplan also discusses in his Bergman article.[44] Patocka was a member of Charter 77 and died after a very long and brutal interrogation in 1977. Responsibility and faith go together, writes Derrida, 'however paradoxical that might seem to some, and both should in the same movement, exceed mastery and knowledge. The gift of death would be this marriage of responsibility and faith. History depends on such an excessive beginning.'[45]

Could it be that, for a contemporary global form of faith and a practice of mutual broad-minded responsibility to develop, certain 'expressions' of 'Denmark' (and other welfare states) would have to 'die' – at least symbolically? The Nordic countries may be described as communities of belief or as traditional communities, besides having been 'modern states', strongly influenced by Lutheran Christianity.[46] Will these societies have to transform radically to realize their responsibilities related to the 'radical interdependence' in a changing understanding of community? Or is the secret of European responsibility a secret of individual responsibility? Kaplan speaks about the role of traditions, and we may consider both legal and religious traditions in Europe and their mutual and strong historical interrelationships.

> Patocka asserts the triumph of the Christian over the Greek in the metaphysics of responsibility, not as a sectarian matter, but as a historical fact. Bernard Yack noted that, postmodern discourse notwithstanding, certain traditions have maintained themselves through history, through uninterrupted argumentation, clarification, commentary and the like.[47]

> Patocka's point is that God's transformation to human form, forced to experience human passion, suffering and finitude, provided a model of human responsibility more intimate and less cerebral than the Greek good ... He argues that there is much to develop in Christian responsibility. He fears that technocracy invaded human consciousness to such an extent that the Christian moment of revelation becomes nugatory.[48]

According to Derrida:

> [...] the concept of responsibility has, in the most reliable continuity of its history, always implied involvement in action, doing, a *praxis*, a *decision* that exceeds simple conscience or simple

---

43   G Hunt, 'Human rights or human responsibilities? Remembering Florence Nightingale', Nursing Ethics, 8/3 (2001).

44   J Derrida, 'Secrets of European responsibility', in *The Gift of Death* (Chicago, IL and London: University of Chicago Press, 1996).

45   Ibid., at 6.

46   H Petersen and KÅ Modeer, *Believing in Norway and Beliefs in Norway*. Report for the Norwegian Helsinki Committee and the Norwegian Institute of Human Rights (Oslo: University of Oslo, 2010).

47   Kaplan above, n, 13, at 1190.

48   Ibid., at 1192.

theoretical understanding, it is also true that the same concept requires a decision or responsible action to answer for itself *consciously*, that is with knowledge of a thematics of what is done, of what action signifies, its causes, ends, etc. In debates concerning responsibility one must always take into account this original and irreducible complexity that links theoretical consciousness (which must also be a thetic or thematic consciousness) to "practical" conscience (ethical, legal, political), if only to avoid the arrogance of so many "clean consciences".[49]

Would this mean that local development of a global sense of responsibility will take place as act and *praxis*? Could the modest memorandum on dress code at Danish courts be interpreted as an act of global responsibility? And could the public pleading by the Danish People's Party to return the local community back be interpreted as an appeal to an activation of responsibility in order to secure the protection of many who feel loss and have lost locally, those who have been described as belonging to a tribe and act according to a tribal logic?[50] And could the young individual wanting the honest, broad-minded, free and colourful community back and singing about it also be part of that development of a multifaceted responsibility, as well as the almost satirical local radio programme setting up a fashion show on scarves?

What kinds of acts may we perform, what kind of praxis may we develop as individuals, professionals and groups of professionals?

---

49   Derrida, ibid., at 25.

50   A Laubjerg, 'Magtens midte er under forandring' [The centre of power is changing] in *Information*, 2 May 2008.

Index

Author Index